Assessing Infants and Preschoolers with Handicaps

Assessing Infants and Preschoolers with Handicaps

Donald B. Bailey, Jr.
University of North Carolina

Mark Wolery
University of Kentucky

Merrill Publishing Company
A Bell & Howell Information Company
Columbus   Toronto   London   Melbourne

Cover Art: David Butts, Early Childhood Education Center, Franklin County
Board of Mental Retardation and Developmental Disabilities,
Columbus, Ohio

Published by Merrill Publishing Company
A Bell & Howell Information Company
Columbus, Ohio 43216

This book was set in Quorum Book.

Administrative Editor: Vicki Knight
Production Coordinator: Carol Driver
Cover Designer: Cathy Watterson

Chapter 15 was supported by Grant No. G 008730527
awarded by the Department of Education to Vanderbilt
University and the University of Minnesota.

Library of Congress Catalog Card Number: 88-61657
International Standard Book Number: 0-675-21008-9
Printed in the United States of America
1 2 3 4 5 6 7 8 9—93 92 91 90 89

Preface

Early childhood special educators and other professionals working with infants and preschoolers with handicaps must constantly make decisions about the nature and amount of services to be provided. Often these decisions are based on clinical judgment—a fundamental component of any human service. It is clear, however, that systematic assessment is an essential aspect of any planning process. Although such assessment is time-consuming, the information gained can help pinpoint intervention needs and ultimately can lead to a more effective and efficient program of services.

This text addresses issues, considerations, and procedures in assessing infants and preschoolers with handicaps. Its development was stimulated by the recognition that assessing very young children is a process that requires different skills and knowledge than does the process of assessing school-aged children. The focus of this text is assessment for the purpose of instructional or intervention program planning.

This book is organized into three major sections. The first addresses fundamental issues and considerations in assessment. Assessment is described and a comprehensive rationale is presented. Tests and their construction are reviewed, and various ways of summarizing test performance are described and compared. Special considerations in assessing infants and preschoolers are addressed, as well as are procedures for assessing young children with sensory or motor impairments. Finally, direct observational procedures and informal assessments are described. The importance of combining tests, interviews, and naturalistic observational data is emphasized.

The second section addresses specialized assessment issues, beginning with a discussion of assessing environments in order to understand more fully children's behavior. Screening procedures are described and characteristics of effective screening are discussed. Finally, three chapters address unique considerations in assessing very young children, including neurobehavioral assessment of the newborn, assessing infant state and behavioral organization, and assessing temperament and behavioral characteristics.

The third section discusses assessment within the context of key curricula/developmental domains. Included are chapters on assessing infant cognitive development, preschool cognitive skills, motor skills, communication skills, social interaction skills, play skills, and self-care skills. The text concludes with a chapter on using assessment information for program planning.

When writing this text, we and our contributors were constantly challenged by the large amount of important information that needed to be condensed into a usable format. Thus, several comments regarding the content limits of this text are appropriate.

First, this book is not about diagnosis and is not written for diagnosticians. It is designed specifically for professionals who are responsible for designing and implementing individualized intervention programs for handicapped infants, toddlers, and preschoolers.

Second, this is not a book on testing *per se* nor is it a review of tests; rather, it is a description of the overall information-gathering process we believe is essential for appropriate planning of services. Although we describe and give introductions to various tests, the reader should not assume that the text provides sufficient information for using or evaluating specific instruments.

Third, we recognize the importance of family assessment in early intervention. However, we did not include a chapter on it for three reasons: (1) the first author just completed an entire book on the topic and thus the information is already available (Bailey & Simeonsson, 1988); (2) it is too big an issue to address in one or two chapters; and (3) at this time a cursory treatment of the topic would be inappropriate because of the complexity of the topic. We have, however, stressed the importance of gathering information from family members and of involving parents in the decision-making process.

Fourth, it should be clear that reading this text will not make one a competent evaluator of children. Clinical skills can only be acquired through experience or supervised practice. This book is designed to provide the foundation upon which experience can be built more meaningfully.

Finally, we recognize that assessment of infants, toddlers, and preschoolers with handicaps will involve multiple disciplines. No one discipline is likely to be able to assess and meet the complex needs of these children,

and students should be encouraged to work together with other professionals as they learn assessment skills.

Acknowledgments

We would like to recognize the contributions of several individuals in the preparation of this text. First, of course, are the chapter contributors. Each was selected because of his or her expertise in specific areas of assessment. We appreciate their contributions and diligent efforts to meet tight deadlines. Second, we acknowledge the reviewers of various drafts of this manuscript: Robert G. Harrington, University of Kansas; David Sexton, University of New Orleans; Sarah Robertson, Arizona State University; Evelyn Lynch, Moorhead State University; Eugene Edgar, University of Washington; Sharon Raver-Lampman, Old Dominion University; Linda McCormick, University of Hawaii; and Kathleen S. Shank, Eastern Illinois University. The authors of chapter 15 wish to thank Micki Ostrosky and Tracy Evans for their helpful comments on an earlier draft of the chapter. We recognize that there is little reward in reviewing texts, but hope that the reviewers realize our deep appreciation of their time and comments. We hope we were able to respond appropriately to their suggestions, and we are convinced that the text is better because of their efforts. Third, we express our appreciation to Vicki Knight for her continued support of our work, and her diligent management of this project. Finally, Joan Holder helped by typing parts of the manuscript, and the following students helped with library searches, proofing drafts, and developing the index: Jan Wilbers, Debra Billings, Jackie Kues, and Richard Granowski.

We dedicate this book to our wives—Pam and Ruth—and our children—Lara, Rebecca, Nathaniel, Steve, and Tim. They continue to be supportive and have patiently endured the pressures and deadlines of yet another project.

Don Bailey
Mark Wolery

Contents

Chapter 1
Assessment and Its Importance in Early Intervention   **1**

The Rationale for Assessment   2
Barriers to Child Assessment   4
Characteristics of Effective Child Assessment   8

Chapter 2
Tests and Test Development   **22**

Test Standardization   23
Test Content   23
Summarizing Test Performance: Norm-Referenced Measures   27
Summarizing Criterion- and Curriculum-Referenced Measures   36
Test Reliability   38
Test Validity   41

Chapter 3
**Procedural Considerations in Assessing Infants
and Preschoolers with Handicaps**   **47**

Special Considerations in Assessing Infants and Preschoolers   47
Assessing Children with Sensory or Motor Impairments   54
Alternative Assessment Strategies   58

Chapter 4
Using Direct Observation in Assessment   64

Definition and Use of Direct Observation   65

Basics of Direct Observation   68

Using Direct Observations to Identify Relationships
Between Child Behavior and Environmental Stimuli   92

Chapter 5
Assessing Environments   97

Rationale for Environmental Assessment   97

Procedural Considerations in Assessing Environments   98

Representative Methods for Assessing Environments   107

Using Environmental Assessment Information   114

Chapter 6
Child Find and Screening Issues   119

Child Find Issues   119

Screening Issues   122

Chapter 7
Screening and Assessing Sensory Functioning   144

Assessing Auditory Functioning of Infants and Preschoolers   145

Assessing Visual Functioning of Infants and Preschoolers   153

Chapter 8
Neurobehavioral Assessment of the Newborn Infant   166

Rationale   167

Historical Perspective   168

Dimensions of Assessment   175

Procedural Guidelines   178

Representative Methods   180

Translating Assessment Data into Intervention   191

Chapter 9
Assessment of Behavioral State Organization   202

Rationale for Assessing Behavioral States 203
Dimensions of Behavioral States 205
Procedural Considerations in Assessing Behavioral States 212
Representative Methods for Assessing Behavioral States 215
Applications of the Assessment of Behavioral States 217

Chapter 10
Assessing Behavioral Characteristics   225

Rationale for Assessing Behavioral Cues, Style, and Characteristics 225
Dimensions of Child Behavior 226
Considerations for Assessment of Child Characteristics 232
Representative Measures or Procedures 235
Translating Assessment Information into Instructional Goals 241

Chapter 11
Assessing Infant Cognitive Development   249

Sensorimotor Assessment Rationale 250
Piagetian Sensorimotor Stages 251
Procedural Considerations in Assessing Sensorimotor Intelligence 254
Representative Methods for Assessing Sensorimotor Abilities 258
Translating Assessment Information into Instructional Goals 267

Chapter 12
Assessment of Cognitive Skills in the Preschool-Aged Child   275

Dimensions of Cognitive Assessment 276
Procedural Considerations When Assessing Cognitive Skills 279
Representative Methods for Assessing Preschool Cognitive Skills 281
Translating Assessment Information into Instructional Goals 291
Summary and Conclusions 295

Chapter 13
Assessing Motor Skills   301

Rationale 302
Overview of the Domain of Motor Development 303
Dimensions of Motor Evaluation and Assessment Procedures 304
Representative Methods for Assessing Motor Skills 321
Translating Assessment Information into Instructional Goals 323

Chapter 14
Assessing Communication Skills   339

Rationale for Assessing Communication 340
Dimensions of Communication Assessment 341
Representative Methods for Assessing Communication 352
Translating Assessment Information into Instructional Goals 377
Conclusion 385

Chapter 15
Assessing Social Interaction Skills   390

Nature of the Social Interaction Development 391
A Sketch of Early Social Development 392
Social Development of Infants and Young Children with Handicaps 392
Dimensions of Social Interaction Assessment 394
Procedural Considerations in Assessing Social Interaction 397
Methods for Assessing Social Interactions 398
Using Social Interaction Assessment Information 417

Chapter 16
Assessing Play Skills   428

Rationale for Assessing Play Skills 428
Dimensions of Play 431
Methods of Assessing Play 433
Using Assessment Information When Planning Intervention 442

Chapter 17
Assessing Self-Care Skills   447

Rationale for Assessing and Teaching Self-Care Skills   447
Description and Characteristics of Self-Care Skills   448
Procedures for Assessing Self-Care Skills   450
Using Self-Care Assessment Information   472

Chapter 18
Using Assessment Information to Plan Instructional Programs   478

Rationale for Linking Assessment Information and Instructional Program Planning   479
Writing Reports from Instructional Program Planning Assessments   479
Translating Assessment Information into Instructional Objectives   481
Translating Instructional Objectives into Instructional Realities   490
Involving the Parent in Using Assessment Information   492

Author Index   497
Subject Index   509

Chapter 1

Assessment and Its Importance in Early Intervention

Donald B. Bailey, Jr.
University of North Carolina
at Chapel Hill

KEY TERMS

- Assessment
- Screening
- Diagnosis
- Placement
- Planning
- Evaluation
- Developmental Milestones Approach
- Stage of Development

- Functional Approach
- Cognitive Skills
- Motor Skills
- Communication Skills
- Play and Social Skills
- Self-Care Skills
- Direct Testing
- Naturalistic Observation

- Direct Observation
- Interviewing
- Multidisciplinary Team
- Interdisciplinary Team
- Transdisciplinary Team
- Arena Assessment
- Ecologically Valid Assessment
- Ecological Approach

Assessing infants and preschoolers with handicaps is a necessary and fundamental activity for teachers, therapists, and other professionals in early intervention. Its importance is evidenced in state and federal legislation, in the rapidly growing number of assessment tools for use with young handicapped children, and in the amount of time devoted to assessment in early intervention programs. This text provides an overview of issues, considerations, and procedures in assessing such infants and preschoolers. The primary focus is on assessment for the purpose of instructional planning. Other purposes of assessment are described, however, and guidelines for achieving them are suggested. This chapter provides a rationale for assessment in early childhood intervention programs and an overview of the assessment process. Various purposes of assessment are presented, barriers to effective assessment are described, and characteristics of effective child assessment are proposed.

The Rationale for Assessment

Assessment may be defined as the process of gathering information for the purpose of making a decision. At least five reasons for assessing infants and preschoolers with handicaps exist: screening, diagnosis, placement, planning, and evaluation.

Screening
One purpose of assessment is to identify infants and preschoolers who may be handicapped or at risk for developmental delay. **Screening** is the process of assessing a large number of children in order to determine which children should participate in a more comprehensive evaluation. Because of the large number of children usually assessed in a screening program, these procedures typically are brief and relatively inexpensive to administer.

Screening is based on the assumption that early identification and treatment of particular problems is important. From a practical perspective, screening is essential in the context of early intervention because handicapped infants and preschoolers are not already enrolled in a comprehensive service delivery system designed to serve all children, such as public schools. Consequently, federal legislation (in the form of Public Law 94-142, the Education for the Handicapped Act, and Public Law 99-457, the 1986 amendments to Public Law 94-142) mandates that states develop and implement public awareness programs focusing on early identification of handicapped infants and toddlers and a comprehensive "child find" system for referring and screening children to identify those who

should participate in a more extensive evaluation. Guidelines and considerations for screening for developmental delays are presented in Chapter 6 and screening and assessing sensory functioning are discussed in Chapter 7.

Diagnosis
A second purpose for conducting child assessments is the **diagnosis** of handicapping conditions or the determination of the extent and nature of developmental delay. When a screening procedure indicates that a child is at high risk for developmental delay or when parents refer their children for perceived developmental problems, a comprehensive, multidisciplinary evaluation should be conducted. Generally, this evaluation would address medical issues, general developmental status, sensory and motor functioning, and social development. The evaluation may lead to a definitive diagnosis as to etiology of the developmental delay or condition, such as a genetic disorder, cerebral palsy, or an identified syndrome. In many cases, however, a specific cause of the delay cannot be identified. In such cases, the result of the diagnostic assessment is simply the determination of whether a child is, in fact, developmentally delayed.

Placement
A third use of child assessment information is to assist in making **placement** decisions about children. The most basic of these decisions is whether a child qualifies for early intervention services. With school-aged children, schools are required to report children by disability category (e.g., learning disabled, mentally retarded, emotionally disturbed); thus, the extent to which a child meets state and federal guidelines for the specific disability category will determine whether that child is eligible for special education services and which type of services will be provided.

Public Law 99-457, however, makes it clear that states do not have to report or serve handicapped infants, toddlers, or preschoolers by disability category. Legislative provisions related to handicapped infants and toddlers define the eligible population as all children from birth through age 2 who fall into one of three categories. First, children who demonstrate documented developmental delays in one or more of the following areas are considered eligible: cognitive, physical, language and speech, psychosocial, or self-help skills. The legislation, however, does not specify the extent of delay required, leaving it to individual states to make that decision. Second, children who have a diagnosed physical or mental condition that has a high probability of resulting in developmental delay also are eligible. For example, an infant with Down syndrome may not appear developmentally delayed on an assessment scale. It is quite likely, however, that such a child ultimately will experience delays in skill acquisition and limitations in skill use. Thus, the legislation does not require a currently existing delay for eligibility purposes. Finally, the legislation provides that states may, at their own discretion, serve infants and toddlers "who are at risk of having substantial developmental delays if early intervention services are not provided."

Likewise, the legislative provisions for handicapped children ages 3 through 5 indicate that states are not required to label these children categorically. Each state must adopt a set of criteria specifying precisely how eligibility for services will be determined. For example, some states may define a delay in terms of number of months (e.g., a 6-month delay or a 12-month delay), whereas others will define delay in terms of number of standard deviations away from the mean. States also will have to decide if the delay can be in only one developmental area or if it must cross multiple domains. Issues pertaining to specific scores and their use for decisions regarding eligibility and placement are discussed in Chapter 2.

In addition to determining whether infants, toddlers, and preschoolers are eligible for services, assessment for placement should address which service option will best meet the needs of the individual child and family. For school-aged children, the decision of placement traditionally has been made on the basis of diagnostic category. Because determining eligibility rather than diagnostic labeling is required by P.L. 99-457, making the placement decision on the basis of diagnostic category is not warranted. If a community has services for infants, toddlers, and preschoolers who have handicaps in home-based, special centers/classrooms, and in regular child-care programs, then the interdisciplinary team (including the parents) must determine which of these options or combinations of options will be used. This decision is best made by considering the needs and abilities of the child and family, the types of services available, and the match between the two. This consideration requires assessment of the child, family, and potential placement options. Decisions about placement should be dynamic; that is, they should be viewed as easily changed. Inasmuch as the purpose of determining placement is to make services available to those in need, placements that do not fulfill this purpose should be changed quickly. The case managers in the infant and toddler programs should play a key role in assessing potential placements, monitoring the adequacy and appropriateness of those placements, and initiating a process for changing placements when needed.

Program Planning

A fourth use of child assessment information is for **planning** intervention programs. From the perspective of a teacher or therapist, this function of assessment is likely to be considered the most essential. Both the Individualized Educational Plan (IEP) for preschoolers and the Individualized Family Services Plan (IFSP) for infants and toddlers require a statement of the child's present levels of development. The infant/toddler legislation specifies that this statement must include present levels of physical development, cognitive development, language and speech development, psychosocial development, and self-help skills. From these and other assessments, individualized goals are drawn for the purpose of instructional planning. Guidelines for instructional planning within each developmental domain are described throughout this text. Additionally, Chapter 18 describes procedures and models for using assessment results to plan and write individual intervention plans.

Evaluation

Finally, assessment information is used for **evaluation** purposes. At the individual level, assessment data can be used to determine the child's rate of progress and to verify the effectiveness of specific intervention strategies with respect to specific target behaviors. Data may also be aggregated across children to determine overall program impact.

Although teachers and therapists often feel they are not involved in or responsible for evaluation activities, such activities are essential for the effectiveness of any program. Through monitoring and evaluating program effectiveness, teams demonstrate a level of accountability for their services to children, families, and the community at large. Evaluation allows teams to identify whether or to what extent progress is being made and can be used to identify when and what changes must be made in either individual interventions or in the program as a whole.

Barriers to Child Assessment

Although child assessment is generally recognized as a fundamental component of early intervention, numerous barriers exist that make it a difficult and imperfect process.

Among these are conceptual, measurement, child, staff, and institutional barriers.

Conceptual Barriers

One of the major barriers to effective child assessment is current limitations of our understanding and conceptualization of the way children grow and develop (Fewell, 1983; Kopp, 1982). Several approaches have been offered, each with its own distinct characteristics. One approach, often referred to as the **developmental milestones approach,** conceptualizes development as the sequential attainment of highly salient developmental "markers." These skills, such as walking, building a block tower, drawing a person, or using two-word combinations, have been shown to discriminate statistically between children of different ages and are assumed to be important as indicators of child growth and development (Egan & Brown, 1986). Thus, many tests select items because of their statistical abilities to discriminate among children.

The developmental milestones approach has been criticized by numerous authors (e.g., Bailey & Wolery, 1984; Brooks-Gunn & Lewis, 1981; Keogh & Sheehan, 1981) because of the questionable relevance of many items to instruction. As Gaussen (1984) suggests,

> the milestones of development which are so much a part of the common currency of clinical practice, and indeed of parenthood, are at risk of becoming conceptual millstones hung round the necks of parents, professionals, and infants alike. As such they serve to restrict the process of assessment and remediation by focusing on aspects of developmental change which are more fixed and less open to intervention. (p.103)

The alternative to the developmental milestones approach is to select items because they are meaningful or important. One basis for the determination of importance is whether the item describes a key behavior representative of a particular **stage of development**. The most well-known version of this approach is Piaget's theory, which postulates a sequence of universal stages of cognitive development. Skills such as imitation, object permanence, means-end behavior, and understanding of causality are assumed to be important indicators of the child's stage of development and, thus, constitute the basis for developing the content of some tests or subtests. A second basis for determining importance is whether the item represents a skill that is necessary for success in daily functioning, either now or in the future. Often referred to as a **functional approach**, this perspective assumes that the major purpose of assessment is to determine the child's proficiency in critical functional skills in order to determine important instructional targets.

The three conceptual approaches to assessment just described are not necessarily mutually exclusive. An object permanence item may be a readily identifiable developmental milestone that is a key skill in Piagetian theory and also an important functional behavior. In reality, many tests combine each approach by incorporating items characteristic of each.

The lack of a common conceptual base and existing limitations of our understanding of the development of infants and preschoolers has resulted in the development of assessment tools that vary, sometimes dramatically, in item content. Examples of such variability are displayed in Table 1.1, in which social development items from two commonly used assessment tools are presented. Although some items are similar, each instrument has conceptualized development in a different fashion and has incorporated different indicators as test items. This variability in content ultimately might not matter if only test scores were used. Two different items might very easily have the same power to differentiate children of different ages or abilities. But are they equally important instructional targets? Furthermore, the items as presented do not necessarily represent logical teaching sequences, inasmuch as items were selected based solely on statistical criteria (Fewell, 1983; Garwood, 1982). Because many early intervention professionals use missed items as a basis for identifying intervention targets, these questions are of critical importance. Guidelines for evaluating test content and for identifying

TABLE 1.1
A Comparison of the First Nine Social Items Beginning at the 24-Month Level of Two Assessment Tools

Hawaii Early Learning Profile	*Early Intervention Developmental Profile*
1. Distinguishes self as a separate person; contrasts self with others	1. Independently chooses toy and begins to play
2. Displays shyness with strangers and in outside situations	2. Pretends to be engaged in familiar activities (being asleep, telephoning)
3. Holds parent's hand outdoors	3. Prefers to play near, but not with, other children
4. Feels strongly possessive of loved ones	4. Discriminates between boys and girls
5. Displays dependent behavior, clings and whines	5. Identifies self in mirror
6. Enjoys a wide range of relationships, meets more people	6. Plays with other children
7. Says no, but submits anyway	7. Separates from familiar person in strange environment for 5 minutes
8. Tends to be physically aggressive	8. Identifies own sex
9. Enjoys experimenting with adult activities	9. Shares toy with adult prompts

skills of importance within each developmental domain are described in Chapters 8 through 17.

Measurement Barriers

A second type of barrier to effective child assessment is a lack of appropriate assessment instruments and procedures. Although many measures have been developed in the past 20 years, these measures often suffer a number of limitations. One is that most were developed for a specific purpose and thus their usefulness is limited to that purpose. Although this is not necessarily a limitation of the instrument, the lack of acceptable instruments occasionally results in practitioners using instruments for purposes for which they were not intended. For example, a screening measure might be used to label a child, or an intelligence test might be used to plan instructional programs. Such practices are inappropriate but continue to occur in part because of other limitations in existing measurement procedures. For example, the lack of an agreed-upon conceptual base for developing instrument content has meant that often measures are not educationally useful.

Also, many of the instruments used in early intervention programs have not undergone the rigorous evaluation procedures required of a good measurement tool. For example, any instrument should be able to produce a relatively consistent pattern of responses from a given child (test reliability) and be useful in regard to its purpose (test validity). Yet data regarding these two aspects of assessment procedures frequently are lacking. The importance of reliability and validity and guidelines for interpreting these data are described in Chapter 2. Also, many instruments allow the generation of developmental age scores when, in fact, the instrument itself was never standardized on a representative sample of children, thus raising significant questions about the believability of such scores. A discussion of "norm-referenced" scoring also is presented in Chapter 2.

A third measurement barrier is that many existing measures are weak in assessing certain critical skill areas. Although most comprehensive measures include traditional domains such as self-help, communication, or motor skills, several areas usually receive inadequate attention. These areas include the behavioral characteristics of children (e.g., attending and task-orientation skills, persistence, consolability, goal-directedness), skills related to social interactions with peers, and inappropriate behaviors such as aggression or rhythmic habit patterns. Yet these domains represent some of the most challenging and important outcomes of early intervention. A further barrier is that most measures fail to consider the specialized assessment needs of young children with handicaps. These needs are described briefly in the next section of this chapter and are elaborated in Chapter 3.

Brooks-Gunn and Lewis (1981) identified a number of other measurement barriers, among which are the use of single age-equivalent scores rather than score profiles, emphasis on only a few developmental domains, and the lack of attention to patterns of interaction among developmental domains. They described a battery of 13 measures used in their Competency Assessment Project and presented clinical case studies describing how profiles were used to examine multiple strengths and weaknesses and to determine interactions among domains.

Child Barriers

Effective child assessment also is hampered by certain characteristics of infants and preschoolers with handicaps. Some of these characteristics are associated with age. Infants and young children are likely to be distractible and inconsistent in their behavioral performance. Limited or nonexistent verbal abilities mean that the teacher or examiner often must make inferences about whether a child has a certain concept or cognitive skill on the basis of overt motor behaviors. Also, young children are likely to be wary of unfamiliar adults, often necessitating a period of warm-up activities or requiring the presence of a parent to ensure familiarity. Finally, neonates and premature infants pose unique issues about both the content of assessment and the procedures by which assessments are conducted. Issues and considerations in assessing young children are described in Chapter 3, and conducting neonatal assessments is discussed in Chapter 8 of this text.

In addition to the limitations imposed by age, handicapping conditions pose further barriers to effective assessment, especially for children with sensory or motor impairments. Visually impaired or hearing-impaired children may learn basic skills through different modalities and thus may require adaptations to the assessment process. Children with motor impairments and limited verbal skills may not give a true indication of their abilities because many items for young children rely on motoric indicators. DuBose (1981) described the unique problems associated with the assessment of severely impaired young children. Strategies for assessing children with sensory or motor impairments are discussed in Chapter 3.

Dunst and Rheingrover (1981) reviewed the literature on stability and continuity in early development and concluded that early development (defined as individual change in behavior over time) is generally discontinuous and unstable. This conclusion is consistent with that offered by others (e.g., McCall, 1979) and poses important issues for infant and preschool assessment. They offer several implications of this finding for assessment of young handicapped children: (a) Do not expect the same types of intellectual skills to be displayed at all ages; (b) be sure to use items that go together or assess similar types of skills across different ages; (c) examine pat-

terns of performance as opposed to individual item performance; (d) do not expect the same level of competence within different skill domains; and (e) do not characterize overall performance on the basis of a single scale of development.

Furthermore, it has been argued that many young children with handicaps display developmental sequences that differ considerably from those observed in nonhandicapped children. While the development of some skills, such as smiling in infants with Down syndrome (Cicchetti & Sroufe, 1976), may follow a normal developmental progression but at a delayed rate, other skills and other children may not be typical. Keogh and Sheehan (1981) suggest that the "nonsequential development of atypical children might be overlooked or disregarded by adhering strictly to normal developmental comparisons" (p. 43). Deviations in developmental sequence are especially likely in children with sensory or physical impairments.

Another consideration in assessing young handicapped children is the fact that many of these children may be on medication. Although all children have the usual range of childhood medications, including occasional antibiotics, handicapped children are more likely to be on drugs used to control seizures or behavior. Simeonsson and Simeonsson (1981) reviewed these medications and concluded that side effects (e.g., drowsiness) from their use may influence performance in assessment situations. Teachers and other professionals working with young handicapped children should be aware of any medications taken by children and observe for potential side effects. If a child's performance during assessment is suspected to be influenced negatively by medication, scores obtained under such conditions should not be used, and the child should be retested at a later time.

Thus, characteristics of the children themselves make assessment a difficult process. These characteristics and guidelines for accommodating them are further described in Chapter 3.

Staff Barriers

A fourth barrier to effective child assessment is the limited assessment skills of many early interventionists, early childhood special educators, and other personnel working with handicapped youngsters. These limitations fall in several categories. First, many early childhood special educators have had extensive training in teaching young handicapped children and informal assessment of skills, but have less training in conducting more formal testing. An example of this problem was reported by Bailey, Vandiviere, Dellinger, and Munn (1987), who found that teachers of young handicapped children made many errors in scoring a standardized assessment tool. Second, although related services personnel, such as speech-language pathologists, physical therapists, or occupational therapists, usually have received training in formal assessment procedures, often their expertise with very young children is limited. Consequently, they may not have the clinical skills to determine the precise abilities and limitations of infants and preschoolers. Third, almost all professionals receive a rather narrow focus in their professional training program. Few have the training or experience to work collaboratively with other professionals to conduct truly interdisciplinary assessments that focus on the whole child.

Institutional Barriers

Finally, institutional barriers limit effective child assessment. For example, many programs have limited resources for purchasing assessment tools. If staff members are not located near a regional resource center with a library of assessment tools for review, they may have to resort to using whatever instruments their program owns. Also, some program administrators may themselves have

limited assessment skills and thus not be able to provide the supervision and training necessary to ensure quality and accurate assessments. Finally, the time constraints and pressures of providing direct services to children often require programs to place less emphasis on the assessment process and thus do not allow sufficient time for assessments to be conducted in a thorough fashion.

Characteristics of Effective Child Assessment

Despite the barriers that exist, assessment of infants and preschoolers with handicaps is a critical component of any early intervention program. This section describes characteristics of an effective model of assessment as evidenced in current statements regarding best practice. Of paramount importance is that the assessment instruments and procedures selected must match the purpose of the assessment, for different purposes warrant different procedures. Guidelines for making such decisions are presented throughout this text. In addition, an effective assessment component (a) covers important developmental and behavioral domains, (b) involves parents as significant partners in the assessment process, (c) incorporates multiple sources and multiple measures, (d) involves multiple disciplines in an interdisciplinary fashion, (e) is ecologically valid, (f) is nondiscriminatory, and (g) evaluates child progress on a regular basis.

Important Developmental Domains

The first characteristic of an effective child assessment program is that it is comprehensive, covering all important domains of development and behavior. This coverage is important both for seeing the whole child as well as for identifying the broad range of child strengths and needs. If important domains are not included, intervention efforts may be only partially successful.

Most professionals would agree that there are five or six developmental domains that should be assessed with any handicapped infant or preschooler. **Cognitive skills** are those related to children's mental development and include basic sensorimotor skills, such as object permanence, causality, means-end behavior, spatial relationships, and imitation, as well as pre-academic skills, including concept development, prereading skills, and premath skills. Strategies and considerations for assessing infant cognitive skills are discussed in Chapter 11, while assessment of preschool cognitive skills is addressed in Chapter 12.

Motor skills are those related to the development and use of muscles or limbs. The two broad areas of motor assessment are gross motor skills, which require movement of large muscles (e.g., walking, throwing, crawling, climbing), and fine motor skills, which require use of small muscles (e.g., grasping, writing, cutting, stacking). Motor skills assessment may also focus on reflexes, reactions, muscle tone, positioning, and use of adaptive equipment. Often these areas are assessed by a physical or occupational therapist. Guidelines and considerations for assessing motor skills are discussed in Chapter 13.

Communication skills are those skills related to exchanging information or feelings. The two broad areas of communication assessment are receptive communication and expressive communication. Communication assessment focuses heavily on the social aspects of communicating. Communication assessment may also focus on the mode of communication and may include gestural communication, speech development, and the need for augmentative communication strategies. Often communication skills are assessed by a speech-language pathologist. Guidelines and considerations for assessing communication skills are found in Chapter 14.

Play and social skills are those skills related to toy use or social interactions with peers. Play skills assessment often involves a combination of cognitive, motor, and communication assessment. Guidelines and considerations for assessing play and social skills are discussed in Chapters 15 and 16.

Self-care skills are those skills related to independent daily functioning and include toileting, feeding, dressing, tooth-brushing, and other similar tasks. These skills often are assessed by special educators, but other professionals, such as occupational therapists, therapeutic recreation specialists, or psychologists, may be involved in one aspect or more of the assessment process. Guidelines and considerations for assessing self-care skills are discussed in Chapter 17.

The assessment domains just described correspond with the domains specified by the components of P.L. 99-457 pertaining to services for handicapped infants. The regulations stipulate that the IFSP must include a statement of the infant's or toddler's present levels of physical development, cognitive development, language and speech development, psychosocial development, and self-help skills.

Skills in each of the domains described could be assessed by using individual tests for each domain or by selecting an instrument that addressed multiple domains. Examples of single-domain measures are described throughout this text and are often used by specialists in related services. Examples of multiple-domain measures often used by early interventionists and early childhood special educators to plan early intervention and preschool programs are displayed in Table 1.2. This table includes a list of the subdomains included in each instrument and the age range addressed.

Most early intervention and early childhood special education programs incorporate each of the aforementioned developmental domains in the assessment process. Other

TABLE 1.2

Some Multiple-Domain Measures Frequently Used in Early Childhood Special Education

Instrument	Domains	Age range (years)
Battelle Developmental Inventory (Newborg, Stock, Wnek, Guidubaldi, & Svinicki, 1984)	Personal-social, adaptive, motor, communication, cognitive	0–8
Brigance Diagnostic Inventory of Early Development (Brigance, 1978)	Psychomotor, self-help, speech and language, general knowledge and comprehension, early academics	0–6
Callier-Azusa Scale (Stillman, 1978)	Motor, perceptual, daily living, cognition/communication/language, social	0–6
Carolina Curriculum for Handicapped and At-Risk Infants (Johnson, Jens, & Attermeier, 1986)	Tactile integration, auditory localization and object permanence, visual pursuit and object permanence, object permanence, reaching and grasping, hand watching, space localization, functional use of objects, control over physical environment, gestural communication, gestural imitation and imitative play, feeding, vocal imitation, vocal communication, responses to communication from others, social skills, gross motor–prone, gross motor–supine, gross motor–upright	0–2
Early Intervention Developmental Profile (Rogers et al., 1981)	Perceptual/fine motor, cognition, language, social/emotional, self-care, gross motor	0–3

domains, however, are likely to be important but may not be included because of the lack of appropriate measures. For example, certain behavioral characteristics of children clearly influence children's functioning and affect both family and program responses to children. Behaviors such as consolability, endurance, goal-directedness, and task-orientation are important skills likely to be emphasized in early intervention programs. Also, inappropriate behaviors such as aggression or rhythmic habit patterns should be assessed and the effects of intervention on those domains documented. Issues and guidelines for assessing state, temperament, and behavioral characteristics of young children are described in Chapters 9 and 10 of this text. Interventionists may also need to assess

factors that are likely to influence the effectiveness of services or that may need to be adjusted for in-service delivery. Among these include environmental assessments (Chapter 5) and assessment of sensory functioning (Chapter 7).

Finally, a critical area for assessment is that of family needs and strengths. Historically, early intervention has been a child-focused endeavor. Increasingly, however, the importance of family needs, both as they relate to the handicapped child and as they have an impact on the family itself, are being recognized as legitimate domains for assessment and targets for intervention services. In fact, the infancy component of P.L. 99-457 specifies that the IFSP should include a statement of family strengths and needs, thus necessitat-

TABLE 1.2
Continued

Instrument	Domains	Age range (years)
Early Learning Accomplish-ment Profile (Glover, Preminger, & Sanford, 1978)	Gross motor, fine motor, cognitive, language, self-help, social, emotional	0–3
Hawaii Early Learning Profile (Furuno et al., 1979)	Cognitive, language, gross motor, fine motor, social, self-help	0–3
HICOMP Preschool Curricu-lum (Willoughby-Herb & Neisworth, 1983)	Communication, self-care, motor skills, problem solving	0–5
Learning Accomplishment Profile (Sanford & Zelman, 1981)	Gross motor, fine motor, cognitive, language, self-help	0–6
Preschool Developmental Profile (Brown et al., 1981)	Perceptual/fine motor, cognitive, speech and language, social/emotional, self-care, gross motor	3–6
Portage Project Checklist (Bluma et al., 1976)	Infant stimulation, socialization, language, self-help, cognitive, motor	0–6
Uniform Performance Assessment System (White et al., 1981)	Preacademic, communication, social/self-help, gross motor	0–6
Vulpé Assessment Battery (Vulpé, 1977)	Basic senses and functions, gross motor, fine motor, language, cognitive, organizational behaviors, activities of daily living, assess-ment of environment	0–5

ing a family component in the assessment process. Although we recognize the importance of this family focus, this text focuses on issues and procedures related to child assessment. The reader is referred to Bailey and Simeonsson (1988) for a review of considerations and procedures in family assessment in early intervention.

Parent Involvement in Child Assessment

The role of parents in child assessment often is limited to that of recipient of information gathered by professionals. Public Law 94-142 specifies that parents must give permission for assessment procedures to be conducted, must be informed of the results of such assessments, are to participate on the inter-disciplinary team in which assessment information is used to plan instructional objectives and program placement, have the right to appeal any decision they disagree with, and have the right to inspect their child's records at any time. The legislation does not mandate a full-er involvement of families in the assessment process. Such involvement, however, may be useful from both a parental and professional perspective.

Parents often feel that professionals do not respect or desire information about their child from their perspective. This situation creates problems when parents feel that they must relinquish a great deal of control to professionals, creating resentment and reducing subsequent participation in the interdisciplinary team process. By involving parents in the assessment process from the beginning, professionals can instill a sense of both trust and competence in families, and may increase parent/professional collaboration.

Also, involving parents in the assessment process is likely to provide important information for professionals. Parents can describe children's behavior at home or in situations such as shopping trips or the church nursery that professionals are not likely to observe. The consistency of a child's performance with parents and with professionals is of potential importance in determining whether skill generalization is a problem for a particular child. Parental involvement in assessment also can provide important information regarding parent priorities for intervention services. For example, the professional may decide that an infant who appears unpredictable is posing a tremendous problem to the mother and may determine that strategies to improve infant rhythmicity and participation in routines are of utmost importance. This goal, however, may not necessarily be of importance to the parent.

Evidence in support of family involvement in the entire assessment process was reported in a study by Brinckerhoff and Vincent (1986). Prior to the IEP meeting, parents of handicapped children ages 3 and 4 completed a family profile, a description of their typical home routine, and a developmental inventory describing their child's performance on typical developmental milestones. Parents also met with a professional who discussed the IEP process with them and how the assessment information they provided might fit into the IEP. When compared with parents who did not participate in this fashion, experimental families made more contributions to the team meeting and made more decisions. More goals were parent-generated; more decisions were characterized as "joint" decisions in the experimental group; and more home-programming suggestions evolved in the experimental group meetings.

Another procedure for increasing the potential for parental involvement is to organize the meeting according to skill areas and discuss first areas of high importance to families, such as self-help or motor skills. In each area, the parents are asked to describe how they perceive their child's skills and needs in the area being considered, such as toileting or feeding. An open-ended question, such as "Could you tell us about how Dani eats at home now?" is used to initiate the discussion. If necessary, professionals can prompt parents for additional or more precise information through use of specific closed-ended questions, such as "Does she pick up a spoon on her own?" Once parents have provided detailed information about the skill being discussed, professionals supplement that information from their own assessments. Any discrepancies in perception of ability are discussed, and then parents are asked to identify priorities for intervention within that skill domain. Professionals attend to and reinforce those priorities whenever possible by establishing goals related to each. If additional goals are deemed important by professionals, they are then mentioned and discussed. This process sends a clear message to parents that they are important members of the decision-making team and that their perspectives and priorities for their children are valued by professionals seeking to provide the most appropriate early intervention services possible.

Use of Multiple Sources and Multiple Measures

The use of multiple sources and multiple measures is important for both legal and practical reasons. Public Law 94-142 specifies that decisions regarding the labeling and placement of handicapped children cannot be made on the basis of a single test or score. From a broader professional perspective, it is increasingly argued that a comprehensive assessment procedure with young handicapped children must ascertain children's performance using multiple sources and multiple measures (Mott, Fewell, Lewis, Meisels, Shonkoff, & Simeonsson, 1986; Neisworth & Bagnato, 1986). These multiple sources include standardized testing conditions, observation in naturalistic situations, and determination of the perceptions of other significant persons.

Direct Testing. **Direct testing** is used when the professional wants to know how an infant or preschooler responds to a standardized stimulus, a request, or a specific set of materials. Direct testing is essential in determining a specific score for a child and in comparing a child's performance with that of other children. Direct testing is often used to assess children's cognitive, motor, and receptive communication skills.

Direct testing using standardized procedures and materials has been criticized as providing a restricted picture of a child's abilities under artificial conditions. Also, because most tests do not allow the examiner to vary item presentation, test the limits of performance, or provide reinforcement or assistance, they have been criticized as being unfair for handicapped children, particularly those with sensory or motor impairments. However, when used appropriately and when all parties involved recognize their limitations, direct tests can be very useful. Not only do they provide a means for evaluating a child's developmental status, but they also can be used to evaluate child progress in a standardized fashion and to evaluate the effectiveness of broad intervention efforts. Examples of standardized tests within each of the major developmental domains and guidelines for determining the conditions under which they should be used are described throughout this text.

Naturalistic Observation. A second major method of gathering information about children's abilities is referred to as **naturalistic observation** or **direct observation.** In general,

naturalistic observation requires the professional or parent to observe the infant or preschool child in natural situations and to record various aspects of the child's behavior. For example, one could observe expressive communication, play and social behaviors, gross motor skills, attending and task persistence, or self-help skills such as toileting, feeding, or dressing.

Direct observation is a critical component of any assessment procedure because it provides information about the way children actually use or do not use certain skills. For example, a child may know how to greet another person or respond to initiations but may not do so in the preschool play group. Because one of the ultimate goals of early intervention is to help children acquire skills that will be useful to them, assessment procedures must be incorporated that reflect the extent to which skills are used in real world situations. Also, some skills, such as play skills, can only be assessed meaningfully in the context of other peers and in typical play environments.

Fewell and Rich (1987) argued that traditional testing procedures often tend to divide skills artificially into domains such as language or motor skills, when in fact these skills almost always are used in combination with each other. They suggested that by using play-assessment procedures, the professional can obtain information about cognitive, communication, and social skills in multihandicapped children and more adequately determine the extent to which those skills are integrated. In a study of 17 deaf/blind preschool children, the authors found high correlations between play observational data and multiple measures of cognition, language, and social behavior. They suggested that not only is such an approach to assessment more efficient, inasmuch as it assimilates data about multiple skill domains, but also it may (a) result in increased cooperation by the child, (b) be easier to administer, and (c) provide a context for observing the child's preferred learning strategies. A more detailed description of play-assessment procedures is provided in Chapter 15, and guidelines and procedures for conducting direct observation and other informal assessment procedures are described in Chapter 4.

Parental Interviews and Assessments by Parents.   A third mode of gathering information is by asking parents. This information can be gathered in at least two ways: by **interviewing** parents or by asking parents to complete standardized measures, rating scales, or checklists.

Interviews are particularly useful when professionals are interested in family perceptions of children's abilities, events such as transitions or medical procedures, and priorities for services. The rationale for interviewing as well as guidelines and a framework for conducting family interviews are described by Winton (1988) and Winton and Bailey (in press). Interviews may be structured or open-ended, and are best used in conjunction with other, more formalized assessment procedures. Their flexibility allows the professional to explore areas of concern as they arise (Odom & Shuster, 1986), and face-to-face discussions using effective communication skills convey a message to parents that their opinions are valued and respected.

Parent participation in the assessment process by completing standardized measures, rating scales, or checklists has been a topic of considerable discussion in the professional literature. In particular, numerous publications have addressed the extent to which parents and professionals agree on ratings of children's abilities. The current status of that research can best be described as contradictory (Sexton, Miller, & Rotatori, 1985). Although studies generally report a high correlation between parent and professional ratings (e.g., Blacher-Dixon & Simeonsson, 1981; Sonnander, 1987), when the actual scores are compared, the results are less clear.

Some studies have concluded that parents generally rate their children's abilities higher than professionals rate them (e.g., Gradel, Thompson, & Sheehan, 1981; Sexton, Hall, & Thomas, 1983), some have reported differences in agreement levels but no consistent directional effects (e.g., Handen, Feldman, & Honigman, 1987), and some have reported no differences at all (e.g., Sexton, Kelley, & Scott, 1982). Sexton, Miller, and Rotatori (1985) suggested that this variability in research findings may be accounted for, in part, by demographic variables and presented data suggesting that agreement is influenced by maternal age and family income. Handen et al. (1987) also found that agreement varied according to the skill area assessed, with greatest agreement in the areas of eating skills and specific behavior problems and lowest agreement in speech and language. Gradel et al. (1981) found greater parent/professional agreement with preschool-aged handicapped children than with infants.

Variables associated with parent/professional agreement will continue to be explored in the professional literature. An important issue, however, is whether parent/professional agreement is always an outcome to be desired. It is quite likely that parents and professionals hold different perspectives on behavior, have different criteria for determining competence, and view children in different contexts. Disagreement on test items may reflect limitations of the assessment tool more than limitations of parents in rating their children's abilities. Gradel et al. (1981) suggest the possibility that instead of interpreting score differences as "parental overestimations," an equally plausible conclusion is "professional underestimation" of children's abilities, due in part to a narrow professional focus, limited time, and a possible orientation to deficits rather than strengths. Handen et al. (1987) conclude that "the judgments of neither parents nor teachers can be relied upon with complete confidence. Practitioners, whose need is for accurate, complete information, should routinely obtain multiple assessments of children's level of functioning" (p. 143). Because of the importance of involving families in the decision-making process and the need for descriptions of children's skills in a variety of situations, parent completion of standardized instruments probably should be viewed as a valid and important component of a broader assessment component in early intervention.

Interdisciplinary Assessments

Federal legislation requires that assessments for handicapped infants, toddlers, and pre-schoolers be conducted by a multidisciplinary team and that the team, as a group and in co-operation with the parents, must be responsible for developing the IEP or the IFSP. Several reasons have been offered in support of assessments by multiple disciplines. Given the complex needs of young children with handicaps, particularly those with severe or multiple impairments, it is unlikely that any one individual possesses all of the clinical skills necessary to develop an appropriate plan for all children. It has been suggested that the interdisciplinary process should reduce erroneous placement decisions (Pfeiffer, 1982), should help ensure that assessments are non-discriminatory (Bailey & Harbin, 1980), and should result ultimately in more appropriate goals and more effective interventions for handicapped youngsters (Allen, Holm, & Schiefelbusch, 1978). Support for the use of teams has been provided by Hochstadt and Harwicke (1985), who found that services recommended by a multidisciplinary team for victims of child abuse and neglect were more likely to be obtained than for those cases in which a multidisciplinary evaluation did not occur.

In reality, teams differ along a number of dimensions. One source of variability is team membership. Professionals most typically included on early intervention teams include special educators, speech-language pathol-

ogists, occupational therapists, and physical therapists. Depending upon the setting, local resources, and individual child and family needs, other team members may include psychologists, social workers, nurses, nutritionists, audiologists, physicians, or regular early childhood educators. A second source of variability is the way in which teams are organized and operate. Traditionally the literature has classified teams of multiple professionals as multidisciplinary, interdisciplinary, or transdisciplinary teams (Fordyce, 1981). The **mutidisciplinary team** contains members from multiple disciplines, but each remains relatively independent and is affected very little by the actions of other team members. The **interdisciplinary team** involves greater interactions among team members, with each member relying on the others for important information and suggestions. The final product is an integrated plan of services that involves significant cooperation between disciplines. The **transdisciplinary team** is one in which multiple disciplines work together in the initial assessment, but the provision of services is conducted by one or two team members. Professionals from each of the disciplines relinquish their roles to the direct service providers and train them in how to perform those responsibilities (Lyon & Lyon, 1980). Generally, professionals agree that the interdisciplinary team is superior to the multidisciplinary team. However, arguments about the relative advantages and disadvantages of the transdisciplinary team persist.

The research on the interdisciplinary team process suggests that true interdisciplinary collaboration, while a desirable goal, is difficult to achieve (Bailey, 1984). Effective interdisciplinary assessment is characterized by (a) active individual participation (Bailey, Helsel-DeWert, Thiele, & Ware, 1983), (b) effective leadership (Orlando, 1981), (c) equality of membership and respect for the contributions of others (Bailey, Thiele, Ware, Helsel-DeWert, 1985), (d) organization and a common understanding of purpose, and (e) group and individual commitment to quality programming as opposed to discipline territoriality.

Although interdisciplinary collaboration has focused primarily on the interdisciplinary team meeting, collaborative efforts can and should occur during the actual data-collection phase prior to the meeting. One strategy is for the team to adopt an assessment tool that addresses multiple domains and then to have each team member be responsible for conducting the assessments in one or more domains. For example, the Battelle Developmental Inventory consists of five domains: cognitive, personal-social, communication, adaptive, and motor. One possible assessment strategy would be for the psychologist to conduct the cognitive assessments, the special educator to assess personal-social skills, the speech-language pathologist to assess communication skills, the occupational therapist to assess adaptive skills, and the physical therapist to assess motor skills. By using components of the same assessment tool, a common assessment protocol and scoring format are developed, facilitating cross-disciplinary communication.

Wolery and Dyk (1984) describe the **arena assessment** approach as one strategy for enhancing collaborative assessment:

> A temporary facilitator, generally the team member with the most expertise in the child's area of need, is assigned prior to the actual assessment activities. The facilitator serves as the primary assessor while other team members and parents sit away from the child and record observations and score portions of assessment tools relevant to their discipline. As the assessment progresses, team members may ask the facilitator to administer certain items relevant to the observer's discipline. Occasionally, an observer may assist the assessor or administer the items directly. Parents are present during the assessment to provide information, administer items if necessary, and validate the child's performance. (pp. 231–232)

In a study comparing the arena assessment procedure with a more typical interdisciplinary assessment of handicapped infants and preschoolers, the authors found that parents greatly preferred the arena procedure, rating it as more effective and providing a more accurate picture of their child's abilities. Professionals participating in the assessments also indicated a preference for the arena model, rating it as more effective in child assessment and as resulting in more positive interactions between team members and greater team consensus on issues.

Ecologically Valid Assessments

What does it mean to say that the assessment of infants and preschoolers with handicaps must be an **ecologically valid assessment**? Bronfenbrenner (1977) characterized contemporary developmental psychology as "the science of the strange behavior of children in strange situations with strange adults for the briefest possible periods of time" (p. 513). He went on to argue that

> the understanding of human development demands going beyond the direct observation of behavior on the part of one or two persons in the same place; it requires examination of multiperson systems of interaction not limited to a single setting and must take into account aspects of the environment beyond the immediate situation containing the subject. (p. 514)

He described such a focus as an **ecological approach** and argued for an increased ecological focus in the study of child development. Similar arguments pertain to the clinical assessment of young children with handicaps. To the extent that such assessments are conducted by strangers, using irrelevant tasks and in isolated settings, they will be limited in their usefulness.

An ecologically valid assessment would incorporate several components. First, as described earlier, assessments should include parents as significant partners in the assessment process. This ensures that the home ecology is considered when identifying skills of importance for intervention purposes. Second, assessments should focus heavily on naturalistic observation of children's behaviors in the context of normally occurring routines, such as when eating, playing with peers, or performing other regular activities, to ensure that professionals are aware of the extent to which children actually use skills. Included in these observations should be an analysis of how skills are integrated for functional purposes. Third, assessments should be nondiscriminatory. Professionals must take a child's cultural background, economic status, and family value systems into consideration when conducting assessments. This is important to ensure that test performance is not unfairly biased because of culture-specific items. It also is important to prevent professionals from identifying instructional targets that either are not important to individual families or that directly conflict with family values. Finally, ecologically valid assessment plans for the next most probable placement when conducting assessments (Vincent, Salisbury, Walter, Brown, Gruenewald, & Powers, 1980). In the infant-toddler component of P.L. 99-457, a transition plan for movement to the next program placement is mandated in the IFSP. Others have described a comprehensive rationale and provided guidelines for planning transitions, and these suggestions are described in Chapter 5. The point to be made in this chapter is that assessment procedures must take into consideration the skills that will be required of a child in a future environment, assess the extent to which the child currently demonstrates those skills, and incorporate instruc-

tion relevant to their attainment in the context of early intervention programs.

Nondiscriminatory Assessments

Bias can occur in the assessment process if a child's performance on a test is unfairly influenced by race, sex, cultural background, or religious affiliation. Bailey and Harbin (1980) summarized the criticisms that have been directed toward the use of standardized tests with minority children:

> In has been variously claimed that most standardized tests (a) are highly loaded with items based on White, middle-class values and experiences; (b) penalize children with linguistic styles differing from that of the dominant culture; (c) sample cognitive styles directly opposed to those found in many children from low income families or culturally diverse groups; (d) are often administered in an atmosphere that may penalize culturally diverse children (e.g., White examiner, group administration); and (e) are scored based on norms derived from predominantly White middle-class standardization groups. (p. 590)

Biased assessment may result in a child being labeled as disabled, handicapped, or retarded when in fact the test itself contributed to the low score received.

Unfortunately, it is not likely that a truly unbiased test ever will be developed. Thus, early childhood specialists involved in the assessment process will need to take care to ensure that asssessments are as fair as possible. In order to accomplish this goal, the following strategies are recommended:

1. Use multiple measures and gather data in naturalistic contexts to ensure that the best picture of the child has been obtained.
2. Use a multidisciplinary team approach to evaluation.

3. Involve parents as significant partners in the assessment process and focus intervention goals and objectives on those areas viewed as particularly important to parents.
4. Focus on skills rather than labeling a child.
5. Provide services in mainstreamed environments in order to avoid the additional stigmatization of self-contained programs.
6. Examine test items to ensure that they are not biased against children of a certain sex or cultural background.
7. Examine test manuals to determine if evidence is presented supporting the fair use of the test with minority children and both boys and girls.

Evaluating Progress on a Regular Basis

A final characteristic of effective assessment in early intervention is that it is conducted on a regular basis. Assessment information is needed for initial program planning but also is essential for documenting child progress, determining whether intervention efforts are effective, and making decisions about changing the amount or type of intervention. Fuchs and Fuchs (1986) conducted a meta-analysis of research on monitoring behavior and found that when teachers frequently assessed child progress and examined the data for the purpose of instructional decision making, children made greater achievement gains.

SUMMARY OF KEY CONCEPTS

- Assessment of young children with handicapping conditions is an important and necessary activity. The information gained from systematic assessment procedures is necessary for identifying children who need early intervention services, for planning appropriate intervention programs for those children, and for evaluating the effectiveness of services.

- Although assessment is an important process, it is a complex one made difficult by current limitations in theoretical concepts of development, measurement instruments, and professional skills.

- When designing assessment procedures, early intervention professionals should take care to ensure that assessments are comprehensive, involve parents, use multiple sources and multiple measures, involve multiple disciplines, and are ecologically valid.

- Assessment information should be gathered periodically and used to make program decisions.

REFERENCES

Allen, K.E., Holm, V.A., & Schiefelbusch, R.C. (1978). *Early intervention—A team approach.* Baltimore, MD: University Park Press.

Bailey, D.B. (1984). A triaxial model of the interdisciplinary team and group process. *Exceptional Children, 51,* 17–25.

Bailey, D.B. & Harbin, G.L. (1980). Nondiscriminatory evaluation. *Exceptional Children, 46,* 590–596.

Bailey, D.B., Helsel-DeWert, M., Thiele, J.E., & Ware, W.B. (1983). Measuring individual participation on the interdisciplinary team. *American Journal of Mental Deficiency, 88,* 247–254.

Bailey, D.B. & Simeonsson, D.B. (1988). *Family assessment in early intervention.* Columbus, OH: Merrill.

Bailey, D.B., Thiele, J., Ware, W.B., & Helsel-DeWert, M.J. (1985). Participation of professionals, paraprofessionals, and direct care staff in the interdisciplinary team meeting. *American Journal of Mental Deficiency, 89,* 437–440.

Bailey, D.B., Vandiviere, P., Dellinger, J., & Munn, D. (1987). The Battelle Developmental Inventory: Teacher perceptions and implementation data. *Journal of Psychoeducational Assessment, 3,* 217–226.

Bailey, D.B. & Wolery, M. (1984). *Teaching infants and preschoolers with handicaps.* Columbus, OH: Merrill.

Blacher-Dixon, J. & Simeonsson, R.J. (1981). Consistency and correspondence of mothers' and teachers' assessments of young handicapped children. *Journal of the Division for Early Childhood, 3,* 64–71.

Bluma, A., Shearer, M., Frohman, A., & Hilliard, J. (1976). *Portage guide to early education.* Portage, WI: The Portage Project, CESA 12.

Brigance, A.H. (1978). *Brigance Diagnostic Inventory of Early Development.* Woburn, MA: Curriculum Associates.

Brinckerhoff, J.L. & Vincent, L.J. (1986). Increasing parental decision making at the individualized educational program meeting. *Journal of the Division for Early Childhood, 11,* 46–58.

Bronfenbrenner, U. (1977). Toward an experimental ecology of human development. *American Psychologist,* 513–531.

Brooks-Gunn, J. & Lewis, M. (1981). Assessing young handicapped children: Issues and solutions. *Journal of the Division for Early Childhood, 2,* 84–95.

Brown, S.L., D'Eugenio, D.B., Drews, J.E., Haskin, B.S., Lynch, E.W., Moersch, M.S., & Rogers, S.J. (1981). *Preschool Developmental Profile.* Ann Arbor: University of Michigan Press.

Cicchetti, D. & Sroufe, A. (1976). The relationship between affective and cognitive development in Down's syndrome infants. *Child Development, 46,* 920–929.

DuBose, R.F. (1981). Assessment of severely impaired young children: Problems and recommendations. *Topics in Early Childhood Special Education, 1*(2), 9–22.

Dunst, C.J. & Rheingrover, R.M. (1981). Discontinuity and stability in early development: Implications for assessment. *Topics in Early Childhood Special Education, 1*(2), 49–60.

Egan, D.F. & Brown, R. (1986). Developmental assessment: 18 months to $4\frac{1}{2}$ years. Performance tests. *Child: Care, Health and Development, 12,* 339–349.

Fewell, R.R. (1983). Assessing handicapped infants. In S.G. Garwood & R.R. Fewell (Eds.), *Educating handicapped infants* (pp. 257–298). Rockville, MD: Aspen.

Fewell, R.R. & Rich, J.S. (1987). Play assessment as a procedure for examining cognitive, communication, and social skills in multihandicapped children. *Journal of Psychoeducational Assessment, 2,* 107–118.

Fordyce, W. (1981). On interdisciplinary peers. *Archives of Physical Medicine, 62*(2), 51–53.

Fuchs, L.S. & Fuchs, D. (1986). Effects of systematic formative evaluation: A meta-analysis. *Exceptional Children, 53,* 199–208.

Furuno, S., O'Reilly, K.A., Hosaka, C.M., Inatsuka, T.T., Allman, T.L., & Zeisloft, B. (1979). *The Hawaii Early Learning Profile.* Palo Alto, CA: VORT.

Garwood, S.G. (1982). (Mis)use of developmental scales in program evaluation. *Topics in Early Childhood Special Education, 1*(4), 61–69.

Gaussen, T. (1984). Developmental milestones or conceptual millstones? Some practical and theoretical limitations in infant assessment procedures. *Child: Care, Health and Development, 10,* 99–115.

Glover, M.E., Preminger, J.L., & Sanford, A.R. (1978). *Early Learning Accomplishment Profile.* Winston-Salem, NC: Kaplan School Supply.

Gradel, K., Thompson, M.S., & Sheehan, R. (1981). Parental and professional agreement in early childhood assessment. *Topics in Early Childhood Special Education, 1*(2), 31–40.

Handen, B.L., Feldman, R.S., & Honigman, A. (1987). Comparison of parent and teacher assessments of developmentally delayed children's behavior. *Exceptional Children, 54,* 137–144.

Hochstadt, N.J. & Harwicke, N.J. (1985). How effective is the multidisciplinary approach? A follow-up study. *Child Abuse and Neglect, 9,* 365–372.

Johnson, N.M., Jens, K.G., & Attermeier, S.A. (1986). *Carolina Curriculum for Handicapped and At-risk Infants.* Baltimore, MD: Paul H. Brookes.

Keogh, B.K. & Sheehan, R. (1981). The use of developmental test data for documenting handicapped children's progress: Problems and recommendations. *Journal of the Division for Early Childhood, 3,* 42–47.

Kopp, C.B. (1982). The role of theoretical frameworks in the study of at-risk and handicapped young children. In D.D. Bricker (Ed.), *Intervention with at-risk and handicapped infants: From research to application* (pp. 13–30). Baltimore, MD: University Park Press.

Lyon, S. & Lyon, G. (1980). Team functioning and staff development: A role release approach to providing integrated educational services for severely handicapped students. *Journal of the Association for the Severely Handicapped, 5*(3), 250–263.

McCall, R. (1979). The development of intellectual functioning in infancy and the prediction of later IQ. In J. Osofsky (Ed.), *Handbook of infant development.* New York: Wiley.

Mott, S.E., Fewell, R.R., Lewis, M., Meisels, S.J., Shonkoff, J.P., & Simeonsson, R.J. (1986). Methods for assessing child and family outcomes in early childhood special education programs: Some views from the field. *Topics in Early Childhood Special Education, 6*(2), 1–15.

Neisworth, J.T. & Bagnato, S.J. (1986). Curriculum-based developmental assessment: Congruence of testing and teaching. *School Psychology Review, 15,* 180–199.

Newborg, J., Stock, J., Wnek, L., Guidubaldi, J., & Svinicki, J. (1984). *Battelle Developmental Inventory.* Allen, TX: DLM Teaching Resources.

Odom, S.L. & Shuster, S.K. (1986). Naturalistic inquiry and the assessment of young handicapped children and their families. *Topics in Early Childhood Special Education, 6*(2), 68–82.

Orlando, C. (1981). Multidisciplinary team approaches in the assessment of handicapped preschool children. *Topics in Early Childhood Special Education, 1*(2), 23–30.

Pfeiffer, S.I. (1982). The superiority of team decision making. *Exceptional Children, 49,* 68–69.

Rogers, S.J., Donovan, C.M., D'Eugenio, D.B., Brown, S.L., Lynch, E.W., Moersch, M.S., & Schafer, D.S. (1981). *Early Intervention Developmental Profile.* Ann Arbor: University of Michigan Press.

Sanford, A.R. & Zelman, J.G. (1981). *The Learning Accomplishment Profile.* Winston-Salem, NC: Kaplan School Supply.

Sexton, D., Hall, J., & Thomas, P.J. (1983). Multisource assessment of young handicapped children: A comparison of a diagnostician, teachers, mothers, and fathers. *Diagnostique, 9,* 3–11.

Sexton, D., Kelley, M.F., & Scott, R. (1982). Comparison of maternal estimates and performance-based assessment scores for young handicapped children. *Diagnostique, 7,* 168–173.

Sexton, D., Miller, J.H., & Rotatori, A.F. (1985). Determinants of professional-parental agreement for the developmental status of young handicapped children. *Journal of Psychoeducational Assessment, 4,* 377–390.

Simeonsson, R.J. & Simeonsson, N.E. (1981). Medication effects in handicapped preschool children. *Topics in Early Childhood Special Education, 1*(2), 61–76.

Sonnander, K. (1987). Parental developmental assessment of 18-month-old children: Reliability and predictive value. *Developmental Medicine and Child Neurology, 29,* 351–362.

Stillman, R. (Ed.). (1978). *The Callier-Azusa Scale.* Dallas: Callier Center for Communication Disorders, University of Texas at Dallas.

Vincent, L.J., Salisbury, C., Walter, G., Brown, P., Gruenewald, L.J., & Powers, M. (1980). Program evaluation and curriculum development in early childhood/special education: Criteria of the next environment. In W. Sailor, B. Wilcox, & L. Brown (Eds.), *Methods of instruction for severely handicapped students* (pp. 303–328). Baltimore, MD: Paul H. Brookes.

Vulpé, S.G. (1977). *Vulpé Assessment Battery.* Toronto: National Institute on Mental Retardation.

White, O.R., Edgar, E., Haring, N.G., Affleck, J., Hayden, A., & Bendersky, M. (1981). *Uniform Performance Assessment System.* San Antonio: Psychological Corp.

Willoughby-Herb, S.J. & Neisworth, J.T. (1983). *HICOMP Preschool Curriculum.* San Antonio: Psychological Corp.

Winton, P.J. (1988). The family-focused interview:

An assessment measure and goal-setting mechanism. In D.B. Bailey & R.J. Simeonsson (Eds.), *Family assessment in early intervention.* Columbus, OH: Merrill.

Winton, P.J & Bailey, D.B. (in press). The family-focused interview: A collaborative mechanism for family assessment and goal setting. *Journal of the Division for Early Childhood.*

Wolery, M. & Dyk, L. (1984). Arena assessment: Description and preliminary social validity data. *Journal of the Association for the Severely Handicapped, 3,* 231–235.

Chapter 2

Tests and Test Development

Donald B. Bailey, Jr.
H. Ann Brochin
University of North Carolina at Chapel Hill

KEY TERMS

- Test
- Standardization
- Item Score
- Raw Score
- Norm-Referenced Test
- Developmental Age Score
- Developmental Quotient
- Standard Score
- Standard Deviation
- Z Score

- T Score
- Percentile Rank
- Extrapolate (a score)
- Criterion-Referenced Measures
- Curriculum-Referenced Testing
- Performance Standard
- Reliability
- Procedural Reliability
- Scoring Reliability
- Test-Retest Reliability

- Alternate Forms (Parallel Forms) Reliability
- Internal Consistency Reliability
- Standard Error of Measurement
- Validity
- Content Validity
- Instructional Utility
- Criterion Validity
- Construct Validity

Child assessment is most commonly associated with the administration of tests. Although it should be recognized that testing is but one of several strategies for gathering information about children, when properly used and interpreted, tests perform important functions. This chapter describes the process of test construction, procedures for summarizing test performance, and considerations in evaluating assessment tools. This information is important for at least three reasons. First, early childhood special educators and other related professionals should be able to evaluate and select, from a variety of options, a test that will achieve the goals for assessment adequately. Second, professionals should be aware of the limitations of existing measures so that any results obtained from them may be interpreted accordingly. Finally, all professionals should be able to understand test scores as reported by other members of the interdisciplinary team, to recognize their limitations, and to explain those scores to parents or others.

Test Standardization

A **test** is a set of standardized tasks presented to a child. The purpose of testing is to determine how well a child performs on the particular tasks presented. **Standardization** includes several components: standard materials, administrative procedures, scoring procedures, and score interpretation. The purpose of standardization is to ensure that all children taking the test receive essentially the same experience, are expected to perform the same tasks with the same set of materials, receive the same amount of assistance from the evaluator, and are evaluated according to a standard set of criteria. If the same materials, procedures, or scoring criteria are not used across all children, the results will have limited comparability across children.

For example, assume that an item on a test was "Puts together a three-piece puzzle." If no further instructions were provided, it would be up to each evaluator to decide how to administer and score this item. Some might use a simple snowman puzzle, consisting of three circles of different sizes, whereas others might choose an interlocking puzzle. Some would show the child the puzzle as it should look, disassemble it, and ask the child to put it back together, whereas others would simply place the three pieces in front of the child and ask her to put the puzzle together. Some would impose a 1-minute time limit, whereas others would give the child unlimited time. Obviously, variations in administrative procedures will influence a child's success with this task. The child who receives the snowman puzzle, is shown how it is supposed to look, and is given unlimited time to complete it has a very different task from the one who receives three pieces of an interlocking puzzle, is not shown how it is supposed to look, and is given only one minute to complete it.

Standardized procedures are essential if test performance is to be compared across children. Strict adherence to standardized procedures is a fundamentally important skill, and a recognition of its contribution to testing is necessary. In testing handicapped youngsters, however, rigid application of standardized procedures may result in erroneous conclusions about a child. For example, a test of cognitive skills may require the child to perform many motor or verbal tasks. A child with cerebral palsy may not be able to perform the motor or verbal components of those tasks, in spite of having the cognitive skills needed to do so. In such a case, the tester might conclude erroneously that the child had mental retardation. Thus, standardization can have serious limitations for handicapped children. Also, standardized procedures often are difficult to apply to very young children who are distractible and sometimes reluctant to participate in a testing session.

This chapter focuses on testing in its standardized form, inasmuch as it is essential that anyone who engages in the assessment process understand that perspective. Chapter 3 of this text addresses issues and considerations in adapting or modifying standardized procedures for very young children with sensory or motor impairments.

Test Content

Any test consists of a set of tasks to which children must respond. How is the content of an assessment tool determined? What are the important tasks that should be included on any assessment of child functioning? In part, these answers are determined by the purpose of the assessment. A screening measure might have a different test content from that of a diagnostic measure. A test of communication skills certainly would have content different from that of a test of self-help skills. At least two approaches may be followed in determining test content: conceptual and statistical. Usually they are both incorporated in any item-selection process; however, some instruments may weigh one criterion over another, and in some cases, only one dimension is considered.

Conceptual Criteria

The first consideration in selecting test items usually is whether they are conceptually related to the goal of testing or to the domain being assessed. Tinkelman (1971) emphasizes the importance of item content being consistent with the goals and objectives of testing. For example, if a test developer wanted to create a measure of fine motor skills, several questions would need to be addressed. First, the broad domain of fine motor skills would be defined to determine which skills are and are not representative of the domain. For example, *fine motor* might be defined as "any skill involving the use of small muscles." However, this definition might be too broad, for behaviors such as blinking, licking, and toe-wiggling all might fit this category. For educational purposes, *fine motor* may actually be defined as "skills requiring use of the hands or fingers." Regardless of how the domain is conceptualized, it must be defined so initial decisions can be made regarding the appropriateness of item inclusion.

Second, the developer must consider the major dimensions or subdomains within the domain to be assessed. For example, fine motor skills would probably include grasping and releasing objects, stacking objects, and using tools such as pencils, scissors, or a spoon. Third, important developmental milestones within each subdomain must be identified. For example, there is a well-defined sequence of milestones in grasping small objects. Finally, the developer may want to at-tend to functionally important skills within the domain to be assessed. This type of content analysis would focus on fine motor skills likely to be important to the infant's or preschooler's success in home or school environments.

Varying degrees of sophistication and rigor could be applied in the identification of test content. For example, one strategy would be for the developer simply to include items he believed to be important in the domain to be assessed. At a more advanced level, other professionals could be consulted to determine professional consensus as to whether the item was conceptually consistent with the domain under consideration. For example, "experts" in fine motor development could rate a set of items or tasks according to their fit within a given domain or subdomain. Other strategies are described in the reliability and validity section of this chapter.

Statistical Criteria

Once a large pool of potential items has been identified, how are individual items selected for inclusion in a given test? Many tests incorporate statistical criteria for item inclusion. To employ statistical criteria, the test developer must conduct an item tryout on a sample of subjects similar to the children for whom the test is designed. For developmental scales, or those in which a child's age is taken into consideration when deciding where to place items, the most commonly used statistical criterion is to select items passed by 50% of the children at a given age level. In the test construction literature this concept is referred to as "item difficulty level" and often is reported as $p = .5$, which means that the probability of an individual child of a certain age passing the item is 50%. For example, if approximately half of normally developing children walk by age 12 months, walking would be an item assigned to the 12-month age level.

For an item to be selected based on statistical criteria, it must develop in a predictable sequence and within a relatively well-defined time frame. Egan and Brown (1986), for example, studied several performance tasks to determine whether a predictable developmental sequence emerged. Their data supported use of tasks such as building a tower with 1-inch cubes, copying cube models, copying geometric shapes, and drawing a person in the developmental assessment of children between ages 18 and 54 months. Table 2.1 shows the ages at which 50% of the children in their sample (425 children in both urban and rural areas of Great Britain) were able to perform certain tasks.

Statistical criteria are essential in developing tests that provide some indication of a child's developmental status relative to normally developing children. For example, the Bayley Scales of Infant Development (Bayley, 1969) were developed to evaluate "a child's developmental status in the first two and one-half years of life"(p. 3). Items initially were selected to "take into account recent

TABLE 2.1
Sample Use of Statistical Criteria to Determine Item Levels

Task	Age at Which 50% of Children Passed Task (months)
Block Tower	
3–4 cubes	before 18
5–7 cubes	18–19
8 or more cubes	24–27
Color Matching	31
Copying Cube Models	
bridge	34
train	39
3 steps	53.5
Copying Shapes	
circle	34
cross	41
square	51

Source: Egan & Brown, 1986

theoretical contributions dealing with the nature of early childhood development" (p. 1). Items actually used in the final test were arranged in order of age placement and assigned an age level based on the age at which 50% of sample children passed the item.

Integrating Conceptual and Statistical Criteria

Conceptual and statistical criteria may be used independently or in concert with each other. In an example of combined use, an item pool might be developed based on conceptual criteria and professional validation, and specific items selected from the pool on the basis of statistical criteria. Sometimes, although rarely, items could be chosen merely on the basis of statistical criteria with only minor attention to conceptual criteria. For example, if a developer was interested only in screening for overall developmental delay, the most important question may be which items are most likely to identify accurately those children who should be referred for more extensive testing. In such cases, conceptual criteria may be of minimal importance, as long as the screening function is accurately performed. On the other hand, other test constructors may not be interested in statistical criteria at all in selecting items. For example, if the purpose of an assessment tool is to determine a child's ability to complete certain tasks that are necessary for success in a preschool environment, then certain items will be included regardless of how well they discriminate among children.

Problems in Procedures for Developing Test Content

In evaluating a particular measure, professionals working with young handicapped children should examine carefully the content of the test to determine (a) how the items were derived and (b) whether the content is consistent with programmatic goals for assessment. This information will be critical in deciding whether a particular test will be appropriate for a given purpose. Bailey, Jens, and Johnson (1983) reviewed assessment tools associated with infant curricula and found that many instruments currently used by early childhood special educators provide little in the way of data or description to support the inclusion of items in the measure. The following is a sample statement from one such measure:

> Item selection began with a review of well-known standardized infant evaluation instruments, including general developmental scales, motor scales and language scales. The selection criteria for items included the following: first, an item must either have appeared in at least two recognized scales, or must be the original item, appearing in no other scale. The latter stipulation allowed the authors to develop original items based on current developmental theories. Second, each item was scrutinized by the project staff member most highly trained in each area of development (e.g., psychologist for the cognition scale; physical therapist for the gross motor scale, etc.) to determine whether it represented a major developmental milestone rather than an unimportant or incidental skill acquisition. Third, the items selected for each section had to represent all aspects of development for that section. For example, the language scale had to include both receptive and expressive items (both gestural and oral modes). And finally, several items had to represent the developmental accomplishments acquired during each age range appearing in the profile. (Rogers, D'Eugenio, Brown, Donovan, & Lynch, 1981, p. 2)

The purpose of this particular instrument is to provide sufficient assessment data to design instructional programs for young handicapped children. However, the criteria as stated for selecting test content leave much to be desired from a consumer's perspective.

Who were the specialists who determined test content? Does the motor section represent only one physical therapist's perspective or was the content for that section based on the consensus of experts? What criteria were employed to decide whether an item was a major as opposed to an incidental skill? Why does inclusion of items from "well-known standardized measures" make them any more appropriate as instructional targets? Furthermore, is the criterion that the item not appear on any other scale really a criterion? This measure opens up the possibility of infinite inclusions of other items based on the developers' concept of new and original items of importance for inclusion.

The Battelle Developmental Inventory (Newborg, Stock, Wnek, Guidubaldi, & Svinicki, 1984) incorporated both conceptual and statistical criteria in item selection. In regard to conceptual criteria, four were used in the selection of items:

> (1) the importance of the behavior in the child's development toward normal functioning in life; (2) the degree of support among professionals and in the literature for identifying the behavior as a milestone in early development; (3) the acceptance of the skill or behavior among educational practitioners as a critical one for the child to possess or acquire; and (4) the degree to which the behavior is amenable to educational intervention. (p. 9)

No data are presented, however, to demonstrate how these decisions were made. Bailey, Vandiviere, Dellinger, and Munn (1987) asked 79 teachers who had used the instrument to estimate, by domain, the percentage of items they considered to be functional instructional targets, skills that had the potential of being useful now or in the future, or were prerequisites for important skills. Overall, the teachers indicated that they considered only about 68% of the items to be good instructional targets. Thus, just because a test developer says the instrument's content is useful for a given purpose does not mean that consumers necessarily agree.

A unique feature of the Battelle Developmental Inventory is the procedure used to select final items. From the pool of items meeting the aforementioned criteria, final items were selected and assigned an age based on statistical criteria. On this particular instrument, the age at which 75% of the children passed an item was the criterion used. Thus, it cannot be assumed that every measure will incorporate the 50% criterion.

The point of this section is to encourage professionals to examine closely the procedures used to determine what items were included on a particular measure. It is tempting to assume that because the items are part of a published measure, somehow they must be important. However, the items may or may not be consistent with the aims of the local assessment project, and thus a careful analysis of content is warranted.

Summarizing Test Performance: Norm-Referenced Measures

When a test is administered, the child's performance on each item is recorded and assigned a value, referred to as the **item score.** On some tests, the item score is binary, with 0 = fail and 1 = pass. Other tests may allow a range of scores that captures partial or assisted performance. Upon completing administration of an assessment instrument, a **raw score** is derived by summing the item scores. A raw score can usually be computed for subtests as well as for the entire instrument. Although a child's performance on individual items provides important information about specific skills and deficits, raw scores alone are meaningless, except for providing the number of points a child has earned or the number of items passed. Raw scores could be compared across several administrations of a test with a single child, but these scores do not provide information that

can be used to determine how a child performs in any other relative sense. For this reason, raw scores are often converted into some other type of score. The score summary used depends on whether the instrument is a norm-referenced or a criterion-referenced measure.

When a single child's performance is compared to a representative sample of children, the result is a **norm-referenced test**. Such instruments are usually developed by administering the measure to a sample of children who are representative of the population to be tested. The examinee's scores can then be compared to those of the norm group, allowing an understanding of where the child's performance falls relative to that of other children of the same age.

The Normative Group

When evaluating the usefulness of a norm-referenced measure, professionals should examine carefully the basis from which norm-referenced scores are derived and characteristics of the normative sample. Some measures, such as the Learning Accomplishment Profile (Glover, Preminger, & Sanford, 1978; Sanford & Zelman, 1981), the Hawaii Early Learning Profile (Furono, O'Reilly, Hosaka, Inatsuka, Allman, & Zeisloft, 1979), and the Early Intervention Developmental Profile (Rogers et al., 1981), allow the generation of developmental age scores, but the instrument itself was never normed. A developmental age is assigned to each item based on sources such as the Bayley Scales of Infant Development (Bayley, 1969), the Denver Developmental Screening Test (Frankenburg & Dodds, 1969), or the Gesell Developmental Schedules (Knobloch, Stevens, & Malone, 1980). As Bailey et al. (1987) suggest, this approach can be problemmatic:

> Since the norms for these measures were gathered in different years and on different populations, their equivalence is uncertain.

Furthermore, even if individual item ages may be generally accurate, the summation of individual item scores to obtain a developmental age is more suspect, since total score analyses were never conducted on the particular reconfiguration of items. (p. 2)

If the test developers administered the instrument to a normative sample, several aspects of that process should be evaluated. First, the year that testing was done should be noted. As society advances, expectations for children change and so too does their typical performance. The older a set of norms, the less likely it is to be representative of children today. To compare a child's performance today with the average 4-year-old of 25 years ago would be misleading. For example, recent articles have evaluated the accuracy of norms on two measures frequently used with young handicapped children and have called for renorming to ensure the validity of results. Hanson and Smith (1987) compared current administrations of the Griffiths Scales of Mental Development (Extension) (Griffiths, 1970) with the average scores of children in the normative group, which was assessed in 1960, and found that the current sample scored more than 11 general quotient points higher than the children in the original standardization sample. Likewise, Campbell, Siegel, Parr, and Ramey (1986) recommend a renorming of the Bayley Scales of Infant Development after finding higher than average scores in a current sample of 12-month-old infants.

In addition to the year of testing, characteristics of the normative sample should be inspected. Ideally, the sample should be stratified, with proportionate representation of various racial groups, geographic regions, sex, income levels, and urban/rural distribution. If the normative group failed to consider one or more of these variables, its representativeness must be questioned. For example, the Developmental Profile II (Alpern, Boll, & Shearer, 1980) collected normative data primarily in Indiana and Washington, raising concerns about its general applicability across the United States.

Mardell-Czudnowski and Goldenberg (1984) describe in detail the standardization procedures employed with the DIAL-R, a preschool screening test. The original norming population was located only in Illinois and consisted of just 320 children. The restandardization involved 2,447 children. Approximately equal numbers of boys and girls were included, and data were gathered proportionately from the four major geographic regions in the United States based on 1980 data from the United States Bureau of Census. Of the total sample, 44.5% were nonwhite in order to create a large and representative subsample of minority children.

It should be noted that handicapped children are rarely included in any normative group. The rationale for this practice is that norms should provide an indication of normal developmental sequences and milestones. It is assumed that the purpose of testing is to determine the nature and extent of deviation from the norm. However, as discussed in Chapter 3, there are some valid arguments suggesting that there is some degree of unfairness inherent in comparing the development of a hearing-impaired child, for example, with that of hearing children.

Norm-referenced Scores

The collection of normative data provides a basis for comparing a child's performance with that of the normative group. At least four types of scores can be used to make such comparisons: developmental age scores, developmental quotients, standard scores, and percentile ranks.

Developmental Age Scores. A **developmental age score** tells the average age at which 50% of the normative sample achieved the same raw score as did an individual child. For example, on a given test, 50% of the normative sample may have achieved a raw score of 75 by age 36 months. Any child whose raw score totaled 75 could then be said to be functioning at a 36-month developmental level. A developmental age score may be reported for an entire measure or for individual subdomains or subscales of a test. A primary advantage of developmental age scores is that they are easily interpretable by parents and professionals. To say that a child is functioning at a 24-month level has a certain degree of simplicity and face validity. A second advantage of developmental age scores is that they usually do reflect positive change or growth in children (Fewell & Sandall, 1986). If a child has a higher raw score total in the spring than she did in the fall, the result will be a higher developmental age. As will be discussed shortly, however, improvements in raw score performance may not necessarily be reflected by improvements in other types of scores. For parents of handicapped children, who are often informed of their child's delay or slow progress, such information as that provided by developmental age scores may confirm developmental gains where other measures may not.

Salvia and Ysseldyke (1985), however, identify four potential problems when using and interpreting developmental age scores. The first difficulty is that two children with the same developmental age score on a measure may have performed completely differently. Because the developmental age score depends solely on the raw score and is a global summary of performance, patterns of performance are obscured. For example, the performance of two children on a set of items is displayed in Table 2.2. Both children earned the same number of raw score points and thus would receive the same developmental age score. However, they clearly possess different skills.

A second problem is that most developmental ages are extrapolated scores. This means that children of a particular age may not actually have been tested as part of the normative process. The test developer instead used a statistical procedure to extrapolate such scores. Development often is uneven (Keogh & Sheehan, 1981), posing a potential problem. Third, as with all summary scores, to state that a child functions like an average 3-year-old is misleading, inasmuch as 3-year-olds are quite variable in their abilities. Also, it must be remembered that by definition, 50% of the population will score below the identified age level and 50% above. Very few

TABLE 2.2
Example of How Two Children With Different Profiles Can Receive the Same Raw Score

Child A		Child B	
Item Number	Raw Score	Item Number	Raw Score
1	2	1	2
2	2	2	2
3	2	3	1
4	1	4	0
5	2	5	1
6	0	6	2
7	2	7	1
8	0	8	1
9	0	9	1
10	0	10	0
11	0	11	0
12	0	12	0
Score:	11	Score:	11

children actually performed precisely at the targeted age level. Developmental ages are best interpreted as an estimate within a range of performance. However, because developmental ages do not include standard deviation data, the range and variability of performance in typical children is almost impossible to ascertain. Finally, Sattler (1982) points out that the differences between developmental ages are not necessarily equal. At younger ages, a 1-year delay may be more significant than at older ages, where one year is not as great a proportion of the child's total age.

Developmental Quotient Scores. A **developmental quotient** (DQ), or ratio score, is computed by dividing a child's developmental age by his chronological age and multiplying the result by 100. The average child who is progressing at an average rate would receive a DQ score of 100 as illustrated below:

$$\frac{37 \text{ months (developmental age)}}{37 \text{ months (chronological age)}} \times 100 = 100$$

Because a DQ is a ratio of developmental to chronological age, taking into account the child's age at the time of the test, it is usually a relatively stable score. For this reason, developmental quotients are seen by some as a more desirable unit of measurement than developmental age scores when assessing the effects of intervention (Snyder-McLean, 1987).

A primary limitation of the DQ is that as children get older, equal increases in developmental age represent smaller proportions of chronological age and thus result in smaller DQ changes. Furthermore, calculating the DQ tells us nothing about the range and standard deviation of scores. Because of this problem, ratio scores are rarely used, for example, in standardized intelligence tests, since a DQ of 85 at one age is not directly comparable to a DQ of 85 obtained at another age (Bailey & Rosenthal, 1987). However, they are quite common in the early intervention field.

Standard Scores. To compensate for problems associated with developmental quotients, most standardized tests now use standard scores for interpreting child performance. A **standard score** is one that has been transformed to fit a normal curve, with a mean and standard deviation that remain the same across ages. To understand standard scores first requires an understanding of the normal curve and the standard deviation.

The normal curve is a theoretical distribution of scores that is the model against which actual performance is interpreted. As displayed in Figure 2.1, the normal curve is bell shaped. It assumes that on any given variable, most individuals will score at or near the mean. As scores deviate from the mean (either greater or less than), fewer instances of those scores will be observed. A **standard deviation** is a number that helps in inter-

FIGURE 2.1
The normal curve, with percentages of the population expected within standard deviation units

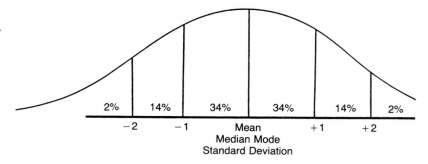

preting where any particular score falls within a larger distribution of scores by describing how far a score is from the mean. Within the normal curve model, it is assumed that one standard deviation encompasses approximately 34% of the individuals in a group, whereas two standard deviations would encompass 48% of the individuals in a group. A standard deviation is always reported as being above or below the mean. Thus, to say that a child's score was 1 standard deviation below the mean would be interpreted to mean that the child's performance was better than 16% of the total population. A score of 1 standard deviation above the mean would be interpreted to mean that the child's performance was better than 84% of the population. This type of information is not available when using developmental quotient scores.

For any given test, the mean and standard deviation of standard scores will be defined by the publisher and developed according to specified criteria. Probably the most well-known version of the standard score or deviation score has a mean of 100 and a standard deviation of 15, as found in the Bayley Scales of Infant Development or the Battelle Developmental Inventory. Using this scoring system, a child with a score of 85 would be said to have a score that was 1 standard deviation below the mean (100 − 15). Other instruments, such as the McCarthy Scales of Children's Abilities and the Stanford-Binet Intelligence Test have a mean of 100 and a standard deviation of 16. Thus, from a population perspective, a score of 70 on the Battelle inventory would be interpreted similarly to a score of 68 on the Stanford-Binet test, for both scores are 2 standard deviations below the mean.

Occasionally a test may report other versions of standard scores, the most common being a Z score or a T score. These scores are interpreted in exactly the same fashion as any other standard score, the only difference being in the defined parameters of the score.

A **Z score** is a standard score distribution with a mean of 0 and a standard deviation of 1, whereas a **T score** is a standard score distribution with a mean of 50 and a standard deviation of 10. Using the above examples, then, a deviation score of 115, a z score of + 1, and a T score of 60 all mean that performance was 1 standard deviation above the mean.

Percentile Ranks. A **percentile rank** is another score that provides information regarding an individual's performance relative to the rest of the population. Specifically, percentile ranks tell what percentage of the population performed at or below a given score. Thus, a percentile rank of 50 would be in the average range and is interpreted to mean that the individual's performance exceeded that of 50% of the normative sample. When the norm group is divided into fourths, each percentile group is called a *quartile;* when a group is divided into tenths, percentile ranks are called *deciles.* These terms are usually used in a general descriptive fashion, such as "Juan's performance was in the top decile," which means the top 10%.

The major limitation of percentile ranks is that they are not on an equal interval scale. The difference between percentile ranks at the extremes is more significant than the difference between percentile ranks closer to the mean, as illustrated by Bailey and Rosenthal (1987). For this reason, percentile ranks should never be used to determine the success of an intervention, nor should they be submitted to any type of data analysis without first converting them to some type of standard score (Sattler, 1982).

Using Extrapolated Scores
Often when calculating score for handicapped children, the examiner finds the child's raw score to be too low for the range of scores covered by the specific test. In such cases,

two options are available. One is simply to report the child's performance as below the lowest obtainable score on the instrument. For example, a child cannot receive a deviation score below 50 on the Bayley Scales, so many reports would simply state "below 50" as the child's obtained score. A second alternative is to **extrapolate** a score by performing additional calculations. For example, Naglieri (1981) published a table for extrapolating scores on the Bayley Scales down to 28. The Battelle Developmental Inventory provides a formula by which extreme scores may be calculated. The examiner finds the mean and standard deviation for the age level and domain of interest, subtracts the mean from the obtained raw score, and divides the resulting figure by the standard deviation, resulting in a z score. To obtain a deviation score, the z score is multiplied by 15 and then added to 100.

The use of extrapolated scores is often necessary when testing handicapped children, particularly those with severe handicaps. However, caution should be exercised when interpreting extrapolated scores for they literally are estimates of performance. No children scoring that low were included in the normative sample, and thus the accuracy of extrapolated scores is uncertain. Additionally, extrapolated scores should only be used when a minimum level or score is earned. Wechsler (1974), for example, warned against calculating IQ scores on the Wechsler Intelligence Scale for Children—Revised when the raw scores are not above 0 on three verbal and three performance subtests. Bailey et al. (1987) found that when extrapolation procedures were used for handicapped children assessed with the Battelle Developmental Inventory, 28% of the children in their sample who required score extrapolation received negative deviation quotients, a theoretically impossible score. When writing test reports, the examiner should always indicate when scores included in the report were obtained through extrapolation procedures.

Using Norm-Referenced Scores for Evaluating Progress

Almost all procedures for summarizing child performance have limitations with respect to their use for demonstrating program or intervention effectiveness. Professionals in early intervention programs need to be aware of these limitations. While a developmental age score may document improvement, it is difficult to determine what proportion of that improvement is due to maturation. Developmental quotients, while able to account for the proportion of variance due to maturation, may not show statistically significant differences between a pretest and posttest score, particularly with older children, because the number of months or years gained becomes a smaller percentage of the child's overall chronological age as he gets older. This problem is illustrated in Figure 2.2, which demonstrates how a gain of 6 months in developmental age influences change in the developmental quotient of a child whose developmental age at 12 months was 6 months. As may be seen, as the child gets older, the 6-month gain results in smaller changes in the developmental quotient. Thus, two children who gained exactly the same skills and demonstrated the same amount of gain in developmental age would show very different levels of change in developmental quotient scores if they were of different ages.

Variations in conclusions made on the basis of various ways of reporting child progress are evident in two case examples of data we have gathered as part of our work with young children. In the first, 15 handicapped children participating in local early intervention programs were selected for testing. All children were below 30 months chronological age and most were severely or profoundly delayed. Children were assessed twice using the Bayley Scales and the Carolina Curriculum for Handicapped Infants (CCHI) (Johnson-Martin, Jens, & Attermeier, 1986), a criterion-referenced measure. The two assessments were four months apart. Because most of the children

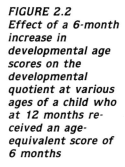

FIGURE 2.2
Effect of a 6-month increase in developmental age scores on the developmental quotient at various ages of a child who at 12 months received an age-equivalent score of 6 months

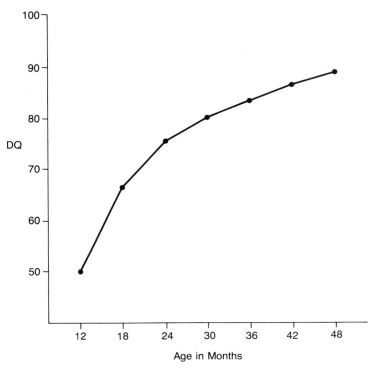

DQ

Age in Months

scored "below 50" on both the mental and psychomotor parts of the Bayley Scales, Naglieri's (1981) method of extrapolating developmental indices for such scores was used. Scores for 13 of the handicapped infants were subjected to the extrapolation, and in each case, infant scores either decreased over the 4-month time period or remained at a "below 28" score on both sections. When raw scores were examined on both the Bayley Scales and the CCHI, however, all children passed significantly more items at the posttest assessment. Thus, although children were improving in their skills, this improvement was not reflected in their standardized scores.

In a second example, a sample of 129 handicapped preschoolers were assessed three times (at 4-month intervals) using the Battelle Developmental Inventory. The results of the assessments when using developmental quotient scores (Figure 2.3a) and developmental age scores (Figure 2.3b) are displayed in Figure 2.3. As may be seen, developmental age scores displayed a steady growth or increase in total and domain scores across the 8-month period. Deviation scores showed more fluctuation across assessments, but actually remained relatively stable from Time 1 to Time 3 assessments. These data may be interpreted to mean that, while children in the sample were not changing their status relative to other children, they were increasing in their ability to perform developmental skills.

In order to describe children's progress in the context of early intervention programs, several formulas have been proposed. Each involves the use of developmental age scores along with additional information. The Intervention Efficiency Index (IEI) (Bagnato & Neisworth, 1980) is the proportion of the

FIGURE 2.3(a)
Change in
developmental
quotient scores of
129 handicapped
preschoolers at
4-month intervals

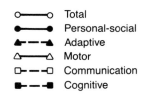

○——○ Total
●——● Personal-social
▲——▲ Adaptive
△——△ Motor
□——□ Communication
■——■ Cognitive

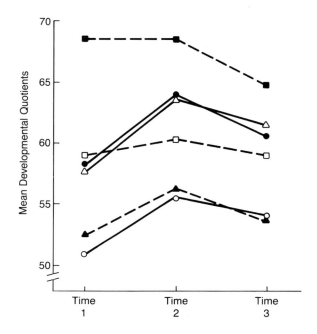

developmental gain to time in intervention and is computed as follows:

Developmental gain
Time in intervention

Using this formula, a child who makes nine months of progress during a 9-month intervention period would receive an IEI score of 1.0. The IEI provides a standardized way of summarizing performance relative to time in intervention, but has been criticized because it does not take into consideration the child's previous rate of development.

Two formulas that take previous development into consideration are the Efficiency In-

dex (Simeonsson & Wiegerink, 1975) and the Proportional Change Index (Wolery, 1983). The Efficiency Index (EI) is calculated according to the following formula:

$$\frac{\text{Actual gain}}{\text{Ideal gain}} \div \frac{\text{Deviation quotient}}{100}$$

The Proportional Change Index (PCI) is calculated according to the following formula:

$$\frac{\text{Developmental gain}}{\text{Time in intervention}} \div$$

$$\frac{\text{Pretest developmental age}}{\text{Pretest chronological age}}$$

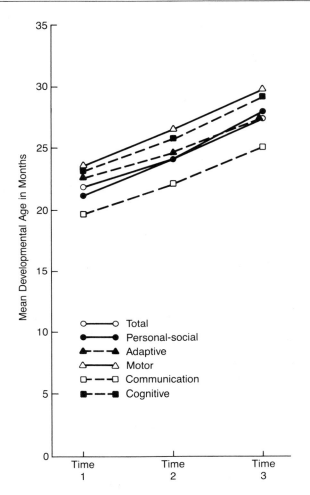

FIGURE 2.3(b)
Change in developmental age scores of 129 hand-icapped preschoolers at 4-month intervals

Both of these indices utilize the data obtained from the IEI, but then divide it by some in-dication of the child's previous rate of development. Both the EI and the PCI will result in scores of 1.0 for any child who, dur-ing an intervention period, displays the same rate of progress as she did prior to interven-tion. Improved rates of progress are reflected in scores above 1.0 and decreased rates are reflected in scores below 1.0. The difference between the two procedures is that the EI incorporates a global measure of pretest de-velopment that is used across all domains, whereas the PCI uses pretest rates of develop-ment that vary according to the domain interest.

Rosenberg, Robinson, Finkler, and Rose (1987) compared formulas for use in evaluating early intervention program impact and concluded that the rate-of-development formulas such as those described here plus others (e.g., Irwin & Wong, 1974) all produce essentially the same rank order of children and thus provide similar information. They all differ, however, from the data obtained when using the Bagnato and Neisworth (1980) for-mula. As Snyder-McLean (1987) suggests, all these procedures are based on the concept of actual change in comparison to predicted change. Snyder-McLean cautions, however, using pretest developmental quotients because of possible fluctuations in child development, raising questions about the extent to which the pretest developmental quotient is representative of the child's overall pattern of development. She suggests that one solution to this problem is to use two or more pretest measures prior to intervention in order to determine a pattern of responses. A second issue is how to use the EI or the PCI after a child has been in intervention for some time. Should the pretest developmental quotient be based on the most recent previous assessment or should it be based on assessment at program entry?

Summarizing Criterion- and Curriculum-Referenced Measures

Tests that measure success or failure in meeting some previously determined objectives are called **criterion-referenced measures.** Criterion-referenced tests are made up of items selected because of their importance to school performance or daily living. Because of their importance, they typically become teaching targets when missed. Criterion-referenced tests do not provide information about where a child's performance falls relative to his peers. Rather, they indicate ability with respect to specific skills. For example, rather than reporting that a child has earned an age equivalent of 38 months on an assessment instrument (as would be possible with a norm-referenced test), one could report that this same child knows three shapes, can name four colors, and can put on a shirt independently.

Criterion-referenced tests have the advantage of attempting to understand the child's strengths and weaknesses without comparing her to others and are appropriate whenever a norm-referenced score is not needed. For example, if a preschool teacher is trying to measure progress toward objectives in a center-based program, the criterion-referenced approach offers behavioral, concrete information.

Usually criterion-referenced tests cannot be used alone to make decisions regarding placement or eligibility for services, inasmuch as those decisions often are based on the nature and extent of the child's developmental delay. However, criterion-referenced tests aid in the understanding of a child's abilities and needs and should be used in placement decisions to complement findings from norm-referenced measures. When determining placement, the primary question should be "Which placement option will best meet a child's needs?" rather than "Which placement option does the child qualify for according to test scores?" Criterion-referenced measures frequently do a better job of identifying functional needs than do norm-referenced tests. Also, reporting results from criterion-referenced tests often is more desired by parents, because such results can focus on specific strengths and needs rather than emphasizing the child's delay.

A special form of criterion-referenced tests is referred to as **curriculum-referenced testing** or curriculum-based assessment (Neisworth & Bagnato, 1986). Curriculum-referenced testing involves the assessment of a child's abilities in the context of a predetermined sequence of curriculum objectives. Assessment covers the same materials presented during instruction. Curriculum-referenced tests are, in reality, criterion-referenced tests; however, they differ from other forms of criterion-referenced testing in that a predetermined criterion is not necessarily set and the test is always related to what was taught in the classroom. While the goal of norm-referenced testing is to compare a child to a norm or standard group and the goal of criterion-referenced testing is to ascertain whether or not a child has acquired a predetermined set of skills, the goal of curriculum-referenced testing is to assess the percentage of material mastered in a given curriculum. Thus, curriculum-referenced tests compare a child's performance to the curriculum.

Curriculum-referenced assessment is a commonly used approach in infant and preschool settings (Bailey et al., 1983). Its utility lies in the fact that there is a direct correspondence between assessment procedures and intervention goals. Missed items in the curriculum become subsequent instructional objectives. The primary limitations relate to potential overreliance on the existing curriculum and overly specific interpretation of individual items. In regard to overreliance on the curriculum, it is clear that handicapped children are extraordinarily variable in their individual needs. Early intervention professionals invariably will need to expand upon preset curricula to tailor assessment demands for individual children. Also, teachers and other professionals must realize that individual curricula items are representative of complex, broad skills. For example, an item such as "puts together a three-piece puzzle" includes cognitive, visual, and motor skills. Instructional activities should not focus merely on putting together a puzzle, but also on relevant functional tasks requiring similar skills.

Criterion-Referenced Scoring

Criterion-referenced and curriculum-referenced tests are scored by first counting the number of items passed. That number itself, equivalent to a raw score, may be the score summary, as in the case of the Evaluation and Programming System for Infants and Young Children (EPS-I) (Bailey & Bricker, 1986). The same limitations as described with raw scores for norm-referenced tests, however, pertain to criterion-referenced measures, because the raw score alone is difficult to interpret. The raw score often is converted into a percentage value, computed by dividing the raw score by the total possible raw score obtainable. The resulting score is an indication of the percentage of items passed.

With school-aged children, performance standards often are set on criterion-referenced tests. A **performance standard** is a specified criterion of performance, such as

8 out of 10 items or 85% of items. According to Berk (1986), these standards frequently are set unsystematically, and thus they often are controversial. Berk's article reviews and describes existing methods for establishing performance standards on criterion-referenced tests and discusses the importance of standard setting for classroom teachers:

What are the consequences of mistakenly

- prescribing new or enrichment materials for a student who is not prepared to handle them?
- prescribing remedial materials and activities for a student who has already mastered that content?
- placing a student in an instructional group that is either too slow or too advanced for that student?
- assigning a student too low a letter grade at the end of the marking period or semester?
- placing a student in a class or course that is too advanced for that student? (p. 164)

Generally speaking, early intervention tests have not formally established performance standards, except within individual items.

Evaluating Progress Using Criterion-Referenced Scores

Progress on criterion-referenced and curriculum-referenced tests may be described in terms of change in either raw score or percentage scores. When interpreting criterion-referenced scores, however, professionals should be cautioned that such scores probably are only ordinal in nature, not equal interval. An equal-interval scale is one in which the difficulty level of each item is equivalent, thus each item requires approximately the same amount of effort to achieve. Unfortunately, equality of item difficulty is rarely documented in criterion-referenced tests, making it difficult to interpret change. For example, one child could achieve several relatively easy items during a period of intervention and demonstrate a sizable increase in percentage of items passed, whereas another child may achieve only one very difficult item and demonstrate only a small increase in percentage of items passed.

Bagnato and Neisworth (1983) propose the use of a Curricular Efficiency Index (CEI), a measure conceptually similar to the change indices described in the context of norm-referenced measures. The CEI is computed according to the following formula:

$$\frac{\text{Number of objectives attained}}{\text{Months in intervention}} \div$$

$$\frac{\text{Mean Nonhandicapped objectives attained}}{\text{Months in intervention}}$$

The formula requires the use of a criterion-referenced or curriculm-referenced measure that has been administered to "comparable" nonhandicapped children and for whom progress data are available. According to the authors, this formula "provided a local standard or norm (mean objectives/month) against which the handicapped's progress could be compared. This ratio of the gain of the handicapped group to the gain of the nonhandicapped 'standard' reflects the relative efficiency of curriculum-based intervention" (p. 190). However, the accuracy of this type of measure is suspect and difficult to ascertain, both because of the unequal nature of criterion-referenced scores and the difficulties inherent in finding and assessing a "comparable" group of nonhandicapped children.

Test Reliability

When evaluating a particular assessment tool, one concern is whether the instrument is reliable. **Reliability** refers to the consistency of test performance. One way to ask a question about reliability would be if several children were administered the same test and each received a different score, how much of that variability is attributable to true differences in children's abilities and how much is due to what is referred to as "error variance"? Another way to ask a question about reliability is if a child took a test over and over again and no practice effect occurred, what would be the variability in the child's performance? The less error variance associated with either of these questions, the greater the test's reliability. Professionals in early intervention should understand the concept of reliability; recognize sources of error in measurement; and be able to read, interpret, and evaluate reliability data.

Sources of Error in Measurement
Measurement error may stem from several sources. The most common are characteristics of the test itself, variation in administrative conditions and child characteristics, and aspects of the examiner.

Test Characteristics. A major source of variability is the test itself, which is often the focus of reliability studies. Items on a test should be clear in regard to the materials required and administrative procedures. If not, one examiner might administer the item in one way and another might use different administrative procedures. Also, a test should have clear scoring procedures. If not, one examiner might give a child credit for a particular response whereas another might credit a failure for precisely the same response. Finally, test reliability can be affected by test length; extremely short or extremely long tests are likely to be less reliable.

Administrative and Subject Conditions. A second major source of error variance is associated with aspects of the subjects taking the test and the conditions under which the test is administered. Stanley (1971) describes several characteristics of the individual child that might result in score variance on a particular test. Among these include lasting and general characteristics of the child (e.g., general ability to comprehend instructions, test-taking skills), lasting but specific characteristics of the child (e.g., skill "scatter," response tendencies in certain specific domains, unfamiliarity with certain item types), temporary but general characteristics of the child (e.g., health, fatigue, motivation, emotional strain), or temporary and specific characteristics of the individual (e.g., fluctuations in attention, use of specific tricks or strategies to respond to an individual test item). Performance may also vary by chance associated with "lucky" responses to items. For example, a child may be asked to point to the red block. A child who does not know colors still has a 25% chance of being correct if she has four blocks from which to choose.

Aspects of a particular test administration may also affect a child's performance and result in score variability. For example, the room may be too cold, poorly lit, or stuffy. The child may not interact well with the particular adult administering the test due to unfamiliarity or characteristics of the adult such as personality style, race, or sex.

The Examiner. Finally, the skill of the examiner in administering and scoring the test influences the reliability of administration. A test may have perfectly clear and precise administrative and scoring procedures, but an individual examiner may not have read them all or may have forgotten one guideline or more. Furthermore, adults make mistakes, for example, in score calculations and transformations. The more complex the scoring procedure required and the more calculations that are necessary, the greater the likelihood of error.

Assessing Test Reliability

When examining the reliability of a given test, the professional generally has two options for source information. First, the administrative

manual of a particular instrument should provide detailed reliability data. Second, reliability studies of particular measures often are published in the professional literature. This body of information, however, is generally much less accessible to most practicing professionals working with young handicapped children.

As Stanley (1971) suggests, "there is no single, universal, and absolute reliability for a test" (p. 363). Just as there are many sources of error variance, so too are there many ways of documenting test reliability. Among these are procedural and scoring reliability, test/retest reliability, alternate forms reliability, the standard error of measurement, and internal consistency reliability. The reliability measure used varies according to the question of interest.

Procedural and Scoring Reliability. **Procedural reliability** refers to the extent to which the examiner follows the precise administrative procedures required by a particular test, whereas scoring reliability refers to the extent to which the score calculations and score summaries are accurate. Both must be assessed by having another individual check the examiner. For example, procedural reliability could be assessed by having one person observe another person administer a test. For each item, the observer notes whether the examiner used the proper materials, placed them in the proper positions, gave the proper directions, and in general followed test protocol accurately. In this case the reliability measure would be the percentage of items administered correctly. **Scoring reliability** consists of two major aspects. First, did the examiner give the proper credit for the child's response? Generally, this crediting will require observation and simultaneous scoring, for testing young children does not usually result in a permanent product such as a written word. Second, did the examiner correctly calculate the child's total score? This question does not require observation. Rather, two individuals must independently score a test. The reliability measure is the extent to which the individuals agree on the final score calculation, or the number of errors made by one individual.

One example of observer reliability was provided by Bailey and Bricker (1986). Two persons independently observed a child participating in routine classroom activities and scored items on the Evaluation and Programming System. A correlation coefficient was used to determine the extent of interobserver agreement. (A correlation coefficient is a statistical measure of how two variables relate to each other. It ranges from -1 to $+1$, with coefficients near -1 or $+1$ considered high correlations and coefficients near 0 considered low correlations. Generally in reliability studies, one would expect that correlations be high and positive.) The results of the study indicated that the two observers were much more likely to agree on some domains than others. For example, the correlations for the gross motor (.95), communication (.85), and social (.85) domains were much higher than those for the fine motor (.64) and cognitive (.23) domains.

An example of assessing the reliability of score calculations was provided by Bailey et al. (1987). Some 79 teachers of 247 handicapped preschoolers administered the Battelle Developmental Inventory and sent the results to the authors. Graduate research assistants subsequently checked each protocol for accuracy in score calculation and summaries. Only 11 teachers (14.5%) and 50 protocols (20.2%) had no scoring errors. The most common errors included simple math miscalculations, failure to establish a basal level, and errors in crediting the child for points below the basal.

Test-retest Reliability. A second form of reliability is referred to as test/retest reliability. **Test-retest reliability** requires administering the same test to a group of children on two different occasions and assessing the

extent to which their scores are comparable and stable over time. For example, Bailey and Bricker (1986), after assessing 28 children, observed and assessed those children again one or two weeks after the initial testing period. The correlation between total test scores in first and second administration was .84. Test/retest reliability for individual subdomains ranged from .46 to .93.

Alternate Forms Reliability. Some instrument creators will develop alternate forms of the same measure. **Alternate forms** or **parallel forms reliability** assesses the extent to which a child's performance on one measure is consistent with his performance on the other. Therefore, it requires that the same child be administered both forms of the test. For example, Boehm (1971) developed two forms of the Boehm Test of Basic Concepts. A median alternate form reliability coefficient of .76 is reported in the administrative manual of the instrument. In a sample tryout of the measure, the mean scores on Form A (42.4) and Form B (42.9) were almost equivalent.

Internal Consistency. A fourth form of test reliability is **internal consistency reliability,** which seeks to determine whether a child's responses on a given administration of a test are internally consistent. In other words, to consider whether there was considerable variability in performance across items or whether the child's performance was relatively consistent. This type of question can be asked only if an instrument is assumed to assess a unitary construct; a child's performance across very different domains (e.g., communication and motor) might be expected to vary.

Internal consistency may be assessed using several procedures. One of the simplest is referred to as split-half reliability, a procedure in which the test essentially is divided into two parts (usually odd versus even items). The reliability measure then is the correlation between the two parts. At a more complex level, formulas such as the Kuder-Richardson procedure or Cronbach's Alpha could be used, in which all possible splits are assessed. For example, McLean, McCormick, Bruder, and Burdg (1987) assessed the internal consistency of the Battelle Developmental Inventory using Cronbach's Alpha with data collected on 40 handicapped children under age 30 months. Internal consistency was high in all five domains of the measure, ranging from .887 to .963.

Standard Error of Meaurement. A final measure of test reliability is referred to as the **standard error of measurement**. This procedure seeks to answer the hypothetical question of how stable a child's performance on a test would be if she could take the test over and over again. Assume that this retesting was done, resulting in a large number of scores for the same child on the same test. That set of scores would have a mean and a standard deviation. The standard error of measurement is the standard deviation of that hypothetical distribution and is thus an estimate of that variability. It is reported in units of the test score itself. For example, the administrative manual of the Battelle Developmental Inventory reports that the standard error of measurement for the total Battelle Developmental Inventory score for children in the 6–11-month age range is 3.28. This finding is interpreted to mean that 68% of the time (because, as displayed in Figure 2.1, 1 standard deviation above and below the mean encompasses 68% of a normal distribution) a child's total raw score would fall within a range of ± 3.28 points.

Summary Comments Regarding Reliability. Clearly test reliability is an important concern in selecting any measure. Although no one score is the "right" reliability, professionals should examine the evidence available for any given measure. Instruments should be selected that have reliability coefficents greater than .80 and preferably greater than .90, and for which there is a small standard error of measurement. Examiners using the test should be familiar with all aspects of test administration and scoring, and periodic checks of both administrative and scoring procedures should be conducted. If a test is known to have low reliability but is still used by a program, results should be interpreted cautiously. For unclear items, a program should adopt local standards for those items and ask each staff person to adhere to them. However, when reports of such administrations are shared with other agencies, any such standards should be fully explained.

Test Validity

In addition to test reliability, professionals using tests must also be concerned about test validity. **Validity** refers to the extent to which a test performs the function for which it was intended. At least four types of validity should be considered: content, instructional, construct, and criterion.

Content Validity. **Content validity** refers to the extent to which the content of the test accurately represents the domain to be tested. For example, a test of cognitive skills should cover the major cognitive attainments of young children and should reflect current theories of cognitive development. According to the Standards for Educational and Psychological Tests (American Psychological Association, 1985), "to demonstrate the content validity of a set of test scores, one must show that the behaviors demonstrated in testing constitute a representative sample of behaviors to be exhibited in a desired performance domain. . . . An investigation of content validity requires that the test developer or test user specify his objectives and carefully define the performance domain in light of those objectives" (p. 28).

In evaluating the content validity of a given test, professionals first should examine the rationale for item selection as described in the technical manual accompanying the test. A very broad test of content validity would be the extent to which the test developer convinces the reader that a thorough and systematic process has occurred in the selection of of test items and test content. This should include a discussion of the theoretical basis for item selection, the source of items, and any data to support the extent to which test content is reflective of the domain assessed. Data supporting content validity typically would consist of the judgment of experts as to the appropriateness of the content. Essentially, content validity is assessed through a logical analysis of the item development process and of the actual items.

Instructional Utility. A second type of validity, and one that is closely related to content validity, is **instructional utility.** In this regard, the user would seek to determine the extent to which an instrument provides useful information for planning intervention programs for young handicapped children.

One way to assess instructional utility is to ask test users to rate the appropriateness of the items for instruction. As described earlier, Bailey et al. (1987) asked teachers to rate the instructional utility of the Battelle Developmental Inventory. They also asked teachers to rate the extent to which standardized adaptations for children with sensory or motor impairments allowed an individual child to demonstrate her optimal skills. Bailey and Bricker (1986) asked staff members using the EPS-I to fill out a form regarding the usefulness and appropriateness of items for designing instructional programs. Such information, particularly when provided at the item level, can be useful in revising instruments as well as in evaluating their overall utility.

Criterion Validity. **Criterion validity** assesses the extent to which a test corresponds to some other independent measure. Two types of criterion validity have been described. Concurrent validity refers to the extent to which a test correlates with another measure administered close in time to the first, whereas predictive validity refers to the extent to which a test relates to some future measure of performance. An example of concurrent validity was provided by Bruder (1984) who compared infants' scores on the communication section of the Revised Gesell Schedules of Infant Development with the same infants' scores on the Snyder Imperative Tasks test to determine the extent to which the two instruments correlated. An example of predictive validity ws provided by Diamond (1987), who conducted a four-year follow up of the Denver Developmental Screening Test to determine the extent to which it identified children who later displayed severe learning problems in school.

Concurrent and predictive validity are particularly important for screening tests. Screening tests that lack concurrent validity are likely to result in children being referred for assessment that will not be diagnosed as delayed. Concurrent validity is also critical in tests used for diagnosis.

Construct Validity. A construct is a hypothetical attribute, such as intelligence or creativity, that is designed to account for variability in behavior. The following statements summarize the essence of **construct validity**:

Evidence of construct validity is not found in a single study; rather, judgments of construct validity are based upon an accumulation of research results. In obtaining the information needed to establish construct validity, the investigator begins by formulating hypotheses about the characteristics of those who have high scores on the test in contrast to those who have low scores. Taken together, such hypotheses form at least a tentative theory about the nature of the construct the test is believed to be measuring. In a full investigation, the test may be the dependent variable in some studies and the independent variable in others. Some hypotheses may be "counter-hypotheses" suggested by competing interpretations or theories. (American Psychological Association, 1985, p. 30)

A sample construct validity question would be to ask whether a particular instrument was, in fact, a measure of intelligence. Mahoney (1984) provided an example of testing the construct validity of the Receptive-Expressive Emergent Language Scale with mentally retarded children. In this study, he demonstrated that the instrument provided a developmental sequence of data about children's communicative behavior, and it correlated well with another measure designed to assess the same construct. However, a thorough documentation of construct validity should also show that the measure in question has a low correlation with measures from other domains. For example, a communication measure should correlate highly with established communication measures and have lower correlations with social and cognitive measures. Although these skills are interrelated, the question is whether the instrument successfully isolates and differentiates those abilities or skills.

Comments About Validity

Questions about validity are of ultimate importance for early childhood special educators and related service personnel because they ask whether an instrument fulfills the function for which it was intended. Validity is both separate from and tied to reliability. Although conceptually they ask very different questions, it is a well-accepted axiom in test development that test validity can be no higher than the test's reliability, and usually is considerably lower. This statement makes sense, for how could an unreliable or inconsistent measure have any accuracy? However, just because a test is reliable does not mean it has any validity to it for certain purposes. For example, a screening test may be perfectly reliable but be of no use in planning instructional programs.

Finally, it must be noted that the vast majority of validity studies conducted on norm-referenced measures have failed to examine the validity of these instruments for use with handicapped individuals, as evidenced in a review by Fuchs, Fuchs, Benowitz, and Barringer (1987) of 27 aptitude and achievement tests. They concluded:

Tests without validation data on handi-capped people simply should not be used with this group to determine diagnoses, classifications, placements, and evaluations of academic progress. Further, because the handicapped population is heterogeneous, we believe handicapped students par-ticipating in validation efforts should be described whenever possible in terms of type and degree of handicapping conditions as well as being characterized by more con-ventional data, including age, race, SES, and sex. (p. 270)

Obviously, it will be difficult for early interventionists to adhere to this suggestion because of the lack of measures validated with young handicapped children. However, they should be aware of these issues, and incorporate the procedures described in Chapter 3 to ensure optimal performance when assessing young children.

SUMMARY OF KEY CONCEPTS

- Testing is the assessment of children's abilities through the presentation of standardized tasks and application of standardized procedures for interpreting children's performance. It is probably the most widely used, and widely misused, form of assessment, and thus an understanding of the process underlying testing is essential.

- Standardized administration and scoring of tests is important when test scores are used. Standardized procedures may penalize some handicapped children, however, and results from standardized testing should be interpreted with caution.

- Teachers and other professionals should examine how test content was derived to ensure that content is adequate for the intended purpose.

- Norm-referenced tests compare a child's performance with that of other children, using developmental age scores, developmental quotients, standard scores, or percentile ranks. Each score has advantages and disadvantages. Clinicians should examine the norm group from which these scores were derived, be able to interpret each, and recognize the limitations of each.

- Criterion-referenced measures document children's attainment of predetermined objectives or curricula items and generally are more useful than norm-referenced measures for instructional purposes.

- Reliability refers to the consistency of test performance. Several factors can influence test reliability.

- Validity refers to the extent to which a test performs the functions for which it was intended.

REFERENCES

Alpern, G.D., Boll, T.J., & Shearer, M.S. (1980). *Developmental Profile II.* Aspen, CO: Psychological Development Publications.

American Psychological Association. (1985). *Standards for educational and psychological tests.* Washington, DC: Author.

Bagnato, S.J. & Neisworth, J.T. (1980). The intervention efficiency index: An approach to preschool program accountability. *Exceptional Children, 46,* 264–269.

Bagnato, S.J. & Neisworth, J.T. (1983). Monitoring developmental progress of young exceptional children: The curricular efficiency index. *Journal of Special Education, 17,* 189–193.

Bailey, D.B., Jens, K.G., & Johnson, N. (1983). Curricula for handicapped infants. In S.G. Garwood & R.R. Fewell (Eds.), *Educating handicapped infants* (pp. 387–415). Rockville, MD: Aspen.

Bailey, D.B. & Rosenthal, S.L. (1987). Basic principles of measurement and test development. In W.H. Berdine & S.A. Meyer (Eds.), *Assessment in special education.* Boston: Little, Brown.

Bailey, D.B., Vandiviere, P., Dellinger, J., & Munn, D. (1987). The Battelle Developmental Inventory: Teacher perceptions and implementation data. *Journal of Psychoeducational Assessment, 3,* 217–226.

Bailey, E.J. & Bricker, D. (1986). A psychometric study of a criterion-referenced assessment instrument designed for infants and young children. *Journal of the Division for Early Childhood, 10,* 124–134.

Bayley, N. (1969). *Bayley Scales of Infant Development.* New York: Psychological Corp.

Berk, R.A. (1986). A consumer's guide to setting performance standards on criterion-referenced tests. *Review of Educational Research, 56,* 137–172.

Boehm, A.E. (1971). *Boehm Test of Basic Concepts.* New York: Psychological Corp.

Bruder, M.B. (1984). The validation of a scale to measure early social-communicative behavior. *Journal of the Division for Early Childhood, 9,* 67–75.

Campbell, S.K., Siegel, E., Parr, C.A., & Ramey, C.T. (1986). Evidence for the need to renorm the Bayley Scales of Infant Development based on the performance of a population-based sample of 12-month-old infants. *Topics in Early Childhood Special Education, 6*(2), 83–96.

Diamond, K.E. (1987). Predicting school problems from preschool developmental screening: A four-year follow-up of the revised Denver Developmental Screening Test and the role of parent report. *Journal of the Division for Early Childhood, 11,* 247–253.

Egan, D.F. & Brown, R. (1986). Developmental assessment: 18 months to $4\frac{1}{2}$ years. Performance tests. *Child: Care, Health and Development, 12,* 339–349.

Fewell, R.R. & Sandall, S.R. (1986). Developmental testing of handicapped infants: A measurement dilemma. *Topics in Early Childhood Special Education, 6,* 86–99.

Frankenburg, W.K. & Dodds, J.B. (1969). *Denver Developmental Screening Test.* Denver: University of Colorado Medical Center.

Fuchs, D., Fuchs, L.S., Benowitz, S., & Barringer, K. (1987). Norm-referenced tests: Are they valid for use with handicapped students? *Exceptional Children, 54,* 263–271.

Furuno, S., O'Reilly, A., Hosaka, C.M., Inatsuka, T.T., Allman, T.L., & Zeisloft, B. (1979). *The Hawaii Early Learning Profile.* Palo Alto, CA: VORT.

Glover, M.E., Preminger, J.L., & Sanford, A.R. (1978). *The Early Learning Accomplishment Profile.* Winston-Salem, NC: Kaplan.

Griffiths, R. (1970). *The abilities of young children. A comprehensive system of mental measurement for the first eight years of life.* High Wycombe, England: The Test Agency.

Hanson, R. & Smith, J.A. (1987). Achievement of young children on items of the Griffiths Scales: 1980 compared with 1960. *Child: Care, Health and Development, 13,* 181–195.

Irwin, J. & Wong, S. (1974). Compensation for maturity in long range intervention studies. *Acta Symbolica, 5,* 33–45.

Johnson-Martin, N., Jens, K.G., & Attermeier, S.M. (1986). *Carolina Curriculum for Handicapped Infants and Infants at Risk.* Baltimore, MD: Paul H. Brookes.

Keogh, B.K. & Sheehan, R. (1981). The use of developmental test data for documenting handicapped children's progress: Problems and recommendations. *Journal of the Division for Early Childhood, 3,* 42–47.

Knobloch, H., Stevens, F., & Malone, A.F. (1980). *Manual of developmental diagnosis.* New York: Harper & Row.

Mahoney, G. (1984). The validity of the Receptive-Expressive Emergent Language Scale with mentally retarded children. *Journal of the Division for Early Childhood, 9,* 86–94.

Mardell-Czudnowski, C. & Goldenberg, D. (1984). Revision and restandardization of a preschool screening test: DIAL becomes DIAL-R. *Journal of the Division for Early Childhood, 8,* 149–156.

McLean, M., McCormick, K., Bruder, M.B., & Burdg, N.B. (1987). An investigation of the validity and reliability of the Battelle Developmental Inventory with a population of children younger than 30 months with identified handicapping conditions. *Journal of the Division for Early Childhood, 11,* 238–246.

Naglieri, J.A. (1981). Extrapolated developmental indices for the Bayley Scale of Infant Development. *American Journal of Mental Deficiency, 85,* 548–550.

Neisworth, J.T. & Bagnato, S.J. (1986). Curriculum-based developmental assessment: Congruence of testing and teaching. *School Psychology Review, 15,* 180–199.

Newborg, J., Stock, J.R., Wnek, L., Guidubaldi, J., & Svinicki, J. (1984). *The Battelle Developmental Inventory.* Allen, TX: DLM/Teaching Resources.

Rogers, S.J., D'Eugenio, D.B., Brown, S.L., Donovan, C.M., & Lynch, E.W. (1981). *Early Intervention Developmental Profile.* Ann Arbor: University of Michigan Press.

Rosenberg, S.A., Robinson, C.C., Finkler, D., & Rose, J.S. (1987). An empirical comparison of formulas evaluating early intervention program impact on development. *Exceptional Children, 54,* 213–219.

Salvia, J. & Ysseldyke, J.E. (1985). *Assessment in special and remedial education.* Boston: Houghton Mifflin.

Sanford, A.R. & Zelman, J.G. (1981). *The Learning Accomplishment Profile.* Winston-Salem, NC: Kaplan.

Sattler, J. (1982). *Assessment of children's intelligence and special abilities.* Boston: Allyn & Bacon.

Simeonsson, R.J. & Wiegerink, R. (1975). Accountability: A dilemma in infant intervention. *Exceptional Children, 41,* 474–481.

Snyder-McLean, L. (1987). Reporting norm-referenced program evaluation data: Some considerations. *Journal of the Division for Early Childhood, 11,* 254–264.

Stanley, J.C. (1971). Reliability. In R.L. Thorndike (Ed.), *Educational measurement* (2nd ed.) (pp. 356–442). Washington, DC: American Council on Education.

Tinkelman, S.N. (1971). Planning the objective test. In R.L. Thorndike (Ed.), *Educational measurement* (2nd ed.) (pp. 46–80). Washington, DC: American Council on Education.

Wechsler, D. (1974). *Manual for Wechsler Intelligence Scale for Children—Revised.* New York: Psychological Corp.

Wolery, M. (1983). Proportional change index: An alternative for comparing child change data. *Exceptional Children, 50,* 167–170.

Chapter 3

Procedural Considerations in Assessing Infants and Preschoolers with Handicaps

Donald B. Bailey, Jr.
T. Lee Rouse
University of North Carolina at Chapel Hill

KEY TERMS

- Activity Level
- Distractibility
- State
- Flexibility
- Planning

- Rapport
- High-interest Materials
- Positive Reinforcement
- Critical Function
- Standardized

- Test the Limits
- Affective Development
- Information-Processing Techniques
- Co-occurrences

The process of assessing infants and preschoolers with handicaps often requires special procedural considerations, first, because the children are very young, and second, because many children have sensory or motor impairments likely to influence their ability to respond to standardized items. This chapter describes special considerations in assessing infants and preschoolers and in assessing children with sensory or motor impairments. Characteristics of these children are presented and guidelines for altering or arranging assessment procedures are discussed.

Finally, new, nontraditional alternatives to typical assessment procedures are described.

Special Considerations in Assessing Infants and Preschoolers

The testing of infants and preschoolers can be a gratifying and enjoyable experience. On the other hand, early childhood assessment also presents a number of challenges not encountered in the evaluation of older children.

For example, infants are unlikely to separate willingly from their parents, have limited attention spans, and may show initial anxiety when confronted with the unfamiliar examiner. The preschool child, while able to function in a more independent manner, is usually unfamiliar with the "rules" of being a good test subject, and when placed in this context will frequently make an effort to determine limits of acceptable behavior. As a result, the examiner is simultaneously faced with the tasks of properly administering test items, establishing a relationship of trust with the child, and on occasion, setting limits on the child's behavior. In this section, pertinent child characteristics that influence the testing process are discussed. Specific procedural guidelines for conducting infant and child assessment are also offered.

Characteristics of Infants and Preschoolers

Successful evaluation of infants and preschoolers requires an accurate understanding of cognitive and behavioral phenomena unique to each developmental period. Knowing what behaviors are typical for infants and preschoolers allows the examiner to anticipate necessary adjustments in his interaction with the child and affords a clearer distinction between normal and abnormal behavior for each period. At least four behavioral characteristics of infants and preschoolers make assessment challenging: activity level/distractibility, variable states/attention span, wariness of strangers, and inconsistent performance due to setting variables. Several qualifications apply to this discussion. First, the list is certainly not exhaustive; rather it is intended as a guide to child characteristics most commonly encountered in testing. Second, age markers, where provided, should be interpreted as general guidelines, not absolute criteria for performance.

Activity Level/Distractibility. Thomas and Chess (1977) define **activity level** as the proportion of active to inactive periods in the child's daily functioning. Among infants and toddlers, activity level may be observed in daily routines such as bathing, dressing, eating, and handling, as well as motility during play and the sleep/wake cycle. **Distractibility,** on the other hand, is defined in terms of the child's ability to maintain an ongoing behavior in the face of competing environmental stimuli. Compared to the school-aged child, preschoolers, and particularly infants, exhibit generally higher activity levels and are more easily distracted by competing contextual stimuli. These are normal developmental phenomena that tend to diminish with age (due to neurological maturation). In addition, individual differences in child temperament and intelligence and immediate influences such as child health status or setting variables also may influence activity levels.

Variable States/Attention Span. A powerful influence on infant attending behavior at any given time is the infant's state of consciousness. (**State** as a domain for potential assessment is discussed extensively in Chapter 9.) In this chapter, state is addressed briefly in regard to its influence on children's behavior during testing. The most obvious states are sleep and awake; however, finer gradations may also be applied. For example, Prechtl (1974) delineated six levels of state: quiet sleep, active sleep, drowsy, quiet awake, active awake, and distress. Those states ranging from drowsy to distressed are most pertinent to testing behavior, and the examiner should be thoroughly familiar with each:

1. Drowsy—eyes open and close; eyes are "heavy lidded" and have dull, glazed appearance. Infant may respond to sensory stimuli although responses are usually delayed.
2. Quiet awake—eyes wide open; limited motor activity; child is quite alert to en-

vironment, primarily through visual modality.

3. Active awake—eyes wide open with accompanying motor activity; occasional periods of fussiness; increased sensitivity to disturbing contextual stimuli.
4. Distress—characterized by crying, grimacing, and increased motor activity.

In general, infants progress through these states sequentially; for example, moving from drowsy to quiet alert, or drowsy back to sleep. On the other hand, a small proportion of infants show extreme state changes, spending much of their time either asleep or in distress.

With infants, it is critical to ascertain from the parent ahead of time when the most alert times of the day are and, if possible, to arrange testing time accordingly. For example, the child who routinely naps in the early afternoon usually will display greater sustained attention and less irritability if tested in the morning.

Wariness of Strangers. Beginning at a developmental age of 6–8 months and continuing through approximately 18 months, infants show varying degrees of distress when approached by unfamiliar adults. The intensity of this distress may be mediated by both constitutional (e.g., temperament) and environmental factors. With regard to the latter, studies suggest that the intensity of the infant's initial response is inversely related to the physical distance between the infant and stranger (i.e., the closer the stranger's initial approach, the greater the likelihood of an unfavorable reaction) (Lewis & Brooks-Gunn, 1972). In addition, infants appear more likely to respond favorably to strangers when held by their caregiver, as opposed to being separated by even a few feet (Morgan & Ricciuti, 1969). Fuchs (1987) describes a series of studies in which he and his colleagues consistenty have found that certain handicapped children obtain higher test scores when

tested by examiners familiar to them. This finding did not seem to apply to testing nonhandicapped children, causing the author to conclude that "examiner unfamiliarity is a source of systematic error or bias that invalidates test-related diagnostic, classification, and program placement decisions" (p. 98). These findings have important implications for establishing rapport during the test session, a subject addressed later in this chapter.

Inconsistent Performance in Unfamiliar Environment. While infants frequently show initially unfavorable reactions to strange environments, it appears that given ample opportunity for adaptation, reliable and valid test results can be obtained outside the home setting. Using a sample of 9- and 15-month-old infants, Horner (1980), for example, compared test/retest characteristics of the Bayley Scales of Infant Development Mental Scale administered in a clinic and one week later in the child's home. Results revealed that raw scores and standard scores were not affected by setting differences.

General Guidelines for Assessing Infants and Preschoolers

Knowledge of child characteristics pertinent to the test setting is an important step in achieving reliable and valid test results. An equally important consideration relates to the power of the examiner as a modifying agent of the child's behavior. The effective examiner is able to recognize characteristics of the child that may impede validity and to apply techniques of behavioral change that will reduce the potency of such threats.

Flexibility. One of the most critical examiner characteristics necessary for reliable and valid assessment is **flexibility** (Ulrey, 1982a, b). Flexibility is important in a variety of contexts, ranging from scheduling considerations, to data collection, to making allowances for individual child needs in the test session. With regard to scheduling, it is important to remember that infants and some preschoolers may need an extended warm-up period to become acclimated to the examiner and the testing environment. Consequently, the examiner should be prepared on occasion to extend the test session beyond its originally scheduled time, or if necessary, plan a second session for another day.

Flexibility in gathering information about the child's abilities is also important. Particularly in infant testing, reports of the parent or another clinician who is familiar with the child's abilities may be utilized when the desired behavior cannot be elicited directly. Whether such reports may be substituted for actual performance depends upon the rules for the specific instrument being administered. Yet even where substitution is not allowed, information acquired in a nonstandardized manner can yield insight into the child's abilities and the reliability of formal test results.

Finally, flexibility is necessary within the context of the individual testing session. For example, when interacting with the child, the examiner must be alert to the need to vary the rate of item presentation, alter the type of activity being administered, and give immediate reinforcement or set limits, all according to the child's varying levels of attention, interest, and motivation.

The Importance of Planning. The testing of young children, more than that of children at any other age, is unforgiving of lapses of attention, indecision in the examiner, and lack of **planning.** Whereas the school-aged child is expected to tolerate lulls in item administration, the preschooler or infant often will not. Consequently, it is important that the examiner give thoughtful attention ahead of time to testing requirements for the child.

Often the examiner will have access to parent application forms, teacher questionnaires, or medical records well in advance of the child's assessment. Careful review of these materials can yield valuable insight into the child's suspected level of functioning, areas of strength or weakness, specific handicapping conditions, and behavioral style. Such information can be used directly as a guide for the examiner's initial interaction with the child, as an aid in selecting appropriate tests and reinforcers, and for estimating an entry level for initial test items. Careful record review is particularly important when the examiner has not had the opportunity to observe the child beforehand.

Immediately prior to the test session, testing materials should be collected and arranged in a systematic manner, thus allowing easy access once testing begins. This is particularly important for infant test kits, which are famous for containing numerous small objects that somehow manage to "disappear" when needed. Any other materials that the examiner anticipates will be used during the session should also be collected ahead of time; for example, special reinforcers, a small toy, tissues, or a chair for the parent (if the parent is to be present during testing). With regard to furniture for the testing of preschool children, Paget (1983) recommends a chair appropriate to the child's size and a table approximately 36 inches long, 20–24 inches wide, and adjustable in height for the child to work comfortably.

Establishing Rapport. One of the most common mistakes made by new examiners is to underestimate the amount of time the child will need to adapt to the testing environment (Rogers, 1982b). All children, but particularly infants, must be given time to become accustomed to and trusting of the examiner. In effect, the examiner's first job is to establish **rapport,** or a trusting relationship with the child.

Rogers (1982b) provides excellent suggestions for building rapport with infants. In the process of establishing rapport, she notes, the examiner moves from a position of little interaction to active involvement with the child. Young infants (i.e., 6 months or younger) may warm to the examiner rapidly, so that the examiner can approach the child almost immediately (e.g., using a simple interactive game such as peek-a-boo). Conversely, the older infant or toddler may show initial wariness of the examiner. Under these circumstances, the examiner should, after placing an interesting toy before the child, turn his attention to the parent and make no direct demands upon the child. During conversation with the parent, the examiner may comment positively and smile in response to the child's manipulation of the toy. As the child becomes accustomed to the setting, the examiner moves toward a role of more active involvement, first tentatively demonstrating an activity to the child (e.g., block stacking) and inviting her to join in, and only gradually making more direct demands.

As with infants, preschool children vary greatly in their level of preparation for the testing experience. The relatively nonverbal child should be approached with positive yet moderate affect. At first there should be few questions; instead, the examiner should use an interesting toy or nontest activity to serve as a medium for rapport building. Conversely, the verbally expressive child will usually enjoy conversation and the opportunity to talk to someone new. In general, it is best to start formal testing with intrinsically interesting activities within the child's mastery level. For a 2-year-old, this might mean assembling a formboard, stacking blocks, or using crayon and paper. Verbal activities may be phased in gradually as the child becomes acclimated to responding to examiner directives. One technique that can be effective for the shy or hesitant child involves the examiner feigning inability to solve some simple problem that the child has clearly mastered. For example, the examiner may attempt to complete a series of nested boxes, repeatedly inserting boxes in the wrong order while maintaining a perplexed expression. Such behavior will

usually gain the child's attention and often will result in the child coming to the examiner's aid.

For the older preschool child being evaluated by a multidisciplinary team, it is often helpful to begin the day's appointments by offering the child and parent a brief tour of the areas where testing is to take place and allowing the child to meet several of the clinicians "who'll be playing games with you today." The child should also be shown where the parent will be during their separation. The emotional tone of this period should be positive and upbeat so as not to overwhelm the child.

It is of the utmost importance that the examiner approach the child, regardless of age, with an air of confidence (Sattler, 1982). Even small children can detect when the examiner is tense or indecisive and may respond by showing increased reticence or noncompliance. And, while very young infants may not be so perceptive, any tension sensed by the parent may be passed on to the child.

Parent Presence. Whenever possible, infants should be tested in the company of a parent, or at least a familiar person. Not only does this reassure the child, but it also provides the examiner with a valuable information resource concerning the child's skills and ways to elicit desired behaviors. Haskins, Ramey, Stedman, Blacher-Dixon, and Pierce (1978) found that maternal presence during testing resulted in significantly higher mental index scores on the Bayley Scales of Infant Development. They concluded that maternal presence was important to ensure optimal infant performance but cautioned that their findings meant that researchers using infant assessment instruments must control this factor carefully when evaluating intervention efforts. Bayley (1969) suggests that a parent always be present for infant assessment and that she be asked to administer items when the examiner meets with resistance. Actively encouraging parent participation also communicates that the examiner values a parent's knowledge and skills and provides one medium for building examiner/parent rapport. When a parent is to be present, it is important to give clear instructions about matters such as how much help she can give to the child and whether or not she should talk to the child. A few minutes should be set aside after the evaluation to respond to any preliminary questions the parent may have about the testing process (Rogers, 1982b).

In contrast to infant testing, every effort should be made to test the preschool child without the presence of a significant other (Paget, 1983; Sattler, 1982). At this age, a parent's presence is usually more distracting than facilitating to performance. There are, of course, exceptions to this statement, as with the extremely fearful or shy child. In cases where a parent must be present, he should remain in the background, perhaps reading or engaged in some other solitary activity. After the examiner has succeeded in establishing rapport with the child, the parent may slip out quietly. Sometimes a child may separate easily from her parent, only to become anxious suddenly during the evaluation. Under these circumstances, the examiner should reassure the child that the parent is close by and will be waiting for her when she has finished. In rare cases, it may be necessary to take a short break from testing and allow the child to spend a few minutes with the parent. This procedure should be used with caution, as the child may subsequently take the opportunity to ask repeatedly for the parent, thus disrupting testing.

As previously noted, flexibility in testing procedures is critical to ensure the child's continued interest and attention during the session. While flexibility does not imply deviation from standardized test procedure, it does require that the examiner vary item type, rate of item presentation, and reinforcement schedules in response to the child's moment-to-moment affective and physical states.

High-Interest Activities. All infant and preschool measures that require direct participation of the child rely on **high-interest materials** to help maintain attention. Materials for such activities are colorful and manipulative and may stimulate several sensory modalities simultaneously (e.g., a small, brightly colored rubber doll that squeaks when pressed). Child-specific factors such as age, modality preference, and learning style also influence what is interesting to a particular child. For the young infant, almost any brightly colored object that can be grasped and mouthed will be at least momentarily interesting. For the older infant and preschooler, manipulative games ranging from pegboards to nested boxes and puzzles are often intrinsically interesting.

Alternating Items. Alternating the type of item presented may be helpful in maintaining attention. The McCarthy Scales of Children's Abilities (McCarthy, 1972), for example, provides a good example of how this technique may be applied to verbal and manipulative activities. The test begins with the colorful, manipulative tasks of puzzle assembly and block building, which place limited verbal demands on the child. Language activities are gradually introduced into the testing sequence, moving from items requiring limited to increased verbal expression. Approximately halfway through the battery, the child is introduced to several gross motor activities (e.g., throwing and catching a ball), which offers a constructive outlet for the child's growing restlessness and flagging attention. The child is then reintroduced to table items through pencil and paper tasks, and moves progressively into tasks requiring increased attention.

Regardless of the particular test selected, similar adjustments may be made in the test sequence depending on the needs of the child. Earlier tasks should be alternated with later, more difficult ones. High-concentration tasks, such as visual matching or memory items, may be alternated with less demanding ones like drawing, stringing beads, or completing formboards. (Note that what is defined as *high concentration* will vary from child to child dependent upon individual learning style.) Item modality can also be manipulated. For example, the examiner may alternate items that emphasize visual attention with those requiring auditory attention.

Dealing with High Activity and Impulsivity. The examiner confronted with a young infant or unusually active preschooler must rely on more than simply varying item type to ensure attention. A technique that may prove useful in such cases is presenting items at an accelerated pace with minimal delay between tasks. To be successful in this technique, the examiner must be thoroughly familiar with the test being used and be able to gain access to particular materials immediately; thus, the importance of arranging materials beforehand. When attempting to change from one activity to the next, it is advisable to introduce the new item before removing the old one, thereby shifting the child's attention and limiting frustration. Distractibility should be countered by keeping all materials out of sight (i.e., in the examiner's lap or beside her chair on the floor) except those necessary for the item at hand. In particular, any edible reinforcers being used must be kept hidden and away from the reach of the child. Attention should be given to the arrangement of the testing room. Extra toys should be put away, and the work table should face a blank wall rather than a window (Paget, 1983). To limit excess gross motor activity, it may be helpful to seat the very active child against a wall or in a corner during formal testing activities.

Reinforcement Procedures. One of the most powerful ways in which the examiner can influence a child's behavior is by the judicious use of positive reinforcement. **Positive reinforcement** is the presentation of a stimulus after a behavior that increases the likelihood of the behavior being performed again. It can take many forms, ranging from social praise, to opportunity to engage in preferred activities, to the use of edible rewards.

Social praise can be a strong motivator for children of all ages (Paget, 1983). Praise should be offered frequently but not to the point that the child becomes satiated. Particularly with infants and to some degree with preschoolers, the examiner's tone of voice is as critical to success as the particular words being used. Spontaneity and enthusiasm are necessary; praise delivered in a perfunctory manner is usually ineffective. On the other hand, the examiner can also err by being too enthusiastic. For example, the shy child who has not yet acclimated to the examiner may be overpowered and retreat in response to the overly enthusiastic examiner. The easily distracted child, on the other hand, may be overstimulated by highly energetic praise. Thus, effective praise should be tailored to the immediate needs of the child.

As the session progresses and the child is confronted more frequently with failure, it will be necessary to "create" opportunities to deliver praise. Earlier, successfully completed test items should be reintroduced and mixed with more difficult ones; the child might also be asked to demonstrate something successful such as counting or reciting the alphabet (Ulrey, 1982b). Kaufman and Kaufman (1977) recommend that the examiner assist the child in completing failed items such as puzzles, letting the child fit in the last piece without assistance. This procedure provides the child with a sense of accomplishment and gives the examiner another opportunity to praise good effort.

Over the course of the evaluation, the child will often express, either verbally or through actions, a clear preference for particular test activities. Contingent opportunities to repeat these activities may be used to elicit compliance with less-preferred activities. In addition, high-interest activities not part of the regular test kit may be useful for promoting appropriate behavior. Items such as soap bubbles and small wind-up toys may be particularly effective with noncompliant preschoolers. Regarding the latter, the child should first be shown the toy, which the examiner subsequently demonstrates. He is then promised brief access to the toy in exchange for completing a specific activity. Compliance gained, the child is allowed to wind the toy, which is retrieved as soon as it runs down. The examiner may then repeat the procedure, promising the child another opportunity for access upon completion of several more items.

A frequently used form of concrete reinforcement is the edible reward. Numerous studies have shown its effectiveness. For example, Edlund (1972) compared pretest and posttest scores on the Stanford Binet for 5- to 7-year-old children under positive reinforcement versus control conditions. Children in the treatment group were rewarded immediately with an M&M® candy for each correct test response. Comparison of pretest and posttest scores revealed a significant difference between the two groups, with the treatment group showing an 11-point gain in mean IQ compared to a 1-point gain for the control group.

Edible rewards may be particularly useful for the younger, immature child who requires immediate reinforcement for appropriate behavior or who is overly distracted by extraneous activities. In choosing particular rewards, it is important to avoid assumptions about what the child will find rewarding or aversive. Consequently, when using edibles, the examiner should try to have several types of treats on hand (Baker, 1983). Small bite-sized foods such as raisins, dry sweetened cereals, chips, or nuts are easy to ration and store. Chocolates such as M&M®s are also effective, although the child may become more quickly satiated to these. Parents should be consulted in regard to effective reinforcers, and the examiner should make sure that the

reinforcer does not present a health hazard (e.g., choking on a nut) or produce allergic reactions.

Environmental Considerations. Finally, assessments of infants and preschoolers is enhanced when certain environmental variables are considered. For example, positioning and seating may influence performance. Infants may sit in a parent's lap. When seated at a table, chairs should be of appropriate height, and children should be able to reach the table comfortably. Some activities may be best conducted on floors or mats. Generally these variables will need to be individualized according to child age, item demands, and individual children's characteristics.

Assessing Children with Sensory or Motor Impairments

Just as behavioral characteristics associated with children's ages influence test performance, so too do factors associated with children's unique handicapping conditions. A common theme underlying much of the professional literature is that most standardized tests do not consider these handicaps and thus are likely to be inappropriate or unfair for many children (Fuchs, Fuchs, Benowitz, & Barringer, 1987). Problems most frequently occur when a child's performance on a particular item is inappropriately influenced by a handicapping condition. The determination of whether the child's performance was thus inappropriately influenced depends upon the basic purpose of the item or test. Consider the following examples:

- A visually impaired child fails a vision screening test. This is not an example of inappropriate influence because the test was specifically designed to assess an ability the child does not possess.
- A child with cerebral palsy receives a low

score on the fine motor domain of a developmental scale. This, too, is not an example of inappropriate influence because the child does, in fact, have deficits in fine motor development.

- A child with cerebral palsy receives a low score on an intelligence test because she cannot perform many of the tasks that require fine motor skills, such are stacking blocks, putting pegs in a pegboard, or drawing a person. This is an example of inappropriate influence because the test was intended to assess cognitive not motor skills. The examiner in this case might incorrectly conclude that this child displayed mental retardation.
- A visually impaired infant cannot track a ball or look for an object that has disappeared from sight. To conclude, however, that this child does not have object permanence (the ability to know that objects still exist even when their immediate presence cannot be perceived) would be incorrect, inasmuch as the child cries when she hears her mother walk out of the room.

These examples illustrate the importance of carefully analyzing the intent of assessment tools as well as specific test items and determining their appropriateness for individual children. White (1980) describes this process as one of identifying the **critical function** of the item or instrument, defined as the "the purpose the behavior is supposed to serve, rather than the specific form of the motor act used to achieve that effect" (p.49). This section addresses general considerations in assessing handicapped children and then describes specific guidelines for use when assessing children with visual, auditory, or motor impairments.

General Considerations

As described in Chapter 2, many tests are **standardized.** This means that the items are meant to be administered using standard materials, procedures, administrative directions, and scoring. This format places the professional assessing handicapped youngsters in a dilemma. On the one hand, to alter standardized procedures in any way violates the basic assumptions underlying the instrument and thus makes any score derived from a nonstandard administration virtually uninterpretable. On the other hand, to test a child using procedures that inappropriately penalize performance also is inappropriate. What are the alternatives?

Several guidelines are offered in this regard. First, if the score on a particular test is of importance, then the item must be administered in the prescribed format. Otherwise, the meaning of the derived scores is unknown. However, it is essential that the examiner exercise professional judgment in reporting derived scores. If the examiner does not judge the derived scores to be representative of the child's true abilities, he must append a statement to that effect to any report of test performance. That statement should be supported by observational data, parent report, or other confirmatory evidence, such as observed performance under modified test conditions.

Second, the examiner should be aware of and use, for all children, strategies that increase the likelihood of obtaining optimal performance in response to test items. For example, the procedures described above for use in assessing very young children, including considerations regarding item sequences, pacing of activities, and use of reinforcement in testing should be used whenever necessary. Also, several specific guidelines are applicable for children with sensory or motor impairments, as described in the next section of this chapter.

Third, once tests have been administered in a standardized fashion for the purpose of reporting scores, professionals should **test the limits** of performance in order to obtain information relevant for instructional purposes and to validate the accuracy of data obtained from standardized administrations. One way to test the limits is to make the item simpler than its original format. For example, rather than having a child select the red block from a set of six that includes orange and yellow, have the child select from a group of three that includes red, black, and green. Another way to test the limits is to provide additional assistance to the child in order to see how much support is necessary before the child can perform the task. This assistance may include providing a prompt, a model, or partial physical assistance. Knowing the child's level of independence on a particular task should help the professional decide whether or not the skill is one that is emerging. A third example of testing the limit is for the examiner to test beyond the basal level or ceiling when appropriate. Because handicapped children are more likely to display "scattered" performance on many tests, such extended testing could help determine the full extent of a child's abilities (by testing beyond the ceiling) or to discover possible gaps in prerequisite skills (by testing below the basal).

A fourth example applies to tests that have timed items. In the standard administration the examiner should adhere to response times specified for each item. When testing the limits of children's skills, however, items could be presented without time constraints. This procedure is particularly applicable for children with motor disabilities when using tests that require manual dexterity and with visually impaired children when the item uses primarily visual materials.

Finally, examiners may need to alter some items in order to assess children with specific disabilities. White's (1980) notion of critical functions is helpful in this regard. Following this approach, the professional first examines each item to determine its purpose or critical function. Sometimes an item's intent is clear; in other cases, however, inferences must be drawn to determine critical functions. For example, an item such as stringing beads according to a specified color pattern requires several different skills, including fine motor coordination, color recognition, and sequencing abilities. If the item, however, is located in a fine motor domain of a test, then it can be assumed that the intent of the item is to assess motor skills. The professional then can take into consideration a child's unique impairments to determine if item failure was inappropriately influenced by the impairment and then to decide if item modification is warranted. For example, if the bead stringing item were located in the cognitive section of a test, fine motor coordination would be irrelevant to the assessment of color recognition and sequencing abilities. The examiner could then modify the item for a child with motor impairments to eliminate the need for fine motor skills.

In addition to general considerations in assessing handicapped youngsters, special considerations pertain to the assessment of children with sensory or motor impairments. The following sections describe some of those considerations.

Assessing Children with Visual Impairments

The development of children with visual impairments is generally characterized by delays in certain areas, qualitative differences in performance, and scattered strengths and deficits. An understanding of the normal developmental pattern of children with visual impairments is essential for any professional assessing such children.

A comprehensive review of the development of children with visual impairments is beyond the scope of this chapter. The reader is referred to specific studies or reviews of such development (e.g., DuBose, 1979; Fewell, 1983; Fraiberg, 1977). Fraiberg's research (1968, 1971, 1977) has provided insights into the development of children with visual impairments. In some areas of development, a clear pattern of delay typically emerges. For example, blind infants typically attain gross motor skills, such as creeping and walking, at a delayed rate. Also, the process of attachment and separation anxiety often is delayed, including behaviors such as smiling and exploring the caregiver's face. In other areas of development, blind infants accomplish certain functions using forms that differ from those observed in sighted infants. For example, blind infants often attempt to communicate through use of subtle hand gestures (Fraiberg, 1977). Finally, in some areas of development, blind children may appear to be more advanced than they actually are. For example, although very young blind children typically exhibit some delays in language, older visually impaired children may hear and use words for which they have no concrete or conceptual referent, such as color words.

When assessing visually impaired children, several principles are agreed upon as essential (Davidson & Legouri, 1986; Hansen, Young, & Ulrey, 1982). First, the child's visual acuities must be assessed. Very few children are totally blind, and it is important to know whether and to what extent a child can perform tasks requiring visual skills. Screening procedures for visual skills are described in Chapter 7 of this text, and a review of assessment of visual functioning is provided by Fewell (1983). Second, if a child has some vision, the examiner should take steps to increase the likelihood that the child can make use of residual vision. These steps may include high illumination (coming from behind the child or indirectly), high-contrast visual stimuli, increased size of the image presented, and close presentation of the stimuli (often 1–2 inches from the child) so the child can see (Fewell, 1983).

Third, the examiner should plan sufficient time to conduct the assessment, allowing the child time to explore the test environment and materials. Hansen et al. (1982) report that it generally takes longer for children with visual impairments to become familiar with objects because they often will utilize tactile, oral, olfactory, and auditory channels

for explanation. Fourth, Hansen et al. also suggest that the examiner be familiar with both normal expectations for the development of children with visual impairments as well as the abnormal behaviors that may be displayed, among which are "hand flapping, moving hands repeatedly in front of the eyes, persistent mouthing in a nonexploratory pattern, repetitive banging of a hand or objects against the mouth, parts of the body, or other surfaces, poking fingers at the eyes, and rocking of the head and/or body" (p. 112).

Finally, examiners should be familiar with assessment tools specifically designed or modified for use with visually impaired children. A version of the Stanford-Binet Intelligence Test, the Perkins-Binet (Davis, 1980), has been adapted for use with children ages 3 and up. Reynell (1979) published an instrument for use with visually impaired children ages 0–5 years that includes six age scales for cognitive and linguistic development. The Battelle Developmental Inventory (Newborg, Stock, Wnek, Guidubaldi, & Svinicki, 1984) provides general guidelines for adapting the instrument for visually impaired children and specific adaptation for selected items. For example, the following adaptation is provided for visually impaired children on the item "strings four large beads," an item at the 24- to 35- month level:

> Before giving the demonstration, allow the child to feel the string and the beads. Position yourself behind the child and hold both of his or her hands in your hands. Demonstrate stringing the four beads guiding the child's hands with your hands. Give clear verbal directions during the demonstration, describing what is being done.
>
> After the demonstration, place the beads on the table or in a small box next to the child. Place one of the child's hands on the pile of beads and place the string in the other hand, and give the child the verbal in-

structions to begin. While the child is stringing the beads, you may assist the child in locating and picking up each additional bead that is to be strung. Do not help the child put the beads on the string. (p. 53)

Assessing Children with Hearing Impairments

In contrast to visually handicapped children, children with hearing impairments generally follow a normal motor developmental pattern. The most obvious area of deficit typically is in language and communication skills, with possible accompanying delays in cognitive and social skills.

When assessing hearing-impaired children, the examiner must know the nature and extent of the child's hearing loss. A brief description of procedures to assess auditory functioning is provided in Chapter 7 of this text and detailed descriptions are provided by Shah and Clay (1983). Because very few children have a complete hearing loss, the amount of usable hearing and the extent to which amplification should be used is essential information in planning the assessment process.

Reviews by Rogers and Soper (1982) and Simeonsson (1986) yield several guidelines for assessing children with hearing impairments. First, children should be allowed to use their hearing aids in order to maximize optimal performance. Second, tasks should be presented in a clear and systematic fashion. Third, the examiner must be skilled in total communication and able to incorporate multiple modes of communication (e.g., signs and gestures). Fourth, tasks requiring verbal responses should be minimized for some hearing-impaired children. When giving an intelligence test, for example, it is generally recommended that the examiner administer the performance section and make a determination on an individual-child basis as to whether the verbal scales are appropriate.

Assessing Children with Motor Impairments

Children with motor impairments, such as cerebral palsy, pose unique challenges to professionals desiring to complete a comprehensive developmental assessment. Because of the nature and extent of their motor impairments, it is often difficult to ascertain their language and cognitive skills.

Because an entire chapter of this text is devoted to the assessment of motor skills (Chapter 13), the topic is addressed only briefly here. Reviews of the assessment of children with severe motor impairment (Rogers, 1982a; Wilhelm, Johnson, & Eisert, 1986) suggest several considerations. First and foremost, the examiner must make sure that the child is positioned or placed in such a fashion as to allow maximum use of available motor skills. Second, if the child needs adaptive equipment, such as a walker or a wheelchair, or some augmented communication system, such as a computer or communication board, the equipment should be allowed and its use noted in any assessment report. Third, the examiner must be aware of the type and extent of motor impairment and the unique response patterns of individual children. For example, some children may respond with an eye gaze whereas others may answer a question with a smile or a frown. Also, some children will be very slow in responding and must be given adequate time to complete their answers. Finally, some items may need to be altered in order to eliminate the motor components. This approach is appropriate when the intent of the item is not to assess a specific motor skill but rather some other developmental domain.

Alternative Assessment Strategies

The challenges posed by infants and preschoolers with handicaps have forced infant and preschool specialists to recognize that traditional approaches to assessing behavioral performance and abilities may be inadequate in providing insight to a child's true capabilities. As a result, several alternative assessment strategies have been developed and evaluated in recent years. Unfortunately, these strategies are not well known and their clinical implications are as yet uncertain. Professionals should be aware of their existence, however, and recognize their potential contribution to a greater understanding of children's abilities. Each of the procedures has demonstrated that there are aspects of children's development and abilities not often tapped when using traditional assessment procedures. This finding should caution professionals to recognize the limitations of their understanding of children and challenge professionals to conduct clinical experiments of alternative assessment procedures with difficult-to-assess children.

Affective Assessment Procedures

One alternative approach to assessment is to examine children's **affective development** as an indicator of cognitive abilities. Cicchetti and Sroufe (1976) demonstrated a strong relationship between affective and cognitive development in infants with Down syndrome. Using a series of tactile (e.g., tickling or bouncing), auditory (e.g., unusual sounds), visual, and social stimuli, the authors demonstrated that normal infants displayed a definite developmental sequence of affective responses to various stimuli. Down syndrome children demonstrated the same sequence but at a delayed rate.

Jens and Johnson (1982) suggest that such a procedure may provide a "window" to view the cognitive development of children who may not have the motor or sensory abilities to complete a more traditional test. Johnson (1982), for example, asserts that by using this procedure, "it may be possible to identify youngsters who perform more than two standard deviations below the mean on a norm-referenced 'mental' test but smile and laugh to stimuli appropriate to his or her age level. For these youngsters the label *retarded* and its particular implications for future development may not be applicable" (pp. 67–68). Johnson goes on to caution that while such a procedure provides important insight into children's abilities, it does not define the child's problem. Furthermore, normal affective development does not necessarily mean that a child is not retarded, nor does it mean that the child will not experience problems in functional adaptation. Jens and Johnson (1982) also caution that the educational implications of such data have yet to be identified. However, "their major value in an intervention paradigm may currently come from using them to change caretaker attitudes toward children's capacity for learning" (p. 22).

Processing of Visual and Auditory Information

A second type of alternative assessment seeks to document how children process information or stimuli presented. Vietze and Coates (1986) defined **information-processing techniques** as "those in which the infant must analyze some aspect of the situation and make a specific behavioral response" (p. 75), and described seven techniques for measuring information-processing skills in infants: classical conditioning, instrumental conditioning, visual fixation, preference for novelty, habituation paradigm, exploration of objects, and cross-model perception. The first two assess the infant's response to two different kinds of conditioning. The next three assess the infant's attentional responses to stimuli, whereas the last two focus on how long and how often infants manually explore objects. Vietze and Coates concluded that, while these procedures show promise in identifying children's disabilities, none has been developed adequately or validated for clinical use. They suggested several steps necessary before such instruments will be useful.

Zelazo (1982) has developed a paradigm for assessment that examines the extent to which an infant can develop a prediction for events and then notice discrepancies in behavior that differ from what is expected. The following describes a sample sequence of activities:

> In the car-doll sequence, a toy car is released from its resting position at the top of a ramp, allowed to roll down and to tap over a brightly colored styrofoam object upon contact. During the discrepant variation, the car taps the object, but it does not fall. There are six presentations in which the object falls when tapped by the car, three presentations when the object does not fall when tapped, and three reappearances of the original event.
>
> The child observes this sequence in a room resembling a puppet theater. The visual events are presented on a brightly lit stage, in front of the child who is seated on the mother's lap. The durations of visual fixation, smiling, vocalizing, and fretting are coded on a button box by an observer seated behind the other wing of the stage. Surface leads attached to the infant's chest are used to produce an electrocardiogram that is converted to a beat-by-beat recording of heart rate using a cardiotachometer. (pp. 115–116)

Zelazo (1982) also suggested that such a procedure is advantageous in comparison to traditional assessment procedures because it focuses on dynamic (rather than static) performance, subtle elicited responses, and clusters of types of behaviors (rather than a single specific motor act). Furthermore, the procedure does not require examiner rapport and should be less biased for children with sensory or motor impairments because it focuses on patterns of response rather than specific developmental pinpoints. He presented a case study and preliminary research

data documenting the clinical usefulness of such a procedure and the presence of an apparent developmental sequence in infant responses to these events.

Obviously, the use of a procedure such as this is exacting and costly in terms of staff time. As with affective measures, the main benefit of this procedure appears to be the possibility of obtaining a more optimistic view of the child's abilities than might be obtained by the sole reliance on more traditional measures.

Brinker and Lewis (1982) asserted that another important competence for infants is the extent to which they detect and utilize **co-occurrences,** defined as two events that occur together. They suggested that handicapped infants have fewer opportunities to experience co-occurrences due to physical or sensory impairments or alterations in parents' interaction styles, but argued that by assessing the infant's abilities to process co-occurrences, the infant specialist can discover the "competent handicapped infant" (p. 9). Brinker and Lewis describe the implications of such an approach for both testing and teaching a skill such as raising the infant's head when lying on its stomach:

> A process approach to the problems of head and trunk control would require simultaneous analysis of head raising in several physical positions. It would also require an analysis of the events to which the child orients and attends and the objects and people involved in such events. Thus the motor components would be separated from the attention components in a process analysis of head raising while prone. This process approach, which requires a continual hypothesis-testing dialogue between assesser/teacher and infant, not only provides information about whether a child can do a certain thing in a certain situation, but it also provides clues as to how and why the child performs in this way. These clues

should be useful guides to teaching other skills in other situations. (p. 9)

In conclusion, it may be stated that alternative assessment procedures such as those described perhaps best serve to emphasize the limitations of our understanding of the skills of children with sensory or motor impairments. At present they are not widely available for clinical use, and the implications of their findings for intervention purposes are largely unknown. Teachers and other early childhood specialists should be aware of their existence, but more importantly, should seek to incorporate creative assessment strategies with individual children to avoid false conclusions regarding the limitations of their competence.

SUMMARY OF KEY CONCEPTS

- Infants and preschoolers with handicaps present assessment problems because they are young and generally not responsive to testing procedures.

- Infants and preschoolers with sensory and physical handicaps present assessment problems also because their impairments may hide their competence when tested with traditional procedures.

- Infants and preschoolers may have high activity levels, be easily distracted, display variable states and attention spans, be wary of strangers, and display inconsistent performance in strange situations.

- To counter the characteristics of young children with handicaps, assessors should be knowledgeable of child characteristics, be flexible in administering the tests and obtaining information, engage in preplanning activities, establish rapport with the infant/child, and involve parents at appropriate levels.

- Assessors should also use high-interest materials, alternate the presentation of item types, pace item presentation appropriately, and use positive reinforcement whenever such measures are allowed in testing protocols..

- Assessors must analyze the intent of tests, purpose of assessment, and intent (or critical function) of items when adapting items for infants and children with motor and sensory handicaps; adaptations of test procedures and materials should be noted in the assessment report.

- After following standard administration procedures, assessors should "test the limits" of children's performance by adapting and varying testing procedures and materials.

- Alternative assessment strategies are emerging that may hold promise for infants and preschoolers with handicaps; these include using affective development as an indicator of cognitive development, determining how the children use sensory information, and focusing on the process of development rather than on the products of development.

REFERENCES

Baker, A. (1983). Psychological assessment of autistic children. *Clinical Psychology Review, 3*(1), 41–59.

Bayley, N. (1969). *Manual for the Bayley Scales of Infant Development.* New York: The Psychological Corp.

Brinker, R.P. & Lewis, M. (1982). Discovering the competent handicapped infant: A process approach to assessment and intervention. *Topics in Early Childhood Special Education, 2*(2), 1–16.

Cicchetti, D. & Sroufe, A. (1976). The relationship between affective and cognitive development in Down's syndrome infants. *Child Development, 47,* 920–929.

Davidson, P. & Legouri, S.A. (1986). Assessment of visually impaired children. In R. J. Simeonsson (Ed.), *Psychological and developmental assessment of special children* (pp. 217–239). Boston: Allyn & Bacon.

Davis, C.J. (1980). *Perkins-Binet Tests of Intelligence for the Blind.* Watertown, MA: Perkins School for the Blind.

Dubose, R.F. (1979). Working with sensorily impaired children, Part I: Visual impairments. In S. G. Garwood (Ed.), *Educating young handicapped children: A developmental approach* (pp. 323–360). Germantown, MD: Aspen.

Edlund, C.V. (1972). The effect on the behavior of children, as reflected in the IQ scores, when reinforced after each correct response. *Journal of Applied Behavior Analysis, 5,* 317–319.

Fewell, R.R. (1983). Assessment of visual functioning. In K.D. Paget & B.A. Bracken (Eds.), *The psychoeducational assessment of preschool children* (pp. 359–386). New York: Grune & Stratton.

Fraiberg, S. (1968). Parallel and divergent patterns in blind and sighted infants. *Psychoanalytic Study of the Child, 23,* 264–300.

Fraiberg, S. (1971). Intervention in infancy: A program for blind infants. *Journal of the Academy of Child Psychiatry, 10,* 381–405.

Fraiberg, S. (1977). *Insights from the blind: Studies of blind and sighted infants.* New York: Basic Books.

Fuchs, D. (1987). Examiner familiarity effects on test performance: Implications for training and practice. *Topics in Early Childhood Special Education, 7*(3), 90–104.

Fuchs, D., Fuchs, L. S., Benowitz, S., & Barringer, K. (1987). Norm-referenced tests: Are they valid for use with handicapped students? *Exceptional Children, 54,* 263–271.

Hansen, R., Young, J., & Ulrey, G. (1982). Assessment considerations with the visually handicapped child. In G. Ulrey & S. J. Rogers (Eds.), *Psychological assessment of handicapped infants and young children* (pp. 108–114). New York: Thieme-Stratton.

Haskins, R., Ramey, C.T., Stedman, D.J., Blacher-Dixon, J., & Pierce, J.E. (1978). Effects of repeated assessment on standardized test performance by infants. *American Journal of Mental Deficiency, 83,* 233–239.

Horner, T.M. (1980). Test-retest and home-clinic characteristics of the Bayley Scales of Infant Development in nine- and fifteen-month old infants. *Child Development, 51,* 751–758.

Jens, K.G. & Johnson, N.M. (1982). Affective development: A window to cognition in young handicapped children. *Topics in Early Childhood Special Education, 2*(2), 17–24.

Johnson, N.M. (1982). Assessment paradigms and atypical infants: An interventionist's perpective. In D. Bricker (Ed.), *Intervention with at-risk and handicapped infants: From research to application* (pp. 63–76). Baltimore, MD: University Park Press.

Kaufman, A. & Kaufman, N. (1977). *Clinical evaluation of young children with the McCarthy Scales.* New York: Grune & Stratton.

Lewis, M. & Brooks-Gunn, J. (1972, April). *Self, other and fear: The reaction of infants to people.* Paper presented at the meeting of the Eastern Psychological Association, Boston.

McCarthy, D.A. (1972). *Manual for the McCarthy Scales of Children's Abilities.* New York: Psychological Corp.

Morgan, G.A. & Ricciuti, H. (1969). Infants' responses to strangers during the first year. In B. M. Foss (Ed.), *Determinants of infant behavior, 4.* London: Methuen.

Newborg, J., Stock, J.R., Wnek, L., Guidubaldi, J., & Svinicki, J. (1984). *The Battelle Developmental Inventory.* Allen, TX: DLM/Teaching Resources.

Paget, K. (1983). The individual examining situation: Basic considerations for preschool children.

In K. Paget & B. Bracken (Eds.), *The psychoeducational assessment of preschool children* (pp. 51–62). New York: Grune & Stratton.

Prechtl, H.F.R. (1974). The behavioral states of the newborn. *Brain Research, 6,* 185–212.

Reynell, J. (1979). *Reynell-Zinkin Scales: Developmental Scales for Young Visually Handicapped Children.* Windsor, England: NFER Publishing Co.

Rogers, S. J. (1982a). Assessment considerations with the motor-handicapped child. In G. Ulrey & S.J. Rogers (Eds.), *Psychological assessment of handicapped infants and young children* (pp. 95–107). New York: Thieme-Stratton.

Rogers, S. J. (1982b). Techniques of infant assessment. In G. Ulrey & S. Rogers (Eds.), *Psychological assessment of handicapped infants and young children* (pp. 59–64). New York: Thieme-Stratton.

Rogers, S. J. & Soper, E. (1982). Assessment considerations with hearing-impaired preschoolers. In G. Ulrey & S.J. Rogers (Eds.), *Psychological assessment of handicapped infants and young children* (pp. 115–122). New York: Thieme-Stratton.

Sattler, J. (1982). *Assessment of children's intelligence and special abilities* (2nd ed.). Boston: Allyn & Bacon.

Shah, C.P. & Clay, W.A. (1983). Assessment of auditory functioning. In K.D. Paget & B.A. Bracken (Eds.), *The psychoeducational assessment of preschool children* (pp. 321–358). New York: Grune & Stratton.

Simeonsson, R.J. (1986). Assessment of hearing-impaired children. In R.J. Simeonsson (Ed.), *Psychological and developmental assessment of special children* (pp 195–216). Boston: Allyn & Bacon.

Thomas, A. & Chess, S. (1977). *Temperament and development.* New York: Brunner/Mazel.

Ulrey, G. (1982a). Influences of infant behavior on assessment. In G. Ulrey & S.J. Rogers (Eds.), *Psychological assessment of handicapped infants and young children* (pp. 14–24). New York: Thieme-Stratton.

Ulrey, G. (1982b). Influences of preschoolers behavior on assessment. In G. Ulrey & S.J. Rogers (Eds.), *Psychological assessment of handicapped infants and young children* (pp. 25–34). New York: Thieme-Stratton.

Vietze, P.M. & Coates, D.L. (1986). Using information processing strategies for early identification of mental retardation. *Topics in Early Childhood Special Education, 6*(3), 72–85.

White, O.R. (1980). Adaptive performance objectives: Form versus function. In W. Sailor, B. Wilcox, & L. Brown (Eds.), *Methods of instruction for severely handicapped students* (pp. 47–69). Baltimore, MD: Paul H. Brookes.

Wilhelm, C., Johnson, M., & Eisert, D. (1986). Assessment of motor-impaired children. In R.J. Simeonsson (Ed.), *Psychological and developmental assessment of special children* (pp. 241–278). Boston: Allyn & Bacon.

Zelazo, P.R. (1982). Alternative assessment procedures for handicapped infants and toddlers: Theoretical and practical issues. In D. Bricker (Ed.), *Intervention with at-risk and handicapped infants: From research to application* (pp. 107–128). Baltimore, MD: University Park Press.

Chapter 4

Using Direct Observation in Assessment

Mark Wolery
University of Kentucky

KEY TERMS

- Observation
- Functional Relationship
- Behavior
- Form
- Effect
- Function
- Frequency
- Intensity
- Duration
- Latency
- Endurance
- Accuracy
- Anecdotal Records

- Running Record
- Specimen Descriptions
- Event-Sampling Recording
- Permanent Products
- Calibrated System
- Data Collection Sheets
- Time-Sampling Recording
- Momentary Time Sampling
- Partial-Interval Time Sampling

- Whole-Interval Time Sampling
- Category-Sampling Recording
- Exhaustive
- Mutually Exclusive
- Levels-of-Assistance Recording
- Task-Analytic Recording
- Chained Skills
- Observer Bias
- Observer Drift
- Functional Analysis
- Analogue Analysis

Assessment, as defined in Chapter 1, is the process of gathering information to make decisions. Testing, described in Chapters 2 and 3, is perhaps the most common method educators, special educators, speech-language pathologists, occupational therapists, and physical therapists have used to obtain needed information. Another means is direct, naturalistic observation. Although direct observation has a rich history in the study of child behavior (Bijou, Peterson, Harris, Allen, & Johnston, 1969), it frequently is ascribed less value than testing in the assessment of child behavior. This chapter defines observation, describes the rationale for using it, and discusses procedures for employing various direct observation methods. The intent of the chapter is that direct observation and testing will not be viewed as competing methodologies, but as integral, inextricably tied components of the assessment of infants, toddlers, and preschoolers for specific purposes.

Definition and Use of Direct Observation

Definition
Observation is a term that needs little formal definition; it involves watching children's behavior and making a record of their responses. In reality, appropriate use of observation is more complex. Some have differentiated naturalistic observation, which occurs in the natural environment, from clinical observation, which occurs in a laboratory or contrived setting (Thurman & Widerstorm, 1985). For purposes of this chapter, *observation* refers to situations in which the interventionist watches and records child behavior, but does not present stimuli to which the child must respond as in direct testing. Observation is a means of discerning what behaviors are performed by children, under what conditions those behaviors appear, and which stimuli are related to those behaviors.

Observation has been used to meet a number of the assessment purposes outlined in Chapter 1. For example, direct observation has been used as a supplement to direct testing in diagnostic assessments (Peterson, 1987). It has been proposed as a means for screening preschoolers in child-care settings but is not realistic for mass screenings. Direct observation is rarely employed in assessments for the purpose of placement but has been described as one of the primary means of collecting data on potential placement environments when planning transitions (Vincent, Salisbury, Walter, Brown, Gruenwald, & Powers, 1980). Most authors, when discussing instructional program planning assessment, recommend the use of direct observation (Thurman & Widerstrom, 1985). When evaluating the effects of specific intervention procedures, direct observation is frequently used (Berdine & Meyer, 1987; White & Haring, 1980; Wolery, Bailey, & Sugal, 1988). Finally, direct observation repeatedly has been employed as a data-collection method in research with infants, toddlers, and preschoolers. In keeping with the intent of this book, this chapter focuses primarily on two purposes of assessment: instructional program planning and monitoring the effects of those programs. When conducting assessments for instructional program planning, interventionists should seek to answer the following questions: (a) what behaviors or skills does the child do independently, (b) what behaviors does the child do with support, adaptation, or assistance, (c) what behaviors does the child need to learn, and (d) what intervention strategies are likely to be successful with this child? When monitoring the effects of programs, interventionists should ask: Is the child making adequate progress, and if not, what changes should be made in the intervention? Direct observation is useful for answering these questions.

Rationale for Direct Observation
At least five reasons exist for integrating direct observation into assessment activities for infants and young children. The rationale provided here applies primarily to assessments for instructional program planning and modification, but may be applicable to other assessment purposes (e.g., screening, placement, and diagnosis).

Assessing Difficult-to-Test Behaviors and Skills. Much of the content of the infant and early childhood special education curriculum remains to be identified and empirically documented; however, it is clear that many of the important developmental skills needed for independent functioning are not easily tested. Difficult-to-test behaviors include those that occur primarily in social contexts or are embedded in routines. For example, it is difficult to design a test or even a testing situation that would tap adequately children's ability to initiate social interactions, demonstrate competence in toileting skills, display functional movement patterns, anticipate a usual routine, or comment on the environment. Nonetheless, these skills are needed by many infants and preschoolers with handicaps, and interventionists must have a means to assess those needs precisely. In addition to skills for which tests are probably impossible to design, there are skills that are testable but for which tests have not been developed. In such cases, interventionists continue to require methods for assessing children's instructional needs. Direct observation can be used with such behaviors.

Validating Information Collected from Other Measurement Strategies. As noted in Chapter 1, early interventionists use three measurement strategies: testing, observation, and interviews. Testing is advantageous because it can be used to assess many skills efficiently. However, testing frequently requires some artificial structuring and needs adherence to prescribed procedures for presentation. It is also episodic. As a result, information gained in testing can be misleading; children's performance may be enhanced or deflated by the testing requirements and may not reflect children's usual behavior patterns. Direct, systematic observation can be used to validate or invalidate information acquired through direct testing. Likewise, interviews are particularly efficient means of gathering information, but the results may be invalid due to the biases of the interviewer and/or interviewee. Similarly, subtle differences in definitions during the interview can lead to invalid information. For example, if the interviewer asks whether a child does a given behavior, and the inter-

viewee interprets the question to mean the child *has* done that behavior, then information very different from that intended is likely to be obtained. Direct systematic observation can be used to confirm or call into question information obtained through interviews.

Extending Assessment Activities to Additional Situations and Conditions. There are at least two areas where direct observation can be used to extend assessment activities outside the traditional school settings: assessment of generalization settings, and assessment of behavioral competence in routines. The purpose of public education is to help individuals learn skills they can use in nonschool situations (Hilgard & Bower, 1975). The true test of what needs to be learned and whether learning has occurred is how the learner functions outside the school or intervention environment. If this is the ultimate purpose, then assessment activities should identify skills that are needed in those situations and the child's ability to perform those skills in those contexts. Careful analysis of generalization environments (Stremel-Campbell & Campbell, 1985) and ecological analyses and inventories (Brown, 1987; Snell & Grigg, 1987) should be used to identify needed skills in generalization environments. These issues are described in Chapter 5 and throughout this text. Warren (1985) describes a process for developing and measuring generalization plans for language behaviors, but it is applicable across skill areas. The process includes (a) writing generalization objectives, (b) recruiting individuals across situations to measure generalization, (c) assessing generalization regularly and each time children learn a step of a skill, (d) conducting generalization checks where generalized responding is actually needed, and (e) ensuring that the measurement system is reliable. Direct observation is the primary means for determining which skills are needed in the natural environment and for assessing whether children actually perform those skills when they are needed.

Many of the skills toddlers and preschoolers need to function independently are performed during routines. Examples of routines are toileting, eating, playing, dressing/undressing, and coming and going from one place to another. To be useful to children, the skills needed for routines must occur in chains (i.e., several behaviors are sequenced together to form a complex skill). Direct testing of chained behavior is quite difficult and may be misleading because appropriate performance of chains is highly dependent upon responding to natural stimuli. Direct observation during routines allows assessment to be extended to these important skill areas.

Identifying Functional Relationships Between Environmental Stimuli and Child Behavior. A **functional relationship** exists when a change in one variable reliably produces a change in another. In this case, the relationships between environmental stimuli and children's behavior are important. At least four "generic" functional relationships exist: (a) reinforcing functions, in which the contingent presentation of a stimulus (positive reinforcement) or withdrawal of an aversive stimulus (negative reinforcement) results in maintenance of, or an increase in, the occurrence of the behavior; (b) punishing functions, in which the contingent presentation of an aversive stimuli (Type I) or withdrawal of a positive reinforcer (Type II) produces a decrease in the occurrence of the behavior; (c) eliciting functions, in which the presentation of a specific environmental stimulus results in a specific response as in reflexive behavior; and (d) discriminative stimulus functions, in which a specific stimulus cues the child that reinforcement is probable if a given behavior occurs. Although the functions performed by some stimuli can be directly tested, identifying the existing relationships between natural environmental stimuli and the child's behavior is an important assessment activity.

Direct observation is the primary means of accomplishing this task. Procedures for conducting this type of assessment are described later in the chapter.

Monitoring Intervention Effectiveness. The results and assumptions derived from the assessment of infants and young children with handicaps should be viewed as tentative. Frequently, they will require modification as intervention is initiated; thus, assessment activities ideally should be ongoing. Continual testing of children is impractical and inappropriate, but some means are needed to determine whether to modify the assumptions about target skills and strategies for intervention. Direct observation is well suited for such a purpose. A literature is growing that guides interventionists in determining whether children are making progress and what changes should be made if progress is not forthcoming (cf. Haring, Liberty, & White, 1980).

Summary of Rationale. Direct observation should be used in assessment activities because it allows (a) assessment of difficult-to-test skills, (b) validation of information collected through other measurement strategies, (c) extension of assessment activities to generalization situations and routines, (d) identification of functional relationships between child behavior and environmental stimuli, and (e) ongoing assessment of intervention effectiveness. Also, direct observation is more flexible than direct testing. Children with sensory or motor impairments are less likely to be penalized, because direct observation does not require standardized item presentation and scoring procedures. Thus, interventionists should be skilled in using it. It should be noted that direct observation, despite its advantages, also has some limitations. Direct observation can be time consuming. Skill is required to design useful observational systems and to analyze data collected from those procedures. Further, some

skills can be assessed more easily and accurately with direct testing, either designed
by teachers or through available tests. In the
remainder of this chapter, procedures for using direct observation are described. In
Chapters 11–17, information is provided on
using direct observation and direct testing for
developing curriculum content in various
developmental areas.

Basics of Direct Observation

The process of collecting data on behavior
using human observers and direct observation
has several definite steps. These steps include
defining the behaviors and identifying the
relevant dimensions of those behaviors, selecting appropriate data-collection systems
and data sheets, selecting appropriate times
and situations for observation, checking the
accuracy of data collection, and using the
results for decision making. For more complete discussions of these issues, see White
and Haring (1980), Wolery et al. (1988), and
Cooper, Heron, and Heward (1987).

Defining Behaviors and Identifying
Relevant Dimensions

With testing, the test authors specify the
stimuli to be presented and define acceptable
child responses. The responses children make
are compared to the descriptions in the test
manuals/protocols, and the tester makes a
determination about the accuracy of the
response. In direct observation and informal
assessment, interventionists must define the
behaviors to be observed. As noted in any
applied behavior analysis text, a **behavior** is
an event that involves movement, has a
definite beginning and end, can be performed
repeatedly, and can be measured reliably. The
reasons for defining behaviors are well understood and include increased precision in
measurement and increased accuracy in com-

munication with others. The manner in which
the behavior is defined and the identification
of a relevant dimension or characteristic of
the behavior will vary depending upon the
focus of the assessment.

Many of the descriptions we use of children
are not really behaviors, and many of the
appropriate intervention goals are not specific
behaviors. For example, when we say children
are eager, curious, creative, cooperative,
playful, social, task directed, communicative,
or persistent, we are describing desirable
characteristics, but are not describing precise
behaviors. Similarly, many of the descriptions
we use for the undesirable qualities of
children's behavior (e.g., withdrawn, impul-
sive, uncooperative, aggressive, disruptive, or
hyperactive) are not behaviors. These descriptions require definition before meaningful
measurement can occur. For example, if an
interventionist wanted to define cooperative,
a number of behaviors could be identified that
indicate this trait. These behaviors might include compliance with adult requests, changing tasks quickly when asked, doing planned
activities, and absence of inappropriate
behaviors such as screaming, hitting others,
throwing toys, and so on. With precise definition of behaviors, the general descriptions can
be measured.

When preparing for an observation, the
interventionist should determine whether the
form or the effect of the behavior is of
primary concern (White, 1980). **Form** refers
to the specific behaviors performed by the
student, and the **effect**, also called **function**,
refers to the outcome of those behaviors. A
form for a greeting response may be saying
hi or good morning or making eye contact and
waving. The effect is that the child communicates that she is greeting another person, that is, the other person perceives being
greeted. Interventionists must determine
whether the form (specific behavior) is important or whether the effect is critical. For
example, the interventionist may want to
know whether a child can initiate social

interactions in a play setting with other children. In such a case, the interventionist is less concerned about the form of the initiation (i.e., the precise behavior used) than whether initiations occur (i.e., the effect). To initiate a social interaction, a number of different behaviors can be used. A child could speak to others, touch them, move close to them, offer a toy, smile, or use some gesture. Each of the forms (behaviors) may result in an initiation. In such cases, the interventionist must define what constitutes an initiation and then develop a measurement system that allows data to be collected on the number of initiations, to whom the initiation was made, the variety of behaviors used to make the initiation, and the conditions that appear to be related to making or not making initiations.

On the other hand, sometimes the form of the behavior is important, particularly if a given effect is accomplished by a narrow range of forms or if particular forms will result in greater assimilation of the child in normalized environments. If an interventionist is concerned, for example, about children's ability to play with a specific toy, feed themselves with spoons, put on their coats, or initiate a verbal greeting response, the precise forms of the behaviors need definition. Forms of behavior are particularly important when monitoring the effects of intervention programs. For example, a child may initiate interactions frequently enough, to a variety of other children, and in appropriate situations; however, all initiations may only involve one or two behaviors. The goal of intervention, then, may be to teach the student to use specific, additional behaviors for initiating interactions. In such cases, the precise behaviors require definition.

All behavior has a number of different dimensions or characteristics that can be measured. These characteristics include the frequency with which the behaviors occur, the intensity or magnitude of their occurrence, their duration, in some cases their latency, and, in others the endurance.

Frequency (or *rate*) refers to how often a behavior occurs. Rate technically refers to how often a behavior occurs for a given time period. **Intensity** refers to the amount of force with which the behavior occurs.
Duration refers to the length of time a given behavior lasts. **Latency** refers to how long it takes a child to initiate a behavior once a cue has occurred. **Endurance** refers to the length of time a given behavior can be repeatedly performed. Another related dimension of behavior is accuracy. **Accuracy** refers to the extent to which a child's behavior conforms to the defined topography of a given behavior. For example, accuracy is particularly important when measuring pre-academic and language behaviors. If an interventionist is attempting to teach a child to name common objects, the accuracy of naming is more important than the frequency, intensity, latency, duration, or endurance.

When defining a behavior either for initial assessment or for monitoring intervention effectiveness, the appropriate dimension should be selected and measured. When selecting the dimension, two questions should be asked. First, if the child is to be more independent, developmentally advanced, or more socially acceptable, which dimension(s) of the behavior should be changed? Second, which dimension can be measured most accurately and easily? For example, if a child is hitting others with his fist, the frequency and intensity of the hitting should be changed to make the child more socially acceptable. The duration of the hits, latency from some cue, the endurance, and accuracy of hits are less important dimensions. When frequency and intensity are applied to the second question, the frequency of hits is measured more easily and accurately than the intensity.

The important dimension for measurement will vary from behavior to behavior. For example, accuracy may be most important with a naming task, frequency with an aggressive behavior, intensity with a behavior such as speaking loudly enough, duration with behaviors such as eye contact or holding up one's head, latency with behaviors such as responding to others' initiations, and endurance with behaviors such as walking or other responses that must be performed repeatedly. The dimension of behavior also is important when writing objectives. The criterion statement in objectives should be written to conform to the most relevant dimension of the behavior. This issue is described in Chapter 18.

Selecting Data Collection Systems and Designing Data Sheets

At least six different data-collection systems are used in direct observation and informal assessment: narrative descriptions, event-sampling, time-sampling, category-sampling, levels-of-assistance, and task analytic systems (Berdine & Meyer, 1987; Wolery et al., 1988). In this section these systems are described, and data-collection sheets are presented. Data-collection sheets and special applications of these systems are described in chapters throughout this text.

Narrative Descriptions. Thurman and Widerstrom (1985) describe three types of narrative descriptions: anecdotal records, running records, and specimen descriptions. **Anecdotal records** are brief statements of events important to child performance. They can be obtained during initial assessment for instructional program planning and then used to guide later assessment activities. For example, an interventionist may administer a test or conduct an observation and notice some behavior that may be indicative of a seizure disorder. An anecdotal record of that behavior is important. It can be used when comparing notes with other team members and in deciding whether evaluation by a neurologist is warranted. Anecdotal records also can be used for monitoring the effects of intervention. It is unlikely that interventionists will have sufficient time to design

formal data-collection systems on all children's objectives. Regularly writing anecdotal records about objectives that are not being measured in other ways allows the interventionist to develop a record of progress and accountability. Such notes are frequently used in hospitals, clinics, and other settings where problem or goal-oriented record keeping systems are in place. Thurman and Widerstrom (1985) suggest the following guidelines: (a) the anecdote should be written soon after the event occurs; (b) the basic action or flavor of the event and key persons should be described; (c) the setting, time, and activity should be listed; (d) the sequence of the event should be described (beginning, middle, and end); and (e) the main event, specific information about the main event, and qualitative description of the event should be included. Anecdotal reports allow information to be gathered efficiently with little effort; however, that information is limited, is not rigorously collected, may not be quantified, and is open to observer bias and inference.

A **running record** is a type of narrative description that is less episodic than anecdotal reports and involves recording all of the child's behavior and relevant events for a period of time (Thurman & Widerstrom, 1985). Although running records are used infrequently, they are appropriate when collecting a language sample, determining how a child's time is spent, and identifying variables that influence children's behavior. When conducting running records, the times and places of observation should be selected, and the setting and situation described. The primary body of the running record is a thorough description of what the child does and how she does it. Events that result in changes in child behavior, or events that should but do not, also are recorded. The behavior of others that is directed toward the child should be described thoroughly. Any inferences or interpretative statements should be noted as such. When running records are used, they should be transcribed into a usable form soon after completion of the observation. Transcription is facilitated by listing three columns: antecedent events, child behavior, and consequent events. The advantage of running records is that a lot of information is gathered about the child's behavior and events surrounding it. The disadvantages are that it is time consuming, requires considerable skill in analysis, may yield relatively little new information, and is open to observer bias and inference.

Specimen descriptions are similar to running records and follow similar procedures (Thurman & Widerstrom, 1985). However, specimen descriptions are designed to portray specific episodes or a series of episodes. Thus, the description is tied more to a given event than to all the behavior that may occur as in a running record. More objective descriptions are written here than in anecdotal records. The advantage of these specimen descriptions is that information can be collected on specific events or episodes. The disadvantages are similar, however, to those of running records.

Naturalistic Research. Recently, special educators have become interested in a research methodology called ethnographic or naturalistic research. This methodology relies heavily on participant observation and structured and unstructured interviews. "The participant observer listens closely, observes behavior in the natural settings, asks questions when events are unclear, and even participates in the setting" (Odom & Shuster, 1986, p. 71). The goal of naturalistic inquiry is to view the world through the perspectives of the individuals in their naturalistic setting. As such, it has ramifications for identifying the relationships that exist between individuals' behavior and events or circumstances that exist in their settings. Odom and Shuster present an example of its use for studying families' perspectives of their handicapped infants.

Event-Sampling Recording. **Event-sampling recording** occurs when the child's behavior signals the interventionist that recording should occur. The simplest form of this system is when an interventionist records a tally each time a behavior occurs; for example, counting the number of hits, correct responses to a pre-academic task, toys with which a child plays, persons to whom the child initiates, steps taken, questions asked, and bites taken. This type of data collection is best used with discrete responses that are relatively brief and have a stable duration and definite beginning and end. Generally, event-based recording is done by human observers who count the number of times the behavior occurs during the observation session. When possible, however, permanent products should be used to record events. **Permanent products** are the results of behavior that can be counted after it occurs. Obvious examples are written products from students, but in early childhood settings, such products are unlikely. However, permanent products can still be used; examples include completed construction materials, putting the cups and napkins out for snack, putting on a coat, shelving toys, and number of used diapers. The advantage of permanent products is that they can be counted at the interventionist's leisure as compared to while the behavior is occurring.

Several issues should be addressed when designing event-sampling recording systems. The behavior that constitutes the event must be defined. This definition of the behavior should be precise so that no questions exist about what is being measured. Also, the interventionist should be sure to consider the dimension of behavior (accuracy, frequency, duration, latency, intensity, endurance) that is most relevant and easily recorded. Collecting data and interpreting it for each of these dimensions requires slightly different procedures. Accuracy data are frequently collected during instructional sessions where children have an opportunity to respond to target stimuli. In such cases, children's responses are recorded as correct or incorrect based on specific definitions, and data are analyzed in terms of percentage correct and incorrect. Percentage is calculated by dividing the number of each type of response by the number of opportunities provided. Percentage data have some distinct advantages. They are easy to calculate, especially when the number of opportunities are 5, 10, 20, 25, 50, or 100. Most people readily understand percentage data; thus, the results of the observation are easily communicated to others. However, percentage data have limitations; the primary one is that an artificial ceiling is placed on performance. For example, two students could be at 100% correct, but one could have performed the same number of responses in half the time required by the other. Many behaviors must be performed quickly before they will be useful to children. Percentage data do not provide information on the response speed. To deal with this problem, the rate of responding can be calculated with accuracy data. *Rate* refers to the number of responses that occur in a given time period, for example, a week, day, or minute. Using minutes as the time unit is useful because it is sensitive to change and can be recorded quickly; however, any standard period can be used if data are collected for the entire period. Rate is calculated by dividing the number of responses (e.g., number correct) by the number of time units (e.g., minutes). Thus, with accuracy data, correct and error rates can be calculated as well as percentage. Another disadvantage of using percentage data is that they may be insensitive measures unless a large number of opportunities is provided. For example, if only five opportunities are provided, then each response is worth 20 percentage points. A rule of thumb is that percentage should not be used unless there are at least 20 opportunities to respond. However, many examples exist in the literature where as few as 10 opportunities existed.

Frequency data can be collected on almost any discrete behavior; however, it is important that the behavior be of consistent duration. For example, frequency data could be collected on the number of crying episodes displayed by an infant, but the duration of episodes could vary considerably. For example, on one day the infant could cry three times and each episode could last 30–40 minutes. On another day the same infant could cry six times with each episode lasting about 2 minutes. Although the infant had more episodes of crying on the second day, the crying behavior would likely be a greater problem on the first. Frequency data can be recorded in a number of ways, including putting a tally mark on a data-collection sheet, using a golf counter or other counting devices, or putting a bean in a jar on the shelf. The number of ways to record frequency data is limited only by an interventionist's creativity. What is important is that an accurate record be maintained with a minimum of effort and time. When collecting frequency data, the duration of the observation session also should be recorded. To say that a child displayed three social initiations on one day and six on another is not useful unless the time allowed on both days was equal. By recording the length of the observation, frequency data can be meaningfully interpreted. When the length of the observation is known, the data can be converted to rate. Further, dividing the observation into several intervals will help in interpreting the data. For example, if the interventionist is going to count the number of initiations during a 20-minute free-play period, then the observation could be divided into ten 2-minute intervals, allowing the interventionist to determine when during the 20 minutes the initiations occurred.

Duration data can be collected on most behaviors occurring longer than a few seconds. Duration data, unlike accuracy and frequency data, require each response to be timed. Although any clock can be used, stop watches greatly increase the precision with which duration data are collected. Duration data can be analyzed in three ways: total duration, duration per occurrence, and percent of time. *Total duration* refers to the total amount of time an infant or child engages in the target behavior during the observation session. Some stop watches are designed to start and stop and start again without being reset. The teacher simply starts and stops the watch each time the behavior occurs and then reads the time at the end of the session. *Duration per occurrence* refers to the average length of time that the child engages in the behavior. Duration per occurrence requires the teacher to record the duration of each instance of the behavior and divide the total time by the number of occurrences. *Percent of time* refers to the percentage of the session in which the student performs the behavior. When data are collected so that the average duration per occurrence is recorded and the length of the observation session also is recorded, then each of the three types can be calculated.

Latency data also require the interventionist to time the behavior, and use of a stop watch is recommended. The timing should occur from the end of the cue to the initiation of the response. As with duration, the total latency for an observation session or the average latency per occurrence can be calculated. Generally, the average latency is more meaningful because the measure is tied to the number of cues provided. Latency data may be used to collect important assessment information. As noted above, assessment should identify potential intervention strategies. An important dimension of intervention planning is knowing the child's typical response time; that is, how long it takes the child to initiate a response after a cue.

Intensity or magnitude of a response is relatively difficult to measure for most responses. Exceptions include such things as how high or far a child can jump. In most cases, however, measurement of intensity requires special instrumentation such as noise or pressure gauges. As a result, intensity is rarely measured. Similarly, endurance data, although infrequently used in early childhood settings, can be collected in a number of ways. For example, an interventionist can time how long a child repeatedly can perform a discrete behavior such as running. Other ways to determine endurance are through measures of distance and use of special instrumentation.

In addition to defining the behavior and considering the important dimension of behavior, event-sampling systems should be well calibrated (White & Haring, 1980). This issue primarily is important when assessing intervention effectiveness. A well-**calibrated system** is one in which each occurrence of the behavior represents relatively equal amounts of the behavior. For example, if the teacher is monitoring children's ability to work puzzles, the number of pieces inserted or the number of puzzles completed could be counted. The number of pieces would be a better measure, because one puzzle may have four pieces and another may have sixteen. If only the number completed were counted, then these two puzzles would represent very different amounts of the behavior. A well-calibrated system also is sensitive to change; that is, it should detect small changes in the behavior. Also, interventionists should be careful to select behaviors that are relatively easy to record, particularly when the effects of intervention are being monitored. If the requirements of monitoring are costly in terms of interventionists' time and effort, it is likely that relatively little monitoring will occur, ineffective intervention will continue longer than necessary, and changes in behaviors being taught will not occur as frequently as possible.

Data-collection sheets must be designed. **Data-collection sheets** are simply the forms on which the record of the observation is written. Tawney and Gast (1984) state that data-collection sheets should contain three types of information: situational, performance, and summary. *Situational information* refers to data that establish who was observed, what behavior was measured, when the observation occurred, and who conducted it. Specifically, it should include the child's name, date, activity, beginning and ending times of the observation, instructional strategies being used, behaviors that are targeted for observation, and observer's name. *Performance information* refers to the actual record of behavior that is generated from the observation. This section of the data sheet varies considerably depending upon the type of data being recorded. For example, if data are being collected to monitor the effects of a direct instruction program, then correct responses, error responses, and no responses may be counted. The data-collection sheet could have a column for each of these types of responses, and when one of them occurred, a check could be placed in the appropriate column. However, if data were being collected on the frequency with which an infant spits up, then a space for tally marks may be sufficient. The third type of information that should be included on the data-collection sheet is *summary data*. This section, at a minimum, should include the total time of the observation, totals for the data recorded (by type, if used), and anecdotal comments made by the observer to explain the data or to describe a related event or issue. Summary data are important because they will reduce the time required when analyzing performance across a number of days and will be useful for transferring that data to graphs. Examples of event-sampling data-collection sheets for frequency (occurrence) and accuracy data are shown in Figure 4.1, data sheets for duration are shown in Figure 4.2 (p. 76), and data sheets for latency are shown in Figure 4.3 (p. 77). These data sheets are samples; interventionists should design their own data sheets to match their situation but should be sure that the three components are included.

Time-Sampling Recording. Unlike event-sampling where the occurrence of a behavior cues the interventionist to record the response, time cues recording in **time-sampling systems.** The interventionist records which response occurred at a given time. Time-sampling procedures, like event sampling, can be used with discrete behaviors (e.g., behaviors of relatively short duration) or with categories of behaviors (see pp. 80–86). In its simplest form, time-sampling involves the interventionist recording at prespecified times whether a behavior is or is not occurring. For example, the interventionist may check the infant at 9:00 and record whether she is asleep or awake or may see which toddlers are playing with toys. The advantages of time-sampling procedures are that they can be used with behaviors that are difficult to count or time and that the same behavior of several children can be collected at once.

Using time-sampling procedures requires some of the same considerations as event-sampling procedures; however, some special considerations also exist. The behaviors to be measured should be defined, and the relevant dimensions of those behaviors should be identified.

The type of time-sampling procedure also should be selected. At least three types of time sampling have been described: momentary, partial-interval, and whole-interval time sampling (Cooper et al., 1987). With these procedures, the observation session is divided into intervals. With **momentary time sampling,** the observer records at a specific time whether the behavior is occurring. For example, the five-hour day may be divided into twenty 15-minute intervals. If the day began at 8:00, the observer would check the target child at 8:00, 8:15, 8:30, 8:45, 9:00, and so on. At each time (e.g., 8:15), the observer would record whether the behavior was occurring *at that instant*. With the **partial-interval** method, the observation period would be broken into intervals, and the

FORM A

Name _____ Date: _____

Behavior/Objective: _____

Time _____ to _____ Total Time: _____

Observer: _____

Trial	C	E	No Response
1			
2			
3			
4			
5			
6			
7			
8			
9			
10			
Total #/%	/	/	/

Comments: _____

FORM B

Name _____ Date: _____

Behavior/Objective: _____

Observer: _____

Day	Time Observed	Record of Behavior	#	Rate
Monday				
Tuesday				
Wednesday				
Thursday				
Friday				

Comments: _____

FORM C

Name _____ Date: _____

Behavior/Objective: _____

Time _____ to _____ Total Time: _____

Observer: _____

Occurrences

Comments: _____

Total # occurrences: _____

Rate of occurrences: _____

FORM D

Name _____ Date: _____

Behavior/Objective: _____

Time _____ to _____ Total Time: _____

Observer: _____

Trial	Response		Trial	Response
1			6	
2			7	
3			8	
4			9	
5			10	

Total Correct _____   Total Errors _____

Correct Rate _____   Error Rate _____

Comments: _____
− = correction, + = error, 0 = no response

FORM E

Name _____ Date: _____

Behavior/Objective: _____

Time _____ to _____ Total Time: _____

Observer: _____

2-min Interval	# of Behavior	Rate
Total		

FIGURE 4.1
Examples of Event-Sampling Data Collection Sheets for Frequency and Accuracy Data

Form A could be used to record the accuracy of students' responses; the teacher would place a check in the appropriate column for each trial. Form B could be used to record frequency (rate) for five days; teacher would place tally mark for each occurrence of behavior. Form C could be used to record frequency (rate); the teacher would place a tally mark for each occurrence of the behavior. Form D would be used for accuracy data; teacher would mark − for correct, + for error, and 0 for no response. Form E could be used to record the rate of behavior during four 2-minute intervals; teacher places tally mark for each occurrence of behavior during each interval.

FORM A

Name _____ Date: _____

Behavior/Objective: _____

Time _____ to _____ Total Time: _____

Observer: _____

Start Time	Stop Time	Total

Comments: _____

Total Number of Occurrences: _____

Total Duration: _____

Average Duration per Occurrence: _____

FORM B

Name _____ Date: _____

Behavior/Objective: _____

Time _____ to _____ Total Time: _____

Observer: _____

Occurrence	Time

Comments: _____

Total Number of Occurrences: _____

Total Duration: _____

Average Duration per Occurrence: _____

FIGURE 4.2
Examples of Two Event-Sampling Data-Collection Sheets for Duration Data
In Form A, the start and stop time of each occurrence is recorded; in Form B only the duration is recorded per occurrence. With both, the total duration, average duration, and percent of time can be calculated.

observer would observe for the entire interval (e.g., from 8:00 to 8:15 and from 8:30 to 8:45). If the behavior occurs during the interval, it is scored as having occurred. With the **whole-interval** method, the observation period is also divided into intervals, and the observer must watch for the entire interval. However, for a behavior to be scored as occurring, it must occur for the *entire* interval. The whole-interval method tends to underestimate the true occurrence of a behavior, and the partial-interval method tends to overestimate the occurrence. Both of these

procedures are quite demanding of teacher-time because the teacher must observe for the entire interval. However, when observation sessions are short (e.g., 10 minutes), these sampling methods can be used. The momentary time sample is probably the easiest and most useful when teachers are monitoring the effects of intervention, because they can be involved in other activities between observation points. This method, however, is not sensitive to behaviors that last for relatively short durations. With each of these methods, the data

FORM A

Name _____ Date: _____

Cue: _____

Behavior: _____

Objective: _____

Observer: _____

Cue Time	Initiate Behavior	Total

Comments: _____

Total Number of Cues: _____

Total Latency: _____

Average Length of Latency _____

FORM B

Name _____ Date: _____

Cue: _____

Behavior: _____

Objective: _____

Observer: _____

Cue Number	Latency
1	
2	
3	
4	
5	
6	
7	

Comments: _____

Total Number of Cues: _____

Total Latency: _____

Average Length of Latency _____

FIGURE 4.3
Examples of Two Event-Sampling Data-Collection Sheets for Latency Data
In Form A, the time the cue was presented and the time the behavior was initiated are recorded; in Form B, the number of cues and the length of the latency are recorded.

are analyzed in terms of the percent of intervals in which the behavior occurs.

Selecting a time-sampling procedure requires consideration of the duration and frequency of the behavior and the length of the observation interval. If a behavior is of short duration, the partial-interval method should be used, although long intervals will overestimate the behavior's occurrence. If the behavior is of long duration, then momentary time sampling or the whole-interval method should be used. The average duration of the behavior should be considered when the whole-interval method is used, and the observation interval should be similar to the average duration. For behaviors that occur frequently and are of moderate or variable duration, the momentary method is better than the others because less observation time is required. For behaviors that occur infrequently (e.g., less than once every 15 or 20 minutes), time-sampling procedures may not be appropriate. Finally, the ease with which the different methods can be integrated into the interventionist's other activities should be considered.

When using the time-sampling procedures, a data-collection sheet must be designed. A variety of forms can be used and vary depending on whether the momentary, whole-interval, or partial-interval method is employed. A sample data-collection sheet for a momentary time sample is shown in Figure 4.4. The behaviors or children being measured are listed on the top, and the times are listed down the left side of the sheet. When the time arrives, the teacher simply notes the occurrence or nonoccurrence of the behavior. In Figure 4.5, a data-collection sheet for partial-interval and whole-interval methods is

Date: _____   Behavior/Name _____

Children's Names or Behaviors Being Recorded

Time								
9:00								
9:10								
9:20								
9:30								
9:40								
9:50								
10:00								
10:10								
10:20								
10:30								
Total								
% of Interval								

✔ = occurrence; X = nonoccurrence

Comments: _____

_____

FIGURE 4.4
Example of a Momentary Time-Sampling Data-Collection Sheet
Behaviors or children being observed are listed across the top of the graph; times for observations are listed on the left-hand side of graph. Occurrence or nonoccurrence of the behavior is recorded.

Name _____ Date: _____

Behavior: _____

Objective: _____

Observer: _____ Observation Time _____ to _____

Minute 1:

Intervals

1	2	3	4	5	6

Minute 2:

Intervals

1	2	3	4	5	6

Minute 3:

Intervals

1	2	3	4	5	6

Minute 4:

Intervals

1	2	3	4	5	6

Minute 5:

Intervals

1	2	3	4	5	6

Minute 6:

Intervals

1	2	3	4	5	6

Minute 7:

Intervals

1	2	3	4	5	6

Minute 8:

Intervals

1	2	3	4	5	6

Minute 9:

Intervals

1	2	3	4	5	6

Minute 10:

Intervals

1	2	3	4	5	6

FIGURE 4.5
Example of Partial-Interval or Whole-Interval Time-Sampling Data-Collection Sheet
Each minute of a 10-minute observation session is divided into six 10-second intervals. Teacher records whether behavior occurred or did not occur by marking O for occurrence and N for nonoccurrence.

displayed. On this sheet, each minute of a 10-minute observation is divided into six 10-second intervals. As with event-sampling recording sheets, numerous variations of these models exist, and interventionists should design sheets that are most appropriate to their situations.

With time-sampling procedures, interventionists need a signal that cues them to record. Sometimes, naturally occurring times such as transitions or 30-minute intervals are sufficient. However, many important behaviors either occur between transitions or require more frequent observation. A timer with a relatively unobtrusive alarm or a digital watch that beeps can be used. Tape recorders with tapes that signal when to observe and record are frequently used with whole-interval and partial-interval systems.

Category-Sampling Recording. **Category-sampling** procedures involve collection of data on behaviors that are placed into categories. The categories are defined, and frequently, several different behaviors could fit into each category. Category-sampling procedures can be used in an event-sampling format or in a time-sampling format, although time sampling is more frequent. For example, if an interventionist was interested in an infant's interactive behavior, the categories may include initiating interactions, responding to others' initiations, and terminating interactions. These categories are not behaviors, they are descriptions of the effects of a variety of behaviors. The infant could use eye gaze, cooing and vocalizations, movement of the limbs, smiles, and other behaviors separately and in combination to initiate interactions. The infant could use looking away, making fussy noises, and decreasing activity to terminate interactions. If a time-sampling procedure was used, a 6-second, partial-interval recording technique could be employed during a play session with the infant's father. The observer would look at the infant for 6 seconds and score any categories for which any of the

defined behaviors occurred. The observations would continue until the end of the sessions. One advantage of category systems is that a variety of behaviors serving the same effects can be measured. Further, a number of different but related categories of responses can be recorded.

Several factors are important when constructing a category-sampling recording system. The categories and behaviors must be clearly defined. The coding system should be **exhaustive,** meaning that any behavior observed should fit into one of the categories. Because it is nearly impossible to anticipate all behaviors, most category-sampling systems employ a category called "other." In some cases, interventionists may be interested only in a certain type of response (e.g., communicative behaviors), and other behaviors such as play would simply be noted as "play" or "other." However, if the "other" category constitutes the majority of the recording, then a revision of the categories may be necessary. In addition to being exhaustive, the categories should be mutually exclusive. **Mutually exclusive** categories means that no behavior could fit into more than one category. If behaviors fit into more than one category, then errors in recording will occur, and the data will be useless for making decisions. To save time, teachers should consider using existing category-sampling systems. Some examples are presented in later chapters of the text and others occur in the research literature. When developing the system, attention must be given to the relevant dimensions of the target behaviors.

Category-sampling systems should include only the number of categories necessary to gather information for the decision being made. If irrelevant categories are included, the accuracy of recording may be affected and interpretation complicated. However, one of the advantages of category sampling is that covariation between different classes of behavior can be detected. For example, Tina's aggressive behavior may vary with her play behavior: When she engages in play she appears to be less aggressive, and when she is not playing, her aggressions increase. Brian, on the other hand, appears to be more aggressive when the frequency of social initiations from other children increases. Category-sampling procedures allow interventionists to identify such relationships, develop intervention plans based on those relationships, and monitor the effects of the intervention. For example, with Tina, the interventionist should develop a plan to increase her engagement with toys rather than use a punishment procedure to decrease her aggression. Similarly, Brian's teacher should teach him to respond positively to peers' initiations. Category-sampling procedures also allow interventionists to measure the effects of the behavior of one person on another. For example, in parent/infant interactions, the behaviors of the parent and infant each may influence the behavior of the other. An interventionist may have a hypothesis that an infant is more fussy and less playful when the parent is more directive. The interventionist could measure four categories of behavior: parental directiveness, parental responsiveness, child play behavior, and fussiness. Such data could indicate whether the hypothesis about parental directiveness and child behavior appeared to be true, and allow an appropriate intervention to be developed.

When category systems are used, interventionists must choose between event- or time-sampling procedures. Children's responses prompt recording with event-sampling procedures and time prompts recording with time-sampling procedures. With category sampling, time-sampling methods are more frequently used, but exceptions occur. Category sampling may be used in an event-sampling format when a child displays a category of behaviors that requires careful measurement, occurs relatively infrequently, and where multiple behaviors appear to produce the same effect. For example, a child

may hit, bite, and pull the hair of other children and may use these actions to express frustration. To ensure that every instance of these behaviors is noted, the interventionist must define each and record them as a category called "aggressive behavior." Similarly, children may be learning specific communicative or social functions, and the interventionist may want a record of the number of requests they make throughout the day. The form of the request or the object being requested may be unimportant. In such cases, the teacher could define behaviors for a "requesting" category and record that category when each request occurs. In both of these examples, the behavior (aggressive behavior or requests) would prompt the teacher to record.

The more usual method of category sampling involves time-sampling formats. For example, the interventionist may be interested in the types of play behaviors being displayed. The categories of different types of play would be developed, and a momentary time-sampling procedure in which the type of play is recorded every 20 seconds could be used. When time-sampling procedures are used, some response should be recorded in each interval. When the categories represent a subset of the total possible behaviors, the interventionist should devise a category that would represent the absence of those behaviors. For example, if solitary, on-looker, parallel, associative, and cooperative play were being measured, it is possible that none of these types of play would be observed in a given interval. In such cases, a category called "nonplay" behaviors could be used. The percent of intervals in which this category is marked may be important in specifying the amount of time the child is actually playing.

Data-collection sheets that facilitate easy recording are needed with category sampling procedures and range from relatively simple to quite complex. Two simple data-collection sheets for recording the occurrence of aggressive and disruptive behaviors are dis-

FORM A

Name _____ Date: _____ Observer: _____

Aggressive Behaviors: _____

Disruptive Behaviors: _____

Time _____ to _____ Total Time: _____

Time	Activity	Aggression	Disruption
	Total		

Comments: _____

FIGURE 4.6
Examples of Category-Sampling Data-Collection Sheets for Two Types of Responses:
Aggressive Behavior and Disruptive Behavior
In form A, the sheet is designed for use with an event-sampling procedure. The teacher would write the time the aggressive or disruptive behavior occurred, note the activity that was occurring, and then put a check mark in the appropriate column. In form B, the sheet is designed for use with a time-sampling procedure. The teacher would observe at each interval, and note whether aggression or disruption occurred.

played in Figure 4.6. Data-collection sheet A is designed for an event-sampling procedure, and data sheet B is designed for a time-sampling procedure. A more complex time-sampling data sheet for measuring levels of social play is displayed in Figure 4.7 (p. 84). Sometimes, data are collected simultaneously on several children and for several behaviors. For example, an interventionist may want to collect data on the percent of time children are engaged in planned ac-

tivities, waiting, or behaving inappropriately. A momentary time-sampling procedure could be used. At the designated time, the observer would scan the classroom and record the category for each child. A sample data-collection sheet for this example is shown in Figure 4.8 (p. 85). The times are written on the left-hand column and the children's names are written across the top. At each time, the observer would write a symbol indicating which behavior was being displayed

FORM B

Name _____ Date: _____ Observer: _____

Aggressive Behaviors: _____

Disruptive Behaviors: _____

Time _____ to _____ Total Time: _____

Time	Activity	Aggression	Disruption
9:05			
9:10			
9:15			
9:20			
9:25			
9:30			
9:35			
9:40			
9:45			
9:50			
9:55			
10:00			
	Total		

Comments: _____

Percent of Intervals of Aggression _____

Percent of Intervals of Disruption _____

FIGURE 4.6
Continued

by each child. Although this system may seem complex, interventionists can learn to record such behavior reliably with practice.

Care should be taken when interpreting data from category-sampling procedures. The percentage of intervals that each category was recorded should be calculated and compared across categories. Few norms exist, however, that tell how frequently different categories of behavior should occur. It is unlikely that each category of behavior will occur at the same proportion of time, and it is likely that such equality would be inappropriate. For example, it would be undesirable to have children waiting the same percentage of time that they are engaged in activities; it is also unlikely that all children would be engaged 100% of the time. Thus, professional judgment is required in interpreting the results of category-sampling

Name _____ Date _____

Area: _____ Activities: _____

Types of Play

Time	Solitary	Onlooking	Parallel	Associative	Cooperative	None
:30						
1:00						
1:30						
2:00						
2:30						
3:00						
3:30						
4:00						
4:30						
5:00						
5:30						
6:00						
6:30						
7:00						
7:30						
8:00						
8:30						
9:00						
9:30						
10:00						
Total % Interval						

✔ = occurrence; X = nonoccurrence

Comments: _____

_____

FIGURE 4.7
Example of a Category-Sampling Data-Collection Sheet for Use with a Time-Sampling Recording System to Determine the Percent of Intervals in Which the Student Engages in Various Levels of Social Play During a 10-Minute Observation

Date: _____ Activities: _____

Time: _____ to _____

Children's Names

Time	Kim	Rodney	Hector	Ian	Larry	Dawn	Joy
2:02							
2:04							
2:06							
2:08							
2:10							
2:12							
2:14							
2:16							
2:18							
2:20							
2:22							
2:24							
2:26							
2:28							
2:30							
2:32							
2:34							
2:36							
2:38							
2:40							
Total % Interval							

E = engaged in activities; W = waiting; I = inappropriate behavior

FIGURE 4.8
Example of a Category-Sampling Data-Collection Sheet for Use with a Momentary Time-Sampling Recording System to Determine the Percent of Time Children Are Engaged Appropriately in Activities, Waiting Behaviors, and Inappropriate Behaviors
Children's names are listed across the top of the sheet and observation times are listed on the left-hand side of the sheet. The teacher records an E for engaged in activities, a W for waiting, and an I for inappropriate behavior for each child and each observation time.

procedures. As noted above, covariation of different behaviors can be detected with category-sampling procedures. Many times this covariation cannot be noted by analyzing the totals of the observation session but requires analysis of patterns of behavior throughout the observation. If one category frequently is recorded after another, then some sequential pattern may be present.

Levels-of-Assistance Recording. As noted earlier, one of the questions that is asked during initial instructional program planning assessments is: What behaviors does the child do with support, adaptation, or assistance? This information can be used to identify the level of support that must be removed before the child can perform independently. It also can be used to plan activities and events where the child can participate with support—that is, the principle of partial participation (Baumgart, Brown, Pumpian, Nisbet, Ford, Sweet, Messina, & Schroeder, 1982). **Levels-of-assistance recording** is a variation of event sampling where the occurrence or nonoccurrence of the behavior is noted at different levels of support. In many, but not all, cases, this type of recording occurs during informal testing rather than naturalistic observation and, in fact, has been used in some tests.

Support or assistance can take many forms, such as adaptive or assistive devices and direct assistance from the teacher. The type of support varies based on the behavior being assessed, the disabilities of the child, and the resources available to the interventionist. However, some common types of assistance are verbal cues, gestural prompts, models, partial physical prompts, and full physical manipulations. Verbal cues may include specific instructions on how to do a behavior, instructions on how to do part of a behavior, rules that help the child do the response, and indirect verbal cues such as hints. Gestural prompts are arm and facial movements that communicate to the child

that a specific behavior is wanted. Models are demonstrations of the behavior to be performed. Partial physical prompts are nudges, pushes, and taps that get the child to do the behavior, and full physical manipulations involve the teacher holding the child's hands and actually putting her through the desired actions.

To conduct such assessments, interventionists initially should present the child with the opportunity to do the behavior independently and then at varying levels of assistance. If the response is not forthcoming, then some minimal level of support (e.g., verbal cue) should be presented. Again, if a response is not forthcoming, then some more intrusive level of assistance should be provided. This process would continue until the child performed the behavior. As such, it is similar to an instructional strategy called the system of least prompts, which has been used successfully in teaching a variety of behaviors to a broad range of children with handicapping conditions (Doyle, Wolery, Ault, & Gast, 1988). The level of assistance needed by the child should be recorded. Interventionists should present multiple trials when using levels-of-assistance recording because many children may not initially know what the assessor wants them to do. Three recording forms for levels-of-assistance data are presented in Figure 4.9. Data sheet A has space to write down the type of assistance needed across trials. Data sheet B includes a list of assistance types, ordered from no assistance to the most intrusive level of assistance, and a row of numbers representing trials. The interventionist circles the number that corresponds to the level of assistance needed by the child on that trial. The advantage of data sheet B is that it can be used for monitoring during intervention. Data sheet C is similar, but the levels of assistance are presented in columns across the top. The number of trials are listed on the left-hand side of the sheet, and the interventionist places a check mark in the level of assistance presented and

FORM A

Name _____ Date: _____

Behavior/Objective: _____

Time ___ to ___ Total Time: ___

Observer: _____

Trial	Write: Level of Assistance Needed
1	
2	
3	
4	
5	

FORM B

Name _____ Date: _____

Behavior/Objective: _____

Time ___ to ___ Total Time: ___

Observer: _____

Level of Assistance Needed	Trial
Independent	1 2 3 4 5
Verbal Prompt	1 2 3 4 5
Model	1 2 3 4 5
Partial Physical Prompt	1 2 3 4 5
Full Physical Manipulation	1 2 3 4 5

FORM C

Name _____ Date _____ Observer _____

Behavior/Objective: _____

Time _____ to _____ Total Time: _____

Levels of Assistance

Trial	Independent	Verbal Prompt	Model	Partial Physical Prompt	Full Physical Manipulation
1					
2					
3					
4					
5					
Total					

Comments: _____

FIGURE 4.9
Example of Three Data-Collection Forms for Levels-of-Assistance Data

Data collection sheet A has space for the tester to write the type of assistance needed across trials. Data-collection sheet B includes a list of assistance types, and a row of numbers representing each trial; the tester circles the number that corresponds to the level of assistance needed on each trial. Data-collection sheet C includes the levels of assistance written across the top of the form, and the trials on the left-hand side; the teacher checks the level of assistance needed on each trial.

another symbol in the level where the child was correct.

Levels-of-assistance recording frequently is used when children are learning to perform a new behavior such as eating with a spoon, putting on a coat, or playing with a new toy. However, it can also be used to assess and teach behaviors that are in the child's repertoire but are not performed when they are needed. For example, a child may be able to comment using two- and three-word combinations, but does so infrequently or fails to do so when appropriate. The levels-of-assistance recording techniques can be used to identify the amount of prompting needed to produce such behaviors at appropriate times.

Task-Analytic Recording. Task analysis is a process of breaking a skill into teachable parts and is described in Chapter 18. Although any behavior can be task analyzed into its component parts, **task-analytic recording** is particularly important with chained skills. **Chained skills** involve a number of discrete behaviors that are performed in a sequence; each step of the chain serves as the stimulus for the child to do the next behavior. Examples of such behaviors include: feeding one's self; going to the bathroom; playing with many toys such as puzzles, blocks, table-top games; riding a tricycle; climbing up a slide and sliding down; dressing and undressing; engaging in social interactions; and speaking in complex and compound sentences. Such skills can be difficult to assess because they may involve multiple behaviors that occur in a sequence.

In the simplest form of task-analytic data collection, the steps of the task analysis are simply checked as occurring or not occurring. Unfortunately, failure to do one step of the task analysis may preclude performance of other steps. For example, a task analysis could be devised for putting on a front-opening shirt, but failure to put the arm in the armhole will preclude completion of the remaining steps. This problem can be solved in two ways and depends in part on the purpose of assessment. First, the teacher can simply complete the step the child cannot do and then assess the remaining steps. Second, the task-analytic recording can be combined with levels-of-assistance recording. If a child fails to complete a step, the teacher could assess the level of assistance needed on that step and then allow the child to progress independently with the remaining steps. Each step that is not completed independently would receive an assessment of the level of assistance required. Both of these procedures work well when children do not know how to do a given skill. In other cases, the child may be able to do all the steps in the task analysis, or response chain, but does not do them in the appropriate sequence. In this case, the interventionist should record the sequence with which the chain is completed. This analysis is frequently done by presenting the child with the task and then writing down the sequence with which the task was performed.

Designing data-collection sheets for task-analytic recording can be difficult; three examples are shown in Figure 4.10. Data form A is designed for recording only whether the child could do each step of the task analysis. This sheet would be used when the teacher was not interested in the level of assistance required. Data sheet B is designed for identifying the incorrect steps and the levels of assistance required at each step. Data sheet C is designed to identify the sequence with which the child does a task analysis. This form would only be used if the child could do all the steps independently, but needed to learn the order in which to do them. The teacher would present the task, watch the child do it, and then write down the sequence (1 for the first step completed, 2 for the second, and so on).

With some skills the form is important and with others the effect is important. Sometimes the end product, rather than the order of steps taken to get to that product,

Name _____ Date: _____

Behavior/Objective: _____

Time _____ to _____ Total Time: _____

Observer: _____

Steps of Task Analysis	Response	
	Correct	Error
Totals		

Comments: _____

Name _____ Date: _____

Behavior/Objective: _____

Time _____ to _____ Total Time:_____

Observer: _____

Steps of Task Analysis	Write Order Child Did Steps (1 = 1st, 2 = 2nd, 3 = 3rd, etc.)

Comments: _____

Name _____ Date _____ Observer _____

Behavior _____

Steps of Task Analysis	Trials			
	1	2	3	4
_____	I V M PP FM	I V M PP FM	I V M PP FM	I V M PP FM
_____	I V M PP FM	I V M PP FM	I V M PP FM	I V M PP FM
_____	I V M PP FM	I V M PP FM	I V M PP FM	I V M PP FM
_____	I V M PP FM	I V M PP FM	I V M PP FM	I V M PP FM
_____	I V M PP FM	I V M PP FM	I V M PP FM	I V M PP FM
_____	I V M PP FM	I V M PP FM	I V M PP FM	I V M PP FM

I = Independent, V = Verbal, M = Model, PP = Partial Physical, FM = Full Manipulation

Circle the level of assistance required for each step.

FIGURE 4.10
Example of Three Task-Analytic Data-Collection Sheets

In data-collection form A, the tester records only the correctness or incorrectness of each step of the task analysis. With data-collection sheet B, the tester records the levels of assistance needed by the child on each step of the task analysis. For data-collection sheet C, the tester writes a numeral for each step in the order in which it occurred (e.g., 1 for first step completed, 2 for second step, and 3 for third step).

is important. For example, setting the table can be done by placing all the plates, then all the forks, and so on, or it can be accomplished by doing each place setting before beginning the next. The end result, a completely set table, occurs with both. When task-analytic recording is used, interventionists should be sure they are not rigid about the sequences of steps when the effect rather than form of a skill is important. For example, the steps used when people tie their shoes vary greatly across individuals. The steps used are not important, but whether the shoes stay tied is. Thus, interventionists should identify the sequence of steps that are easiest for each child.

Summary of Recording Systems. Six different recording systems have been described in this section. These include narrative descriptions, event-sampling, time-sampling, category-sampling, levels-of-assistance, and task-analytic recording. Early interventionists should be fluent in using each system and in designing data sheets for each.

Selecting Times and Situations for Observation

In addition to defining behaviors and selecting a data-collection system and relevant data-collection forms, interventionists should carefully select times and situations for observation. When the purpose of the measurement is assessment for instructional program planning, the observation should occur in situations where the behavior is likely to occur. This applies even when conducting informal testing sessions. For example, if social interactions are going to be observed, then the child should be with peers who will respond to the target child's initiations and may even initiate interactions to the target child.

The contexts where the child is likely to need the skill also should be selected as a situation for assessment. For example, communication and social skills should be assessed in situations such as free play (as compared to situations such as group instruction, where children should be attending to the teacher and following directions). Further, dressing and undressing skills may show very different patterns in the corner of the classroom in the middle of the day as compared to getting ready to go outside and play, go swimming, or take a bath. Ideally, assessment also should occur in generalization settings. Chapters 11–17 describe contexts and situations where assessment activities are most appropriate for given skills.

An issue closely related to when to conduct the observation is how much observation should occur. Two general rules of thumb are offered: "Collect enough data to answer the question being asked, but do not waste time by collecting too much information," and "the more important the decision the greater the need for additional data." Translating these rules into hard and fast recommendations is difficult. When the purpose of the assessment is instructional program planning, at least two to three observations are needed; however, if the data are quite different across these observations, then more data collection may be needed. Similarly, if, after a couple observations or informal assessments (e.g., when using level-of-assistance recording or task-analytic recording), the child clearly cannot do the behavior or a given step, then more data collection probably is not warranted. In part, the extent of the initial observation depends upon the interventionist's skill in conducting ongoing assessment. If recommendations from the assessment will be followed but will not be monitored or modified frequently, then more information is needed during assessment. However, if the recommendations will be followed but will be monitored and modified on an ongoing basis, then fewer data may be needed.

If the purpose of the data collection is to monitor the effects of intervention, then frequent assessment is needed. The use of probes, which are short instances of measurement, can greatly reduce ongoing data-collection demands. This issue has been given considerable attention in a number of sources (e.g., White & Haring, 1980; Wolery et al., 1988).

Checking the Accuracy of Data Collection

A pervasive characteristic of the human condition is the tendency to make errors; in fact, we are familiar with the saying that "to err is human." Because most direct observation assessment activities are conducted using human observers, errors are likely. Kazdin (1977) has identified two major types of errors: observer bias or expectations and observer drift. **Observer bias** refers to changes in the data collection that occur because of the observer's expectations, feelings, and so on, rather than on actual changes in the behavior. Observer bias is an important consideration in both initial assessment for program planning and monitoring intervention effectiveness. **Observer drift** refers to unspecified changes in the definitions that observers apply to data collection over time. Drift is a particular problem when monitoring program effectiveness. If an interventionist has been teaching a child for a number of days or weeks with a preferred strategy, then she could unwittingly collect data that indicate a change is occurring when indeed it is not. Or, the change may not be as great as is recorded by the interventionist. To control for these problems, reliability checks are conducted where two or more observers collect data on the same behavior during the same observation sessions using the same observation techniques. Their data are then compared and a percentage of agreement is calculated. Calculating agreement percentages for event-sampling data involves dividing the smaller score by the larger and multiplying by 100. With time-sampling and category-sampling data, the records of both observers should be compared at each interval and their responses should be scored as an agreement

or a disagreement. The number of agreements are then divided by the number of agreements plus the number of disagreements and then multiplied by 100. Procedures for conducting and calculating reliability estimates are described in detail by Cooper et al. (1987) and Wolery et al. (1988). Conducting reliability checks is difficult in some early childhood settings, but it is possible. In part, if the decisions based on the data are critical and if there is a suspicion that bias or drift may be occurring, then reliability checks should be made. Retraining observers, clarifying the definitions, and practicing with the observation procedures are frequently sufficient for correcting problems of reliability.

Using the Data for Decision Making. An underlying assumption of this text is that measurement of children's behavior should occur for specific purposes. Assessing children and collecting data should not occur simply for the sake of measurement. All measurement activities, including data collection through direct observation, should occur for some reason. While data collection can occur for accountability reasons and to communicate with others, the primary purpose is to gather information for making decisions. A number of different decisions can be made with information gathered through direct observation and informal assessment. These decisions include determining what behaviors the child does independently or does with adaptations, support, and assistance or does not do; the general conditions under which behavior occurs or does not occur; which events in the environment are related to the occurrence of the behavior; what interventions may be successful; whether progress is being made; and what modifications in intervention strategies should occur.

Using the data to make decisions can be facilitated by summarizing the data and graphing it. When the purpose of assessment is for planning instructional programs, then totaling the results of the observation and calculating the percentage, rate, or total time may be sufficient levels of data summary. Calculating the mean, median, range, and trend of data may be useful in some cases. Graphing data is an extremely useful summary technique when the purpose of assessment is monitoring intervention effectiveness. Several sources describe procedures for graphing data (cf., Parsonson & Baer, 1978; White & Haring, 1980). Fuchs and Fuchs (1986) suggest that when teachers graph data (rather than simply collecting and recording it), student performance may be higher. This finding probably occurs because: (a) graphing may help indicate when the desired increases or decreases in performance are not occurring, (b) graphing may indicate subtle characteristics of the data that are obvious only when the data are presented graphically (e.g., decreases in performance after absences and weekends, increased in correct responses but no concomitant decrease in error responses, increasing trend in the data that is too slow), and (c) performance patterns displayed on graphs may suggest the type of intervention change needed. Haring et al. (1980) describe several data patterns and data decision rules that can be used when monitoring intervention effectiveness. Many of the patterns indicate not only that a change in intervention is needed, but also what that change should be (cf., Wolery et al., 1988, chap. 8).

Summarizing the Basics of Direct Observation

The process of using direct observation involves several steps: (a) defining the behaviors and identifying the relevant dimensions of that behavior, (b) selecting appropriate data-collection systems and data sheets, (c) selecting appropriate times and situations for observation, (d) checking the accuracy of data collection, and (e) using the results for decision making. Each of these steps requires con-

siderable attention and can influence the quality and usefulness of the information collected.

Using Direct Observations to Identify Relationships Between Child Behavior and Environmental Stimuli

Direct observation can be used in at least three ways: first, to identify behaviors relevant to instructional program planning; second, to monitor the progress children make or the effectiveness of interventions; and third, to identify the relationships that exist between children's behavior and environmental stimuli. This section addresses the third purpose. The application of information derived from such assessments is particularly helpful in designing interventions. In this section, procedures are described for identifying which stimuli appear to function as reinforcers for conducting functional analyses and analogue analyses.

Reinforcer Assessment

The activities and routines planned for infants, toddlers, and preschoolers should have reinforcing properties. Nonetheless, an important component of nearly any intervention strategy is the feedback or consequences that result from correct or appropriate performance. The conditioned social reinforcers, such as praise and smiles, used with older students may not have been acquired by infants, toddlers, and preschoolers; therefore, identification of reinforcers is a legitimate assessment activity. Three means for identifying reinforcers are described in this section; for additional information see Kazdin (1980), Striefel (1974), and Wolery et al. (1988).

Interviewing Significant Others. Family members and other individuals who have frequent contact with the child may be aware of useful reinforcers. When asking them about reinforcers, the interviewer should ask questions such as "What does he like?", "What does he ask for?", "When given a choice, what does he take or do?", "Does she like tickling, rough and tumble play?", "What foods, liquids, noises, does she like?", "What activities or games (peek-a-boo, etc.) does she like to play?" Such questions help focus individuals' responses better than general questions.

Observing the Student. Interviewing others may result in few useful reinforcers for some children. In such cases, a useful means of identifying reinforcers is to observe the child when no demands are placed on him. The observer should attempt to determine what behaviors occur frequently and what consequences follow those behaviors. Further, the observer should determine which objects, activities, and movements the child chooses when different selections are available.

Providing a Reinforcer Menu. After identifying some initial stimuli, the teacher might engage the child in a structured activity and provide a choice of reinforcers after each correct response. Three or four options can be presented after each response. The interventionist should record which stimulus is selected each time to see if a preference exists for one over the others.

Conducting a Functional Analysis

A **functional analysis** is a process whereby the relationships that exist between stimuli and children's behavior are identified. Functional analyses are conducted by observing children's behavior in some natural setting, and collecting four types of information. First, as with a running record, the setting events should be described. The setting information should include a brief description of the physical setting including the design of the environment such as the size, pieces

of significant equipment, the type and amount of materials, temperature in the room, noise level, the activities, the number of adults and their roles, and the number of children and a description of their behavior. The setting information is described at the beginning of the observation, and notes about significant changes (e.g., activity changes, entry of additional children or adults) should be noted as the observation continues. The data-collection sheet is divided into three columns: antecedent events, behavior, and consequent events. The titling of these three columns has resulted in functional analyses being called the "ABC Analysis." Any event that precedes the child's behavior is noted in the "antecedent" column. The child's behavior is noted in the "behavior" column, and events that follow the child's behavior are noted in the "consequent" column. During the observation, the observer simply writes a description of these various events in the respective columns. Abbreviations should be used and a check mark placed in the antecedents column when a consequent event serves as an antecedent for a new behavior. The written descriptions should be objective and free of any inferences. Verbal and nonverbal behavior should be recorded, and attention should be paid to any social behavior directed toward the target child and/or any behavior that appears to occur as a result of the child's behavior.

Functional analyses can be used for at least two purposes: first, to describe the relationships between environmental stimuli and all of the child's behavior; and second, to describe the relationships between environmental stimuli and a specific child behavior (e.g., some antisocial response). Functional analyses for the first purpose should occur across a variety of settings and over multiple sessions. A substantial amount of data are needed to identify and then confirm the presence of many functional relationships. If the latter purpose is intended, then fewer sessions are needed but should occur when the target behavior is most likely. In either case, the results of a functional analysis can be used to identify a large number of behaviors the child does independently; thus, it has value beyond identifying functional relationships with environmental stimuli.

Conducting an Analogue Analysis

Analogue analysis is similar to functional analysis but is conducted in brief, controlled assessment sessions that occur in artificially designed rather than natural settings. The purpose of analogue analysis is to identify the relationships between stimuli that set the stage for a given behavior and/or stimuli that maintain the behavior. Analogue analyses should be used to confirm or refute specific hypotheses an interventionist holds about relationships between environmental stimuli and child behavior. Usually, analogue analyses are employed with behavior problems rather than adaptive behaviors. The interventionist designs artificial situations that test the hypothesis. For example, Ronnie is a four-year-old child who cries frequently. His teacher suggests that he may be crying to get adult attention or to escape from activities he does not like. To test these two hypotheses, the teacher designs a series of situations where only these two things vary. For example, data are collected in a 15-minute activity that Ronnie likes and where adult attention is given regularly every 2 minutes. After one or two sessions in this condition, the variables are changed: data are collected in the same activity, but attention is only given if Ronnie cries. Later, these two conditions are repeated in a 15-minute activity that Ronnie does not like. If crying is highest only in conditions where adult attention is provided contingent upon crying, or only in the condition that Ronnie does not like, then one of the hypotheses is confirmed and the other refuted. Examples of such assessments can be found in the literature (cf. Carr & Durand, 1985; Iwata, Dorsey, Slifer, Bauman, & Richman, 1982). Several findings are apparent from such studies: (a) specific relationships between environmental stimuli and behavior can be identified, (b) information about the relationships are useful in planning interventions, (c) one variable can control more than one inappropriate behavior, and (d) a single inappropriate behavior can be controlled by more than one variable. Considering such information is critical to planning interventions that are ethically defensible and socially valid.

SUMMARY OF KEY CONCEPTS

- Direct observation should be used in assessment activities because it allows (a) assessment of difficult-to-test behaviors, (b) validation of information collected in other situations, (c) extension of assessment activities to generalization settings and routines, (d) identification of functional relationships between environmental stimuli and children's behavior, and (e) intervention effectiveness to be monitored on an ongoing basis.

- Direct observation is useful primarily in instructional program planning assessment and in monitoring the effects of intervention.

- Use of direct observation in assessment activities requires (a) definition of the behaviors and identification of their relevant dimensions, (b) selection of appropriate data-collection systems and data sheets, (c) selection of appropriate times and situations for observation, (d) assessment of the accuracy of data collection, and (e) use of the results for decision making.

- *Behavior* is a movement, has a definite beginning and end, is repeatable, and can be measured reliably.

- Behaviors have various dimensions that can be measured including frequency (rate), intensity (magnitude), accuracy, duration, and latency.

- Several data-recording systems exist including narrative descriptions, event-sampling, time-sampling, category-sampling, levels-of-assistance, and task-analytic recording. Each of these has unique requirements and uses in assessment.

- Direct observation can be used to identify reinforcers and identify functional relationships between stimuli and behavior using functional analyses and analogue assessments.

REFERENCES

Baumgart, D., Brown, L., Pumpian, I., Nisbet, J., Ford, A., Sweet, M., Messina, R., & Schroeder, J. (1982). Principle of partial participation and individualized adaptions in educational programs for severely handicapped students. *The Journal of the Association for the Severely Handicapped, 7*(2), 17–27.

Berdine, W. H. & Meyer, S. A. (Eds.). (1987). *Assessment in special education.* Boston: Little, Brown.

Bijou, S. W., Peterson, R. F., Harris, F. R., Allen, K. E., & Johnston, M. S. (1969). Methodology for experimental studies of young children in natural settings. *Psychological Reports, 19,* 177–210.

Brown, F. (1987). Meaningful assessment of people with severe and profound handicaps. In M. E. Snell (Ed.), *Systematic instruction of persons with severe handicaps* (pp. 39–63). Columbus, OH: Merrill.

Carr, E. G. & Durand, V. M. (1985). Reducing behavior problems through functional communication training. *Journal of Applied Behavior Analysis, 18,* 111–126.

Cooper, J. O., Heron, T. E., & Heward, W. L. (1987). *Applied behavior analysis.* Columbus, OH: Merrill.

Doyle, P. M., Wolery, M., Ault, M. J., & Gast, D. L. (1988). System of least prompts: A literature review of procedural parameters. *Journal of the Association for Persons with Severe Handicaps, 13,* 28–40.

Fuchs, L. S. & Fuchs, D. (1986). Effects of systematic formative evaluation: A meta-analysis. *Exceptional Children, 53,* 199–208.

Haring, N. G., Liberty, K. A., & White, O. R. (1980). Rules for data-based strategy decision in instructional programs. In W. Sailor, B. Wilcox, & L. Brown (Eds.), *Methods of instruction for severely handicapped students* (pp. 159–192). Baltimore, MD: Paul H. Brookes.

Hilgard, E. R. & Bower, G. H. (1975). *Theories of learning.* Englewood Cliffs, NJ: Prentice-Hall.

Iwata, B. A., Dorsey, M. F., Slifer, K. J., Bauman, K. E., & Richman, G. S. (1982). Toward a functional analysis of self-injury. *Analysis and Intervention in Developmental Disabilities, 2*(3), 3–20.

Kazdin, A. E. (1977). Artifact, bias, and complexity of assessment: The ABC's of reliability. *Journal of Applied Behavior Analysis, 10,* 141–150.

Kazdin, A. E. (1980). *Behavior modification in applied settings* (2nd ed.). Homewood, IL: Dorsey Press.

Odom, S. L. & Shuster, S. K. (1986). Naturalistic inquiry and the assessment of young handicapped children and their families. *Topics in Early Childhood Special Education, 6*(2), 68–82.

Parsonson, B. S. & Baer, D. M. (1978). The analysis and presentation of graphic data. In T. R. Kratochwill (Ed.), *Single subject research:*

Strategies for evaluating change (pp. 101–165). New York: Academic Press.

Peterson, N. L. (1987). *Early intervention for handicapped and at-risk children: An introduction to early childhood-special education.* Denver: Love.

Snell, M. E. & Grigg, N. C. (1987). Instructional assessment and curriculum development. In M. E. Snell (Ed.), *Systematic instruction of persons with severe handicaps* (3rd ed.) (pp. 64–109). Columbus, OH: Merrill.

Stremel-Campbell, K. & Campbell, C. R. (1985). Training techniques that may facilitate generalization. In S. F. Warren & A. K. Rogers-Warren (Eds.), *Teaching functional language: Generalization and maintenance of language skills* (pp. 251–288). Baltimore, MD: University Park Press.

Striefel, S. (1974). *Managing behavior-behavior modification: Teaching a child to imitate (part 7).* Lawrence, KS: H & H Enterprises.

Tawney, J. W. & Gast, D. L. (1984). *Single-subject research in special education.* Columbus, OH: Merrill.

Thurman, S. K. & Widerstrom, A. H. (1985). *Young children with special needs: A developmental and ecological approach.* Boston: Allyn & Bacon.

Vincent, L. J., Salisbury, C., Walter, G., Brown, P., Gruenwald, L. J., & Powers, M. (1980). Program evaluation and curriculum development in early childhood/special education: Criteria of the next environment. In W. Sailor, B. Wilcox, & L. Brown (Eds.), *Methods of instruction for severely handicapped students* (pp. 303–328). Baltimore, MD: Paul H. Brookes.

Warren, S. F. (1985). Clinical strategies for the measurement of language generalization. In S. F. Warren & A. K. Rogers-Warren (Eds.), *Teaching functional language: Generalization and maintenance of language skills* (pp. 197–221). Baltimore, MD: University Park Press.

White, O. R. (1980). Adaptive performance objectives: Form versus function. In W. Sailor, B. Wilcox, & L. Brown (Eds.), *Methods of instruction for severely handicapped students* (pp. 47–70). Baltimore, MD: Paul H. Brookes.

White, O. R. & Haring, N. G. (1980). *Exceptional teaching* (2nd ed.). Columbus, OH: Merrill.

Wolery, M., Bailey, D. B., & Sugal, G. M. (1988). *Effective teaching principles and procedures of applied behavior analysis with exceptional students.* Boston: Allyn & Bacon.

Chapter 5

Assessing Environments

Donald B. Bailey, Jr.
University of North Carolina
at Chapel Hill

KEY TERMS

- Normalized
- Least Restrictive
- Environment
- Physical Space
- Open-plan Facility
- Closed-plan Facility
- Modified Open-plan Facility
- Accessible Space

- Inaccessible Environment
- Organization and Supervision of Space
- Peer Environments
- Responsiveness
- Functions
- Forms
- Schematic
- Checklists

- Rating Scales
- Engagement
- Nonengagement
- Ecobehavioral Assessment
- Molar Descriptions
- Molecular Descriptions
- Process-product Analysis
- Environmental Neonatology

At first glance, a chapter on assessing environments seems out of place in a book on assessing children. However, environmental assessments are important within the broad context of making decisions regarding children's placement and the goals for intervention programs. This chapter provides a rationale for environmental assessment, describes procedural considerations in assessing environments, and gives examples of representative issues and methods for assessing typical environments in which handicapped infants and preschoolers are placed.

Rationale for Environmental Assessment

Interest in environments has increased dramatically in recent years as early interventionists have grown to realize the importance of the environment in shaping the behavior of both children and adults (Phyfe-Perkins, 1980; Rogers-Warren, 1982; Weinstein & David, 1987). The relationship between the quality of home environments and the developmental progress of both normally developing (e.g., MacPhee, Ramey, & Yeates, 1984) and handicapped children (e.g., Piper &

Ramsay, 1980) is well documented. Likewise, several studies have documented a clear relationship between environmental provisions in daycare and children's language and cognitive development (McCartney, 1984; McCartney, Scarr, Phillips, & Grajek, 1985). Thus, a primary rationale for environmental assessment is to determine the extent to which a given environment is likely to facilitate children's development.

A second reason for assessing environments is to determine the extent to which they are safe, warm, and generally comfortable places for the care of children. Studies to be reviewed later in this chapter have documented disconcerting aspects of center-based environments for handicapped preschoolers (e.g., Bailey, Clifford, & Harms, 1982) and hospital environments for premature and very-low-birthweight neonates (e.g., VandenBerg, 1982; Wolke, 1987a;b). Systematic assessment of these nebulous but important dimensions of environments should lead to the provision of more enjoyable and comfortable surroundings.

David and Weinstein (1987), in a review of the physical environment and children's development, summarize these first two rationales for environmental assessment by asserting that all environments should fulfill certain basic functions for children. These include fostering personal identity through stable interactions within a pleasant environment, fostering the development of competence by engaging in a facilitative environment, providing opportunities for growth, fostering a sense of security and trust, and providing a balance of opportunities for social interactions and privacy. Through environmental assessment, professionals can describe the presence or absence of variables that are likely to fulfill these functions and plan appropriate environmental changes.

A third reason for assessing environments is to determine the extent to which environments are **normalized** or **least restrictive.** Public Law 94-142 mandated that handicapped children be served in the least restric-

tive environment appropriate to meet their educational needs. Restrictiveness was conceptualized on a continuum with self-contained residential programs at one extreme and regular classrooms at the other extreme. Broader conceptualizations of restrictiveness have also been offered. For example, Kenowitz, Zweibel, and Edgar (1979) assessed restrictiveness in regard to the extent to which nonhandicapped peers are available, the environment is accessible, and teaching strategies are effective. Recent court rulings and statements from the U.S. Department of Education clearly indicate that the least restrictive environment provisions of P.L. 94-142 do, in fact, apply to the new preschool programs mandated under P.L. 99-457. Thus, a third rationale for assessing environments is to determine, across multiple dimensions, the extent to which they are normalized or least restrictive.

A final reason for assessing environments is to determine the extent to which certain skills are required for successful placement in those environments. This is an important issue for both families and children, particularly when transitions are upcoming and a move from one program to another is being planned. In fact, P.L. 99-457 specifies that the Individualized Family Service Plan for infants and toddlers must include a statement of the steps needed to support the transition of the child to a preschool program. By determining the skills necessary to succeed in an environment, teachers and parents can work together to facilitate skill acquisition in order to maximize the likelihood of successful transitions (Bailey & Simeonsson, 1988).

Procedural Considerations in Assessing Environments

The effective assessment of environments requires a knowledge of important dimensions of the environment. This section describes those dimensions and provides broad guidelines or considerations when planning for environmental assessments.

Dimensions of Environments

What is an environment? Broadly construed, the **environment** includes everything that surrounds us and experiences to which we are exposed. A more narrow concept of the environment focuses only on the built, or physical, environment. For the purpose of this text, we adopt a broad view of environments that includes space, materials, organization, scheduling, social aspects, and contingency experiences.

The Physical Space. The **physical space** refers to the amount of space that is available and the way that space is arranged. In regard to amount of space, an apparent relationship has been noted between small amounts of space per person and aggressiveness in social interactions (Weinstein, 1979). Most states have regulations pertaining to the minimum amount of square footage necessary per child in any child-care program. According to the accreditation criteria and procedures of the National Academy of Early Childhood Programs (1984), a center should have at least 35 square feet of usable indoor space and 75 square feet of outdoor play space for each child in the program. These figures may need to be altered in programs serving children who require adaptive or supportive equipment such as wheelchairs or proneboards. Not only does such equipment take up space not usually needed in child-care programs, but it also requires additional space for adequate use.

In regard to arrangement of space, Moore (1987) described three basic types of designs. An **open-plan facility** has "unpartitioned space with few or no internal walls," whereas a **closed-plan facility** has "self-contained classrooms usually arranged along corridors or as in a house with several small interconnecting rooms" (p. 51). In contrast, a **modified open-plan facility** is the "organization of space into a variety of large and small activity spaces open enough to allow children to see the play possibilities available to them while providing enough enclosure for the child to be protected from noise and visual distractions" (p. 52). In a study of these three environments with normally developing children ages 2–6, Moore found that the modified open-plan centers resulted in greater use of activity settings, smaller group sizes, increased engagement in cognitively oriented behaviors, and increased child-initiated behaviors. Open-plan centers were likely to result in more "random" behavior, whereas closed-plan facilities resulted in greater amounts of time spent in transitions from one activity or setting to another and increased observations of withdrawn behavior in children. Moore argued that the use of modified open-plan facilities is important for children's development, and thus professionals engaged in the assessment of environments should examine spatial arrangement.

An additional dimension of the physical space important to handicapped youngsters is the extent to which space is accessible. This issue is particularly important for children with visual or motor impairments. **Accessible space** is space that children can get to and make use of independently. An **inaccessible environment** is one in which the child's internal freedom within that environment is restricted (Kenowitz et al., 1979) or in which some portion of the environment is unattainable without teacher assistance. For example, if a room contains multiple levels separated by stairs, a child in a wheelchair will not be able to move from one level to another. Likewise, if the dramatic play center is located in a loft, it may be difficult for visually impaired children or children with motor impairments to gain access to that center. Thus, professionals should assess the extent to which children's movements are inappropriately restricted by some dimension of the physical environment.

Organization and Supervision of Space. A related dimension of the environment is the **organization and supervision of space.** Several authors have argued that space must be organized and well defined according to use or functions (Moore, 1987; Olds, 1979). For example, Moore (1987) examined the extent to which child-care centers incorporated spatial definition (e.g., appropriateness of storage, work surfaces and display space, separation of activities, degree of area definition and enclosure) in environmental design and use and found that the degree or level of engagement in activities was higher in spaces that were well defined. Olds (1987) suggests that a well-defined activity area should have five attributes: a specific location, visible boundaries, surfaces for both work and sitting, adequate space for storing and displaying materials, and a "mood" or "personality" that is achieved by use of color and soft materials.

Of course children's use of space is mediated by the amount and type of teacher supervision and involvement. For example, LeLaurin and Risley (1972) compared two procedures for teacher supervision of activity areas. The *zone* procedure, in which adults were assigned to activity areas and children were allowed to move at their own pace, resulted in higher levels of engagement than did a "man-to-man" procedure, in which teachers were assigned a group of children and the group had to stay together at all times.

Materials. An environment should contain sufficient materials for the number of children who will use the environment. The materials should be colorful and appealing to children, appropriate for children's developmental levels, and developmentally facilitative. They should be planned and available, recognizing that different kinds of toys and materials are likely to encourage different kinds of behavior. For example, Quiltich and Risley (1973) demonstrated that some toys, such as crayons, are likely to promote "iso-late" behavior (children playing by themselves), whereas other toys, such as games or dress-up clothes, are likely to promote social interactions between two or more children. Materials should be in good repair and, for many materials, it is essential that multiple pieces of the same toy or material be available in order to prevent arguments and facilitate parallel and cooperative play activities.

Peer Environments. A fourth dimension of the environment is the children who are available to serve as peers and playmates. Most state regulations focus on the *number* of peers in a group, with specific guidelines provided for allowable group size. For example, staff-child ratios recommended for different ages by the National Academy of Early Childhood Programs (1984) are displayed in Table 5.1. Two other dimensions of **peer environments** could be assessed, however. One is the extent to which nonhandicapped children are available and used as playmates. Observers should be careful not to assume that just because nonhandicapped children are enrolled in a program, mainstreaming experiences occur. Grouping and scheduling considerations may mean that normally developing children infrequently are grouped with handicapped peers. Guidelines for assessing social interactions are described in Chapter 15. A second dimension to assess is the age of available peers. Programs can be grouped according to either same-age or mixed-age groupings. An important question regarding an environment is the extent to which the selection and assignment of peers to groups results in a situation that is appropriate for an individual handicapped child.

Organization and Scheduling. A fifth dimension of the environment is the level of organization and scheduling of activities and teacher roles in the program. An excellent physical environment can be neutralized if it is poorly managed or organized. Hart (1982) emphasizes that specific roles need to be

TABLE 5.1
Recommended Staff-Child Ratios within Group Size

Age of children*	6	8	10	12	Group size 14	16	18	20	22	24
Infants (birth–12 mos.)	1:3	1:4								
Toddlers (12–24 mos.)	1:3	1:4	1:5	1:4						
Two-year-olds (24–36 mos.)		1:4	1:5	1:6**						
Two- and three-year-olds			1:5	1:6	1:7**					
Three-year-olds					1:7	1:8	1:9	1:10**		
Four-year-olds						1:8	1:9	1:10**		
Four- and five-year-olds						1:8	1:9	1:10**		
Five-year-olds						1:8	1:9	1:10		
Six- to eight-year-olds (school age)								1:10	1:11	1:12

*Multi-age grouping is both permissible and desirable. When no infants are included, the staff-child ratio and group size requirements shall be based on the age of the majority of the children in the group. When infants are included, ratios and group size for infants must be maintained.
**Smaller group sizes and lower staff-child ratios are optimal. Larger group sizes and higher staff-child ratios are acceptable only in cases where staff are highly qualified.

Source: From *Accreditation Criteria and Procedures of the National Academy of Early Childhood Programs* (p. 24) by National Academy of Early Childhood Programs, 1984, Washington, DC: The National Association for the Education of Young Children. Copyright 1984 by NAEYC. Reprinted by permission.

assigned to adults, and each adult needs to be aware of those roles. Children and staff should be assigned to primary groups. The National Academy of Early Childhood Programs (1984) suggests that continuity of adults is important, especially for infants and toddlers, and that infants should spend the majority of time interacting with the same person each day. It is also essential, however, that adults in the program work together as a professional team.

Safety. A sixth dimension of the environment is its safety. Safety includes many aspects. An environment should be free of hazards. Equipment should be in good repair and appropriate for the ages of the children in the center. Adequate supervision of children must occur at all times, and adults should know basic emergency procedures.

Responsiveness. A seventh dimension of the environment is its **responsiveness.** An en-

vironment should contain many forms of responses to children's behavior. Wachs (1979) argued that a physically responsive environment may help teach children that their behavior can, in fact, influence the environment. This ability should enhance feelings of competence (Olds, 1979) and help children become more independent. Responsiveness may come from reactive toys, peers, or adults. For example, Goldberg (1977) emphasized the importance of social reciprocity to the enhancement of feelings of social competence.

Promoting Independence. A good environment promotes independence in children. Independence is partially facilitated by an accessible environment. It also can be aided by a variety of environmental provisions. For example, in a center containing some children with visual impairments, toy shelves could be labeled using raised figures or shapes to indicate where toys should be returned when not in use. Teachers facilitate independence by providing just enough assistance (e.g., models, prompts, physical assistance) to ensure the child is successful but not so much as to promote overreliance on teacher assistance. Adults also promote independence by waiting, allowing children sufficient time to perform specific behaviors independently.

General Guidelines for Assessing Environments

Assessing environments is in many ways a very different process from assessing children. In conducting environmental assessments, professionals should be aware of these unique issues and be able to design individualized assessments appropriate for a variety of environments.

Be Aware of Published Guidelines for Environmental Provisions. Although few assessment tools exist to measure environments, published guidelines are often available that allow professionals to design and conduct their own assessments. One of the most well-known and visible of these guidelines is the *Accreditation Criteria and Procedures* published by the National Academy of Early Childhood Programs (1984), a division of the National Association for the Education of Young Children. The criteria were developed in order to facilitate a process by which early childhood programs could become accredited according to criteria established for high quality center-based programs. Although primarily developed for centers serving normally developing infants, toddlers, and preschoolers, the guidelines are also appropriate for handicapped children's programs. It is likely, however, that additional criteria may need to be examined when evaluating environments for handicapped youngsters. The published criteria for high quality early childhood programs cover 10 areas: interactions among staff and children, curriculum, staff/parent interactions, staff qualifications and development, administration, staffing, physical en-

vironment, health and safety, nutrition and food service, and evaluation. The nine criteria for the physical environment are displayed in Table 5.2.

Although most state agencies have guidelines for programs serving nonhandicapped children, there is no comparable set of accreditation criteria for early intervention programs for handicapped youngsters. Thus professionals will need to individualize and tailor assessments to individual programs.

Recognize the Complexity of Environmental Assessment. Wachs (1987) suggested that research to date has failed to recognize the complexity of environments and the nature of environmental influences. The effects of a given environment will depend in part upon the built space, but also will vary according to the individuals in that space and how they continually react to and modify the environment over time. Environmental assessments must be conducted with the realization that it is always an interactive context. This means that environmental assessment cannot be done completely in the absence of children. Walking into a room and examining the materials, equipment, and arrangement is an important first step. However, until the observer has had an opportunity to see how the environment is used and how adults and children in the environment behave, the overall picture will be incomplete.

Focus on Functions Not Forms. A third important guideline is to recognize that the bottom line in environmental assessment is the care of children in environments that fulfill certain basic **functions** or needs (e.g., safe, warm, developmentally facilitative, independence-promoting, enjoyable, normalized). Environmental assessments should focus primarily on whether these functions are achieved, not whether specific **forms** of the environment are available. Consider, for example, the contrast between a daycare center for children of executives in a major corpora-

TABLE 5.2
Criteria for the Physical Environment

1. The indoor and outdoor environments are safe, clean, attractive, and spacious. There is a minimum of 35 square feet of usable playroom floor space indoors per child and a minimum of 75 square feet of play space outdoors per child.
2. Activity areas are defined clearly by spatial arrangement. Space is arranged so that children can work individually, together in small groups, or in a large group. Space is arranged to provide clear pathways for children to move from one area to minimize distractions.
3. The space for toddler and preschool children is arranged to facilitate a variety of small group and/or individual activities including block building, socio-dramatic play, art, music, science, math, manipulatives, and quiet book reading. Other activites such as sand/water play and woodworking are also available on occasion. Carpeted areas and ample crawling space are provided for nonwalkers. Sturdy furniture is provided so nonwalkers can pull themselves up or balance themselves while walking. School-aged children are provided separate space arranged to facilitate a variety of age-appropriate activities.
4. Age-appropriate materials and equipment of sufficient quantity, variety, and durability are readily accessible to children and arranged on low, open shelves to promote independent use by children.
5. Individual spaces for children to hang their clothing and store their personal belongings are provided.
6. Private areas are available indoors and outdoors for children to have solitude.
7. The environment includes soft elements such as rugs, cushions, or rocking chairs.
8. Sound-absorbing materials are used to cut down on excessive noise.
9. The outdoor area includes a variety of surfaces such as soil, sand, grass, hills, flat sections, and hard areas for wheel toys. The outdoor area includes shade; open space; digging space; and a variety of equipment for riding, climbing, balancing, and individual play. The outdoor area is protected from access to streets or other dangers.

Source: From *Accreditation Criteria and Procedures of the National Academy of Early Childhood Programs* (pp. 25–27) by the National Academy of Early Childhood Programs, 1984, Washington, DC: The National Association for the Education of Young Children. Copyright 1984 by NAEYC.

tion and a family daycare home in a rural mountain community. The appearance of those two environments is likely to be quite different. One will have many of the most modern toys and play equipment, whereas the other is likely to have only a few toys, many of which are older. However, it would be a mistake to assume that the corporate daycare environment automatically is superior. In fact, the family daycare home could be superior in achieving many of the desired outcomes of child care. Likewise, it is tempting to be critical of the environments provided children raised in low-income families. Professionals, however, should seek to look behind the first image of an environment to identify positive and facilitative aspects that might be in a very different form from that expected yet which fulfill the same developmentally facilitative functions.

Be Familiar with and Use a Variety of Assessment Strategies. As described in Chapter 1, effective assessment of children incorporates multiple sources and multiple measures. Likewise, a number of strategies may be used to assess environments. Although information about environments can be obtained by interviewing adults who work in that environment, direct observational assessment is preferred, because it often is difficult for adults to be objective about rating their own environment. One strategy is to draw a **schematic** diagram depicting the environmental arrangement in a room. A sample schematic from a preschool classroom is displayed in Figure 5.1. Ideally, a schematic drawing should be proportionally accurate, with room and equipment size in proportion to reality. Using various symbols and labeling areas and equipment can facilitate any visual analyses of the schematic.

Drawing a schematic allows the professional to analyze the environment in terms of spatial arrangement and priority. Such analyses can be enhanced by using the schematic in conjunction with an observational analysis of activity patterns of children. For example, at selected intervals notations could be made

as to how many children were in a given area. Several of these observations could provide an indication of which are the most popular activity areas and which are infrequently used. Also, a single child's use of the environment could be documented by simply drawing lines to represent the child's movement during a defined time period. As displayed in Figure 5.2, such an analysis could help differentiate children who wander around an environment from activity to activity from those who become seriously involved in one or two activities for extended periods of time. If few children spend a lot of time in activities, the environment probably needs modification. If more detailed information is needed, a momentary time-sampling procedure such as that described in Chapter 4 can be used to note where each child is at each observation

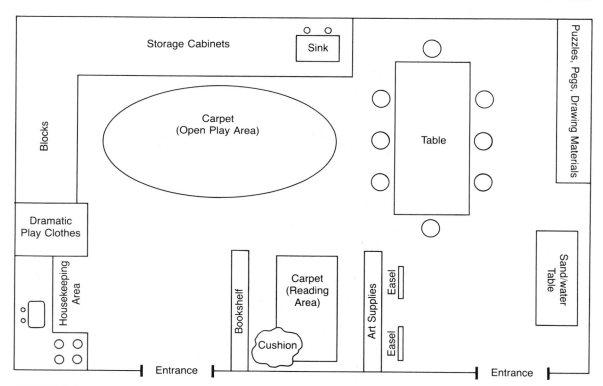

FIGURE 5.1
Schematic Depicting a Preschool Environment

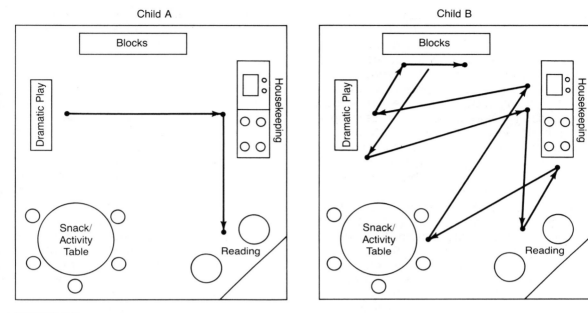

FIGURE 5.2
Schematic Comparing the Activity/Movement Patterns of Two Children During a 30-Minute Free-Play Period

point. This procedure will allow assessment of the proportion of time each child in the center spends in each area.

A second strategy for evaluating environments is to document environmental quality through use of **checklists.** A checklist is simply a list of environmental provisions that someone considers important. By studying the environment, asking adults who work in the environment, or observing interactional patterns, the checklist can be completed. Numerous examples of checklists for various dimensions of infant and toddler centers (e.g., nap and potty charts, activity records) have been described by Herbert-Jackson, O'Brien, Porterfield, and Risley (1977) and O'Brien, Porterfield, Herbert-Jackson, and Risley (1979).

Third, environments can be evaluated using **rating scales.** Probably the most common format utilized, a rating scale generally consists of a number of items organized into sev-

eral dimensions of environmental provisions. The items may be scored in a binary (yes/no) fashion similar to a checklist or may require the use of a rating scale with several values possible depending upon the quality of the environment observed. Ideally, a rating scale is based on substantial professional expertise and evaluation regarding scale content, with supporting data indicating the scale's validity for various purposes. Several examples of rating scales are described in subsequent sections of this chapter.

Assess the Effects of Environments. Because environments are interactive, the ultimate test of an environment is how it influences the behavior of children and adults. For example, an environment with inadequate space and insufficient or inappropriate toys and materials is likely to result in higher levels of aggressive behavior. If one were to evaluate the effects of improving such an environment, documenting changes in aggressive behavior may be appropriate.

One of the most frequently used and fundamental measures of environmental effectiveness is documenting child engagement within environments. **Engagement** refers to the extent to which children are actively and appropriately involved with materials, people, or activities in the environment. Numerous studies conducted with older children have documented the importance of engagement in relation to academic achievement (e.g., Berliner & Rosenshine, 1977; Borg, 1980). Likewise, numerous studies have documented changes in engagement as a function of various environmental provisions (e.g., Krantz & Risley, 1977; Montes & Risley, 1975; Twardosz, Cataldo, & Risley, 1974).

Engagement is assessed by observing children and documenting the extent to which they are engaged in appropriate activities. Obviously the precise definition of engagement will vary according to the classroom situation and expectations for children in each activity area (Bailey, Harms, & Clifford, 1983). Instances of **nonengagement** include self-stimulatory behavior, nonattending, aggressive behavior, aimless wandering, or inappropriate use of materials. The first step in assessing engagement is to develop a definition of the behaviors considered on-task or appropriate within various activity areas. A time-sampling procedure (see Chapter 4) is used to identify levels of engagement either for an individual child or for the whole group. For example, at 30-second intervals the teacher could record the number or percentage of children who are at that moment engaged in appropriate activities. A useful extension of this approach is to add a third category to record the percentage of children who are waiting, either in line, for a turn, for help, or for materials.

McWilliam, Trivette, and Dunst (1985) investigated the possible utility of behavior engagement as a measure of the efficacy of early intervention. Using engagement assessments in two different types of programs,

they showed that the two program types could be distinguished on the basis of child engagement, with one model resulting in higher levels of engagement within certain activities than another.

A second broad strategy for assessing the interactive effects of environmental provisions has been referred to as **ecobehavioral assessment,** "a means of assessing program variables through systematic observation and measuring the moment-to-moment effects of an array of variables upon student behavior" (Carta & Greenwood, 1985, p 92). In evaluating early intervention programs, these authors have focused on three levels of analysis, all based on direct observational data. **Molar descriptions** of programs are used to show how adults and children spend their time during the day, in general terms (e.g., engaged vs. nonengaged) or more specific terms (e.g., direct instruction, location of play, peer interaction). **Molecular descriptions** of programs are determined by computing conditional probabilities. For example, given that the teacher is reading a story, what is the likelihood that a child or group of children is listening or participating? Finally, a **process-product analysis** looks at the relationship between molecular relationships, molar descriptions, and children's subsequent outcomes, such as enhanced developmental progress.

By way of summarizing this section, Landesman-Dwyer's (1985) guidelines for environmental assessment are appropriate:

(1) Objective environmental features believed to have an effect on program integrity and success should be listed; (2) Key informants believed to be able to provide insights . . . should be asked to provide both objective and subjective accounts; (3) If standardized tools are used, investigators should consider analyzing the individual items for their relevance to the particular types of environments under assessment; and (4) To the extent possible, indicators of program "success" or "outcome" should be selected that can be separated from the description

of the environment per se. Ideally, these indicators should reflect what is expected as a function of particular environmental variables. (p. 194)

Representative Methods for Assessing Environments

A variety of measures and procedures have been proposed for assessing various environments related to the care of children. This section describes representative methods and procedures for assessing home environments, center environments, and hospital environments. The section concludes with a discussion of the assessment of skills needed for successful participation in a given environment. Such assessment is important for placement purposes as well as for instructional activities likely to facilitate successful transitions.

Assessing Home Environments
One environment in which infants and preschoolers spend considerable time is the home, and several authors have addressed measurement issues related to assessing home environments. Early interventionists, particularly those working in home-based infant programs, may be interested in assessing the home environment to determine the extent to which it is safe, warm, and developmentally facilitative. A detailed description of considerations and procedures in assessing family environments is presented by Simeonsson (1988), and thus assessment of the home environment is only briefly addressed here.

Home Observation and Measurement of the Environment. By far the most well-known and commonly used measure of the home environment is the Home Observation and Measurement of the Environment (HOME) (Caldwell & Bradley, 1972). The HOME scale

was designed to assess the quantity and quality of the physical environment of the home as well as the social, emotional, and cognitive support provided children in their own homes. Two versions of the scale exist, one for rating homes of children ages 0–3 years, the other for children ages 3–6. The infant version contains 45 items organized into 6 subscales: (1) emotional and verbal responsiveness of mother; (2) avoidance of restriction and punishment; (3) organization of physical and temporal environment; (4) provision of appropriate play materials; (5) maternal involvement with child; and (6) opportunities for variety in daily stimulation. The preschool version contains 55 items organized into 8 subscales: (1) stimulation through toys, games, and reading materials; (2) language stimulation; (3) physical environment; (4) pride, affection, and warmth; (5) stimulation of academic behavior; (6) modeling and encouraging of social maturity; (7) variety of stimulation; and (8) physical punishment. Both instruments are completed on the basis of a home visit by a trained observer. Each item contains a statement about the environment (e.g., "Child has some muscle activity toys or equipment") which is scored as either yes or no on the basis of observation and interviews with the parent. Raw scores may be generated for each subscale and for the total score. No norms or score transformations are available.

Numerous studies have examined the reliability of the HOME scales and their utility in regard to their primary purpose, which is to serve as a screening measure to identify high-risk home environments. In regard to reliability, Elardo, Bradley, and Caldwell (1977) reported high interrater agreement, and Mitchell and Gray (1981) found total scores to be consistent over time, although subscales were not. The relationship between HOME scores and subsequent testing of cognitive and language development has been documented repeatedly (Bradley & Caldwell, 1977; Elardo, Bradley, & Caldwell, 1977). Also,

Piper and Ramsay (1980) found a relationship between the quality of the home environment as indicated by ratings on the HOME scale and changes in the developmental status of infants with Down syndrome.

Although designed primarily as a screening tool, Powell (1981) suggests that the HOME scale can serve as a mechanism for feedback to parents and as a teaching tool to promote high-quality interpersonal interactions between parent and child. However, the interventionist using the HOME scale in this fashion should take care to communicate a positive impression of parenting skills and to build on parent priorities for services (Bailey, 1987). Also, there is considerable variability in the importance of individual items, and interventionists should examine the pattern of scores and not just the individual items. Individual items may reflect values that the parent does not hold or may not be sensitive to qualitative issues. For example, one item on the infant scale is "Family has a pet." Obviously it would be quite inappropriate to suggest that owning a pet is an important goal for all families. Furthermore, some families may have a pet, but it could be inappropriate for the age of the child (e.g., a snake or an aggressive dog) and thus not fulfill the function for which it was intended.

Purdue Home Stimulation Inventory. The Purdue Home Stimulation Inventory (Wachs, 1977) was developed to assess the infant's physical environment provided in the home. The instrument consists of 30 items gathered through interviews and observations within the home environment. According to the author, the instrument was not developed with the intent of being theoretically consistent, but rather with the purpose of tapping as many relevant dimensions of the physical environment as possible. Items assess dimensions such as routines, number of adults and siblings living in the home, materials available, and activity levels. In a study of 39 normally developing infants from a range of environ-

mental arrangements, Wachs found that 6 items on the instrument were consistently associated with children's cognitive development:

> a physically responsive environment, an adequate degree of personal space as defined by the presence of a stimulus shelter and a lack of overcrowding, the degree to which the physical set-up of the home permits exploration, and the degree of temporal regularity in the home. In addition, there is a high noise-confusion level in the home which is negatively related to development. Certain items such as the presence of strangers, the presence of a mobile, changes in available toys and objects, and amount of floor freedom are also related to development but not with the same consistency or frequency as the above items. (p. 30)

Assessing Infant and Preschool Center Environments

A second environment in which handicapped infants and preschoolers spend time is in out-of-home caretaking environments. These environments may include a center in which several staff care for children, or a family day home in which an adult cares for several children in his or her own home. Several instruments for rating the quality of these environments are described in this section.

Early Childhood Environment Rating Scale. The Early Childhood Environment Rating Scale (ECERS) (Harms & Clifford, 1980) "was designed to give an overall picture of the surroundings for children and adults in preschool settings, including the use of space, materials, and activities to enhance children's development, daily schedule, and supervision" (Harms & Clifford, 1983, p. 262). It is designed for use across environments serving typical infants and/or preschoolers. The 37 items are organized into 7 subscales: (1) personal care routines, (2) furnishings and display, (3) language-reasoning experiences, (4) fine and gross motor activities, (5) creative activities, (6) social development, and (7) adult needs. Scoring the entire instrument generally requires a morning's observation and interviews with staff. Each item is scored on a scale from 1 (inadequate) to 7 (excellent), with criteria provided for ratings of 1, 3, 5, and 7. Two example items from the ECERS are displayed in Table 5.3 (p. 110).

Items on the scale were developed based on an extensive literature review and input from practicing caregivers and supervisors. Their importance was validated by a panel of seven experts in early childhood education. Studies reported by the authors indicate that scores on the scale correlate well with broader ratings by experts of program quality. Interrater reliability was .88 and test/retest reliability was .96 (Harms & Clifford, 1983).

Several studies have documented the utility of the ECERS in evaluating important dimensions of environmental quality. A series of studies have examined the relationship between ECERS ratings and various developmental outcomes for children. McCartney, Scarr, Phillips, Grajek, and Schwarz (1982), McCartney (1984), and McCartney, Scarr, Phillips, and Grajek (1985) found significant relationships between overall ratings of environmental quality and measures of both intellectual and langauge development in children. Children in high-quality centers generally were rated by both parents and caregivers as more considerate and more sociable than children attending other daycare programs. Bjorkman, Poteat, and Snow (1986), however, found no clear-cut association between ECERS ratings and observed social behavior of 4-year-olds in four daycare centers, two with high ECERS scores and two with low ECERS scores.

Bailey, Clifford, and Harms (1982) used the ECERS to compare environments in 56 classrooms for normally developing preschoolers with 25 classrooms for handicapped preschoolers. Overall scores for nonhandicapped classrooms were significantly higher than those for handicapped preschoolers, with 12 individual items rated higher: furnishings for relaxation and comfort, room arrangement, child-related display, space for gross motor practice, scheduled time for gross motor activities, art, blocks, sand/water, dramatic play, space to be alone, free play, and cultural awareness. The authors suggested that the data indicated these preschool environments were significantly different from those normally provided for young children and apparently were less normalized. The extent to which these differences represented appropriate modifications for handicapped children was not known.

The authors of the ECERS have recently developed two additional measures that incorporate the same approach and framework for environmental assessment, but which focus more specifically on two types of environments. The Infant/Toddler Environment Rating Scale (ITERS) (Harms, Cryer, & Clifford, in press) is designed to assess the quality of care provided for children under age 30 months, while the Famly Day Care Rating Scale (FDCRS) (Harms & Clifford, in press) is designed to assess the quality of care provided in a family daycare home. A comparison of subscales and items on the ECERS, ITERS, and FDCRS is displayed in Table 5.4 (p. 111).

The Early Childhood Physical Environment Scales. The Early Childhood Physical Environment Scales (Moore, 1982) were developed in order to describe the arrangement and atmosphere of early childhood programs and consist of two scales. One rates the organization of the space of the center as a whole, whereas the other rates the organization and character of individual rooms or areas. The whole-center scale assesses 10 dimensions: visual connection between spaces, closure of spaces, spatial separation, mixture of large and small spaces, separation of staff and children's areas, separation of functional versus activity areas, separation of age groups, circulation, visibility, and connection

TABLE 5.3
Two Sample Items from the Early Childhood Environment Rating Scale

	Inadequate 1	2	Minimal 3	4	Good 5	6	Excellent 7
Room arrangement	No interest centers defined. Room inconveniently arranged (Ex. traffic patterns interfere with activities). Materials with similar use not placed together.		One or two interest centers defined, but centers not well placed in room (Ex. quiet and noisy activities near one another, water not accessible where needed). Supervision of centers difficult, or materials disorganized.		Three or more interest centers defined and conveniently equipped (Ex. water provided, shelving adequate). Quiet and noisy centers separated. Appropriate play space provided in each center (Ex. rug or table area out of flow of traffic). Easy visual supervision of centers.		Everything in 5 plus centers selected to provide a variety of learning experiences. Arrangement of centers designed to promote independent use by children (Ex. labeled open shelves, convenient drying space for artwork). Additional materials organized and available to add to or change centers.
Informal use of language	Language outside of group times primarily used by staff to control children's behavior and manage routines.		Staff sometimes talks with children in conversation, but children are asked primarily "yes/no" or short answer questions. Children's talk not encouraged.		Staff-child conversations are frequent. Language is primarily used by staff to exchange information with children and for social interaction. Children are asked "why, how, what if" questions, requiring longer and more complex answers.		Staff makes conscious effort to have an informal conversation with each child every day. Staff verbally expands on ideas presented by children (Ex. adds information, asks questions to encourage child to talk more).

Source: From *Early Childhood Environment Rating Scale* (pp. 17, 21) by T. Harms and R.M. Clifford, 1980, New York: Teachers College Press. Copyright 1980 by T. Harms and R.M. Clifford. Reprinted by permission.

TABLE 5.4

Comparison of Items and Subscales from the ECERS, ITERS, and FDCRS

ECERS	ITERS	FDCRS
Personal Care Routines	**Personal Care Routines**	**Basic Care**
Greeting/departing	Greeting/departing	Arriving/leaving
Meals/snacks	Meals/snacks	Meals/snacks
Nap/rest	Nap	Nap/rest
Diapering/toileting	Diapering/toileting	Diapering/toileting
Personal grooming	Personal grooming	Personal grooming
Furnishings and Display	Health	Health
for Children	Safety	Safety
For routine care	**Furnishings and Display**	**Space and Furnishings for**
For learning activities	**for Children**	**Care and Learning**
For relaxation and comfort	For routine care	For routine care and learning
Room arrangement	For learning activities	For relaxation and comfort
Child-related display	For relaxation and comfort	Child-related display
Language-Reasoning	Room arrangement	Indoor space arrangement
Experiences	Child-related display	Active physical play
Understanding of language	**Listening and Talking**	Space to be alone
Using language	Informal use of language	**Language and Reasoning**
Using learning concepts	Books and pictures	Informal use of language
Informal use of language	**Learning Activities**	Helping children understand
Fine and Gross Motor	Eye-hand coordination	language
Activities	Active physical play	Helping children use language
Perceptual/fine motor	Art	Helping children reason
Supervision (fine motor)	Music and movement	**Learning Activities**
Space for gross motor	Blocks	Eye-hand coordination
Gross motor equipment	Pretend play	Art
Scheduled time for gross	Sand and water play	Music and movement
motor	**Interaction**	Sand and water play
Supervision (gross motor)	Peer interaction	Dramatic play
Creative Activities	Adult-child interaction	Blocks
Art	Discipline	Use of T.V.
Music/movement	Cultural awareness	Schedule of daily activities
Blocks	**Program Structure**	Supervision of play
Sand/water	Schedule of daily activities	**Social Development**
Dramatic play	Supervision of daily activities	Tone
Schedule	Staff cooperation	Discipline
Supervision	Provisions for exceptional	Cultural awareness
Social Development	children	Provision for exceptional
Space to be alone	**Adult Needs**	children
Free play	Adult personal needs	**Adult Needs**
Group time	Opportunities for professional	Relationship with parents
Cultural awareness	growth	Balancing personal and
Tone	Adult meeting area	caregiving responsibilities
Provisions for exceptional	Provisions for parents	Opportunities for professional
children		growth
Adult Needs		
Adult personal area		
Opportunities for personal		
growth		
Adult meeting area		
Provisions for parents		

between indoor and outdoor spaces. Each item is rated on a 5-point scale. The scale rating individual rooms or areas also assesses 10 dimensions: spatial definition of activity centers, visual connections to other centers, size, storage and work space, concentration of same-use resources, softness, flexibility, variety of seating and working positions, amount of resources, and separation of activity centers from circulation paths.

Moore (1982) recommends that these scales be used in conjunction with other measures to gain a more complete picture of the environment. He developed two measures to assess teachers, one focusing on teacher style and one on educational philosophy. Both are self-ratings completed by teachers. Additionally, an Environment/Behavior Observation Schedule is used to code the behavior of children and adults in early childhood settings. Before observation begins, a schematic is drawn of the environment, which is then divided into cells representing approximately 60 square feet. A time-sampling system is recommended, in which several categories of behavior are coded according to the cell in which they occurred. An example of the scale's use was reported by Moore (1986), who found that differences in engagement were related to the amount of spatial definition in a given area.

Preschool Assessment of the Classroom Environment. The Preschool Assessment of the Classroom Environment Scale (PACE) (McWilliam & Dunst, 1985) consists of 70 items organized into four categories: (1) program organization (including program management, integration, and parent involvement); (2) environmental organization (including the physical environment, staffing patterns, classroom scheduling, and transitions); (3) instruction (including child growth and development, curriculum, plans for intervention, method of instruction, and behavior management); and (4) program outcomes (including program evaluation plan and child

engagement). In contrast to the ECERS, which was designed primarily to assess programs serving normally developing children, the PACE instrument was designed primarily to assess environments serving handicapped children from age 0–6. Each item is scored on a 5-point rating scale that is completed after observing the classroom environment, interviewing staff, and reviewing written materials.

Dunst, McWilliam, and Holbert (1986) assessed 20 preschool programs, including those for both handicapped and nonhandicapped children. Reliability of two independent ratings using the PACE instrument was 82%. The instrument was able to differentiate program types, and ratings of the management, organization, and operation of environments were significantly related to child outcomes of engagement and behavior characteristics as well as caregiver style of interaction.

Assessing Hospital Environments

A third environment in which handicapped infants and preschoolers spend time is in hospitals, usually the neonatal intensive care unit (NICU) or a pediatric unit. When hospital stays are required, the primary concern is the health of the child, and medical routines and procedures generally take first priority. The importance of the child's developmental and emotional needs in such environments, however, is increasingly recognized (See Chapter 8). Of particular concern relative to this chapter is the nature of hospital environments. VandenBerg (1982) described the rapidly changing technology in neonatal intensive care nurseries (ICNS) and its contribution to increased survival rates for low birthweight and otherwise high-risk infants. She suggested that "the same technical advances have brought with them a host of new problems. The modern ICN environment is replete with negative stimuli for infants and their caregivers" (p. 83). It is an inherently stressful environment for infants, caregivers, and parents, due to the serious nature of the infants' health status, the nature of treatment procedures used, high noise levels, frequent changes of caregivers, disruptions in the parent/child relationship, and work-related stresses for staff. She argued that the ICN should have one or more developmental specialists to provide infant care that is coordinated and responsive to infant developmental needs and ensure a "humanization" of the intensive care nursery.

Wolke (1987a;b) describes an emerging field referred to as **environmental neonatology:**

> a multidisciplinary field concerned with the systematic study of special care facilities for the newborn and their impact on the medical and developmental state of sick infants. The crucial questions are: what is the environment of the special care baby unit like today; and how can we best provide for the bio-behavioral well-being of the preterm infant? (Wolke, 1987b, p. 987)

While this field has not yet yielded standardized rating scales such as those designed for rating home and center environments, several important dimensions of the NICU environment have been identified around which professionals from multiple disciplines can conduct informal assessments and recommend developmentally facilitative changes. Wolke (1987b), for example, describes four key problem areas.

Noise Levels. The level of noise in the hospital environment is usually high because of the number of people in the room at any one time, telephones, doors slamming, various alarms and buzzers associated with monitoring equipment, and other stimuli such as staff radios. Also, Wolke (1987b) describes short but intense sound associated with events such as closing the incubator doors, which could result in a sound level of up to 115 decibels. The high noise level in the NICU environment is potentially problematic because it may result in sleep disturbances in children, interrupting patterns of sleep and awake cycles. Human speech is masked, and the source of sounds is often impossible for the infant to discern. Also, some sudden, high-level noises may actually have negative physiological consequences.

Light. Light levels are usually high in the NICU, both to facilitate caregiving responsibilities and to provide treatment for some infants. Furthermore, light levels are likely to remain constant 24 hours a day. At least two problems may result from high light levels. First, they may actually damage the retinas of low birthweight infants (Glass, Avery, Subramaniou, Keys, Sostek, & Friendly, 1985). Also, constant light levels make it almost impossible for an infant to establish any sense of a regular day/night cycle.

Handling. Patterns of care can also be disruptive, as evidenced in the high frequency of handling sick infants. Usually handling occurs as a result of some procedure performed by a nurse or pediatrician. Not only can such handling be painful and disrupt sleep patterns, it has also been demonstrated that unusually high levels of medical complications occur during or immediately after routine handling of preterm infants (Murdoch & Darlow, 1984).

Early Learning. Finally, both VandenBerg (1982) and Wolke (1987a;b) suggest that the NICU is not usually an environment that facilitates early learning. Social interactions are brief and often precluded by necessary medical procedures. Many experiences are unpleasant, and opportunities to experience predictable, response-contingent relationships are few. Perhaps by adapting the ecobehavioral approach to assessment (Carta & Greenwood, 1985) professionals in the NICU could evaluate how infants spend their time and the behavioral and developmental consequences of that engagement.

Assessing Environmental Demands

A final dimension of environmental assessment is the process of determining the skills that an environment requires in order for a child to be successful within it. This is an important issue at the time of initial placement of children into programs, and subsequently at transition points when children move from one program to another. For example, a multidisciplinary team is working with parents to identify the most appropriate placement for their 3-year-old son with Down syndrome. One option is placement in a regular preschool program for normally developing children, with periodic consultation by specialists. Will this be an appropriate learning environment, and is the child likely to succeed in it? These questions can be answered in part by using rating scales such as the ECERS or the PACE to determine the quality of environmental provisions. But such an assessment is not likely to provide complete information regarding the child's ability to be successful in that environment. Thus, further assessment of environmental demands for success may be necessary.

Some programs have developed criteria or identified formal checklists indicating the behaviors or skills expected within that environment. This rating most frequently occurs at the kindergarten level, and Polloway (1987) provided a review and examples of inventories of kindergarten survival skills. These inventories are useful as assessment tools in identifying a child's strengths and deficits relative to a placement under consideration. However, such inventories are not always available, and so other strategies may be needed. Vincent, Salisbury, Walter, Brown, Gruenewald, and Powers (1980) suggest four strategies for determining survival skills. These include trial placement (placing the child in the new environment for a short period of time to determine functional abilities), follow-up studies (studying children who have already made the transition to determine if they were successful), skill generation (asking teachers to identify important behaviors or skills), and direct observation (observing programs and using coding procedures to identify the range and types of skills needed and the contexts within which they are used).

Using Environmental Assessment Information

Once environmental assessments are conducted, how can they be used in program planning and evaluation? Several guidelines are discussed in this section.

First, it must be recognized that while standardized measures of environments have been developed, the ultimate question is whether a particular environment is appropriate for a particular child; often the professional will need to rely on a combination of standardized and individualized assessments to determine if there is a "goodness of fit" between the child and the environment. It is this fit that is of utmost importance, rather than the characteristics of the child or the environment in isolation of each other.

Second, it must be recognized that persons responsible for environments may not always be receptive to suggestions regarding environmental changes, particularly if those suggestions require major changes or embrace values or lifestyles not held by that individual. Although this problem may occur in any environment, it is most likely to occur in the evaluation and attempted modification of home environments. Assessment of environments should be conducted in recognition of this important consideration, and suggestions for environmental changes should be made only after the modification is deemed important by both caregivers and consultants.

Third, professionals should recognize the limitations of existing standardized measures of environments and use them only as intended. For example, the HOME scale was designed as a screening measure. As indicated in Chapter 6, screening measures are not designed for planning interventions. Each instrument should be examined in regard to the intervention implications of items. Also, professionals should recognize that many items on existing measures are "indicator" items. That is, they describe a specific aspect of the environment that serves as an indicator of something bigger. For example, the Purdue Home Stimulation Inventory asks whether the child is fed supper at a regular time or whenever the child seems hungry. Wachs (1977) suggests that this item reflects the broader construct of "temporal regularity in the home." A naive interventionist might set as an intervention goal to change supper to a regular time. If the rest of the child's life is irregular, however, such an environmental modification is likely to have little influence.

In many cases, however, environmental assessments, when conducted appropriately, provide extremely important information in planning effective intervention programs for young children. To be most effective, an environmental assessment and development of a plan for environmental modification should be a systematic process involving several steps. For example, Dunst, McWilliam, and Holbert (1986) suggest five steps. First, the classroom teacher or other caretaker responsible for an environment should conduct a self-evaluation of environmental provisions, using an instrument with content similar to standardized rating scales. Included in the self-evaluation should be the caregiver's indication of whether he would like assistance with changing various environmental dimensions. Second, an independent evaluation is conducted by an outside evaluator. Third, both evaluations are used to discuss the existing environment and possible changes. Fourth, a systematic plan is developed that reinforces existing program strengths and builds up weak or inadequate areas. The plan should be developed recognizing that the measures used may not necessarily have been designed to plan changes in environments, and thus additional data may be needed. Finally, once plans are developed they should be considered tentative. Changes in children's behavior and functioning within environments should be monitored and evaluated to determine the effectiveness of environmental modifications. As Bailey, Harms, and Clifford (1983) note, such an evaluation must be conducted so that the child behaviors measured (e.g., independence, engagement, aggression, social play) are consistent with the goals of the environmental change. As implementation proceeds, adjustments may be needed. Further, the extent to which the plan actually is implemented should be documented.

SUMMARY OF KEY CONCEPTS

- Environments should be assessed to determine whether they (a) facilitate children's development, (b) are safe, warm, and comfortable places, (c) are normalized and least restrictive, and (d) require particular skills.

- Environments should be defined broadly, and dimensions of the environment include the physical space, materials, social variables, organization and scheduling, safety, responsiveness, and the manner in which independence is promoted.

- When assessing environments, teachers should (a) be aware of the complexities of environmental assessments, (b) appreciate the dynamic and interactive nature of environments, (c) focus on functions rather than forms, and (d) be familiar with a variety of assessment strategies.

- Multiple sources of information and multiple measurement strategies should be used when assessing environments.

- Environmental assessment information should be used for planning and implementing environmental changes.

REFERENCES

Bailey, D.B. (1987). Collaborative goal-setting with families: Resolving differences in values and priorities for services. *Topics in Early Childhood Special Education, 7*(2), 59–71.

Bailey, D.B., Clifford, R.M., & Harms, T. (1982). Comparison of preschool environments for handicapped and nonhandicapped children. *Topics in Early Childhood Special Education, 2*(1), 9–20.

Bailey, D.B., Harms, T., & Clifford, R.M. (1983). Matching changes in preschool environments to desired changes in child behavior. *Journal of the Division for Early Childhood, 7*, 61–68.

Bailey, D.B. & Simeonsson, R.J. (1988). *Family assessment in early intervention.* Columbus, OH: Merrill.

Berliner, D.C. & Rosenshine, B. (1977). The acquisition of knowledge in the classroom. In R. Spiro & W. Montague (Eds.), *Schooling and the acquisition of knowledge.* Hillsdale, NJ: Erlbaum.

Bjorkman, S., Poteat, G.M., & Snow, C.W. (1986). Environmental ratings and children's social behavior: Implications for the assessment of day care quality. *American Journal of Orthopsychiatry, 56*, 271–277.

Borg, W.R. (1980). Time and school learning. In C. Denham & A. Lieberman (Eds.), *Time to learn.* Washington, DC: U.S. Department of Education.

Bradley, R.H. & Caldwell, B.M. (1977). Home observation for measurement of the environment: A validation study of screening efficiency. *American Journal of Mental Deficiency, 81*, 417–420.

Caldwell, B.M. & Bradley, R.H. (1972). *Home observation and measurement of the environment inventory.* Center for Child Development and Education, University of Arkansas at Little Rock, 33rd and University Avenues, Little Rock, AR 72204.

Carta, J.J. & Greenwood, C.R. (1985). Ecobehavioral assessment: A methodology for expanding the evaluation of early intervention programs. *Topics in Early Childhood Special Education, 5*,(2), 88–104.

David, T.G. & Weinstein, C.S. (1987). The built environment and children's development. In C.S. Weinstein & T.G. David (Eds.), *Spaces for children: The built environment and child development* (pp. 3–20). New York: Plenum.

Dunst, C.J., McWilliam, R.A., & Holbert, K. (1986). Assessment of preschool classroom environments. *Diagnostique, 11*, 212–232.

Elardo, R., Bradley, R., & Caldwell, B.M. (1977). A longitudinal study of the relation of infants' home environments to language development at age three. *Child Development, 48*, 595–603.

Glass, E., Avery, G.B, Subramaniou, K.N.S., Keys, M.P., Sostek, A.M., & Friendly, D.S. (1985). Effect of bright light in the hospital nursery on the incidence of retinopathy of prematurity. *New England Journal of Medicine, 313*, 501–504.

Goldberg, S. (1977). Social competence in infancy: A model of parent-infant interaction. *Merrill-Palmer Quarterly, 23*, 163–177.

Harms, T. & Clifford, R.M. (1980). *Early childhood environment rating scale.* New York: Teachers College Press.

Harms, T. & Clifford, R.M. (1983). Assessing preschool environments with the Early Childhood

Environment Rating Scale. *Studies in Educational Evaluation, 8,* 261–269.

Harms, T. & Clifford, R.M. (in press). *The family day care rating scale.* New York: Teachers College Press.

Harms, T., Cryer, D., & Clifford, R.M. (in press). *Infant/toddler environment rating scale.* New York: Teachers College Press.

Hart, B. (1982). So that teachers can teach: Assigning roles and responsibilities. *Topics in Early Childhood Special Education, 2*(1), 1–8.

Herbert-Jackson, E., O'Brien, M., Porterfield, J., & Risley, T.T. (1977). *The infant center.* Baltimore: University Park Press.

Kenowitz, L., Zweibel, S., & Edgar, G. (1979). Determining the least restrictive educational opportunity. In N.G. Haring & D.D. Bricker (Eds.), *Teaching the severely handicapped* (Vol. III). Columbus, OH: Special Press.

Krantz, P.J. & Risley, T.R. (1977). Behavioral ecology in the classroom. In K.D. O'Leary & S.G. O'Leary (Eds.), *Classroom management: The successful use of behavior modification* (2nd ed.) (pp. 349–367). New York: Pergamon.

Landesman-Dwyer, S. (1985). Describing and evaluating residential environments. In R.H. Bruininks & K.C. Lakin (Eds.), *Living and learning in the least restrictive environment* (pp. 185–196). Baltimore: Paul H. Brookes.

LeLaurin, K. & Risley, T.R. (1972). The organization of day-care environments: "Zone" versus "man-to-man" staff assignments. *Journal of Applied Behavior Analysis, 5,* 225–232.

MacPhee, D., Ramey, C.T., & Yeates, K.O. (1984). Home environment and early cognitive development: Implications for intervention. In A.W. Gottfried (Ed.), *Home environment and early cognitive development* (pp. 343–369). New York: Academic Press.

McCartney, K. (1984). Effect of quality of day care environment on children's language development. *Developmental Psychology, 20,* 244–260.

McCartney, K., Scarr, S., Phillips, D., & Grajek, S. (1985). Day care as intervention: Comparisons of varying quality programs. *Journal of Applied Developmental Psychology, 6,* 247–260.

McCartney, K., Scarr, S., Phillips, D., Grajek, S., & Schwarz, J.C. (1982). Environmental differences among day care centers and their effects on children's development. In E.F. Zigler & E.W. Gordon (Eds.), *Day care: Scientific and social policy issues* (pp. 126–151). Boston: Auburn House.

McWilliam, R.A. & Dunst, C.J. (1985). [Preschool assessment of the classroom environment]. Unpublished rating scale. Family, Infant and Preschool Program, Western Carolina Center, Morganton, NC.

McWilliam, R.A., Trivette, C.M., & Dunst, C.J. (1985). Behavior engagement as a measure of the efficacy of early intervention. *Analysis and Intervention in Developmental Disabilities, 5,* 59–71.

Mitchell, S.K. & Gray, C.A. (1981). Developmental generalizability of the HOME inventory. *Educational and Psychological Measurement, 41,* 1001–1010.

Montes, F. & Risley, T.R. (1975). Evaluating traditional day care practices: An empirical approach. *Child Care Quarterly, 4,* 208–215.

Moore, G.T. (1982). *Early childhood physical environment scales.* Center for Architecture and Urban Planning Research, P.O. Box 413, Milwaukee, Wisconsin 53201.

Moore, G.T. (1986). Effects of the spatial definition of behavior settings on children's behavior: A quasi-experimental field study. *Journal of Environmental Psychology, 6,* 205–231.

Moore, G.T. (1987). The physical environment and cognitive development in child-care centers. In C.S. Weinstein & T.G. David (Eds.), *Spaces for children: The built environment and child development* (pp. 41–72). New York: Plenum.

Murdoch, D.R. & Darlow, B.A. (1984). Handling during neonatal intensive care. *Archives of Disease in Childhood, 59,* 957–961.

National Academy of Early Childhood Programs (1984). *Accreditation criteria and procedures.* Washington, DC: National Association for the Education of Young Children.

O'Brien, M.O., Porterfield, J., Herbert-Jackson, E., & Risley, T.R. (1979). *The toddler center.* Baltimore, MD: University Park Press.

Olds, A.R. (1979). Designing developmentally optimal classrooms for children with special needs. In S.J. Meisels (Ed.), *Special education and development: Perspectives on young children with special needs* (pp. 91–138). Baltimore, MD: University Park Press.

Olds, A.R. (1987). Designing settings for infants and toddlers. In C.S. Weinstein and T.G. David (Eds.), *Spaces for children: The built environment and child development* (pp. 117–138). New York: Plenum.

Phyfe-Perkins, E. (1980). Children's behavior in preschool settings—A review of research concerning the influence of the physical environment. In L.G. Katz (Ed.), *Current topics in early childhood education* (vol. III) (pp. 91–125). Norwood, NJ: Ablex.

Piper, M.C. & Ramsay, M.K. (1980). Effects of early home environment on the mental development of Down syndrome infants. *American Journal of Mental Deficiency, 85,* 39–44.

Polloway, E.A. (1987). Transition services for early age individuals with mild mental retardation. In R.N. Ianacone & R.A. Stodden (Eds.), *Transition issues and directions* (pp. 11–24). Reston, VA: Council for Exceptional Children.

Powell, M.L. (1981). *Assessment and management of developmental changes and problems in children.* St. Louis: Mosby.

Quiltich, J. & Risley, T. (1973). The effects of play materials on social play. *Journal of Applied Behavior Analysis, 6,* 573–578.

Rogers-Warren, A.K. (1982). Behavioral ecology in classrooms for young, handicapped children. *Topics in Early Childhood Special Education, 2*(1), 21–32.

Simeonsson, R.J. (1988). Assessing family environments. In D.B. Bailey & R.J. Simeonsson (Eds.), *Family assessment in early intervention* (pp. 167–183). Columbus, OH: Merrill.

Twardosz, S., Cataldo, M.F., & Risley, T.R. (1974). Open environment design for infant and toddler day care. *Journal of Applied Behavior Analysis, 7,* 529–546.

VandenBerg, K.A. (1982). Humanizing the intensive care nursery. In A. Waldstein, G. Gilderman, D. Taylor-Hershel, S. Prestridge, & J. Anderson (Eds.), *Issues in neonatal care* (pp. 83–105). Chapel Hill: TADS, University of North Carolina.

Vincent, L.J., Salisbury, C., Walter, G., Brown, P., Gruenewald, L.C., & Powers, M. (1980). Program evaluation and curriculum development in early childhood/special education. In W. Sailor, B. Wilcox, & L. Brown (Eds.), *Methods of instruction for severely handicapped students* (pp. 303–328). Baltimore, MD: Brookes.

Wachs, T.D. (1979). Proximal experience and early cognitive-intellectual development: The physical environment. *Merrill-Palmer Quarterly, 25,* 3–41.

Wachs, T.D. (1987). Developmental perspectives on designing for development. In C.S. Weinstein & T.G. David (Eds.), *Spaces for children: The built environment and child development* (pp. 291–308). New York: Plenum.

Weinstein, C.S. (1979). The physical environment of the school: A review of the research. *Review of Educational Research, 49,* 577–610.

Weinstein, C.S. & David, T.G. (1987). *Spaces for children: The built environment and child development.* New York: Plenum.

Wolke, D. (1987a). Environmental and developmental neonatology. *Journal of Reproductive and Infant Psychology, 0,* 17–42.

Wolke, D. (1987b). Environmental neonatology. *Archives of Diseases in Childhood, 62,* 987–988.

Chapter 6

Child Find and Screening Issues

Mark Wolery
University of Kentucky

KEY TERMS

- Child Find
- Screening
- Reliability
- Procedural Reliability
- Scoring Reliability
- Validity
- Concurrent Validity
- Predictive Validity

- Sensitivity
- Specificity
- Economy (of Screening Tests)
- Coverage (of Screening Tests)
- Appropriateness (of Screening Tests)

- Acceptability (of Screening Tests)
- Serial Use
- False Positives
- False Negatives
- Single-Stage Model
- Two-Stage Model

Unlike older children, infants, toddlers, and preschoolers are not required to participate in publicly supported educational programs. In fact, relatively few programs are available for infants and young children other than those designed specifically for children from economically disadvantaged environments and children with handicapping conditions. These programs do not require participation and in some cases may not be available. Therefore, early intervention programs for young children with handicaps must obtain their participants from the population at large. This process is known as child find and frequently involves screening activities. This chapter defines and describes issues related to child find programs, defines screening, discusses issues that must be addressed in implementing a screening program, and describes common screening instruments.

Child Find Issues

Definition of Child Find

The term *child find* has been used as a synonym for screening, public awareness, and tracking children. However, **child find** is a systematic process of identifying infants and children who are eligible or potentially eligible for enrollment in intervention programs, tracking those individuals , and making them known to appropriate service providers. Child find is a method of ensuring early identification of children. Child find activities are required by P.L. 94–142, P.L. 98–199, P.L. 99–457, and other statutes such as the Social Security Act through the Early Periodic Screening, Diagnosis, and Treatment (EPSDT) program (Tucker, 1979). However, child find programs frequently are not active or effective, particularly in states where infant and preschool services have not been required.

Rationale for Child Find Services

Traditionally, the rationale for child find activities and screening efforts has been based on the belief that early identification of children and subsequent intervention will prevent later problems and help children reach their maximum potential (Hayden & McGinness, 1977). While this rationale remains appropriate, at least three others exist. First, if children currently have needs, those needs should be identified and addressed. This statement suggests that current needs, as well as prevention of future needs, are a legitimate reason for intervention and early identification. Second, early identification and the resulting early intervention may have value for parents. Clearly, parents are influenced by the birth of an infant with handicaps and early identification and subsequent intervention address some of the difficulties faced by families. A third rationale for child find activities is more pragmatic: It is required by several laws. Thus, the rationales for child find and screening are to identify children and provide intervention (a) to prevent later problems, (b) to address current difficulties, (c) to assist families, and (d) to comply with the law. It is critical to note, however, that child find and screening are only the first steps of a comprehensive service system; without subsequent intervention, few benefits will accrue to children and families.

Components of Child Find Programs

Bourland and Harbin (1987) argue for a broad definition of child find and maintain that it includes at least 10 components. These components and a description of each are shown in Table 6.1. In addition to these components, Bourland and Harbin (1987) and Cross (1977) raise several issues that influence decisions related to establishing a comprehensive child find program. They suggest that the child find program should be an ongoing, year-round program rather than a once-a-year effort. The advantages of an ongoing program are opposite those for once-per-year programs. Families can enter service systems at any time throughout the year in ongoing programs but only yearly from once-per-year programs. Referrals to diagnostic assessment services are made regularly with ongoing programs, but tend to result in delays from once-per-year programs (Lichtenstein & Ireton, 1984). Once-per-year programs, however, can receive considerable publicity and thereby increase participation. To minimize the lack of visibility that can be associated with ongoing programs, emphasis can be placed on the publicity given to the program at various points throughout a year (e.g., quarterly or semiannually), or special efforts can be initiated at given times such as kindergarten registration.

Interagency involvement and coordination are needed to avoid duplication of efforts, to use personnel and other resources efficiently, and to avoid giving parents a fragmented view of available services. In states where the program for children aged 0–2 years is in an agency other than education, the child find efforts of both agencies should be carefully coordinated. Further, other agencies such as public health, maternal and child health, crippled children's services, mental health and mental retardation services may have child find responsibilities. The child find activities of all these agencies should be coordinated; Bourland and Harbin (1987) describe procedures for facilitating interagency coordination, and examples of interagency programs

TABLE 6.1

Components of Comprehensive Child Find Programs

Component	Description
Definition of target population	The population to be identified must be defined and described.
Screening and prescreening	Procedures should exist for informal screening information being disseminated to the public (e.g., listing of developmental skills on a brochure) and formal screening available to individuals and groups.
Public awareness	Information about services and how to access them is described through the mass media and other communication mechanisms.
Referrals	A mechanism must exist for different agencies and professionals to be informed about making appropriate referrals to other agencies.
Data management, registries and tracking systems	A means of tracking children, ensuring follow-up and maintaining records must be established.
Case management	Some person or agency must be responsible for maintaining contact with identified children and ensuring they obtain necessary services.
Diagnostic assessment	Services must be available for conducting diagnostic assessments and for identifying the intervention services needed.
Coordination	Coordination of child find activities across agencies must occur to ensure efficient use of resources.
Financial resources	The limited financial resources available for child services must be reviewed to ensure efficient use.
Trained personnel	Personnel must be trained to implement the child find program.

Source: Based on information from *START resource packet: Child find* by B. Bourland and G. Harbin, 1987, U. S. Department of Education, Grant No. G00-84C-3515. Copyright 1987 by the Frank Porter Graham Child Development Center, University of North Carolina, Chapel Hill.

exist in the literature (Lombard, 1980; Roscoe, 1979).

Child find approaches and activities should be implemented so that they meet the needs of individual communities. Kurtz (1980) suggests that referral and screening are the two distinct approaches to early identification. Referral systems rely on the awareness of potential problems on someone's part and subsequent referral for assessment. Screening systems attempt to screen the mass population and make referrals based on the results. Although programs vary considerably with each approach, program planners should consider several issues. Information should be collected on existing child-care services in a community, existing screening programs, lines of communication between agencies, availability of diagnostic services, demographic characteristics of the community, geographic location of services, geographic location of high-risk groups, and adequacy of the health-care services. The system selected and the subsequent program should accommodate the information that is gathered. Consideration also should be given to establishing a "single-portal of entry" so that families can go to one specific location and find information on the available programs, including screening and diagnostic services. Such programs require considerable interagency coordination during both initial planning and operation, and the efficacy of this option over more traditional options should be evaluated.

Procedures must be established to maintain the privacy of families by having records treated confidentially. High-risk registries and tracking systems must be designed so that the confidentiality of the children and families is protected. Yet, the system has to be sufficiently open so that persons who have need of the information can have access to it.

Finally, the program must find effective ways of communicating with professionals who may have contact with families and to the public at large. Prior to informing professionals or the public, Cross (1977) states that the target population in terms of age and handicapping conditions should be clearly defined, the geographic boundaries served should be identified, and procedures for making referrals or receiving screening should be clearly specified.

Professionals such as physicians, other health-care providers, child-care professionals, social workers, and others need to receive information about the program. Families are likely to turn to health-care professionals when problems are suspected with their children; thus, it is critical that health-care providers be aware of child find and screening services (Kurtz, Devaney, & Strain, 1983).

Unfortunately, reliance on physicians to make referrals to child find programs may result in under-referral (Kurtz, 1980). Provision of written information, face-to-face description of the program, and presentations to professional groups (e.g., local pediatric association) may result in some referrals to the program. However, continued contact with various professionals may be an important variable in increasing the number of referrals.

Many techniques such as brochures, posters in public places, public service announcements in the electronic media, feature articles in newpapers, presentations at parent-teacher association meetings, presentations to civic groups, letters, and written notices sent home with school-aged children are common ways to inform the public about the availability of child find services (Bourland & Harbin, 1987). Unfortunately, little information exists about the effectiveness of such approaches. Some data suggest that, at least for rural areas, brief parent group instruction (e.g., at PTA meetings) was more effective in increasing parents' awareness of early identification than was a thorough, multidimensional, mass media effort lasting for three months (Kurtz, Devaney, Strain, & Sandler, 1982). Another means of getting children to screening is to use mobile screening units that go where children are. Examples include conducting screening at shopping malls, events such as county fairs, and other places where parents of young children are apt to congregate. In such instances, appointments for screening may need to be made for children where problems are suspected.

Screening Issues

Definition of Screening

Screening infants and children is an important part of most comprehensive child find programs. **Screening** is a process of measuring infants and children (usually in large numbers) to identify those needing further assessment to determine whether they exhibit a condition or are at risk to do so in the future (Bailey & Rosenthal, 1987; Lillie, 1977). The question asked in screening is, "Should this child be referred for diagnostic assessment?" Planning screening programs requires consideration of several issues, which are discussed in this section: (a) the focus of screening, (b) target population and schedule of screening, (c) sources of developmental delays, (d) characteristics of effective screening programs, (e) decision models for acting on screening data, and (f) description of common screening instruments. Prior to discussing these issues, information on the EPSDT program is provided.

Early and Periodic Screening, Diagnosis, and Treatment

The Early and Periodic Screening, Diagnosis, and Treatment (EPSDT) program is a nationwide screening and referral-to-service program that was established in 1972. The EPSDT program has two primary goals: to increase early case finding and to connect children from low-income families with needed medical services (Margolis & Meisels, 1987). Ideally, child find activities initiated under P.L. 99–457 will be coordinated with each state's EPSDT program. Recent evaluations of the program indicate that in many cases the program has failed to meet either of its objectives, particularly with children who have developmental disabilities. These problems are noteworthy because those who are designing child find programs should attempt to ensure that their programs avoid these difficulties. Margolis and Meisels, in a sobering and thoughtful article, identified three factors that have interfered with goal achievement in the EPSDT program. First, many of the screening instruments and procedures used in the program do not appear to be effective in screening children at risk for developmental delays or medical conditions.

In some cases, the developmental measures were ineffective in identifying half of the children with developmental disabilities; in other cases, some of the prescribed medical tests were not even completed. Second, facility and personnel barriers existed. Public awareness of the program was low, transportation to the service sites was lacking in some cases, equipment was inadequate in some centers, staff vacancies existed, and staff training (particularly in developmental disabilities) was needed. Third, referral barriers existed, including lack of service providers to whom families could be referred, transportation problems, and lack of funds to pay for needed diagnostic and treatment services. These findings indicate that the EPSDT program does not meet the needs of children with developmental disabilities as it was intended to do. These problems are not unique to EPSDT and should be avoided by new child find programs and activities.

Focus of Screening Efforts

Screening can occur for many suspected problems, but in early intervention, screening efforts typically target infants and children who are at risk for developmental delays or handicapping conditions. Thus, the screening measures usually address a number of developmental areas such as communication, social/emotional, motor, and cognitive development (Brooks-Gunn & Lewis, 1983). As described later in this chapter, several measures have been used for screening multiple developmental domains. Tests also exist for screening individual developmental domains, and some are mentioned in subsequent chapters. Generally, the goal of screening is to identify infants and children who currently are experiencing delays in development, but another goal of some programs is to identify children who will experience later school failure or problems. This chapter focuses primarily on screening for current developmental delays rather than screening for success/failure in kindergarten or first grade. For information on kindergarten screening see Simmer (1983).

In addition to developmental status, screening activities should include a developmental history, a physical exam, and measurement of visual and auditory functioning (Lichtenstein & Ireton, 1984). The developmental history should include information on the pregnancy, perinatal factors and insults, and the course of development (Mercer & Trifiletti, 1977). However, some authors have questioned the wisdom of extensive developmental histories because the information is rarely used in making decisions (cf., Gallerani, O'Regan, & Reinherz, 1982). The best tactic is to collect the information that will be useful and will help in the interpretation of children's status. The physical examination should be obtained from a pediatrician or other health-care provider through well-baby check-ups or systematic efforts to monitor children's health. Any current or past medical conditions (e.g., seizures, diseases, or high fevers), treatments of such conditions, physical anomalies, and growth patterns should be noted. Some screening programs also include a nutritional screening and dental check (Lombard, 1980). Visual and auditory functioning can be assessed through a variety of methods that are discussed in Chapter 7 and other sources (cf. Cress, Spellman, DeBriere, Sizemore, Northam, & Johnson, 1981; Langley & DuBose, 1976; Mandell & Johnson, 1984; Thompson, 1979; Wilson, 1978).

Environmental factors commonly are credited with influencing children's developmental progress, and these factors should be considered when attempting to understand children's functioning (cf. Bronfenbrenner, 1979). Recently, ecological models have appeared for conceptualizing intervention (Dunst, 1985; Rogers-Warren, 1984) and assessment issues (Paget & Nagle, 1986). Some authors have suggested that measurement of children's home environments might

provide useful screening information (cf. Caldwell & Bradley, 1982; Harrington, 1984).

Target Population and Schedule of Screening

Target Screening Population. Inasmuch as the purpose of screening is to identify children who should be referred for further assessment, children who are obviously handicapped (e.g., child with severe handicaps) should *not* be screened, rather they should be referred directly to diagnostic or program eligibility assessments (Harrington, 1984). Of the remaining children, children who are at risk for developmental delays should be given priority in screening activities. Several factors place children at risk for delays and are discussed in the next section. Another group that should be a high priority for screening is children whose parents are concerned about their developmental progress. Although data are somewhat mixed, it appears that parents can be reliable judges of their child's developmental status (Blacher-Dixon & Simeonsson, 1981), may tend to rate their child's performance slightly higher than professionals (Gradel, Thompson, & Sheehan, 1981), and tend to agree with professionals' ratings of their child's status (Meltzer, Levine, Hanson, Wasserman, Schneider, & Sullivan, 1983). Given the general agreement between parents and professionals, parents who report concerns should receive screening for their child. Authors have argued about the advisability of identifying preschoolers who may have learning disabilities (cf. Kirk, 1987; Senior, 1986). Although no diagnosis can be made on the basis of screening, attention should be given to children who are developmentally delayed and whose development appears uneven across different domains of development. In short, screening activities should be initiated on the referral from almost any source—parents, physicians, public health nurses, and other child-care professionals.

Schedule of Screening. As noted above, child find activities, including screening, should be available throughout the school year. The schedule of screening also refers to whether a given child receives multiple screenings during the preschool years. Clearly, screening should be serial. At a minimum, it should occur during infancy in well-baby clinics and upon entry in the public school system. However, screening should also occur between infancy and public school enrollment (Caldwell & Bradley, 1982). Having multiple points of screening allows delays that begin later in the preschool period (e.g., ages 3–4) to be identified. Scheduling developmental screening with receipt of childhood immunizations is a structure that increases the probability of regular screening throughout the preschool years. Having screening available to children in regular child-care programs also increases the probability of screening between infancy and school entry.

Sources of Developmental Delays

Several authors have attempted to categorize the sources of developmental delays. Tjossem (1976) identified three categories of factors that placed children at risk for delays: established, environmental, and biological. The *established risk category* includes those diagnosed conditions in which the outcomes are fairly well established. Examples are children with Down syndrome or cerebral palsy. The *environmental risk category* includes children who are living in environmental conditions that are apt to produce delayed development. Examples, according to Bijou (1981), include environments with (a) poor economic conditions, (b) deviant parental practices, (c) strong and frequent aversive contingencies (e.g., child abuse), (d) meager social contacts and/or contacts with uncaring persons, (e) factors that strengthen anti-

social or anti-intellectual behavior, (f) factors that promote helplessness, and (g) persons who treat children as ill or abnormal. The *biological risk category,* called *suspect risk* by Keogh and Kopp (1978), includes those "children whose early developmental histories and conditions were suggestive of possible biological insult, e.g., extremely low birthweight, perinatal anoxia" (Keogh & Daley, 1983, p. 8).

Meier (1979) suggested two categories: intra-individual, and inter-individual/extra-individual sources. *Intra-individual sources* are conditions from within the child such as metabolic, genetic, or central nervous system dysfunctions or health conditions that may result in developmental delays. *Inter-individual/ extra-individual sources* are factors that are primarily a result of environmental variables (e.g., poor economic conditions) and social interaction patterns (e.g., abuse or neglect).

From these suggested sources, four comments are appropriate. First, a variety of factors from different sources can produce developmental delays. Second, factors from different sources can interact with one another resulting in increased risk for delays. Third, children are likely to experience these factors in varying levels of intensity, frequency, and for various durations. This variability in exposure may be related to the presence or degree of delay. Therefore, a perfect relationship does not exist between the presence of any of these factors and developmental delays. Fourth, when these factors are present (alone and in combination), interventionists cannot assume that delays will be evident, rather they should be aware that the possibility of delays is increased and may progressively increase over time.

Characteristics of Effective Screening Programs

Several characteristics of effective screening programs have been postulated (cf. Frankenburg, Coons, & Ker, 1982; Meisels, Wiske, &

Tivnan, 1984). When planning and operating a screening program, interventionists should evaluate their procedures and the instruments they use against these characteristics.

Reliability of Screening Tools and Procedures. **Reliability,** as described in Chapter 2, is a critical dimension of tests and other measurement activities; it refers to the consistency and stability of the measures. Screening measures are usually norm-referenced tests for which reliability estimates can be obtained. However, presence of acceptable reliability estimates and studies by the test author or other researchers is only the beginning step in ensuring that screening procedures are reliably implemented. Several sources of error exist in screening. First, the test itself could have unacceptable reliability. When establishing a screening program, interventionists should read the test manual carefully, consult measurement indices (e.g., Buros, 1978), and review research articles that have assessed the reliability of the measure in question. Second, the **procedural reliability** of the test administration is critical and refers to the extent to which the tester complies with the procedures described by the test manual or protocol. Procedural reliability is assessed by having someone observe the administration of the test and determine the extent to which the examiner complies with the described procedures. Many factors in screening programs increase the possibility of inappropriate test administration. For example, using paraprofessionals with limited training and administering the same instrument repeatedly within a day may set the occasion for incorrect test administration. Third, **scoring reliability** is important. A test may have acceptable reliability, it may be administered perfectly, but the tester may score the responses incorrectly. Again, when a measure is being used repeatedly over a short period of time, scoring errors are likely to increase.

Scoring reliability is assessed by having two individuals score the same test administration and then comparing their results. Fourth, reliability errors can occur in the interpretation of the scoring. Although a test may be scored correctly, the examiner can add the scores incorrectly, use the wrong tables, write down the incorrect score, or make incorrect judgments based on the scores.

Two problems can arise when reliability errors are present. First, children who should not be referred to diagnostic assessments may be referred, and second, children who should be referred may not be referred. While many issues other than reliability affect referral rates, it is clear that the multiple sources of error in administration, scoring, and interpretation can affect referral rates. A recent report on Minnesota's state-wide preschool screening program revealed an interesting finding: "Some school districts found problems in all children they screened; others did not find problems in any children. Referral rates showed similar variability, ranging from 0 to 86 percent of the children screened" (Thurlow, O'Sullivan, & Ysseldyke, 1986). While this finding probably is not totally due to reliability issues, it clearly is an area of potential problems. Any screening program must select measures that are reliable, plan and implement periodic evaluations of reliability, and make adjustments based on the evaluation results.

Validity of Screening Tools and Procedures. As also noted in Chapter 2, **validity** is a critical dimension of tests and deals with the extent to which measures can be used for specific purposes. Two types of criterion validity are important for screening measures: concurrent validity and predictive validity. **Concurrent validity,** as it relates to screening measures, refers to the extent to which the screening test agrees with more thorough measures (usually diagnostic tests) at about the same point in time. Because the focus of screening frequently is development, the screening tests should have high agreement with more thorough dvelopmental measures that would be administered within a few days. **Predictive validity**, as it relates to screening measures, refers to the extent to which the screening test agrees with children's performance on outcome measures later in time. For example, predictive validity is seen when a screening measure given to 4-year-old children accurately predicts success or failure in first grade. The validity of commonly used screening tests is addressed later in this chapter.

When discussing validity, several issues are important. First, measures do not have inherent validity, rather they are valid for specific purposes. With screening measures, the issue is: Can the test be used for answering the question, "Should this child be referred to diagnostic or eligibility assessments?"; i.e., is it valid for this purpose? Screening tests are not valid for answering questions such as, "What effects were produced by this intervention program?", "Does this child have mental retardation?", "Does this child have developmental delays?", "What should we teach this child?", among others. Second, validity for given purposes assumes that reliability exists. If a test has acceptable test reliability, but is administered, scored, or interpreted inaccurately, then the validity is suspect. This fact underscores the need for periodic assessment of the reliability with which measures are administered, scored, and interpreted. Third, existence of either concurrent *or* predictive validity does not ensure that the other exists. A test could have concurrent validity with developmental status as measured by an indepth assessment of development, but this validity does not ensure that it can be used to predict later outcomes. Similarly, a test with predictive validity may not have concurrent validity. Fourth, the concurrent and predictive validity of measures are established through conducting research related to the performance of specific tests on each of these two issues. Of par-

ticular importance is whether tests have sensitivity and specificity (Lichtenstein, 1981). **Sensitivity** refers to the ability of the screening test to identify a high proportion of the children who are indeed developmentally delayed or have handicapping conditions. **Specificity** refers to the screening test not resulting in referrals of children who do not have handicaps or developmental delays. In other words, the tests should sort those who should and should not be referred to diagnostic and program eligibility assessments. As discussed later in this chapter, evaluation of these two characteristics is important in determining the cut-off score for making referrals. Frequently, concurrent validity is established by correlational studies; for example, the results of the screening test for a group of children are correlated to the results on a criterion measure. This approach has an inherent weakness, because the real issue is how well a screening test selects given students who will also score poorly on the criterion test. Thus, the real issue is not the correlation coefficient, by the "hit rate," which is determined by calculating a test's sensitivity and specificity. Fifth, to be valid, screening measures should be free from bias due to age, sex, geographic factors, economic background, and racial or ethnic status (Lichtenstein & Ireton, 1984). Interventionists should evaluate carefully the test manuals and the research that has been conducted on various measures to determine whether the standardization population included children from the ages to be screened, had an equal distribution of males and females, included children of different racial and ethnic groups, included families from a variety of economic backgrounds, and sampled geographic regions similar to those for which the measures are being considered.

Cost of Screening Procedures. As noted previously, child find and screening are first steps in a comprehensive service delivery system. Other important activities include determining eligibility for program placement, conducting assessments to develop intervention plans, implementing intervention plans, and evaluating that implementation and its effects. The financial resources available to the program must be distributed across these activities. The help given to families and their children primarily comes from the intervention aspects of the program. Therefore, most of the resources should be spent on those activities. Thus, the **economy** of the screening program is an important issue; screening activities should be done as economically as possible. Because paraprofessionals are paid less than professionals, several authors have recommended using them to conduct screening activities (Frankenburg et al., 1982; Meier, 1979). However, as Lichtenstein and Ireton (1984) point out, paraprofessionals must be trained and supervised, and this process may be expensive. Thus, the cost of having professionals conduct screening activities must be compared with the cost of hiring, training, and supervising paraprofessionals. Utilizing paraprofessionals probably is warranted only when a large number of children will be screened. Also, when concentrated mass screenings occur, the economic benefits increase for using paraprofessionals and/or part-time staff. The point of this characteristic is that the screening efforts should consume a small amount of the total program budget.

Ease of Administration of Screening Procedures. The goal of screening is to measure as many children as possible and to identify those who should be referred for comprehensive assessment. To do this screening as efficiently and as inexpensively as possible, paraprofessionals frequently are used. If the tests are simple to use, then training the paraprofessionals will be less expensive. Further, the reliability of the screening will likely be increased if the measure is easily given and is relatively short (e.g., less than 30

minutes). By using short, quick procedures, the team can screen more children in a day, and financial resources can be devoted to more thorough assessment and intervention activities.

Coverage and Appropriateness of Screening Tools and Procedures. This characteristic addresses the items on screening tests. **Coverage** for developmental screening tests refers to the extent to which the items address relevant areas of development; for example, the social/emotional, motor, communication, and cognitive domains. A careful balance must be made between thoroughly addressing relevant domains and keeping the screening efficient. Coverage also refers to how well a measure addresses the target age range. Some measures may address birth through age 5 or 6 but have relatively few items at the first 12–18 months. Interventionists should review the coverage of the instrument for the ages of children that are targeted for screening.

Appropriateness refers to the extent to which the items and test administration consider the characteristics of infants and children. For example, a screening test that required extensive paper and pencil work would be inappropriate for 4-year-old children, and group administration would be inappropriate for toddlers. The manner in which the tests are administered should be reviewed carefully prior to selection.

Acceptability of Screening Tools and Procedures. **Acceptability** refers to the extent to which the population being screened will participate willingly in the program. Screening programs can be evaluated on several dimensions to determine their acceptability, but in the end, the extent to which people participate is the true test of acceptability. Screening tests and procedures should be enjoyable to the infants, children, and families, and, when possible, direct testing should be in a game format. The atmosphere should be relaxed, unhurried, and pleasant (Powell, 1981). The activities should not be time consuming and should be conveniently accessible. *Accessibility* refers to having the screening activities occur in geographically convenient locations as well as having screening procedures that do not require calling a number of people and so forth to have a child screened. Thus, the procedures for getting a child screened should be easy to negotiate. Providing child care or a play area for siblings or for children waiting to be screened will increase acceptability. Allowing parents to be present and participate in screening frequently will increase acceptability.

Serial Use of Screening Tools and Procedures. **Serial use** of screening tests and procedures refers to the ability of the measures to be used repeatedly with a child during the preschool years. As noted earlier, screening should occur at several points during the preschool period. Ideally, the same measures could be used at the various screening points. Serial screening allows delays that occur later in the toddler and preschool years to be identified, allows better decision making because of the multiple data points, and assits in providing parents with information about child development and rearing.

Screening Tools and Procedures as Vehicles for Training Parents. Powell (1981) suggests that periodic developmental screening can be used to provide parents with information on (a) varying rates of development exhibited by children, (b) the sequential nature of development, (c) the notion that different children require different types of interactions, and (d) that the same child will require different types and amounts of stimulation at various times throughout the preschool years. Further, developmental screening can be used to teach parents about problem solving with their children and can provide assurances to

families that the experiences they are providing appear to facilitate positive development.

To obtain these benefits, the parents' role in developmental screening should be analyzed (Powell, 1981). First , parents are entitled to receive information about the screening in general. For example, parents should be told that the screening is to identify children who may need further assessment and that children cannot be diagnosed on the basis of these measures. Parents also should be told of the value of having developmental screening on a regular basis and should be informed of the procedures for securing that service. Second, parents are entitled to receive information about the tests being used at any particular screening. This information should include a short description of the areas that will be tested and a discussion of the types of items that will be used. Also, if the test begins with less advanced items and proceeds to more advanced items, then parents should be warned that their child will not be expected to respond correctly to all items. Third, depending upon the measures used, parents may be key participants. For example, some measures use parent interviews (e.g., Developmental Profile II [DP II], Alpern, Boll, & Shearer, 1980) and others allow parents to administer some of the items (e.g., Denver Developmental Screening Test [DDST], Frankenburg, Dodds, & Fandal, 1975). In either case, the parents should be fully aware of what is expected of them. Fourth, parents should be encouraged to make comments and ask questions before, during, and after the screening. Parents should be given opportunities to express their concerns about their child's development and about child-rearing practices. As Powell (1981) suggests, interventionists' responses to these questions should help parents solve problems rather than simply providing solutions or answers. Thus, if parents express concern about a given problem, the interventionist might help them design a method of collecting more information about it and then bring that information back for analysis and recommendations. The goal is to make parents independent rather than dependent upon service providers in addressing concerns about their child's developmental progress. Finally, as noted above, interventionists should praise parents liberally for engaging in appropriate child-rearing practices.

Regular Evaluation of Screening Programs. In their discussion of the inadequacies of the EPSDT program, Margolis and Meisels (1987) state that lack of evaluation data has contributed to the problems of the program. Thus, it appears that a characteristic of effective screening programs is regular evaluation of program operation and effects. Several issues should be addressed in such evaluations; these include the percent of children screened, the percent referred, the time-lag between referral and diagnostic assessment, and the identification of factors that interfere with program effectiveness. Parents' satisfaction with the screening program and their suggestions for improvement also should be solicited.

Comments on Screening Program Characteristics. Characteristics of good screening programs include using (a) reliable tests and reliable administration, scoring, and interpretation; (b) measures that have concurrent validity with current development or can predict later outcomes; (c) economical procedures; (d) tests and procedures that can be administered quickly and easily; (e) measures that are comprehensive and appropriate to the population; (f) measures and procedures that are acceptable to the population; (g) procedures that can be used repeatedly; (h) screening procedures to provide parents with training and information; and (i) regular program evaluation.

Decision Models for Acting on Screening Results

Potential Screening Outcomes. The purpose of screening is to identify children who should be referred for diagnostic or program-eligibility assessments. Ideally, only children with handicaps or developmental delays would be referred; however, errors are likely. Because children either are or are not developmentally delayed (as defined by some criteria) and children either are referred for assessment or are not referred, four potential outcomes can occur. First, the screening procedures may indicate a child is not delayed and later assessment would confirm this conclusion; ideally this child would not be referred for assessment. Second, the screening procedures may indicate another child is delayed and later assessment also would confirm this conclusion; ideally this child would be referred for assessment. Third, the screening procedures may indicate that a child may have a delay when indeed he does not, but the child may be referred for assessment. This referral is an error (overreferral), and is known as **false positive.** The consequences of false positives are (a) children's families may become anxious about potential problems during the time the referral is being processed (however, upon indepth assessment, it would be determined that the child was not delayed or handicapped and that the screening results were in error) and (b) assessment resources are consumed by children who do not need them. Fourth, the screening procedures may indicate that children do not have developmental delays or handicaps when they actually do (underreferral); this error is known as **false negative.** The results of false negatives are more serious. Children who are in need of diagnostic assessments and intervention programs will not be referred to those services, and their delays may become more severe. Further, parents may have the false assumption that their child is developing normally when in fact she is not. Thus, the referral decision is an important one.

Issues to Consider in Establishing Referral Criteria. In making referrals, a balance must be established between false positives and false negatives. Generally, programs attempt to err on the side of false positives. Several factors affect this balance. A decision should be made concerning whether the referral will be based on the results of the screening test(s) only or will be supplemented with professional judgment (Lichtenstein & Ireton, 1984). Ideally, use of test results and professional judgment is desirable because a child may appear "normal" on a screening test, but professionals may have additional information that would lead them to believe that further assessment is warranted. However, use of professional judgment alone probably is inappropriate.

Another issue to consider is whether referrals will be based on one tool/procedure or whether multiple tools/procedures will be used (Lichtenstein & Ireton, 1984). Generally, multiple tools/procedures are more desirable, but they also are more expensive, require more administration time, necessitate more monitoring of reliability, and require more staff training. When two or more measures are used, programs should consider using a combination of measures that secure information from different sources. For example, some measures are administered through direct testing (e.g., the DDST), and other measures rely on parents' reports (e.g., DP II; or the Minnesota Child Development Inventory [MCDI], Ireton & Thwing, 1974). A combination of these probably is more desirable than using two that rely on direct testing or two that rely on parents' reports.

Programs also need to determine what level of performance is needed to make a referral. Several means can be used for setting the referral criteria. Some screening tests include interpretation procedures that can be used. For example, the DDST (Franken-

burg et al., 1975) allows for the classification of profiles in three ways: "normal," "questionable," and "abnormal," and the Developmental Indicators for the Assessment of Learning–Revised (DIAL-R) (Mardell, Czudnowski, & Goldenberg, 1983) allows classification of profiles by "potential problem," "OK," or "potential gifted." With such measures, teams could refer children based on the classification of profiles. For example, with the DDST the questionable or abnormal profiles could be referred and with the DIAL-R, potential problem profiles could be referred.

Another means for establishing criteria is to compare the child's score to that of the standardization population. For example, referrals could be made on any child whose developmental age is 25% below her chronological age, or on children whose development is 1 or 2 standard deviations below the mean. Such calculations are easily made on such measures as the DP II and the MCDI. Another method for calculating the referral criteria is to refer a given percentage of the children screened. Lichtenstein and Ireton (1984) suggest establishing the cut-off score so that the number of children referred is similar to the number receiving special services in school. For example, if a local system serves about 12% of their school population in the special education program, then 12% of the children screened would be referred for further assessment. Gallagher and Bradley (1972) suggest adjusting the cut-off score so that it will overrefer children and thereby reduce the chance of not referring children who need intervention. This method is only recommended when nearly the entire population of preschool children are screened.

As states establish their definitions for developmental delay, this information should influence the criteria by which students are referred for assessments to demonstrate the existence of a delay. For example, if a state uses a very broad definition of developmental delay that would include all children who have mild delays or are at risk for delays, then the criteria for referral from screening should be more liberal than in a state where the definition only addresses children with severe developmental delays.

Consideration of Single- or Two-Stage Decision Models. In the most basic form, children can be screened and a referral decision can be made based on those results. This is known as a **single-stage model** and is depicted in Figure 6.1.

To make screening efforts more efficient and cost-effective and to reduce the number of false positives, more than one screening point can occur. This is called a **two-stage model,** and two examples are shown in Figure 6.2. For example, after the initial assessment, some children would be allowed to exit the system. Children who present borderline results to the first screening would be screened again in one or two months after the first screening. If their responses continue to be borderline, then referral for comprehensive assessment should be initiated. If their performance on the second screening is satisfactory, then they are monitored, but not referred for additional assessment. As shown in Figure 6.2, in some two-stage models, children can be referred directly to follow-up assessments if their responses on the initial screening indicate a clear need to do so. The two-stage model can take many forms, and the same instrument or different instruments can be used at the two stages.

Frankenburg, Van Doorninck, Liddell, and Dick (1976) developed a short screening measure from the DDST called the Denver Prescreening Developmental Questionnaire (PDQ) for use in the two-stage model. Items on the PDQ were taken from the DDST and converted to yes/no questions. Ten questions were developed for each of several age ranges. In the first stage, parents answered ten questions about their child's development using the PDQ. Based on their responses, children who were suspect for developmental delays were screened (stage two) with the full DDST. After screening, children were either referred for diagnostic assessment or determined not to need additional assessment. They found that this two-stage process was more efficient than a single-stage model for parents who had at least a high school education, but was not successful with parents who had less education. Bruder (1987), however, modified the PDQ by adding open-ended questions and pictures, and used it during a monitoring program for at-risk infants with single mothers whose average age was 16.4 years and who had not completed high school. In the context of the monitoring program, mothers were reliable in completing the PDQ, and it was useful in making decisions about referral for assessment.

Teska and Stoneburner (1980) present an interesting variation of the two-stage model. They trained paraprofessionals to use the DDST to screen children in a Head Start program. All children who did not pass the first stage were then screened by professionals with a variety of assessment instruments. Children who did not pass the second stage were referred for diagnostic evaluations. This two-stage model produced a substantial decrease in the amount of time and money spent administering diagnostic assessments to children who were not handicapped. For more information on the two-stage models consult Lichtenstein and Ireton (1984).

Regardless of the criteria used for making referrals and of the type of decision model

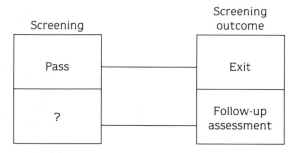

FIGURE 6.1
Example of Single-stage Model of Screening

FIGURE 6.2
Two Examples of
Two-Stage Screening Programs
(Source: From
Preschool screening:
Identifying young
children with
developmental and
educational prob-
lems *(p. 220) by*
R. Lichtenstein and
H. Ireton, 1984;
Orlando, FL: Grune
& Stratton. Copy-
right 1984 by
Grune & Stratton.
Reprinted by
permission.)

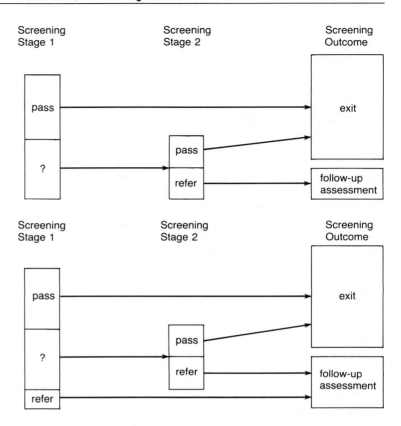

used, teams should evaluate the results of the screening program. Over the course of a couple of years, programs should attempt to determine whether children who passed screening later needed intervention services, whether a large proportion of the children referred to diagnostic assessments resulted in no diagnosis or lack of program eligibility, whether referred children were actually followed up by diagnostic personnel, and how long the delay was between referral and diagnostic assessment.

Description of Common Screening Instruments

Many instruments exist for screening early development, and descriptions of these can be found in many sources (e.g., Bettenburg, 1985; Fallen & Umansky, 1985; Lichtenstein & Ireton, 1984; Peterson, 1987). These measures are implemented in at least three ways: direct observation, parent reports, and direct testing. The most frequently used are combinations of parent reports and direct testing. However, some evidence suggests that with some guidance (e.g., a form identifying particular behaviors), teachers of preschool children can make judgments that agree highly with the results of screening instruments (e.g., Stoner & Purcell, 1985), and, with such ratings, teachers can identify children who are socially withdrawn (Greenwood, Walker, Todd, & Hops, 1979).

Five measures are described here for two reasons. First, they sample the range of available instruments, and second, they are widely used. Several other measures exist and may be as adequate as those described below; examples include the Early Screening Inventory (Meisels & Wiske, 1983), Developmental Activities Screening Inventory - II (Fewell & Langley, 1984), Miller Assessment of Preschoolers (MAP) (Miller, 1982), Minneapolis Preschool Screening Instrument (Lichtenstein, 1980), Comprehensive Identification Process (CIP) (Zehrbach, 1975), and A Developmental Screening Inventory (Knobloch, Pasamanick, & Sherard, 1966). Miller and Sprong (1986) followed the lead of McCauley and Swisher (1984) and evaluated screening measures on the basis of ten psychometric standards that were taken from the Standards for Educational and Psychological Tests (APA, 1974). These dimensions are shown in Table 6.2. Early interventionists should use these dimensions when reviewing test manuals.

Denver Developmental Screening Test (DDST). The DDST was originally published in 1967, and minor revisions were made later (Frankenburg et al., 1975; Frankenburg, Goldstein, & Camp, 1971). The DDST is probably the most widely known and used of all the developmental screening measures. It covers four areas—personal-social, fine motor-adaptive, language, and gross motor— and is designed for screening children from ages 2 weeks to 6 years. It can be administered through direct testing in 15-20 minutes, although interviews can be used on some items. For a comprehensive description of the DDST, see Powell (1981).

Although the revised DDST is used extensively, criticisms of the test's sensitivity in identifying children with delays (cf., Bettenberg, 1985; Margolis & Meisels, 1987; Nugent, 1976) and in predicting success in kindergarten as determined by teacher ratings have appeared (Cadman, Chambers, Walter, Feldman, Smith, & Ferguson, 1984). The revised DDST can be made more sensitive by referring children who have "questionable" as well as "abnormal" ratings; however, this results in increased overrefer-

ral rates (i.e., less specificity) (German, Williams, Herzfeld, & Marshall, 1982). The lack of sensitivity has been identified in a number of studies. Meisels (in press), in a review of these studies, states that the problem is of sufficient magnitude that the "DDST . . . can NO longer be recommended for me in mass developmental screening" (p. 15). Further, use of the DDST in addition to regular observations by nurses resulted in greater identification of infants with delays (Jaffe, Harel, Goldberg, Rudolph-Schnitzer, & Winter, 1980). Diamond (1987) analyzed the ability of the Revised DDST to predict school problems four years after screening. She found that an "abnormal" rating on the DDST was a good predictor of school problems including special class placements. However, a "questionable" rating on the DDST was a poorer predictor than parents' written concerns about children's learning. Standardization of the measure has occurred in several countries outside of the United States. Such standardization is necessary to make the measure useful in different cultures (e.g., Ueda, 1978; Williams & Williams, 1987). Interventionists should be familiar with the DDST because of its extensive use by pediatricians, public health nurses, and other health-care professionals.

Developmental Profile II (DP II). The DP II is a revision of the Developmental Profile published in 1972; it has been used widely in intervention programs but has received little research attention as a screening measure in the literature. The DP II covers five developmental areas—physical (motor), self-help, social, academic (cognitive), and communication—and includes the age range of birth through age 9 (Alpern, Boll, & Shearer, 1980). The test is administered through direct interview with someone who knows the child well, and requires 20–40 minutes. Scoring the measure is particularly easy and can be completed quickly. Tables are provided as referral guidelines that list scores for each age

TABLE 6.2
Dimensions by Which Screening Tests Can Be Evaluated

Dimension	Description
Norming sample described	Test manual should clearly define the standardization or normative sample enabling the test user to examine its suitability for a particular population.
Adequate sample size	An adequate sample size for each subgroup examined during standardization is a minimum of 100 children.
Item analysis	Systematic item analysis should occur during item construction and item selection; test manual should describe the quantitative methods used to study and control item difficulty and item validity.
Central tendency and variability	Test manual should report measures of central tendency and variability of test scores for each subgroup examined during objective evaluation of the test.
Concurrent validity	Test manual should describe concurrent validity studies.
Predictive validity	Test manual should describe predictive validity studies.
Test/retest reliability	Test manual should describe test/retest reliability estimates and should obtain a correlation coefficient of .90 or better that is statistically significant at or beyond the .05 level.
Interexaminer reliability	Test manual should describe interexaminer reliability estimates and should obtain a correlation coefficient of .90 or better that is statistically significant at or beyond the .05 level.
Test procedures described	Test manual should describe the administration and scoring procedures in sufficient detail to allow users to duplicate administration and scoring used during standardization.
Examiner qualifications	Test manual should state who is qualified to administer the test.

range in terms of "significant delay," "borderline range: Inconclusive," and "normal development." The DP II was standardized in Washington state and Indiana. Although 89% of the sample was from large cities, the test is well constructed in terms of social class and racial origin. For a comprehensive description of the measure, see Powell (1981).

Outside of that reported in the manual, little research exists on the use of the DP II as a screening tool. German et al. (1982) compared the sensitivity and specificity of the DDST and the DP II using the Bayley Scales of Infant Development (Bayley, 1969), McCarthy Scales of Children's Abilities (McCarthy, 1972), and Sequenced Inventory of Communication Development (Hendrick, Prather, & Tobin, 1975) as criterion measures. They found that the DP II could be made more sensitive if children in the "borderline range" were referred than if only children with "significant delay" profiles were referred. However, as with the DDST, if children with "borderline range" profiles were included, overreferrals increased. Further, the DP II tends to overrefer fewer children than does the DDST. Clearly, additional research needs to be conducted with the DP II. The ease with which it can be implemented is a strength. Interventionists should be familiar with the measure because of its use in many intervention programs. In the past, it has served as a dependent measure in program evaluation studies; however, such use may be inappropriate. The best use of this measure is as a screening tool.

Developmental Indicators for the Assessment of Learning–Revised (DIAL-R). The DIAL-R (Mardell-Czudnowski & Goldenberg, 1983) is a revision of the original DIAL published in 1975. The DIAL-R includes three major areas—motor, concepts, and language—and covers the age range of 2-6 years (Mardell-Czudnowski & Goldenberg, 1984). The DIAL-R is administered through direct testing and requires about 20–30 minutes. Separate scores for each of the three assessed areas

and a total score are possible. Children can be classified as "potential problem," "OK," or "potential gifted." Separate norms exist for white and nonwhite populations.

Although relatively little research has been conducted with the DIAL-R, two factors speak well for its use. First, the standardization procedures used were quite extensive (cf. Mardell-Czudnowski & Goldenberg, 1984). "The sample population was stratified according to age, sex, ethnicity, geographic region, and size of community" (Bettenberg, 1985, p. 65). Further, the DIAL-R was rated better than the CIP, DDST-R, or MAP on having the psychometric properties suggested by the American Psychological Association (Miller & Sprong, 1986). Second, the DIAL-R is based on the DIAL, which had considerable research exposure (cf. Docherty, 1983; Mardell-Czudnowski, 1980; Obrzut, Bolocofsky, Heath, & Jones, 1981; Sarachan-Deily, Hopkins, & DeVivo, 1983). However, clearly additional research on the sensitivity and specificity of the DIAL-R is warranted.

Minnesota Child Development Inventory (MCDI). The MCDI inventory has eight scales—general development, gross motor, fine motor, expressive language, comprehension-conceptual, situation comprehension, self-help, and personal social (Ireton & Thwing, 1974). It addresses children from ages 6 months to 6 years. The MCDI is unique in the manner in which it is administered. There are 320 items that are questions requiring yes/no answers. The items are randomly organized and are not listed by age or developmental domain. The items are printed in a booklet for parents to read and score as yes or no on an accompanying answer sheet. The answer sheet is then scored either mechanically or with templates. It requires 20–30 minutes to complete the questionnaire, and scoring is easily accomplished. A profile for each area assessed can be used to display the child's performance. This measure was standardized on a suburban sample that is not particularly representative of the U.S. population.

Despite the inadequacies of the norming sample, the concurrent validity of the MCDI has some support. For example, the MCDI general development, expressive language, and comprehension-conceptual scales were positively and statistically related to the cognitive scales of the McCarthy Scales of Children's Abilities. However, the gross and fine motor scales of the MCDI did not correlate significantly with the motor scales of the McCarthy nor did the self-help scale (Gottfried, Guerin, Spencer, & Meyer, 1983). Further, the MCDI identified children who were performing below normal in general cognitive development (Gottfried et al., 1983). Gottfried, Guerin, Spencer, and Meyer (1984) followed 98 preschoolers longitudinally and found that the MCDI general development scale was a valid predicator of later McCarthy scores. Kenny, Hebel, Sexton, and Fox (1987) also found that the MCDI scales (with the exception of the MCDI self-help scale) were highly related to the McCarthy scales, and that the MCDI had a hit rate of about 80%. Colligan (1981) found that MCDI scores at the beginning of kindergarten could reliably predict second grade reading achievement. Saylor and Brandt (1986) found that for infants and toddlers (8–30 months), the MCDI correlated highly with the mental scale of the Bayley Scales of Infant Development. The MCDI is not without problems. For example, parents must be able to read and score the questions, and it may not identify the developmental status of infants as well as it does that of preschoolers (Byrne, Backman, & Smith, 1986).

Battelle Developmental Inventory Screening Test. The Battelle Developmental Inventory (BDI) is a developmental scale that also contains a screening test (Newborg, Stock, Wnek, 1984). The BDI Screening Test covers the five areas assessed with the full BDI—that is,

personal-social, adaptive, motor, communication, and cognitive domains. The BDI Screening Test covers age ranges from birth through 8 years. The manual reports that administration through direct testing, observation, and interview requires 10–30 minutes. Scoring and administration procedures are similar to the full BDI, and adaptations are included for children with handicaps. Cut off scores for the screening test are listed by five probability levels that correspond to different standard deviations below the mean for each age group.

Little research with this screening test has occurred, but Newborg et al. (1984) report that it is highly correlated with the full BDI scores. Given the high concurrent validity of the full BDI with other accepted criterion measures (cf. McLean, McCormick, Bruder, & Burdg, 1987), it would be desirable if the screening test also had such validity. One study, however, suggests caution: McLean, McCormick, Baird, and Mayfield (1987) found that (a) the concurrent validity of the BDI Screening Test with the full BDI may not be as high as reported, (b) the screening test may overrefer children (at least as compared to the DDST, and (c) administration time was longer (about 45 minutes) than reported in the manual.

Concluding Comments on Screening Tests. German et al. (1982), in their study of the revised DDST and the DP II, state, "the data suggest that the [tests] are imperfect yet useful screening instruments" (p. 323). This statement could be made about all of the measures just described and listed. Several reasons for their lack of perfection could be postulated. Screening measures sample only a small part of the child's total behavior, may be given only once or twice during the preschool period, and are administered quickly. The authors of nearly all the measures would likely welcome additional research on the validity and reliability of the measures, yet, this research is often underfunded, difficult to conduct, and time consuming. Further, the criterion measures to which the screening instruments' performances are compared are less than perfect. Given these factors, it may be unreasonable to expect any screening measure to refer all children who will be diagnosed as having problems and to refer only those children. Likewise, it may be unreasonable for any screening measure to predict adequately the future performance of all screened children.

A more salient reason that screening measures are (and are likely to remain) imperfect is that they measure the product of development rather than the variables that influence development. For example, environmental factors and parent/child interactions clearly influence children's development. Ideally, screening could include these two factors. Some progress in this direction has occurred. For example, the Home Observation and Measurement of the Environment (HOME) scales have been positively correlated with later development (Caldwell & Bradley, 1982; Elardo & Bradley, 1981; also, see Chapter 5). The HOME also is a fairly accurate predictor of later school success. However, it requires a home visit of 30–60 minutes and, of course, travel time to and from the home visit (Powell, 1981). Thus, it is not a mass screening measure, and two Home Screening Questionnaires (HSQ) have been developed. These are completed by parents when their child receives developmental screening (Frankenburg et al., 1982). The HSQ scales correlate moderately with the HOME scales; however, the HSQ scales are able to identify accurately homes where low HOME scores would be found, but overrefer homes where high HOME scores would be obtained (Harrington, 1984). The HSQ identifies about 89% of the children as being at risk who were also identified using the full HOME (Brooks-Gunn & Lewis, 1983) and overreferrals could be identified using the full HOME (Harrington, 1984). In the future, use of measures such as the HSQ in conjunction with measures of developmental status and parent/child interactions could increase the success rate of screening programs.

SUMMARY OF KEY CONCEPTS

- Child find is a systematic process of identifying infants and children who are eligible or potentially eligible for enrollment in intervention programs, tracking those individuals, and making them known to appropriate service providers.

- Child find programs involve several components that should be fully explored during the planning of local child find activities.

- Screening involves measurement of children to identify those who need further referral to diagnostic or program eligibility assessments.

- Screening programs should focus on children's current developmental status, visual and auditory functioning, and their physical status.

- Children who are at risk for developmental delays because of environmental or other factors should be screened, as should all children whose parents are concerned about their development.

- Screening should be available throughout the year and should occur at multiple times between birth and age 6.

- Several characteristics of screening programs (tests and procedures) have been identified. They should be reliable, valid (with current and future performance), inexpensive, administered easily and quickly, comprehensive and appropriate to the population, accessible to the population, capable of serial use, used to train parents, and evaluated regularly. Intervention programs should compare their efforts to these characteristics.

- Screening programs must specify the criteria and decision model that will be used to decide which children are referred.

- Several screening tests are available and have varying strengths and weaknesses.

REFERENCES

Alpern, G. D., Boll, T. J., & Shearer, M. S. (1980). *Manual Developmental Profile II.* Aspen, CO: Psychological Development Publications.

American Psychological Association. (1974). *Standards for educational and psychological tests.* Washington, DC: Author.

Bailey, D. B. & Rosenthal, S. L. (1987). Assessment in early childhood special education. In W. H. Berdine & S. A. Meyer (Eds.), *Assessment in special education* (pp. 111–140). Boston: Little, Brown.

Bayley, N. (1969). *Bayley Scales of Infant Development.* New York: Psychological Corporation.

Bettenburg, A. (1985). *Assessment: Instruments and procedures for assessing young children.* St. Paul, MN: Minnesota Department of Education.

Bijou, S. W. (1981). The prevention of retarded development in disadvantaged children. In M. J. Begab, H. C. Haywood, & H. L. Garber (Eds.), *Psychosocial influences in retarded performance. Volume I: Issues and theories in development* (pp. 24–46). Baltimore, MD: University Park Press.

Blacher-Dixon, J. & Simeonsson, R. J. (1981). Consistency and correspondence of mothers' and teachers' assessments of young handicapped children. *Journal of the Division for Early Childhood, 3,* 64–71.

Bourland, B. & Harbin, G. (1987). *START resource packet: Child find.* (U.S. Department of Education, Grant No. G00-84C-3515). Chapel Hill, NC:

Frank Porter Graham Child Development Center, University of North Carolina.

Bronfenbrenner, U. (1979). *The ecology of human development.* Cambridge, MA: Harvard University Press.

Brooks-Gunn, J. & Lewis, M. (1983). Screening and diagnosing handicapped infants. *Topics in Early Childhood Special Education, 3*(1), 14–28.

Bruder, M. B. (1987). *An infant monitoring project for at-risk inner city families.* Manuscript submitted for publication.

Buros, O. K. (1978). *The eight mental measurements yearbook.* Highland Park, NJ: Gryphon Press.

Byrne, J. M., Backman, J. E., & Smith, I. M. (1986). Developmental assessment: The clinical use and validity of parent report. *Journal of Pediatric Psychology, 11,* 549–559.

Cadman, D., Chambers, L. W., Walter, S. D., Feldman, W., Smith, K., & Ferguson, R. (1984). The usefulness of the Denver Developmental Screening Test to predict kindergarten problems in a general community population. *American Journal of Public Health, 74,* 1093–1097.

Caldwell, B. M. & Bradley, R. H. (1982). Screening for handicapped environments. In E. B. Edgar, N. G. Haring, J. R. Jenkins, C. G. Pious (Eds.), *Mentally handicapped children: Education and training* (pp. 49–64). Baltimore, MD: University Park Press.

Colligan, R. C. (1981). Prediction of reading difficulty from parental preschool report: A 3-year follow-up. *Learning Disability Quarterly*, *4*, 31–37.

Cress, P., Spellman, C., DeBriere, T., Sizemore, A., Northam J., & Johnson, J. (1981). Vision screening for persons with severe handicaps. *Journal of the Association for the Severely Handicapped*, *6*, 41–50.

Cross, L. (1977). Casefinding. In L. Cross & K. Goin (Eds.), *Identifying handicapped children: A guide to casefinding, screening, diagnosis, assessment, and evaluation* (pp. 9–15). New York: Walker.

Diamond, K. E. (1987). Predicting school problems from preschool developmental screening: A four-year follow-up of the Rivised Denver Developmental Screening Test and the role of parent report. *Journal of the Division for Early Childhood*, *11*(3), 247–253.

Docherty, E. M. (1983). The DIAL: Preschool screening for learning problems. *Journal of Special Education*, *17*(2), 195–202.

Dunst, C. J. (1985). Rethinking early intervention. *Analysis and Intervention in Developmental Disabilities*, *5*, 165–201.

Elardo, R. & Bradley, R. (1981). The Home Observation for Measurement of the Environment: A review of research. *Developmental Review*, *1*, 113–145.

Fallen, N. & Umansky, W. (1985). *Young children with special needs* (2nd ed.). Columbus, OH: Merrill.

Fewell, R. R. & Langley, M. B. (1984). *Developmental Activities Screening Inventory—II*. Austin, TX: Pro-Ed.

Frankenburg, W. K., Coons, C. E., & Ker, C. (1982). Screening infants and preschoolers to identify school learning problems (Denver Developmental Screening Test and Home Observation and Measurement of the Environment Inventory). In E. B. Edgar, N. G. Haring, J. R. Jenkins, & C. G. Pious (Eds.), *Mentally handicapped children: Education and training* (pp. 11–27). Baltimore: University Park Press.

Frankenburg, W. K., Dodds, J. B., & Fandal, A. W. (1975). *Denver Developmental Screening Test*. Denver, CO: LADOCA Project and Publishing Foundation.

Frankenburg, W. K., Goldstein, A. D., & Camp, B. W. (1971). The revised Denver Developmental Screening Test: Its accuracy as a screening instrument. *The Journal of Pediatrics*, *79*, 988–995.

Frankenburg, W. K., Van Doorninck, W. J., Liddell, T. N., & Dick, N. P. (1976). The Denver Prescreening Developmental Questionnaire (PDQ). *Pediatrics*, *57*, 744–753.

Gallagher, J. J. & Bradley, R. H. (1972). Early identification of developmental difficulties. In I. Gordon (Ed.), *Early childhood education*. Chicago: University of Chicago Press.

Gallerani, D., O'Regan, M., & Reinherz, H. (1982). Prekindergarten screening: How well does it predict readiness for first grade? *Psychology in the Schools*, *19*, 175–182.

German, M. L., Williams, E., Herzfeld, J., & Marshall, R. M. (1982). Utility of the revised Denver Developmental Screening Test and the Developmental Profile II in identifying preschool children with cognitive, language, and motor problems. *Education and Training of the Mentally Retarded*, *17*, 319–324.

Gottfried, A. W., Guerin, D., Spencer, J. E., & Meyer, C. (1983). Concurrent validity of the Minnesota Child Development Inventory in a nonclinical sample. *Journal of Consulting and Clinical Psychology*, *51*, 643–644.

Gottfried, A. W., Guerin, D., Spencer, J. E., & Meyer, C. (1984). Validity of the Minnesota Child Development Inventory in screening young children's developmental status. *Journal of Pediatric Psychology*, *9*, 219–230.

Gradel, K., Thompson, M., & Sheehan, R. (1981). Parental and professional agreement in early childhood assessment. *Topics in Early Childhood Special Education*, *1*(2), 31–39.

Greenwood, C. R., Walker, H. M., Todd, N. M., & Hops, H. (1979). Selecting a cost-effective screening measure for the assessment of preschool social withdrawal. *Journal of Applied Behavior Analysis*, *12*, 639–652.

Harrington, R. G. (1984). Preschool screening: The school psychologist's perspective. *School Psychology Review*, *13*, 363–374.

Hayden, A. H. & McGinness, G. D. (1977). Bases for early intervention. In E. Songtag (Ed.), *Educational programming for the severely and profoundly handicapped* (pp. 153–165). Reston, VA: Division on Mental Retardation, Council for Exceptional Children.

Hedrick D., Prather, E., & Tobin, A. (1975). *Sequenced Inventory of Communication Develop-*

ment. Seattle: University of Washington Press.

Ireton, H. & Thwing, E. (1974). *Manual for the Minnesota Child Development Inventory.* Minneapolis, MN: Behavior Science Systems.

Jaffe, M., Harel, J., Goldberg, A., Rudolph-Schnitzer, M., & Winter, S. T. (1980). The use of the Denver Developmental Screening Test in infant welfare clinics. *Developmental Medicine and Child Neurology, 22,* 55–60.

Kenny, T. J., Hebel, J. R., Sexton, M. J., & Fox, N. L. (1987). Developmental screening using parent report. *Developmental and Behavioral Pediatrics, 8*(1), 8–11.

Keogh, B. & Daley, S. (1983). Early identification: One component of comprehensive services for at-risk children. *Topics in Early Childhood Special Education, 3*(3), 7–16.

Keogh, B. & Kopp, C. B. (1978). From assessment to intervention: An elusive bridge. In F. Minifie & L. Lloyd (Eds.), *Communication and cognitive abilities—Early behavioral assessment* (pp. 523–547). Baltimore, MD: University Park Press.

Kirk, S. A. (1987). From my perspective: The learning disabled preschool child. *Teaching Exceptional Children, 19*(2), 78–80.

Knobloch, H., Pasamanick, B., & Sherard, E. S. (1966). *A Developmental Screening Inventory.* Albany, NY: Albany Medical College.

Kurtz, P. D. (1980). Early identification of rural, handicapped preschool children. *Human Services in the Rural Environment, 5*(2), 4–11.

Kurtz, P. D., Devaney, B., & Strain, P. (1983). Rural parents' attitudes and knowledge regarding handicapped preschool children: Implications for developing an early indentification program. *Child Care Quarterly, 12*(1), 71–82.

Kurtz, P. D., Devany, B., Strain, P., Sandler, H. (1982). Effects of mass-media and group instruction on increasing parent awareness of early identification. *The Journal of Special Education, 16,* 329–339.

Langley, B. & DuBose, R. F. (1976). Functional vision screening for severely handicapped children. *New Outlook for the Blind, 70,* 346–350.

Lichtenstein, R. (1980). *Minneapolis Preschool Screening Instrument.* Minneapolis, MN: Minneapolis Public Schools.

Lichtenstein, R. (1981). Comparative validity of two preschool screening tests: Correlational and classificational approaches. *Journal of Learning Disabilities, 14*(2), 68–72.

Lichtenstein. R. & Ireton, H. (1984). *Preschool screening: Identifying young children with developmental and educational problems.* Orlando, FL: Grune & Stratton.

Lillie, D. L. (1977). Screening. In L. Cross & K. Goin (Eds.), *Identifying handicapped children: A guide to casefinding, screening, diagnosis, assessment, and evaluation* (pp. 17–24). New York: Walker.

Lombard, T. J. (1980). A lesson for every state from Minnesota's Preschool Screening Program. *The Journal of School Health, 50,* 459–462.

Mandell, C. J. & Johnson, R. A. (1984). Screening for otitis media: Issues and procedural recommendations. *Journal of the Division for Early Childhood, 8*(1), 86–93.

Mardell-Czudnowski, C. D. (1980). Validity and reliability studies with DIAL. *Journal for Special Educators, 17,* 32–45.

Mardell-Czudnowski, C. D. & Goldenberg, D. (1983). *DIAL (developmental indicators for the assessment of learning—revised).* Edison, NJ: Childcraft Education Corp.

Mardell-Czudnowski, C. D. & Goldenberg, D. (1984). Revision and restandardization of a preschool screening test: DIAL becomes DIAL-R. *Journal of the Division for Early Childhood, 8*(2), 149–156.

Margolis, L. H. & Meisels, S. J. (1987). Barriers to the effectiveness of EPSDT for children with moderate and severe developmental disabilities. *American Journal of Orthopsychiatry, 57,* 424–430.

McCarthy, D. (1972). *Manual for the McCarthy Scales of Children's Abilities.* New York: Psychological Corporation.

McCauley, R. & Swisher, L. (1984). Psychometric review of language and articulation tests for preschool children. *Journal of Speech and Hearing Disorders, 49,* 34–41.

McLean, M., McCormick, K., Bruder, M. B., & Burdg, N. B. (1987). An investigation of the validity and reliability of the Battelle Developmental Inventory with population of children younger than 30 months with identified handicapping conditions. *Journal of the Division of Early Childhood, 11*(3), 238–246.

McClean, M., McCormick, K., Baird, S., & Mayfield, P. (1987). *A study of the concurrent validity of the Battelle Developmental Inventory Screening*

Test. Unpublished manuscript, Auburn University, Auburn, AL.

Meier, J. H. (1979). Developmental screening overview. In B. L. Darby and M. J. May (Eds.), *Infant assessment: Issues and applications* (pp. 47–63). Seattle, WA: WESTAR.

Meisels, S. J. (In press). Can developmental screening tests identify children who are developmentally at-risk? *Pediatrics.*

Meisels, S. J. & Wiske, M. S. (1983). *The Early Screening Inventory.* New York: Teachers College Press.

Meisels, S. J., Wiske, M. S., & Tivnan, T. (1984). Predicting school performance with the Early Screening Inventory. *Psychology in the Schools, 21,* 25–33.

Meltzer, L. J., Levine, M. D., Hanson, M. A., Wasserman, R., Schneider, D., & Sullivan, M. (1983). Developmental attainment in preschool children: Analysis of concordance between parents and professionals. *The Journal of Special Education, 17,* 203–213.

Mercer, C. D. & Trifiletti, J. J. (1977). The development of screening procedures for the detection of children with learning problems. *The Journal of School Health, 47,* 526–532.

Miller, L. J. (1982). *Miller Assessment for Preschoolers.* Littleton, CO: Foundation for Knowledge in Development.

Miller, L. J. & Sprong, T. A. (1986). Psychometric and qualitative comparison of four preschool screening instruments. *Journal of Learning Disabilities, 19,* 480–484.

Newborg, J., Stock, J. R., & Wnek, L. (1984). *Battelle Developmental Inventory: Examiner's manual.* Allen, TX: DLM Teaching Resources.

Nugent, J. H. (1976). A comment on the efficiency of the revised Denver Developmental Screening Test. *American Journal of Mental Deficiency, 80,* 570–572.

Obrzut, J. E., Bolocofsky, D. N., Heath, C. P., & Jones, M. J. (1981). An investigation of the DIAL as a pre-kindergarten screening instrument *Educational and Psychological Measurement, 41,* 1231–1241.

Paget, K. D. & Nagle, R. J. (1986). A conceptual model of preschool assessment. *School Psychology Review, 15,* 154–165.

Peterson, N. (1987). *Early intervention for handicapped and at-risk children: An introduction to early childhood-special education.* Denver, CO: Love.

Powell, M. L. (1981). *Assessment and management of developmental changes and problems in children* (2nd ed.). St. Louis, MO: C. V. Mosby.

Rogers-Warren, A. K. (1984). Ecobehavioral analysis. *Education and Treatment of Children, 7,* 283–303.

Roscoe, D. (1979). Preschool screening in Hawaii. *Educational Perspectives, 18*(4), 3–7.

Sarachan-Deily, A. B., Hopkins, C., & DeVivo, S. (1983). Correlating the DIAL and the BTBC. *Language, Speech, and Hearing Services in Schools, 14*(1), 54–59.

Saylor, C. F. & Brandt, B. J. (1986). The Minnesota Child Development Inventory: A valid maternal-report form for assessing development in infancy. *Developmental and Behavioral Pediatrics, 7,* 308–311.

Senior, E. M. (1986). Learning disabled or merely mislabled? The plight of the developmentally young child. *Childhood Education, 62*(3), 161–165.

Simmer, M. (1983). The warning signs of school failure: An updated profile of the at-risk kindergarten child. *Topics in Early Childhood Special Education, 3*(3), 17–28.

Stoner, S. & Purcell, K. (1985). The concurrent validity of teachers' judgments of the abilities of preschoolers in a daycare setting. *Educational and Psychological Measurement, 45,* 421–423.

Teska, J. A. & Stoneburner, R. L. (1980). The concept and practice of second-level screening. *Psychology in the Schools, 17,* 192–195.

Thompson, M. (1979). Assessment of the young hearing-impaired child. In B. L. Darby and M. J. May (Eds.), *Infant assessment: Issues and applications* (pp. 181–197). Seattle, WA: WESTAR.

Thurlow, M. L., O'Sullivan, P. J., & Ysseldyke, J. E. (1986). Early screening for special education: How accurate? *Educational Leadership, 44*(3), 93–95.

Tucker, J. (1979). *Implementing child find services: A resource handbook for educators.* Des Moines, IA: Mid-West Regional Resource Center.

Tjossem, T. D. (1976). (Ed.). *Intervention strategies for high-risk infants and young children.* Baltimore, MD: University Park Press.

Ueda, R. (1978). Standardization of the Denver Developmental Screening Test to Tokyo children.

Developmental Medicine and Child Neurology, 20, 647–656.

Williams, P. D. & Williams, A. R. (1987). Denver Developmental Screening Test norms: A cross-cultural comparison. *Journal of Pediatric Psychology, 12*(1), 39–55.

Wilson, W. R. (1978). Sensory assessment: Auditory-behavioral assessment of auditory function in infants. In F. Minifie & L. Lloyd (Eds.), *Communication and cognitive abilities—Early behavioral assessment.* Baltimore, MD: University Park Press.

Zehrbach, R. (1975). *Comprehensive Identification Process: Screening administrator's manual.* Urbana-Champaign: University of Illinois.

Chapter 7

Screening and Assessing Sensory Functioning

Patricia Kinney
University of Kentucky
Teri Ouellette
Lexington Hearing and Speech Center
Mark Wolery
University of Kentucky

KEY TERMS

- Outer Ear
- Ear Canal
- Middle Ear
- Tympanic Membrane
- Ossicles
- Eustacian Tube
- Inner Ear
- Cochlea
- Audiology
- Frequency
- Hertz
- Intensity
- Decibels
- Hearing Threshold
- Conductive Hearing Loss

- Otitis Media
- Sensorineural Hearing Losses
- Mixed Loss
- High-Risk Register
- Auditory Brainstem Response (ABR)
- Impedance Audiometry
- Tympanometer
- Tympanogram
- Audiogram
- Behavior Observation Audiometry (BOA)
- Conditioned Orientation Response (COR)
- Visual Reinforcement Audiometry (VRA)
- Play Audiometry
- Pure Tone
- Aided Response
- Vision

- Visual Acuity
- Blindness
- Visual Impairment
- Ophthalmologist
- Optometrist
- Preferential Looking Procedure
- Visually Evoked Potential
- Refraction
- Binocularity
- Strabismus
- Visual Field
- Color Vision
- Functional Vision Assessment

Early interventionists frequently screen infants and preschoolers for developmental delays and assess them for instructional program planning. In addition, early interventionists may be among the first professionals who consider the sensory abilities of young children. They should be able to screen sensory functioning, make referrals to audiologists and ophthalmologists or optometrists, and interpret the reports written by those professionals. Early interventions also should gather or use others' information on sensory functioning when planning instructional programs. The purpose of this chapter is twofold: to discuss auditory and visual screening of infants and young children and to describe the measures, terms, and procedures used by professionals who assess visual and auditory functioning. Assessment of auditory functioning is described first, followed by assessment of visual functioning.

Assessing Auditory Functioning of Infants and Preschoolers

One of the major capacities that binds us together as a society is communication. The full development of this capacity is largely dependent on our ability to use hearing to interpret speech and language. By hearing the pragmatically appropriate speech of others in various situations, children develop sound-symbol relationships and linguistic structures. Also, hearing allows a feedback loop for the development and refinement of language and speech. Several studies suggest that the diagnosis and remediation of hearing losses in children under age 3 is an important factor in maximizing their chances for near-normal language and speech development (Garrity & Mengle, 1983; Mischook & Cole, 1986; Pollack, 1985). In fact, some sources indicate that an undiagnosed and untreated hearing impairment in infancy or early preschool causes sensory deprivation resulting in the functional or physiological

atrophy of neural channels (Mischook & Cole, 1986; Pollack, 1985). While experts agree on the need for early diagnosis and intervention, no completely reliable method exists for screening infants and mildly affected preschoolers, although improvements are being made.

Types of Hearing Losses

To understand various types of assessment procedures and issues related to diagnosis, it is necessary to know the basics of aural anatomy and audiology and the various types of hearing losses. The ear consists of three major divisions: the outer ear, middle ear, and inner ear. The **outer ear** consists of the auricle, the visible portion of the ear that serves to direct sound waves into the ear, and the external auditory meatus, or **ear canal.** The **middle ear** consists of the **tympanic membrane,** or ear drum, and three small bones known as **ossicles.** These structures of the middle ear serve to change sound waves to mechanical energy and conduct that energy to the inner ear. The middle ear is connected to the back of the throat by the **eustacian tube,** which equalizes ear pressure and drains fluids. The organ of the **inner ear** is the **cochlea.** The cochlea is a spiral organ filled with sensory hair cells that transform the mechanical energy into electrochemical energy, which is sent as impulses through the auditory nerve to the brain (Clark, 1980).

Audiology is the science of hearing measurement. Most states require audiologists to obtain a masters degree and successfully pass professional examinations prior to practicing. The basics of the science are relatively straightforward. The two properties of sound most often measured are frequency and intensity. **Frequency** refers to the pitch of the sound and is measured in **Hertz** (Hz). Low numbers (125, 250, 500 Hz) refer to low-pitched tones, and higher numbers (4000, 8000 Hz) refer to high-pitched sounds. **Intensity** refers to the loudness of the sound and is measured in **decibels** (dB). Audiologists generally begin testing with a sound of sufficient decibel level to be sure it is easily heard (30–40 dB). They gradually present softer sounds, until they discover the softest tones the individual can hear. This is referred to as the **hearing threshold.** In the average adult, the hearing threshold is 0 dB. Some people hear in the negative decibel range, but thresholds up to 10–15 dB are usually considered normal for children. Conversational speech is about 50–60 dB. Most equipment cannot test above 120 dB.

There are three basic types of hearing losses; the most common among children is a **conductive loss.** These losses originate in the outer or middle ear due to interference with the conduction of sound from the outer ear to the cochlea. In this type of loss, the cochlea and auditory nerve are unaffected. Conductive losses are mild to moderate in nature and are often treatable through medication and/or surgery. Some disorders resulting in conductive losses are atresia (congenital absence of the ear canal), occlusion (blockage of the canal), breaks in the ossicular chain, and perforations of the tympanic membrane (Clark, 1980). The most common causes of loss in infants and preschool children are those connected with ear infections— negative pressure in the middle ear, fluid (or effusion) in the middle ear, and otitis media.

Otitis media, infection of the middle ear, affects more than two thirds of all children before the age of 3, and 50% of those children experienced three or more infections. On the average, each episode is preceeded and/or followed by 40 days of middle ear effusion (fluid) (Giebink, 1984; Klein, 1986). The infections vary in duration from as short as one week to as long as six months, and hearing may be affected for the entire period. Middle ear problems are especially prevalent in children with Down syndrome, cleft palate, and immune abnormalities; they are also prevalent among children who spend time in daycare facilities, have frequent upper respiratory problems, or live with adults who smoke (Pukander, Sipila, & Karma, 1984; Todd, 1986).

For many years recurrent otitis media was viewed as a normal event of childhood. Infections were generally treated with antibiotics with little or no follow up and little concern for subsequent effusion. Only the most recurrent and severe cases were treated with ventilation tubes. Ventilation tubes are small plastic or metal tubes placed in the tympanic membrane to help maintain normal middle ear pressure and avoid fluid accumulation and infection. Treatment is provided to control the course of the disorder and to prevent medical complications and possibly developmental delays. Recent research suggests that chronic otitis media in children under age 3 may result in deficits in speech, language, and intellectual development (Silva, Kirkland, Simpson, Stewart, & Williams, 1982; Stewart, Kirkland, Simpson, Silva, & Williams, 1984). Zinkus and Gottlieb (1980) found children had delays in the acquisition of most language skills, lower verbal intelligence scores, and lower reading scores. Further, auditory processing, auditory perception, and spelling problems have been noted (Sak & Ruben, 1981). The intelligence test scores of children with recurrent middle ear infections are about 15 points lower than children who did not experience recurrent middle ear problems (Gdowski, Sanger, & Decker, 1986). Studies on this issue, however, generally have been criticized on methodological grounds (Paradise & Rogers, 1986), and other studies have failed to support these findings (cf., Fischler, Todd, & Feldman, 1985; Roberts, Sanya, Burchinal, Collier, Ramey, & Henderson, 1986). Nonetheless, these results have raised sufficient concern to stimulate the medical and educational community to look for more aggressive methods of diagnosis, treatment, and rehabilitation for children with chronic otitis media.

Sensorineural hearing losses are generally considered to be the most serious. They are due to damage in the inner ear and/or the auditory nerve, which can cause profound losses, some with little measurable residual hearing. Sensorineural losses in chldren are usually moderate to profound (50–120 + dB), can vary greatly across frequencies, and are often more severe at higher frequencies. The only medical treatment available for sensorineural losses is the cochlear implant. Implants are surgically inserted in the cochlea and supply direct electronic stimulation of the auditory nerve. At present, they require externally worn support equipment similar in size to a portable radio. Implants are useful only for the profoundly impaired who cannot benefit from hearing aids. They are considered experimental at this time, especially with young children.

The third type of hearing loss is a **mixed loss**. It occurs when a person who has sustained sensorineural damage also suffers from a conductive loss. Transitory mixed losses are common among children with sensorineural losses. They often suffer from recurrent otitis media as do other children.

Screening and Auditory Assessment Tests

This section contains information on screening infants' hearing, impedance audiometry, other auditory screening procedures, and brainstem evoked response procedures.

Infant Screening and Testing. While all professionals agree that early diagnosis and intervention are of paramount importance, diagnostic services for infants and children with multiple handicaps are not universally available. For screening, most professionals agree that a **high-risk register** followed by direct testing of infants who are at risk for hearing impairment is the most feasible strategy (Amochaev, 1987). In 1982, the Joint Committee on Infant Hearing of the American Speech-Language-Hearing Association recommended that the following seven factors be considered in identifying infants who are at risk for hearing impairment:

1. Family history of childhood hearing impairment.
2. Congenital perinatal infections.
3. Anatomical malformations of the head or neck.
4. Birth weight less than 1500 gm.
5. Hyperbilirubinemia at a level exceeding indications for exchange transfusion.
6. Bacterial meningitis, especially from *Hemophilus influenzae.*
7. Sever asphyxia, which may include infants with Apgar scores of 0 to 3 who fail to institute spontaneous respiration by 10 minutes and those with hypotonia persisting to 2 hours of age. (Mahoney & Eichwald. 1987, p. 156)

Relatively few states have government sponsored high-risk registers to identify each newborn who may have a hearing impairment, and it is estimated that fewer than half of the identified infants are actually tested (Mahoney & Eichwald, 1987). Such high-risk registers generally refer 8–15% of all infants screened and about 10% of those infants will prove to have some degree of hearing loss (Fitch, Williams, & Etienne, 1982; Mahoney & Eichwald, 1987).

Many hospitals, however, screen newborns before release from the nursery using special devices that produce sounds of varying frequency and intensity. Newborns are observed by physicians or nurses for the auropalpebral response (APR) or eye blink, or for arousal from the sleep state in response to sound (Garrity & Mengle, 1983). Some hospitals use a more sophisticated device, called the "Crib-o-gram." This device uses motion-sensitive detectors embedded in the crib and connected to a polygraph. It measures the movements of the infant immediately before and after the introduction of a loud sound (92 dB) of mixed frequencies. Measurements are taken a minimum of 20 times per child (Garrity & Mengle, 1983; McFarland, Simmons, & Jones, 1980). This method eliminates the need for a human observer and allows repeated measures on each child, but it is costly and thus may not be used in all hospitals. Other hospitals use **Auditory Brainstem Response** (ABR) procedures, which have been made more feasible with recent technological advances (Amochaev, 1987). The ABR is an abbrieviated form of the brainstem evoked response described later in this chapter. The Telephone Pioneers Project has been using volunteers to administer ABR screening to high-risk neonates. The group uses portable testing devices brought into newborn nurseries. If the test can be timed to take place during a normal sleep state no sedation is required. It is administered much as the full brainstem evoked responses, but yields only screening results (Pollack, 1985). This method is more objective than behavioral observation, but is not widely available. It has been reported to yield a high proportion of false positives (Pollack, 1985), although this can be reduced with retesting (Jacobson & Morehouse, 1984). Comparisons of various screening methods and issues are discussed by Jacobson and Jacobson (1987).

The difficulty in defining a universally applicable response topography for children under age 3 makes screening outside the newborn nursery difficult. While many pediatricians attempt to screen such children during well-baby visits, maternal reports or informal means (hand clapping, noise makers, etc.) are frequently employed. Because such sounds are not controlled for frequency or intensity and are presented under poorly controlled circumstances (the child may be responding to visual cues, maternal responses, or even vibrations), they often yield a high number of false negatives. Even testing under controlled circumstances is difficult, and identification of mild to moderate losses (especially sensorineural or unilateral losses) in infants is unusual. Frequently, a child older than 1 year can be taught some sort of conditioned response that produces more reliable results.

Impedance Audiometry. One testing method that is often used with infants and children is **impedance audiometry,** which measures the resistance of the middle ear system to sound energy. It is most useful in identifying middle ear problems. A complete impedance battery includes three tests: tympanometry, static compliance, and acoustic reflex thresholds. By far the most common among children, especially for screening, is tympanometry.

A **tympanometer** is a probe about the size of a large pen containing three appliances: a loudspeaker, pressure pump, and microphone. The probe is placed in the child's ear canal and when an adequate seal is obtained, a series of beeps is produced. The microphone serves to measure how much of the sound energy is reflected back from the ear drum. This procedure is repeated across varying degrees of pressure created by the pump. The less compliant, or movable, the ear drum is, the less sound is transmitted through the middle ear system, and more sound will be reflected back into the canal. Under normal testing circumstances, when the pressure in the ear canal is higher or lower than the pressure in the middle ear, the ear drum is less movable and therefore reflects more sound. The point at which the least sound is reflected is the point at which the pressure in the ear canal is equal to that in the middle ear. Thus, this method can be used to identify the amount of pressure in the middle ear and the degree to which the ear drum can move (compliance) (Clark, 1980; Pappas, 1985; Roeser & Price, 1981).

This test yields two important pieces of information. The first is a **tympanogram,** which is a graph of the compliance of the ear drum and middle ear system. Tympanograms are classified into three basic types, and examples are shown in Figure 7.1. Type A is a "normal" result, showing a definite peak of compliance at near 0 pressure (normal atmospheric pressure). Type B shows no peak and indicates little or no movement of the ear drum

FIGURE 7.1
The Three Major Types of Tympanograms
Type A shows normal functioning; Type B shows fluid in the middle ear or a patent (open) ventilation tube; Type C shows negative middle ear pressure.

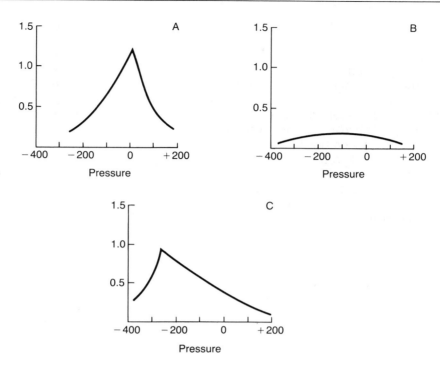

under any degree of pressure. This result usually indicates middle ear effusion (fluid) or patent (open) tubes in the ear drum. Type C tympanograms show a definite peak, but at negative pressure (− 150 or less). This finding indicates that the eustachian tube is not functioning adequately. Type C tympanograms often precede or follow incidences of effusion or otitis media. The other important piece of information usually included in a tympanogram is the volume of the ear canal. The machine measures the volume of the canal from the tip of the probe to the ear drum. If there is a perforation (hole) or a patent ventilation tube in the ear drum, the machine will measure the volume of the middle ear in addition to that of the ear canal. Thus, very large volumes can help to pinpoint perforations or clarify the findings of a Type B tympanogram.

The test can be done easily, quickly, and with little cooperation from the child. Some tympanometers are lightweight and automatic enough to be used with relatively little training. As such, this method is ideal for screening large groups of preschoolers for middle ear problems. It provides information on how well the middle ear is conducting sound, but yields no information on how well the child actually hears. A child may have a profound sensorineural hearing loss and have normal tympanograms. Best practice involves ruling out middle ear complications with tympanograms immediately before proceeding to any other hearing tests.

Other Audiometric Tests. A number of variations on the basic audiometric tests are used to evaluate young children. Portable audiometers are often used in preschools for hearing screenings. Due to the relatively high noise levels and number of distractors in such surroundings, these tests are accurate for screening purposes only. The younger the child, the less reliable the results. Very young children and many older children with multiple handicaps cannot be tested with earphones, as the pressure from the device causes their ear canals to collapse temporarily. Thus the only reliable method of testing such children, even for screening purposes, is in a sound-proof booth designed for that purpose. However, when this type of testing occurs, the hearing threshold may reflect only that of the better ear.

The testing process for children is similar to that used with adults. The child is presented with a sound of sufficient decibel level to be sure it is easily heard. The child, through some arbitrary response, must communicate to the tester when a sound is heard. When this response topography is established, the intensity of the sound is gradually decreased until the child fails to respond. The threshold is established at the least intense sound that consistently elicits a response. Responses are graphed on an **audiogram;** a sample is shown in Figure 7.2. Responses for the right ear are graphed with circles; responses for the left are graphed with Xs.

For children with a mental age of 4 years

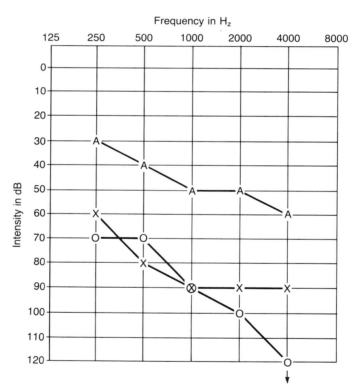

FIGURE 7.2

A Sample Audiogram

The frequency of sound, measured in Hertz (Hz), is shown across the top of the audiogram; the intensity of sound, measured in decibels (dB), is shown on the left of the audiogram. Responses from the left ear are shown by Xs and responses from the right ear are shown by Os. The As indicate aided responses; that is, responses found when the subject wears a hearing aid. The data in this audiogram show a severe to profound hearing loss with the loss being most severe at high frequencies.

or older, this process is simple. The child is instructed to raise his hand or press a button when he hears the tone. Other methods are necessary for younger children. Testing for infants under age 1 begins with **Behavioral Observation Audiometry** (BOA) (Garrity & Mengle, 1983; Pappas, 1985). The infant is tested in a sound-proof booth, using speakers (sound field testing) rather than earphones. The order of sound presentation is reversed, beginning with quieter sounds and getting louder while watching for reactions such as a change in sucking patterns, the APR (eye blink), a change in activity level, or an attempt to localize (look for) the sound. This method will pinpoint serious losses but is less reliable for mild to moderate losses because normal infants frequently do not respond to sounds under 40–50 dB. As soon as the child is old enough to localize a sound (approximately 7 months), children may be tested using **Conditioned Orientation Response** (COR) or **Visual Reinforcement Audiometry** (VRA) (Garrity & Mengle, 1983; Hasenstab & Horner, 1982; Pappas, 1985; Pollack, 1985). These procedures are similar and depend on conditioning the child to turn in the direction of an auditory stimulus in a sound field, using some form of visual reinforcement, such as a lighted doll. VRA occurs in a sound-proof booth equipped with speakers to the left and the right. An attractive toy is placed on top of the speakers. During testing, the child is held by an adult or seated in the middle of the room. Another adult attempts to keep the child's visual attention directed at midline. When a sound is introduced, the audiologist observes whether the child turned in the direction of the sound. If the child turns, the toy is lighted or activated and serves as a reinforcer for turning to sound. These procedures can be highly successful until the child outgrows interest in the reinforcer. At this age (18 months to 5 years, depending on the child), play audiometry is used. In **play audiometry** the child is conditioned to indicate that she hears a sound by initiating a response to a repetitive game, such as putting a block in a container or a ring on a stick (Garrity & Mengle, 1983; Pollack, 1985). Play audiometry may be used in a sound field or with earphones.

There are several other variations of testing procedures. Testing is usually done with pure tones. The term **pure tone** refers to sounds of only one frequency. Audiologists sometimes test with warble tones (mixed frequencies with a warbling sound) and with amplified speech as well (Clark, 1980). Speech awareness is often used with infants. In fact, some sources indicate that because the mother's voice is the most salient sound for an infant, speech awareness using the mother's voice may be the most reliable hearing test for the young infant (Pollack, 1985). This test yields a speech awareness threshold. In children who possess language, speech discrimination testing also is used. This requires the child to repeat or point to pictures of specific words presented by the audiologist. This test yields a percentage score (Clark, 1980). Children who wear hearing aids also should be tested with their hearing aids on, yielding what is known as an **aided response** (see Figure 7.2).

It is considered best practice to have at least one other person with the child in the testing booth. The mother may be asked to hold the child during testing, but she may be needed to speak through the microphone in order to assess the infant's response to her voice. Thus, the teacher may be called upon to hold the infant. In the case of BOA or VRA testing, the teacher may be asked to provide mild distraction, bringing the child's head back to midline between stimulus presentations. In play audiometry, the teacher may provide a model of the expected response, manipulate play materials to keep the child's attention, and/or dispense reinforcers. In any of these roles, the teacher must be careful not to respond in any way to the auditory stimuli. Startles, gestures, or eye movements may trigger false responses in the child.

Because much of this testing is done in a sound field, ear protection should be provided for persons in the booth who are not being tested.

Brainstem Evoked Response. Brainstem evoked response audiometry (also known as brainstem auditory evoked potential) is an important testing method for infants and handicapped children (Garrity & Mengle, 1983). Using a process similar to that of an electroencephalogram, the child is placed under sedation, and electrodes attached to the skin are used to record the brainstem response to auditory stimuli. Inasmuch as this procedure requires no cooperation from the child, it is valuable for use with children who have few response topographies. However, it yields results only from 1500 to 4000 Hz (Hasenstab & Horner, 1982; Pappas, 1985) and will not pinpoint low-frequency or mild hearing losses. When used with neonates the results must be confirmed through other means, as they are often influenced by the immaturity of the brainstem.

Indicators of a Hearing Loss

Teachers are often the professionals who have the longest and most intimate contact with handicapped infants and preschoolers. As a result, teachers may be in the best position to spot indicators of possible hearing losses. Conductive losses may be suspected when the child shows a sudden change in responsiveness to everyday sounds. Persistent ear infections, running ears, red or hot ears, and poking or pushing at the ears also are indications of a conductive loss. Children with long-term conductive losses sometimes drop the initial consonants in words, especially voiceless consonants (e.g., *f, s, p, h*), for these sounds carry less power in running speech.

Sensorineural losses may be suspected when a child shows marked delays in developing speech and language. Sensorineural losses can be frequency specific (a loss of 30–50 dB at one or two frequencies only). They sometimes "slope" to higher frequencies, with near-normal hearing of low-pitched sounds but little hearing of high frequencies. Thus, they may be indicated by speech in which certain high frequency sounds are consistently absent. Voiceless sibilants and fricatives such as *s, f,* and voiceless *th* (as in *thick*) are high-frequency sounds that may be absent in children with sensorineural losses, particularly when they appear in initial or final positions.

In children who already have developed speech and language skills, some general indications of possible hearing problems are shown in Table 7.1. A child who consistently shows more than one of these behaviors should be referred for further audiological testing (Roeser & Northern, 1981). In prelingual children, the earliest indications will be seen in developmental delays specific to

TABLE 7.1
Potential Indicators of Hearing Loss in Children with Speech and Language

Requests frequent repetition (huh?)

Watches the speaker's mouth

Tires easily

Speaks too loudly or softly

Turns one ear toward the sound source

Strains to hear

Is inattentive

Makes frequent or unusual mistakes in directions

Is isolated or passive

Exhibits tension

Has any speech defect

Changes in achievement after an illness

Breathes through the mouth

Experiences dizziness

Has frequent ear infections

Complains of ringing or buzzing in the ears

Gives inconsistent responses to questions

Makes inappropriate comments in conversation

speech and hearing milestones. Teachers must use their judgment in estimating the developmental abilities of severely handicapped children. The sequences shown in Table 7.2 (p. 154) can serve as a guideline. Children who show delays in any of these behaviors, especially if they are inconsistent with delays in other developmental areas, should be referred for testing (Pappas, 1985).

Assessing Visual Functioning of Infants and Preschoolers

The ability to use vision is important for independent functioning and performing many behaviors within each developmental area. For example, visual skills are involved when children find hidden objects; respond to a familiar face with a smile; point to a desired toy; imitate the play of other children; name familiar objects in books; match shapes, letters, and numbers; and crawl to a toy out of reach. The sense of vision is regarded as the primary sensory modality (Smith & Cote, 1982). **Vision** is the process by which information is received by the eye from light rays reflected off objects and then sent to the brain for interpretation. For vision to occur, light must be available.

Beginning with a brief overview of visual development and vision impairments, this section emphasizes the importance of early detection and treatment of vision problems. Clinical as well as teacher-administered functional assessment of vision are discussed. Finally, considerations for translating results from clinical and functional vision assessments into educational goals also are presented.

Visual Development
Visual skills appear to develop in an orderly sequence. At birth, visual behaviors are primarily reflexive, and vision is not as sharp as that of an adult. **Visual acuity,** the ability

to detect fine detail, may be at about 20/400 for a newborn (Morse & Trief, 1985). At this point the infant can detect only light, movement, and gross form. A developmental sequence of selected visual behaviors is presented in Table 7.3. By 18 months, children's visual acuity may reach 20/20, the acuity of an adult with normal vision (Harrell & Akeson, 1987). For normal visual development to occur, anatomical and physiological processes are necessary. These processes are believed to be dependent on early visual experiences as well as physical maturation. Several authors suggest that a critical period for visual development occurs between the early months of life and the ages of 6 or 7 years (Lockman, 1983; Morse & Trief, 1985).

Vision Impairments
Legal definitions of visually impaired and blind are based on measures of visual acuity. A visual acuity indicates the smallest object that the individual is able to identify at a specific distance. Visual acuity is reported as a fraction, in which the distance at which the individual could detect the smallest item presented is the numerator and the distance at which a person with normal vision could detect the item is the denominator. For example, a visual acuity of 20/200 indicates that an individual can detect at 20 feet what a person with normal vision can detect at 200 feet. Normal visual acuity is 20/20, and **blindness** is defined as a visual acuity of 20/200 or greater in the best eye after correction. **Visual impairment** is defined as a visual acuity between 20/70 and 20/200 in the best eye after correction. It is important to note that an estimated 85% of the population diagnosed as legally blind has usable vision (Jose, 1983). Examples of common eye disorders in young children with vision impairments are presented in Table 7.4. For a more thorough discussion of these types of disorders, the reader is referred to Harrell and Akeson (1987) and Smith and Cote (1982).

TABLE 7.2
Language, Auditory, and Speech Milestones for Prelingual Infants and Toddlers

Age	Milestones
3 Months	Wakes or startles to loud sounds
	Reacts to mother's voice even when she is not visible
	Changes sucking patterns to loud sounds
	Develops differentiated cries
	Smiles
	Vocalizes vowel sounds (cooing)
	Laughs
6 Months	Turns head toward source of sound
	Vocalizations include 6–8 consonant sounds
	Makes "happy" sounds while playing or in anticipation of eating
	Shows enjoyment of musical toys
	Stops crying upon hearing mother's voice more than 50% of the time
9 Months	Reacts to salient environmental sounds
	Attempts to imitate sounds others make
	Responds to name and 2–3 familiar words (*bye-bye, no, mama*)
	Enjoys peek-a-boo
	Focuses on source of sound or speech
	Increases number of speech sounds
	Reacts to voice tones (angry, friendly, happy)
12 Months	Uses at least three words consistently and with meaning
	Receptively identifies familiar objects
	Uses inflection to ask a question
	Uses appropriate voice tone to convey emotion
	Uses jargon (string of sounds with correct intonation and rhythm of speech)
	Vocalizes (without crying) to gain attention
18 Months	Repeats two-word strings
	Points to 3–5 body parts after verbal request
	Participates in vocal games (peek-a-boo, so big) without gestural cues
2 Years	Follows simple verbal commands (3–5 words)
	Points to objects or pictures on request
	Refers to self by name
	Uses 2–5 word sentences
	Says short nursery rhymes or sings short songs
	Has a vocabulary of 50–100 words (minimum)

TABLE 7.3
Visually Related Tasks in Developmental Sequence

Age	Visual Tasks
0–1 month	Pupillary response to light Visually fixates on near objects Prefers to look at contours, simple patterns
1–3 months	Tracks moving objects to midline Tracks moving objects past midline Shifts gaze between two objects Moves eyes together Tracks objects vertically Begins to look within designs
4–12 months	Visually fixates on objects at 3 feet Reaches for and grasps objects Imitates facial expressions, gestures Has color vision Discriminates forms
1–3 years	Marks and scribbles with crayon Points to pictures Finds objects hidden—invisible displacement Matches shapes
3–5 years	Copies shapes Names colors

Source: Adapted from *Preschool Vision Stimulation: It's More than a Flashlight*, by Lois Harrell and Nancy Akeson, 1987, New York: American Foundation for the Blind. Copyright 1987 by American Foundation for the Blind.

Prevalence of Vision Disorders

Individuals with handicaps are at a greater risk for vision impairments than the general population. It is estimated that 50–90% of individuals with cerebral palsy have some type of vision impairment, particularly those with spasticity; more than 33% of individuals with hydrocephaly have vision disorders; individuals with Down syndrome are likely to have refractive errors, strabismus, or astigmatisms; and children with mental retardation are at greater risk for vision impairments than other children (Ellis, 1986; Warburg, 1986). Premature infants and infants of low birthweight (less than 1500 g) also are at a high risk of vision impairments. The types of vision impairments found to occur more frequently in these populations include retrolental fibroplasia (RLF), amblyopia, diabetic retinopathy, and strabismus (Morse

& Trief, 1985). RLF is damage to the retina resulting from excessive oxygen administered to premature infants (Langley, 1980). Morse and Trief (1985) indicated a recent increase in the incidence of RLF due to the improved survival rate of low birthweight infants. Other high-risk factors for vision impairments are medical complications at birth, infections during pregnancy (e.g., syphilis, toxoplasmosis, and rubella), and history of visual impairments in the family (Baird & Hemming, 1982; Morse & Trief, 1985). Certain medications, such as phenobarbital or dilantin, can affect visual performance. The types of side effects include increased sensitivity to light, limited vision, abnormal pupillary responses, and nystagmus (Baird & Hemming, 1982).

Children within any of the high-risk groups should be screened periodically for vision impairments. Warburg (1986) suggested that

TABLE 7.4
Types of Vision Disorders

Type	Description
Cataracts	Opaque or cloudy lens that may reduce visual acuity and visual field
Cortical blindness	Eye appears normal, but the part of the brain responsible for visual function is damaged
Nystagmus	Involuntary, rapid movement of the eye
Refractive errors	Light rays are not focused on the retina, resulting in blurred vision; includes astigmatisms, myopia, and hyperopia
Strabismus	Misalignment of the eyes, caused by muscle imbalance

the most common cause of low vision in individuals with mental retardation is the lack of prescribed spectacles. Visual deprivation early in life may lead to permanent visual loss (Fellows, Leguire, Rogers, & Bremer, 1986). Disorders such as strabismus and amblyopia can be corrected if detected and treated at an early age, otherwise irreversible damage may result (Morse & Trief, 1985). Additionally, visual efficiency can be improved with systematic visual training (Barraga & Morris, 1980).

Clinical Assessment of Vision

Clinical assessment of vision is conducted by an ophthalmologist or optometrist. An **ophthalmologist** is a medical doctor who specializes in the diagnosis and medical treatment of eye disorders. An **optometrist** detects eye diseases, prescribes corrective lenses, and evaluates vision. The visual evaluation may include measures of near and distant visual acuity, field of vision, color vision, binocularity, and refraction (Jose, 1983).

Visual Acuity. Assessment of visual acuity for older children and adults requires the ability to name the letters on a standard (Snellen) eye chart. For preschool children, acuity instruments have been designed that require the ability to name or match symbols. Among

these are the *Flash-Card Vision Test* (New York Association for the Blind, 1966) and the *Stycar Vision Tests* (Sheridan, 1973). The Flash-Card Vision Test requires children to identify or match an apple, house, and umbrella. The Stycar Vision Tests include the miniature toy test, which consists of familiar toys to be identified or matched (Fewell, 1983).

Infants and young children frequently are unable to perform the responses required for adminisration of eye charts or matching activities. Therefore, procedures such as preferential looking, forced-choice preferential looking, and visual evoked potential can be used to evaluate their visual acuity (Morse & Trief, 1985; Atkinson, 1986). Research has demonstrated that infants prefer to look at patterned rather than nonpatterned designs. The **preferential looking procedure** involves presenting pairs of screens, one with a striped pattern and the other with no pattern. The patterns are graduated according to width of the stripe. As each pair is presented, the duration of the infant's gaze is recorded for each trial. A visual acuity threshold is determined when children show no preference for either screen, indicating that no difference is perceived. The width of the stripes at this point indicates the visual acuity measure. An illustration depicting this procedure is presented in Figure 7.3. With the forced-

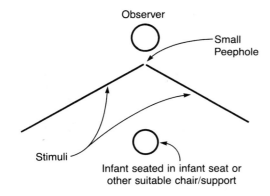

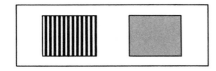

Stimulus with a series of black and white stripes   Solid gray stimulus

FIGURE 7.3
Bird's-Eye View of the Forced-Choice Preferential Looking Procedure (top); Example of the Stimuli That Children Would See (bottom)

choice preferential looking procedure, the observer frequently does not know which screen is patterned. Preferential looking also has been used to measure the acuity of toddlers and preschoolers (Atkinson, 1986; Morse & Trief, 1985).

Visually evoked potential is a procedure that indicates the presence or absence of electrical activity in the part of the brain that receives visual information, the occipital cortex. This procedure can be used to determine visual acuity levels but requires specialized personnel and technical equipment (Atkinson, 1986; Morse & Trief, 1985).

Measures of visual acuity may be used for diagnosis (e.g., blindness), to determine

eligibility for specific services, to identify a need for further visual evaluation, and to determine some of the information needed for treatment such as corrective lenses or surgery. For educational intervention, it provides information concerning the distance at which children can see certain sizes of objects (Jose, Smith, & Shane, 1980). Because visual acuity may differ according to the distance at which an item is presented, measurement should include near vision and distance vision, approximately 14 inches and 20 feet (Harley & Lawrence, 1977). It is important to note that a visual acuity measure of 20/400 is normal for a newborn.

Refraction. **Refraction** is the ability of the eyes to bend light rays; that is, the focusing power. An eye with normal refractive ability bends light rays so that an image is focused on the retina at the back of the eye. An eye with abnormal refractive ability may cause an image to focus in front of or behind the retina, resulting in blurred and distorted vision. Treatment for refractive errors may consist of prescriptive lenses (Harley & Lawrence, 1977).

Binocularity. The ability of the eyes to work together is **binocularity.** Evaluation of binocularity consists of observing the eye movements during certain tasks. Atkinson (1986) reported that binocular visual evoked potentials may be used with infants over age 3 months. If children are not using both eyes together, **strabismus** might be present. Surgery and/or vision training may be used to correct this disorder if detected and treated by age 9 (Smith & Cote, 1982).

Field of Vision. The range of vision that is possible when the eyes are fixed on a target is the **visual field.** Specific eye conditions, such as tunnel vision, may restrict visual fields. An individual with tunnel vision has a visual field that is limited to central vision only. A child's field of vision may be indicated on the eye

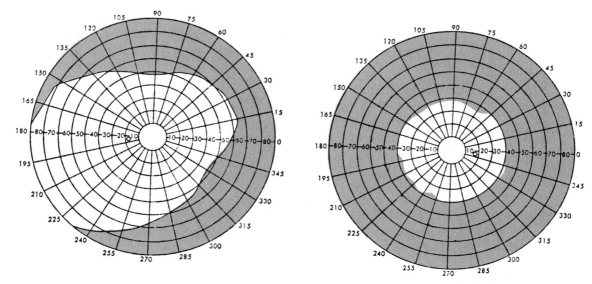

FIGURE 7.4
Normal and Abnormal Fields of Vision
The illustration on the left indicates a normal field of vision for the left eye. The illustration on the right indicates a restricted field of vision that is limited to central vision only.

report with a diagram such as the one in Figure 7.4 where an example of normal and abnormal field of vision is provided.

Color Vision.   Because many preschool educational materials rely on a child's ability to discriminate colors, evaluation of **color vision** is important. This evaluation is done through matching, sorting, or identification activities (Hritcko, 1983).

The clinical eye report should provide the child's diagnosis, near and distant visual acuity, field of vision, color vision, and recommendations for intervention. To aid in acquiring more information concerning implications of children's visual loss, a list of sample questions to ask the vision specialist is presented in Table 7.5.

Nonclinical Assessment of Vision
Nonclinical assessment of vision can be conducted by educational interventionists and in-cludes vision screening and functional vision assessment. Vision screening is conducted to identify children who should be referred to a vision specialist. **Functional vision assessment** is conducted to evaluate children's use of vision with everyday activities (Hritcko, 1983).

Vision Screening. Schools routinely may screen children's vision on an annual basis with tests of visual acuity, such as the Snellen chart. Vision screening of children within any of the high-risk groups for vision impairments should occur more frequently, perhaps twice per year. Harley and Lawrence (1977) suggested that the identification of children with vision disorders should include four components. These are (a) periodic administration of a screening test; (b) ongoing observation for behavioral and physical indicators of a visual problem; (c) referral to vision specialists when a vision disorder is suspected; and (d) integration of recommendations into the child's individualized program.

TABLE 7.5
Questions Interventionists Should Ask the Vision Specialist

1. What is the child's diagnosis?
2. What is the cause of the vision problem?
3. Is the condition stable? Will it deteriorate? Will it improve?
4. Are there any other problems associated with the vision problem to be aware of?
5. Are there any particular behaviors that would indicate a need to contact a vision specialist?
6. What can the child see?
7. What type of lighting is best for this child?
8. Are there any restrictions on activity?
9. How frequently should the child see the vision specialist?

Source: Adapted from *Preschool Vision Stimulation: It's More than a Flashlight,* by Lois Harrell and Nancy Akeson, 1987, New York: American Foundation for the Blind. Copyright 1987 by American Foundation for the Blind.

Two types of instruments for screening vision in infants and young children with handicaps are available. The first type provides a measure of the individual's visual acuity. Tests that can be used to screen the visual acuity of infants and young children with handicaps include the *Teller Visual Acuity Cards* (Vistech Consultants, 1986), *Home Eye Test* (Boyce, 1973), *Stycar Vision Tests* (Sheridan, 1973), *Flash-Card Vision Test for Children* (New York Association for the Blind, 1966), and the *Parsons Visual Acuity Test* (Cress, Spellman, DeBriere, Sizemore, Northam, & Johnson, 1981). The second type provides a quick review of the child's functional vision abilities. A test for screening functional vision is included in the *Functional Vision Inventory* (Langley, 1980).

Screening Visual Acuity. The *Teller Visual Acuity Cards* (Vistech Consultants, 1986) consist of 16 cards that are used to measure visual acuity using the preferential looking procedure. These cards consist of one white card and 15 cards with vertical black stripes that are ordered by the width of the stripe. Visual acuity norms for birth to 36 months and suggestions for testing infants, preschoolers, and individuals with handicaps are provided.

The *Home Eye Test* (Boyce, 1973) consists of an E-chart. The child must indicate which direction the *E* is pointing for occurrences of the letter from large to small. This test is designed for preschoolers and has been described as reliable, inexpensive, and simple to administer (Fewell, 1983; Harley & Lawrence, 1977).

The *Stycar Vision Tests* (Sheridan, 1973) and the *Flash-Card Vision Test for Children* (New York Association for the Blind, 1966) were designed for young children with handicaps (Langley, 1980). The Stycar includes the miniature toys test and the rolling balls test. For the miniature toys test, the child identifies or matches toys that are 2–5 inches high presented from about 10 feet. The rolling balls test consists of balls that are ordered by size. The child is requested to retrieve the ball as it is rolled horizontally across the child's vision. The *Flash-Card Vision Test* consists of 12 cards in which the child must match or identify a house, apple, or umbrella. The flashcards are presented from a distance of 10 feet.

The *Parsons Visual Acuity Test* (PVAT) was designed for children whose response is limited to points, eye gazes, or yes/no responses (Cress et al., 1981). The PVAT includes a pretraining program that uses an errorless training (stimulus shaping/fading) procedure for teaching discriminations. The PVAT test materials consist of a set of cards in which pictures of a bird, cake, and hand are presented for the child to discriminate.

Screening Functional Vision.   The *Functional Vision Inventory for the Multiple and Severely Handicapped* (Langley, 1980) includes the *Functional Vision Screening Test.* The presence or absence of behaviors such as reflexive reactions, fixation, shifting gaze, and visual tracking are determined. The results from scoring are used to determine whether a more comprehensive evaluation of functional vision is warranted. Baird and Hemming (1982) provided a description of materials found useful for screening functional vision of infants. For example, vertical tracking can be assessed with the use of a red ball attached by an elastic string on a ping-pong paddle.

In addition, interventionists should employ direct observation when screening visual skills. Information acquired through such observations can be useful in making a referral for additional assessment. Indicators of possible vision problems are provided in Table 7.6. It should be noted that the presence of some of the behaviors in any one child may not indicate a need for referral. The child's developmental level must be taken into con-

sideration. However, the persistence of any of these behaviors provides justification for referral to a vision specialist.

Assessing Functional Vision.   Prior to conducting a functional vision assessment, several types of information should be consulted. First, if clinical reports of the child's visual status are available, they should be obtained for review to determine the child's diagnosis, prescription, and prognosis. However, these reports should be read with caution for children's functional visual performance may not always coincide with clinical visual performance. For example, the clinician may not have recognized a child's reactions to visual stimuli because those responses were subtle. Second, the parent should be interviewed and invited to participate in the assessment. Information to be obtained during the interview should include behaviors that parents have noticed that may indicate specific visual strengths or weaknesses, whether the child is on medication, and any special cautions (e.g., child has seizures when flashing light is presented). Third, children's developmental level should be considered, because the developmental level may be correlated to levels of visual functioning. For example, a child may be able to track an object visually to midline but not past midline. This may be due to the child's overall developmen-

TABLE 7.6
Indicators of Possible Vision Problems

Physical Symptoms	Behavioral Indicators
Frequently tearing eyes	Does not move eyes together
Rapid, involuntary eye movements	Tilts head when viewing an object
Crusty eyelids	Bumps into objects when moving
No pupillary response to light	Holds objects close to eyes for visual examination
No blink reflex	
Reddened eyes or lids	Does not respond to familiar faces
	Does not reach directly for objects
	Squints eyes frequently
	Visually scans or tracks by moving head

tal level and not be indicative of a vision deficiency. Because an accurate assessment of
functional vision requires that children be in
an alert state, several observation sessions
may be needed. Selection of visual materials,
optimal positions, and environmental conditions should be considered to facilitate best
responses.

Selection and use of *materials* is a critical
consideration when conducting functional vision assessments. Types and degrees of vision
loss will vary among children, so a range of
visual materials should be presented systematically. For some children with visual
handicaps, the clearest visual response may
be to a fluorescent object under a blacklight.
This provides a high contrast and eliminates
other visual distractions. To guide selection
of a range of visual materials, Goodrich and
Kinney (1985) identified six dimensions of
visual materials that are presented in Table
7.7.

Proper *positioning* during a functional vision assessment is important, particularly for
infants and children with motor involvement.
Infants tend to be more alert when positioned
upright. If the infant or young child does not
separate easily from his parents, Baird and
Hemming (1982) recommend that the parent
hold the child over her shoulder during the
assessment activities. For children with
motor impairments, consultation with a
physical therapist is advised. During the

assessment, the child's head should be in normal alignment with the rest of the body.
Children with a high frequency of reflexive
movements may perform best while lying on
their sides (Baird & Hemming, 1982). However, the best position must be determined
individually and may require experimenting
with different positions.

Consideration should be given to several
environmental variables when conducting
functional vision assessments. Lighting conditions should be analyzed; certain conditions
such as dull lighting, glare from windows, or
lights that are too bright may interfere with
children's visual performance. In addition, as
much of the assessment as possible should be
conducted in the context of everyday activities. For example, children can be observed
during snacks and mealtimes, outdoor play,
and fine motor tasks.

When conducting functional vision assessments, children's *behavioral state* (see
Chapter 10) and the *behaviors* they exhibit
should be observed carefully and noted.
Children with limited motor ability or with
severe cognitive delays may react to visual
materials with behaviors that are very subtle. These behaviors include eye widening,
body movement, startles, and cessation of activity. Observation of the child for a minimum
of 15 seconds prior to presenting the stimulus
may be necessary to note any behavioral
changes (Goodrich & Kinney, 1985).

TABLE 7.7
Dimensions of Visual Materials

Dimensions	Examples
High contrast	Yellow on black; red on white
Reflective	Mirrors, foil
Illuminated	Illumination by blacklight, tensor lamp
Lighted	Flashlight with colored-disk penlight
Size	4-inch cube → beach ball
Motion	Wind-up mobiles; spinning tops

Source: Adapted from *Adaptips: Adapting curricula for students who are deaf-blind and
function in the sensorimotor developmental stage* (p. 199) by J. Goodrich and P. Kinney, 1985,
Lexington, KY: University of Kentucky. Copyright 1985 by University of Kentucky (ERIC Document Reproduction Service No. ED 276 225).

During administration of the functional vision assessment, the presence or absence of each behavior should be recorded as well as the room illumination, visual quality of objects used (e.g., color, size), distance of object, and child's position (Jose et al., 1980). For most items, the child should be given at least three different opportunities to respond. Materials should be varied to avoid satiation. It is important to observe and note how the child approaches visual tasks. For example, does the child reach directly for objects or does she reach over the object? Does the child use both eyes or turn his head to use the left eye?

The types of visually related behaviors that should be included in the functional vision assessment are eye movements, gross and fine motor skills, near and distant vision, visual field, and visual perception. Many of these behaviors are within the domains covered by early childhood developmental assessments. An analysis of those behaviors that are visually related within each developmental area (e.g., motor, communication) may provide a basis for selection of items for assessment and intervention. Categories of visual skills and examples of behaviors are provided in Table 7.8.

A few resources for functional vision assessment and intervention planning are available. The *Functional Vision Inventory for the Multiple and Severely Handicapped* (Langley, 1980) is a comprehensive measure for assessing the vision of children who are developmentally young. Seven areas of vision assessment are evaluated, which include (a) structural defects/behavioral abnormalities; (b) reflexive reactions; (c) eye movements; (d) near vision; (e) distance vision; (f) visual field preference; and (g) visual perception. Guidelines for vision intervention are provided as well as strategies to improve visual functioning. The *Program to Develop Efficiency in Visual Functioning* (Barraga & Morris, 1980) includes an assessment of vision with an emphasis on visual perceptual skills. A curriculum for training visual efficiency is included, which consists of 150 lessons in eight areas. Another functional vision inventory with vision stimulation activities for developmentally young children is included in *Look at Me* (Smith & Cote, 1982).

A critical task after an assessment is the analysis of the information gathered to be translated into goals for intervention. The summary from a vision assessment may include the findings and recommendations from the clinical assessment; identification of best materials, best presentation distance and field restrictions; optimal positions, environmental conditions for vision training intervention; and identification of priorities for vision programming.

TABLE 7.8
Functional Assessment of Vision: Examples of Categories and Behaviors

Category	Behaviors
Eye movements	Tracks objects Shifts gaze between two objects Moves eyes together
Near vision	Reaches for objects presented at 16 inches
Distance vision	Reaches for objects presented beyond 16 inches Points to and names objects at 3 feet
Visual field	Looks or reaches for objects presented at midline, to the right, left, top, and bottom Walks without bumping into objects
Visual perception	Reaches directly for objects Matches, names colors, shapes, photos Copies shapes, letters

SUMMARY OF KEY CONCEPTS

- The auditory and visual senses are critical ones in interacting with the physical and social world; early detection and treatment of auditory and visual impairments is a critical concern of early interventionists.

- Three types of hearing losses exist: conductive losses, sensorineural losses, and mixed losses.

- Several factors have been identified that indicate an infant should be screened for hearing impairments; infants with these risk factors should be placed on a high-risk register, and their hearing should be screened.

- Impedance audiometry can easily be conducted and indicates whether the middle ear is functioning properly.

- Several methods can be used to assess hearing function, including behavioral observation audiometry, conditioned orientation response procedures, visual reinforcement audiometry, and play audiometry; these procedures should be conducted by audiologists, but teachers can assist in their implementation.

- Teachers also should observe children to determine whether they behave as though they have hearing impairments.

- Several visual disorders exist including poor acuity, restricted field of vision, eyes not working together, and failure to see differences in colors.

- Individuals with handicapping conditions are at greater risk for visual impairments than is the general public; the greatest cause of low vision in children with handicapping conditions is the lack of appropriate corrective lenses.

- Clinical assessment of visual functioning should be conducted by an ophthalmologist or optometrist and should include an evaluation of visual acuity, refraction, binocularity, field of vision, and color vision.

- Several procedures beyond the standard Snellen eye chart can be used to assess visual acuity, including matching controlled stimuli and the preferential looking procedure.

- Teachers should participate in screening students for deficits in visual acuity using a variety of measures and can observe students for signs of visual impairments.

- Teachers should conduct functional vision assessments that indicate how children are using their vision.

- When conducting a functional vision assessment, teachers should consult reports from vision specialists, interview parents, consider the child's developmental level, carefully control the materials presented to the child, position the child properly during the assessment, attend to environmental variables such as lighting, and carefully note the child's responses to visual stimuli.

REFERENCES

Amochaev, A. (1987). The infant hearing foundation—a unique approach to hearing screening of newborns. *Seminars in Hearing, 8*(2). 165–168.

Atkinson, J. (1986). Methods of objective assessment of visual functions in subjects with limited communication skills. In D. Ellis (Ed.), *Sensory impairments in mentally handicapped people* (pp. 201–217). San Diego: College-Hill Press.

Baird, A. S. & Hemming, A. M. (1982). Neonatal vision screening. *Journal of Visual Impairment and Blindness, 76,* 182–185.

Barraga, N. C. & Morris, J. E. (1980). *Program to develop visual efficiency in visual functioning.* Louisville, KY: American Printing House for the Blind.

Boyce, V. S. (1973). The home eye test program. *Sight Saving Review, 43,* 43–48.

Clark, J. (1980). *Audiology for the school speech-language clinician.* Springfield, IL: Charles C. Thomas.

Cress, P. J., Spellman, C. R., DeBriere, T. J., Sizemore, A. C., Northam, J. K., & Johnson, J. L. (1981). Vision screening for persons with severe handicaps. *Journal of the Association for the Severely Handicapped, 6,* 41–50.

Ellis, D. (1986). The epidemiology of visual impairment in people with a mental handicap. In D. Ellis (Ed.), *Sensory impairments in mentally handicapped people* (pp. 3–34). San Diego: College-Hill Press.

Fellows, R. R., Leguire, L. E., Rogers, G. L., & Bremer, D. L. (1986). A theoretical approach to vision stimulation. *Journal of Visual Impairment and Blindness, 80,* 907–909.

Fewell, R. R. (1983). Working with sensorily impaired children. In S. G. Garwood (Ed.), *Educating young handicapped children: A developmental approach* (pp. 235–280). Rockville, MD: Aspen Systems Corporation.

Fischler, R. S., Todd, N. W., & Feldman, C. M. (1985). Otitis media and language performance in a cohort of Apache Indian children. *American Journal of Diseases of Children, 139*(4), 355–360.

Fitch, J. L., Williams, T. F., & Etienne, J. E. (1982). A community based high risk register for hearing loss. *Journal of Speech and Hearing Disorders, 47*(4), 373–375.

Garrity, J. & Mengle, H. (1983). Early identification of hearing loss: Practices and procedures. *American Annals of the Deaf, 128*(2), 99–106.

Gdowski, B. S., Sanger, D. D., & Decker, N. T. (1986). Otitis media: Effect on a child's learning. *Academic Therapy, 21*(3), 283–291.

Giebink, G. S. (1984). Epidemiology and natural history of otitis media. In D. Lim, C. Bluestone, J. Klein, & J. Nelson (Eds.), *Recent advances in otitis media with effusion* (pp. 5–8). Philadelphia: B. C. Decker.

Goodrich, J. & Kinney, P. (1985). *Adaptips: Adapting curricula for students who are deaf-blind and function in the sensorimotor developmental stage.* Lexington, KY: University of Kentucky. (ERIC Document Reproductive Service No. ED 276 225)

Harley, R. K. & Lawrence, G. A. (1977). *Visual impairment in the schools.* Springfield, IL: Charles C. Thomas.

Harrell, L. & Akeson, N. (1987). *Preschool vision stimulation: It's more than a flashlight.* New York: American Foundation for the Blind.

Hasenstab, M. & Horner, J. (1982). *Comprehensive intervention with hearing-impaired infants and preschool children.* Rockville, MD: Aspen Systems Corporation.

Hritcko, T. (1983). Assessment of children with low vision. In R. T. Jose (Ed.), *Understanding low vision* (pp. 105–137). New York: American Foundation for the Blind.

Jacobson, J. T. & Jacobson, C. A. (1987). Application of test performance characteristics in newborn auditory screening. *Seminars in Hearing, 8*(2), 133–141.

Jacobson, J. T. & Morehouse, C. R. (1984). A comparison of auditory brainstem response and behavioral screening in high-risk and normal newborn infants. *Ear and Hearing, 5,* 247–253.

Jose, R. T. (1983). The eye and functional vision. In R. T. Jose (Ed.), *Understanding low vision* (pp. 2–42). New York: American Foundation for the Blind.

Jose, R. T., Smith, A. J., & Shane, K. G. (1980). Evaluating and stimulating vision in the multiply impaired. *Journal of Visual Impairment and Blindness, 74,* 2–8.

Klein, J. O. (1986). Risk factors for otitis media in children. In J. Kavanagh (Ed.), *Otitis media and child development* (pp. 45–51). Parkton, MD: York Press.

Langley, B. (1980). *Functional vision inventory for the multiple and severely handicapped.* Chicago: Stoelting Co.

Lockman, J. L. (1983). Infant perception and cognition. In S. G. Garwood & R. R. Fewell (Eds.), *Educating handicapped infants* (pp. 117–164). Rockville, MD: Aspen Systems Corporation.

Mahoney, T. M. & Eichwald, J. G. (1987). The ups and "Downs" of high-risk hearing screening: The Utah statewide program. *Seminars in Hearing, 8*(2), 155–163.

McFarland, W. H., Simmons, F. B., & Jones, F. R. (1980). An automated hearing screening technique for newborns. *Journal of Speech and Hearing Disorders, 45,* 495–502.

Mischook, M. & Cole, E. (1986). Auditory learning and teaching of hearing impaired infants. In E. Cole and H. Gregory (Eds.), *Auditory learning. Volta Review Monogragh, 88*(5), 67–82.

Morse, A. R. & Trief, E. (1985). Diagnosis and evaluation of visual dysfunction in premature infants with low birth weight. *Journal of Visual Impairment and Blindness, 79,* 248–251

New York Association for the Blind. (1966). *A flashcard vision test for children.* New York: Author.

Pappas, D. (1985). *Diagnosis and treatment of hearing impairment in children: A clinical manual.* San Diego: College-Hill Press.

Paradise, J. L. & Rogers, K. D. (1986). On otitis media, child development, tympanostomy tubes: New answers or old questions? *Pediatrics, 77*(1), 88–92.

Pollack, D. (1985). *Educational audiology for the limited-hearing infant and preschooler* (2nd ed.). Springfield, IL: Charles C. Thomas.

Pukander, J., Sipila, M., & Karma, P. (1984). Occurrence of and risk factors in acute otitis media. In D. Lim, C. Bluestone, J. Klein, & J. Nelson (Eds.), *Recent advances in otitis media with effusion* (pp. 9–12). Philadelphia: B. C. Decker.

Roberts, J. E., Sanya, M. A., Burchinal, M. R., Collier, A. M., Ramey, C. T., & Hendersen, F. W. (1986). Otitis media in early childhood and its relationship to later verbal and academic performance. *Pediatrics, 78*(3), 423–430.

Roeser, R. & Northern, J. (1981). Screening for hearing loss and middle ear disorders. In R. Roeser and M. Downs (Eds.), *Auditory disorders in school children* (pp. 120–150). New York: Thieme-Stratton.

Roeser, R. & Price, D. (1981). Audiometric and impedance measures: Principles and interpretation. In R. Roeser & M. Downs (Eds.), *Auditory disorders in school children* (pp. 71–101). New York: Thieme-Stratton.

Sak, R. & Ruben, R. (1981). Recurrent middle ear effusion in childhood: Implications of temporary auditory deprivation for language and learning. *Annals of Otology, Rhinology, and Laryngology, 90,* 546–551.

Sheridan, M. D. (1973). *Manual for the Stycar Vision Tests.* Windsor, Ontario: NFER Publishing Co.

Silva, P. A., Kirkland, C., Simpson, A., Stewart, I. A., & Williams, S. M. (1982). Some developmental and behavioral problems associated with bilateral otitis media with effusion. *Journal of Learning Disabilities, 15*(7), 417–421.

Smith, A. J. & Cote, K. S. (1982). *Look at me: A resource manual for the development of residual vision in multiply impaired children.* Philadelphia: Pennsylvania College of Optometry Press.

Stewart, I., Kirkland, C., Simpson, A., Silva, P., & Williams, S. (1984). Some developmental characteristics associated with otitis media with effusion. In D. Lim, C. Bluestone, J. Klein, & J. Nelson (Eds.), *Recent advances in otitis media with effusion.* Philadelphia: B. C. Decker.

Todd, N. W. (1986). High risk factors for otitis media. In J. Kavanagh (Ed.), *Otitis media and child development* (pp. 52–59). Parkton, MD: York Press.

Vistech Consultants. (1986). *Teller acuity cards handbook.* Dayton, OH: Author.

Warburg, M. (1986). Medical and ophthalmological aspects of visual impairment in mentally handicapped people. In D. Ellis (Ed.), *Sensory impairments in mentally handicapped people* (pp. 93–114). San Diego: College-Hill Press.

Zinkus, P. & Gottlieb, M. (1980). Patterns of perceptual and academic deficits related to early chronic otitis media. *Pediatrics, 66*(2), 246–253.

Neurobehavioral Assessment of the Newborn Infant

Karen J. O'Donnell
Jerri M. Oehler
Duke University Medical Center

KEY TERMS

- Neurobehavioral Assessment
- Neonatal Intensive Care Unit (NICU)
- Stress
- Support
- Behavioral Organization
- Temperament
- Neurological Reflexes

- Autonomic Stability
- Motor Status
- State Organization
- Attention
- Caregiving Context
- Developmental Milestones
- Behavioral Subsystems
- Self-regulation

- Synactive Model
- Irritability
- Sensory Thresholds
- Neonatology
- Naturalistic Observation
- Gestational Age
- Habituation
- Consolability

The assessment of the newborn infant is a relatively new area of interest for the early childhood special educator. It presents a body of knowledge, clinical challenges, and intervention implications that may be unfamiliar. Indeed, the major constructs and measurement strategies used in the newborn neurobehavioral assessment have their roots in developmental neurology and pediatrics, not in education. On the other hand, assessment of the developmental status and needs of the young infant is relevant to early educa-tional intervention and to educational outcomes. Both research with medically high-risk infants (such as very low birthweight infants) and federal legislation mandating the early education of special-needs infants, toddlers, and their families emphasize that relevance. Early childhood and special education training programs have begun to address this area, challenging many of the existing boundaries around education, psychology, and medicine. Certainly, the infant who is at high risk for mental retardation or central nervous system

(CNS) dysfunction warrants our coordinated effort.

This chapter describes the history and current status of a rapidly developing area, the behavioral assessment of the human neonate. It is written for educators in early intervention who may be consumers of test information from the neonatal period and for those who may, subsequently, obtain further training and work in neonatal settings. Primarily, this chapter serves as a broad introduction for the individual new to the major constructs and strategies involved in assessing a newborn. Of course, entire textbooks and courses are available and necessary for training in this area.

A secondary goal of the chapter is to place neonatal assessment in its historical and contemporary context. In this respect, the chapter is different from others in this book. Newborn assessment is seen as a highly specialized area and not simply a downward extension of preschool and school-aged educational testing. For that reason, more attention is given to medical and psychological origins, suggesting that only with the integration of these aspects of the young infant's functioning with behavioral assessment and with their application to educational strategies is very early intervention feasible.

The chapter is organized into six sections. A rationale for and various approaches to evaluating the newborn are introduced, and the historical roots of current assessment strategies are reviewed. The dimensions important in evaluating newborns are addressed: the infant's status and aspects of the physical and social environment. Procedural guidelines for good clinical practice in the assessment of the newborn infant are described, including the needed prerequisites in training and experiences in newborn settings. Brief descriptions of the more commonly used newborn assessments are included. Various approaches to translating assessment data into interventions for the infant and family are outlined.

Rationale

Consider the following infants for whom **neurobehavioral assessment** (the assessment of the behavioral and developmental status of the newborn as it relates to the maturity and integrity of the central nervous system) might be recommended. Baby Boy Brown is in an isolette in the **neonatal intensive care unit** (NICU) of the hospital. At present, he is at 37 weeks post conception, having been born at 32 weeks of gestation. The infant is recovering from the respiratory illness that often occurs in premature infants. Presently he is doing well, feeding from a nipple, and not receiving supplemental oxygen. After two days of adjusting to an open crib in the nursery, discharge home is planned. As a developmental specialist in the nursery, you may be asked to evaluate Baby Brown and to provide information about him to his physicians, his parents, and to the community early intervention program. Primary questions for the assessment include his current behavioral and developmental status, needs for follow-up assessments, and specific needs for caregiver interventions that support further recovery and optimal developmental outcome. How would you go about this? Or, if you were the educational specialist in the early intervention program, how would you utilize the information provided by the developmental specialist?

Baby Girl Lucas, on the other hand, is the full-term newborn daughter of a young girl in the alternative high school program for teenaged parents. Baby Lucas and her mother are preparing to go home from the hospital to the mother's parents' home. The mother's teachers have been concerned about her interest in the infant and about her hints that she is afraid to care for the baby. The mother and infant have been referred to your early intervention program, and you would like to use newborn assessment techniques as an intervention to demonstrate to the mother her infant's behavioral capabilities. Your goal is that this mother see her daughter as a unique person and to facilitate the mother's awareness of the infant's needs and her ability to respond to them. What are some of the dimensions of the infant's behavior that can be observed and used in the intervention?

Baby Boy Mitchell is also in the NICU. At 30 weeks post conception, he still requires supplemental oxygen delivered by mechanical ventilation. His medical caregivers are concerned because he is so restless and irritable that adequate mechanical ventilation is very difficult. As a clinician trained in the behaviorial assessment of the newborn, you are in a position to evaluate this infant to assist his nurses and physicians with strategies for calming him and for providing environmental support for improved respiratory functioning. What can you observe about this infant's behavior that provides information about his responses to **stress** and what he needs for **support**? How can you do so without additional handling of this fragile infant?

These infants represent three instances in which a child-development professional might evaluate a newborn infant or be in a position to use information from a behavioral assessment for intervening with the child, the family, or community services. In fact, the three assessments likely will have much in common; they will address the infants' neurological integrity, **behavioral organization** and needs, and individual personalities or **temperament.** The assessments also will differ substantially. The infants are at different ages with different medical conditions, and the nature of the information requested for each is different.

As is implied in the three examples, particularly in the instance of Baby Lucas, the newborn infant can be assessed to describe the individuality of the infant and/or to evaluate the infant's contribution to the critical beginnings of relationships with caregivers. The assessment can provide the basis for intervention with the caregiving system before patterns of behavior, expectations, and attributions are well established.

In this way, the assessment can be used to enhance the parent's understanding of the infant as an individual and to underline their mutual influences.

As in the case of Baby Brown, neonatal assessment also is used to provide an index of neurological integrity and developmental status. It can be used to determine needs for follow-up assessments or intervention programs and to provide a baseline from which to assess behavioral recovery from a biomedical event or condition (e.g., birth asphyxia, very low birthweight). For Baby Mitchell, newborn assessment strategies can be employed to determine the infant's current needs from the environment (e.g., "How, when, how much to touch fragile preterm infants," Gorski, 1984) and to design a physical and social environment supportive of the developing central nervous system and recovery from illness. Newborn infants also are systematically evaluated to research the effects of a specific biomedical event or process on behavioral organization and developmental level or to evaluate the effects of medical or environmental intervention strategies. In other words, there is a wide range of reasons to assess a newborn infant and more than one approach to the task.

An understanding of the historical context of neonatal assessment is considered critical to the use and application of contemporary methodologies, particularly given that neonatal assessment did not develop from an educational tradition. For this reason, a review of the origins of specific components of contemporary methods of neonatal assessment are presented in some depth. Figure 8.1 depicts a preterm infant being assessed in an isolette in an NICU setting.

Historical Perspective

The assessment of the newborn infant is often associated with the Neonatal Behavioral Assessment Scale (NBAS) (Brazelton, 1973; 1984). In fact, the introduction of the NBAS

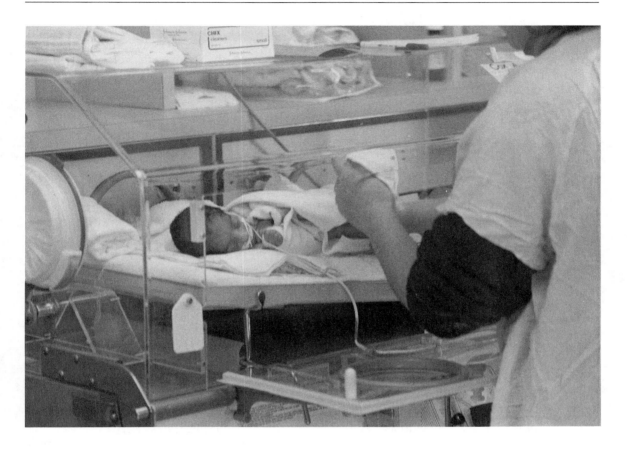

FIGURE 8.1
Preterm Infant Being Examined in an Isolette (Photograph used with permission of James M.
Helm, 1988)

marked a wave of interest in the behavioral status of the newborn for clinicians and researchers concerned with early development. The popularization of the NBAS heightened awareness of the newborn's behavioral capabilities and individual differences including but extending beyond the traditional focus on **neurological reflexes.** This heightened awareness led the way to a burgeoning of literature on early infant development, focusing on the importance of and strategies for assessment.

Trends in current assessment techniques, such as the NBAS, are readily apparent in the works of various clinicians and researchers throughout the 20th century. It is difficult to identify a single line of clinical and research efforts leading to the current state of the art, however. As pointed out in St. Clair's (1978) review of neonatal assessment, newborns have been tested from different perspectives by different disciplines, often attempting to measure different basic constructs seen as important in the behavior of the newborn. Indeed, it can be said that the currently popular assessments of the newborn (e.g., Brazelton, 1984; Als, Lester, Tronick, & Brazelton, 1982; Dubowitz & Dubowitz, 1981) involve the logical integration of disparate historical traditions. Three of these traditions are described below with emphasis on those components evident in current assessment approaches: developmental neurology, behavioral pediatrics, and developmental psychology.

Contributions from Developmental Neurology

One major component of the behavioral assessment of the newborn infant is rooted in the tradition of neurological assessment with emphasis on evaluating reflexes. The first identified reflex, the pupillary reflex, is credited to Magitat in 1903 (St. Clair, 1978), and Moro described the well-known startle reflex in 1918 (St. Clair, 1978). However, there was no comprehensive description of infant reflexes until the late 1920s. The works of several European developmental neurologists, in particular, mark the evolution of hypotheses about infant neurological development and about strategies for examining the level or integrity of the newborn's central nervous system by observing and eliciting reflex behavior. In a review of the contributions of four of these individuals—Peiper, Andre-Thomas, Saint Anne-Dargassies, and Prechtl—Parmelee (1962) outlined developmental neurology's early contributions to neonatal behavioral assessment.

Albrecht Peiper (1928) provided the first comprehensive description of reflex behavior in the human infant. This East German neurologist drew substantially from the work of Magnus (e.g., 1924), a neurologist in Holland who documented the persistent asymmetric tonic neck reflex (ATNR) (the classic fencing reflex) as well as other obligatory movement patterns in adults with brain injuries. Magnus hypothesized that the same reflexes are present in the human newborn and disappear with the development of higher brain centers.

Peiper then studied the reflex behavior of the human newborn and young infant as an index of brain development. He devised a scheme for observing the newborn's control of posture and movement, demonstrating that innate newborn postural responses disappear as the central nervous system matures. Peiper did not develop a systematic assessment for diagnosing neurological difficulties in the newborn, and he made no attempt to correlate his observations about stages of neurobehavioral development with chronological age. With Isbert (Peiper & Isbert, 1927), however, he provided a model for changes in infant posture and movement over time.

In France, Andre-Thomas and his colleagues also were studying newborn movement patterns as an index of development and as they related to the integrity of the central nervous system. This group is given credit for the first systematic neurological examination for the neonate (Andre-Thomas, Chesni, & Saint Anne-Dargassies, 1960; Saint Anne-Dargassies, 1960). Andre-Thomas's major interest was in the primary reflexes, not the postural responses that intrigued Magnus and Peiper. Andre-Thomas and his colleagues studied, in particular, the Moro reflex (the startle), the rooting reflex, automatic walking, incurvation of the spine, and the grasp reflex. They hypothesized that the primary reflexes would decrease in intensity over the first three months of life and become integrated into voluntary movement patterns.

Several of Andre-Thomas's contributions can be found in contemporary strategies used for newborn assessment. He approached the assessment of the newborn by observing spontaneous movement, eliciting reflexes, and assessing the extent to which developmentally less mature reactions were still present in movement. He compared different parts of the body in terms of movement patterns and muscle tone, introducing the concepts of active (in spontaneous movement) versus passive (when manipulated by an examiner) muscle tone and "extensibility" (i.e., degree of increased muscle tone; spasticity) versus "flaccidity" (i.e., low muscle tone; hypotonia). Also relevant to current trends in newborn assessment, Andre-Thomas's (1959) observations extended beyond posture and movement; he indicated that even newborn infant behavior is "governed by affect" and that the full-term newborn's behavior is well organized. With his student Saint Anne-Dargassies, he published two texts on neonatal neurology and assessment (Andre-Thomas & Saint Anne-Dargassies, 1952; Andre-Thomas, Chesni, & Saint Anne-Dargassies, 1960).

Saint Anne-Dargassies (1965) made several of her own contributions to the neurobehavioral assessment of the newborn. She studied the prognostic value of Andre-Thomas's assessment techniques and found fairly successful prediction of abnormal development at age 2 years. Importantly, she also examined neurobehavioral differences between preterm and full-term infants and found that the behavior of the preterm infants came closer to that of full-term infants as they approached 40 weeks post conceptional age (Saint Anne-Dargassies, 1955; 1957). From this work, she proposed a developmental scale for evaluating the preterm infant prior to term age; the exam focuses on muscle tone, primary reflexes, and the infant's general adaptive ability.

Saint Anne-Dargassies's assessment of the newborn begins with the close observation of the undisturbed infant's behavior, attending to the infant's **autonomic stability** (e.g., respiratory regularity, temperature control), **motor status** (movement and posture), and **state organization** (i.e., control over level of arousal). Examiner manipulations include testing visual responses, muscle tone, and primary reflexes. Repeated exams and the importance of the persistence of abnormal responses in indicating neurological dysfunction are emphasized. Dargassies's exam was designed specifically to differentiate brain-injured infants from non-brain-injured infants by the presence or absence of expected or abnormal responses.

Heinz Prechtl was born and trained medically in Austria and did most of his work in the Netherlands. His interest was in developing an evaluation of the newborn in order to study the effects of various obstetric conditions. Although Prechtl was trained with Konrad Lorenz (the founder of ethology; see Lorenz, 1965), his approach emphasizes more subtle aspects of movement than do his predecessor's approaches; for example, close attention to the symmetry of motor responses. Prechtl's exam (1977; Prechtl & Beintema, 1964) was first in this tradition to be well conceptualized and well standardized and to have well-defined scoring. Further, he specified the importance of the physical environment and the infant's posture and state to the infant's responses to test items.

The Prechtl and Beintema (1964) exam has two parts. The examiner first observes the infant's state of arousal, posture, movements, skin color, and respiratory regularity. Then, the exam moves to the elicitation of reflexes and to other examiner maneuvers. State is seen as very important to the infant's responses and, therefore, to the timing of examiner maneuvers. Brazelton (1973) utilized this organizing concept of state in the development of the NBAS. In 1977, a 10-minute screening version of the Prechtl exam was developed for use in clinical practice. No well-designed, specific studies of the exam's reliability and validity are reported, but examples of use of the assessment with infants with prenatal or perinatal complications versus normal infants can be found elsewhere (e.g., Prechtl, 1965 a;b).

Paine (1960; 1961) was one of the first American physicians to develop a neurological examination for infants and young children. The exam includes tests of neuromotor behavior (e.g., muscle tone, primitive reflexes, deep tendon reflexes), sensory abilities, the cranial nerves, and speech and mental state. Relevant to current neonatal assessment strategies, Paine described several methods for assessing muscle tone, including resistance to movement (similar to Brazelton's passive movement items) and muscle palpation (examining by touch).

Other neurological exams for the newborn and young infant, most notably that of Amiel-

Tison and Grenier (1983) have emerged. An increase in multidisciplinary approaches to the clinical care of infants seems to have resulted in the gradual inclusion of more behavioral test items, such as the assessment of visual responses. These neurologically based exams have in common the view that infant behavior is an index of neurological status and that the maturation of the central nervous system results in behavioral change (DiLeo, 1967).

The focus of developmental neurologists, by and large, has been the identification of gross brain dysfunction by the assessment of reflexes. Few studies tested which reflexes or responses individually or in combination were most predictive of brain damage. In many cases, the meaning of the presence or absence of a particular response is not clear, and many authors have indicated that the neurological examination does not, by itself, capture the sum of infant behavioral organization. Although there are hints of interest in the newborn's sensory capabilities and overall organizational competence, the exams are not focused in this way. No substantive attempts have been made to assess behavioral capabilities and individual differences in infant **attention,** or ability to manage and respond to social and nonsocial stimuli, and responses to social stimuli. Further, no models are suggested that include the effects of neonatal behavior on caregivers, interactions with caregivers, and the infant's own caregiving. The neurological examination, by itself, does not reflect a model of development that includes the contribution of the **caregiving context,** that is, personal qualities of the caregivers as well as aspects of the broader sociocultural context, to infant behavior and development.

Contributions from Behavioral Pediatrics
In his text, *The Development of the Infant and Young Child,* Illingworth (1960) credits Charles Darwin (1944) with the first major attempt to document the sequence of development in a child. Darwin described in detail the developmental milestones of one of his ten children, perhaps marking the beginning of significant public and scientific interest in the nature of growth and change in early childhood.

More known for his pioneering work in this area is Arnold Gesell. Gesell's work, first published in 1925, represents his several decades of observing and documenting **developmental milestones** for the first five years of life and developing a system for the diagnosis of developmental delay. Gesell's group focused initially on the first year of life (see Gesell & Thompson, 1938). Subsequently, they provided developmental schedules over the preschool years (Gesell, 1940), emphasizing the continuity between infancy and the preschool years.

Gesell's (1940) view of early development is, essentially, a maturational one: "The environment inflects preliminary patterns; it determines the occasion, the intensity, and the correlation of many aspects of behavior; but it does not engender the basic progressions of behavior development. These are determined by inherent, maturational mechanisms" (p. 13). His focus, then, was the continuity in and the age-related sequence of developmental change. When he described the individuality of the fetus and newborn, he emphasized his view that individual differences in physiological processes and behavioral functioning were the result of individual differences in the growth of the central nervous system.

Gesell's contribution to newborn assessment lies largely in the definition of steps and stages in developmental change. Gesell's norms were established on a large group of children seen monthly, beginning at age 4 weeks. The work has been expanded by his colleagues (e.g., Knobloch, Stevens, & Malone, 1980) and others (e.g., Bayley, 1969) to include markers of developmental status relevant to the newborn period as well. Developmental diagnosis in the most recent revision of the "Gesell" scales (Knobloch, Stevens, & Malone, 1980) includes observations of posture and movement (e.g., the ATNR, hands being predominantly fisted versus open, right head turning preference), visual responses to a red ring, and responses to animate (the examiner's voice) and inanimate (a rattle) auditory stimuli. The revision includes normative data on many more subjects than did the original, and these authors view the work as less maturation-based than Gesell's, stressing the social context in which developmental change occurs.

The most widely used developmental assessment and screening tools today draw heavily on the Gesell schedules, in particular The Bayley Scales of Infant Development (Bayley, 1969) and the Denver Developmental Screening Test (Frankenburg & Dodds, 1967). Current strategies for newborn assessment include this type of normative approach, especially in the examination of visual and auditory responses to animate and inanimate stimuli.

The Contribution of Developmental Psychology

Contemporary approaches to newborn assessment are seen as more complex than the mere addition of age-normed milestones to neurological assessment. It is suggested that more recent approaches reflect the evolving models for understanding human development found, primarily, in the fields of psychology and education. In several of her papers, Als (e.g., Als, Lester, Tronick, & Brazelton, 1982) traces the theoretical underpinnings of behavioral assessment from the history of developmental psychology; her work is a substantial attempt to reconcile developmental processes with the manner in which development and behavior are assessed. In general, over the past two decades views of human development have become more complex in terms of both determinants and mechanisms. The importance of the care-

giving context and the transactional nature of the infant and context relationship are emphasized (Sameroff & Chandler, 1975).

What are these contemporary views of newborn behavior and development? How are they incorporated into assessment techniques? These questions are largely beyond the scope of this chapter, and the reader is referred to Als and co-workers (1982) for a more comprehensive review of the assumptions about development implicit in current assessment techniques. Several popular assumptions about development are summarized here, however, because they are seen as central to understanding newborn behavior and being able to attach meaning to assessment findings. Three principles are identified and discussed briefly: a) development is hierarchical; b) development is dialectical; and c) development is teleological.

Development is Hierarchical. Development has order, steps or stages; there is mutual dependence from one step or stage to the others. Each step or developmental task is seen as more complex than the preceding one because it incorporates the preceding one. The hierarchical notion is well known in developmental psychology from Piaget's descriptions of stages in cognitive development (see Ginsburg & Opper, 1969).

Relevant to the newborn, Als and colleagues (1982), for example, define the infant's development as a hierarchy of tasks or as developing **behavioral subsystems** (i.e., organized, mutually dependent components of behavior) of overall organization. The developing subsystems are identified, in order, as physiological stability and autonomic control; freedom and control in movement; differentiation of and control over states of arousal; social interactive competence through attention and response to social stimuli; and **self-regulation,** that is, the ability to manage complex environmental demands with minimal expense to lower subsystems.

For an infant like Baby Brown, overall

developmental status would be assessed not only by indicators of the status of individual subsystems but also by the way in which each affects the others. He may, for example, have achieved physiological stability but still be struggling to control movements in his arms and legs when placed on his back. Incomplete development in the motor area, then, may compromise the development of well-defined states of arousal and responses to social stimuli.

Development is Dialectical.   Sameroff (1983) offers one of the best descriptions of the dialectic in development. In brief, this principle assumes that, at each developmental step or stage and with each developmental task, the achievement and its integration into overall functioning is subject to the relationship between the infant and the context or environment in which development occurs. Descriptions of the dialectic in development can be found at the level of the cell (e.g., Palay, 1979, cf. Als et al., 1982) and at the level of the family or community (e.g., O'Donnell, 1986). The assumption involves more than a simple interaction; the infant and the physical and social context are seen in mutual, ongoing transactions, each contributing to change in the other and to itself through the transaction.

This view of development suggests a different meaning for the assessment of the newborn than did that of Gesell, for example, who viewed test responses as reflecting maturation or the interruption of maturation by brain damage. In contrast, Als's **synactive model** (e.g., Als, 1986) incorporates the assumption of a hierarchy of subsystem development with the notion that the subsystems develop through transactions with one another and with the environment. In other words, newborns bring behavior patterns to their experiences, affecting those experiences, which, in turn, influence the infant's behavior patterns.

Baby Lucas and her mother offer a good example of the dialectic principle, that is, that

the behavior of each is shaped by the other in an ongoing manner. If the infant should begin her life as an active, difficult to console infant, the mother's low self-confidence might be reinforced. If she then feels helpless in calming her infant and withdraws, the infant is deprived of the environmental support that would help improve her overall behavioral organization. The infant may become even more disorganized and unresponsive, further exacerbating the young mother's despair and withdrawal.

Development is Teleological.   Teleology is the view that developmental changes are guided not only by mechanical forces but by movement toward certain goals. It is suggested that the view of the human infant as developing in a hierarchical and dialectical manner carries with it the notion of direction. Infant development is seen as progressing from diffuse, general functioning to the differentiation of specialized components of behavior to an organization of these components into a system that functions as a whole. Teleological assumptions are not new to newborn development and assessment. Werner (1957), for example, indicated that all development moves from globality to increased differentiation and hierarchical integration. The principle is particularly helpful in newborn assessment, however, in developing a model for the infant's current status and needs for future developmental progress.

Baby Mitchell, the very young sick infant mentioned previously, may be so vulnerable to the stimulation in the nursery because of his "all or nothing" responses to touch, light, or sound. In other words, stress for this infant may result in decreased physiological stability, motor disorganization, and **irritability.** As he recovers and matures and with the help of a supportive caregiving environment, we expect that these subsystems of behavior will become increasingly differentiated from one another and, subsequently, contribute to controlled and organized behavioral responses.

In summary, these three assumptions underpin many of the current techniques for the assessment of the newborn. Assessment is seen as an opportunity for the examiner and the infant to act out the dialectic between the infant and the caregiving context. Tests are constructed, using many items from traditional age-norm and neurological approaches, to elicit from the infant indicators of current functioning and individual responses to and needs from the environment. The meaning of the assessment lies in the ability to generalize beyond the assessment itself to the infant's status and needs at this time and in anticipation of future development.

Dimensions of Assessment

The domain of neonatal assessment is infant behavior. Neonatal testing makes the assumption that infant behavior is both meaningful and organized. The question of how behavior is organized has been answered in different ways; subsequently, tests were constructed to reflect different models. In the newborn neurological examinations, behavior is seen as having meaning for the integrity of the central nervous system; the presence or absence of specific reflexes and reactions indicates the presence or absence of brain damage. Therefore, evaluation studies focus on the neurological examination's prediction of a subsequent normal versus abnormal diagnosis. Similarly, assessment of the newborn and young infant on a developmental schedule is based on the assumption that behavior has meaning for the child's maturity, for whether or not the child is delayed or comparable to same-aged children in a normative group. Evaluation efforts are designed to test for continuity between performances at earlier and later dates.

Contemporary approaches to the assessment of the newborn combine test items from the neurological and age-norm approaches, but they define meaning in the in-

fant's behavior in a very different way. The infant's behavior is seen as having meaning not only about the infant but also about the physical and social context and the transactions between infant and context. Contemporary developmental theories suggest, then, that assessment should address the child, the environment, and transactions between the child and the caregiving context. Clinicians and researchers in infant assessment have been struggling with these new complexities in the assessment task, especially with test evaluation concepts like reliability and validity. Given these models, do we presume continuities in development? If development involves more than the infant's maturation, few simple continuities over time would be found.

Several commonly used instruments focus primarily on the infant's status per se; the theoretical perspective may include the importance of the context, but the assessment is directed to the infant and her behavior at a single point in time. There also are well-known examinations of the newborn that attempt to capture the dialectic between infant behavior and context. These authors and users emphasize that the infant's response is subject to the infant's biologic status, behavior organizational agenda, and support or disruption from the context. Finally, there are assessment strategies designed to evaluate the developmental context, primarily. Several dimensions of the physical and social context have been explored with the goal of identifying more or less optimal environments. The major constructs or dimensions of infant behavior and relevant aspects of the physical and social context are identified below.

Dimensions of Infant Behavior
Neonatal assessment can be seen as addressing three broad dimensions of infant behavior: neurological integrity, behavioral organization, and individual differences in temperament. These dimensions are seen as major constructs of concern to the clinician

or researcher; assessment is the task of identifying concrete or quantitative indicators of the more abstract constructs. For the most part, current neurobehavioral assessment approaches to the newborn include some indicators of each of these three major constructs.

As noted above, one of the early uses of neonatal assessment was for the identification of the brain-damaged infant. This focus is still a major area of concern, with the infant's behavior providing a view of the functioning of the central nervous system. Indicators of neurological integrity include reflexes and postural responses, skill achievement on a developmental schedule, and behavioral organization congruent with gestational age. Unfortunately, the infant's performance on any of these areas can be difficult to interpret; poor performance can represent a transient process in the brain (e.g., recovery from swelling), and good performance could mask an insult not yet evident in behavior. For this reason, it is generally recommended that repeated assessments and the construction of a curve of infant functioning over time be used (Brazelton, 1973). For example, neurobehavioral changes in an asphyxiated (lack of oxygen at birth) newborn over the first 7–14 days of life likely provide more information about prognosis than any single exam. For an infant being followed for the possibility of hydrocephalus (enlarged ventricles in the brain), changes in behavior can support other indicators of a nonoptimal process. Neurobehavioral status is only one indicator of brain injury, and these data are best combined with information about neurostructural change (from brain scanning techniques) and neurofunctional impairment (e.g., EEG, brainstem evoked-potential testing).

Beyond the concern of brain injury versus no brain injury are more complex questions about the behavioral organization of the newborn infant. The full-term, healthy newborn is seen as a competent individual with the abilities to attend and respond in social interactions as well as to influence those in-

teractions (Brazelton, 1973; 1984). This level of competence is based on well-organized and coordinated behavioral subsystems (Als et al., 1982). That is, for a newborn infant to attend to his mother's voice and reinforce her interactions with him, he must be able to maintain alertness, control arm and leg movements, continue to breathe, control his body temperature and skin color, and so on. The notion here is that difficulty on any level will affect the other levels; trouble controlling movements likely will challenge his ability to stay alert and attentive; energy expended in breathing cannot be used for functioning in other subsystems.

Als's (1986) synactive model of subsystem organization is well described elsewhere, but it is noted here to underline this significant contribution to the field of newborn assessment. From this perspective, behavioral assessment is able to address more of the complexities in behavioral organization, not just whether or not injury has occurred. In Als's model, the infant is assessed on the hierarchy of subsystems: autonomic stability, motor maturity, state organization, attention and orientation, and self-regulation. Indicators are identified for each area, and test findings address each area individually and as they affect one another. In addition, the perspective permits the examiner to view the infant and context together, seeing how functioning in each subsystem is affected by the physical and social context.

The third area of concern identified for newborn assessment is temperament. The NBAS, for example, is based on a model of the full-term newborn as a well-organized social partner. Relative strengths and weaknesses in subsystem organization may underpin behavioral differences, and one original intent of the assessment was to identify individual constitutional differences (Brazelton, 1973; 1984) and to appraise the way in which these differences influence caregivers. One goal of assessing individual differences in newborns as social partners is to facilitate intervention with caregivers and infants, if needed, before dysfunctional patterns of interaction become established. The assessment can be used to describe the newborn's individuality to a parent and to emphasize their mutual effects. Neurobehavioral assessment, in particular the NBAS, has often been used as an intervention for parents, designed to support the attachment process. Baby Lucas's mother could learn that she did not cause her infant's irritability and that she can help her baby to become calm.

Dimensions of the Infant's Caregiving Context. If newborn assessment strategies are to reflect the theoretical notions about the dialectic between the infant and the caregiving context, an important area of concern is the nature of that context, how it affects and is affected by the infant. Specifically, two dimensions of the context relevant to the assessment and understanding of newborn behavior are the physical environment and the social environment. Assessment strategies for the hospital environment, the home, and the parent/infant relationship are beyond the scope of this chapter. Chapter 5 provides an overview of environmental assessment, and assessing the parent/infant relationship is widely addressed elsewhere. Several comments about the effects of aspects of the infant's environment are warranted, however, to underline their relevance to the infant's behavior and to determine sources of stress and support for the infant.

Literature on infant development for the past two decades has included in its scope the effects of nonoptimal physical environments. Various studies have demonstrated the full-term and preterm infant's vulnerability to differences in environmental input; behavioral organization appears to be dependent on support from the outside as well as maturation from the inside. A major focus of research on the effects of the physical environment has been the NICU, and it is well accepted that components of this environment experienced by sick and immature infants can affect their behavioral functioning and, perhaps, their subsequent developmental outcome. The nature of the environmental effects is still argued, however. The NICU has been seen as sensorily deprived (e.g., Rice, 1977; Scarr-Salapatek & Williams, 1973) and as providing excessive stimulation (e.g., Cornell & Gottfried, 1976). Some investigators claim that there is an inappropriate pattern of stimulation rather than an inadequate amount (Gottfried, Wallace-Lande, Sherman-Brown, King, & Coen, 1981; Lawson, Daum, & Turkewitz, 1977). Most clinicians and researchers conclude that we still do not know enough about the physiological and sensory needs and thresholds of infants or about the effects of various levels or durations of stimulation to make substantial environmental changes with confidence.

This literature may be incomplete, but it is compelling and suggestive for newborn assessment. In these studies, some environmental sources of stress and possibilities for support stand out. For example, excessive lighting in the NICU has been associated with increased incidence of visual deficits in premature infants (Glass, Avery, Kolinjavadi, Subramanian, Keys, Sostek, & Friendly, 1985). While a single study does not suffice to indict excessive lighting, it deserves careful attention and further study. Certainly, excessive lighting interferes with the infants' ability to open their eyes, look at their caregivers, and explore the environment.

In addition, numerous studies have documented excessive noise in the NICU (Kellman, 1982; Bess, Peck, & Chapman, 1979; Gottfried et al., 1981) and its association with negative effects on the infant's physiological stability, such as decreased oxygen levels in the blood (Long, Lucey, & Philip, 1980; Martin, Herrell, Rubin, & Fanaroff, 1979). Medical procedures are very expensive for sick infants; infants often show distress for up to five minutes after a 1-minute procedure (Gorski, 1983).

In terms of social stimuli, gentle stroking of the infant's extremities and chest was found to increase significantly body movement and avoidance behaviors (such as yawning, grimacing, crying) in very low birth-weight infants (Oehler, 1985). In contrast, soft talking was noted to increase significantly eye opening and eye movement, whether the infant was asleep or awake prior to stimulation (Oehler, Eckerman, & Wilson, 1988).

For more information about the NICU environment, the reader is referred to Gottfried and Gaiter (1985); *Infant Stress Under Intensive Care* is an edited volume that includes studies of the nursery setting and its effects on infants, parents, and medical caregivers. These and other authors suggest strongly that we have enough evidence about the effects of the NICU environment that close assessment of an infant and her responses to perturbations in the environment is warranted. Ideally, for an individual infant, sources of stress, methods of support, and **sensory thresholds** could be identified and managed, as feasible, to enable improved organization and development.

Procedural Guidelines

The assessment of a newborn infant is very different from testing an older child or adult. Previous training in the standardized and informal testing of older children will apply to testing strategies, in general; but the occasion of testing a newborn infant in a newborn setting presents several new demands. Guidelines for good practice in testing newborns are indicated for the examiner's training and experience, for the infant's status in testing, and for the testing environment. Fortunately, many of the current neurobehavioral approaches define specifically who, how, and when to test.

The Examiner
Educators and other developmental specialists are generally well trained in the close observation of behavior, and this observation is the essence of newborn assessment. You are familiar with having a model for the meaning of behavior, observing an individual, organizing the data back into the model, developing hypotheses about the status of the individual in specified areas of concern, and drawing conclusions about behavior in terms of diagnosis, prognosis, or needs for intervention in the present. This procedure also is the task of the examiner of the newborn infant.

The examiner of the newborn will need to be knowledgeable in several areas, however. Training programs in infancy and infant assessment usually include in their curricula rather extensive material on brain-behavior relationships, motor development, and biomedical risk factors for the premature or ill newborn—areas heretofore not commonly taught in education departments. The infant's behavior is seen as having meaning about the functioning of the central nervous system, so newborn assessment requires some understanding of neonatal neurology and neuropathology. The clinician is referred to several excellent texts on **neonatology** or neonatal nursing (e.g., Volpé, 1981; Avery, 1987; Fanaroff & Martin, 1987; Oehler, 1981); chapters on the central nervous system and neurologic problems in the newborn are excellent introductions to this area.

The second area of knowledge needed for newborn assessment and relatively unfamiliar to the educator is that of motor development and the assessment of movement. In addition to coursework and direct supervision, it is recommended that you work with physical or occupational therapists in a number of assessments. Qualitative aspects and subtle components of movement are important in newborn assessment and cannot be learned from a textbook only. Similarly, if you will be doing assessments in a newborn nursery, particularly an NICU, you will find that you need to become comfortable in that setting and knowledgeable about equipment and procedures. In most nursery settings, there are very important rules about behavior: When do you wash? What can you touch? Can you wear your ring? You may find that your nursery has a procedure manual you can review to learn appropriate handling of infants and equipment. At first, your ignorance may be embarrassing and overwhelming. You likely will find that nursery personnel would rather educate you than be uncomfortable with you in their setting.

The Infant

The theoretical basis of neurobehavioral assessment presumes close attention to the responses, thresholds, and needs of the infant being tested. In particular, most exams ask for close monitoring of state; many map the order of items by the infant's minute-to-minute state of arousal. Some exams are to be given at specified times (e.g., halfway between feedings) as an attempt to minimize different states of arousal at the beginning of the exam.

This attention to state is an excellent example of one of the basic differences between newborn and older child assessment; that is, what you do in the assessment is determined, by and large, by what the infant does. You want to experience a range of the infant's responses; so, you attempt to elicit the best response as well as observe the average one. You do what you have to do to elicit these responses. For example, if an infant's motor disorganization is interfering with visual tracking, you likely will stop, swaddle, and hold the infant in a contained position, and try again. This approach requires a thorough knowledge of the exam and much experience in handling infants. Unlike standardized tests for older children, infant assessment lets you know only where you are going; you are not always certain how you will get there.

Sick and premature infants require even more flexible procedures. A good newborn examiner will derive as much data from observations of the undisturbed infant as possible and as much from necessary interventions or procedures as possible. We know that han-

dling and various positions can negatively affect sick and premature infants' physiological status (e.g., heart rate, respiratory regularity, oxygen saturation). Minimizing aversive input is one goal of assessment; it also should be the method of good assessment. When handling is required, close attention to the infants' responses is necessary. Stress responses are respected, recovery time and support are given. Testing is terminated if the infant indicates continued stress. We want information about an individual infant's thresholds; we do not want to take the infant beyond them.

In general, the method of assessment is determined by the infant's status. A full-term, healthy newborn may readily engage with an examiner for a NBAS assessment in the infant's home. A growing preterm infant may require the tempered, well-modulated assessment described by Als (e.g., 1986). A sick newborn, still being mechanically ventilated, might benefit from an assessment of his responses to environmental stimuli but will require a minimally intrusive measure, such as the **naturalistic observation** system provided by Als (1984).

The Physical Environment

Newborn environments, nurseries and homes, usually are the settings of the assessment. When possible, most test developers recommend an environment with reduced external stimuli. You may get very different responses to an exam administered in the center of a noisy, brightly lit nursery versus in a quiet, nearly dark room with a rocking chair and a place for the examiner to prop his feet. Developmental clinicians have gotten very clever at finding corners, closets, or rooms adjacent to nurseries for their assessments.

Another issue to consider about the context of testing is the presence or absence of the parent. With the parent present, the assessment is an intervention; there is no way for it to be otherwise. It is an opportunity for the parent to get to know and understand the individuality of the child and the meaning in her behavior. Testing with the parent can be distracting for the examiner, however. There are many reasons to examine an infant with parents present or without; the goal and results of the testing will differ. You also can choose to do two exams or to see the infant alone and report, in detail, your findings to the parent.

Representative Methods

Representative newborn assessment strategies are described in this section. For purposes of organization, the exams are divided into two categories: those focused on the infant per se and those that, to some extent, assess mutual influences of the infant and caregiving context. Each exam is described in terms of its theoretical perspective, the major constructs of concern, indicators of the major constructs, specific procedures for administration and scoring, research and evaluation information, and general comments.

Assessment of Infant Status

The assessment results most likely of interest and use to the special or early childhood educator are the Apgar score and the assessments of **gestational age.** Both are systems for describing the infant's status at birth; they usually are done by physicians or nurses.

The Apgar Scoring System. The Apgar scoring system (Apgar, 1953) was devised as an index of the effects of obstetrical procedures, such as medication for the mother during labor and delivery or resuscitation efforts. The score also is used as a measure of the infant's immediate need for assistance with cardiopulmonary adaptation (Oehler, 1981). For this reason, it is seen as an index of the degree of and persistence of birth asphyxia.

To obtain the Apgar score, the infant's physiologic stability is observed in five areas: heart rate, respiratory effort, reflex irritability, muscle tone, and color. Scoring criteria are shown in Table 8.1. The physician or nurse in the delivery room observes the infant in the five areas, assigning a score of 2, 1, or 0 in each area for a maximum total score of 10.

TABLE 8.1
The Apgar Scoring Criteria

Sign	0	1	2
Heart rate	Absent	Slow (below 100)	Over 100
Respiratory effort	Absent	Weak cry, hypoventilation	Good, strong cry
Muscle tone	Limp	Some flexion of extremities	Well-flexed
Reflex response			
1. response to catheter in nostril (tested after oropharynx is clear)	No response	Grimace	Cough or sneeze
2. tangential foot slap	No response	Grimace	Cry and withdrawal of foot
Color	Blue, pale	Body pink, extremities blue	Completely pink

Source: Based on Apgar, 1953.

A total score is assigned at 1 minute after birth and again at 5 minutes. Sometimes, especially in instances of low initial scores, the infant is assessed at 10 and 20 minutes as well.

No studies of interrater reliability for the Apgar score were found. Test/retest reliability is, of course, not an applicable construct; change in infant status from one observation to the next is anticipated and desirable. The criteria used for scoring suggest the content validity of the system.

It is important to point out that predictive validity studies of the Apgar score often test the effectiveness of the exam for purposes for which it was not designed. The majority of studies reported in this literature address the relationship between the Apgar score and subsequent infant mortality and morbidity. The results are interesting; they are relevant to the care and planning for the high-risk infant. They are not true validity tests, however; the Apgar was designed to document the newborn's immediate status and need, not to predict the future.

Studies of the prediction of mortality in the neonate from the Apgar score are fairly consistent. For example, Apgar, Holaday, James, Weisbrot, and Berrien (1958) found a mortality of 0.13% with an initial Apgar score of 10 versus 15% for an initial score of 0, 1, 2, or 3. A low Apgar score, then, does not predict mortality well; but it predicts mortality better than does a high score.

In contrast, findings about the Apgar and morbidity are very inconsistent, and results seem related to which outcome measures are used at what age and to the variation in scores for the groups studied. For example, Serunian and Broman (1975) were able to discriminate high (7–10) versus low (0–3) Apgar-scoring children on the Bayley Scales at age 8 months. However, Shipe, Vandenberg, and Williams (1968) found no relationship between neonatal Apgar scores and scores on the Stanford-Binet Intelligence Scale at age 3. Some investigators contend that, if

the Apgar is to be used as a predictor of developmental outcome, the scores assigned later (e.g., at five or ten minutes) are better. Illingworth (1960) argues that if a measure of asphyxia is needed, the length of time until the onset of regular respirations is at least as adequate as the Apgar score.

Although the notion that birth asphyxia and other perinatal risk factors predict poor development is longstanding (e.g., Little, 1862), it is apparent that their effects may be eclipsed by the child's transactions with the caregiving context (Sameroff & Chandler, 1975). If we do not expect a simple relationship between birth events and developmental outcome, we certainly would not expect to find one with a measurement strategy not intended for that purpose. On the other hand, the Apgar score may be an important source of information for the developmental clinician. An indicator of a stressful labor and delivery often is enough evidence to warrant careful attention to the infant's subsequent adaptation and organization and to the potential from the caregiving environment to optimize recovery.

Gestation Age Assessment. The goal of the Gestational Age Assessment (Dubowitz, Dubowitz, & Goldberg, 1970) is to provide a reliable method of determining gestational age in the newborn infant. It is recognized that weight alone is not a sufficient indicator of age; an infant can be larger than average for gestational age or small for gestational age. Further, distinguishing between prematurity and growth retardation as well as identifying the large-for-age infant have implications for medical care and follow up (Oehler, 1981). In fact, there is some evidence that for the preterm infant the Apgar score does not reflect physiological well being but developmental maturity (Catlin, Carpenter, Brann, Mayfield, Shaul, Goldstein, & Oh, 1986). Therefore, knowing the infant's gestational age or maturity is important in interpreting other behavioral assessments as well as in anticipating medical needs.

The Dubowitz assessment claims as its roots the neurological assessment strategies of Andre-Thomas and Saint Anne-Dargassies. The exam has two parts: neurological criteria and an assessment of external criteria. The external characteristics are adapted from Farr, Mitchell, Neligan, and Parkin (1966), and include skin texture, skin color, skin opacity, edema (swelling), lanugo (body hair), ear form, ear firmness, genital appearance, breast size, nipple formation, and plantar skin creases. The neurological criteria were selected from a pilot study of items derived from various neurological exams (e.g., Amiel-Tison & Grenier, 1983; Robinson, 1966). Items were chosen to be easily definable, reliable among observers, and least affected by the infant's state of arousal or the presence of neurological abnormalities.

Administration of the gestational age exam requires rather extensive experience observing and handling newborn infants; it is usually done by nurses and physicians. Individual test items are listed on the test form from less disturbing to the infant to more disturbing, but no recommendations about the best state of arousal for the exam are made. The neurological criteria include 10 items, scored from 1 to 5, from less mature to more mature. The 11 external criteria items are scored from 1 to 4, also from less mature to more mature. Scores from both parts of the exam are summed, then combined for determining a gestational age estimate.

Interrater agreement for the selected neurological items was found to be 89% in a study of 167 infants (Dubowitz et al., 1970). For the external criteria, the Dubowitz (1970) group adapted the work by Farr et al. (1966), who obtained gestational age norms from a study of 280 infants of mothers who were certain of their pregnancy dates. In the Dubowitz reliability work, with 167 infant subjects, interrater agreement on external criteria was 91%. In their study, infant weight did not seem to affect scoring.

In an attempt to examine the validity, the group (Dubowitz et al., 1970) examined 150 infants, 87 of whom had had very reliable due dates. Scores from external characteristics were more highly correlated with known gestation than the neurological criteria; however, the highest correlation was obtained with the total score of external and neurological characteristics.

Data from the assessment of gestational age are very useful for the developmental clinician, for discriminating immaturity from dysmaturity, in particular, and for arriving at more reasonable expectations for the infant's behavioral organization. For example, you may be asked to evaluate a 37-week infant who is not feeding well by nipple. You may determine that the infant is, in fact, closer to 34–35 weeks post conception and is having age-appropriate difficulty maintaining an alert state. The gestational age of an infant is so important that one measure often is not adequate; the "best guess" about gestational age likely comes from information about dates, from the exam, and (if available) from ultrasound findings. Most recently, examinations of lens vascularity have been used to estimate gestational age, particularly for infants less than 28 weeks.

Assessment of Newborns and Context

This group of five assessments comprises the most commonly used tests of neurobehavioral status in the newborn. The newest, the *Assessment of Preterm Infant Behavior* (Als et al., 1982), is, to date, the most overt attempt to assess the infant and to put the results in dialectic context. The other assessment approaches lend themselves to interpretation from this perspective.

The Graham Rosenblith Behavior Test for Neonates. Graham's (1956) exam was initially developed to distinguish brain-injured from normal newborns. Rosenblith's (1961a) revision of the original scale was intended to identify high-risk infants, those who warrant medical and psychological attention and follow up, and to make selecting a group of low-risk infants possible for use in adoption cases (Rosenblith, 1974). The theoretical perspective of both efforts appears to have been eclectic, incorporating age-normed data, measures of muscle tone, and behavioral responses to stimuli.

There were five discrete areas in the original Graham (1956) exam. A pain threshold test involved a mild electrical stimulus applied to just below the infant's knee, intensity varied to elicit movement of the limb. Impaired sensory functioning was considered one indicator of brain damage. The maturation scale included nine items drawn from various developmental schedules (e.g., Gesell & Amatruda, 1941). A variety of stimuli or conditions were included, such as observations of posture, auditory responses, reactions to aversive stimuli, and strength of grasp. The vision scale examined eye movements, fixation, and tracking with scoring adapted from Gesell and Ilg (1949). The muscle tension rating was designed to quantify deviations in muscle tone, and an irritability rating was derived from the infant's sensitivity to stimuli during the exam as a whole. The Rosenblith (1961b) revision of the Graham Scales eliminated the pain threshold test. Otherwise, most items were retained. The new scales yield two scores (motor and tactile-adaptive) and two ratings (muscle tone and irritability).

Administration of the Graham Rosenblith Behavior Test requires 30 minutes to 1 hour. Infant state is not controlled but is noted. No special training is said to be required for administration; but, again, familiarity with newborns and the close observation of behavior and movement patterns is essential. It is interesting to note that Rosenblith, in the 1961 manual of the revised scales, suggested that the infant's best performance, not modal performance, be used for scoring. Brazelton (1973) followed this lead in developing the NBAS.

Graham, Matarazzo, and Caldwell (1956) provided standardization, reliability, and validity data on the original Graham Scales by studying 176 normal and 81 high-risk infants (either asphyxiated, with infections, or otherwise traumatized at birth). In brief, measures of split-half and test/retest reliability were acceptable, and mean scores discriminated normal from high-risk infants. Interrater agreement on the maturation and vision tests were 0.97 and 0.90, respectively. Percentages of perfect agreement on scoring muscle tension and irritability were 68 and 79, respectively. No reliability scores between raters were computed on the pain threshold tests. Lower rater agreement scores have been found elsewhere (Rosenblith & Lipsitt, 1959), however.

Validity studies of the Graham scales are unimpressive. Concurrent criterion-related validity was tested by Graham, Pennoyer, Caldwell, Greenman, and Hartmann (1957); they essentially failed to discriminate asphyxiated from normal infants by the exam. Predictive validity also was examined in the three-year follow-up study. Correlations between the Graham scores and IQ were weak for the normal infants; no correlation was found between the scores for the asphyxiated group.

Rosenblith (1961b) modified the Graham scales, in part, to improve reliability and internal consistency. New data regarding reliability were provided, and test/retest reliabilities in the new scale were better for maturation and vision scores and worse for irritability and muscle tension ratings. In a validity test, comparing Graham Rosenblith scores and ratings with 8-month outcome measures using the Bayley Scales, Rosenblith's (1961b) results are confusing. Many significant relationships are identified, but often they vary among the four samples studied. In general, however, infants with more optimal scores on the maturational index did better on nearly all 8-month scores. In a follow up of 4-year-olds, Rosenblith (1975) reported several significant relationships; the predominant impression was that various measures of motor status were most successful at predicting development across areas at age 4 years.

The Graham Rosenblith exam is not frequently used. Its major importance lies in that it marks the beginning of a behavioral or neurobehavioral approach to newborn testing. In these scales many threads of more contemporary assessment aproaches are found.

The Neurological Assessment of the Preterm and Full Term Newborn Infant. The Neurological Assessment of the Preterm and Full Term Newborn Infant (Dubowitz & Dubowitz, 1981) also claims its roots in the neurological tradition. The intent of this exam is to measure the functional neurological status of the newborn, to document abnormal behavior, and to provide a means for comparing full-term and preterm infants.

There are four major areas of concern in the assessment. They include **habituation** (the ability to manage environmental input), assessment of muscle tone and movement patterns, testing of reflexes (primitive and deep tendon reflexes), and several neurobehavioral items. Habituation is tested to repetitive flashlight and rattle stimuli and can be administered in drowsy or sleep states. Sixteen items measure muscle tone and movement patterns; they include assessment of posture, resistance to movement, head control, posture in prone and ventral suspension, spontaneous movement, tremors, and startles. Deep tendon reflexes and four primitive reflexes are tested, including palmar grasp (hand grasp) and the Moro reflex. Neurobehavioral items are very similar to the state organization and orientation items on the NBAS. State of arousal and asymmetry of responses are seen as important in interpreting results, and they are documented for each item.

The exam was designed specifically not to require extensive training, to be brief (15 minutes or less), and to be easy to administer.

The exam can be done in an isolette if necessary. Optimal timing for the infant, for consistency in state of arousal, is seen as $\frac{2}{3}$ of the way between feedings. Materials are simple: a light, a rattle, and a red yarn ball.

The exam is easy to administer and score. Items are grouped on two pages with diagrams and brief scoring instructions. Most items are scored on a 5-point scale, 1 to 5 for minimal to maximal response. No summary scores are derived. The test manual suggests and provides examples for interpretation of various response patterns.

The exam was constructed with items from Saint Anne-Dargassies (1965), Prechtl (1977), and Parmelee and Michaelis (1971) as well as with items adapted from the NBAS (Brazelton, 1973). Items were piloted over a two-year period and on more than 500 infants, and the test underwent several revisions. No reliability data are provided in the manual; however, two studies of rater agreement with an earlier version of the exam were reported (Dubowitz, Dubowitz, Morant, & Verghole, 1980). In the first, 11 infants were seen by 2 observers; for the 352 items scored, there was one 3-point discrepancy, two 2-point differences, and 24 1-point disagreements. Higher disagreement rates were found in the second study with 12 infants, 2 raters, and 340 items: 10 3-point differences, 12 2-point differences, and 82 1-point differences.

Concurrent criterion-related validity was examined by the same group (Dubowitz et al., 1980). The criterion was an ultrasound assessment of the presence or absence of intraventricular hemorrhage (IVH) in the 32–35 weeks post-conception infant. The Dubowitz exam was able to discriminate between the two groups of infants, IVH versus no-IVH. Of 31 infants with IVH, 24 had 3 or more abnormal signs on the exam; only 2 of 37 infants without IVH had 3 or more abnormal signs. Signs most frequently associated with IVH were decreased muscle tone, decreased motility, and increased tightness in the popliteal angle.

Predictive criterion-related validity was examined by comparing the newborn assessment with normal versus abnormal diagnoses and a neurological assessment at 1 year. Of infants who were normal at one year, 91% were assessed as normal at term gestational age. Only 35% of the normal 1-year-olds had tested abnormal at term age.

This exam is quick and easy to administer and score. The claim that no special training is needed is misleading; in fact, rather extensive experiences with reflex testing and handling newborn infants is essential. This assessment often is compared, favorably and unfavorably, with the NBAS. The two exams have much in common; there are a number of NBAS items on the Dubowitz, but the NBAS scoring is not used. The clinician should probably make a decision between the exams based on the specific information needed about the infant. On a continuum of neurobehavioral exams being less or more congruent with the notion of dialectical, hierarchical, and teleological development, the Dubowitz likely falls after the Graham Rosenblith Scales and before the NBAS. Interpretations of exam findings in terms of reciprocal infant-environmental effects are not stressed.

The Neonatal Behavioral Assessment Scale. The NBAS (Brazelton, 1973; 1984) was designed to measure "interactive behavior," "the infant's available responses to his environment, and so, indirectly, his effect on the environment" (Brazelton, 1973, p. 4). The focus of the exam is individual differences in the behavioral organization of full-term newborn infants. The newborn is seen as active and interactive, capable of shaping social interactions. The theoretical perspective is an organismic view of infant development and of the infant assessment: "It is obvious that a baby's responses should not be seen as static but that each one will lead to and become the background for the next one—and, as a result, the processes through which infants go as we interact with them become the best measure of their potential" (Brazelton, 1973; p. 4).

Several major constructs are assessed in the NBAS. For example, a major concept in the approach is the importance of state of arousal to infant responses. Brazelton uses states as described by Prechtl and Beintema (1964) to direct the examiner for administration of items. State organization also is assessed by measures of lability and control of state. (A more complete description of state can be found in Chapter 9). Also, Brazelton (1973; 1984) emphasizes the infant's capacity to manage input, to cut it out (habituation) and to attend (orientation). This major construct sounds much like infant temperament (see Chapter 10), and Brazelton acknowledges the assessment of temperamental differences to be one of the goals of his exam. Further, he contends that the NBAS is not a neurological exam; but there is a reflex component to the exam.

In the NBAS, the infant is seen as an active, not passive, contributor to his caregiving through individual differences in behavioral organization. Areas in which individual differences are found include autonomic control, neurological or motor maturity, state organization, and orientation and habituation capacities. Indicators of each area comprise the exam.

The NBAS is recommended for the full-term newborn or the preterm infant after 37 weeks post conception in a stable medical condition. Desired environmental conditions include quiet, comfort, and dim lights. Test equipment consists of a flashlight, rattle, bell, red ball, and a sterile stick (for habituation to pin prick). A sequence for item administration is presented in the manual. The sequence is designed to elicit a range of states from sleep to alertness, gradually, with perturbations from less to more intense and stimuli presented in a distal to proximal manner. The examiner is counseled, however, to attend well to the infant's state and to shift the administration sequence as needed to elicit optimal performance from the infant.

Behavior Scoring Sheet

Initial state

Predominant state

Scale (Note State)	1	2	3	4	5	6	7	8	9
1. Response decrement to light (1,2)	—	—	—	—	—	—	—	—	—
2. Response decrement to rattle (1,2)	—	—	—	—	—	—	—	—	—
3. Response decrement to bell (1,2)	—	—	—	—	—	—	—	—	—
4. Response decrement to tactile stimulation of foot (1,2)	—	—	—	—	—	—	—	—	—
5. Orientation—inanimate visual (4,5)	—	—	—	—	—	—	—	—	—
6. Orientation—inanimate auditory (4,5)	—	—	—	—	—	—	—	—	—
7. Orientation—inanimate visual and auditory (4,5)	—	—	—	—	—	—	—	—	—
8. Orientation—animate visual (4,5)	—	—	—	—	—	—	—	—	—
9. Orientation—animate auditory (4,5)	—	—	—	—	—	—	—	—	—
10. Orientation—animate visual and auditory (4,5)	—	—	—	—	—	—	—	—	—
11. Alertness (4 only)	—	—	—	—	—	—	—	—	—
12. General tonus (4,5)	—	—	—	—	—	—	—	—	—
13. Motor maturity (4,5)	—	—	—	—	—	—	—	—	—
14. Pull-to-sit (4,5)	—	—	—	—	—	—	—	—	—
15. Cuddliness (4,5)	—	—	—	—	—	—	—	—	—
16. Defensive movements (3,4,5)	—	—	—	—	—	—	—	—	—
17. Consolability (6 to 5,4,3,2)	—	—	—	—	—	—	—	—	—
18. Peak of excitement (all states)	—	—	—	—	—	—	—	—	—
19. Rapidity of build-up (from 1,2 to 6)	—	—	—	—	—	—	—	—	—
20. Irritability (all awake states)	—	—	—	—	—	—	—	—	—
21. Activity (3,4,5)	—	—	—	—	—	—	—	—	—
22. Tremulousness (all states)	—	—	—	—	—	—	—	—	—
23. Startle (3,4,5,6)	—	—	—	—	—	—	—	—	—
24. Lability of skin color (from 1 to 6)	—	—	—	—	—	—	—	—	—
25. Lability of states (all states)	—	—	—	—	—	—	—	—	—
26. Self-quieting activity (6,5 to 4,3,2,1)	—	—	—	—	—	—	—	—	—
27. Hand-to-mouth facility (all states)	—	—	—	—	—	—	—	—	—
28. Smiles (all states)	—	—	—	—	—	—	—	—	—
29. Alert responsiveness (4 only)	—	—	—	—	—	—	—	—	—
30. Cost of attention (3,4,5)	—	—	—	—	—	—	—	—	—
31. Examiner persistence (all states)	—	—	—	—	—	—	—	—	—
32. General irritability (5,6)	—	—	—	—	—	—	—	—	—
33. Robustness and endurance (all states)	—	—	—	—	—	—	—	—	—
34. Regulatory capacity (all states)	—	—	—	—	—	—	—	—	—
35. State regulation (all states)	—	—	—	—	—	—	—	—	—
36. Balance of motor tone (all states)	—	—	—	—	—	—	—	—	—
37. Reinforcement value of infant's behavior (all states)	—	—	—	—	—	—	—	—	—

FIGURE 8.2
NBAS Scoring Sheet

Behavioral and Neurological Assessment Scale

Infant's name					
Sex	Age				
Mother's age	Father's age				
Examiner(s)					
Conditions of examination:					
Birthweight					
Time examined					
Time last fed					
Type of delivery					
Length of labor					
Type, amount and timing of medication given mother					

Date	Hour
Born	
Father's S.E.S.	
Apparent race	
Place of examination	
Date of examination	
Length	
Head circ.	
Type of feeding	
Apgar	
Birth order	
Anesthesia?	
Abnormalities of labor	

Initial state: observe 2 minutes

1	2	3	4	5	6
deep	light	drowsy	alert	active	crying

Predominant states (mark two)

1	2	3	4	5	6

Elicited Responses

	O*	L	M	H	A†
Plantar grasp		1	2	3	
Hand grasp		1	2	3	
Ankle clonus		1	2	3	
Babinski		1	2	3	
Standing		1	2	3	
Automatic walking		1	2	3	
Placing		1	2	3	
Incurvation		1	2	3	
Crawling		1	2	3	
Glabella		1	2	3	
Tonic deviation of head and eyes		1	2	3	
Nystagmus		1	2	3	
Tonic neck reflex		1	2	3	
Moro		1	2	3	
Rooting (intensity)		1	2	3	
Sucking (intensity)		1	2	3	
Passive movement		1	2	3	
Arms R		1	2	3	
L		1	2	3	
Legs R		1	2	3	
L		1	2	3	

Descriptive paragraph (optional)				
Attractive	0	1	2	3
Interfering variables	0	1	2	3
Need for stimulation	0	1	2	3

What activity does he use to quiet self?
hand to mouth
sucking with nothing in mouth
locking onto visual or auditory stimuli
postural changes
state change for no observable reason

COMMENTS:

O* = response not elicited (omitted)
A† = asymmetry

Source: From *Neonatal Behavioral Assessment Scale* (2nd ed.) by T. B. Brazelton, 1984,
Philadelphia: J. B. Lippincott. Copyright 1984 by J. B. Lippincott.

The Brazelton group emphasizes the importance of examiners being reliable with one another in administration and scoring. Training includes extensive experience in handling newborn infants, observing trained examiners, and doing several supervised exams. All examiners using the test for research purposes are required to obtain the formal reliability training available in several sites around the country.

In the NBAS, the examiner and the infant engage in an approximately 30-minute interaction; scoring occurs after the exam. Scoring includes 28 behavioral items, each rated on a 9-point scale; and 18 elicited responses from the reflex profile of Prechtl and Beintema (1964) are scored on a 3-point scale. In the 1984 revision, nine supplementary items are included also. Many clinicians and researchers use a 5-point scale instead for the reflex assessment as suggested by Sostek and Anders (1977). The NBAS can be found in Figure 8.2 (pp. 186–187).

There are several ways to condense NBAS data. Initially, Als, Tronick, Lester, and Brazelton (1979) presented a system of a priori clusters for items. Optimal versus worrisome scores for interactive processes, motoric processes, organizational processes: state control, and organizational processes: response to stress can be derived. Several factor-analytic studies have emerged; the most commonly used factor analytically determined clusters are those by Lester, Als, and Brazelton (1982): range of state, regulation of state, motor status, autonomic stability, orientation, and habituation. As an example, the items contributing to one factor, regulation of state, are (a) self-quieting activity, (b) hand-to-mouth facility, (c) **consolability**, and (d) cuddliness.

The NBAS is, at present, the most studied of neurobehavioral exams for the newborn infant. Several reviews or annotated bibliographies, such as the one by Sostek (1978) are available. Several studies can be cited that are rather representative. In terms of reliability,

the Brazelton group found that interrater reliability after training to be greater than 90% if an item score within 1 point was considered to be an agreement (Als et al., 1979). This level of reliability is intended to hold up for two years, but no studies of interrater agreement several months after training were found. In general, test/retest reliability studies found low to moderate correlations between scores. Brazelton (e.g., 1978) would contend that a significant amount of the variability is in the infant, not in the test. He suggests that the continuities in behavior likely would be found between the infant and the caregiving system, not in the infant over time.

One group (Sameroff, Krafchuk, & Bakow, 1978) compared 35 infants 24 hours apart to assess short-term stability for individual items, factors, and a priori clusters. The best stability was in scores for muscle tone and motor maturity ($r = .57$, $r = .78$, respectively). Interestingly, only the initial habituation task was stable, that is, the light versus rattle, bell, and pin prick ($r = .46$ versus $r = .05$, $r = .05$, and $r = .07$). Irritability measures were unstable. Factor scores showed better stability than cluster scores; however, the motor cluster scores correlated .56 with one another. Asch, Gleser, and Steichen (1986) examined the sources of variance for repeated measures of the NBAS, concluding that measurement error is too high for one exam on one occasion with one examiner to have meaning for the individual infant. For clinical prediction, this group agrees with several other authors (e.g., Lester, 1984) that at least two test occasions and, possibly, two raters, are necessary.

Validity questions for the NBAS generally are approached by predictive criterion-related tests. Again, some of the best predictive success has been with recovery curves, or repeated exams, at 40, 42, and 44 weeks post conception when compared to the 18-month Bayley scores (Lester, 1984). In this particular study, recovery curve scores were significantly related to mental and motor performance on the Bayley Scales for both term and preterm infants; from 42% to 63% of the variance on 18-month scores was predicted by the NBAS scores.

Sostek and Anders (1977) examined concurrent and predictive validity with the NBAS. The exam was accomplished between 5 and 12 days of life with an interrater reliability of .85 on the a priori clusters. Simultaneously, nurses completed an adaptation of the Carey (1970) measure of infant temperament; that is, they used 35 out of the original 70 items that seemed appropriate for the newborn. The temperament factor distractibility was significantly associated with the a priori motor score and total score on the NBAS. At age 4 months, NBAS scores did not predict motor scores on the Bayley Scales of Infant Development. Rather, mental scores were associated with the NBAS state organization and overall score. These findings underline not only the complex issues involved in infant assessment but also the complexity of models of early infant development.

The NBAS has become a very popular approach to newborn assessment. The exam has been judged negatively for its low to moderate stability and mixed predictive findings. Its contribution is significant, nonetheless. Compared with its predecessors, the exam provides an organized view of the newborn infant's behavioral competence and the infant's possible effects on caregivers. The exam does emphasize individual differences, as intended, and it is seen as an effective mode for intervention with parents. When assessments are used over time, there also seems to be some continuity between newborn behavior and developmental progress, at least during the first 4 months.

The Assessment of Preterm Infant Behavior (APIB). Als's original intent for the APIB (Als et al., 1982) was to be the refinement and extension of the NBAS for use with preterm and ill newborn infants. In addition, she has used

the NBAS framework to design an instrument that reflects her developmental model, the synactive model. The primary goal of the APIB is to examine the infant's behavioral organization within each evolving subsystem in the model's hierarchy. Table 8.2 describes these subsystems and the indicators used to assess the infant's status in each.

The synactive model for the development of the newborn specifies a "continuous intraorganizational subsystem interaction seen in continuous interaction with the environment" (Als, 1986, p. 17). Key features of the model are the hierarchy of behavioral subsystem, behavioral organization, and continuous interaction with the environment. As Als says, the assessment is directed at "the way the individual infant appears to handle his experience of the world around him, rather than on the assessments of skills per se" (p. 18).

The APIB is designed so that the examiner provides systematic sensory and handling input to the infant in order to assess each behavioral subsystem. The intervention with

TABLE 8.2
Behavioral Subsystems and Their Indicators

Behavioral Subsystem	Examples of Indicators
Autonomic stability	Heart rate, lability of color, respiratory regularity, visceral signs
Motor status	Posture, tone, movements
State organization	Definition and range of states, control of states
Attention and orientation	Attention, quality of responsiveness
Self-regulation	Maintenance and recovery of behavioral organization

Source: Adapted from Als et al., 1982.

the infant is by "packages" or graded maneuvers. Like the NBAS, items are planned to be distal to proximal and provide less to more intense stimulation; the general sequence of the exam is very similar to the NBAS. With exception of the attention/interaction maneuvers, all packages contribute items to all subsystems. Scores are derived that reflect her basic subsystem scheme.

The exam usually takes about 30 minutes, but administration is more variable than the NBAS; with the premature infant, the examiner often must stop and offer "time out" or support for stress reactions. At the beginning of the exam, the infant is to be asleep and midway between feedings. The examiner moves through the sequence of packages, observing the infant's responses to the stimuli, the infant's coping with stressful stimuli, and the infant's need for and use of external support. Scoring the exam takes approximately 1 hour.

Administering the APIB requires the examiner to be very skilled in handling premature newborn infants and experienced in examining in an isolette if necessary. Extensive training experience is recommended to be able to observe infant responses at this subtle and detailed a level as the examiner is required to modulate her input, minute-by-minute, to the infant's thresholds. Training with Dr. Als is available and is seen as necessary for safe as well as valid administration.

Little research, except from the authors themselves, is available on the APIB. Als (1985a) found good stability in APIB scores in both full-term and preterm infants examined two weeks after their expected due dates. Validity studies come from two directions of research. First, concurrent criterion-related validity was indicated with electrophysiological correlates of patterns of behavioral organization (Duffy, 1985). Second, predictive validity of patterns of behavior to 9 months and to 5 years (Als, 1985a; 1985b) were found. Specifically, the overall disorganized, easily distressed newborn be-

havior was predictive of disorganized behavior in the older child.

There still is relatively little known about the APIB assessment. It is not easy to administer; the examiner must be constantly alert to the infant's most subtle responses and modulate input accordingly. Scoring is extraordinarily time consuming. Whether the results of the exam are worth the expense to the infant, clinician, or researcher is not clear.

Newborn assessment consumers need more information about the meaning of the APIB assessment and its possible contribution to various clinical and research tasks. The model it provides for viewing newborn behavior and the approach to assessment by participation in the infant and context dialectic are very attractive. Observations of infant stress, self-regulation, and response to support appear to lend themselves directly to intervention strategies for improved medical care and psychological outcome (Als et al., 1986).

Naturalistic Observation of the Preterm Neonate. This behavioral observation method (Als, 1984) was designed to document observations of preterm newborn infants' responses to stress and support from the environment. Observations are based on the conceptual framework for the APIB; in this assessment, however, the infant's well being in each behavioral subsystem is assessed without actually handling the infant.

Major areas of concern are infant responses to and recovery from stress in the neonatal setting, such as sound, lighting changes, and procedures. Stress and defense behaviors (from the APIB, Als et al., 1982) are identified and observed; they include autonomic and visceral stress signals, motoric stress signals, and state-related stress signals. Indicators of autonomic and visceral stress signals, for example, include sighing, yawning, hiccoughing, sneezing, coughing, and changing color.

The method of this system involves observing the infant in 2-minute epochs, scoring heart rate and oxygen levels from the monitor, counting respiratory rate, noting the infant's posture and position, and observing the stress and defense behaviors in the areas described above. The infant is observed for a period of time before a procedure (feeding, vital signs, etc.), during the procedure, and during recovery from the procedure. A sample score sheet is presented in Figure 8.3 (p. 192).

There is no score per se. Results are reported in written descriptions of the infant's stress and defense reactions and recommendations for interventions that support increased overall organization, particularly cardiopulmonary and autonomic stability.

The major research done with the naturalistic observation system was not designed to test reliability and validity per se. Als, Lawhon, Brown, Gibes, Duffy, McAnulty, and Blickman (1986) used the system to design individual care plans for very low birthweight infants. The observations were completed on infants in the study with a greater than 85% agreement between two observers. The infant's care and physical environment were modified according to an individual plan derived from the observations and shared with the nursing staff and the parents. Study outcome measures are seen as reflecting the individualized care that resulted from the observations. Findings indicated significant differences with individualized care in time for recovery from respiratory illness and developmental assessments. There were no differences between the groups on weight gain.

Translating Assessment Data into Intervention

Various assessment strategies for the newborn infant are seen as addressing one or more dimensions of behavior: neurological integrity, individual differences and needs in behavioral organization, and the infant in relationships with caregivers. Whether or not these are the important dimensions of infant behavior to assess and whether or not our test strategies measure them well are still widely discussed. Further, tests of how well infant assessment predicts developmental outcome offer mixed and complex findings. The area of neonatal assessment is an evolving one, and it is clear that we still have much to learn about meaning in newborn behavior and how to measure important dimensions of it.

The task of translating assessment data into interventions for the infant and family is equally complex. It is suggested that this area has grown and will continue to evolve with increased knowledge about newborn behavior, its organization, and its needs from the caregiving context. Given our current state of the art, newborn assessment is seen as offering information about intervention and planning needs in the three major dimensions addressed. Is this child at high risk for mental retardation and/or CNS dysfunction? If so, how can we plan for the child and family? How is this individual infant developing on the hierarchy of developmental tasks? What in the caregiving context supports or interferes with optimal development? What would it be like to care for this infant? What is her temperament like?

Assessment Data Regarding Neurological Integrity

This is, perhaps, the oldest reason to test newborn infants behaviorally; it also may be the least effective one for the individual infant. However, combined information about the infant's biological risk status (possible insults to the nervous system) and neurobehavioral status in the neonatal period can be very relevant to planning for the infant and family. For an infant like Baby Boy Brown, for example, behavioral information can support recommendations for immediate

OBSERVATION SHEET Name: _____ Date: _____ Sheet Number _____

	Time:	0-2	3-4	5-6	7-8	9-10
Resp:	Regular					
	Irregular					
	Slow					
	Fast					
	Pause					
Color:	Jaundice					
	Pink					
	Pale					
	Webb					
	Red					
	Dusky					
	Blue					
	Tremor					
	Startle					
	Twitch Face					
	Twitch Body					
	Twitch Extremities					
Visceral/Resp:	Spit up					
	Gag					
	Burp					
	Hiccough					
	BM Grunt					
	Sounds					
	Sigh					
	Gasp					
Motor:	Flaccid Arm(s)					
	Flaccid leg(s)					
	Flexed/Tucked Arms Act.					
	Flexed/Tucked Arms Post.					
	Flexed/Tucked Legs Act.					
	Flexed/Tucked Legs Post.					
	Extend Arms Act.					
	Extend Arms Post.					
	Extend Legs Act.					
	Extend Legs Post.					
	Smooth Mvmt Arms					
	Smooth Mvmt Legs	I				
	Smooth Mvmt Trunk					
	Stretch/Drown					
	Diffuse Squirm					
	Arch					
	Tuck Trunk					
	Leg Brace					
Face:	Tongue Extension					
	Hand on Face					
	Gape Face					
	Grimace					
	Smile					

	Time:	0-2	3-4	5-6	7-8	9-10
State:	1A					
	1B					
	2A					
	2B					
	3A					
	3B					
	4A					
	4B					
	5A					
	5B					
	6A					
	6B					
	AA					
Face (cont.):	Mouthing					
	Suck Search					
	Sucking					
Extrem.:	Finger Splay					
	Airplane					
	Salute					
	Sitting On Air					
	Hand Clasp					
	Foot Clasp					
	Hand to Mouth					
	Grasping					
	Holding On					
	Fisting					
Attention:	Fuss					
	Yawn					
	Sneeze					
	Face Open					
	Eye Floating					
	Avert					
	Frown					
	Ooh Face					
	Locking					
	Cooing					
	Speech Mvmt.					
Posture:	(Prone, Supine, Side)					
Head:	(Right, Left, Middle)					
Location:	(Crib, Isolette, Held)					
Manipulation:						
	Heart Rate					
	Respiration Rate					
	TcPO$_2$					

2002-02 1M (12/83)
H.Als 1981

FIGURE 8.3

A Behavioral Score Sheet *(Source: From "Individualized Behavioral and Environmental Care for the Very Low Birth Weight Preterm Infant at High Risk for Bronchopulmonary Dysplasia: Neonatal Intensive Care Unit and Developmental Outcome" by H. Als et al., 1986, Pediatrics, 78 pp. 1123–1132.)*

intervention (e.g., demonstrating his attention abilities to his mother), long-term intervention (e.g., if there are consistent concerns about muscle tone and assymmetry in movement, a referral to physical therapy may be considered), and long-term follow-up of developmental and behavioral functioning.

Helpful in evaluating the use of behavioral assessment for this identifying brain injury is a paper by Gardner, Karmel, Magnano, and Norton (article submitted for publication). They stress that quantification of behavioral data can contribute to our understanding of the consequences of brain injury for an individual infant; to do so, though, the assessment should reflect the deficits resulting from the brain insult. Few studies of the neurobehavioral instruments available have attempted to identify the relationship between behavioral test results and specific, identified brain injury; so this kind of validity data is rarely available to the clinician.

Gardner and her colleagues identified a group of very low birthweight infants; they were assessed for brain injury using cranial ultrasonography to identify structural pathology and brainstem auditory evoke potential testing (brainstem response to auditory stimuli) to identify functional pathology. Prior to discharge, the infants were examined using a neurobehavioral instrument developed by this group that emphasizes muscle tone, symmetry in movement, and visual and auditory attention. The findings indicated that behavioral testing contributed significantly to the identification of infants with documented brain injury. These findings support the utility of converging assessments for the assessment of neurological integrity; they also underline the contribution of behavioral assessment to identifying those infants who may benefit from therapy or intervention.

The Assessment of Behavioral Organization

Models from which we assess an infant's individual differences in behavioral organization

(e.g., Als et al., 1982) are predicated on the notion of developmental intervention. That is, examining indicators of an infant's functioning on a hierarchy of behavioral subsystems tells us about the infant's status and needs. Specific interventions in the physical and social context can be mapped to her status and needs in each area. The major focus of this approach to intervention is the individualization of the physical environment and social interactions for the infant with a goal of increased behavioral organization, which is seen as facilitating physical recovery, supporting the developing central nervous system, and providing reinforcement for caregivers.

The approach to intervention from this perspective follows the hierarchial scheme provided by Als and her colleagues (e.g., 1982); the assessment provides the framework for defining sources of stress and support for the infant in each area and determining priorities for intervention strategies. Figure 8.4 (p. 194) provides an overview of the hierarchy of behavioral subsystems with a focus for intervention for each.

It is important to discriminate this developmental approach from an earlier infant stimulation model. The latter approach to preterm infants, in particular, was based on the notion that the NICU environment was sensorily deprived and/or that input for the infant was to be modeled from the physical and social environment of the full-term, healthy newborn. Further studies of the NICU environment and the development of the fetal neonate do not support that approach (e.g., Gottfried and Gaiter, 1985). Developmental or individualized intervention strategies have not been systematically validated either (with the exception of the study by Als et al., 1986) and remain vulnerable to research findings (Harris, 1986).

Baby Boy Mitchell, if assessed from a developmental model, could be seen the following way:

The infant's pulmonary pathology along with immaturity makes him very

FIGURE 8.4
Hierarchy of
Developmental
Tasks for the High-
risk Newborn
(Source: Adapted
from Als et al.,
1982)

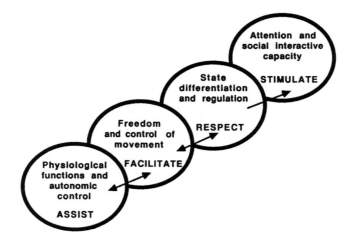

vulnerable to environmental stimulation. His autonomic instability is manifested by mild color changes, oxygen desaturation, decreased heart rate, and tachypnea during tactile stimulation and conversation around his isolette. In terms of motor status, he maintained a flexed position in both upper and lower extremities. Arching and diffuse squirming were observed with tactile and/or auditory stimulation. His attempts to move away from the stimulation and "tuck" himself in was hampered by the physical restraints used. Fairly rapid shifts in states of arousal from sleep to high activity with stimulation were noted, resulting in an "all or nothing" response to being perturbed. No alert or drowsy states were observed; there was no cry.

Given the observations that stimulation is, in fact, very threatening to Baby Mitchell's overall stability, intervention recommendations likely would focus on protecting the infant from overwhelming input. It may be suggested, for example, that conversation that is not directed at the infant should take place away from the bedside. Oxygen levels should be allowed to return to baseline between procedures, allowing time for recovery between manipulations. Grouping procedures, as feasi-

ble, to every three or four hours can be recommended to support more quiet sleep. Prone or sidelying positions may help stabilize the infant motorically. Sidelying, in particular, allows the infant to get his hands to his mouth and provides at least one avenue for self-consoling. Foot rolls, lamb's skin, and other bedding arrangements can be made for "nesting" to contain and support the infant. Light and environmental noise can be reduced somewhat by covering the top of the isolette. Many of these suggestions can be found in the paper by Als and her colleagues (1986); training in the assessment and intervention strategies is available from this group.

Again, the research in this area is not conclusive. We do have evidence that overstimulating a medically fragile infant can have negative physiological and developmental effects. We think that individualizing the environment to the infant's specific competencies and needs will promote immediate and longer-term outcomes. Again, what we do not know yet is—*which* infant can benefit from *which* intervention. Indeed, we do not know yet which intervention may be harmful to which infant. It is essential that the clinician in this area be armed with information from ongoing research in the area and with a great deal of humility about our current models for trying to influence a developing human being.

Assessment of Newborn Infant Temperament and Relationships with Caregivers

Since its development, the NBAS has been extensively used and studied as an intervention with caregivers. The behavioral exam is seen as an opportunity for the clinician to join with caregivers in observing, discovering, and discussing the newborn's individuality, in particular, the infant's competencies and characteristic responses to caregiver behavior. Indeed, this type of intervention has substantial face validity: Any relationship requires two individuals, each responding to and perceiving a response from the other. A parent's becoming acquainted with his infant's needs and responses could facilitate a view of the infant as separate, as having individual characteristics, and as influencing and being influenced by the parent. At least in theory, the intervention could support a more optimal beginning relationship for vulnerable infants and caregivers.

In fact, several studies support the theory. Outcome measures of qualities of the developing parent/child relationship such as sensitivity, involvement, responsiveness, and reciprocity have been associated with the NBAS being used as an intervention. Worobey (1984) has provided a comprehensive review of these studies. One study, in particular, is relevant to our concerns about Baby Girl Lucas and her mother. Widmayer and Field (1981) demonstrated the NBAS to a group of teenaged mothers from lower socioeconomic groups. The intervention seemed to be associated with higher infant performance at one year on the Mental Scale of the Bayley Scales of Infant Development.

The manner in which effects like those from the Widmayer and Field study are mediated is not clear and probably is quite complex. One scenario might be that Baby Lucas's mother does not appear interested in the infant because of her own low self-esteem and lack of confidence that she can care for her baby. In addition, the infant's temperament may be predominately quiet, not intense, and not demanding. The couple may be the kind of "fit" that could produce neglect, increased infant lethargy, increased maternal withdrawal, and so on. The experience of the infant as having needs and as positively responding to her caregiving could provide a foundation for a long-term relationship of mutual awareness, need, and response.

Several works are available to guide the clinician for using neurobehavioral assessment to identify individual differences and to intervene with families. Nugent (1985) has provided an excellent text that includes descriptions of individual test items from the NBAS, interpretations that can be used with caregivers, and implications for caregiving.

SUMMARY OF KEY CONCEPTS

- The assessment of the newborn infant presents an area of knowledge, clinical challenges, and intervention implications that may be relatively new to the special or early childhood educator.

- The origins of various components of contemporary methods of newborn assessment can be found in the areas of developmental neurology, behavioral pediatrics, and developmental psychology.

- One major component of the behavioral assessment of the newborn is rooted in the tradition of neurological assessment with emphasis on evaluating reflexes.

- A pioneer in the field of behavioral pediatrics, Arnold Gesell, observed and documented developmental milestones for the first five years of life. Aspects of the normative approach can be found in current strategies for newborn assessment.

- Recent approaches to newborn assessment reflect the evolving models for child developmental processes, emphasizing not only the infant's behavior but also the infant's physical and social context and transactions between infants and context.

- Contemporary views of newborn behavior and development can be summarized with three principles: developmental processes are described as hierarchical, dialectical, and teleological.

- Newborn testing makes the assumption that infant behavior is meaningful and that it is organized. Different models for organization have resulted in different assessment approaches, specifically: the neurological exam; the normative approach; and, more recently, approaches that integrate both with a view of the infant in an ongoing, dynamic relationship with the caregiving context.

- Neonatal assessment can be seen as addressing three major dimensions of the infant's functioning: neurological integrity, behavioral organization, and temperament.

- Neonatal assessment also addresses aspects of the infant's physical and social environment that influence and are influenced by the infant's behavior.

- Testing a newborn infant in newborn settings is seen as highly specialized, requiring training in brain behavior relationships, motor development, and biomedical risk factors as well as extensive experience handling full-term and preterm infants.

- Newborn infants, especially sick and preterm ones, require flexible test procedures. A good examiner derives as much data from observations of the undisturbed infant as possible. When handling the infant, close attention to and respect for the infant's stress signals are necessary.

- With the parent present, the assessment is an intervention. It provides an opportunity for the parent to get to know and understand the individuality of the child and to find meaning in her behavior.

- The assessment of gestational age and the Apgar score are systems for describing the infant's status at birth; they usually are done by physicians and nurses.

- The Graham Rosenblith exam marks the beginning of a behavioral or neurobehavioral approach to newborn testing.

- The Dubowitz neurobehavioral assessment addresses four areas of concern: habituation, muscle tone and movement, reflexes, and behavioral responses to stimuli.

- With the NBAS, the infant is assessed as an active, not passive, contributor to his caregivers through individual differences in behavioral organization. In particular, state is seen as the mediator of behavioral responses in the areas of autonomic control, neurological or motor maturity, state organization, and orientation and habituation capacities.

- The APIB examines systematically the infant's behavioral organization within each evolving subsystem in the synactive model's hierarchy of developmental tasks.

- The major constructs from the APIB can be assessed by observation only by using the systematic scoring system developed by Als and her colleagues (1986).

REFERENCES

Asch, P., Gleser, G., & Steichen, J.J. (1986). Dependability of Brazelton neonatal behavioral assessment cluster scales. *Infant Behavior and Development, 9,* 291–306.

Als, H. (1984). *Manual for the naturalistic observation of newborn behavior (preterm and full term).* Unpublished manuscript, Child Development Unit, Children's Hospital Medical Center, Boston, MA.

Als, H. (1985a). *Newborn behavior in preterms and full terms.* (Paper presented at the biannual meeting of the Society for Research in Child Development, Toronto.)

Als, H. (1985b). Patterns of infant behavior: Analogs of late organizational difficulties? In F.H. Duffy & N. Geschwind (Eds.), *Dyslexia: Current status and future directions* (pp. 67–92). Boston: Little, Brown.

Als, H. (1986). Assessing the neurobehavioral development of the premature infant and the environment of the neonatal intensive care unit: A synactive model of neonatal behavioral organization. *Physical and Occupational Therapy in Pediatrics, 6,* 3–53.

Als, H., Lawhon, G., Brown, E., Gibes, R., Duffy, F., McAnulty, G., & Blickman, J. (1986). Individualized behavioral and environmental care for the very low birth weight preterm infant at high risk for bronchopulmonary dysplasia: Neonatal intensive care unit and developmental outcome. *Pediatrics, 78*(6), 1123–1132.

Als, H., Lester, B.M., Tronick, E.Z., & Brazelton, T.B. (1982). Toward a research instrument for the assessment of preterm infants' behavior (APIB). In H. Fitzgerald, B.M. Lester, & M.W.

Yogman (Eds.), *Theory and research in behavioral pediatrics: Vol. 1* (pp. 35–132). New York: Plenum.

Als, H., Tronick, E., Lester, B.M., & Brazelton, T.B. (1979). Specific neonatal measures: The Brazelton neonatal behavioral assessment scale. In J. Osofsky (Ed.), *Handbook of infant development* (pp. 185–215). New York: John Wiley & Sons.

Amiel-Tison, C. & Grenier, A. (1983). *Neurologic evaluation of the newborn and the infant.* New York: Masson.

André-Thomas (1959). Integration in the infant. *Cerebral Palsy Bulletin, 1,* 3–12.

André-Thomas, Chesni, Y., & Saint Anne-Dargassies, S. (1960). *The neurological examination of the infant.* London: Medical Advisory Committee of the National Spastics Society.

André-Thomas & Saint Anne-Dargassies, S. (1952). *Etudes neurologiques sur le nouveau-né et le jeune nourrisson.* Paris: Masson.

Apgar, V. (1953). A proposal for a new method of evaluation of the newborn infant. *Current Researches in Anesthesia and Analgesia, 32,* 260–267.

Apgar, V., Holaday, D., James, L., Weisbrot, I., & Berrien, C. (1958). Evaluation of the newborn infant: Second report. *Journal of the American Review Medical Association, 168,* 1985–1988.

Apgar, V. & James, L. (1962). Further observations on the newborn scoring system. *American Journal of Diseases of Children, 104,* 419–428.

Avery, G.B. (Ed.). (1987). Neonatology: *Pathophysiology and management of the newborn* (3rd ed.). Philadelphia: Lippincott.

Bayley, N. (1969). *The Bayley scales of infant development.* New York: The Psychological Corporation.

Bess, F.H., Peck, B.F., & Chapman, J.J. (1979). Further observations on noise levels in infant incubators. *Pediatrics, 63,* 100–106.

Brazelton, T.B. (1973). *Neonatal behavioral assessment scale.* (Clinics in Developmental Medicine No. 50). Philadelphia: J.B. Lippincott.

Brazelton, T.B. (1978). Introduction. In A. Sameroff (Ed.), Organizational and stability of newborn behavior: The Brazelton neonatal behavioral assessment scale. *Monographs of the Society for Research in Child Development, 43* (5–6), 1–14.

Brazelton, T.B. (1984). *Neonatal behavioral assessment scale* (2nd ed.). (Clinics in Developmental Medicine No. 88). Philadelphia: J.B. Lippincott.

Carey, W.B. (1970). A simplified method for measuring infant temperament. *Journal of Pediatrics, 77,* 188–194.

Catlin, E.A., Carpenter, M.W., Brann, B.A., Mayfield, S.R., Shaul, P.W., Goldstein, M., & Oh, W. (1986). The Apgar score revisited: Influence of gestational age. *Journal of Pediatrics, 109,* 865–868.

Cornell, E.H. & Gottfried, A.W. (1976). Intervention with premature human infants. *Child Development, 47,* 32–39.

Darwin, C. (1944). A biographical sketch of an infant. Cited in R. Illingworth (1960), *The development of the infant and young child: Normal and abnormal.* New York: Churchill Livingstone.

DiLeo, J. (1967). Developmental evaluation of very young infants. In J. Hellmuth (Ed.), *Exceptional infant, Vol. 1.* (pp. 121–142). New York: Brunner/Mazel.

Dubowitz, L. & Dubowitz, V. (1981). *The neurological assessment of the preterm and full term newborn infant.* (Clinics in Developmental Medicine No. 79). London: Heinemann.

Dubowitz, V., Dubowitz, L., & Goldberg, S. (1970). Clinical assessement of gestational age. *Journal of Pediatrics, 77,* 1–10.

Dubowitz, L.M.S., Dubowtiz, V., Morante, A., & Verghote, M. (1980). Visual fixation in the preterm and full term infant. *Developmental Medicine and Child Neurology, 22,* 465–475.

Duffy, F.H. (1985). *Evidence for hemispheric differences between full terms and preterms by electrophysiological measures.* (Paper presented at the biannual meetings of the Society for Research in Child Development, Toronto.)

Fanaroff, A.A. & Martin, S. (1987). *Neonatal-prenatal medicine.* St. Louis: C.V. Mosby.

Farr, V., Mitchell, R.G., Neligan, G.A., & Parkin, J.M. (1966). The definition of some external characteristics used in the assessment of gestational age in the newborn infant. *Developmental Medicine and Child Neurology, 8,* 507.

Frankenburg, W. & Dodds, J. (1967). The Denver Developmental Screening Test. *Journal of Pediatrics, 71*(2), 181–191.

Gardner, J.M., Karmel, B.Z., Magnano, M.A., & Norton, K. (1988). Neurobehavioral indicators of early brain insult. Manuscript submitted for publication.

Gesell, A. (1925). *The mental growth of the preschool child: A psychological outline of normal development from birth to the sixth year, including a system of developmental diagnosis.* New York: Macmillan.

Gesell, A. (1940). *The first five years of life: A guide to the study of the preschool child.* New York: Harper.

Gesell, A. & Amatruda, C. (1941). *Developmental diagnosis.* New York: Hoeber.

Gesell, A.L. & Ilg, F.L. (1949). *Child development, an introduction to a study of human growth.* New York: Harper.

Gesell, A. & Thompson, H. (1938). *The psychology of early growth.* New York: Macmillan.

Ginsburg, H. & Opper, S. (1969). *Piaget's theory of intellectual development.* Englewood Cliffs, NJ: Prentice-Hall.

Glass, P., Avery, G., Kolinjavadi, N., Subramanian, S., Keys, M., Sostek, A., & Friendly, D. (1985). Effect of bright light in the hospital nursery on the incidence of retinopathy of prematurity. *The New England Journal of Medicine, 313* (7), 401–404.

Gorski, P. (1984). Caring for immature infants—a touchy subject. In C.C. Brown (Ed.), *The many facets of touch* (pp. 84–91): Johnson & Johnson.

Gorski, P.A. (1983). Premature infant behavioral and physiological responses to caregiving interventions in the intensive care nursery. In J. Call, E. Galenson, & R. Tyson (Eds.), *Frontiers of infant psychiatry.* New York: Basic Books.

Gottfried, A.W. & Gaiter, J. L. (1985). *Infant stress under intensive care.* Baltimore, MD: University Park Press.

Gottfried, A.W., Wallace-Lande, P., Sherman-Brown, S., King, J., & Coen, C. (1981). Physical and social environment of newborn infants in special care units. *Science, 214,* 637–675.

Graham, F.K. (1956). Behavioral differences between normal and traumatized newborns: I. The test procedures. *Psychological Monographs, 70* (20, Whole No. 427).

Graham, F.K., Matarazzo, R.G., & Caldwell, B.M. (1956). Behavioral differences between normal and traumatized newborns: II. Standardization, reliability, and validity. *Psychological Monographs, 70* (21, Whole No. 428).

Graham, F.K., Pennoyer, M.M., Caldwell, B.M., Greenman, M., & Hartmann, A.F. (1957). Relationship between clinical status and behavior test performance in a newborn group with histories suggesting anoxia. *Journal of Pediatrics, 50*(2), 177–189.

Harris, M. (1986). Stimulation of premature infants: The boundary between believing and knowing. *Infant Mental Health Journal, 7*(3), 171–188.

Illingworth, R.S. (1960). *The development of the infant and young child: Normal and abnormal.* New York: Churchill Livingstone.

Kellman, N. (1982). Noise in the intensive care nursery. *Neonatal Network, 1,* 81–87.

Lawson, K., Daum, C., & Turkewitz, G. (1977). Environmental characteristics of a neonatal intensive care unit. *Child Development, 48,* 1633–1639.

Lester, B.M. (1984). Data analysis and prediction. In T.B. Brazelton, *Neonatal behavioral assessment scale* (2nd ed.). (Clinics in Developmental Medicine No. 88). Philadelphia: J.B. Lippincott.

Lester, B.M., Als, H., & Brazelton, T.B. (1982). Regional obstetric anesthesia and newborn behavior: A reanalysis toward synergistic effects. *Child Development, 53,* 687–692.

Little, W.J. (1862). On the influence of abnormal parturition, difficult labor, premature birth, and asphyxia neonatorum on the mental and physical condition of the chid, especially in relation to deformities. *Transaction of the Obstetric Society of London, 3,* 293–344.

Long, J.G., Lucey, J.F., & Philip, A.G.S. (1980). Noise and hypoxemia in the intensive care nursery. *Pediatrics, 65,* 143–145.

Lorenz, K. (1965). *The evolution and modification of behavior.* Chicago: University of Chicago Press.

Lydic, J.S. & Nugent, J.K. (1982). Theoretical background and uses of the Brazelton neonatal assessment scale. *Physical and Occupational Therapy in Pediatrics, 2*(2/3), 117–131.

Magitat, A. (1903). L' apparition prococe reflexe photomeur au cours du development foetal. *Annales d'oculistique, 141,* 161.

Magnus, R. (1924). *Korperstellung.* Berlin: Julius Springer.

Martin, R.J., Herrell, N., Rubin, D., & Fanaroff, A. (1979). Effect of supine and prone positions on arterial oxygen tension in the preterm infant. *Pediatrics, 63,* 528–531.

Moro, E. (1918). Das erste Trimenon. *Münchener medizinische Wochenschrift, 65,* 1147–1150.

Nugent, J.K. (1985). *Using the NBAS with infants and their families: Guidelines for intervention.* White Plains, NY: March of Dimes Birth Defects Foundation.

O'Donnell, K. (1986). The family system in neonatal care. In D. Slaton (Ed.), *Special care for special babies.* Chapel Hill: University of North Carolina.

Oehler, J.M., Eckerman, C., & Wilson, W. (1988). Social stimulation and the regulation of premature infants' state prior to term age. Manuscript submitted for publication.

Oehler, J.M. (1985). Examining the issue of tactile stimulation. *Neonatal Network, 4,* 25–33.

Oehler, J.M. (1981). *Family-centered neonatal nursing care.* Philadelphia: J.B. Lippincott.

Paine, R. (1960). Neurological examination of infants and children. *Pediatric Clinics of North America, 8,* 577–610.

Paine, R.S. (1961). The early diagnosis of cerebral palsy. *Rhode Island Medical Journal, 44,* 522–527.

Palay, S. L. (1979). *Introduction to the nervous system: Basic neuroanatomy.* (Lecture delivered at Harvard Medical School.)

Parmelee, A.H. (1962). European neurological studies of the newborn. *Child Development, 33,* 169–180.

Parmelee, A.H. (1985). Sensory stimulation in the nursery: How much and when? *Journal of Developmental and Behavioral Pediatrics, 6,* 242–243.

Parmelee, A.H. & Michaelis, R. (1971). Neurological examination of the newborn. In J. Hellmuth (Ed.), *Exceptional infant, Vol. 2* (pp. 3–23). New York: Brunner/Mazel.

Peiper, A. (1928). *Die Hirntatigkeit des Sauglings.* Berlin: Julius Springer.

Peiper, A. & Isbert, H. (1927). Uber die Korperstellung des Sauglins. *Jahrbuch der Kinderheilkunde, 115,* 142.

Prechtl, H. (1965a). Problems of behavioral studies in the newborn infant. In D. Lehrman, R. Hinde, & E. Shaw (Eds.), *Advances in the study of behavior, Vol. 1* (pp. 75–98). New York: Academic Press.

Prechtl, H. (1965b). Prognostic value of neurological signs in the newborn infant. *Proceedings of the Royal Society of Medicine, 58,* 3–4.

Prechtl, H.F.R. (1977). *The neurological examination of the full term newborn infant.* (Clinics in Developmental Medicine No. 63). London: Heinemann/Spastics International Medical Publications.

Prechtl, H.F.R. & Beintema, D. (1964). *The neurological examination of the full term newborn infant.* London: Heinemann/Spastics International Publications.

Rice, R.D. (1977). Neurophysiological development in premature infants following stimulation. *Develomental Psychology, 13,* 69–76.

Robinson, R.J. (1966). Assessment of gestational age by neurological examination. *Archives of Diseases of Children, 41,* 437.

Rosenblith, J.F. (1975). Prognostic value of neonatal behaviors. In B.Z. Friedlander, G.M. Sterritt, & G.E. Kirk (Eds.), *Exceptional Infant, Vol. 3* (pp. 157–172). New York: Brunner-Mazel.

Rosenblith, J.F. (1961a). *Manual for behavioral examination of the neonate as modified by Rosenblith from Graham.* Unpublished manuscript, Brown University, Institute for Health Sciences.

Rosenblith, J.F. (1961b). The modified Graham Behavior Test for neonates: Test-retest reliability, normative data, and hypotheses for future work. *Biologia Neonatorum, 3,* 174–192.

Rosenblith, J.F. (1974). Relations between neonatal behaviors and those at eight months. *Developmental Pychology, 10,* 779–792.

Rosenblith, J.F. & Lipsitt, L. (1959). Interscorer agreement for the Graham Behavior Test for neonates. *Journal of Pediatrics, 54,* 200–205.

Saint Anne-Dargassies, S. (1955). La maturation neurologique du prematuré. *Etudies Neo-Natales, 4,* 71.

Saint Anne-Dargassies, S. (1957). Hematome extra dural diagnostique, operé et gueri chez un nouveau-né. *Etudies Neo-Natales, 11,* 165.

Saint Anne-Dargassies, S. (1960). Neurologic development of the infant: The contribution of Andre-Thomas. *World Neurology, 1,* 71–77.

Saint Anne-Dargassies, S. (1965). Neurologic examination of the neonate. *Proceedings of the Royal Society of Medicine, 58,* 5.

Saint Anne-Dargassies, S. (1977). *Neurological development in full term and preterm neonates.* Amsterdam: Elsevier.

Sameroff, A. J. (1983). Developmental systems: Contexts and evolution. In Vol.1: History, theory, and methods. In P. Mussen (Ed.), *Handbook of child psychology,* New York: Wiley.

Sameroff, A. & Chandler, M. (1975). Reproductive risk and the continuum of caretaking casualty. In F. Horowitz, M. Hetherington, S. Scarr-Salapatek, & G. Siegel (Eds.), *Review of child development research, Vol. 4* (pp. 187–244). Chicago: University of Chicago Press.

Sameroff, A., Krafchuk, E., & Bakow, H. (1978). Issues in grouping items from the neonatal behavioral assessment scale. In A. Sameroff (Ed.), Organization and stability of newborn behavior: A commentary on the Brazelton neonatal behavioral assessment scale. *Monographs of the Society for Research in Child Development, 43,* 46–59.

Serunian, S. & Broman, S. (1975). Relationship of Apgar scores and Bayley mental and motor scores. *Child Development, 46,* 969–700.

Shipe, D., Vandenberg, S., & Williams, R. (1968). Neonatal Apgar ratings as related to intelligence and behavior in preschool children. *Child Development, 39,* 861–866.

Sostek, A.M. (1978). Annotated bibliography of research using the neonatal behavioral assessment scale. In A. Sameroff (Ed.), Organization and stability of newborn behavior: A commentary on the Brazelton neonatal behavioral assessment scale. *Monographs of the Society for Research in Child Development, 43,* 124–135.

Sostek, A.M. & Anders, T.F. (1977). Relationships among the Brazelton neonatal scale, Bayley infant scales, and early temperament. *Child Development, 48,* 320–323.

St. Clair, K.L. (1978). Neonatal assessment procedures: A historical review. *Child Development, 49,* 280–292.

Volpé, J.J. (1981). *Neurology of the newborn.* Philadelphia: W.B. Saunders.

Werner, H. (1957). The concept of development from a comparative and organismic point of view. In D.B. Harris (Ed.), *The concept of develop-*

ment (pp. 125–148). Minneapolis: University of Minnesota Press.

Widmayer, S.M. & Field, T.M. (1981). Effects of Brazelton demonstrations for mothers on the development of preterm infants. *Pediatrics, 67,* 711–714.

Worobey, J. (1984). A review of Brazelton-based interventions to enhance parent-infant interaction. *Journal of Reproductive and Infant Psychology, 3,* 64–73.

Chapter 9

Assessment of Behavioral State Organization

James M. Helm
Wake County Medical Center
Rune J. Simeonsson
University of North Carolina at Chapel Hill

KEY TERMS

- **Behavioral States**
- **Mediate**
- **Bidirectional Influences**
- **Synactive Theory**
- **Clarity (of states)**
- **Lability (of states)**
- **Rhythmicity (of states)**

Behavioral states and their organization reflect the integrity and maturity of the developing child's central nervous system (CNS). They are important because they mediate behavior and reflect the child's ability to respond to various forms of stimulation. Evaluation of behavioral states can provide a context for understanding behavior. Behavioral states have been defined in a variety of ways, but are separated into two main categories: sleep states and awake states. Sleep states may be quiet or active, whereas awake states include alert, active/fussy, or crying states. Drowsiness is usually identified as an awake but transitional state. Parameters of state organization include clarity of states, lability of states, patterns of occurrence, and influences upon states.

Given the fact that CNS dysfunction is a common characteristic of at-risk and handicapped infants, consideration of behavioral states and their organization is important in assessment and intervention efforts. This chapter (a) presents a rationale for assessment of behavioral state organization, (b) describes important dimensions of behavioral state organization, (c) reviews procedural considerations and representative methods for assessing behavioral states, and (d) identifies implications of such assessment for intervention with at-risk and handicapped infants and young children.

Rationale for Assessing Behavioral States

In assessment and intervention activities with infants and young children with handicaps, it is important for practitioners and parents to attend to variables that influence behavior and development. **Behavioral states** are expressions of the maturity, status, and organization of the central nervous system. They **mediate** the child's ability to respond to the environment and to stimulation. Although states are defined by a group of characteristic behaviors, they are expressed individually. They can be affected by influences intrinsic or extrinsic to the child. Variation in behavioral states—their stability, patterns, and clarity—accounts for significant differences within and between individual children. Such variation needs to be systematically documented and taken into account when individualizing intervention.

Parents, infant development specialists, and those working with parents of very young children are likely to be keenly aware of the variability of behavioral states. An infant's ability to sleep for extended periods and the quality of the awake/alert states (e.g., bright eyed and curious or irritable) are important components of parental adjustment to a new baby and the developing parent/child relationship. The range and quality of states, as well as the ability of the infant to maintain states, reflect current status of development and behavioral organization and possibly predict later functioning. Further, the presence, intensity, and quality of reflexes, the occurrence and characteristics of self-generated behaviors, and behavioral responses to stimulation vary systematically as a function of state.

Although state is a concept that has received widespread attention in research on neonatal development, its significance as a focus for assessment by interventionists working with infants and preschoolers with handicaps has received less attention (Simeonsson, Huntington, & Parse, 1980). State-related behaviors are, however, likely to be of practical importance to parents, in that the quality of alertness and sleep patterns, for example, influences caregiving patterns. Further, quiet alertness, a behavioral state, provides the context for learning many skills.

The realization that the interaction of state and stimulation must be systematically considered to understand infant behavior better (Brazelton, 1973) is a central reason for the importance of assessing state. The **bidirectional effects** of the environment and infant maturation are evident. Each affects states (e.g., patterns or clarity), which, in turn, affect the responsiveness of the infant. The importance of state has been demonstrated in a variety of contexts, including the effects of hunger on behavior (Feldman, 1978), the differentiation of normal infants and those at risk for sudden infant death syndrome (Harper, Leake, Hoppenbrouwers, Sterman, McGinty, & Hodgman, 1978), the effects of drug history on infant postnatal development (Turner & MacFarlane, 1978), the effect of states on reflexes (Lenard, von Bernuth, & Prechtl, 1968), and the differential effects of nursery routines upon the relative time in sleep states and later growth and sleep patterns (Mann, Haddow, Stokes, Goodley, & Rutter, 1986). The predictive value of state assessment has also been examined. Sostek and Anders (1977) found state-related scores to be predictive of Bayley mental scores at age 10 weeks, and Becker and Thoman (1981) predicted development at age 1 year from recurrent periods of very rapid eye movement (REM storms). Beyond this specific examination of state much of the literature on learning and facilitation of development with young children assumes alertness or attentive behavior. Quiet alertness is influenced by numerous factors, and the better these factors are understood, the more likely it is that interventionists can help facilitate states appropriate for learning.

Simeonsson, Huntington, and Parse (1980)

discuss the use of state as an important domain when assessing handicapped children
and suggest that, although assessment of
state has been focused primarily on neonates,
the concept seems relevant to handicapped
infants and children beyond the newborn
period. This assumption is based on the
premise that state variability may continue
to be a characteristic of handicapped infants
and young children due to neurological insults
and/or drugs that influence level of arousal
or activation. Thus, careful examination of
behavioral states and influences upon them
is important to understand behavior across
the early childhood period.

Presented in Table 9.1 is a list of factors
supporting the systematic assessment of
states of at-risk and handicapped infants and
young children. The table draws on Korner's
(1972) presentation of state as an obstacle,
as a variable, and as a mediator of stimulation. Seen as an obstacle, state variability may
account for error in observation and/or

assessment (i.e., reflexes may be expressed
differentially in different states, or fussy or
sleepy infants will not attend optimally). As
a variable in its own right, it may be important to understand sleep patterns or effects
of the environment on alertness, particularly for severely handicapped infants whose
behavioral repertoires are often very limited.
State could thus be assessed in terms of its
distinctiveness, range, predictability, and
alterability. State also mediates responsiveness to stimulation, and it is important
to identify the optimal states during which
specific types of stimulation are effective.
The importance of state as a variable is also
apparent in the context of recent work with
premature infants (e.g., Als, 1986) and with
new parents (Nugent, 1985). Observation of
state provides a window into a child's ability
to control stimulation and respond to it
(Brazelton, 1985). Finally, research suggests
that assessment of states can reflect the integrity of an infant's central nervous system

TABLE 9.1
Importance of Assessing Behavior State Organization

State as an Obstacle	
Source of error	(a) reflexes differentially elicited
	(b) tired infant not performing well
	(c) excited, active infant noncompliant
Handicapped infant may have limited alert time	(a) alert time may not be convenient
	(b) alertness may be easily disrupted
State as a Variable	
CNS insults and/or drugs may influence state	(a) unique sleep patterns
	(b) lethargic alert state
State may be a sensitive variable in its own right	(a) importance of maintaining attention
	(b) importance of sleep patterns
	(c) effects of environment on states
	(d) effects of social stimulation
State as a Mediator	
Infant responsiveness different in each state	(a) reflexes can be different
	(b) ability to attend differs
Rhythmicity of states influences family routines	(a) unpredictable sleep disrupts routines
	(b) state organization can be predictive

Source: The data are from "State as Variable, as Obstacle, and as Mediator of Stimulation
in Infant Research" by A. F. Korner, 1972, *Merrill-Palmer, 18,* 77–94.

and can be predictive of later development (Thoman, Denenberg, Sievel, Zeidner, Becker, 1981).

States are influenced by context. They develop within the maturing child and are supported or challenged by both internal and external factors. The **synactive theory** developed by Als and colleagues (Als, Lester, Tronick, & Brazelton, 1982; Als & Duffy, 1982) provides an organizing frame for assessment and understanding of states in infants and young handicapped children. (Also see Chaper 8.) The theory has been developed in the context of work with premature infants but is applicable to early development in general. In the synactive theory, the child's behavior is seen as the product of maturation in continuous interaction with internal and external influences. An infant's behavior represents an effort to maintain balanced organization while responding to challenges. The synactive theory posits a hierarchy of five interdependent subsystems. The most primitive response of an organism is on the physiological level, which includes heart rate, respiration, temperature control, digestive system, and so on. Physiological responses are behaviorally observable from respiration rates and patterns, color changes, visceral responses, and autonomically controlled movements (i.e., startles). The second level is the motor subsystem, which includes muscle tone, posture, and movement. The third is the state subsystem that includes clarity of states and lability, range, and patterns of states. The fourth level is the attention/social interactional subsystem, which includes the ability to attain and maintain an alert state, orient to stimuli, and respond in a socially reciprocal manner. The fifth subsystem is the ability of the infant to self-regulate, that is, to respond to stimuli without losing physiological stability or motor control and without rapid fluctuations of state. Each subsystem has self-regulatory mechanisms that both reflect the child's efforts and allow the child, within capabilities, organized receptivity of stimulation and other environmental

challenges. The synactive theory explains subsystem differentiation and early child behavior as a developmental process whereby all subsystems develop, stabilize, and integrate in simultaneous negotiation with one another and the environment (Als et al., 1982). The hierarchical nature of the subsystems and behavioral indices of the organization of four subsystems are depicted in Figure 9.1 (p. 206). The self-regulatory subsystem is expressed as part of each subsystem, and examples of balanced behaviors are listed. The value of the synactive theory is that it provides a framework for understanding infant behavior and the relationship of behaviors to one another. As represented in Figure 9.1, behavioral state reflects one hierarchical level of the organization of behavior and shows its relationship to development and the complexity of behavior.

Behavioral states of infants are important determiners of their response to stimulation. Professionals working with infants and their families need to understand states, their influence on behaviors, how they are expected to change over time, and the interactive effect of the environment and biological status on an infant's regulation of state. In this chapter, infant states are reviewed to provide a basis and context for understanding observations of infant behaviors and states. The research provides a framework to understand how regulation of states reflects an infant's current level of maturity and CNS organization and shows in one way that there is a continuity of organization. The implications of state assessment are examined as to how intervention directed toward helping infants organize and control states might affect infant development, parent/child relationships, and later functioning.

Dimensions of Behavioral States

In infants and young children behavioral states are an expression of biological maturi-

FIGURE 9.1
Representation of the hierarchical relationship and behavioral indices of each subsystem in the synactive theory of development (Source: Model adapted from O'Donnell, 1987; for more information see Als et al., 1982.)

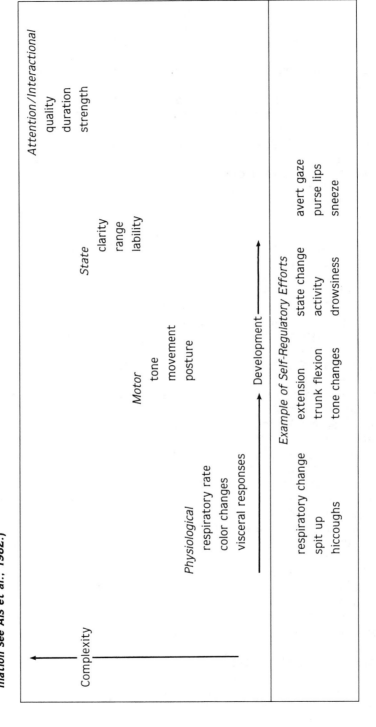

ty and CNS organization and are both influenced by the environment and mediate responses to stimulation. As emphasized throughout this chapter, states occur within context; it is therefore important to evaluate several dimensions of behavioral state organization, including **clarity, lability, rhythmicity,** and influences upon state. In order to provide a broader understanding of state, the following topics are considered: (a) definitions of state, (b) ontogeny of state development, (c) influences upon state, and (d) the mediating effects of state.

Definitions of Behavioral States

Definitions and descriptions of states and the behaviors that mark different states have varied according to purpose and method of observation (Als et al., 1982; Ashton, 1971; 1973; Prechtl, 1974; Thoman, 1975; Wolff, 1966), but generally behavioral states are considered a "configuration of functional parameters that remain relatively stable for predictable periods and occur repeatedly" (Wolff & Ferber, 1979, p. 292). States are defined by characteristic parameters of respiration, eye movements, movement, and heart rate. The basic categorization is sleep or awake states; more refined definitions are often tied to specific research or clinical purposes.

The definitions developed by Brazelton (1973) are probably the most frequently used with infants. In this system there are six states recognized as easily distinguishable through behavioral observations: deep (quiet) sleep, light (active) sleep, drowsy, quiet alert, active alert, and crying. They are sometimes referred to by number, states 1, 2, 3, 4, 5, and 6, respectively.

Although states appear to be a continuum of arousal, behavioral observations as well as confirming EEG readings demonstrate that states are qualitatively different from one another (Hack, 1987; Lenard, von Bernuth, & Prechtl, 1968; Wolff & Ferber, 1979). States

are "qualitatively highly specific with a distinct type of internal organization and brain center control" (Hack, 1987, p. 474). Behavioral states and state changes have been defined by Brazelton (1973) as occurring if the characteristic behaviors of a state are exhibited for 15 seconds, but the amount of time deemed adequate to indicate a state change has also varied from 3 seconds (Als, 1984) to 3 minutes (Prechtl, 1974).

In Table 9.2 are the behavioral descriptions of two methods to categorize states that have been used for clinical work and are provided as examples. The categories used in Brazelton's Neonatal Behavioral Assessment Scale (Brazelton, 1984) are summarized here as in Nugent's guide for clinical use of the NBAS (1985, p. 17). The Carolina Record of Infant Behavior (CRIB) (Simeonsson, 1979) is an example of a scale that uses states as part of an instrument designed to document the unique behavioral responses of children in the sensorimotor stages of development (Simeonsson, Huntington, Short, & Ware, 1982).

As mentioned, others have defined behavioral states differently, depending on research or clinical interests. For example, Als and colleagues (1982) use Brazelton's six states to describe the states of infants but classify the diffuse behaviors of premature infants (immature states) as A states and the well-modulated behaviors of full-term or more mature infants as B states; Becker and Thoman (1981) describe a particular aspect of light sleep where there are periods of intensely rapid eye movements (REM) as "REM storms"; and Sammons and Lewis (1985) use three or four classifications to describe clinically the states of premature infants depending upon the purpose.

Ontogeny of Behavioral States

The behaviors characteristic of each state evolve from global, diffuse expression, which over time cluster together and begin to oc-

TABLE 9.2
Examples of Descriptions of Behavioral States Used in Two Assessment Procedures: Brazelton Neonatal Behavioral Assessment Scale (NBAS) and the Carolina Record of Individual Behavior (CRIB)

	NBAS
State 1:	Deep sleep with regular breathing, eyes closed, no spontaneous movement, no rapid eye movement. Startles may appear.
State 2:	Light sleep with eyes closed, irregular respirations, more modulated motor activity. Rapid eye movements are present (often called REM sleep).
State 3:	Drowsy or semi-alert, eyes may be open or closed, activity levels are variable.
State 4:	Alert with bright look, minimal activity.
State 5:	Eyes open, considerable motor activity. Fussing may or may not be present.
State 6:	Crying state.

cur rhythmically. These rhythms and differentiated behaviors develop separately and independently of one another and later combine into clusters of behaviors associated with states (Berg & Berg, 1979; Dreyfus-Brisac, 1968; 1970; Prechtl, Fargel, Weinmann, & Bakker, 1979).

Movements become differentiated into active and quiet episodes by 28 weeks gestational age; eye movements are differentiated into quiet and rapid periods by 30 weeks gestational age (Dreyfus-Brisac, 1968); regular and irregular respirations are clearly differentiated by 34 weeks gestational age; EEG patterns are differentiated by 36 weeks gestational age; and muscle tone suppression occurs in different states by 40 weeks gestational age (term age) (Anders, 1982). The earliest differentiation of these behaviors into active and quiet sleep is at about 30 weeks

gestational age with active sleep fully differentiated by 35 weeks, and quiet sleep differentiated by 36 weeks. Eye opening before 34–36 weeks gestational age occurs for short periods (briefly to 5 minutes). After 34 weeks gestational age these short periods become less frequent, but the eyes stay open for longer periods and become associated with awake states (Wolff & Ferber, 1979). Als's method for definition allows one to identify emerging states, inasmuch as their immature form is recognized.

The clustering of behaviors into states and the establishment of state rhythms continues for many years. For example, states do not reflect diurnal patterns until about 5–6 weeks post term age (45-46 weeks gestational age) (Berg & Berg, 1979), at which time the longest sleep period tends to be at night; it is not until about 4–6 months of age that

TABLE 9.2
Continued

CRIB

State 1:	Deep sleep, eyes closed, regular respiration, no body movements.	State 5:	Quiet awake, relatively inactive, eyes open and appear bright and shiny, respiration regular.
State 2:	Intermediate sleep, eyes closed, few minor facial, body, and/or mouth movements; respiration is "periodic" alternating periods of shallow and deep breathing.	State 6:	Active awake, eyes open, diffuse motor activity of limbs or whole body, vocalizations of a content nature.
State 3:	Active sleep, eyes closed, irregular respiration, some gross motor activity (stirring, writhing, grimacing, mouthing, or other facial expression).	State 7:	Fussy awake, eyes open, irregular respirations, diffuse motor activity, vocalizations of fussy, cranky variety.
State 4:	Drowsiness, eyes open and closed intermittently, fluttering eyelids, eyes have glassy appearance, frequent relaxation followed by sudden jerks.	State 8:	Mild agitation, eyes open, diffuse motor activity, moderate crying, tears may or may not be present.
		State 9:	Marked uncontrollable agitation, screaming, eyes open or closed, tears may or may not be present.

Source: The data in column 1 are from J. K. Nugent (1985); the data in column 2 are from R. J. Simeonsson (1979).

sleep states occur primarily at night (Coons & Guilleminault, 1984), and it is several years before adult EEG patterns of sleep are fully developed and differentiated (Anders, 1982; Roffwarg, Muzio, & Dement, 1966).

Sleep/wake cycles change rapidly throughout infancy and early childhood and more slowly through adulthood. The near-term fetus spends about 90% of the time in either quiet sleep or active sleep (Nijhuis, Prechtl, Martin, & Bots, 1982). Newborns, at term age, sleep about 16–17 hours per day, with about 50% being REM sleep or active sleep (Ferber, 1985; Roffwarg et al., 1966). By age 2–3 children sleep about 12–13 hours per day, and REM sleep is only 25%; adults (20–45 years) sleep about 6 to 8 hours, and REM sleep is 20%; REM sleep occurs only for about 15% of the 5–7 hours of sleep in persons 50 years or older (Roffwarg et al., 1966). The total time of REM sleep per day changes from 8–9 hours in infancy to about 1–2 hours as an adult. During the first two years of life, children develop the four stages of non-REM (NREM) sleep and sleep patterns that continue through adult life (Anders, 1982; Ferber, 1985).

Until about 3–4 weeks post term, a newborn's sleep over the 24-hour day is approximately in equal segments between feedings (about four hours). By age 3 months, sleep, particularly REM sleep, predominates at night (Coons & Guilleminault, 1982; Fagioli & Salzarulo, 1982). By age 3–4 months, the longest sleep is preceded by the longest awake period, and between 3 and 6 months a pattern of being awake during the day and asleep at night is firmly established (Coons & Guilleminault, 1984; Ferber, 1985).

Influences on States

There are biological and environmental influences on the expression of states as well as on an infant's ability to maintain states. As mentioned above, states mediate responsiveness; therefore, when behavior is assessed, the mediating effects of states need to be considered. Factors influencing states and some behaviors influenced by states are presented in Figure 9.2.

A review of Figure 9.2 reveals that the environment can influence infant states and their maintenance by stimuli that support or elicit responding. Furthermore, the same stimulus can differentially influence states depending on intensity, frequency, and dura-

tion of stimulation (Wolff, 1966; Gardner, Karmel, & Dowd, 1985). At the same time, the supports offered in the environment, such as swaddling (Korner, 1972) or nonnutritive sucking (Wolff & Simmons, 1967), have an impact on how much stimulation can be tolerated. It should be remembered also that infant states do not influence responsiveness to stimulation in isolation; that is, other infant characteristics influence state-related behaviors, including gestational age (Als et al., 1982), body positions (e.g., head position) (Brazelton, 1973), visceral or health status (e.g., hunger or asphyxia) (Dubowitz & Dubowitz, 1981), or CNS status (Prechtl, Theorell, & Blair, 1973). The transactions between the infant's maturity and status along with environmental demands determine the mediating effects of states. The child's age, status of the child's central nervous system, and the extent to which the environment supports or challenges the child affect the clarity, lability, and rhythmicity of state expression.

The synactive theory (Als et al., 1982), as shown in Figure 9.1, provides a framework to understand some of these relationships.

FIGURE 9.2
Factors influencing state organization and the mediating role of state organization on behavior

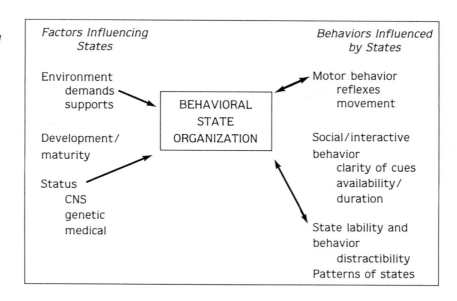

The environment can support or challenge the infant's ability to self-regulate systems. If an infant is to attain an alert state and maintain social responsivity, the physiological, motor, and state subsystems must be stable enough that stimulation does not overwhelm the infant. Infants who have been or are physiologically unstable or who have had some trauma have a more difficult time regulating all systems in order to maintain alertness. More mature or better-organized infants can self-regulate with a minimum of environmental supports. They can more easily gain and maintain alertness and thereby engage the world. Researchers are studying the effectiveness of interventions based on the synactive theory (Als, 1986; Als & Duffy, 1982; Als, Lawhon, Brown, Gibes, Duffy, McAnulty, & Blickman, 1986) and need to examine further the effects of a compromised central nervous system or atypical genetic profile on self-regulatory efforts.

Conclusions from both research and clinical accounts vary as to whether premature infants have more difficulty regulating states than full-term infants. For example, although Anders and Keener (1985) found few differences in length of time in different states, patterns of sleep, and length of longest sleep when comparing a group of preterm and full-term infants over their first year, many clinical reports suggest preterm infants tend to be more irritable, less able to maintain bright-eyed alertness, reverse day and night, and more often are less social than full-term infants (Michaelis, Parmelee, Stern, Haber, 1973; Goldberg & DiVitto, 1983; Harrison & Kositsky, 1983; McGehee & Eckerman, 1983). As Parmelee (1975) suggests, most studies examine group differences but also find variability within groups.

It is well documented that infants with brain dysfunction show highly variable and unusual sleep patterns (Prechtl et al., 1973). Of concern are both atypical behaviors in states and atypical patterns of state cycles. Research with autistic children, for example,

has shown that the development of sleep patterns is delayed (Tanguay, Ornitz, Forsythe, & Ritvo, 1976). Babies who are small for gestation age show an immature (sometimes abnormal) EEG (Thoman, Denenberg, Sievel, Zeidner, & Becker, 1981); that is, their EEG recordings in all states are similar to EEG recordings of younger babies or can have unusual aspects. Children with Down syndrome have been found to have delayed development in patterns of eye movements during sleep and different patterns of state occurrence (Prechtl et al., 1973). Children with PKU or hypothyroidism show deviations in sleep patterns, and babies with brain malformation and/or chromosomal anomalies are poor sleepers (Monod & Guidasci, 1976).

Researchers also are examining whether or not either unusual patterns of sleep or highly varied patterns can be predictive of later functioning (Lombroso & Matsumiya, 1985; Anders, Keener, & Kraemer, 1985).

State as a Mediator of Behavior

An infant can respond to stimulation by changing states, but behavior states also mediate responsiveness to stimulation (Brazelton, 1973; Korner, 1972; Prechtl, 1974; Wolff, 1966). Some reflexes are differentially expressed in different states (Lenard, von Bernuth, & Prechtl, 1968). For example, externoceptive reflexes, those elicited from external manipulation, are elicited most reliably during the quiet alert state but can also be elicited in active sleep and drowsiness. These include the palmar and plantar grasp, Babkin reflex, the palmomental reflex, rooting, and tonic components of the glabella reflex and the lip-tap reflex. Proprioceptive reflexes, reactions occurring within the organism, are equally strong during both quiet sleep and wakefulness. They are weak or absent during irregular sleep. These responses include the Moro reflex, knee and bicep jerk, and ankle clonus. A third class of reflexes that appear to be relatively independent of state are the nociceptive reflexes, or protective reflexes, which include the Babinski reflex and abdominal reflex (Lenard et al., 1968; Prechtl, 1974). It should be noted that the influence of states on the elicitation of reflexes can be altered by other factors, for example, nonnutritive sucking by an infant during elicitation of reflexes may result in a more pronounced palmar grasp and less pronounced skin reflexes (Lenard et al., 1966).

Wolff (1966) summarized infant responses to a variety of stimuli while in different states. Generally, the babies were much less sensitive to external stimulation during quiet sleep and crying. Visual or auditory stimulation can modify drowsy, waking activity or crying states, and monotonous stimulation (white noise) lowers the infant's activity level even when crying and can induce sleep states, but babies in these sleep states do not show the same spontaneous or elicited movements as when in "restful sleep." Wolff summarized that responsiveness is jointly determined by the modality involved and the quality of stimulation (intensity and frequency).

State also influences the movements and postures of infants. Muhiudeen, Melville-Thomas, Ferguson, and Mohan (1984) observed infants at age 3 days and found that the most postures were observed when infants were in the active awake state and in a seated, reclined position; generally, infants showed the fewest postures in the supine position. Berg and Berg (1979) and Hack (1987) provide comprehensive reviews of other research related to infants' states.

Procedural Considerations in Assessing Behavioral States

As with any domain of behavior, assessment procedures need to be appropriate for the purpose. When considering behavior states, numerous procedures may be appropriate if one is to describe a child fully. This discussion will focus primarily on procedural questions that might be considered by interventionists who are observing for purposes of designing interventions. There are several aspects of states that might be considered, and the following are discussed: (a) organization of states, especially sleep and quiet alertness; (b) maintenance of an appropriate state for the situation, for example, staying awake during feeding; (c) effect of stimulation on states; and (d) patterns of the occurrence of states, for example, sleep patterns. Of course, these become differentially important depending upon the child's age, ability to organize and maintain states, and again, the purpose of the evaluation. This section ends with a brief discussion on procedural considerations on assessing states with severely handicapped children.

A hypothetical example, following a premature infant over the course of several months, will demonstrate how issues change depending upon the child's age, environmental demands, and expectations. In preterm infants younger than 36 weeks gestational age, behavioral states are not well differentiated, and descriptions of the behaviors of these infants often emphasize the difficulty of classifying the observed behaviors as states (Dreyfus-Brisac, 1968; Prechtl et al., 1979).

As mentioned previously, Als and colleagues (1982) developed a system to classify preterm infant behaviors into states. Classifications are based on those used in the Neonatal Behavioral Assessment Scale (NBAS) (Brazelton, 1973). According to Als's system, behaviors displayed for three seconds can delimit a state. There are six states classified as in the NBAS and each state can be described as immature (A states) or as mature (B states). A states are characterized by diffuse movements and very irregular respirations. The quiet alert A state is also seen as either low (4AL), with dull, unfocused eyes, or hyper (4AH), with eyes wide open accompanied by an expression that gives the impression of "panic or fear" (Als, 1984). B states are the same as those described by Brazelton (1973).

Research suggests that premature infants have lower oxygen demands and use fewer calories when in quiet states (either quiet sleep or quiet alert); therefore, a reasonable goal might be to determine positions or handling techniques that facilitate quiet states (Als, 1986). To facilitate this process, an interventionist might observe infant behaviors carefully, including state and changes in states, during a regular caregiving activity (Als et al., 1986). State might be recorded using the six A or B states described above and recommendations discussed with nursing staff. At the same time the infant's parents may be trying to figure out how to help their baby nurse better. The interventionist may describe and evaluate states according to one of Sammons's and Lewis's (1985) descriptions (see Table 9.3). This evaluation might help parents more easily observe their infant's cues and may yield approaches for increasing endurance during feeding.

After an infant's discharge from the hospital, her parents may be concerned with several state-related situations; for example, the baby might be very irritable, or she may have problems with sleep patterns. It is important to be familiar with approaches to evaluate both situations. For the first problem, irritability, it might be most appropriate for the interventionist to observe the infant during times when alertness or social interaction is demanded and use a system like that of Als (Als et al., 1982) or Sammons and Lewis (1985). For sleep-pattern problems, it might be most effective to ask the parents to chart daily activities, including sleep/awake patterns, for a week (Ferber, 1985).

Approaches suggested in the preceding example can also be applied to young children with handicaps, but other techniques can also be used. For example Simeonsson, Huntington, Short, and Ware (1982) present an observation instrument, the Carolina Record of Individual Behavior (CRIB) (Simeonsson,

1979), to record individual behaviors of children. A component of the CRIB assessment includes recording the infant's predominant state as well as all the states observed during an activity. Nine states are designated to provide a description of the child's behavior (see Table 9.2). These state observations can be used either to formulate goals or to characterize behaviors more completely. State ratings can elaborate one's understanding of handicapped children by emphasizing individual differences. An example might be with two young Down syndrome children who perform at the same developmental level but exhibit different states during a typical play activity. They may have the same range of behaviors, but one might be predominantly in a quiet awake state and the other in a fussy awake state. Intervention activities may need to vary considerably with this information.

Another approach to recording state-like behaviors was used by Landesman-Dwyer and Sackett (1978) to describe sleep and activity levels of profoundly mentally retarded individuals. The four-level scale (sleep, low, moderate, and high level of activity) could be used to characterize a child's general pattern of activity during a school day or part of a day. It may also be useful to extend the concept of state to a more general one of predictable patterns of responsivity to environmental stimulation (Simeonsson et al., 1980). Those familiar with premature infants have observed infants going to sleep when overstimulated (Nance, 1982), or those familiar with severely and profoundly handicapped children may have observed patterns of "tuning out," "tuning in," or "shutting down" to external sensory or social stimulation (Simeonsson et al., 1980). The degree to which such patterns or clusters of behavior are regular and predictable may make them an important index of development. As such, they may represent the emergence of the child's adaptation to an environmental demand in terms of timing of actions (Ashton,

TABLE 9.3
Representative Methods for Assessing Behavioral States

Measure or Procedure	State Categories	Reported or Suggested Clinical Applications of State Observations
APIB (Als et al., 1982)	Same as Brazelton with A and B states. A = immature (diffuse movement), B = mature; Two 4A states, L = low intensity, H = hyper (wide-eyed, fearful look); AA states = too stressed (i.e., apnea)	Document behavioral states of premature or sick infants whose states may not be mature or well-organized
NBAS (Brazelton, 1973)	1. Deep (quiet) sleep 2. Light (active) sleep 3. Drowsy 4. Quiet alert 5. Active awake 6. Crying	Document range, strength, and lability of states in neonates Use states to discuss infant behaviors Record states during event
Ferber, 1985	Sleep Chart: Record asleep, awake, bed/nap time daily for 1–2 weeks	Document sleep patterns Document sleep-related behaviors in household
Landesman-Dwyer & Sackett, 1978	Sleep Low-level activity Moderate-level activity High-level activity	Document different levels of activity within limited range Document states of profoundly handicapped children
Sammons & Lewis, 1985	Sleep Awake Fussy	Discuss with parents states of premature/sick infants

1971), rhythms of infant/adult interactions (Field, 1979), or sleep patterns (Ferber, 1985).

The emphasis here is that the appropriate method of assessing behavioral states is dependent upon the child (e.g., age, status), the nature of the concern (e.g., sleep patterns, general behavior during play), the purpose of the evaluation (e.g., keep child awake during feeding, help parents develop a bed-time routine), and the context of the proposed intervention (e.g., hospital nursery, home, or preschool classroom). The better the understanding of behavioral states, the better the understanding of both the effect of the environment on state and the mediating effects of state on behavior. From this basis one can best decide appropriate methods to assess states.

TABLE 9.3
Continued

Measure or Procedure	State Categories	Reported or Suggested Clinical Applications of State Observations
	Deep sleep Light sleep Overload Playing possum	Discuss with parents behaviors of premature/sick infants
CRIB (Simeonsson, 1979)	1. Deep sleep 2. Intermediate sleep 3. Active sleep 4. Drowsiness 5. Quiet awake 6. Active awake 7. Fussy awake 8. Mild agitation 9. Marked agitation	Record states during specific activities Document individual differences between children Document a wide range of awake and active behaviors
Thoman, 1975	Quiet sleep A Quiet sleep B Active sleep without REMs Active sleep with REMs Active sleep with dense REMs Drowsy Alert inactive Waking active Fussing Crying Indefinite	Document states (these procedures mostly used with video recordings)
Wolff, 1966	Regular sleep Irregular sleep Periodic sleep Drowsiness Alert inactivity Waking activity Crying	Document states (these procedures are not part of extended evaluation)

Representative Methods for Assessing Behavioral States

Many of the procedures used for assessing infant behavioral states have been for research purposes. These research interests have included examination of state and patterns of occurrence as (a) part of defining individual differences (e.g., Brazelton, 1973), (b) markers of neurobehavioral status (e.g., Als et al., 1982; Becker & Thoman, 1982), (c) developmental markers (Dreyfus-Brisac, 1970), (d) predictors (e.g., Thoman et al., 1981), (e) outcome measures of the effect of procedures on states (e.g., Korner, 1972), and (f) mediators of behavioral responsiveness (e.g., Wolff, 1966). There are also clinical evaluations that have been developed and sometimes overlap with research methods. A range of examples of the different categorizations of behavioral states are presented in Table 9.3 along with reported or suggested clinical applications for each method.

The system used in the Brazelton or NBAS (Brazelton, 1984) is probably the most frequently used system for rating the states of infants. The descriptors are summarized in Table 9.2. In the NBAS, a series of procedures is used to evaluate the child's ability to deal with stimulation from the environment. State is assessed at all times, and if characteristic behaviors of a state are displayed for 15 seconds, the child is rated as being in that state. An infant can exhibit some behaviors characteristic of other states for a short time, but only if behaviors change for 15 seconds is the child considered to have changed states. Also of importance is the range and lability of states. Most newborns have available to them the full range of 6 states and will change states between 3 and 15 times during a 30-minute evaluation. The NBAS was initially developed as a research tool to examine individual differences in newborn behavior and has been used in a wide range of projects (see Brazelton, 1984). The NBAS is also used clinically (Nugent, 1985; Widmayer & Field, 1980).

One clinical use of the NBAS has been to acquaint parents with the behaviors and competencies of newborns by administering the evaluation with parents observing (Nugent, 1985). Throughout the NBAS the examiner can discuss the infant's behavior with the parents. The identification of states provides a format to discuss close observation of the baby's behavior in general as well as issues relating to sleep and waking behavior. Nugent suggests, for example, discussing general information such as how much time a newborn usually sleeps (averages of 16–17 hours a day or at most 4½ hours at a time), how much time a 3-month-old sleeps (about 14 hours), or how there are wide variations in individual patterns. An examiner could also discuss

issues such as schedule feeding or demand feeding when a baby is awake and indicating hunger.

The systems developed by Wolff (1966) and Thoman (1975) have been used mostly in research with newborns or very young infants. The classifications used by Wolff include periodic sleep (see Table 9.3 on pp. 214–215). As stated previously, this type would most likely be active sleep in Brazelton's system. Periodic sleep consists of occasional body movements and breathing that has short periods of regular and irregular respirations. In Thoman's (1975) classifications, sleep and wakefulness are divided into five states each. Of particular note is the classification of active sleep with dense REMs. Research has indicated that this state is found with most babies, but an inordinate amount of time in active sleep with dense REMs may suggest a disorganized baby or a developmental risk (Becker & Thoman, 1981; 1982). Studies of infant sleep in this much detail are not practical for early interventionists, but it is important to note that unusual sleep behavior or patterns may be important predictors of later development and therefore should be examined further when noted by either parents or interventionists.

States discussed by Sammons and Lewis (1985) apply mostly to premature infants. The states of sleep, awake, or fussy are easy for parents to understand and help focus parents on their baby's behavior. The descriptions for deep and light sleep are consistent with others, but *overload* and *playing possum* are unique characterizations. Overload is usually seen when a baby is exhausted, has little muscle tone, and is not very responsive to further stimulation. With playing possum, the baby appears to be asleep, with eyes closed and little movement, but is still very reactive to stimulation. Both states are seen mostly in immature or sick babies and suggest the baby's need for quiet support. Sammons and Lewis (1985) discuss several issues related to the sleep habits and patterns of premature infants and suggest practical ideas as to how to help these babies develop desired sleep patterns.

The CRIB assessment (Simeonsson, 1979) and methods developed by Landesman-Dwyer and Sackett (1978) provide means to document the behavioral states of older children and adults. The CRIB provides a system to describe the behaviors of children in the sensorimotor stage of development, and the Landesman-Dwyer and Sackett system was designed to describe the behavior of severely or profoundly retarded children. States are considered the context in which behavior occurs and can provide important information as to the effect of stimulation or the behavior patterns during the course of a designated time period. When these behaviors are systematically considered, program goals and strategies can directly target states.

The approach by Ferber (1985) provides a systematic method to evaluate sleep behavior. Parents become understandably upset when their child's sleep patterns disrupt the routines of sleep of the household. The sleep chart allows one to examine sleep patterns over time and within the context of daily activity. In clinical settings one often hears parents discussing various methods to change sleep habits in some way. Too often ideas are given without complete information, or they are not applied systematically and therefore are less likely to succeed. Ferber's work provides a basis for understanding sleep and a systematic way to approach problems.

Applications of the Assessment of Behavioral States

There are both research and clinical applications related to the assessment of states. Representative research applications are briefly summarized as an example of how assessment of states relates to broader aspects of behavior and development.

Research applications of the assessment of behavioral states

Efforts have been made to predict later functioning from the quality of states and consistency of state cycles. Thoman (1975) summarized a number of her own studies and those of colleagues and found that babies who were rated as having poorly organized sleep states were similarly rated after an interview with their mothers eight months later. Thoman also suggests that an observed pattern where the rate of state changes increases with age could indicate potential problems such as a higher risk for sudden infant death syndrome. Thoman and colleagues (Becker & Thoman, 1981; 1982; Thoman, Denenberg, Sievel, Zeidner, & Becker, 1981) have also found that consistencies in sleep patterns during the 2nd–5th week of life were highly predictive of later problems. More specifically an unusual frequency of REM storms ("intense REM bursting during active sleep involving eye movements of great amplitude, usually accompanied by raising of the brows and opening of the eyes," Becker & Thoman, 1982, p. 203) was related to less stable state organization during the first two months of life and predicted lower Bayley scores at age 1 year (Becker & Thoman, 1981). These REM storms are occasionally observed in all normal infants during the first five weeks of life.

Lombroso and Matsumiya (1985) found that an indicator of sleep pattern concordance (consistency in patterns over the four measurement times) accurately discriminated outcomes for 11 of 13 infants with abnormal development and 15 of 17 infants with normal development. Anders, Keener, and Kraemer (1985) concluded that state constructs such as "activity, irregularity and dysinhibition—whether measured by neonatal behavioral assessment or by sleep studies—are significant predictors of developmental outcome measured by the Bayley examination at 6 months and 1 year of age" (p. 204).

Research has also examined efforts to encourage quiet alertness. Swaddling has been reported as helpful for soothing crying babies (Harrison & Kositsky, 1983; Nance, 1982; VandenBerg, 1982). It is recommended as a method for obtaining more available alert states during evaluations (Brazelton, 1973) and is suggested as a way to facilitate more modulated and controlled sleep states in young or disorganized infants (Als et al., 1986). Other researchers have found that both auditory and visual stimulation can be used to modify infant states. Infants in a drowsy state, an active awake state, or crying can sometimes be helped into a quiet alert state by providing them with appropriate voice stimulation or interesting visual stimulation (Brazelton, 1973; Harrison & Kositsky, 1983; Wolff, 1966). Premature infants who are in an alert state but indicate they are overstimulated (e.g., averting gaze) can regain focus if auditory or visual stimulation is decreased (Field, 1979; Als et al., 1982).

Korner and Schneider (1983) found vestibular stimulation soothed crying infants more effectively than did a position change or contact, whereas none of the manipulations affected sleep. Barnard and Bee (1983) found a decrease in activity levels and longer sleep/wake cycles for premature infants provided temporally patterned kinesthetic and auditory stimulation with a rocking bed and heartbeat audiotape.

The effects of nonnutritive sucking on behavioral states have also been studied. Wolff and Simmons (1967) observed, as have others (Neeley, 1979; Woodson, Drinkwin, & Hamilton, 1985), that infants engaged in this action were in less active states (increased time in quiet sleep and active sleep and decreased time in active awake and crying states) and showed fewer state changes.

These studies indicate that states, their regulation, and patterns of occurrence are related to CNS organization, and if observed systematically over time, they can reveal developmental continuities. The work also suggests biological and environmental contributions to infant state and motor organization.

Clinical Applications of the Assessment of Behavioral States

Parents have many concerns about infant behaviors and development that are related to states. Many of these concerns can be addressed through environmental manipulations. There is much evidence that the environment, including distal factors such as noise and light and proximal factors such as handling or position, affect the states of infants (Korner, 1972; Korner & Schneider, 1983; Lawson, Turkewitz, Platt, & McCarton, 1985; Mann et al., 1986). Unless a child is unable to demonstrate a particular state, the clinical concern with states is often related to problems such as undue irritability, disturbing sleep patterns, or inability to maintain alertness. In this section we will discuss concerns related to state behavior and ways in which one might address those concerns. Documentation of state organization can be used to improve parental observation and to intervene with infant problems of irritability, poor attention, apparent fatigue or disorganized behavioral responses, and sleep habits.

The cluster of behaviors associated with a particular state occurs in the context of activities or expectations. For example, if a child tends to fall asleep during feeding or becomes active and irritable shortly after beginning to play, the context includes the activity around the event and the child's daily routines, medications, and so forth. In these two contexts, the expectation is for the child to remain awake and actively eat until finished or to stay alert and enjoy playing, respectively. If the context is not understood, issues related to the child's state may not be well addressed.

Using States to Improve Parental Observations. A discussion of states is an appropriate way to help parents or other caregivers closely observe behavior. As stated earlier, Nugent (1985) suggests that if one is demonstrating a NBAS with parents, she can begin by pointing out the baby's state and use that opportunity to discuss sleep habits. One can also use the opportunity that the NBAS affords to point out changes in states and accompanying behaviors, as well as manipulations used by the examiner or efforts by the baby to try to control states. Even without demonstrating a NBAS, one can use sleep behavior or contrasts between quiet alert and active awake, for example, to focus on patterns of infant behavior.

An important issue in facilitating development with handicapped children is responsivity. Much research suggests that development and parent/child relationships are best facilitated within a responsive relationship that includes sensitive reading of infant cues by parents (e.g., Goldberg, 1977; Ramey, Farran, & Campbell, 1979). Focus on state-related behavior is one way to introduce the idea that close observation can clue the observer as to a child's responses to stimulation or their needs.

Dealing with Irritability. An irritable baby is not fun. Talk to any parent whose baby is irritable and the stress is clear. Careful attention to the assessment of states can sometimes help address irritability. First, one must understand that there are numerous reasons for a baby to be irritable, and many may not be affected by simple manipulation of the environment. Some babies are irritable because their digestive systems are not mature, or for reasons that never become clear; the "right trick" for keeping a baby quiet and happy may never be found. But if there are changes that might be helpful, we believe that systematic observation of states, concurrent activity, and noting daily patterns is a good way to approach the problem.

Several methods might be attempted depending on the nature of the irritability. Some fussy behavior may be due to poor or inappropriate sleep habits. An infant or young child may not be able to maintain a pleasant demeanor without a nap. Recording the number of hours and times of daily sleep may indicate this problem (see also the following section).

Irritability may also be caused by overstimulation. Young babies or handicapped infants may not be able to maintain quiet alertness in the face of excessive stimulation (Field, 1979). The amount of stimulation that constitutes excessive could vary considerably as a function of time of day, health status, or the nature or duration of the stimulation. Important considerations might include: (a) health status, (b) time of day when the infant is in a pleasant mood, (c) how the child reacts to the particular stimulation at other times, (d) how the child reacts if the stimulation is systematically varied (e.g., reduced, made less challenging, changed, or stopped), or (e) if there are supports for the child that can be offered which calm the child. Supports would vary depending on the child's age and individual needs and might include specific techniques used in the research discussed previously. They could also include a gentle, comforting embrace, changing the distance from the stimulation, or providing a short time out. The method for recording states might vary depending on the child's age and circumstances observed. For example, with a very young child, the system in the NBAS might be appropriate during a short event such as feeding, whereas with an older child in a play situation the CRIB categories along with a chronicle of events might be more appropriate.

If irritability is a problem with a very young infant, methods to help a baby calm down or self-organize may be important. Following the synactive theory, motor containment through swaddling might be appropriate (Harrison & Kositsky, 1983; Lipton, Steinschneider, & Richmond, 1965) or a reduction of the social demands. For older infants who are irritable, the same principle of providing some structure for a lack of control might be applied. This could be in the form of physical support or emotional support if, for example, a child is overly excited; also reducing the stimulation might be effective (Field, 1979).

Concerns with Attention or Alertness. A concern related to irritability might be a lack of appropriate attention or with a smaller child an inability to maintain a quiet alert state. Issues presented previously also might be appropriate to consider with this problem. Generally though, it would be important to determine whether the child can ever attain a quiet alert state, under what circumstances, and how he attempts to maintain that state. This information could then be used in a behavioral program to increase the child's tolerance and endurance. It also may be the case that a simple behavioral program is not most appropriate, rather it might be important to discover how the child tries to maintain herself and support those efforts. For example, a young infant may not be able to stay in a quiet alert state with social interaction unless her arms and legs are gently contained (as they would be if she were being held with her shoulders rounded, her body slightly flexed, and her feet supported by the holder's hands). Another infant might be able to maintain organized behavior if he were allowed to suck on his fingers or simply be provided a break in the action when he indicates a need for one.

The issue of overstimulation could apply also to older children. Again careful evaluation of the child's ability to attend, under what conditions, and for how long given optimal conditions might determine if the problem is the child's ability or the influence of the environment.

Concerns with Fatigue or Disorganized Behavior. As mentioned before, concern with state-related behavior is usually related to the context, such as the circumstances

when the desired behavior, perhaps quiet attention during feeding, is to occur. One approach to understanding how to address the problem is to assess the state-related behavior both within and separate from the desired circumstances. This assessment might help identify any relationship between the context and behavior. For example, a very young infant might be able to be quiet and alert when quietly held but when fed might always go to sleep. If there were activity in the room during feeding or if there were too much social interaction, the baby might not be able both to eat and manage the stimulation and thus might shut out the environment by going to sleep. The response to overstimulation by one baby might be to go to sleep, while another might become irritable or disorganized.

These problems need to be approached in the manner just described; that is, evaluate the child's ability to maintain states outside of challenging demands, determine if there are identifiable supports that might help the child, and present demands gradually in order to determine the threshold of tolerance. Recommendations then might be to develop a behavioral program to increase desired behavior. The point here is that a clearer understanding of states and influences upon them might allow practitioners to better address state-related problems.

Concerns with Sleep Habits. It is beyond the scope of this chapter to address fully the range of problems children have with sleep. Ferber's (1985) work is recommended as an excellent source for dealing with sleep problems of children of all ages. One overriding recommendation is to provide a pleasant, regular routine around going to sleep and then maintaining the routine. Ferber explains normal sleep patterns and suggests ways to deal with exaggerated or "out of sync" patterns. Sammons and Lewis (1985) also suggest pleasant bedtime routines and add that infants should go to sleep after the routine, not during it, so that they get used to going to sleep by themselves. In their book for mothers of premature infants, Sammons and Lewis suggest that nighttime awakening should be avoided. The infant should be allowed to awaken on her own unless medical considerations dictate otherwise (e.g., for medications or nutritional needs of the infant or to relieve extreme discomforts of breast-feeding mothers).

Premature infants going home from a NICU sometimes have difficulty adjusting to normal home routines and sometimes have day/night reversals, awakening at night and sleeping in the day (Nance, 1982). In a book for parents of premature infants, Nance recommends that, if there are problems, parents keep a strict schedule of feeding during the day and feed only on demand at night, sleep when the baby sleeps, notice if a bath awakens or tires the infant and time them appropriately, go for walks or car rides to induce sleep (if it works), experiment with lighting and white noise, and resist temptation to play or socially interact with the baby at night. Once a sleep schedule is established, a parent should then slowly, over several weeks, adjust room variables (lights or sounds) to desired levels. If feeding is required at night, Ferber (1985) suggests careful calculation of total liquid intake and, after consultation with a physician, a decision whether liquid is needed at night or not,

inasmuch as getting too much food can also cause night wakings.

Ferber (1985) also discusses sleep problems of children with handicaps. His experience indicates that often there are behavioral or habitual problems associated with sleeping that are separate from the handicap and suggests behavioral treatments be tried before any medication solutions are instituted. Prescribed medication schedules should not be altered without consulting a physician. Sometimes the CNS damage associated with many handicaps does affect sleep, and in these cases only partial correction of sleep problems may be achieved through behavioral management. Ferber discusses a wide range of sleep problems, including sleepless children, schedule disturbances, and various interruptions of sleep such as nightmares or sleep apnea.

General Concerns about Behavior. When one has a concern related to the general, underlying behavior being displayed by an infant or young handicapped child, it is recommended that one carefully observe and evaluate the child's behavioral state organization. A systematic approach to the understanding of clarity, robustness, and patterns of behavior states provides one way to understand young children's behavior.

SUMMARY OF KEY CONCEPTS

- Behavioral states are defined by characteristic behaviors that describe a child's awake or sleep status. Sleep states are usually described as quiet or active, and awake states described as drowsy, alert, active, or crying.

- States are important to understand and to assess because they mediate a child's responsiveness and provide a context for understanding behavior. Children respond differently to stimulation in different states.

- A child's age and status (e.g., health or central nervous system) as well as characteristics of the environment (immediate surroundings and daily patterns) can affect the clarity, lability, and rhythmicity of state expression.

- The synactive theory provides a framework to understand the relationship of state-related behaviors to other aspects of biophysical functioning.

- Behavioral state organization reflects a child's current status, helps explain behavior, and possibly predicts development.

- Assessment of states can improve observation skills and the understanding of infant behavior for parents and practitioners, especially when concerns center on an infant's alertness, irritability, sleep habits, or situational behavior (behavior in a particular setting or situation).

REFERENCES

Als, H. (1984). *Manual for the naturalistic observation of newborn behavior.* Boston, MA: The Children's Hospital.

Als, H. (1986). A synactive model of neonatal behavioral organization: Framework for the assessment and support of the neurobehavioral development of the premature infant and his parents in the environment of the neonatal intensive care unit. *Physical and Occupational Therapy in Pediatrics, 6*(3/4), 3–55.

Als, H. & Duffy, F. H. (1982). The behavior of the fetal newborn: Theoretical considerations and practical suggestions for the use of the APIB. In A. Waldstein (Ed.), *Issues in neonatal care* (pp. 21–60). Chapel Hill, NC: WESTAR/TADS Production.

Als, H., Lawhon, G., Brown, E., Gibes, R., Duffy, F. H., McAnulty, G., & Blickman, J. G. (1986). Individualized behavioral and environmental care for the very low birth weight preterm infant at high risk for bronchopulmonary dysplasia: Neonatal intensive care unit and developmental outcome. *Pediatrics, 78*, 1123–1132.

Als, H., Lester, B. M., Tronick, E. Z., & Brazelton, T. B. (1982). Towards a research instrument for the assessment of preterm infants' behavior (APIB). In H.E. Fitzgerald, B.M. Lester, & M.W. Yogman (Eds.), *Theory and research in behavioral pediatrics, 1* (pp. 35–132). New York: Plenum Press.

Anders, T.F. (1982). Annotation; Neurophysiological studies of sleep in infants and children. *Journal of Child Psychology and Psychiatry, 23*, 75–83.

Anders, T.F. & Keener, M. (1985). Developmental course of nighttime sleep-wake patterns in full-term and premature infants during the first years of life. I. *Sleep, 8*, 173–192.

Anders, T.F., Keener, M.A., & Kraemer, H. (1985). Sleep-wake organization, neonatal assessment and development in premature infants during the first year of life. II. *Sleep, 8*, 193–206.

Ashton, R. (1971). Behavioral sleep cycles in the human newborn. *Child Development, 42*, 2098–2100.

Ashton, R. (1973). The state variable in neonatal research: A review. *Merrill-Palmer Quarterly, 19*, 3–20.

Barnard, K.E. & Bee, H.L. (1983). The impact of temporally patterned stimulation on the development of preterm infants. *Child Development, 54*, 1156–1167.

Becker, P.T. & Thoman, E.B. (1981). REM storms at 6 months predict mental development at one year. *Science, 212*, 1415–1416.

Becker, P.T. & Thoman, E.B. (1982). Intense rapid eye movements during active sleep: An index of neurobehavioral instability. *Developmental Psychology, 15*, 203–210.

Berg, W.K. & Berg, K.M. (1979). Psychophysiological development in infancy: State, sensory function, and attention. In J.D. Osofsky (Ed.), *Handbook of infant development* (pp. 283–343). New York: Wiley.

Brazelton, T.B. (1973). Neonatal behavioral assessment scale. *Clinics in developmental medicine No. 50*, Philadelphia: J.P. Lippincott.

Brazelton, T.B. (1984). *Neonatal behavioral assessment scale* (2nd ed.). (Clinics in Developmental Medicine, No. 50) Philadelphia: J.P. Lippincott Co.

Brazelton, T.B. (1985). Introduction. In J.K. Nugent, *Using the NBAS with infants and their families*. White Plains, NY: March of Dimes Birth Defects Foundation.

Coons, S. & Guilleminault, C. (1982). Development of sleep-wake patterns and non-rapid eye movement sleep stages during the first six months of life in normal infants. *Pediatrics, 69*, 793–798.

Coons, S. & Guilleminault, C. (1984). Development of consolidated sleep and wakeful periods in relation to the day/night cycle in infancy. *Developmental Medicine and Child Neurology, 26*, 169–176.

Dreyfus-Brisac, C. (1968). Sleep ontogenesis in early human prematurity from 24 to 27 weeks of conceptual age. *Developmental Psychobiology, 1*, 162–169.

Dreyfus-Brisac, C. (1970). Ontogenesis of sleep in human prematures after 32 weeks of conceptual age. *Developmental Psychobiology, 3*, 91–121.

Dubowitz, L. & Dubowitz, V. (1981). *The neurological assessment of the preterm and full-term newborn infant*. (Clinics in Developmental Medicine No. 79). Philadelphia: J.P. Lippincott.

Fagioli, I. & Salzarulo, P. (1982). Sleep states development in the first year of life assessed through 24-hour recordings. *Early Human Development, 8*, 215–228.

Feldman, J. (1978). Nonelicited newborn behaviors in relation to state and prandial conditions. *Merrill-Palmer Quarterly, 24*, 79–84.

Ferber, R. (1985). *Solve your child's sleep problems*. New York: Simon & Schuster.

Field, T.M. (1979). Interaction patterns of preterm and term infants. In T.M. Field, A.M. Sostek, S. Goldberg, & H.H. Shuman (Eds.), *Infants born at risk: Behavior and development* (pp. 333–356). New York: SP Medical & Scientific Books.

Gardner, J.M., Karmel, B.Z., & Dowd, J.M. (1985). Relationship of infant psychobiological development to infant intervention programs. In M. Frank (Ed.), *Infant intervention programs: Truths and untruths* (pp. 93–108). New York: Hawthorne.

Goldberg, S. (1977). Social competence in infancy: A model of parent-infant interaction. *Merrill-Palmer Quarterly, 23*, 163–177.

Goldberg, S. & DiVitto, B.A. (1983). *Born too soon*. San Francisco: W.H. Freeman.

Hack, M. (1987). The sensorimotor development of the preterm infant. In A. Fanaroff & R. Martin (Eds.), *Neonatal-perinatal medicine: Diseases of the fetus and infant* (4th ed.) (pp. 473–494). Washington DC: C.V. Mosby.

Harper, R.M., Leake, B., Hoppenbrouwers, T., Sterman, M.B., McGinty, D.J., & Hodgman, J. (1978). Polygraph studies of normal infants and infants at risk for the sudden infant death syndrome: Heart rate and variability as a function of state. *Pediatric Research, 12*, 778–785.

Harrison, H. & Kositsky, A. (1983). *Premature baby book*. New York: St. Martin's Press.

Korner, A.F. (1972). State as variable, as obstacle, and as mediator of stimulation in infant research. *Merrill-Palmer, 18*, 77–94.

Korner, A.F. & Schneider, P. (1983). Effects of vestibular-proprioceptive stimulation on the neurobehavioral development of preterm infants: A pilot study. *Neuropediatrics, 14*, 170–175.

Landesman-Dwyer, S. & Sackett, G.P. (1978). Behavioral changes in nonambulatory, mentally retarded individuals. In C.E. Meyers (Ed.), *Quality of life in severely and profoundly mentally retarded people: Research foundations for improvement* (pp. 55–144). Washington, DC: American Association for Mental Deficiency Monograph No. 3.

Lawson, K.R., Turkewitz, G., Platt, M., & McCarton, C. (1985). Infant state in relation to its environmental context. *Infant Behavior and Development. 8*, 269–281.

Lenard, H.G., von Bernuth, H., & Prechtl, H.F.R. (1968). Reflexes and their relationship to behavioural state in the newborn. *Acta Paediatrica Scandinavica, 57*, 177–185.

Lipton, E.L., Steinschneider, A., & Richmond, J.B. (1965). Swaddling, a child care practice: Historical, cultural, and experimental observations. *Pediatrics, 35*, 521–567.

Lombroso, C.T. & Matsumiya, Y. (1985). Stability in waking-sleep states in neonates as a predictor of long-term neurologic outcome. *Pediatrics, 76*, 52–63.

Mann, N.P., Haddow, R., Stokes, L., Goodley, S., & Rutter, N. (1986). Effect of night and day in preterm infants in a newborn nursery: Randomised trial. *British Medical Journal, 293*, 1265–1267.

McGehee, L.J. & Eckerman, C.O. (1983). The preterm infant as a social partner: Responsive but unreadable. *Infant Behavior and Development, 6*, 461–470.

Michaelis, R., Parmelee, A.H., Stern, E., & Haber, A. (1973). Activity states in premature and term infants. *Developmental Psychobiology, 6*, 209–215.

Monod, N. & Guidasci, S. (1976). Sleep and brain malformation in the neonatal period. *Neuropaediatrie, 7,* 228–249.

Muhiudeen, H.A., Melville-Thomas, G., Ferguson, S.D., & Mohan, P. (1984). The postures exhibited by 3-day-old full term neonates. *Early Human Development, 10,* 57–66.

Nance, S. (1982). *Premature babies: A handbook for parents by parents.* New York: Berkley Books.

Neeley, C.A. (1979). Effects of nonnutritive sucking upon the behavioral arousal of the newborn. *Birth Defects: Original Article Series, 15*(7), 173–200.

Nijhuis, J.G., Prechtl, H.F.R., Martin, C.B., & Bots, R.S.G.M. (1982). Are there behavioral states in the human fetus? *Early Human Development, 6,* 177–195.

Nugent, J.K. (1985). *Using the NBAS with infants and their families.* White Plains, NY: March of Dimes Birth Defects Foundations.

O'Donnell, K.J. Personal communication, May 15, 1987.

Parmelee, A.H. (1975). Neurophysiological and behavioral organization of premature infants in the first months of life. *Biological Psychiatry, 10,* 501–512.

Prechtl, H.F.R. (1974). The behavioural states of the newborn infant (a review). *Brain Research, 76,* 185–212.

Prechtl, H.F.R., Theorell, K., & Blair, A.W. (1973). Behavioural state cycles in abnormal infants. *Developmental Medicine and Child Neurology, 15,* 606–615.

Prechtl, H.F.R., Fargel, J.W., Weinmann, H.M., & Bakker, H.H. (1979). Postures, motility and respiration of low-risk pre-term infants. *Developmental Medicine and Child Neurology, 21,* 3–27.

Ramey, C.T., Farran, D.C., & Campbell, F.A. (1979). Predicting IQ from mother-infant interactions. *Child Development, 50,* 804–814.

Roffwarg, H.P., Muzio, J.N., & Dement, W.C. (1966). Ontogenetic development of the human sleep-dream cycle. *Science, 152,* 604–619.

Sammons, W.A.H. & Lewis, J.M. (1985). *Premature babies: A different beginning.* Princeton, NJ: C.V. Mosby.

Simeonsson, R.J. (1979). *Carolina Record of Individual Behavior.* University of North Carolina at Chapel Hill, Frank Porter Graham Child Development Center, Chapel Hill.

Simeonsson, R.J., Huntington, G.S., & Parse, S.A. (1980). Expanding the developmental assessment of young handicapped children. *New Directions for Exceptional Children, 3,* 51–74.

Simeonsson, R.J., Huntington, G.S., Short, R.J., & Ware, W.B. (1982). The Carolina record of individual behavior: Characteristics of handicapped infants and children. *Topics in Early Childhood Special Education, 2,* 43–55.

Sostek, A.M. & Anders, T. (1977). Relationships among the Brazelton neonatal scale, Bayley infant scales and early temperament. *Child Development, 48,* 320–326.

Tanguay, P.E., Ornitz, E.M., Forsythe, A.B., & Ritvo, E.R. (1976). Rapid eye movement (REM) activity in normal and autistic children during REM sleep. *Journal of Autism and Child Schizophrenia, 6,* 275–288.

Thoman, E.B. (1975). Sleep and wake behaviors in neonates: Consistencies and consequences. *Merrill-Palmer Quarterly, 21,* 295–314.

Thoman, E.B., Denenberg, V.H., Sievel, J., Zeidner, L., & Becker, P. (1981). State organization in neonates: Developmental inconsistency indicates risk for developmental dysfunction. *Neuropaediatrie, 12,* 45–54.

Turner, S. & MacFarlane, A. (1978). Localization of human speech by newborn baby and effects of meperidine. *Developmental Medicine and Child Neurology, 20,* 727–734.

VandenBerg, K. (1982). Humanizing the intensive care nursery. In A. Waldstein (Ed.), *Issues in neonatal care* (pp. 21–60). Chapel Hill, NC: WESTAR/TADS Production.

Widmayer, S.M. & Field, T.M. (1980). Effects of Brazelton demonstrations on early interactions of preterm infants and their teenage mothers. *Infant Behavior and Development, 3,* 79–89.

Wolff, P.H. (1966). The causes, controls, and organization of behavior in the neonate. *Psychological Issues, 5* [Monograph 17].

Wolff, P.H. & Ferber, R. (1979). The development of behavior in human infants, premature and newborn. *Annual Review of Neuroscience, 2,* 291–307.

Wolff, P.H. & Simmons, M.A. (1967). Nonnutritive sucking and response thresholds in young infants. *Child Development, 38,* 631–638.

Woodson, R., Drinkwin, J., & Hamilton, C. (1985). Effects of nonnutritive sucking on state and activity: Term-preterm comparisons. *Infant Behavior and Development, 8,* 435–441.

Assessing Behavioral Characteristics

Gail S. Huntington
University of North Carolina at Chapel Hill

KEY TERMS

- Behavioral Cues
- Interpretability
- Behavioral Style
- Difficultness

- Behavioral Characteristics
- Clinical Judgment
- Situational Effects

- Subscales
- Goodness-of-Fit
- Mediating Variable
- Anticipatory Guidance

Rationale for Assessing Behavioral Cues, Style, and Characteristics

Traditionally, handicapped children have been assessed in terms of cognitive, motor, social, self-help and language development using assessment techniques that focus on specific task performance. The strategies children employ in generic tasks, however, also provide useful information for intervention planning. In addition, children's behavioral characteristics, even those of very young children, influence others in their environment. From a transactional point of view, knowledge of individual child characteristics may lead to a better understanding of individual-environment influences. The goal of providing individualized intervention will be greatly enhanced by a view of the child that includes assessment of individual behavorial characteristics. Child development theories and recent research findings have suggested domains that may have potential for documenting the complexities of the behavior of children with handicaps as it affects caregivers and service providers in the child's environment. Three of these domains, summarized in Table 10.1, are behavioral cues, behavioral style, and behavioral characteristics. This chapter describes the relationship of each of these domains to the assessment of infants and toddlers, and the provision of services to handicapped youngsters within a family context.

TABLE 10.1
Behavioral Domains with Relevance to Infant Intervention

Domain	Relevance to Intervention	Assessment Procedures
Behavioral styles	Document variability of child behavioral style; possible index of child's contribution to adult/child interaction	Parent report measures, parental interview, observation of behavior in multiple situations
Behavioral cues	Affects adult feelings of efficacy and competence; affects child's feelings of competence	Parental perceptions of child's responsiveness and predictability; observations of child's reactions to contingent reinforcement
Behavioral characteristics	Excessive caregiving demands increase stress; RHPs affect goal achievement; child's contribution to "goodness-of-fit"	A number of assessment measures available, e.g., IBR (Bayley, 1969), CRIB (Simeonsson, 1978), Child Domain of PSI (Abidin, 1986)

Dimensions of Child Behavior

What are some of the key dimensions of children's characteristics? In Chapter 9, the focus was on the assessment of state. This chapter addresses behavioral cues, behavioral style, and a broadly defined area of child behavioral characteristics.

Behavioral Cues

Parents, caregivers, and service providers are all concerned with maximizing the probability that their interactions with the child will be positive. One way in which this interaction is accomplished is through evaluation of the **behavioral cues** emitted by the infant or toddler, in an effort to match the intervention with the need that is expressed. The success of the intervention is in part a function of "the extent to which an infant's behaviors are clearly defined and produce distinctive signals and cues for adults" (Goldberg, 1977, p. 177).

Interpretability refers to the relative ease with which the parent or teacher can attach meaning to the child's behavior, can observe the child and know he is sleepy, hungry, or wants to be held. Children whose cues are easily interpreted are likely to enhance adult feelings of efficacy and competence because cues that are correctly interpreted lead to interactions that often bring about desired results. Reciprocally, infants whose behavioral cues are correctly interpreted experience caregiving behaviors that are responsive to expressed needs and develop feelings of competence in their ability to influence their surroundings. Unfortunately, handicapped or at-risk children may not strengthen feelings of competence because their behavioral cues may be less clear than those of their nonhandicapped peers (Bailey & Wolery, 1984; McCollum & Stayton, 1985).

The work of Yoder (1987) supports this notion, as he reports observers were able to agree upon the occurrence of a communicative cue significantly less often for severely handicapped infants than for less handicapped infants. McGhee and Eckerman (1983) compared full-term and preterm infants during periods of face-to-face interaction with their mothers and found preterm infants to be less able to maintain their state of arousal and to exhibit frequent startling and jerking movements, making it difficult for parents to respond appropriately to their more erratic behavior. However, the attachment of meaning to behavioral cues occurs only within the context of an interaction and may increase with familiarity. Parents may find their own child's cues to be clearer than do persons unfamiliar with the child's cues. In a longitudinal study of parental perceptions of the clarity of their infants' cues of distress, happiness, interest in toys or social interaction, and understanding/learning, mothers of handicapped and nonhandicapped infants perceived as equally clear their infants' cues having to do with distress and happiness (Goldman & Johnson-Martin, 1987). On the other hand, mothers of handicapped infants were less sure of their infants' cues having to do with learning and interest in social interactions. Opportunity may play a part in this discrepancy, as handicapped infants emit fewer cues of this nature, thus providing the adults in their environment an impoverished context in which to learn their cues. However, at least two conclusions are implicit in these findings: First, despite some degree of familiarity with their cues, mothers still found handicapped infants' cues to be less clear than those of nonhandicapped infants for some behaviors, across ages. Second, behavioral clarity does not appear to be a unitary construct, indicating that intervention to help parents more easily interpret their infants' cues might be more effective if the various types of cues were assessed individually and only those perceived as difficult were targeted for intervention (Goldman & Johnson-Martin, 1987). The implications of cue interpretation for parent/child interaction and subsequent child development are clearly important. Interventions to assist parents to recognize subtle cues and to help infants discriminate the relationship between their own behavior and its results may improve infant adaptation and development.

Parental feelings of efficacy and competence may arise from their evaluations of interactions with their child. Consequently, parents' preceptions of their child's behavior and characteristics are probably more powerful determinants of parent/child interactions than any assessment of the infant (Goldberg, 1977). Thus, any assessment procedure must include verbal or written information concerning the parents' perceptions of the child's **interpretability**, predictability, and responsiveness. In this area, an interview may prove to be of considerable assistance in defining the specific difficulties being experienced by the family. Information from temperament and process behavior assessments (such as the Carolina Record of Individual Behavior, 1982, or the Bayley Infant Behavior Record, 1969) can form the basis of the interview, for they capture many of the particular behaviors that constitute the concepts of predictability and responsiveness. Clarification can be facilitated through observation of the infant alone and within the family, in the home and when possible in other settings.

If opportunity to observe and familiarize oneself with the behavioral cues of the infant or toddler is an important factor in the ability to interpret cues correctly, then service providers may be at a disadvantage. Handicapped infants and toddlers are often in intervention settings for only a few hours each week, affording the intervention staff little opportunity to become familiar with individual behavioral cues. In addition, unlike parents, who must learn the cues of only their own child, service providers must learn the cues of a number of children. Parental expertise can be a great help to interventionists and other service personnel as they attempt to familiarize themselves with children's cues. Parents and other family members can be asked to function as interpreters of the child's cues, in a live situation or from a video tape. They can be asked to explain what it is the child needs or wants, and how the parent knows this. This method not only provides the interventionist with information about the child, but also offers an opportunity for family and staff to discuss any problems the family might have in interpreting the child's cues. When a child is severely handicapped, or has low tone or sensory or motoric involvement, parents may be unable to interpret the cues the child emits, thus leading to a belief that the child is not communicating. For example, it is through the visual modality that humans develop their earliest concepts of self, others, and the world around them. When this sensory modality is unavailable, adult/child interaction can break down with serious consequences for the development of the child (Rogers & Puchalski, 1984). Adults experience difficulties in reading the infant's cues and responses and have a tendency to perceive the infant as unresponsive. However, in work designed to help parents become more attuned to their child's cues, Fraiberg (1977) has described the way in which parents learn to read the preferences and needs of their blind or visually impaired child by watching the active hands rather than the passive face. Behavioral cues are an important area of handicapped infant and toddler behavior that have an impact on the relationship between family members and the handicapped child as well as on the designing of services to meet the needs of the individual child. It is important to include assessment and discussion of the types and clarity of cues in any individualized child evaluation and goal plan.

Behavioral Style

The concept of individual differences in **behavioral style,** or temperament, has been around for a long time, with four types of temperament having been described by Hippocrates as far back as 460 BC and elaborated on by the physician Galen in the 1st century AD. Until lately, however, it was only applied to adults and generally only to adult males.

The study of temperament in children is a relatively recent effort, with the work of Thomas and Chess being given credit for the current interest in the concept as an outgrowth of their research with the New York Longitudinal Study (Thomas, Chess, & Birch, 1968).

Several different theoretical perspectives have been proposed for the concept of temperament. Among these are the EAS (Emotionality, Activity, Sociability) theory of Buss and Plomin (1984), which defines temperament as the inherited aspects of personality; and Eysenck's Extraversion-Introversion and Neuroticism dimensions (Eysenck & Eysenck, 1969), which have been applied to school-aged children but not to young children or infants. The theoretical position of Rothbart and Derryberry (1981) holds that temperament reflects constitutionally based differences in reactivity and self-regulation, while Goldsmith and Campos (1982) see individual differences in the primary emotions as the content of temperament in infancy. As a result of these varied views of temperament, there are points of disagreement, as well as points of agreement, among the major theorists. According to Goldsmith and Rieser-Danner (1986), there are at least seven controversial issues pertaining to the conceptualization of temperament: the actual dimensions of temperament, the amount of emphasis to place on biological factors, the role of motivation, relative emphasis to be placed on the level of definition (behavioral or psychophysiological), whether temperament is regulatory or expressive of behavior, the role of contextual and interpersonal influences, and the relationship between temperament and personality. Areas of relative agreement include the belief that temperament refers to individual differences in behavior, that at least some of these appear in infancy and represent elements of later personality. Furthermore, compared to other aspects of behavior, temperament characteristics are relatively stable, and at least some have a biological substrate. Finally, there is some agreement that the expression of temperamental characteristics can be influenced by environmental conditions (e.g., parenting practices).

In addition to defining temperament as individual differences in behavioral style, that is, the "how" of behavior rather than the "why" (motivation) or "what" (capabilities), Thomas, Chess, and Birch (1968) have interpreted the constellation of irregularity, slow adaptability, withdrawal, and frequent negative mood as describing "difficult" children. Recently, however, the concept of the difficult child has been much criticized on the grounds that temperament characteristics, in and of themselves, are neither good nor bad, easy nor difficult. **Difficultness** and easiness do not reside in the individual, but are evident in the interactions between particular temperament characteristics and particular environmental demands. Any characteristic may appear to a parent to be difficult if it violates their expectations of appropriate behavior. Some parents (and some cultures) prize high activity in children. For these parents, a quiet, relatively inactive child would represent a difficult temperament characteristic. However, whether or not difficultness is a function of expectations/interactions, the cluster identified by Thomas and Chess (1977) seems to be applicable to North American, middle-class, preschool children. For infants, on the other hand, the fussy, hard-to-soothe, labile infant has received the label of *difficult* (Bates, Freeland, & Lounsbury, 1979). Clearly, parental perceptions of the easiness or difficultness of their child will have an impact on the interactions that occur within the family and, consequently, on the development of the child and must be included in a complete assessment procedure.

Within the context of the family, the temperament attributes of the infant or child may describe characteristics of the child with which the family must cope and which in-

fluence the mutual adaptation of the family and infant. As a function of these individual differences, infants and young children elicit different responses from parents and caregivers as early as the neonatal period (Sirignano & Lachman, 1985). In a prospective study of first-time parents and childless couples, self-rating scales were used to obtain both global/trait and situation-specific state measures for efficacy expectations, personal control, anxiety, and depression at two points, 16 weeks apart. The parent group showed more positive change than the nonparent group on efficacy and anxiety. In addition, new parents who perceived their infants as having easier temperaments experienced more positive change, especially in personal control, than did parents whose infants were seen as more difficult. The results of a study of infant and family adjustment in the first year (Sprunger, Boyce, & Gaines, 1985) indicated that infant temperament continues to affect family functioning beyond the neonatal period, but that the type of effect is not unidirectional nor can it be predicted on the basis of child characteristics alone. Examining the notion of infant/family congruence through the construct of rhythmicity (the degree of predictable regularity in both infant and family), Sprunger and colleagues found that the lack of family/infant congruence was significantly predictive of overall family adjustment.

The role of temperament and family interactions in preschool children was examined by Simpson and Stevenson-Hinde (1985) in a study involving more than 40 boys and girls who were assessed at both 42 and 50 months of age. Mothers interviewed in their homes provided information on child temperament characteristics and family interactions. No sex differences were found between boys and girls on assessed temperament characteristics. For both boys and girls, however, moody/intense scores were associated with negative family interactions. An interaction was found showing that shy scores were associated with negative interactions for boys, but with positive interactions for girls, especially at 50 months. The authors suggest that these differences may be an expression of differing behavioral expectations for boys and girls.

The role of temperament in parent/child interaction has been examined extensively among nonhandicapped children (Lerner & Galambos, 1985; Simpson & Stevenson-Hinde, 1985; Thomas & Chess, 1977). Findings indicate that specific temperament traits can affect the attitudes and behaviors of parents in many ways, a finding that can be extended to families of handicapped children. In a study of handicapped infants and toddlers, Huntington, Simeonsson, Bailey, & Comfort (1987) found that the clinically relevant temperament clusters of *easy, difficult*, and *slow-to-warm-up* also could be used to differentiate handicapped children. In addition, child temperament ratings were predictive of the appropriateness and quality of maternal interactions with their children. Mothers whose children were rated as easy had the most optimal scores on both aspects of interaction, compared to mothers whose children fit either of the other two categories.

In addition to their effect on family members, temperament characteristics of young children also influence the provision of educational and intervention services to these children. The influence of temperament on school achievement can be seen in the findings that children who exhibit positive temperament patterns tend to have their intelligence overestimated by teachers (Pullis & Caldwell, 1982) and to receive higher teacher-given grades than their achievement test scores would predict (Keogh, 1983). In an examination of the interpersonal behavior patterns of 105 first-grade children and their teachers, Paget, Nagle, and Martin (1984) found that children's temperament characteristics were related to student/teacher interactions. Specifically, children who were more distractible and socially withdrawn re-

ceived more praise than children who were attentive and adaptable. The authors note that, while the results may appear counterintuitive, the teachers' behavior may be designed to improve the confidence of these young children as they are beginning school and is evidence of the teachers' sensitivity to the individual needs of the children.

Professionals frequently rely on informal ratings of temperament when designing intervention programs. For example, the child who is highly distractible, nonpersistent, and slow to adapt to new situations will require a different set of circumstances in which to learn than will the child who is task-oriented and adaptable. Furthermore, dimensions of behavioral style may be expressed differently in different situations. In a study involving 43 handicapped and nonhandicapped infants ranging in age from 9 to 22 months, Greenberg and Field (1982) found that observers rated the same infants as having easier temperaments during teacher/child and mother/child interactions than when the infants were observed during free-play sessions. These results suggest that, at least for handicapped children, behavioral style may be related to the structure of dyadic interaction. Significant relationships have, in fact, been found between the temperament ratings of high-risk 4-year-olds and teachers' ratings of "teachability" (Keogh, 1982). In addition, child temperament characteristics may affect interactions between handicapped youngsters and their peers as well as teachers. A study examining this question in reference to handicapped and nonhandicapped preschoolers was conducted by Keogh and Burnstein (1988). Teachers rated the temperament characteristics of both groups using the Teacher Temperament Questionnaire (Keogh, Pullis, & Caldwell, 1982), a short form of the Thomas and Chess Teacher Temperament Questionnaire (1977). Teachers rated the nonhandicapped children as displaying more optional temperament characteristics on two of the three factorial dimensions: task orientation and flexibility. In addition, the children, who were in the same classrooms, were observed in three situations: total-group time, small-group time, and outdoors. Handicapped preschoolers in this study, in contrast to their nonhandicapped peers, were found to interact more with adults than with peers and to receive more adult attention if they were perceived as having more negative temperaments. The authors hypothesize that the increased contact may reflect teacher efforts to increase the children's involvement in the program and to manage their behavior. Thus, temperament characteristics appear to have implications for both families and teachers of young handicapped children.

Behavioral Characteristics

In addition to temperament and behavioral cues, there are other basic **behavioral characteristics** that are likely to affect children's interactions with parents, teachers, and peers. These characteristics include such behaviors as social and object orientation, attention span, reactivity, rhythmic habit patterns, and self-help skills. While assessment of behavior in infancy and early childhood has been of theoretical interest for some time, it is increasingly important for diagnostic and clinical implications. Documentation of these types of generic behaviors may thus facilitate the provision of individualized intervention services. The goal of early intervention to ameliorate developmental handicaps has highlighted the need for effective assessment of child behavioral characteristics. Meeting this need, however, has been particularly difficult with handicapped infants and toddlers in light of their limitations. Assessment of behavioral characteristics has also been hampered by the lack of suitable instruments that can accommodate handicaps that complicate the assessment process.

The significance of assessing behavior patterns of handicapped infants and toddlers is

that it provides an index of variability in responding to social and nonsocial objects. Assessment strategies are needed, which bypass the limitations of traditional instruments and the reliance on single measures of functioning, such as the IQ. Assessment should reflect the infant's or young child's exploratory behavior and ways of dealing with the environment. Variability and unevenness of handicapped development should be taken into account in their own right rather than controlled or treated as sources of error in assessment.

Many aspects of child functioning, including behavioral characteristics, have been implicated in the additional stress reported by caregivers. More parental and family problems have been reported in families whose children were socially unresponsive, displayed more repetitive behaviors, and had more caregiving needs (Beckman, 1983). Higher levels of stress have been related to behavioral or attitudinal deficits on the part of the child, such as lack of self-help skills or the inability to communicate with others. Increased severity of the handicap, with its associated physical incapacities, was found to exacerbate the stress (Dyson & Fewell, 1986). Behavioral attributes difficult for families to cope with will also have an impact on the provision of services, as interventionists attempt to contend with the stressful behaviors of the many children they serve. As might be expected, the unique demand characteristics of specific handicapping conditions may be differentially stressful. For example, personal and family functioning has been found to be more disrupted by the presence of a child with autism than by one with Down syndrome (Holroyd & McArthur, 1976). It is assumed that this finding is due to the fact that autistic children, while appearing to be normal, have more conspicuous and difficult behavior problems and present more caregiving demands than do children with Down syndrome. Collectively, these findings indicate that the behavioral characteristics of handicapped children have the potential to exert a negative effect on the social environment.

A conspicuous set of behaviors that may interfere with both the assessment process and goal achievement are those collectively known as rhythmic habit patterns (RHPs). In infancy, RHPs may be developmental precursors of voluntary movement, as has been proposed by Thelen (1981). In nonhandicapped children, RHPs have been shown to be normal in the first years of life, after which they tend to be replaced by more functional behaviors. A number of RHPs have been documented in nonhandicapped infants in the first year of life: body rocking, head banging, hand sucking, and lip biting. However, RHPs appear later in handicapped populations and tend to persist longer. In addition, there are a number of other habitual, repetitive, and/or stereotypic behaviors that are usually seen only in exceptional children and are often considered indicative of pathology. Among these are pica (ingestions of inedibles), breath holding, hair pulling, and tongue thrusting (Short & Simeonsson, 1982). The nature, persistence, and frequency of these RHPs may interfere significantly with the child's ability to respond and function. For example, a child who is preoccupied with persistent body rocking is unavailable to participate in more adaptive actions. In clinical practice, the reduction and/or elimination of RHPs is often a primary goal of intervention in order that more appropriate and adaptive movements can be acquired. Assessment of RHPs thus may be of importance in designing interventions to modify their impact on development.

As can be seen, behavioral characteristics of young handicapped children can exert a strong influence on the assessment process and the provision of services. These behaviors are important to consider not only in terms of general intervention planning, but also as critical instructional targets in their own right. Issues affecting assessment of child characteristics will be discussed in the following section.

Considerations for Assessment of Child Characteristics

Although there is a need for valid assessment of a broad range of behavioral characteristics of young handicapped children, a number of factors, singly or in combination, impose significant limitations on the achievement of this aim. These factors include definitional issues, limitations of the child and the examiner, and problems of measurement (Simeonsson, Huntington, & Parse, 1980). These issues are summarized in Table 10.2.

Regardless of the limiting factors, valid assessment of the temperament and behavior of handicapped youngsters must be considered a realistic goal for those who work with exceptional populations. However, if this goal is to be realized, it seems to be appropriate to consider the means whereby the assessment process can be improved.

Clinical Judgment

Because the interest is on child characteristics as they influence interactions with others and mediate the effectiveness of developmental interventions, assessment procedures must include the perceptions of parents and other care providers. Offered the opportunity, parents can be accurate reporters of their child's behavior and development (Chee, Kreutzberg, & Clark, 1978; Sexton, Miller, & Rotatori, 1985; Sonnander, 1987). In addition, interventionists and other professionals involved with the child and family have the opportunity to exercise their own **clinical judgment** in regard to the effect of the child's behavior on the environment. There has been a disproportionate reliance on formal assessment conducted by professional examiners to the exclusion of the insights, knowledge, and judgments of parents and staff who work directly with children. The very nature of clinical judgment makes it subject to bias, distortion, and inaccuracies, but if precautions are taken, the degree to which con-

TABLE 10.2
Some Effects of Specific Handicapping Conditions on the Interactional Skills of Children

Handicap	Reported Findings	Relevant Studies
Mental retardation	Reduced responsivity to others; decreased vocalizations; lack of, or delayed, smiling; more solitary play; fewer imitations of others; more likely to resist or not respond to cuddling	Cicchetti & Sroufe, 1976; Cunningham, Reuler, Blackwell, & Deck, 1981; Kennedy, 1973; Marshall, Hogrenes, & Goldstein, 1973; Stone & Chesney, 1978
Hearing impairment	Impaired communication; inconsistent responses to communicative attempts; fewer social initiations	Ferris, 1980; Greenberg & Marvin, 1979; Schlesinger & Meadow, 1972; Wedell-Monnig & Lumley, 1980
Visual impairment	Irregular smiling; smiling in response to auditory cues only; child must "maintain contact" by tactile and auditory (rather than visual) cues	Als, Tronick, & Brazelton, 1980; Fraiberg, 1974, 1975; Kastein, Spaulding, & Scharf, 1980; Scott, Jan, & Freeman, 1977
Physical and motor impairments	Limp or physically unresponsive; difficulty in relaxing; decreased ability to laugh or smile; smile may look like a grimace; impaired communication skills; impaired locomotion skills prevent child from independently seeking out parent	Featherstone, 1980; Gallagher, Jens, O'Donnell, 1983; Jens & Johnson, 1982; McCubbin, Nevin, Larsen, Comeau, Patterson, Cauble, & Striker, 1981; Mordock, 1979; Prechtl, 1963; Roskies, 1972

Source: From *Teaching infants and preschoolers with handicaps* by D. B. Bailey and M. Wolery, 1984, Columbus, OH: Merrill. Copyright 1984 by Merrill Publishing Co. Reprinted by permission.

fidence can be attached to clinical judgments of parents and staff can be greatly enhanced. For example, taking care to avoid the elicitation of socially desirable responses through careful wording of questions, replacing value-laden labels such as "retarded" with alternatives like "exceptional" or "special," presenting behaviors along a continuum rather than in a dichotomy, and sensitizing participants to relevant dimensions through discussion and written materials may be important ways to increase the reliability of clinical judgment.

Within the context of early intervention, the importance of parental and staff perceptions cannot be stressed too much. It is the perception of the child's behavior as much as the behavior per se that is the basis of the interactions adults and children conduct with each other, both inside and outside the home. In order to develop appropriate intervention goals and strategies, the perceptions of the family and staff need to be included in assessment procedures and the interview process.

Multiple Sources

A second way in which assessment of child characteristics may be improved is through multiple "windows," that is, the gathering of information from several sources and through several modes. Early intervention has moved away from a model where reliance is placed on a single measure of children's abilities and status to one that incorporates multiple sources of information gathered through multiple measurement strategies (Fewell, 1983; Peterson & Meier, 1987). Given the complex nature of child-environment reciprocity, an approach employing many measures and strategies is essential. When it is the child's effect on family adaptation and functioning that is of interest, parents are clearly a valuable source of information. Parents and other caregivers may be uniquely sensitive to subtle characteristics of the handicapped child that cannot be measured by traditional tests nor are immediately apparent to the casual observer. In the interest of gathering as broad a base of information as possible, mothers and fathers should be considered separate and unique sources of information. Each may bring an individual perspective to observations of their child, thereby adding to the picture of the total child.

Parents represent an important source of information for the evaluation of child characteristics, but they are not the only source. Other family members, particularly siblings, can furnish both corroborative and unique perspectives of the child's impact on the family. Professionals involved with the family also have significant knowledge and perceptions to add to the picture. Although professional contact with the child and family may be more limited than that of family members, training can sharpen their ability to detect and evaluate child characteristics of consequence to child development.

In addition to multiple sources of information, the assessment program should consider using multiple methods. Parental perceptions can be expressed verbally in more-or-less structured situations (e.g., conversations with the therapist or during a structured interview) and in writing, through the use of standard assessment instruments. Initial assessment of temperament and behavior can be gathered through paper-and-pencil measures and validated through interviews or observations. Professional observation of children's behavior in either home settings or in more-structured settings offers additional opportunities both to confirm parental (and professional) perceptions and to gather new information. Observational procedures, such as those described in Chapter 4, furnish information about the behavior in everyday settings, through everyday interactions. Although it is clear that the presence of an observer may disrupt or bias the behavior—a caveat that must also be considered when observing behavior in a structured setting—as one form of information gathering, observational procedures have considerable merit and should be included in an overall assessment program. Odom and Shuster (1986) present suggestions for reducing observer bias and increasing the validity of observer information through naturalistic inquiry by participant observers. This technique can be very time consuming, but it is a source of rich and unique knowledge.

The information obtained from each source can be both overlapping and unique. The inclusion of multiple sources through multiple methods should increase the likelihood of identifying the singular characteristics of each child that influence adaptation and development.

Situational Effects

A third consideration in the assessment of child characteristics is the **situational effect**, or the effect of setting variables on children's behavior. Much assessment of child characteristics is completed in a "testing room," laboratory or clinic situation. This environment is generally one unfamiliar to the child. When this is so, sufficient time needs to be allowed for any child to become acclimated to the surroundings. In addition, specific needs of handicapped infants and toddlers must be met if an accurate evaluation of child behavior is to be made. For example, the child with motor impairments must be positioned correctly. Furthermore, novel environments that have not been tactually explored by the visually impaired child or those which do not support the residual hearing of the hearing-impaired child may inhibit the child, providing a distorted representation of the child's usual behavior. On the other hand, it must be remembered that children may very well behave differently in different settings, and even very young children may adjust their behavior to meet those demands. For that reason, it is essential to have evaluations of the child's behavior in a variety of settings, including the home, and with a variety of persons, including parents, family, and professionals.

Representative Measures or Procedures

Individual behavioral characteristics of handicapped infants and toddlers may be assessed using a variety of procedures. This section describes some representative measures and procedures and discusses advantages and limitations of each.

Behavioral Style

The significance of measuring temperament in young handicapped children is that it provides a way to consider characteristics of the child as they are perceived by or influence the parent or caregiver. Consequently, most temperament scales are parent-report measures. Much of the current interest in temperament is associated with the work of Thomas, Chess, and Birch (1968), who demonstrated the concurrent and predictive utility of nine categories of temperament and three personality clusters that arise from them. The nine categories are: activity, rhythmicity, adaptability, approach, mood, intensity, distractibility, persistence, and threshold. The diagnostic clusters of *difficult, easy,* and *slow-to-warm-up* are derived from these categories. Subsequent research has followed this general model, but substantial effort has gone into the development of simpler, more direct assessment procedures than the interview technique first employed by Thomas et al. (1968). Carey and McDevitt (1978) have developed an Infant Temperament Questionnaire (ITQ) that was standardized on 203 infants, ages 4–8 months. Clinical and research instruments to measure temperament in toddlers between 12 and 36 months (Fullard, McDevitt, & Carey, 1984) and young children from 3 to 7 years (McDevitt & Carey, 1978) also have been developed by Carey and his associates. Each of the measures consists of a series of statements to which the respondent replies on a scale of 1 (almost never) to 6 (almost always), rating the degree to which the statement is true of the child's behavior. For example, an item on the toddler scale reads "The child stops play and watches when someone walks by." The category scores can be grouped into personality clusters of *difficult, easy, slow-to-warm-up,* and *intermediate, high,* or *low.* The clusters have demonstrated some usefulness in predicting later behavior disorders (Thomas & Chess, 1977; Terestman, 1980) and have practical utility as markers of concern in parent child interaction.

Several other temperament scales also have been developed in response to the interest in the concept and to perceived limitations of other instruments. An adaptation of the ITQ is the Short Temperament Scale for Infants (Sanson, Prior, Garino, Oberklaid, & Sewell, 1987) a 30-item scale that measures the temperament factors of approach, cooperation/management, activity/reactivity, rhythmicity, and irritability on a scale identical to that of the ITQ. The sum of the first three factors constitutes a measure of an easy-to-difficult continuum, which was found to be significantly related to such behaviors as crying, colic, and sleep problems. Garside, Birch, Scott, Chambers, Kolvin, Tweedle, and Barber (1975) developed a brief temperament questionnaire, Abbreviated Temperament Questionnaire, that consisted of 30 items administered through a focused interview technique. Each item was rated on a 5-point scale indicating the degree of presence of the behavior. In a study of nursery school children in England, Garside and co-workers found four meaningful components of temperament: (1) withdrawal; (2) high activity, intensity, and distractibility; (3) moodiness/sulkiness; and (4) irregularity. Although the names are somewhat different, the categories are very similar to those of Thomas and colleagues (1977). In another effort designed to avoid the problem of asking parents to make judgments and utilize distant recollections, Rothbart (1981) developed the Infant Behavior Questionnaire (IBQ). This questionnaire is a caregiver report instrument, with the items designed to refer to specific, concrete examples of the infant's behaviors in the immediate past week. The six dimensions assessed by the IBQ are activity level, smiling and laughter, fear, distress to limitations, soothability, and duration of orienting. The

author reports moderate convergence between IBQ ratings and home observations at three ages, as well as stability of temperament ratings over the three age points (Rothbart, 1986). Other investigators (e.g., Pedersen, Anderson, & Cain, 1980) believed some scales were vulnerable to social desirability and acquiescence responses by parents and so developed the Perception of Baby Temperament (PBT) scale based on the nine dimensions of temperament defined by Thomas et al. (1968). The PBT is administered as a 56-statement Q-sort. Respondents sort the items into three response categories indicating how "like" their child the item is, plus a "have no experience" category, based on the child's behavior in the previous two weeks. An additional feature of their scale is that the items were designed to be appropriate for fathers as well as mothers. This reflects an interest in viewing temperament in the larger context of family interactions. The Infant Characteristics Questionnaire (Bates et al., 1979) is a scale designed to measure infant difficultness. The scale contains 24 items rated on a 7-point scale, with 1 representing optimal temperament and 7 representing difficult temperament. In a study of 322 infants from age 4 to 6 months, responses indicated that mothers found fussy, hard-to-soothe, changeable infants as difficult.

Table 10.3 presents a list of questionnaires that have been designed to measure behavioral style in infants and toddlers. Although all were developed for use with nonhandicapped populations, many also have been used with handicapped children. For example, Huntington and Simeonsson (1987) recently conducted a study of the temperament characteristics of 40 youngsters with Down syndrome. The children were between 1 and 3 years of age, and behavioral style was assessed with the Toddler Temperament Scale (Fullard et al., 1984). The Down syndrome group, aged 1–2 years, resembled the nonhandicapped group on all the **subscales**. For older toddlers (2–3 years) the

TABLE 10.3

Questionnaires for Measuring Temperament in Infants and Toddlers

Questionnaire	Age Range	Reference
Baby Behavior Questionnaire	3-10 months	Bohlin, Hagekull, & Lindhagen (1981)
Infant Behavior Questionnaire	3-12 months	Rothbart (1981)
Infant Characteristics Questionnaire	4-6 months	Bates et al. (1979)
Infant Temperament Questionnaire	4-8 months	Carey & McDevitt (1978)
Infant Temperament Questionnaire-French	4-8 months	Maziade, Boudreault, Thivierge, Caperaa, & Cote (1984)
Six-month Temperament Questionnaire-Swedish	5-8 months	Persson-Blennow & McNeil (1979)
Swedish Temperament Questionnaire	12-24 months	Persson-Blennow & McNeil (1980)
Short Temperament Scale for Infants–Australian	4-8 months	Sanson et al. (1987)
Perception of Baby Temperament		Pederson, Zaslow, Cain, & Anderson (1979)
Toddler Behavior Questionnaire	11-15 months	Hagekull & Bohlin (1981)
Toddler Temperament Scale	1-3 years	Fullard, McDevitt, & Carey (1984)
Parent Temperament Scale–Revised	3-5.5 years	Pfeffers & Martin (in press)
Behavioral Style Questionnaire	3-7 years	Hegvik, McDevitt, & Carey (1982)
Parent Temperament Questionnaire	3-7 years	Thomas & Chess (1977)
Dimensions of Temperament Survey	3-adult	Lerner, Palmero, Spiro, & Nesselroade (1982)

children with Down syndrome again were very similar to the reference group, except for two subscales—the handicapped children had scores reflecting lower persistence and requiring greater stimulation to elicit a response. Further, results indicated no significant correlations between temperament subscale scores and chronological or developmental age indices (Huntington & Simeonsson, 1987). These findings indicate that temperament appears to be relatively independent of age markers within the infant and toddler range (Huntington & Simeonsson, 1987). For that reason, it is recommended that the chronologically age-appropriate scales be used with both handicapped and nonhandicapped children.

Behavioral Characteristics

Behavioral characteristics of infants and young children can affect the interactions children experience in the context of the home, clinic, or school. These characteristics can be documented in a number of ways. For example, through parental report, the number of additional or unusual caregiving demands can be ascertained (Beckman, 1983). A second parental source for gathering information aout the child is the Child Characteristics Domain on the Parenting Stress Index (PSI) (Abidin, 1986). The measure has 101 items that yield six subscales that examine the child's contribution to stress in the parent/child system. The subscales are adaptability, acceptability, demandingness, mood, hyperactivity/distractibility, and reinforcement of parent. The instrument is particularly useful for ages birth to 3, although it has been used with children up to age 10. The PSI yields both a total score and domain scores, which provide more information about the specific types and sources of stress being experienced by the family.

In addition to parent reports, there are observational measures to be completed by the interventionist or other program staff that will document behavioral characteristics of the child that are generic in nature and not tied to a particular task or test. One measure designed for this purpose is the Infant Behavior Record (IBR) (Bayley, 1969), the third part of the Bayley Scales of Infant Development. The IBR offers a summary estimate of a wide variety of behaviors observed during a testing situation. It consists of 30 items, 25 of which are 5- or 9-point rating scales. However, the scales are variable in that the optimal score can vary from the mid-point to the end, or somewhere in between. In addition, although modal values are available across different ages, these values were based on a relatively small sample size and are difficult to interpret for comparative purposes (Matheny, 1980; Simeonsson et al., 1980). However, the IBR does seem to tap important infant behaviors and may be useful clinically, despite any methodological limitations. The utility of the IBR to assess behavior was reinforced in a comprehensive investigation by Dolan, Matheny, and Wilson (1974) with infants from the Louisville Twin Study. The distribution of ratings for IBR scores at 3, 6, 9, 12, 18, 24, and 30 months was compared with that of the original standardization sample. Although small differences were found between the two samples, 80% agreement was obtained for modal ratings. Dolan et al. (1974) indicated that the findings supported the IBR's sensitivity to maturational changes, sex differences, and response clusters of behavior.

The characteristics of children with handicaps have prompted the development of behavior inventories designed to be uniquely sensitive to their problems. For example, the Children's Handicaps Behavior and Skills schedule (CHBS) is an instrument developed by Wing and Gould (1978). The CHBS includes 42 sections that assess developmental skills, and 21 sections that evaluate the abnormalities often present in handicapped populations (for example, stereotyped activities). The abnormal behavior items are rated according to the level of severity. In an analysis of 104 children, Wing and Gould found an overall agreement of more than 70% between parents and professionals. Interestingly, greater agreement was found for the absence of abnormalities than for their presence, a finding which should be kept in mind when assessing handicapped children.

A second scale designed particularly to assess the behavior of persons functioning in the sensorimotor level is the Carolina Record of Individual Behavior (CRIB) (Simeonsson, 1979; Simeonsson, Huntington, Short, & Ware, 1982). The scale is observational in nature and was developed, in part, to redress the limitations of the IBR. The scale, which is appropriate for handicapped infants and toddlers, consists of two parts and is completed after a period of observation or interaction with the child. The first part of the CRIB documents the child's state or level of arousal. State, as described in Chapter 9, is an appropriate area to assess in handicapped children not only to document its influence on performance, but also because inconsistency of state organization has been found to be indicative of dysfunction. (Thoman, Denenberg, Sieval, Ziedner, & Becker, 1981).

The second part of the CRIB includes Sections A, B, and C. Section A consists of eight developmental behaviors that are ordinal in nature, with each rated on a 9-point scale that has 1 as the most basic level and 9 as the most developmentally advanced. The eight behaviors assessed in Section A are social orientation, participation, motivation, endurance, receptive communication, expressive communication, object orientation, and consolability.

Section B also has eight behaviors rated on a 9-point scale. These behaviors are normally distributed, and items are developed so that 1 and 9 reflect polar extremes (e.g., hypoactive versus hyperactive), and 5 is the optimal score. The eight behaviors assessed

in this section are activity, reactivity, goal directedness, response to frustration, attention span, responsiveness to caregiver, tone of body, and responsiveness to examiner. Figure 10.1 displays sample scales from Sections A and B.

Section C lists 23 specific behaviors, such as exploratory patterns, communicative styles, and a number of rhythmic habit patterns observed. These are rated on a 4-point scale, indicating an estimate of the frequency with which they are exhibited. The utility of the CRIB in documenting RHPs in a heterogeneous population of handicapped children from age 3 to 89 months (X = 35 months) was demonstrated by Short and Simeonsson (1982). Results indicated that the most frequently exhibited RHPs for the total group were sucking hands/fingers, kicking the feet, arching the body, throwing the head back, and rocking the body. In addition, 5 of the 14 assessed RHPs differentiated children as a function of handicapping condition. For example, orthopedically impaired children engaged in less foot-kicking behavior than any other group, and Down syndrome children were reported to display tongue thrusting more than any other subgroup. The authors suggest that the CRIB can be used to identify the onset and decline of RHPs in the course of normal development as well as to document their abnormal persistence in clinical populations.

A factor analysis of the 16 subscales revealed four factors: communication (A5, A6, A7, A8, B1); interaction (A1, A2, A3, A4, B3, B8); responsivity (B1, B2, B3, B4, B5, B6, B8); and tone (B7). Reliability of the CRIB is determined on the basis of interrater agreement within 1 point (Gaensbauer, 1982). The mean percentage of agreement for the 16 subscales in a recent study with 65 home-based interventionists was 82%, while Beckman, Thiele, Pokorni, and Balzer-Martin (1986) reported a mean percentage of agreement of 97% for a total of 73 observations over three occasions.

Section A:

A5—Expressive Communication

Score for evidence of intentional communication (i.e., movements, babbling and/or other vocalizations should not be scored simply because they are present, but only if they show evidence of intentionality).

Circle One Response:

1. Child gives no evidence of any communication.

2. Child communicates needs/wants by total body movements—gross movements toward or away from source of stimulation.

3. Child communicates needs/wants by partial body movements; e.g., movements of trunk, facial expression, eye movements, etc.

4. Child communicates needs/wants by use of upper extremities—reaches out/pushes away with hands.

5. Child indicates needs/wants by fine motor movements—i.e., pointing, waving, etc.

6. Child communicates with simple vocalizations and/or gestures—e.g., hand to mouth = "eat," etc.

7. Child communicates with idiosyncratic single word or signs.

8. Child can communicate with single words or signs that are generally understood.

9. Child can communicate with phrases using words or formal signs (including Bliss symbols) with persons in general

X = not applicable

Section B:

B1 - Activity

Amount of gross bodily movement

Circle One Response:

1. No self-initiated movement, only responses to intrusive stimuli.

2. Only head or eye movement—very inactive.

3. Some movement, primarily of the extremities, e.g., head rocking, arm waving, leg kicking, etc.

4. Underactive, occasional adjustment to situational demands.

5. Activity level generally appropriate to situational demands and age.

6. Overactive—occasional adjustment to situational demands.

7. Squirms, bounces, fidgets when not allowed to move freely.

8. Extremely active—very difficult to quiet sufficiently to attend to situational demands.

9. Hyperactive—neither caregiver nor examiner can contain child without physical restraint.

X = not applicable

FIGURE 10.1
Sample Subscales from Carolina Record of Individual Behavior

Given the salience of behavioral characteristics for adaptation and development, a question of importance is the stability of these characteristics in infants and young children. Beckman et al. (1986) con- ducted a longitudinal study of 39 high-risk in- fants over the first year of life. Findings with the CRIB indicated that stability was greatest when the time between observations was relatively short, and that the most stability was observed on the A-scale items, which are developmentally based. As has previously been shown, even very young infants exert some influence on their environment. Knowledge of which behavioral characteristics remain stable and which do not may contribute to a better understanding of the mutual child-environment influences.

Translating Assessment Information into Instructional Goals

A major purpose for assessment of child functioning is to derive goals that reflect the program's efforts to enhance the developmental and behavioral achievements of the handicapped child. The derivation of goals is a collaborative process between parents and professionals, which requires cooperation and negotiation. As has been suggested elsewhere (Bailey et al., 1986; Winton & Bailey, 1988), a focused interview offers the opportunity for parents and professionals to discuss assessment results in the context of child development and family adaptation. For example, parents may have rated their infant as having characteristics associated with difficult temperament, and as the interventionist reviews the assessment information, he may reach the conclusion that this is an important dimension to consider when writing goals. However, it may emerge during the interview that the parents do not find the child's behavior to pose a problem for them or their family. Another family whose child presents similar characteristics may, on the other hand, deem such behaviors to be a major problem. The process of collaborative goal setting will reveal these divergent views and ensure that the setting of goals is individualized and appropriate for each child and family.

The transactional nature of developmental outcome in early intervention, while generally assumed, is difficult to put into operation. Intervention goals and activities have often been either generic in nature or developed on an as-needed basis. A conceptual framework that acknowledges the complex nature of child and environment transactions, while offering a way to account for variability in outcome, is **goodness-of-fit,** a concept that has been developed by Thomas and Chess (1977) to explain the role temperament plays in accounting for variability in developmental outcomes in vulnerable children. Goodness-of-fit, or concordance, exists when the characteristics of the child are compatible with the expectations of the environment and lead to an optimal outcome. Dissonance, or poorness-of-fit, between child and environment demands contributes to a less-than-optimal outcome. The utility of the concept has been demonstrated in clinical studies of deaf children. (Chess, Fernandez, & Korn, 1980), as well as in research on academic performance of elementary school-aged children (Lerner, Lerner, & Zabski, 1985; Keogh, 1986), and psychosocial adaptation of adolescents (Lerner, 1983). An extension of this concept to families in early intervention examined the adaptation of mothers of handicapped toddlers as a function of the goodness-of-fit of maternal, child, and support variables (Simeonsson, Bailey, Huntington, & Comfort, 1986).

Within the context of the goodness-of-fit concept, the major goal of early intervention can be defined as attempting to optimize the concordance of child characteristics and environmental demands. As Chess and colleagues (1980) have pointed out, "the central issue is to individualize each child's situation and needs, and delineate concretely those environmental demands and expectations which are consonant with the child's capacities and limitations and which will provide the basis for a healthy developmental course" (p. 66). In a practical sense, this means, for example, adapting a curriculum designed to improve small-motor control both for the child who has a low threshold of response to external stimuli and is easily distracted, as well as for the child who has a good attention span but is irritable and nonadaptable. Each of these children will need a different approach, which must be reflected in the goals and activities established to encourage individual development.

The concept of temperament may function as a **mediating variable**, as in the examples given above, or as an intervention target in its own right. Temperamental characteristics are manifested by particular behaviors, and, when appropriate, these behaviors can be made the target of intervention goals. During the course of goal setting, parents and professionals have the chance to discuss the effect of the child's behaviors on the family. It may be the case that Child A and Child B are both perceived as having difficult temperaments; however, in the case of Child A the specific behavior that is disrupting the family is that of unpredictable sleep patterns, and for Child B it may be finicky eating habits. Interventionists can plan collaboratively with parents to help them take a direct approach in moving a child whose sleep/wake cycle is irregular into one that is more predictable. Other parents can be helped to move more slowly in introducing new foods into the diet of a child who seems to be slow to adapt to new tastes or textures. Parental feelings of stress will be reduced by the very act of making a plan that they are not only comfortable with but feel capable of carrying out. Although temperament functions in large degree as a mediator of the child's responses and the environment's demands, specific aspects of temperament that affect the child's functioning in the larger context can become the target of goals.

Carey (1985) has discussed the interaction of temperament and clinical conditions, from the point of view that temperament can function as either an outcome of various clinical conditions or as a predisposing factor. He concludes that handicapping conditions "do not impose consistent patterns of behavioral style" on the handicapped child (p. 96). However, temperament has been implicated in the development of childhood behavioral problems by a number of researchers and clinicians (Carey, 1974; Dunn, Kendrick, & MacNamee, 1981; Webster-Stratton & Eyberg, 1982). This knowledge has led to efforts to circumvent later problems by providing temperament-related counseling to parents to help them cope with the child's present behavior or to avoid future problem behavior (Webster-Stratton & Eyberg, 1982; Little, 1983). Despite the usefulness of this approach, Rothbart (1982), among others, has cautioned against the widespread use of temperament for screening and counseling of parents of temperamentally high-risk children. One of the main arguments against parental temperament counseling is the desire to avoid mislabeling a child and thereby creating a problem where none existed before. Clearly, one must be extremely sensitive to the issues involved in labeling children. However, the fact remains that clinicians working with young children are called upon frequently for advice concerning a variety of behavioral issues that are temperamental in nature. This is no less true of early intervention service providers than for persons in other clinical settings. The question thus becomes how to improve assessment and counseling services. Cameron and Rice (1986) propose a procedure called **anticipatory guidance** that appears to have relevance to clinical settings. They developed a list of 37 behavioral issues that occur in a majority of infants between the ages of 5 and 12 months and produce stress in parents when they occur with great frequency or intensity, and assigned each a month in which they were likely to occur. They next generated an expected temperament profile (ETP) for each version of each issue. For example, they hypothesized that accident risk, assertiveness, and mealtime issues were more likely to occur among energetic, adjustable infants and sleep problems among low-threshold, energetic, and less adjustable infants. The list of ETPs was based on an examination of the relevant literature, clinical experience, and a pilot study (Cameron & Rice, 1979). Written anticipatory guidance suggestions, sent to the parents, were generated for the 177 infants in the study, based on their ages and ITQ (Carey & McDevitt, 1978) profile. Parents were asked at the 12-month follow up to rate the effectiveness of the anticipatory guidance. More than 90% of the parents felt that filling out the questionnaire had been helpful; more than 80% said the guidance materials helped them to understand the issues that occurred; and more than 70% found the suggestions for handling problems helpful. As a way to furnish guidance in handling temperament-associated behavioral issues, this methodology has considerable promise. It can also help both families and interventionists understand the interaction of temperament and environment in the context of the home and intervention setting.

Specific behavioral characteristics of the infant and young child can affect the way in which the child interacts with the social and physical environment and, as such, are of importance to intervention. Knowing the infant's preferred interaction strategies can influence the way in which materials and curricula are presented and can provide information about the child's likely reaction to diverse teaching methods. At a practical level, it may be necessary to address such behaviors as interfering RHPs before other, more advanced intervention goals can be effective. A program designed to extinguish or reduce the frequency of specific RHPs may be a first step to the development of goals in other areas. As with specific aspects of temperament, specific behavioral characteristics may act as mediating variables or be intervention targets in their own right. For example, the toddler who communicates manually will require different strategies for achieving social-emotional goals than will the child who communicates orally. These strategies may involve expanding the number of persons who can communicate with the child to include extended family and peers.

The child's preferred interaction strategies also have importance for caregiving activities. An irritable infant or toddler with excessive caregiving demands can be a source of stress for parents and family. Although it may be difficult to alter caregiving demands that parents find stressful, parents and other caregivers can be helped to modify their own expectations or behaviors to reduce the associated stress. A creative approach to providing parents with relief from the demands of the child may be valuable. Parents who are unwilling to leave the child may need to develop a plan whereby each provides the other with specific free time each week. For others, extended family can be called on, and community facilities that offer opportunities for respite can be explored. The goal of relief from constant caregiving may be an appropriate one, but efforts to achieve it must be tailored to fit the specific environment in which the child resides, if they are to be realistic.

Providing appropriate early intervention experiences to the young child who exhibits few clear indications of understanding is a difficult task. An initial goal might well be to spend more time observing the child in an effort to document the cues emitted or to ask parents and other caregivers to describe the cues they have determined to be those of learning and understanding. Ensuring that staff members respond appropriately to the more readily interpreted cues of distress and satisfaction may serve two purposes, that of familiarizing staff with the child's signals and that of providing the child with additional opportunities to experience success in affecting her environment. Parents have only one set of cues to learn; interventionists may have half a dozen or more. Having parents keep a written list of their child's behavioral cues will not only focus parental attention on the cues the child is providing but will also give the interventionist a way to review the cues prior to each visit, thereby maximizing the chances that cues will be noted and interpreted correctly.

This chapter has focused on child characteristics that can affect child environment interactions. Characteristics pertaining to the handicapped child, such as behavioral cues, behavioral style, and behavioral characteristics, have been suggested as areas to assess in this regard. These characteristics often function to mediate the child's responses to environmental demands, thus affecting the perceptions of family and pro-fessionals, and through them, the world the child experiences. The key to the provision of individualized services is the incorporation of idiosyncratic signaling routines, unique inter-personal styles, and novel interactive strategies into the development of intervention goals and service plans. Attention given to evaluation of these areas of functioning offers the service provider a window into the individuality of the child and ensures the appropriate modification and adaptation of services to meet the needs of each child.

SUMMARY OF KEY CONCEPTS

- Child characteristics of importance to the success of early intervention are behavioral cues, behavioral style, and behavioral characteristics.

- All children emit behavioral cues; some kinds may be more difficult to interpret than others, particularly for children who are severely, sensorily, or motorically impaired.

- Behavioral style has been implicated in behavior problems in the family (e.g., feeding, colic, and sleep) as well as in provision of education and intervention for young children, particularly through the concept of "difficultness."

- Idiosyncratic behavioral characteristics of young handicapped children, such as rhythmic habit patterns and increased caretaking demands, can interfere with not only the assessment process but also the provision of services.

- Three means whereby the assessment process may be improved are an increased reliance on clinical judgment, the employment of multiple sources of information, and expanded attention to situational effects on children's responses.

- Behavioral style and behavioral characteristics may function as mediating variables in the development of intervention goals or as goals in their own right.

- Individualizing intervention services is an example of operationalizing the concept of goodness-of-fit of environmental demands and individual abilities.

REFERENCES

Abidin, R. R. (1986). *Parenting Stress Index-Manual.* Charlottesville, VA: Pediatric Psychology Press.

Als, H., Tronick, E. & Brazelton, T. B. (1980). Affective reciprocity and the development of autonomy: The study of a blind infant. *Journal of the American Academy of Child Psychiatry, 19,* 22–40.

Bailey, D. B., Jr., & Wolery, M. (1984). *Teaching infants and preschoolers with handicaps.* Columbus, OH: Merrill.

Bailey, D. B., Jr., Simeonsson, R. J., Winton, P. J., Huntington, G. S., Comfort, M., Isbell, P., O'Donnell, K. J., & Helm, J. M. (1986). Family-focused intervention: A functional model for planning, implementing, and evaluating individualized family services in early intervention. *Journal of the Division for Early Childhood, 10*(2), 156–171.

Bates, J. E., Freeland, C. A. B., & Lounsbury, M. L. (1979). Measurement of infant difficultness. *Child Development, 50*(3), 794–803.

Bayley, N. (1969). *Manual for the Bayley Scales of Infant Development.* New York: Psychological Corporation.

Beckman, P. J. (1983). Influence of selected child characteristics on stress in families of handicapped children. *American Journal of Mental Deficiency, 88*(2), 150–156.

Beckman, P. J., Thiele, J. E., Pokorni, J. L., & Balzer-Martin, L. (1986). Stability of behavioral characteristics in preterm infants. *Topics in Early Childhood Special Education, 6*(2), 57–67.

Bohlin, G., Hagekull, B., Lindhagen, K. (1981). Dimensions of infant behavior. *Infant Behavior and Development, 4,* 83–96.

Buss, A. H. & Plomin, R. (1984). *Temperament: Early developing personality traits.* Hillsdale, NJ: Erlbaum.

Cameron, J. R. & Rice, D. C. (1979). *Infant temperament types: Relationship to early development issues and potential utility in preventive mental health programs.* Unpublished manuscript.

Cameron, J. R. & Rice, D. C. (1986). Developing anticipatory guidance programs based on early assessment of infant temperament: Two tests of a prevention model. *Journal of Pediatric Psychology, 11*(2), 221–234.

Carey, W. B. (1974). Night waking and temperament in infancy. *Journal of Pediatrics, 77,* 188–194.

Carey, W. B. (1985). Interactions of temperament and clinical conditions. *Advances in Developmental and Behavioral Pediatrics, 6,* 83–115.

Carey, W. B. & McDevitt, S. C. (1978). Revision of the Infant Temperament Questionnaire. *Pediatrics, 61*(5), 735–738.

Chee, F. K. W., Kreutzberg, J. R., & Clark, D. (1978). Semicircular canal stimulation in cerebral palsied children. *Physical Therapy, 58,* 1071–1075.

Chess, S., Fernandez, P., & Korn, S. J. (1980). Do deaf children have a typical personality? *Journal of the American Academy of Child Psychiatry, 19,* 654–664.

Chess, S. & Thomas, A. (1986). *Temperament in clinical practice.* New York: The Guilford Press.

Cicchetti, D. & Sroufe, A. (1976). The relationship between affective and cognitive development in Down syndrome infants. *Child Development, 46,* 920–929.

Cunningham, E. E., Reuler, E., Blackwell, J., & Deck, J. (1981). Behavioral and linguistic developments in the interactions between normal and retarded children and their mothers. *Child Development, 52,* 62–70.

Dolan, A. B., Matheny, A. P., & Wilson, R. S. (1974). Bayley Infant Behavior Record: Age trends, sex differences, and behavioral correlates. *JSAS Catalog of Selected Documents, 4,* 9 (ms. 551).

Dunn, J., Kendrick, C., & MacNamee, R. (1981). The reactions of firstborn children to the birth of a sibling: Mothers' reports. *Journal of Childhood Psychology and Psychiatry, 22,* 1–18.

Dyson, L. & Fewell, R. R. (1986). Stress and adaption in parents of young handicapped and nonhandicapped children: A comparative study. *Journal of the Division of Early Childhood, 10*(1), 25–34.

Eysenck, H. J. & Eysenck, S. B. G. (1969). *Personality structure and measurement.* London: Routledge and Kegan Paul.

Featherstone, H. (1980). *A difference in the family.* New York: Basic Books.

Ferris, C. (1980). *A hug just isn't enough.* Washington, DC: Gallaudet College Press.

Fewell, R. R. (1983). Assessing handicapped infants. In S. G. Garwood & R. R. Fewell (Eds.), *Educating handicapped infants.* Rockville, MD: Aspen.

Fraiberg, S. (1974). Blind infants and their mothers: An examination of the sign system. In M. Lewis & L. Rosenblum (Eds.), *The effect of the infant on its caregiver.* New York: Wiley.

Fraiberg, S. (1975). The development of human attachments in infants blind from birth. *Merrill-Palmer Quarterly, 21,* 315–334.

Fraiberg, S. (1977). *Insights from the blind.* New York: Basic Books.

Fullard, W., McDevitt, S. C., & Carey, W. B. (1984). Assessing temperament in one- to three-year-old children. *Journal of Pediatric Psychology, 9*(2), 205–217.

Gaensbauer, T. T. (1982). Regulation of emotional expression in infants from two contrasting caretaking environments. *Journal of the American Academy of Child Psychiatry, 21*(2), 163–171.

Gallagher, R. J., Jens, K. G., & O'Donnell, K. J. (1983). The effect of physical status on the affective expression of handicapped infants. *Infant Behavioral Development, 5*, 73–77.

Garside, R. F., Birch, H., Scott, D., Chambers, S., Kolvin, I., Tweedle, E. G., & Barber, L. M. (1975). Dimensions of temperament in infant school children. *Journal of Child Psychology and Psychiatry, 16*, 219–231.

Goldberg, S. (1977). Social competence of infancy: A model of parent-child interaction. *Merrill-Palmer Quarterly, 23*(3), 163–177.

Goldman, B. D. & Johnson-Martin, N. (1987, April). *Understanding babies' cues: A comparison of parents of normally developing and handicapped infants*. Paper presented at the Biennial Meeting of the Society for Research in Child Development, Baltimore, MD.

Goldsmith, H. H. & Campos, J. J. (1982). Toward a theory of infant temperament. In R. N. Emde & R. J. Harmon (Eds.), *The development of attachment and affiliative systems*. New York: Plenum.

Goldsmith, H. H. & Rieser-Danner, L. A. (1986). Variation among temperament theories and validation studies of temperament assessment. In G. A. Kohnstamm (Ed.), *Temperament discussed*. Lisse: Swets Publishing Service.

Greenberg, R. & Field, T. (1982). Temperament ratings of handicapped infants during classroom, mother and teacher interactions. *Journal of Pediatric Psychology, 7*(4), 387–405.

Greenberg, M. T. & Marvin, R. S. (1979). Attachment patterns in profoundly deaf preschool children. *Merrill-Palmer Quarterly, 25*, 265–279.

Hagekull, B. & Bohlin, G. (1981). Individual stability in dimensions of infant behavior. *Infant Behavior and Development, 4*, 97–108.

Hegvik, R. L., McDevitt, S. C., & Carey, W. B. (1982). The Middle Childhood Temperament Questionnaire. *Developmental and Behavioral Pediatrics, 3*, 197–200.

Holroyd, J. & McArthur, D. (1976). Mental retardation and stress on parents: A contrast between Down's syndrome and childhood autism. *American Journal of Mental Deficiency, 80*, 431–436.

Huntington, G. S. & Simeonsson, R. J. (1987). Down syndrome and toddler temperament. *Child: Care, Health and Development, 13*, 1–11.

Huntington, G. S., Simeonsson, R. J., Bailey, D. B., & Comfort, M. (1987). Handicapped child characteristics and maternal involvement. *Journal of Reproductive and Infant Psychology, 5*, 105–118.

Jens, K. & Johnson, N. (1982). Affective development: A window to cognition in young children. *Topics in Early Childhood Special Education, 2*(2), 17–24.

Kastein, S., Spaulding, I., & Scharf, B. (1980). *Raising the young blind child: A guide for parents and educators*. New York: Human Sciences Press.

Kennedy, J. C. (1973). The high-risk maternal-infant acquaintance process. *Nursing Clinics of North America, 8*, 549–556.

Keogh, B. K. (1982). Temperament: An individual difference of importance in intervention programs. *Topics in Early Childhood Special Education, 2*(2), 25–31.

Keogh, B. K. (1983). Individual differences in temperament: A contribution to the personal-social and educational competence of learning-disabled children. In J. D. McKinney & L. Feagans (Eds.), *Current topics in learning disabilities*. New York: Ablex.

Keogh, B. K. & Burnstein, N. D. (1988). Relationship of temperament to preschooler's interactions with peers and teachers. *Exceptional Children, 54*(5), 456–461.

Keogh, B. K., Pullis, M. E., & Caldwell, J. (1982). A short form of the Teacher Temperament Questionnaire. *Journal of Educational Measurement, 19*(4), 323–329.

Lerner, J. V. (1983). The role of temperament in psychosocial adaptation in early adolescents: A test of a "goodness-of-fit" model. *The Journal of Genetic Psychology, 143*, 149–157.

Lerner, J. V. & Galambos, N. L. (1985). Maternal role satisfaction, mother-child interaction, and child temperament: A process model. *Developmental Psychology, 21*(6), 1157–1164.

Lerner, J. V., Lerner, R. M., & Zabski, S. (1985). Temperament and elementary school children's actual and rated academic performance: A test of the "goodness of fit" model. *Journal of Child Psychology and Psychiatry, 26,* 125–136.

Lerner, R. M., Palermo, M., Spiro, A., III, & Nesselroade, J. R. (1982). Assessing the dimensions of temperamental individuality across the lifespan: The Dimensions of Temperament Survey (DOTS). *Child Development, 53,* 149–159.

Little, D. L. (1983). Parent acceptance of routine use of the Carey and McDevitt Infant Temperament Questionnaire. *Pediatrics, 71,* 104–106.

Marshall, N. R., Hogrenes, J. R., & Goldstein, S. (1973). Verbal interactions: Mothers and their retarded children vs. mothers and their nonretarded children. *American Journal of Mental Deficiency, 77,* 415–417.

Matheny, A. P., Jr. (1980). Bayley's Infant Behavior Record: Behavioral components and twin analyses. *Child Development, 51,* 1157–1167.

Maziade, M., Boudreault, M., Thivierge, J., Caperaa, P., & Cote, R. (1984). Infant temperament: SES and gender differences and reliability of measurement in a large Québec sample. *Merrill-Palmer Quarterly, 30*(2), 213–226.

McCollum, J.A. & Stayton, V. D. (1985). Infant/parent interaction: Studies and intervention guidelines based on the SIAI Model. *Journal of the Division for Early Childhood, 9*(2), 125–135.

McCubbin, H. I., Nevin, R. S., Larsen, A., Comeau, J., Patterson, J., Cauble, A. E., & Striker, K. (1981). *Families coping with cerebral palsy.* St. Paul University of Minnesota, Family Social Science.

McDevitt, S. C. & Carey, W. B. (1978). The measurement of temperament in 3–7 years old children. *Journal of Child Psychology and Psychiatry, 19,* 245–253.

McGhee, L. J. & Eckerman, C. O. (1983). The preterm infant as a social partner: Responsive but not readable. *Infant Behavior and Development, 6,* 461–470.

Mordock, J. B. (1979). The separation-individuation process and developmental disabilities. *Exceptional Children, 46,* 176–184.

Odom, S. L. & Schuster, S. K. (1986). Naturalistic inquiry and the assessment of young handicapped children and their families. *Topics in Early Childhood Special Education, 6*(2), 68–82.

Paget, K. D., Nagle, R. J., & Martin, R. P. (1984). Interrelationships between temperament characteristics and first-grade teacher-student interactions. *Journal of Abnormal Child Psychology, 12*(4), 547–560.

Pedersen, F. A., Zaslow, M., Cain, R. L., Anderson, B. J., & Maureen, T. (1980). A methodology for assessing parent perception of baby temperament. *ASJS Catalog of Selected Documents, 10,* 10–11 (ms. 1987).

Persson-Blennow, I. & McNeil, T. F. (1979). A questionnaire for measurement of temperament in six-month-old infants: Development and standardization. *Journal of Child Psychology and Psychiatry, 20,* 1–13.

Persson-Blennow, I. & McNeil, T. F. (1980). Questionnaire for measurement of temperament in one- and two-year-old children: Development and standardization. *Journal of Child Psychology and Psychiatry, 21,* 37–46.

Peterson, N. L. & Meier, J. H. (1987). Assessment and evaluation processes. In N. L. Peterson (Ed.), *Early intervention for handicapped and at-risk children* (pp. 275–326). Denver: Love.

Pfeffers, J. & Martin, R. (in press). Comparison of mother's and father's ratings of referred and nonreferred preschool children. *Journal of Clinical Psychology.*

Prechtl, H. F. R. (1963). The mother-child interaction in babies with minimal brain damage. In B. M. Foss (Ed.), *Determinants of infant behavior, 2.* New York: Wiley.

Pullis, M. E. & Caldwell, J. (1982). The influences of children's temperament characteristics on teacher's decision strategies. *American Research Journal, 19*(2), 165–180.

Rogers, S. J. & Puchalski, C. B. (1984). Social characteristics of visually impaired infants' play. *Topics in Early Childhood Special Education, 3*(4), 52–56.

Roskies, E. (1972). *Abnormality and normality: The mothering of thalidomide children.* Ithaca, NY: Cornell University Press.

Rothbart, M. K. (1981). Measurement of temperament in infancy. *Child Development, 52,* 569–578.

Rothbart, M. K. (1982). The concept of difficult temperament: A critical analysis of Thomas, Chess and Korn. *Merrill-Palmer Quarterly, 28*(1), 35–40.

Rothbart, M. K. (1986). Longitudinal observation of infant temperament. *Developmental Psychology, 22*(3), 356–365.

Rothbart, M. K. & Derryberry, D. (1981). Development of individual differences in temperament. In M. E. Lamb & A. L. Brown (Eds.), *Advances in developmental psychology, 1.* Hillsdale, NJ: Erlbaum.

Sanson, A., Prior, M., Garino, E., Oberklaid, F., & Sewell, J. (1987). The structure of infant temperament: Factor analysis of the revised infant temperament questionnaire. *Infant Behavior and Development, 10,* 97–104.

Schlesinger, H. S. & Meadow, K. P. (1972). Sound and sign: Childhood deafness and mental health. Berkeley: University of California Press.

Scott, E. P., Jan, J. E., & Freeman, R. D. (1977). *Can't your child see?* Baltimore, MD: University Park Press.

Sexton, D., Miller, J. H., & Rotatori, A. F. (1985). Determinants of professional-parent agreement for the developmental status of young handicapped children. *Journal of Psychoeducational Assessment, 4,* 377–390.

Short, R. J. & Simeonsson, R. J. (1982, March). *Rhythmic habit patterns as a function of handicapping condition.* Paper presented at International Conference on Infant Studies, Austin, TX.

Simeonsson, R. J. (1979). *The Carolina Record of Individual Behavior.* University of North Carolina, Chapel Hill.

Simeonsson, R. J. (1987). *Psychological and developmental assessment of special children.* Boston: Allyn & Bacon.

Simeonsson, R. J., Huntington, G. S., & Parse, S. (1980). Expanding the developmental assessment of young handicapped children. In J. J. Gallagher (Ed.), *New directions for exceptional children, 3,* (pp. 51–74).

Simeonsson, R. J., Bailey, D. B., Huntington, G. S., & Comfort, M. (1986). Testing the concept of goodness of fit in early intervention. *Infant Mental Health Journal, 7*(1), 53.

Simeonsson, R. J., Huntington, G. S., Short, R. J., & Ware, W. B. (1982). The Carolina Record of Individual Behavior: Characteristics of handicapped infants and children. *Topics In Early Childhood Special Education, 2*(2), 43–55.

Simpson, A. E. & Stevenson-Hinde, J. (1985). Temperamental characteristics of three- to five-year-old boys and girls in child-family interactions. *Journal of Child Psychology and Psychiatry, 26*(1), 43–53.

Sirignano, S. W. & Lachman, M. E. (1985). Personality change during the transition to parenthood: The role of perceived infant temperament. *Developmental Psychology, 21*(3), 558–567.

Sonnander, K. (1987). Parental developmental assessment of 18-month-old children: Reliability and predictive value. *Developmental Medicine and Child Neurology, 29,* 351–362.

Sprunger, L. W., Boyce, W. T., & Gaines, J. A. (1985). Family-infant congruence: Routines and rhythmicity in family adaptations to a young infant. *Child Development, 56,* 564–572.

Stone, N. W. & Chesney, B. H. (1978). Attachment behaviors in handicapped infants. *Mental Retardation, 16,* 8–12.

Terestman, N. (1980). Mood quality and intensity in nursery school children as a predictor of behavior disorders. *American Journal of Orthopsychiatry, 50,* 125–138.

Thelen, E. (1981). Rhythmical behavior in infancy: An ethological perspective. *Development Psychology, 17,* 237–257.

Thoman, E. B., Denenberg, V. H., Sieval, J., Ziedner, L. P., & Becker, P. (1981). State organization in neonates: Developmental inconsistency indicates risk for developmental dysfunction. *Neuropediatrics, 12,* 45–54.

Thomas, A. & Chess, S. (1977). *Temperament and development.* New York: Brunner/Mazel.

Thomas, A., Chess, S., & Birch, H. G. (1968). *Temperament and behavior disorders in children.* New York: New York University Press.

Webster-Stratton, C. & Eyberg, S. (1982). Child temperament: Relationship with child behavior problems and parent-child interactions. *Journal of Clinical Child Psychology, 11,* 123–129.

Wedell-Monnig, J. & Lumley, J. M. (1980). Child deafness and mother-child interaction. *Child Development, 51,* 766–774.

Wing, L. & Gould, J. (1978). Systematic recording of behaviors and skills of retarded and psychotic children. *Journal of Autism and Childhood Schizophrenia, 8*(1), 79–97.

Winton, P. J. & Bailey, D. B., Jr. (1988). The family-focused interview: A collaborative mechanism for family assessment and goal-setting. *Journal of the Division for Early Childhood, 12*(3), 19–34.

Yoder, P. J. (1987). Relationship between degree of infant handicap and clarity of infant cues. *American Journal of Mental Deficiency, 91*(6), 639–641.

Chapter 11

Assessing Infant Cognitive Development

Mary Beth Langley
Nina Harris Exceptional Student Education Center
Pinellas Park, Florida

KEY TERMS

- Sensorimotor Intelligence
- Reflexive Behaviors
- Piagetian Approach
- Object Permanence

- Piagetian Developmental Stages
- Means-Ends
- Causality
- Spatial Relationships

- Imitation
- Scheme of Object Concept
- Traditional Scales
- Ordinal Scales
- Schemes

The integration and refinement of sensory and motor behaviors to produce adaptive responses to the environment during the first 24 months of life is referred to as **sensorimotor intelligence.** Sensorimotor intelligence is the ability to solve problems through the integration of perception, postural adjustments, and movement prior to the acquisition of language (Casati & Lezine, 1968). In normally developing children, these sensorimotor skills permit the acquisition of increasingly more complex mental behaviors as children respond and adapt to sensory information through motoric interactions with the environment. Sensorimotor intelligence begins with **reflexive behaviors,** expands to refined and coordinated sensory and motor skills, and progresses to using those skills to manipulate tools and eventually mental images for solving problems. The acquisition of sensorimotor abilities affords children the critical skills necessary for achieving higher-level thought and adaptive processes. Children learn goal-directed behavior during these first 24 months. They learn that the world is a permanent place that has order and predictable consequences. Furthermore, they learn that any number of means exist for controlling the actions of others and of events that occur around them. This chapter provides a rationale for sensorimotor assessment, describes key components of sensorimotor abilities, presents strategies for assessing sensorimotor skills, and discusses implications of sensorimotor assessment for early intervention.

Sensorimotor Assessment Rationale

Sensorimotor skills are the foundation for the development of social, communicative, self-care, and play behaviors and should be assessed to determine each child's unique pattern of sensorimotor development (Dunst & Gallagher, 1983). Strengths and weaknesses within and among specific sensorimotor domains and any significant gaps in sensorimotor development that may preclude the acquisition of symbolic behavior, reasoning skills, or adaptive behaviors should manifest themselves during the assessment. An assessment of sensorimotor abilities also yields some insight as to why children may not be progressing in other areas of development, such as communication, play, and independence. An assessment of sensorimotor skills will reflect whether delays in acquiring these other skills is due primarily to cognitive deficits or to a combination of sensory, physical, and environmental influences or deficits. An assessment of these early requisites for more mature learning and thought is essential, particularly when a child manifests sensory and/or motor impairments. It can be used to determine primary learning and response modes, to ascertain which aspects of a child's sensorimotor skills may be compromised by the impairment(s), and to identify any compensatory mechanisms the child has learned to employ, an indication of adaptive behavior. Information provided by an analysis of these variables will enable curricular intervention to be focused on the appropriate behavioral level for each sensorimotor domain and delivered in an approach consis-

tent with the child's primary learning style and mode. Perhaps the most relevant reason for assessing the range and nature of sensorimotor abilities is to predict, for both immediate and future environments, how efficient a child is or will be in adapting to social and environmental demands. Additionally, the assessment of sensorimotor intelligence will provide estimates of rate of learning as well as demonstrate the effectiveness of educational intervention when used as data for program evaluation. Knowledge of the conceptual framework of each of the individual sensorimotor domains and of the characteristic behaviors germane to each stage of sensorimotor progression permits the practitioner to understand the interrelationships between and among the various sensorimotor domains and how, in turn, those domains can influence the development of social, communicative, self-care, and play skills (Ginsburg & Opper, 1979).

The assessment of sensorimotor intelligence should entail a two-pronged approach: (a) assessment of the range and variety of sensorimotor behaviors and (b) assessment of the general level of competence that is most characteristic of children's development in each sensorimotor area as well as of the cumulative sum of their sensorimotor development. As the separate assessment of sensory and of motor behaviors is addressed in Chapters 7 and 13, the assessment of specific sensorimotor intellectual domains will be the primary focus in this chapter. Regardless of the instrument selected for the assessment, similar types of sensorimotor skills will be addressed in each; the nature of the presentation of the items will depend on the philosophical design of the instrument. The underlying conceptual framework is arranged to assess the efficiency with which children use sensory and motor skills for problem solving. Although the following description of sensorimotor intellectual behaviors is based on a **Piagetian approach** (Piaget, 1952), the behaviors will be applicable across assessment instrumentation, and their descriptions will enable the practitioner to analyze children's responses in a manner that facilitates the translation of assessment results into intervention strategies. An understanding of both the horizontal components (i.e., skills such as **object permanence** and behaviors relating to objects) and the vertical hierarchy of sensorimotor stage development (i.e., primary circular reactions and coordination of secondary circular reactions) enables the practitioner to assess sensorimotor concepts and their individual stage of development (Brainerd, 1978). Piaget (1952) divided intellectual development during the sensorimotor period into six ordinal stages, during which each of the concepts described as schemes by Piaget become progressively more complex in form.

Piagetian Sensorimotor Stages

The **Piagetian developmental stages** within the sensorimotor period span the range from birth to 24 months. Although these stages overlap in development and texts report slight differences in the developmental ranges covered by each stage, the general age ranges are consistent. The six stages of the sensorimotor period and the primary learning characteristic associated with each stage follow.

Stage I: Reflexes (birth/1 month to 6 weeks). The child in this stage is dominated by **reflexive behaviors** and simply reacts physiologically to external stimuli. The majority of reflexes at this stage are protective in nature. The child blinks in response to light and air, turns his head to clear his nose from the surface, sucks to take in nourishment, and startles at loud or unexpected sounds. The primary function of the reflexive stage appears to be simply to "get the system ready" for learning. This first stage prepares

the sensory and motor systems for their roles as response and feedback mechanisms.

Stage II: Primary Circular Reactions (1 to 4 months). During this stage children learn to integrate sensory and motor behaviors and begin to interact with their environment. They look for sounds, watch their hands, bring their hands to their mouths, and bring their hands and feet together. The interactions cause a pleasurable effect, but the results produced are accidental in nature. Children's actions are focused on their own bodies and not yet directed towards objects.

Stage III: Secondary Circular Reactions (4 to 8 months). The most important learning that occurs at this stage is that children become aware that they can have an effect on the environment. They notice that their actions produce pleasurable results and begin to repeat behaviors systematically to continue the pleasurable actions. They kick in the crib to keep the mobile moving, shake rattles to hear the sound, and swipe at toys to keep them activated. Casati and Lezine (1968) explain that in Stage III, children's relationship between their perceptions and their manual activities is more accurately felt, with prehension becoming distinct from forearm gestures. While children focus on the results of their actions rather than on the action itself as in Stage II, their discoveries remain random, with no preestablished goal in mind.

Stage IV: Coordination of Secondary Circular Reactions (8 to 12 months). The outstanding feature of this stage is that children learn to become goal-directed. They now can chain behaviors together to achieve a desired goal. However, if their attempts to accomplish a desired result are ineffective, they appear to have no alternative recourse available. They do not try another way of reaching their goal, because at this stage they are limited to familiar behavioral schemes. They rotate their bodies from sitting to crawl for a toy; they grasp and pull to reach a cookie or toy; they grasp a toy and use it to strike a surface, or grasp an adult's hand and push it toward a desired object.

Stage V: Tertiary Circular Reactions (12 to 18 months). The key characteristics of this stage are that children learn new behaviors through trial and error and become adept in instrumental behavior. It is in this stage that the foundations for deductive reasoning emerge. The difference between this stage and the previous one is that now children have the skills to try something different if their first attempt to accomplish a goal is unsuccessful. If the lid does not go on one pot, they try another pot or reach for a different lid and try it. Their actions and thoughts are very flexible and they have many cognitive and motoric alternatives at their disposal.

Stage VI: Combination of New Means through Mental Combinations (18 to 24 months). A primary characteristic of Stage VI is that children acquire insight into problems rather than solving them through trial and error. At this stage children learn to use foresight; they now have a goal in mind prior to physical action and can predict which strategies will be needed to achieve the goal. At this stage, they have enough information about a task to be performed to make a choice about the most appropriate response. Now children can discern which lid among many will fit a specific pot before trying it. Also, at this stage children now can function symbolically; they use one thing to represent another. A croquet mallet becomes a jack-hammer or a ship's rudder, a ladder transforms into a guitar, a stick becomes a galloping horse. Also characteristic at this stage is the emergence of the syndrome of cravings for such toys as Transformers℠, for children can now appreciate the concept of reversibility. It should be noted, however, that their ability to symbolize is quite primitive.

Piagetian Sensorimotor Schemes

Throughout the evolution of these sensorimotor stages, children simultaneously acquire increasingly more complex forms of the six horizontal domains. Piaget (1952) termed these concepts **schemes.** In the normally developing child, these six domains emerge in a somewhat parallel but separate pattern. Assessment of the progression of each of the six concepts is essential if eduational intervention is to enhance integrated development rather than isolated skills. Each of these concepts moves from being motor and sensory skills to symbolic abilities.

Visual Pursuit and Permanence of Objects. The primary function of this scheme is that children learn to attend to critical events in the environment and develop systematic searching, organizational, and memory skills. Visual attending, orienting, tracking, and scanning skills are precursors to the development of the realization that objects no longer in view exist in some other place or form. However, while deficient visual processes may impede the acquisition of this concept, they do not preclude its development. From visually and manually pursuing objects as they move, children learn to scan systematically possible known options in order to produce the most appropriate response. Tasks representative of this scheme are searching for a dropped object, retrieving an object hidden under a container, and recalling in which of three locales an object is hidden. Objectives to achieve in the assessment of **object permanence** include an evaluation of the efficiency of child's attending behaviors, the child's persistence in pursuing a goal, the efficiency and organization of search behaviors, the number of events the child can hold successfully in his memory, and the child's ability to deduce an appropriate response.

Means-Ends Relationships. The acquisition of **means-ends** (sometimes called problem solving, cf., Dunst, 1981) relationships culminates in children's ability to use insight to solve unfamiliar problems. Children watch their hands and observe that they can be used to acquire something they want, and they learn to use objects as tools to achieve desired results. Eventually they learn that symbols (e.g., words) can be used as tools to solve problems, and they gradually acquire a stockpile of behaviors to accomplish desired results through mental rather than physical manipulations. Representative tasks include reaching for an interesting object, switching objects from hand to hand, pulling strings and cloths to retrieve objects, and employing an unattached object as a means of retrieving another object beyond direct reach. Objectives to achieve in the assessment of this scheme include an evaluation of the child's use of motor behaviors to achieve a goal, the child's understanding of tool use, the child's ability to chain behaviors to accomplish a goal, the extent of goal-directed behavior, and the child's ability to reason in light of novel situations.

Causality. The major function of the acquisition of **causality** is instilling in children the ability to search for the causal source or relationship behind the solution of a problem. Causality is initiated as children accidentally create pleasurable feelings with their own bodies by waving their hands, bouncing in their cribs, or kicking their legs. Once they realize they can control their environment effectively through systematic motoric procedures, more complex actions occur by engaging other people. As experiences with pleasurable effects increase, children begin to anticipate results and events and learn to search for the activating or causal mechanism needed to operate toys or produce the anticipated event. Tasks representative of this scheme include increased activity in anticipation of a pleasurable event, shaking a toy in anticipation of an interesting sound, search-

ing for the clapper in a bell, returning a toy to an adult in anticipation that the adult will make the toy work, and looking for the right button to push for a drink at an unfamiliar fountain or for the source of obtaining a favorite piece of gum. Objectives to achieve in the assessment of this scheme include the extent of child's ability to repeat a pleasurable event, the extent of child's understanding of her ability to direct an adult's actions, and the child's ability to deduce the causal source or relationship for solving novel problems.

Construction of Objects in Space. As a result of mastering **spatial relationships** children acquire the understanding of the three-dimensionality of objects and recognition of objects from any angle; they learn that there is a specific end or side of objects that produces desired effects. They learn how to manipulate objects in space in order to use objects together and learn about number, size, and space and begin to understand the relationship of gravity to objects. Eventually, children begin to use reasoning to reach desired locales, events, or objects through the shortest possible route and the quickest way. Representative tasks in the area of construction of objects in space include shifting attention from one event to another, turning to locate sound sources, releasing objects into and dumping objects from containers, fitting lids on containers, imitating strokes with a crayon, and inserting shapes in formboards. Objectives to achieve in the assessment of this scheme include an evaluation of the child's ability to orient to environmental stimuli, the child's ability to discriminate foreground from background, the child's understanding of the functional side or end of objects, the child's appreciation of the limits of space, the child's ability to relate objects to each other, the extent of the child's appreciation of gravity, and the child's ability to make judgments about spatial relationships.

Imitation. Children learn new behaviors through both vocal and gestural **imitation** of the people and events around them. The most important function of imitation is its use as a means for acquiring new information. A critical prerequisite to learning to imitate is attending to social interactions. Eventually, children learn to form mental images of familiar behaviors and objects, which they can then use for play and problem solving. The progression of imitative behaviors is depicted in Table 11.1.

Objectives to achieve in the assessment of this scheme include an evaluation of the extent of complexity and the range of behaviors the child has for interacting with the environment, the child's attention to other people, the child's observation of events, the child's ability to replicate observed actions, and the child's ability to replicate actions observed on previous occasions and in other contexts.

Behaviors (Schemes) Relating to Objects. Mastering the **scheme of object concept** affords children numerous strategies for make-believe play and for succeeding in self-care and other adaptive activities. As they manipulate a wide range of objects of various sizes, textures, and forms, children learn that different behaviors on objects produce different reactions, and they gradually learn to apply the appropriate behavior according to the perceptual attributes of the object. They learn to attract the attention of adults through objects as well as to use adults to obtain desired objects. As experiences with different sets of objects expand, children learn to use objects to substitute for unavailable objects, culminating in the ability to engage in make-believe play with miniature replicas of life-sized objects and situations. This understanding of objects and object behaviors facilitates the ability to classify objects according to attributes and functions. Representative tasks include employing mouthing, shaking, and banging actions on objects, us-

TABLE 11.1
Hierarchy of Imitation Development

1. Children continue behaviors in which they are engaged when imitated by others.
2. Children imitate behaviors they have been observed to perform when another individual initiates the imitation.
3. Children learn to modify behaviors within their repertoire by imitating someone else; the behaviors must be visible to the child and difficulty will be experienced if the behaviors are not in the child's repertoire.
4. Children imitate behaviors new to their repertoire but must still be able to see their body; the new behaviors are imitated through trial and error.
5. Children now can imitate behaviors they cannot see themselves perform but initially do so through gradual approximation.
6. Children can imitate behaviors they observed at a previous time; they engage in representational play behaviors.

ing objects functionally, and selecting familiar objects when named. Objectives to achieve in the assessment of this scheme include an evaluation of the extent and range of behaviors used to manipulate objects, the child's ability to discriminate actions appropriate for the attributes of objects, the child's understanding of the functional use of objects, the child's ability to instigate social interaction with objects, the child's ability to engage in representational play with objects, and the child's ability to use objects as symbols for other objects.

Procedural Considerations in Assessing Sensorimotor Intelligence

Bricker and Campbell (1980) stressed that cognitive development is greatly influenced by sensory, physical, and social mechanisms. Children with profound sensory, motor, social, or intellectual deficits may exhibit insufficient behavior to be measured by more traditional instruments and checklists. For those children with deficits in sensory, physical, social, or intellectual processes, practitioners must reorient their expectations of what to assess and how to conduct the assessment. Gerken (1983) argued that the intellectual level of children functioning within the severe/profound range cannot be measured in the traditional way. She further proposed that attention to early biological development concerning activity levels, perceptual responsiveness, and sleep/wake cycles is necessary to the assessment process of such children (see Chapters 8–10). Sensorimotor assessment of children with sensory, physical, or social deficits must entail judicious selection and adaptation of instruments that provide a comprehensive measure of sensorimotor intelligence while simultaneously avoiding penalizing children's performance because of the nature of handicapping condition(s). Selection of a scale to assess sensorimotor cognitive abilities will depend on the nature of children's handicap, the extent of sensory, social, communicative, and/or physical impairments, the level of integration of the central nervous system (as demonstrated through motoric behavior), and the extent and quality of previous interactions and experiences. Therefore, the practitioner must be prepared to tailor each assessment to the individual and his specific handicapping condition(s) and response mode(s). Griffiths (1954) perhaps most succinctly emphasized the assessment dilemma posed when testing children with impairments when she asked: "How can we give enough weight to those directions in which their effort is unimpaired, and be in a position to assess the effect of specific disabilities on the total test result?" (p. 35). The most critical assumption is that no child is untestable because all behavior reflects some level of adaptive functioning. If children are considered "untestable," teachers may incorrectly assume they also are "unteachable."

A Piagetian approach to assessment of sensorimotor abilities is advocated because of its application across a wide array of developmental scales and checklists. A Piagetian framework can effectively serve as the foundation from which to analyze the majority of cognitive tasks included on instruments of early cognitive behaviors. Assessment instruments available for the investigation of sensorimotor intelligence can basically be assigned to one of two categories: **Traditional scales** and **ordinal scales** of psychological development. Traditional scales, whether norm-referenced or criterion-referenced, provide a sample of behaviors considered characteristic of a specific age range. Typically, the selected items have little relationship to each other and often do not tap the entire range of sensorimotor intelligence. It is not unusual to find that several age levels have lapsed before a specific domain is again addressed. Often, depending on the instrument, certain domains are heavily weighted with minimal or no attention to other sensorimotor domains. Because of these organizational issues and issues related to item selection, the traditional measures are of limited value when conducting assessments for instructional programming purposes.

Ordinal scales of development are based on the assumption that the acquisition of early cognitive and intellectual competencies involves qualitative transitions from lower to higher levels of cognitive functions. Lower levels of behavior serve as the foundation for the emergence of sequentially more sophisticated forms of the same concept. "There is a hierarchical relationship between the achievements at different levels, so that in principle the achievements of the higher level do not incidentally follow, but are intrinsically derived from those at the preceding level and encompass them within the highest level" (Uzgiris & Hunt, 1975, p. 11). Differences between ordinal scales and the more traditional developmental checklist-type as-

TABLE 11.2
Comparison of Traditional and Ordinal Scales

Traditional Scales	Ordinal Scales
Items are additive and represent landmarks; little attention is given to interrelationships among items	Items are ordered by level of difficulty; quality of performance is considered
The notion of general intelligence is assumed as the conceptual underpinning	Infant cognition is assumed to be composed of varied sets of abilities that vary with more progressive levels of behavior
A summary of items depicts the profile of the child's functioning; individual items are not emphasized	The child's level of competence along a developmental continuum is determined in each specific domain assessed
A standard fixed rate of development is assumed; items are distributed according to age levels at which they are attained in the normally developing child	Scales consider influences imposed on development by experience; a range of reactions and behaviors is anticipated
Different children may exhibit very contrasting learning profiles and be assigned the same age placement	Identical scores reflect identical performance within the hierarchy of the same conceptual domains
Profiles may depict a wide scatter in performance; strengths and weaknesses are determined only through an analysis of items	Learning patterns are determined by noting in which domains performance is highest and lowest
Administration procedures are standardized and must be followed exactly	Administration procedures are flexible and designed to meet the needs and interests of the individual child; the primary focus is on eliciting optimal performance

sessment scales delineated by Dunst and Gallagher (1983) are summarized in Table 11.2.

Several of the more recent developmental scales provide for assessment of children's abilities through direct testing, observation, and caregiver interview. The primary advantage of direct testing is that the practitioner can structure situations designed to elicit specific behaviors children may not have demonstrated spontaneously. Being able to pursue children's line of thinking to facilitate their optimal functioning is still another advantage of direct testing that may not be possible nor feasible through informal observation methods. An additional advantage of direct testing is that the conditions for eliciting the same behaviors at a later time may be replicated readily, thus increasing the possibility that children's responses are elicited under similar conditions. This will be particularly critical when assessment data are used as a variable in program evaluation. Disadvantages of direct testing are that (a) children's responses may not be characteristic of how they would respond in more natural settings and contexts, (b) children may not exhibit the behavior being tapped because the situation and/or the materials are not motivating, and (c) children's immediate interests are not addressed, which is more frequently the case when traditional measures are used.

Informal observation of children in familiar settings and routines allows more characteristic views of their abilities and may be actually more reflective of how children can be expected to perform even under the most optimal learning opportunities. When the practitioner analyzes children's interactions with the environment from a Piagetian approach, observation throughout the day can provide an excellent assessment of sensorimotor abilities and may identify behaviors that are difficult to elicit under more structured conditions. For example, it is not unusual for children to lose interest in searching for even the most stimulating toy during the assessment of object permanence, yet be observed in familiar settings to search several locales until a favorite food or play item is found. Disadvantages to informal observation are that children's optimal performance may not be demonstrated, the practitioner loses some control over assessment conditions and, if not familiar with Piagetian theory and concepts, may not recognize the manifestation of a concept when it is couched within the context of self-care, play, or independence activities. For example, the practitioner may wish to discern whether children can stack five blocks but not realize that the child is demonstrating the concept of construction of objects in space as several large cardboard bricks are aligned to make a fence for a make-believe house. Additionally, children's ability to squeeze toothpaste onto a toothbrush may go undetected as representative of the functional use of objects, recognition of the functional end/side of objects, and as a complex level of means-ends behaviors.

By interviewing caregivers with carefully selected questions, information or support can be obtained for the practitioner's hypotheses about the child's sensorimotor abilities that direct testing or informal observations failed to reveal. Caregivers often are able to relate specific examples of individual sensorimotor schemes that represent the same type of tasks attempted during the more formal assessment or they may supply additional data on the quality and consistency of children's responses. Additionally, caregivers may provide examples of behaviors that are more indicative of certain stages of sensorimotor functioning than do tasks presented under isolated conditions. A major disadvantage of the interview method is the high level of skill required both to formulate appropriate interview questions that will evoke specific assessment data and to support qualitative, nonjudgmental interpersonal relationships. The interviewer must be able to discern the underlying data that are provided even when the caregivers appear to be responding appropriately to the practitioner's query. For example, if the caregiver replies "yes" to the question, "Does Jamie search for things she cannot see?", the practitioner still has no evidence of the level on which Jamie's object permanence skills are functional. If the practitioner is searching for some indication that Jamie's search skills are functional at stage VI and the caregiver offers "She oftentimes will continue to look after her parents when they come up behind her and tickle her up the middle"; he should ascertain that, in this instance, Jamie requires a physical stimulus to motivate her and that she has to persist very minimally to locate the source of her pleasure. Therefore, Jamie's searching skills may be limited to stage IV. The investigation by Fewell, Langley, and Roll (1982) supports data that suggest caregivers and teachers alike tend to inflate children's abilities when data are elicited in an interview format.

When selecting the assessment battery and designing assessment contexts, the practitioner should form some hypothesis of the way in which children: take in information, indicate their responses, must be positioned and handled in order to produce optimal responses, respond to unfamiliar people and settings, attend over a period of time, relate to materials representing various forms of sensorimotor domains, and respond to various reinforcers/behavior management strategies.

Additional concerns that should be addressed are whether children have any specific fears that would preclude the use of certain stimuli during the assessment (e.g., lights, unusual noises), and when the child is most alert and responsive, particularly in the case of very young children. If children are taking medication, its effects on their attention and neurological status must be ascertained. Sensory and physical capabilities and the extent of compliance behavior will most significantly influence children's performance of cognitive tasks and should be taken into account. Additional variables that will affect children's cognitive performance as well as the selection of the assessment instruments are the extent and quality of experiences they have been afforded and those in which they will likely participate as well as those from which they potentially will be excluded. The practitioner should analyze assessment tools prior to their administration to discern whether the selected instrument will provide information identified as important in the assessment referral, the instrument will tap efficiently the full range of sensorimotor abilities, specific sensorimotor domains are more heavily weighted than other domains, the nature of the response requirements will significantly limit children's performance because of their impairment(s), and the orientation of the instrument is compatible with the nature of children's handicapping condition(s): (e.g., are the items heavily dependent on social and linguistic behaviors and does the child to be assessed exhibit a number of behaviors characteristic of autistic children?).

Representative Methods for Assessing Sensorimotor Abilities

There is a plethora of instruments designed for assessing the abilities of young children that are both standardized assessment tools and formal/informal checklists. A number of assessment tools have evolved from programs serving children with impairments, due to the lack of appropriate instruments for identifying the needs of this group. Several of these scales are commercially available. Generally, such instruments are recapitula-

tions and reorganizations of the items from other scales deemed inappropriate by the developers of the new instrument with few or inappropriate adaptations provided to compensate for the nature of the handicapping condition(s). Several attempts to provide more efficient and effective assessment measures have resulted, however, in tools that have merit for use with children with impairments. Descriptions of these scales are included in the following discussion. Additional assessment instruments that have been useful in the assessment of more difficult-to-test children are summarized in Table 11.3 Instruments from both the traditional and ordinal orientations that are commonly used in programs serving infants and children with exceptional needs are included. Reviews of the instruments are based on their clinical utility with difficult-to-test infants and young children.

Traditional Instruments

Traditional instruments of sensorimotor behaviors can be divided into two categories: those that are norm-referenced or criterion-referenced with neither overt recognition of children with impairments nor provisions for sensory, physical, or social deficits and those that are norm-referenced or criterion-referenced but have been developed specifically for use with children with impairments and/or have provided strategies for adapting items to accommodate sensory, physical, and/or social deficits. According to Simeonsson (1986), the scale of sensorimotor intelligence most commonly used in programs with infants and children with handicaps is the Bayley Scales of Infant Development (Bayley, 1969). While these scales consist of three independent measures of mental, psychomotor, and social domains, only the Bayley Scale of Mental Development will be discussed here. The primary advantages of the Bayley scale are (a) its well-respected stan-

TABLE 11.3
Instrument Summaries

Instrument	Age Range	Areas Assessed	Unique Features
Adaptive Performance Instrument (Gentry, 1980)	Birth–24 months	Sensorimotor skills; physical intactness, reflexes and reactions, gross and fine motor, social, self-care, and communication skills	Particularly useful with severely and profoundly handicapped children; scoring criteria afford qualitative observations; suggestions for adaptations for physically, hearing-, and visually impaired and deaf/blind
Comprehensive Developmental Evaluation Chart (Cliff, Carr, Gray, Nymann, & Redding, 1975)	Birth–3 years	Reflexes, gross motor manipulation, vision, feeding, receptive and expressive language, cognitive-social, and hearing	May serve as a quick but thorough screening instrument and is particularly sensitive at the earlier ranges; very helpful in a team approach to screening children
Developmental Diagnosis (Knobloch, Stevens, & Malone, 1980)	Birth–3 years	Adaptive, gross motor, fine motor, language and personal-social behaviors	The manual provides excellent descriptions and illustrations of developmental skills; a must for anyone involved in the assessment of infants and young children
Generic Skills Assessment Profile (McLean, Snyder-McLean, Rowland, Jacobs, & Stremel-Campbell, no date)	2 weeks–30 months (approximate)	Object relationships, comprehensions, imitation, expressive communication, representation, and dyadic interaction	A graphic profile of early aspects of communication that may be used to chart the progression of language development; the profile may be scored from informal interactions and observations of children as they participate in developmental assessments; particularly useful in a team approach

dardization qualities, (b) its proven effectiveness in measuring the skills of children with handicaps, and (c) the large number and variety of behaviors tapped at each age level from birth to 30 months. A number of items may be scored on the basis of incidental observation, and there are provisions for scoring omissions, refusals, and caregiver reports of behaviors. A particularly attractive feature of the Bayley scales is the large number of items provided for assessment of visual and auditory behaviors, which comprise approximately the first 48 items on the scale. However, it is the expansive number of items that test cognition via items heavily loaded with sensory and motor behaviors that render the use of the Bayley inappropriate with children with sensory and motor deficits. From 13 through 30 months, the scale is heavily weighted with language items and perceptual motor tasks, many of which are timed.

A helpful feature of the Bayley Scales is the clustering of items of similar behaviors on the protocol, which facilitates both administration and scoring. The raw score is the total number of items passed both above and below the basal level. The raw scores are converted to a Mental Development Index (MDI), and in cases where the MDI is below 50, developmental age equivalents are derived from the normative tables by cross-referencing the child's total raw score with the MDI of 100 and pinpointing the chronological age in which the raw score falls. The Bayley Scales are most appropriately administered by psychologists trained to work with infants and young children and is most appropriate for children with cognitive delays or mild sensory and communication impairments. It is not recommended for use with children with moderate to severe physical impairments. The Bayley is standardized on a population of normally developing children and has no provisions for children with severe impairments. Campbell, Siegel, Parr, and Ramey (1986) recently published

data suggesting a need to renorm the Bayley Scales inasmuch as average scores for a representative current sample of infants ranged from 109 to 114.

A scale of infant intelligence very similar to the Bayley is Cattell's (1960) Infant Intelligence Scale. Spanning the developmental range of 2 to 30 months, the Cattell initially was designed to be a downward extension of the Stanford-Binet test. Although the scope and number of behaviors are not as comprehensive as the Bayley, many items on the Cattell are almost identical to those on the Bayley. Like the Bayley, the Cattell protocol clusters items by behaviors and materials alongside the individual lists of items at each age level. Additionally, the protocol includes items from the Binet through the second half of the fourth year. A unique feature of the Cattell is the provision of two additional items for the majority of age levels to substitute if an item among the first five is spoiled during its administration. The score is reported as developmental age levels in months, and score computation is quickly and easily accomplished. The same applications suggested of the Bayley apply also to the Cattell. This instrument is more appropriately administered, however, by such instructional personnel as teachers than is the Bayley.

An instrument designed specifically to be used with children with delays and deficits of various natures is the Griffiths' Mental Development Scales (Griffiths, 1954). Although the scale extends from birth through 8 years, there is a separate instrument (*The Abilities of Babies*) for the measurement of abilities during the first two years of development. During the first 24 months, five independent scales of behaviors comprise the Griffiths' test: locomotor, personal-social, hearing and speech, eye and hand coordination, and performance. The manual to *The Abilities of Babies* is unique in that there is an entire chapter devoted to the performance of children with communication, severe cognitive, physical, and sensory deficits. The Griffiths' profiles of performance are provided for children exhibiting each of these handicapping conditions. The advantage of the profiles is that the practitioner has a reference point with which to compare the performance of children with handicaps similar to those profiled to determine whether a child's performance on the Griffiths is typical of children with the same nature of impairment. The items on the Griffiths' Scales are quite practical and relate to the types of skills children will need in everyday routines. Any order of item administration is permitted, and the practitioner is encouraged to take advantage of children's interest throughout testing. As in the Bayley, incidental observation of the items is allowed. Smith, Bidder, Gardner, and Gray (1980), however, found higher interrater reliability on the eye-hand, the performance, and the practical reasoning scales; the personal-social, locomotor, and hearing and speech scales were more sensitive to interpretation by raters. These last three scales, however, are more likely to be informally assessed as the evaluator interacts with the child. Although the performance scale covers the breadth of sensorimotor concepts, it is heavily laden with perceptual-motor items, many of which are timed. The locomotor and the hearing and speech scales are weak when administered to children with severe motoric impairments. With the exception of the hearing and speech scale, the Griffiths' test is useful with children with severe emotional and social deficits. A general intelligence quotient may be derived, and developmental ages for each of the five scales can be obtained. Because the Griffiths' test spans such a wide age range, it is a highly desirable instrument to use in programs serving infants and preschoolers. Because of its British origin, several of the items are culturally biased, but these few items usually do not affect the general outcome significantly. It should be noted that it was normed on a British population, and this fact raises concerns about the applicability of norms to U.S. children. Also Hanson and Aldridge-Smith (1987) found a substantial difference on scores of children tested today as compared with those tested in the original standardization. Beail (1985) reported that data collected on 25 profoundly multiply handicapped children suggested that the Griffiths' and the Bayley scales could be used interchangeably but that higher scores consistently were obtained with the Griffiths.

A fairly recent addition to the field of assessment of young children is the Battelle Developmental Inventory (BDI) (Newborg, Stock, Wnek, Guidabaldi, & Svinicki, 1984). The BDI is formatted similarly to the Griffiths in scope of assessment as well as age range. It was constructed to provide for multifactored evaluation of children and consists of five domain scales: cognitive, personal-social, motor, communication, and adaptive. The most attractive features of the BDI are the suggested adaptations of items for specific handicapping conditions, the excellent and extremely comprehensive standardization data compiled on the use of the BDI with normally developing children, and the provision for three methods of assessment: observation, interview, and direct testing. Primary shortcomings of the BDI are the sparsity of items provided in each age range and the lack of items providing comprehensive assessment of the full range of sensorimotor cognitive abilities. The cognitive scale is divided into subscales that assess perceptual discrimination, memory, reasoning, academic, and conceptual behaviors. Within the first 3 years, the BDI provides a total of only 17 cognitive items. Typical of the cognitive behaviors assessed during the first 35 months are: Follows visual and auditory stimuli, inserts circle and square in formboard, matches forms, and repeats two digits. Several of the items appear to be placed within inappropriate age ranges. For example, "repeats a two-digit number" and "selects the hand hiding a toy" are both placed at the 24–35 month range, and the concept of self as a causal agent with a familiar toy is placed in the 2–3 year age range. Many of the suggested adaptations provide for minimal changes in the original items, change the initial conceptual intent of the original item, or simply instruct the practitioner to omit the item. However, for the practitioner unfamiliar with eliciting responses from children with impairments, attempts to provide strategies for adapting items is a welcomed feature. McLean, McCormick, Bruder, and Burdg (1987) found that the BDI demonstrated psychometric integrity when used in programs for young children with identified handicaps but were dissatisfied with the BDI's "developmental milestone approach" (p. 245). McLean et al. indicate

> administration time, training requirements, acquisition of assessment materials, and extrapolation procedures used in calculating extreme standard scores, the requirement to follow the prescribed order of items, insufficiency of the manual to specify training requirement for users of the BDI, and the attainment of negative scores as high as −80 in the motor domain for one child were distinct disadvantages. (pp. 244–245)

Because the BDI is relatively new to the field, it deserves time and study to prove its effectiveness with children with a wide range of handicapping conditions. It is perhaps best used as a screening tool, which is incorporated in the scale. Scores are reported in the form of developmental age equivalents and percentile ranks for each of the scales and for the total instrument. McLean et al. conclude, "When used in conjunction with other measures to child and family functioning, it [Battelle] will serve as a valuable outcome measure for early intervention programs" (p. 245).

Designed specifically to be used in the assessment of visually impaired children with additional handicapping conditions, the Reynell-Zinkin Scales, Part 1 Mental Develop-ment (Reynell, 1979) offers the unique feature of norms provided for sighted, partially sighted, and totally blind children. The Reynell is divided into subscales that measure social adaptation, sensorimotor understanding, exploration of the environment, response to sound and verbal comprehension, vocalization and expressive language (structure), expressive language (vocabulary and content), and communication. The author encourages the practitioner to take advantage of children's interest when administering the items and to score incidental observations of target behaviors. The exploration of environment and sensorimotor understanding scales are particularly relevant and practical for the visually impaired child. A most helpful feature is the division of expressive language into structure and content because the vocalization of many multihandicapped, visually impaired children is echolalic in nature and lacking in content or communicative intent. An unfortunate omission is a means of translating children's performance on the communication scale into developmental ages, although this scale is very appropriate for deaf/blind children and other nonverbal visually impaired children. When the developmental age equivalents of each of the subscales and for the total scale are derived for totally blind children, they are consistently inflated as much as 6 to 18 months when compared with the same performance on other scales of development. The author does not clarify the significance of the different age equivalents established for each of the functional vision levels, and one can only assume that the inflated ages for the blind children were derived as a result of the influence of the visual impairment on development. The sensorimotor understanding scale, however, provides an efficient assessment of children's early cognitive behaviors. All in all, the Reynell test offers a functional approach to the assessment of multihandicapped, visually impaired children functioning within the birth-to-5-year age range.

The following three developmental scales were developed primarily for the assessment of children with impairments, provide strategies for translating assessment results immediately into instructional programming, and provide for a comprehensive assessment of children's progression in the primary developmental domains.

The Early Intervention Developmental Profile (EIDP) (Rogers, Donovan, D'Eugenio, Brown, Lynch, Moersch, & Schafer, 1981) is one of the very few assessment instruments based on specific philosophical approaches. The EIDP assesses development from birth through age 5 in perceptual/fine motor, cognition, language, social-emotional, self-care, and gross motor domains. The authors report that the cognition scale is Piagetian based, although the items are randomly scattered across developmental levels. The motor scales of the EIDP are definite strengths of the scale, while, as in the Griffiths, the language scale is the weakest when used for children with severe impairments. The primary advantages of the EIDP are its comprehensiveness of developmental coverage, its intent for use in a team approach, the efficiency and speed with which it can be administered, and the provision of a graphic means of profiling children's abilities. The major disadvantage is the relatively small number of items in each age range; however, it is this feature of the EIDP that makes it a highly desirable tool for quickly screening a child's developmental progress or to be used to supplement additional assessment measures. Children's development is charted according to three-month age ranges, depending on the highest item accomplished in each assessment domain (e.g., 0–2, 12–15, 32–35 months). Also, it should be noted that age levels were assigned to items based on estimates derived from other measures, thus clinicians should exercise caution when using any scores generated by the EIDP. An activity booklet accompanies the EIDP in which each skill assessed is cross-referenced with suggested instructional strategies supplemented with provisions for adapting the instruction for children with visual, hearing, and physical impairments. Unfortunately, the activities are designed specifically to teach the assessment behaviors. This is, however, an excellent tool to use with new teachers and with paraprofessionals learning to work with children with handicaps.

The Hawaii Early Learning Profile (HELP) (Furuno, O'Reilly, Hosaka, Inatsuka, Allman, & Zeisloft, 1979) is a comprehensive assessment of children's development in cognitive, language, fine and gross motor, self-help, and social domains. The HELP charts provide for a graphic display for the progression of children's abilities from birth through age 3. Children's performance is recorded according to whether they mastered the skill, required an assistive device, accomplished the skill to the best of their abilities but were unable to accomplish the skill fully due to a physical limitation, or demonstrated no acquisition of the target skill. The cognitive section is almost completely dominated by Piagetian sensorimotor items and provides a thorough, sequential approach to assessment of cognition, particularly during the first two years. The social domain is particularly sensitive to subtle attachment and bonding behaviors and to behavior states and is one of the strongest components of the instrument. When the performance of severely handicapped young children on the HELP was compared with their performance on the Infant Psychological Development Scale (IPDS) (Uzgiris & Hunt, 1975), the EIDP, and the Comprehensive Development Evaluation Chart (Cliff, Carr, Gray, Nymann, & Redding, 1975), this practitioner's experience was that the HELP provided for assessment of nearly three times as many behaviors as any of the other assessment measures. Although it initially seems overwhelming in its scope, the nature of the assessment of behaviors permits the scoring of items as they are observed in the course of assessment of other behaviors. The accompaniment of an instructional guide that suggests numerous ways to teach the concepts underlying the assessment behaviors makes the HELP a most appealing and functional assessment to integrate into intervention programs serving young children with a variety of handicapping conditions.

The Vulpé Assessment Battery (Vulpé, 1977) is a "unified approach to developmental assessment, performance analysis, and program planning for atypically developing children" (p. 49). The cognitive processes and specific concepts scale is extremely comprehensive in its sequential presentation of developmental items by category. Concepts assessed within the birth to 24-month range include object, body, shape, size, and space concepts; visual memory; auditory discrimination; auditory attention; comprehension; memory; cause/effect or means/ends behaviors; and categorizing/combining schema. The object concepts scale contains items that assess both the manipulation of objects similar to the object schemes scale of the IPDS and object permanence. Object permanence skills and short-term memory for objects and pictures also are assessed in the visual memory subscale. Within the space scale, children's understanding of the orientation of faces and patterns, physical accommodation of the shape of objects, understanding of shape constancy, and manipulation of formboards are assessed. Children's orientation to sounds and objects in space, to their own body parts, and to other people as well as the ability to relate two or more objects to each other in space are measured in the space concepts section. The categorizing/combining schema subscale encompasses the assessment of children's ability to integrate sensory mechanisms with motoric behaviors, response to weight, understanding of the effects of behavior on others, and of the association of familiar objects with their categories.

The Vulpé has a large number of assessment items in a wide range of areas contributing to concept development within the birth to 5-year range. In addition to the assessment of specific concepts, the Vulpé assesses children's organizational behavior (how they approach and learn tasks); attention and goal orientation; internal behavior control related to recognition and response to environmental limits, problem solving and learning patterns; and dependence/independence. Children's responses are rated according to their quality across a 7-point scale rather than on a pass/fail basis and may be scored as follows: (a) no response; (b) attention to task; (c) physically assisted; (d) socially/emotionally assisted; (e) verbally assisted; (f) independent; and (g) transfers (generalizes). The Vulpé was designed to analyze an individual child's performance rather than to compare children with some normative standard. While a global developmental score is not derived from children's performance, individual subscale scores and a cumulative developmental score may be approximated by referring to the developmental ages that are provided as reference points and are intended to serve as a general developmental guide.

The Vulpé Scale is a competency-oriented assessment tool that allows both for the assessment of children's optimal functioning and for a uniform, reproducible, well-defined coding system for scoring performance, which eliminates ambiguity and variability between observers. Although the Vulpé does not provide specific instructional goals, objectives, and teaching strategies, the hierarchical nature of the items and comprehensiveness of the assessment battery provide guidelines for developing programming and curricular activities. Because of the organization and structure of the Vulpé (items are all grouped within categories of behavior and labeled as such), a pattern of strengths and weaknesses is easily derived. Vulpé (1977) states that the assessment is not a standardized test but a "systematic overview of many aspects of the individual student's pattern of interacting with the world" (p. 4). Reliability data indicate the Vulpé test can be reliably administered by a variety of child-care professionals to children with different handicapping conditions. The major drawback to the use of the Vulpé is the voluminous breadth of skills that are assessed. The author recognizes this disadvantage and suggests that skills may be observed informally and over time. The comprehensive nature of the Vulpé is perhaps the feature that makes it a highly desirable diagnostic-prescriptive assessment tool that can be used to design appropriate instructional activities.

Ordinal/Piagetian Measures. The efficacy of a Piagetian approach to assessment and programming with young children with handicaps has been supported by Best and Roberts (1976), Dunst (1980, 1981), Dunst and Gallagher (1983), Dunst and Rheingrover (1981), Heffernan and Black (1984), Kahn (1976, 1979), Rogers (1977), Sigman and Ungerer (1981), Wachs and DeRemer (1978), Weisz and Zigler (1979), and Woodward (1959). The most frequently used Piagetian assessment tool is the Infant Psychological Development Scales. (Uzgiris & Hunt, 1975), commonly referred to as simply the Uzgiris-Hunt scales (Simeonsson, 1986). The Uzgiris-Hunt scales are based on the concept that intelligence can be partitioned into several distinct but parallel branches of cognitive development. The Uzgiris-Hunt scales assess seven areas of cognitive development over the span of the sensorimotor period: visual pursuit and the permanence of objects, means-ends relationships, causality, gestural imitation, vocal imitation, the construction of objects in space, and behaviors relating to objects. The highest item passed along one of these branches of development signifies the point on a developmental continuum at which the child is functioning. The overall score is the average of the highest items passed across the various domains. The primary advantage of using the Uzgiris-Hunt scales is the degree of flexibility provided in their administration. The immediate interest of

children may be used to structure task presentations, and simply observing children's interactions with a variety of toys and materials can be used to score many of the scale steps. The practitioner can supply materials of interest to children to maintain motivation and thereby elicit target responses. Although novel and exciting toys can be used, familiar objects from children's home or educational setting can be equally valuable. For each concept, the manual specifies the location and position of the child, suggested materials for eliciting the desired responses, specific directions to the practitioner for setting up the eliciting situations, the number of repetitions permitted, and the desired and typical responses to the eliciting situations. An item from the causality scale is presented in Figure 11.1.

Familiarity with the items described in the Uzgiris-Hunt scales facilitates an understanding of the conceptual basis of similar items on more traditional scales of sensorimotor development. The Uzgiris-Hunt scales have been used successfully with autistic (Sigman & Ungerer, 1981), hearing-impaired (Best & Roberts, 1976), visually impaired (Davis & Langley, 1980), physically impaired (Fetters, 1981), and mentally handicapped (Kahn, 1976) children. Heffernan and Black (1984) suggest that the Uzgiris-Hunt scales may not be the best to use with children whose social interaction skills are specifically impaired and that the skills of physically impaired children may be underestimated. These authors also advise caution when using the Uzgiris-Hunt scales with children approaching the end of the sensorimotor period of development. Disadvantages to using the Uzgiris-Hunt scales are the detailed and intricate number of items and responses with which to be familiar and the rather cumbersome protocol. Within some of the domains, there are rather large conceptual leaps between items. An additional limitation of the Uzgiris-Hunt and other Piagetian-based scales is that the extent to which the sequence of the steps is a true picture of a common developmental sequence

FIGURE 11.1
Sample Item from the Uzgiris-Hunt Scales

<table>
<tr><td colspan="2" align="center">***Behavior to a spectacle created by an agent acting on an object***</td></tr>
<tr><td>Location:</td><td>Same as in situation 5 (Infant in seat with working surface—face-to-face with examiner)</td></tr>
<tr><td>Object:</td><td>Any object which can be manipulated to create a spectacle of interest to the infant may be used. For example, a roly-poly toy which can be made to spin around on a surface, a music box that has to be started by pulling a cord, a pendulum toy, or a "slinky" toy create interesting spectacles.</td></tr>
<tr><td>Directions:</td><td>Obtain the infant's attention and set off the object. Once the object stops, wait a few moments to observe the infant's behavior, leaving both the object and your hand within the infant's reach. . . It is important that the examiner's role in creating the spectacle be quite obvious. However, this situation is most successful when the act setting off the object is not an easy one for the infant to perform. Set off each spectacle 2–3 times.</td></tr>
<tr><td>Repeat:</td><td>2–3 different spectacles.</td></tr>
<tr><td>Infant Actions:</td><td>a. Shows interest during the spectacle, but does not attempt to recreate it.
b. Performs some act which can be considered a "procedure" when the object stops.
*c. Touches the object or the examiner's hand lightly when the object stops and waits.
*d. Picks up the object and gives it to the examiner to activate.
e. Attempts to activate the object himself.</td></tr>
</table>

*Responses that receive the highest level of credit

Source: **From *Assessment in infancy: Ordinal Scales of Psychological Development* by I. Uzgiris and J.M. Hunt, 1975, Urbana: University of Illinois Press. Copyright 1975 by University of Illinois. Reprinted with permission.**

is not yet known (Heffernan & Black, 1984). However, for its role in the development of functional, generative instructional objectives, the use of the Uzgiris-Hunt framework is unequaled (Dunst, 1981).

In 1980, Dunst contributed an invaluable adaptation of the Uzgiris-Hunt scales by filling in some of the conceptual gaps with additional Piagetian items arranged along with the original Uzgiris-Hunt items in a very practical format. The Dunst (1980) protocol significantly reduces the confusion often experienced with the use of the original Uzgiris-Hunt format. Heffernan and Black (1984) found that Dunst's addition of sug-

gested developmental ages for each of the items proved valid. Further, Heffernan and Black found that Dunst's version facilitated explaining children's level of achievement across developmental domains to parents. Anyone interested in using the Uzgiris-Hunt scales should become familiar with Dunt's adaptations.

Other Piagetian-based measures include the Albert Einstein Scales (Escalona & Corman, 1966), the Casati-Lezine Scales (Casati & Lezine, 1968), and the Mehrabian and Williams scales (1971). The Einstein Scales of Sensorimotor Development consist of a space scale that encompasses stages III–VI, a manual prehension scale that assesses development in stages I–III, and an object permanence scale that taps behaviors in stages III–VI. The uniqueness of many of the tasks presented in the Einstein scales permits them to be used as refreshing supplements to more traditional Piagetian items. The manual prehension scale, precursor to the assessment of means-ends relationships, provides a systematic, qualitative assessment of behaviors that is not readily available in other scales of development such as tactile exploration, touch-grasp sequence, bilateral hand contact, invisible touch and restraint of hand, and hitting at a suspended toy. Similarly, the Casati-Lezine scales (1968) provide an assessment of only four series of tests in the areas of (a) searching for hidden objects, (b) use of intermediaries, (c) exploration of objects, and (d) the combination of objects. The Casati-Lezine sequences span development from stage III–stage VI. These scales offer additional interesting Piagetian items not included in the Uzgiris-Hunt scales, although some of the items have been selected for inclusion as experimental items on the Dunst (1980) version of the Uzgiris-Hunt scales. Both the Einstein and the Casati-Lezine scales report the level of children's development according to stage placement. Mehrabian and Williams (1971) proposed a Piagetian-based measure of cognitive development that emphasized items that appeared to tap representational ability, including linguistic and nonverbal communication abilities. The proposed scale consists of 28 items that assess abilities in the domains of denotation and representation, observing response, reciprocal assimilation, object stability, imitation, and causality. The authors found that the administration of the total scale took 15–30 minutes and that children's scores expressed the level of cognitive development in months. Because the Mehrabian and Williams scale offers some variance in conceptual approach and type of items, the practitioner may wish to study the items carefully prior to selecting them for inclusion in a battery of other Piagetian tasks.

This scale does not offer the practitioner a readily usable set of items. For those interested in pursuing the development of nonverbal behaviors in children and the cognitive relationship between early "motor-gestural" (p. 125) behaviors and later linguistic development, the Mehrabian and Williams scale suffices as an excellent assessment framework.

Translating Assessment Information into Instructional Goals

The early interventionist who has a thorough understanding of the sensorimotor conceptual domains can ascertain a valid profile of children's abilities and deficits that formulate unique patterns of learning which, in turn, will generate immediate programming needs and appropriate instructional strategies. Integrated, functional programming must be based on integrated, functional assessment. If behavior is randomly sampled, children may be taught random, nonfuctional, isolated skills. It is essential that the teacher be able to analyze items from traditional scales to determine which of the Piagetian concepts is represented by each respective item administered to children. For those practitioners who are not familiar with this type of item analysis, it is suggested that they recruit the assistance of team members and other instructional personnel to analyze completely the traditional scales with which they feel most comfortable. One way to approach the analysis is to use Dunst's (1980) assessment framework as a model for discerning the conceptual nature of the items. Although the majority of items incorporate several behaviors, the Dunst model will enable practitioners to analyze the item according to its most significant concept. For example, if the item under scrutiny is "stacks two blocks," the practitioner will need to locate that or a similar item within Dunst's framework. This item is found in the domain of construction of objects in space as scale step 9: Builds tower of two cubes. If the item being analyzed is "releases cube to take a third," this type of item is found in the domain of means-ends relationships as scale step 5: Drops one or both objects held in hands to obtain a third object. While this is a tedious, exhausting approach, the practitioner will begin to appreciate quickly the similarities among items on different scales, which facilitates immediate recognition of the concept being represented.

A second skill critical to designing functional instructional objectives is to be aware of the primary learning characteristics of each stage of sensorimotor development (primary circular reactions vs. coordination of secondary circular reactions). An awareness of the type of learning that occurs at each stage prevents teaching children static, isolated skills and facilitates the teaching of concepts across developmental domains, settings, and functional materials. Additionally the practitioner needs to understand the subcomponents of each of the six domains in order (refer to the following suggested goals in each domain) to instruct children in the general concept rather than the specific scheme (object permanence). When the teacher can identify children's level of mastery of each of the six sensorimotor domains and the characteristics of the learning period subsequent to the level of mastery of each of the six domains, he can establish strategies that not only integrate children's thinking and allow for inherent generalization of behaviors but incorporate cognitive activities into other aspects of children's development. Such tactics not only avoid teaching the assessment item but afford infinite practical learning opportunities within children's natural environment. For instance, if the task assessed was the ability of a child to locate a cube hidden under a cup, the concept being measured is that of object permanence. If the child achieved mastery at the stage III level of object permanence, appropriate instructional strategies may be developed as depicted in Figure 11.2.

Test Item:	*Retrieves cube hidden under cup*
Conceptual Domain:	*Object permanence*
Stage Placement:	*Stage IV: Coordination of secondary circular reactions*
Child's response:	*Attended primarily to the cup; retrieved block when part of it extended beyond the lip of the cup*
Suggested Instructional Objective:	*Children will retrieve their spoons from under their napkins in order to eat their cereal.*
Generalization Activity:	*Children will retrieve their sneakers from the shoe box in order to play outside after they observe their caregiver remove the lid briefly before replacing it.*
Concomitant Instructional Objectives Addressed	
Self-Care, Eating:	*Children will participate in hand-over-hand self-feeding patterns.*
Self-Care, Grooming:	*Children will participate in simple dressing skills such as pulling on a shirt placed over their head, and a shoe positioned over their toes.*

FIGURE 11.2
Translation of Assessment Item into Instructional Program

The targeted skills incorporate cognitive objectives into self-care settings in which additional objectives can be met and the selected strategies provide for natural reinforcement for performing the desired behavior (eating and playing). Rather than having as an objective that the child will locate a cube displaced under a cup, which is an end in itself, the selected skills facilitate the development of a means of systematic searching and foster concomitant development of additional developmental skills. Examples of goals to be fostered within each of the sensorimotor domains are delineated in Table 11.4.

As much as possible, the goals suggested in Figure 11.2 should be incorporated into ongoing communication, social interactions,

TABLE 11.4
Sensorimotor Goals for Instructional Planning

Domain	Goals
Object Permanence	1. The development of efficient visual, auditory, and tactile/kinesthetic attending behaviors. 2. Extension of children's persistence in searching for displaced objects. 3. The development of efficient and organized search behaviors. 4. Expansion of the length and number of variables with which children can retain events in their memory. 5. The development of the ability to deduce logically the locale of familiar and preferred objects and activities.
Means-Ends Relationships	1. Development of a wide range of behaviors for acting on the environment. 2. Development of the understanding of tool use. 3. Development of the ability to chain behaviors to accomplish a goal. 4. Development of goal-directed behavior. 5. Development of representational problem-solving skills.
Causality	1. Development of behaviors that can be used to create and maintain pleasurable events. 2. Development of the child's understanding of his ability to direct an adult's actions. 3. Development of strategies for searching and deducing causal sources or relationships for solving novel problems.
Construction of Objects in Space	1. Development of the ability to orient to environmental stimuli. 2. Development of the ability to discriminate objects and activities in the foreground relative to children and from objects and activities in the background. 3. Development of the appreciation of the functional side or end of objects. 4. Development of the concept of three-dimensionality and form constancy.

TABLE 11.4
Continued

Domain	Goals
	5. Development of the ability to relate to each other and combine them in logical spatial orientations for purposeful activity. 6. Development of an understanding of the influence of gravity. 7. Development of the ability to make judgments about spatial relationships.
Imitation	1. Facilitation of an increase in the range and extent of complexity of behaviors available for interacting with the environment. 2. Facilitation of an increase in attention to other people. 3. Facilitation of an increase in the extent and quality of observation powers of environmental events. 4. Facilitation of the extent of the ability to replicate observed actions that children can see themselves perform. 5. Facilitation of the extent of the ability to replicate observed actions that children cannot see themselves perform. 6. Facilitation of the extent of the ability to replicate actions observed on previous occasions and in other contexts.
Behaviors Relating to Objects	1. Development of an increase in the extent and range of behaviors used to manipulate objects. 2. Development of the ability to discriminate and apply actions dictated by the attributes of objects. 3. Development of an understanding of the functional use of objects. 4. Development of the ability to instigate social interaction with objects. 5. Development of the ability to engage in representational play with objects and miniature toy sets (e.g., Fisher Price, Little Tykes, Tomy, etc.). 6. Development of symbolic behavior.

self-care, and play routines, and each sensorimotor objective must have as its primary function the integration of all other developmental skills. Particularly when caring for the young child in the home, the caregiver needs minimal responsibilities for implementing isolated, structured intervention tactics. However, when cognitive activities can become an inherent part of routines that must be implemented on a day-to-day basis, the caregiver becomes more observant of children's behaviors, provides more opportunities to practice the skills, and increases the likelihood that the skills will generalize across settings, contexts, people, and materials. The same is true when providing for cognitive intervention in a classroom that houses 10 or more young children with special needs. The teacher has little time, within a limited schedule, to ensure that each child receives individual intervention in each of the sensorimotor areas. The following instructional strategies are contrived to demonstrate how behavioral objectives in the sensorimotor areas can be incorporated into day-to-day routines at home and into social interaction contexts within the classroom. For more extensive descriptions and examples, see Dunst (1981).

Targeted Objectives:
1. Development of the ability to retrieve partially hidden objects
2. Development of the ability to use nonmanual behaviors to control the actions of others
3. Development of the ability to use objects to instigate social and communicative interactions
4. Development of the ability to imitate behaviors they can see themselves perform, using actions within their behavioral repertoire
5. Development of the functional use of objects
6. Development of the ability to combine objects in space

Context: Diaper Change
Instructional Strategies:
1. Near the changing surface, place the container of diapers within easy reach of children. Pull out the diaper so that it is partially exposed to children. Require children to retrieve the diaper and offer it to you to initiate having their diaper changed.
2. Allow children to explore the diaper, the powder container, washcloths/diaper wipes, and their clothing prior to their use or application. Talk to them and show them where each of the objects belongs (diaper on bottom, pants on bottom, powder on table, washcloth or diaper wipes in laundry basket or trashcan.)
3. Demonstrate for children throwing the washcloth, dirty diaper, or wet wipes into the laundry basket or trashcan and offer them the opportunity to dispose of one or more articles.

4. Wait to help children from the changing surface until they establish gaze with you; pause to imitate children's behaviors and encourage them to maintain reciprocal interactions with familiar motor schemes.

Targeted Objectives:
Same as previous objectives

Context: Group Socialization Activity
Instructional Strategies:
1. Select a toy that can be used simultaneously with several children to elicit an array of cognitive, communicative, and fine motor behaviors on several different developmental levels. Games such as Stuff Your Face®, Hungry Hippos®, and Simon® are excellent for fostering a number of developmental behaviors in groups of children. Toys such as the Fisher Price Discovery House® with a number of interactional possibilities also are good to use in social interaction contexts.
2. Place the toy in the center of the table but within easy visual access of the children. Wait for children to look at you to initiate requesting the toy.
3. Allow children to manipulate one aspect of the toy, then encourage children to push the toy to a peer for a turn in imitating the first child's actions on the toy.
4. With each interaction, encourage children first to imitate the actions of the previous child and then to explore the actions of other features of the toy. For example, the Fisher Price House has a toy car in which a doll can ride; the car can be allowed to roll down a ramp, or a spinning mechanism and a bell provide delightful sounds and interesting spectacles when activated.
5. While children watch, release the car or the doll so that it partially disappears from view. Wait to see whether children will search for the toy or whether they

notice the visible part of the toy prior to helping them retrieve it.

6. After children have had several opportunities to pass the toy among themselves, take the toy prior to their passing it to see whether children will attempt to protest or to attract your attention to have the toy returned.

The assessment of sensorimotor intelligence and design of realistic and functional intervention programs for enhancing the progress of sensorimotor skills from a Piagetian framework can be an exciting and challenging task. The wide variety of assessment instruments available for the assessment of sensorimotor skills and a comprehensive knowledge base of the developmental sequence and characteristics of learning patterns at each stage of sensorimotor development arm the teacher with qualitative tools for enriching the young child's competence in adapting to home, school, and community environments.

SUMMARY OF KEY CONCEPTS

- Sensorimotor skills are the foundation for many other skills including behaviors in communication, social, self-care, and later cognitive abilities.

- Sensorimotor skills involve integrating sensory and physical movements that eventually lead to representational or symbolic abilities.

- Sensorimotor abilities appear to progress through six stages originally described by Piaget, including reflexes, primary circular reactions, secondary circular reactions, coordination of secondary circular reactions, tertiary circular reactions, and combination of new means through mental combinations.

- Six concepts appear to develop simultaneously during the sensorimotor period: visual pursuit and object permanence, means-ends relationships, causality, construction of objects in space, imitation, and behaviors for relating to objects.

- Assessment of children's sensorimotor abilities requires prior identification of visual, auditory, and physical impairments.

- Sensorimotor abilities can be assessed through traditional measures (norm-referenced or cirterion-referenced instruments) or ordinal measures.

- Traditional measures include the Bayley Scales of Infant Development, Infant Intelligence Scale, The Abilities of Babies (Griffiths' Mental Development Scales), Battelle Developmental Inventory, and the Reynell-Zinkin Scales, Part I Mental Development.

- Criterion- and curriculum-referenced scales such as the Early Intervention Developmental Profile, Hawaii Early Learning Profile, and the Vulpé Assessment Battery can be used, although they are not thorough assessments of Piaget's sensorimotor concepts.

- Piagetian-based measures such as the Infant Psychological Development Scales, especially with Dunst's adaptions, allow an assessment of the sensorimotor concepts that lead to useful instructional objectives.

- To translate assessment information into useful instructional objectives, interventionists must be skilled in (a) analyzing the intent of test items and identifying which sensorimotor concept is being measured, (b) recognizing the learning characteristics of each sensorimotor stage, and (c) integrating instruction into activities from other curricular areas and into ongoing routines.

REFERENCES

Bayley, N. (1969). *Bayley Scales of Infant Development*. New York: Psychological Corp.

Beail, N. (1985). A comparative study of profoundly multiply handicapped children's scores on the Bayley and the Griffiths' developmental scales. *Child: Care, Health and Development, 11*(1), 31–36.

Best, B. & Roberts, G. (1976). Early cognitive development in hearing-impaired children. *American Annals of the Deaf, 121,* 560–564.

Brainerd, C.J. (1978). *Piaget's theory of intelligence.* Englewood Cliffs, NJ: Prentice-Hall.

Bricker, W. & Campbell, P.H. (1980). Interdisciplinary assessment and programming for mulihandicapped students. In W. Sailor, B. Wilcox, & L. Brown (Eds.) *Methods of instruction for severly handicapped students.* Baltimore, MD: Paul Brookes.

Campbell, S.K., Siegel, E., Parr, C.A., & Ramey, C. (1986). Evidence for the need to renorm the Bayley Scales of Infant Development based on the performance of a population-based sample of 12-month-old infants. *Topics in Early Childhood Special Education, 6*(2), 83–96.

Casati, I. & Lezine, I. (1968). *Les etapes de l'intelligence sensorimotrice.* Paris: Editions de Centre de Psychologie Applique.

Cattell, P. (1960). *Cattell Infant Intelligence Scale.* New York: Psychological Corp.

Cliff, S., Carr, D., Gray, J., Nymann, C., & Redding, S. (1975). *Comprehensive Developmental Evaluation Chart.* El Paso, TX: El Paso Rehabilitation Center.

Davis, J. & Langley, M.B. (1980). *A guide to developing a classroom curriculum for visually impaired, multihandicapped infants.* Chicago: Stoelting.

Dunst, C.J. (1980). *A clinical and educational manual for use with the Uzgiris and Hunt Scales of Infant Psychological Development.* Austin, TX: Pro-Ed.

Dunst, C.J. (1981). *Infant learning: A cognitive, linguistic strategy.* Allen, TX: Developmental Learning Materials.

Dunst, C.J. & Gallagher, J.L. (1983). Piagetian approaches to infant assessment. *Topics in Early Childhood Special Education, 3*(1), 44–62.

Dunst, C.J. & Rheingrover, R. (1981). Discontinuity and instability in early development: Implications for assessment. *Topics in Early Childhood Special Education, 1*(2), 49–60.

Escalona, S. & Corman, H. (1966). *Albert Einstein scales of sensorimotor development.* Unpublished paper. New York: Albert Einstein College of Medicine. Department of Psychiatry.

Fetters, L. (1981). Object permanence development in infants with motor handicaps. *Physical Therapy, 61,* 327–333.

Fewell, R.R., Langley, M.B., & Roll, A. (1982). Informant vs. direct screening: A preliminary comparative study. *Diagnostique, 7,* 163–167.

Furuno, S., O' Reilly, A., Hosaka, C., Inatsuka, T., Allman, T., & Zeisloft, B. (1979). *The Hawaii Early Learning Profile and Activity Guide.* Palo Alto, CA: VORT.

Gentry, D. (Ed.). (1980). *Adaptive Performance Instrument: Book 2: Sensorimotor Development.* Moscow, ID: University of Idaho.

Gerken, K.C. (1983). Assessment of preschool children with severe handicaps. In K.D. Paget and B.A. Bracken (Eds.), *The psychoeducational assessment of preschool children.* New York: Grune & Stratton.

Ginsburg, H. & Opper, S. (1979). *Piaget's theory of intellectual development* (2nd ed.). Englewood Cliffs, NJ: Prentice-Hall.

Griffiths, R. (1954). *The abilities of babies.* London: University of London Press.

Hanson, R. & Aldridge-Smith, J. (1987). Achievements of young children on items of the Griffiths scales: 1980 compared with 1960.

Child: Care, Health and Development, 13, 181–195.

Heffernan, L. & Black, F.W. (1984). Use of the Uzgiris and Hunt scales with handicapped infants. Concurrent validity of the Dunst age norms. *Journal of Psychoeducational Assessment, 2,* 159–168.

Kahn, J.V. (1979). Application of the Piagetian literature to severely and profoundly mentally retarded persons. *Mental Retardation, 17,* 273–280.

Kahn, J.V. (1976). Utility of the Uzgiris and Hunt scales of sensorimotor development with severely and profoundly handicapped children. *American Journal of Mental Deficiency, 80,* 663–665.

Knobloch, H., Stevens, F., & Malone, A.F. (1980). *Manual of developmental diagnosis: The administration and interpretation of the revised Gessell and Armatruda Developmental and Neurologic Examination.* Hagerstown, MA: Harper & Row.

McLean, J.E., Synder-McLean, L., Rowland, C., Jacobs, P., & Stremel-Campbell, K. (no date). *Generic Skills Assessment Inventory: Experimental edition.* Parsons, KS: University of Kansas, Bureau of Child Research.

McLean, M., McCormick, K., Bruder, M.B., & Burdg, N.B. (1987). An investigation of the validity and reliability of the Battelle Developmental Inventory with a population of children younger than 30 months with identified handicapping conditions. *Journal of the Division for Early Childhood, 11*(3), 238–246.

Mehrabian, A. & Williams, M. (1971). Piagetian measures of cognitive development for children up to age two. *Journal of Psycholinguistic Research, 1*(1), 113–126.

Newborg, J., Stock, J., Wnek, Guidubaldi, J., & Svinicki. (1984). *The Battelle Developmental Inventory: Examiner's manual.* Allen, TX: Developmental Learning Materials.

Piaget, J. (1952). *The origins of intelligence in children.* New York: International Universities Press.

Reynell, J. (1979). *The Reynell-Zinkin Scales: Developmental scales for young visually handicapped children.* Windsor, England: NFER Publishing.

Rogers, S. (1977). Characteristics of the cognitive development of profoundly retarded children. *Child Development, 48,* 837–843.

Rogers, S.J., Donovan, C.M., D'Eugenio, D.B., Brown, S., Lynch, E., Moersch, M.S., & Schafer, S. (1981). *Early Intervention Developmental Profile. Revised edition.* Ann Arbor: The University of Michigan Press.

Sigman, M. & Ungerer, J.A. (1981). Sensorimotor skills and language comprehension in autistic children. *Journal of Abnormal Child Psychology, 9,* 149–166.

Simeonsson, R.J. (Ed.). (1986). *Psychological and developmental assessment of special children.* Boston, MA: Allyn & Bacon.

Smith, J.A., Bidder, R.T., Gardner, S.M., & Gray, O.P. (1980). Griffiths' Scales of Mental Development and different users. *Child: Care, Health and Development, 6,* 11–16.

Uzgiris, I. & Hunt, J.M. (1975). *Assessment in infancy: Ordinal Scales of Psychological Development.* Urbana: University of Illinois Press.

Vulpé, S.G. (1977). *Vulpé Assessment Battery.* Toronto: National Institute on Mental Retardation.

Wachs, T. & DeRemer, P. (1978). Adaptive behavior and the Uzgiris-Hunt scale performance of young, developmentally disabled children. *American Journal of Mental Deficiency, 83,* 171–176.

Weisz, J.R. & Zigler, E. (1979). Cognitive development in retarded and non-retarded persons; Piagetian tests of the similar sequence hypotheses. *Psychological Bulletin, 86,* 831–851.

Woodward, M. (1959). The behavior of idiots interpreted by Piaget's theory of sensory development. *British Journal of Educational Psychology, 29,* 60–71.

Assessment of Cognitive Skills in the Preschool-Aged Child

Kathleen D. Paget
University of South Carolina

KEY TERMS

- Cognition
- Cognitive Structures
- Intellectual Functions
- Preoperational Stage
- Preconceptual Phase
- Intuitive Phase
- Information Processing
- Attention
- Persistence
- Social Learning
- Reciprocal Determinism
- Task-intrinsic Motivation

- Metacognition
- Types of Cognitive Competence
- Forms of Cognitive Competence
- Contexts of Cognitive Competence
- Ecological Approach
- Situational Specificity
- Psychometric Approach
- Nonstandardized Administration

- Process Oriented Approach
- Test-Teach-Test Pardigm
- Naturalistic Teaching
- Incidental Teaching
- Perceptual Discrimination
- Memory
- Reasoning
- Problem Solving
- Concept Formation

Various reasons exist to explain why an early childhood special educator or other early intervention personnel would assess preschool children's cognitive functioning. When children are identified through screening efforts as needing special education programs, a cognitive assessment is often needed to help determine eligibility. In addition, a cognitive assessment is useful for understanding a child's strengths and weaknesses in skill areas such as concept formation, memory, and problem solving. To assist teachers or parents in preschool classrooms, Head Start programs, or home-based programs, cognitive assessments may provide information for evaluating children's progress in cognitive skill development or determining appropriate learning activities that are matched to children's developmental levels. Furthermore, there are occasions when a cognitive assessment may be useful for making decisions about early or late entrance into school. An adequate assessment of preschool children's cognitive skills is essential to a complete understanding of their development because cognitive skills are closely intertwined with skills in other domains, especially language, social, and adaptive behaviors.

When early childhood special educators turn to the literature for ideas on how to assess preschool children's cognitive development, the result may be very confusing (cf., Schakel, 1986). The educational and psychological literature contains psychometric techniques, including the familiar Stanford-Binet, the Binet-Fourth Edition, the McCarthy Scales of Children's Abilities, the Kaufman Assessment Battery for Children, and some other alternative measures. The early childhood literature speaks of Piaget and Gesell. The special education literature emphasizes criterion-referenced assessment and comprehensive tools for program planning, which assess several developmental areas in addition to cognition. The current literature on child development focuses on research techniques to assess information-processing abilities in children. The purpose of this chapter is to reduce this confusion by synthesizing various models and dimensions of cognition and by discussing important procedural considerations, assessment methods, and strategies for determining appropriate and functional instructional goals for preschool-aged children who have handicapping conditions.

Dimensions of Cognitive Assessment

A comprehensive understanding of cognition and its multiple components must underlie assessment procedures. Understood as a process, cognition is much broader than the preacademic skills represented on developmental instruments. Broadly conceived, **cognition** is composed of mental processes by which individuals acquire knowledge. Moreover, cognition is the process of acquiring a conscious awareness that helps us *know* and *understand* in a wide spectrum of activities such as remembering, learning, thinking, and attending. As a human phenomenon, cognition is composed of unobservable events, their subsequent comprehension, and resultant response (Flavell, 1982). These covert behaviors characterize the activities of human thought processes and pose definite challenges to any professional interested in the cognitive assessment of preschool-aged children.

In an effort to present general parameters of cognitive development as it pertains to special education, several perspectives must be addressed. Two principles are clear: First, preschool-aged children are active problem solvers who attempt to discriminate, extract, and analyze information; second, their directed, planful action undergoes rapid developmental change. Three comtemporary theoretical orientations are consistent with the theme of a young child as an active problem solver: (a) Piaget's theory of cognitive development; (b) information-processing approaches; and (c) social learning theory.

Piagetian Theory

Piaget views cognitive development as being composed of **cognitive structures** and **intellectual functions.** He uses the term *schema* to describe mental structures used by individuals to represent, organize, and interpret experience. He describes intellectual growth as an active process whereby children are repeatedly assimilating new experiences and accommodating their cognitive structures to their new experiences. The cognitive operations of adaptation and organization facilitate children's ability to construct a progressively better understanding of the world. Three types of cognitive structures have been defined by Piaget: (a) sensorimotor (organized behavior patterns used to represent or respond to objects or experiences); (b) symbolic (internal cognitive images used to represent past experiences); and (c) operational (internal cognitive images that organize thoughts logically (Clarke-Stewart & Koch, 1983).

Children between the ages of 2 and 7 years are thought to be in what Piaget termed the **preoperational stage,** which consists of two phases: the **preconceptual phase** and the **intuitive phase.** During the preconceptual phase, the use of language expands, and limitations in logical reasoning are evident. Three features of this phase are (a) egocentrism (an inability to distinguish easily between a child's own perspective and that of someone else); (b) animism (a belief that inanimate objects have human qualities and are capable of human action); and (c) difficulty with conservation (e.g., understanding that liquid poured from one glass into another remains the same amount despite a difference in the sizes of the glasses). Recent research suggests, however, that preoperational children may be less egocentric and more able to conserve than Piaget had found (cf., Flavell, 1982). Also during this phase, pretend play develops to a level at which children are capable of creating fantasy worlds, inventing imaginary playmates, and participating in role play. In the intuitive phase of the preoperational stage, symbolic thought improves, although children tend to focus on a single aspect of a problem while ignoring others (Clarke-Stewart & Koch, 1983).

Information Processing Theory

As a model of human cognitive development, **information processing** explains decision making, knowing, and remembering as processes. In this approach to the study of cognitive development, the mind is conceived of as a complex cognitive system, analogous in some ways to a computer. Essentially, human cognition becomes what the computer must know in order to produce a behavior. Most of the information-processing research builds directly on Piaget's contributions to the understanding of cognitive develoment. Contrary to Piaget's structural explanation underlying the thought structure of logic in thought processes, however, information processing accounts for and identifies specific mental processes by which cognition is processed. Some researchers, such as Pascual-Leone (1980) and Case (1978), have modified Piagetian theory to take into account information-processing considerations (also called neo-Piagetian theories). One such approach is Siegler's (1981) rule-assessment approach. Essentially, Siegler's work examines a child's problem-solving skills within a domain at different ages. A child's pattern of responses across problems helps to determine which of the information-processing rules the child is using.

Several other information-processing perspectives have examined cognitive development. For example, researchers have found that young children have limited **attention** and **persistence** at tasks (Wellmann, Ritter, & Flavell, 1975), and their curiosity interferes with systematic problem solving. Thus, contrary to Piagetian theory, very young children may fail to solve problems because they are unable to sustain their attention long enough to gather the necessary information. By about age 5, children become more persistent in their attempts to solve problems. Hence, younger children may know to look first at relevant stimuli and label them; whereas older children are better at attending selectively without special training.

Social Learning Theory

Social learning theorists (e.g., Bandura, 1978) suggest that cognitive development is much more than a result of some combination of individual characteristics and environmental influences. These theorists view all three as existing within a mutually interdependent network; they exist as a set of reciprocal determinants. Thus, cognitions, beliefs, and expectations influence behavior and vice versa. Behavior partially determines the nature of the environment, whereas cognition determines the psychological definitions of the environment. Bandura's **reciprocal determinism** model accommodates very well the rapid developmental changes, behavioral fluctuations, and emerging skills that characterize very young children. Learning problems are seen to stem from the interaction among a child's motivation and developmental status, specific situational factors, and differing approaches to socialization. Thus, professionals using the model analyze a child's interactions with people and objects, as well as reactions to events. Direct observation and consultation with significant adults in various settings constitute major activities.

Other Aspects of Cognitive Functioning

According to Haywood and Switzky (1986), cognitive functions include cognitive operations, principles, processes, and strategies, as well as a host of "non-intellective" variables such as attitudes toward learning, work habits, and motives. The most important of these "non-intellective" variables is **task-intrinsic motivation,** generally defined as the disposition to find one's rewards within tasks (e.g., in challenge, information processing for its own sake, creativity, learning, responsibility, and the satisfaction of engaging in task performance and achievement). There is substantial evidence both that individual differences in intrinsic motivation are strongly associated with variations in the effectiveness and efficiency of learning and that intrinsic motivation is, to a large degree, a learned disposition (e.g., see reviews by Haywood & Wachs, 1981; Haywood, Meyers, & Switzky, 1982; Switzky & Haywood, 1984). An important concept that must be considered in any discussion of cognitive skills is

metacognition, which refers to a child's knowledge "about knowing and how to know" (Brown, 1975). With this knowledge, learners allocate and orchestrate their cognitive resources effectively to meet task demands. Metacognition may be viewed as one of many potential domains of knowledge and skill that children may acquire; however, the domain is not reading or arithmetic. Rather, it is thinking and mental organization. The Lock Box (Goodman, 1981) is an instrument designed to assess the metacognitive functioning of young children. Using structured observations of play behaviors, the assessor is able to evaluate a child's mental organization and persistence.

Recent investigations by cognitive psychologists, developmental psychologists, and special educators indicate that youngsters' metacognitive knowledge and skill may play a critical role in school achievement (Brown, Bransford, Ferrara, & Campione, 1983; Goodman, 1981). Metacognitive deficiencies have been identified in special needs children in their performance of a variety of academic, problem-solving, and memory tasks (Brown et al., 1983). Identification of these characteristics has resulted not only in a better understanding of human learning, but in the development of instructional interventions for these children (e.g., Brown & Palinscar, 1982). Skills within the programs include self-review, self-questioning, and clarification of important information. Thus, although many special-needs children with learning problems may evidence specific deficits in rudimentary skills such as letter and number identification, it also has become clear that teaching cognitive skills requires instruction in *how* to think and solve problems.

Dunst and McWilliam (1988) delineate the dimensions of cognitive functioning in terms of the *types, forms,* and *contexts* of interactions with the environment. The **types of cognitive competence** range from conventionalized interactions (with animate and inanimate aspects of the environment) to interactions that are less conventional or normative (e.g., indicating a desire to be picked up and held by moving one's head rather than extending the arms). The **forms of cognitive competence** are social or non-social, and the **contexts** in which competencies should be assessed are home, school, and community. Within this framework, the goal of assessment strategies is to discern the manner in which a child manifests cognitive competencies using whatever behavioral indicators may be interpreted as examples of cognitive capability. This model provides an innovative alternative to traditional methods of cognitive assessment, which have focused on the child's ability to match behavior to the response demands of test items, rather than the assessor's ability to interpret a wide variety of behaviors as indicators of different types and forms of cognitive competence. In addition, it underscores the interrelationships among social and cognitive competencies.

Procedural Considerations When Assessing Cognitive Skills

When assessing the many dimensions of cognitive functioning, early intervention personnel will find an **ecological approach** with **situational specificity** essential to accurate assessment that results in appropriate recommendations. Often, when doing cognitive assessments, the tendency is to look at factors in a child's medical and developmental history and internal characteristics of the child for comprehensive explanations of cognitive functioning. Nevertheless, from a reciprocal determinism perspective (Bandura, 1978), we know that specific features of the situation in which assessments take place must be considered to include the child's personal characteristics and behaviors, as well as environmental influences.

Ecological assessment approaches call for an evaluation of the child's skills in each of the significant environments that influence her functioning. A strong connection has been shown, for example, between characteristics such as maternal IQ and educational level (Ramey & Campbell, 1979; Ramey, Stedman, Borders-Patterson, & Mengel, 1978) and young children's performance on tests of cognitive competence. In addition, variables related to low-income conditions have been shown to be highly correlated with children's cognitive competence at young ages (Ramey & Campbell, 1979). Furthermore, significant relationships are reported between child cognitive competence and such variables as child-rearing practices, parent responsiveness and stimulation, parental teaching and interaction style, and quality of mother/child interaction (Bradley & Caldwell, 1979; Hunt, 1979; Matas, Arend, & Sroufe, 1978; Ramey, Farran, & Campbell, 1979). In fact, contingent verbal responsiveness is so vital to adequate cognitive development that no evaluation would be complete without an assessment of parent/child interaction patterns. In this regard, Bronfenbrenner (1974) observed that "the psychological development of the young child is enhanced through his/her involvement in progressively more complex, enduring patterns of reciprocal contingent interaction with persons with whom he/she has established a mutual and engaging attachment" (p. 31). Procedures designed to structure observation of parent/child interaction include: Home Observation and Measurement of the Environment (HOME) (Bradley & Caldwell, 1976), the Caregiver Styles of Interaction Scales (CSI) (Dunst, 1986a), the Parent-Child Play Scale (PCP) (Dunst, 1986b), Parent/Caregiver Interaction Scale (P/CIS) (Farran, Kasari, & Jay, 1984), the Play Assessment Scale (Fewell, 1984a), and the Maternal Behavior Rating Scale (Mahoney, Powell, & Finger, 1986). Research with these instruments indicates they are even more predictive indices of cognitive abilities than the child's socioeconomic status.

The importance of environment does not

stop with an understanding of the child in his early home setting. Research has suggested that cognitive competence can be affected through center-based intervention, especially if it occurs during the early years (Belsky & Sterinberg, 1978; Ramey & Campbell, 1979). Thus, it is important that assessors consider all aspects of the child's current environments, including child-care settings and preschool programs, not only for understanding current functioning, but for planning intervention strategies (Dunst, McWilliam, & Holbert, 1986). Assisting in the attainment of this goal are instruments such as those described in Chapter 5. Although the case for an ecological, situation-specific approach to cognitive assessment is clear, most of the formal cognitive assessment tools and techniques currently available were not developed within an ecological framework. The early instruments developed from the psychometric tradition in educational psychology (e.g., Stanford-Binet, Wechsler Preschool and Primary Scale of Intelligence) reflect an assumption that intellectual ability is relatively static within age levels and situations (Garwood, 1983; Jens, 1984). These instruments allow comparison of a child's performance to that of other children his age, but they focus on outcome scores rather than the process a child uses to arrive at an answer or the situational influences affecting a response.

The limitations of the **psychometric approach** to understanding the cognition of preschool-aged children have led to the development of alternative tests and techniques by people in other disciplines and with different theoretical backgrounds. Thus, tools for cognitive assessment of preschool children have come not only from psychometric theories, but from Piagetian and other developmental stage theories, behavioral theory, and information-processing theories (cf., Sternberg & Powell, 1983, for an excellent discussion of these different explanations of the development of intelligence). Special educators concerned with

assessing the cognitive status of handicapped children have found the traditional tools to be inappropriate for assessing certain groups of handicapped preschoolers. Some have turned to nonstandard administrations of standardized tests such as the Bayley Scales of Infant Development (Bayley, 1969) or to behavioral theory for assessment techniques.

Behavior checklists, which allow the examiner to observe specific behaviors performed to given standards under given conditions (Walls, Werner, Bacon, & Zane, 1977), have been devised, as well as methods such as anecdotal records, time samples, and rating scales (Cohen, Stern, & Balaban, 1983). Systematic observations can be recorded with pen and paper, audiotape or videotape, or small portable computers. Observation of behaviors such as attention, persistence, and task-intrinsic motivation must supplement observation of absent, emerging, and acquired skills. In addition, interviews with caregivers, conducted from a situation-specific approach, provide valuable information toward understanding environmental conditions that contribute to a child's suboptimal or optimal performance.

The next section of this chapter presents representative methods for assessing preschool cognitive skills. Although the methods discussed focus on child characteristics, it is important to note that the theories behind all these approaches are evolving toward more ecological views. Whereas Piagetian theory is interpreted as identifying fixed, universal stages of cognitive development, neo-Piagetians are responding to evidence that contradicts this view by proposing that children may show cognitive competence beyond a certain stage under certain circumstances and that cognitive stages may not be invariable (see, for example, Gelman & Gaillargeon, 1983). In addition, although behavioral theorists once viewed cognitive development as merely the accumulation of simple stimulus-response connections made by a child, neobehaviorists (e.g., Kendler &

Kendler, 1975) and social learning theorists (Bandura, 1978) view this simplistic process as only explanatory of certain periods of human development and certain types of behavior. In addition, while information processing theories emphasize internal processes, some proponents are beginning to focus on the importance of the child's interaction with the physical and social environment (e.g., Wertsch, 1979). Emphasis also has been placed in some information processing theories on the different processes that may operate at different ages and on different types of tasks (Das, Kirby, & Jarman, 1979; Kaufman & Kaufman, 1983). Thus, procedures from any of these approaches are beginning to lend themselves to interpretation from an ecological perspective.

Representative Methods for Assessing Preschool Cognitive Skills

In this section, a variety of assessment instruments, procedures, and strategies are discussed. As the reader peruses the following information, it should be kept in mind that the assessment methods presented are related to one another in complementary fashion. That is, they can be combined into assessment batteries to meet specified purposes, with each method eliciting unique information from the child.

Instruments from the Psychometric Tradition

Most standardized assessment tools normed on preschool-aged children are based on a psychometric approach (Schakel, 1986). As discussed, these tools have been most useful for making educational placement decisions. Most are administered in an individual assessment situation and, therefore, represent a limited sample of the child's cognitive functioning. This fact should be kept in mind

when any of these tests are used to contribute to a cognitive assessment. The most popular and useful of these standardized tests are described below, although the information does not comprise an exhaustive listing of available tests nor are in-depth reviews provided. Readers should bear in mind that administration of these instruments requires considerable training on the part of properly certified or licensed psychologists.

The Stanford-Binet Intelligence Scale. The 1972 version of the Stanford-Binet (Terman & Merrill, 1973) has been criticized for use with preschoolers because of its outdated norms, its high verbal content, and its emphasis on one global score (Reynolds & Clark, 1983; Salvia & Ysseldyke, 1985; Sattler, 1982). Despite the criticism, it has a long history of use for assessing preschool-aged children and evaluating the effects of programs such as Head Start.

The fourth edition of the Stanford-Binet (Thorndike, Hagen, & Sattler, 1986a) is described by its authors as a "thoroughly modern" test. Unlike earlier versions, this edition was devised using a theoretical model of intelligence. This three-level model of cognitive ability consists of a general reasoning component, which is subdivided into crystallized abilities, fluid-analytic abilities, and short-term memory. *Crystallized abilities* are measured by subtests that assess verbal and quantitative reasoning; *fluid-analytic abilities* involve visualization tasks; and *short-term memory* is assessed by separate items. A total of 15 subtests is on the new test, but only 8 of these are given to children ages 2–5. These subtests are vocabulary, comprehension, absurdities, quantitative, pattern analysis, copying, bead memory, and memory for sentences. The subtests are organized into subscales termed *verbal reasoning, abstract/ visual reasoning, quantitative reasoning,* and *short-term memory.* Subtest raw scores are converted to standard age scores with a mean of 50 and standard deviation of 8, while area standard age scores (e.g., verbal reasoning) and the composite score have a mean of 100 and standard deviation of 16.

The new edition of the Stanford-Binet addresses many of the criticisms that have been leveled against earlier versions of the test, but data are not yet available to show how well they are addressed. This version added many item types that are nonverbal in format, thus making it less language-dependent than the earlier version. In addition, there is movement away from emphasis on a single score. Although it is still possible to obtain a score reflecting a "general" factor, the new edition recognizes the need for looking at different types of abilities. Nevertheless, preliminary factor analytic evidence suggests caution when interpreting the subscale scores (Reynolds, Kamphaus, & Rosenthal, 1988). From an ecological perspective, the new Binet should represent an improved method for assessing preschoolers who have no school experience. It separates out the "scholastic" ability component (crystallized abilities), influenced by school-like experiences, from the other components, thought to depend less on such experiences.

According to the test developers, the fourth edition improves on the format of the earlier version. The examiner is able to focus quickly on the level of tasks appropriate for a young child, which is an attractive feature. Like the earlier version, a vocabulary score and the child's age combine to determine the entry level so that preschool children, who as a group are highly variable in level of ability and are easily distracted, are not subjected to many tasks that are too difficult or too easy. The new Stanford-Binet also retains the advantage of covering an extended age range (ages 2–23 years).

Kaufman Assessment Battery for Children (K-ABC). The K-ABC (Kaufman & Kaufman, 1983), like other instruments reviewed in this section, was devised as an individually admin-

istered test of intelligence. It covers the age range from 2½ through 12½ years and, thus, has caught the interest of professionals who assess preschool-aged children. The manuals for the K-ABC attest to the fact that much careful preparation and validation went into publication of the test.

The K-ABC battery yields standard scores with a mean of 100 and a standard deviation of 15 in four global areas of functioning: sequential processing, simultaneous processing, a mental processing composite (MPC), and achievement. Unlike many intelligence tests, the K-ABC was developed from a theoretical foundation that focuses on the individual's information-processing and problem-solving style. Also unlike the others, the global score (MPC) is obtained entirely from tests that "minimize the role of language and verbal skills for successful performance, and include stimuli that are as fair as possible for children from diverse backgrounds" (Kaufman & Kaufman, 1983, p. 2.). One of the authors' primary goals in developing the K-ABC was "to be sensitive to the other diverse needs of preschool. . .children" (p. 5) and to develop a test that would be useful for making meaningful educational recommendations. As yet, however, the effectiveness of its intervention model has not been researched with preschool children. The inclusion of teaching items for problem-solving tasks on the tests, the nonverbal nature of the items, and the "colorful, child-oriented, and game-like" nature of the test materials are appealing for use with preschoolers. Another useful feature of the test is that out-of-level testing is possible. That is, a gifted 4½-year-old can be assessed using the school-age subtests of the K-ABC, while a delayed 5-year-old can be assessed using a younger level.

Recent research with the K-ABC raises some cautions for preschool assessors. Using data from 5-year-olds in the standardized sample, Keith (1985) suggests sequential-simultaneous interpretations may not apply to preschoolers. His factor analysis suggests that a one-factor solution (a simultaneous factor) may best explain the data for this age group. Keith indicated further that if a two-factor solution is allowed, factor one for 5-year-olds is a reasoning factor (primarily nonverbal reasoning) and factor two is a verbal memory factor.

In addition, Bracken (1985) pointed out other potential problems with the K-ABC, suggesting that the breadth of information attainable for preschool-aged children is limited, requiring administration of additional tests (i.e., to assess cognitive skills related to use of language and social competence). In addition, according to Bracken, the K-ABC lacks an adequate floor for low-functioning preschool children and has no provision for substitute administration if one subtest is spoiled. Understandably, there also is limited information on predictive validity of the test. There is some evidence, however, that the MPC is not measuring the same construct as the Wechsler Preschool and Primary Scale of Intelligence (WPPSI) or Binet IQs.

McCarthy Scales of Children's Abilities. The McCarthy scales were developed to measure "the general intellectual level of children as well as their strengths and weaknesses in important abilities" (McCarthy, 1972, p. 1). The author stated that she chose the content for the battery primarily on the basis of her teaching and clinical experience in developmental psychology. She developed the test to fill a gap in available instruments for assessing the learning of normal and learning-disabled young children. In addition to a global measure of cognitive ability (the general cognitive index, GCI), the test provides measures of several more specific abilities (verbal, perceptual-performance, quantitative, memory, and motor). The mean value for the GCI is 100 and the standard deviation is 16. Subscale means are 50 with standard deviations of 10.

The McCarthy scales have been viewed as a major alternative to the Binet and WPPSI

(Paget, 1986; Salvia & Ysseldyke, 1985). The test was carefully designed and well standardized. Reported reliabilities for the GCI and the verbal scale are excellent, although those for the other scales are somewhat lower. Other strengths reported for the McCarthy scales are its useful profile of abilities, which may be relevant to developmental concerns, and its appeal to children (Sattler, 1982). In addition, the range of ages for which the test can be used (2½–8½) is a positive feature for professionals who work with all ages of preschool children.

There are some practical disadvantages to the McCarthy scales for assessors of preschool-aged children. Unlike the Stanford-Binet and WPPSI, there are no provisions for children's refusals in administering or scoring the test. In addition, the limited floor of the test (lowest possible GCI = 50) makes it inadequate for use with young moderately and severely developmentally disabled children (Kaufman & Kaufman, 1977), although Harrison and Naglieri (1978) have provided extrapolated GCIs for gifted and low-functioning populations.

Validity studies of the McCarthy scales have resulted in several noteworthy findings. Although the test offers a useful framework for diagnostic purposes because of the several different ability scales, factor analytic studies (e.g., Kaufman, 1975) show that for 3- and 4-year-olds, a quantitative factor does not appear, resulting in cautious interpretation of the quantitative scale for this age group. In addition, wider scatter between different scales has been shown to be common, suggesting that differences between subscale scores do not necessarily imply deficiencies. Kaufman and Kaufman (1977) provide useful guidelines for interpreting subtest scatter and scores on individual subtests.

With respect to the McCarthy's utility for assessing preschool handicapped children, the manual asserts that it is useful for assessing children with mental retardation, sensory deficits, speech deficits, giftedness, and learning disabilities. Nevertheless, users should beware that none of these special groups was incorporated into the normative sample. In addition, studies have shown that McCarthy GCIs obtained on preschoolers may be significantly lower than IQs obtained on other norm-referenced tests. Gerken, Hancock, and Wade (1978) reported a mean difference of 10.5 between the GCI and Stanford-Binet IQ for a preschool sample, and Bracken (1981) found a mean difference of 15.7 for a sample of gifted preschool and primary children. Phillips, Pasewark, and Tindall (1978) found a difference of 7 points between the GCI and WPPSI Full Scale IQ, with the WPPSI being higher. Although Kaufman and Kaufman (1977) have interpreted lower GCIs with learning disabled children as evidence that the McCarthy scales more accurately predict "learning disabilities" in young children, others have interpreted the difference as evidence that the McCarthy is measuring something other than intelligence.

Wechsler Preschool and Primary Scale of Intelligence (WPPSI). The WPPSI (Wechsler, 1967) is a downward extension of the *Wechsler Intelligence Scale for Children* (WISC) and was designed to measure a child's global intellectual ability on verbal and performance tasks. The test is composed of verbal and performance subscales and yields three intelligence quotients (verbal, performance, and full scale), each with a mean of 100 and standard deviation of 15. In devising the WPPSI, Wechsler wanted an instrument that would be continuous with the WISC; therefore, he deliberately chose items from the WISC and used the same items or extensions of those items for the WPPSI. Thus, the items did not originate from an emphasis on the cognition of preschool-aged children.

The WPPSI frequently is used for preschool cognitive assessment, but reviews of the test suggest flaws that make it less than ideal. The age range is restrictive (4–6½ years). The test is extremely long (requires 1 to 1½

hours), and some preschoolers find it difficult to attend to the tasks for that length of time. Proper administration is difficult, and scoring is subjective on some items (see Reynolds & Clark, 1983; Sattler, 1982). Strengths of the WPPSI are its excellent standardization sample and its statistical properties. Some professionals find that looking at the verbal-performance discrepancy provides useful information (see Sattler, 1982, for a review of related studies). Nevertheless, readers are cautioned that differences of 11 points between VIQ and PIQ are relatively common on the WPPSI and 12-point differences occur for one out of four children (Reynolds & Gutkin, 1981).

Although good normative data, reliability, and validity of the WPPSI may make it useful for comparisons of an individual child's performance with that of age mates in the standardization sample, the following cautions should be noted. Studies suggest care in interpreting the WPPSI for children who are black, Mexican-American, and of low socioeconomic status (SES), because such children tend to score lower than white children and have greater verbal-performance discrepancies (Crockett, Rardin, & Pasewark, 1976; Henderson & Rankin, 1973; Kaufman, 1973). WPPSI scores do not appear to be good predictors of later school achievement for these children. Another problem is the limited floor and ceiling of the WPPSI, which is especially problematic to age 4. The lowest possible full scale IQ for a 4-year-old is 55, making the results difficult to interpret for low-functioning children. The WPPSI is currently under major revision and will be restandardized in the next few years.

Other Tests of Cognitive Functions. The aforementioned instruments represent the "Big Four" in preschool cognitive assessment from the psychometric tradition (Schakel, 1986). There are other instruments, however, which have proven useful in preschool assessment for special populations of children and deserve mention as appropriate tools for some aspects of cognitive assessment. They are listed in Table 12.1. Readers are referred to Buros (1986), Sattler (1982), Salvia and Ysseldyke (1985), and other compendia of test reviews for further information about these tests.

Adaptations of Traditional Tests

Unless an assessor looks closely at the kinds of tasks a child passes and fails, the tests reviewed thus far will be of very limited use for intervention. Most assessors use subjective interpretations of these tests to obtain more than an end-product score. Scoring and interpretive systems such as those developed by Kaufman (1979) also have been used to examine clusters of subtests so as to glean more specific information. Nevertheless, early intervention personnel interested in linking assessment results to preschool curricula will find that instruments described in later sections of this chapter are likely to yield more functional information regarding a child's cognitive skills.

Frequently, it is useful to administer tests under **nonstandardized conditions,** to modify test materials, or to accept nonstandard responses in an effort to obtain information about a child's best performance, especially if the child is moderately to severely impaired and her impairment is not represented in the comparison or normative sample of the test (see Chapter 3). Kiernan and DuBose (1974) and DuBose and Langley (1977) developed scales for use with deaf/blind children and other handicapped children by adapting items from various scales. Haeussermann (1958) also advocated this adaptive administration approach for young children with cerebral palsy. These adaptations are not norm-referenced; however, norms are not always necessary when the objective is to help understand the process whereby children learn rather than to document their scores. Although adaptations often yield rich infor-

mation, they must be made cautiously, and care should be taken when interpreting differences in performance under standardized and nonstandardized conditions to parents and teachers.

Piagetian-Based Scales

As mentioned earlier, the cognitive developmental theory of Piaget has been popular for explaining intellectual development of normal children from birth onward. Ordinal scales have been developed from this theory to assess children's cognitive development in reference to Piagetian stages. Scales for assessing development in the first stage (sensorimotor) are used mostly for assessing infants (Escalona & Corman, 1969; Uzgiris & Hunt, 1975), although some individuals have advocated using these measures to assess the cognitive development of low-functioning preschoolers (e.g., Rogers, 1977, 1982). There is one commercially available instrument for assessing children ages 4 to 7, who are believed to be in Piaget's preoperational stage of cognitive development (Goldschmidt & Bentler, 1968), which includes tasks related to concepts such as conservation and egocentrism.

Because Piagetian-based tools often do not meet validity and reliability standards and are not norm-referenced in the traditional sense, they have not been used frequently for placement and classification decisions, although they have proven useful in instruction and programming for those who adhere to Piagetian or neo-Piagetian theory (Dunst, 1981). Nevertheless, proponents of Piagetian-based assessment have pointed out their dangers (Dunst & Gallagher, 1983; Dunst & Rheingrover, 1981; Rogers, 1982) and have asserted cautions in interpreting results. Recent evidence indicates that preschool-aged children can function better on certain cognitive tasks than Piaget's theory proposes, if these tasks are presented in a manner suited to preschoolers' interests (Gelman &

TABLE 12.1
Alternative Norm-Referenced Measures

Instrument	Age Range	Unique Aspects	Limitations
Arthur Adaptation of the Leiter International Performance Scale (Arthur, 1952)	3-0 to 7-11	Requires no verbal response or verbal understanding from child; a new handbook has been developed that facilitates administration and interpretation	Cumbersome test, difficult to administer; limited, outdated norm sample; no strong evidence that this test is more "culturally fair" than other norm-referenced tests
Columbia Mental Maturity Scale (Burgemeister, Blum, Lorge, 1972)	3-6 to 10-0	No verbal response required from child; good technical qualities; flexible directions; requires only 15–20 minutes	Only one item type; only one global score can be determined
Extended Merrill-Palmer Scale of Mental Tests (Ball, Merrifield, & Stott, 1978)	3-0 to 5-11	Only instrument based on Structure of Intellect Model (Guilford, 1956); evaluates process as well as content; founded on a theory of intelligence	Inadequate standardization; questionable reliability and validity; no evidence for fit of the model to young children's thinking
Griffiths Mental Development Scales (Griffiths, 1979)	Birth to 8	Comprehensive; enticing, childlike materials; measures a wide range of functioning; yields useful information from nonverbal children	Manual is difficult to read; limited guidelines for interpretation of scores
Nebraska Test of Learning Aptitude (Hiskey, 1966)	3-0 to 16-0	Can be administered entirely via pantomime; requires no verbal response; normed on deaf children	No adequate description of standardization; limited reliability; no mainstreamed deaf children in norm sample

Test	Ages	Comments	Limitations
Perkins-Binet Tests of Intelligence for the Blind (Davis, 1980)	4-0 to 18-0	Flexible administration; only such instrument available for the blind	Children under age 6 underrepresented in norm sample
Pictorial Test of Intelligence (French, 1964)	3-0 to 8-0	Nonverbal format allows pointing or eye movement response; well standardized; good reliabilities reported	Norms dated; no handicapped children in norm sample; format is unvaried and may be boring to some children
Woodcock Johnson Psycho-Educational Battery (Woodcock & Johnson, 1977)	3 to adult	Attractive, well-organized test materials; designed for educational decision making	Not many preschool students in normative sample; limited information on reliability and validity for this age group
British Ability Scale (Elliott, Murray, & Pearson, 1983)	2½ to 17	Comprehensive: 23 scales cover 6 areas: speed of information processing, reasoning, spatial imagery, perceptual matching, short-term memory, retrieval and application of knowledge; oral, written, and performance tasks provided; evidence shows that sex and social class bias is negligible	Only British norms are available at present
Boehm Test of Basic Concepts-Preschool Version (Boehm, 1986)	3 to 5	Brief (10–15 minutes) and easy to administer; requires only a pointing response; measures child's understanding of each concept and situation; resource guide (up to grade 2) for teaching can be purchased	Limited in usefulness for visually impaired children

TABLE 12.1
Continued

Instrument	Age Range	Unique Aspects	Limitations
Bracken Concept Development Series (Bracken. 1986)	2½ to 8	Includes a basic concept scale *and* a concept development program; the Scale measures 285 basic concepts in 11 subtest categories; pointing response appropriate for motorically impaired children; concept development program provides colorful, creative materials with lesson plans for teaching: at-home worksheets suggest ways in which parents can reinforce child's conceptual understanding; normative sample carefully selected; Spanish translations available	Limited in usefulness for visually impaired children
Metropolitan Achievement Tests Sixth Edition (MAT 6). Preprimer and Primer (Prescott, Farr, Hogan. & Balow. 1986)	Grades K.5–1.9	Preprimer level includes three tests: (1) the Reading Test measures visual discrimination, letter recognition, and auditory discrimination; (2) Mathematics Test measures numeration, geometry. measurement. problem solving; (3) Language Test measures listening comprehension;	Norms not available for children with handicapping conditions; not easily adapted to children with handicapping conditions

| | parent folders provide parents with an understanding of the reasons for assessment and the results; scores are explained and recommended ways to improve child's scores are provided; sample items are included; materials are attractive, child-friendly | | |
| Stanford Early School Achievement Test (SESAT): 2nd Edition (Madden, Gardner, & Collins, 1984). | Grades K.0–1.9 | Measures listening comprehension, retention and organization, decoding and comprehension skills, knowledge of world, mathematics concepts and skills; listening test has advance organizers to allow children to organize their thoughts before and during listening process; a guide for classroom planning assists teachers with application of test results | Norms not available for children with handicapping conditions; not easily adapted to children with handicapping conditions |

Source: Adapted and expanded from "Cognitive Assessment of Preschool Children" by J. Schakel. *School Psychology Review,* 1986. *15,* 200–215. Copyright 1986 by National Association of School Psychologists. Expanded and adapted by permission.

Gaillargeon, 1983). In addition, there is evidence that children may show more competence in one aspect of a cognitive developmental stage than another (Dunst & Rheingrover, 1981). Therefore, just as with measures previously discussed, Piagetian tasks, presented in the typical manner, may underestimate a child's true abilities.

Criterion-Referenced and Curriculum-Based Instruments

Instruments that are criterion-referenced and curriculum-based were developed to meet the need for assessment results that would transfer into useful recommendations for curriculum and intervention (Fewell, 1984b; Neisworth & Bagnato, 1986). These tools often are checklists of items drawn from descriptions of normal child development. Some require formal administration of items under standard conditons, while others can be administered informally by observing children and/or questioning parents or caregivers. They comprise several domains of development, including a cognitive or preacademic domain. The cognitive domain usually contains items related to knowledge of concepts, verbal and nonverbal reasoning, and quantitative skills. Examples of some of the most popular tools being used currently are the Learning Accomplishment Profile (Sanford & Zelman, 1981), the Portage Checklist (Bluma, Shearer, Frohman, & Hilliard, 1976), the HICOMP Curriculum (Willoughby-Herb & Neisworth, 1983); the Brigance Diagnostic Inventory of Early Development (Brigance, 1978), the Hawaii Early Learning Profile (HELP) (Furono, O'Reilly, Hosaka, Inatsuka, Allman, & Zelsloft, 1979), and the Arizona Basic Assessment and Curriculum Utilization System (ABACUS) (McCarthy, Bos, Lund, Glatke, & Vaughan, 1984). Items failed on these instruments often are targeted for intervention, as they are based on observable behaviors that translate into skills that can be taught. Nevertheless, this approach is not problem-free.

Items from these scales do not always lead to legitimate or functional instructional goals that would improve children's abilities to function more independently in their ecologies. In addition, like some of the standardized assessment tools, many curriculum-based or criterion-referenced instruments have cognitive skill sequences that are not in true developmental progression for all children (Garwood, 1983). This issue may not pose major problems when making curriculum decisions regarding normal or mildly handicapped preschoolers, but it can be serious in the assessment of children with moderate or severe handicaps. Moreover, as Strain (1984) has suggested, criterion-referenced instruments often are based on normal developmental milestones and are not referenced to handicapped children, nor do they usually present validity or reliability indices. Thus, they are subject to many of the same criticisms as norm-referenced instruments (p. 7). Bearing these caveats in mind, the reader interested in more detailed discussion of specific curriculum-based instruments is referred to Neisworth and Bagnato (1986) and Bagnato, Neisworth, and Capone (1986).

The Battelle Developmental Inventory (BDI) (Newborg, Stock, Wnek, Guidubaldi, & Svinicki, 1984) is an instrument that deserves specific mention because it is both criterion- and norm-referenced, thus providing information on a child's developmental strengths and limitations, as well as comparisons with age-mates. Designed to allow multi-source/multimethod assessment through structured testing, parent interviews, and observations of children in natural settings, the BDI includes a scoring system that takes into account emerging skills as well as fully developed skills. In addition, the instrument offers modifications in administrations for children with various handicapping conditions. Composed of four subdomains, the test obtains information regarding perceptual discrimination, memory, reasoning and academic skills, and conceptual development.

Process-Oriented Assessment Approaches

The main assumption of process assessment is that the identification of cognitive strategies is integral to any full explanation of intelligent performances (Sternberg, 1981). Fewell (1984b) states that most **process-oriented approaches** have stemmed from human information processing models that are based on performance of *normal* children. However, they are beginning to be used to understand handicapped children, as deficient information-processing mechanisms seem to be characteristic of certain handicapping conditions.

One technique appearing as a useful addition to traditional cognitive assessment tools is the **test-teach-test paradigm.** In this approach, assessment is not seen as static; rather, the examiner gives the child an opportunity to learn from the experience and apply that learning to solve the problems presented. The Haeussermann (1958) approach mentioned earlier and the Learning Potential Assessment Device (LPAD) (Feuerstein, Rand, & Hoffman, 1979; 1980) are examples of this technique. The LPAD technique yields information about a child's "cognitive map" and ability to learn and, thus, is seen as useful for intervention planning. Special adaptations of the LPAD for preschoolers are currently underway (Lidz, 1983). Brown and Ferrara (1985) discuss process-oriented techniques from research based on the theory of Vygotsky (1978), whereby children are given a set of increasingly explicit hints toward solution of a problem until they are able to solve it. These techniques are reported to be useful as measures of less-biased cognitive assessment of children from a variety of cultures.

Although developed with infants, there are some experimental approaches to cognitive assessment that may prove useful for assessing severely or multiply impaired preschoolers. Examples include measures designed by Kearsley (1979), Lewis and Goldberg (1969), and Zelazo (1981) to assess a child's understanding of events based on his visual fixation, vocalization, and heart rate. An expectancy is established with the child by presenting the same stimulus or sequence several times, followed by a discrepant event. The child's reaction to the discrepant event in terms of the aforementioned physiological measures provides an idea of his cognitive functioning. Kearsley (1979) has shown that multiply impaired children who show significant delays on standardized tests are more likely to perform at an age-appropriate level on these expectancy tests.

From the above discussion, it is clear that assessment of cognitive competence in young children is a complex process involving a multimeasure/multisource approach. Assessors who attempt to glean an adequate amount of information from the use of one measure in isolation from others will discover the futility of this approach in deriving meaningful information about a child. Bagnato and Neisworth (1981) provide elaboration of this point, and the reader is referred to their book for a more detailed explanation.

Translating Assessment Information into Instructional Goals

The development of functional, developmentally appropriate goals in the cognitive domain is the primary purpose of assessment strategies. Because cognitive processes underlie other aspects of a child's functioning, progress toward the attainment of these goals influences development across these other areas. Thus, an assumption that should be kept in mind by any teacher of young, special-needs children is that cognitive, social, language, and sensorimotor skills are interrelated in unique ways for each child assessed.

The importance of setting goals that are developmentally appropriate cannot be overemphasized. Interviews with caregivers and careful observations across settings of skills that are fully acquired, are emerging, or are not yet present in a child's behavioral repertoire are essential to determining the appropriate amount of challenge that sets the occasion for learning to occur. In addition to the development of appropriate goals, activities must be designed and materials used that provide an adequate blend of familiarity and novelty.

The purpose of this section is to discuss the link between assessment results and instructional strategies across the cognitive subdomains of perceptual discrimination, memory, problem solving, and concept formation. The information is presented with naturalistic teaching as the underlying instructional strategy and with the assumption that assessment and instruction comprise a continual process, wherein changes are made based on children's developmental progress. Rather than describing instructional strategies in detail, this section emphasizes the translation of assessment results into instructional goals. Readers interested in more detailed descriptions of instructional strategies are referred to volumes such as Gearheart, DeRuiter, and Sileo (1986), Lerner, Mardell-Czudnowski, and Goldberg (1987), and Bailey and Wolery (1984).

Naturalistic Teaching

Naturalistic teaching strategies serve as an appropriate mechanism for translating assessment results into instructional goals. These teaching strategies involve (a) brief interactions used for teaching new skills or providing practice on acquired behaviors and (b) child-directed activities based on the child's specified request, focus of attention, or current level of development (Halle, Alpert, & Anderson, 1984). This form of teaching incorporates many of the generalization strategies suggested by Stokes and Baer (1977), such as training in natural settings and using natural reinforcers. An essential principle is that the complexity and frequency with which information is presented is determined by and

accommodates the child's unique repertoire of skills rather than being determined by a fixed set of methods. The flexibility required by teachers who use this strategy reflects the fact that assessment of the child's skill is a continual process that occurs over time.

Incidental teaching (Hart & Risley, 1975) is a specific form of naturalistic teaching applied to the improvement of communication competencies. Dunst and McWilliam (1988) delineate five steps essential to the incidental teaching process, which are important to remember when conducting cognitive assessments and translating the results into instructional goals. These five steps are (a) ensuring the child's responsiveness to the environment through provision of opportunities that secure the child's attention; (b) maintaining the child's attention based on the arrangement of environmental features that function as reinforcers; (c) eliciting and sustaining the child's interactions with the environment; (d) creating elaboration of the child's behavior; and (e) working toward conventionalization of the child's response, thus bringing the child close to adaptive or normalized cognitive competence.

From the above discussion, it should be clear that the goals of naturalistic or incidental teaching strategies are determined through interactions between a child and her environment. Although instruction occurs most frequently between an adult and the child, teachers must be vigilant to interactions the child has with peers for cues relevent to appropriate goals. In addition, interactions with her parent(s) must be included as an essential component of the assessment-intervention process. With a focus on interactions as indicators of cognitive competence, the interrelationships among language, social, and cognitive functioning also are underscored.

With the steps of incidental teaching outlined, we can turn our attention to their application within specific subdomains of cognitive competence. This information will be combined with illustrations of how test-based assessment results may be linked to instructional goals. The reader must bear in mind that, when determining instructional goals from absent or emerging skills reflected in test items, one must not "teach to the test" and interpret successful performance on an item as a true indication of cognitive competence. Rather, behaviors are manifestations of underlying cognitive processes that teachers should seek to develop across various activities, settings, materials, and people. Too often the assumption is made that a failed item from a test should translate verbatim into an instructional goal. This assumption ignores the possibility that the failure may have been influenced by the setting events of the assessment situation, including the materials used, the ways in which the materials were presented, and characteristics of the assessor and his interactions with the child. The use of naturalistic teaching prevents this mistaken translation from occurring because it requires the assessor to attend to behavioral cues from the child and arrange the animate and inanimate environment in ways that accommodate those behaviors. In its positive, proactive approach, this type of instruction stands in contrast to negative, deficit-centered approaches.

Perceptual Discrimination

An item from the BDI (Newborg et al., 1984) designed to assess **perceptual discrimination** at the 3- to 4-year level is "The child identifies simple objects by touch." Rather than attempting to develop this process of perceptual discrimination by introducing unfamiliar objects, the teacher would want to begin with those objects in which the child has already shown interest. Once engagement with the assessor is developed, other objects may be introduced toward attainment of the goals of being able to discriminate among a variety of objects. Thus, using a child's interest in an object in his naturally occurring environment as a point of departure for instructional activity is a competence-enhancement approach. Of course, the teacher must also adapt instruction to the sensorimotor, motor, and language skills of the child and design activities around his capabilities rather than around his disabilities. A limitation of the BDI in this subdomain is that it does not assess auditory discrimination in addition to haptic and visual discrimination. Thus, the teacher interested in truly understanding the process of perceptual discrimination for a particular child must supplement the BDI with other assessment methods (e.g., observations of the child's responses to loud and soft sounds).

Memory

Many measures of cognitive functioning contain items requiring the child to repeat digit sequences and recall familiar objects or sentences (e.g., the McCarthy Scales, the Revised Binet, the WPPSI, and the BDI). Successful performance on these items is based on the assumption that the stimuli are attended to by the child and that the child's sequencing abilities are adequately developed. For preschool-aged children who are multiply impaired, this can be a mistaken assumption. This situation exemplifies the notion mentioned earlier that "deficits" in cognitive functioning, as identified and interpreted by an assessor who is too test-bound, may be setting specific. Rather than requiring the child to repeat an arbitrarily chosen sequence of digits or to recall which object in a sequence was covered by a box, a more useful strategy is to use objects already familiar and of interest to the child. In doing so, a teacher may find intact **memory** processes that can be elaborated using a variety of materials across activities (e.g., group time, free play, snack time). In addition, many tests that assess memory are limited to visual and auditory modalities rather than the full range of modalities. Thus, to understand a child's memory processes, teachers will want to incorporate activities that tap haptic and kinesthetic processes and do not require sequencing skills.

Reasoning/Problem Solving

Most standard assessment procedures designed to measure **reasoning** and **problem solving** skills are heavily dependent on children's ability to remember directions to the tests, their ability to understand the directions, and their ability to express a response verbally or motorically. In addition, the relative emphasis on these abilities often varies from one age level to the next. For example, successful performance at the 4- to 5-year level is entirely dependent on receptive and expressive language skills, while items at the 5- to 6-year level are based entirely on visual abilities. Thus, it would be a mistake to infer faulty reasoning skills without considering the skills necessary to a successful performance. Instructional goals in the reasoning/problem-solving subdomain must be established so as to require responses of which a child is capable. The modified procedures for special-needs children provided in the BDI manual may provide useful information in this respect. Nevertheless, they too may need to be modified further because of a child's specific impairments.

Limitations of test-based assessment results underscore the importance of observing cues from a child in a variety of settings to understand how she reasons and solves problems. Thus, a free-play situation may reveal that a child who "failed" to identify missing parts of pictured objects may be able to point spontaneously to a missing part of a toy. Similarly, a child who is unable to respond verbally to questions such as "Why do we have cars?" may reveal his understanding

through appropriate creative play. The perceptive and flexible teacher will attempt to strengthen such skills by gradually introducing new materials, modeling, and arranging the environment so as to increase the opportunity for the child to demonstrate competence.

Conceptual Development

Both the Boehm Test of Basic Concepts-Revised (Boehm-R) (Boehm, 1986) and the Bracken Concept Development Series (Bracken, 1986) include detailed materials and instructions for translating assessment results on **concept formation** into instructional goals. Nevertheless, because the materials are primarily visual and require the child to point to the correct response, teachers will need to adapt the materials and instructions for visually and hearing-impaired children who also have motoric limitations. Adaptations for children with handicapping conditions presented in the BDI manual are helpful in this respect (see also Chapter 3). Thus, for an item requiring a child to sort forms by shape, children with visual impairments would need to spend time feeling the forms before and during sorting. Children with motor impairments would need to be allowed to tell the examiner which pile to put the objects into, and verbal instructions for children with hearing impairments would need to be accompanied by gestures. With these considerations, an accurate assessment of a child's conceptual development may occur, and appropriate instructional goals may be established. In addition, observation of a child's understanding of concepts in naturally occurring contexts (e.g., the colors of foods at snack time) will frequently provide functional information. Taken further, interactions with the child that are response contingent will set the occasion for refinement and elaboration of learned concepts and the modification of instructional goals based on new learning.

Summary and Conclusions

This chapter has presented an overview of important considerations when assessing the cognitive functioning of preschool-aged children. Adaptations of traditional norm-referenced measures and alternatives to these measures for accurate assessment of special needs children have been emphasized. Alternative measures discussed included Piagetian-based scales, criterion-referenced and curriculum-based instruments, and process-oriented approaches. The relationships among these instruments and various theories of cognitive functioning were discussed, and the need for a multi-measure/multisource perspective on assessment was emphasized. Careful and systematic observation of interactions between young children and their caregivers was introduced as a vital component of assessment procedures, and the importance of situational specificity, or the context in which assessment takes place, was under-scored. Incidental teaching was presented as a framework for establishing and attaining instructional goals, and application of this strategy to goal setting within representative subdomains was made.

SUMMARY OF KEY CONCEPTS

- Reasons for assessing the cognitive skills of preschoolers with handicaps include gathering information to (a) make placement and program eligibility assessments, (b) identify strengths and weaknesses in cognitive processes, (c) match instruction to children's abilities, and (d) identify the interrelations with other developmental domains.

- *Cognition* refers to mental processes by which individuals acquire knowledge.

- Two important principles in understanding children's cognitive abilities are: Preschool children are active problem solvers, and preschool children experience rapid developmental change.

- Three theoretical perspectives are consistent with these principles and are useful in understanding children's cognitive abilities: Piaget's theory, information-processing theories, and social learning theory.

- Assessment of cognitive skills can be viewed from two vantage points: (a) the traditional view, where children are expected to provide specific responses to specific test stimuli, and (b) an ecological view, where the assessor interprets a variety of behaviors as indicators of different types and forms of cognitive abilities. The ecological approach encompasses measures of the child's personal characteristics, behaviors, and environmental influences (e.g., home environment, other frequented environments, and parent/child interactions).

- The strengths, weaknesses, and use of psychometric measures (Stanford-Binet Intelligence Scale, Kaufman Assessment Battery for Children, McCarthy Scales of Children's Abilities, Wechsler Preschool and Primary Scale of Intelligence) are described.

- Alternatives to psychometric measures such as scales based on Piaget's theory of development, criterion- and curriculum-referenced tests, and process-oriented approaches are discussed.

- Use of systematic observation of children's interactions with their caregivers and the materials in their environments is seen as a critical component of cognitive assessment when the purpose is establishing instructional goals.

- Incidental, naturalistic teaching, is seen as a means of using ecologically derived assessment information in intervention programs.

REFERENCES

Arthur, G. (1952). *The Arthur adaptation of the Leiter International Performance Scale.* Chicago: Stoelting.

Bagnato, S. J. & Neisworth, J. T. (1981). *Linking developmental assessment and curricula.* Rockville, MD: Aspen.

Bagnato, S. J., Neisworth, J. T., & Capone, A. (1986). Curriculum-based assessment for the young exceptional child: Rationale and review. *Topics in Early Childhood Special Education, 6,* 97–110.

Bailey, D. B. & Wolery, M. (1984). *Teaching infants and preschoolers with handicaps.* Columbus, OH: Merrill.

Ball, R. S., Merrifield, P., & Stott, L. H. (1978). *Extended Merrill-Palmer Scale.* Chicago: Stoelting.

Bandura, A. (1978). The self system in reciprocal determinism. *American Psychologist, 33,* 344–358.

Bayley, N. (1969). *Bayley Scales of Infant Development.* New York: Psychological Corp.

Belsky, J. & Sterinberg, L. D. (1978). The effects of day care: A critical review. *Child Development, 49,* 929–949.

Bluma, S., Shearer, M., Frohman, A., & Hilliard, J. (1976). *Portage Guide to Early Education Checklist.* Portage, WI: Cooperative Educational Service Agency 12.

Boehm, A. (1986). *Boehm Test of Basic Concepts.* New York: The Psychological Corp.

Bracken, B. A. (1981). McCarthy Scales as a learning disability diagnostic aid: A closer look. *Journal of Learning Disabilities, 14,* 128–130.

Bracken, B. A. (1985). A critical review of the Kaufman Assessment Battery for Children (K-ABC). *School Psychology Review, 14,* 21–36.

Bracken, B. A. (1986). *Bracken Concept Development Series.* New York: The Psychological Corp.

Bradley, R. H. & Caldwell, B. M. (1976). The relation of infants' home environments to mental test performance at 54 months: A follow-up study. *Child Development, 47,* 1172–1174.

Bradley, R. H. & Caldwell, B. M. (1979). Home observation for measurement of the environment: A revision of the preschool scale. *American Journal of Mental Deficiency, 84,* 235–244.

Brigance, A. H. (1978). *Brigance Diagnostic Inventory of Early Development.* Billerica, MA: Curriculum Associates.

Bronfenbrenner, U. (1974). *Is early intervention effective?* Washington, DC: Office of Human Development.

Brown, A. L. (1975). The development of memory: Knowing about knowing, and knowing how to know. In H. W. Reese (Ed.), *Advances in child development and behavior, 10* (pp. 103–152). Hillsdale, NJ: Erlbaum.

Brown, A. L., Bransford, J. D., Ferrara, R. A., & Campione, J. C. (1983). Learning, remembering, and understanding. In J. H. Flavell and E. M. Markman (Eds.), *Handbook of child psychology, Vol. 1: Cognitive development* (pp. 77–166). New York: Wiley.

Brown, A. L. & Ferrara, R. A. (1985). Diagnosing zones of proximal development. In J. Wertsch (Ed.), *Culture, communication, and cognition—Vygotskian perspectives* (p. 5). London: Cambridge University Press.

Brown, A. L. & Palinscar, A. S. (1982). Inducing strategic learning from texts by means of informed, self-control training. *Topics in Learning and Learning Disabilities, 2,* 1–17.

Burgemeister, B., Blum, L. H., & Lorge, I. (1972). *Columbia Mental Maturity Scale.* New York: Harcourt, Brace, & World.

Buros, O. (1986). *Ninth mental measurements yearbook.* Lincoln, NE: Buros Institute.

Case, R. S. (1978). Intellectual development from birth to adulthood: A neo-Piagetian interpretation. In R. W. Siegler (Ed.), *Children's thinking:*

What develops? (pp. 56–78). Hillsdale, NJ: Erlbaum.

Clarke-Stewart, A. & Koch, J. (1983). *Children: Development through adolescence.* New York: Wiley.

Cohen, D. V., Stern, R., & Balaban, N. (1983). *Observing and recording the behavior of young children* (3rd ed.). New York: Teachers College Press.

Crockett, B. K., Rardin, M. W., & Pasewark, R. A. (1976). Relationship of WPPSI and subsequent Metropolitan Achievement Test scores in Head Start children. *Psychology in the Schools, 13,* 19–20.

Das, J. P., Kirby, J., & Jarman, R. F. (1979). Simultaneous and successive syntheses: An alternative model for cognitive abilities. *Psychological Bulletin, 82,* 87–103.

Davis, C. (1980). *Perkins-Binet Test of Intelligence for the Blind.* Watertown, MA: Perkins School for the Blind.

DuBose, R. & Langley, B. (1977). *The Developmental Activities Screening Inventory.* Hingham, MA: Teaching Resources.

Dunst, C. J. (1981). *Infant learning: A cognitive-linguistic intervention strategy.* Hingham, MA: Teaching Resources.

Dunst, C. J. (1986a). *The Caregiver Styles of Interaction Scales.* Unpublished document. Human Development Research and Training Institute, Morganton, NC.

Dunst, C. J. (1986b). *A rating scale for assessing parent-child play opportunities.* Unpublished document. Family, Infant and Preschool Program, Morganton, NC.

Dunst, C. J. & Gallagher, J. L. (1983). Piagetian approaches to infant assessment. *Topics in Early Childhood Special Education, 3,* 44–62.

Dunst, C. J. & McWilliam, R. A. (1988). Cognitive assessment of multiply handicapped young children. In T. Wachs & R. Sheehan (Eds.), *Assessment of developmentally disabled children* (pp. 105–130). New York: Plenum.

Dunst, C. J., McWilliam, R. A., & Holbert, K. (1986). Assessment of preschool classroom environments. *Diagnostique, 11,* 212–232.

Dunst C. J. & Rheingrover, R. M. (1981). Discontinuity and instability in early development: Implications for assessment. *Topics in Early Childhood Special Education, 1,* 49–60.

Elliott, C. D., Murray, D. J., & Pearson, L. S. (1983). *British Ability Scales.* New York: The Psychological Corp.

Escalona, S. K. & Corman, H. H. (1969). *Albert Einstein Scales of Sensorimotor Development.* New York: Albert Einstein College of Medicine of Yeshiva University.

Farran, D., Kasari, C., & Jay, S. (1984, August). *Parent-Caregiver Interaction Scale: Training manual.* Chapel Hill, NC: Frank Porter Graham Child Development Center.

Feuerstein, R., Rand, Y., & Hoffman, M. (1979). *The dynamic assessment of retarded performers.* Baltimore, MD: University Park Press.

Feuerstein, R., Rand, Y., & Hoffman, M. (1980). *Instructional enrichment.* Baltimore, MD: University Park Press.

Fewell, R. R. (1984a). *The Play Assessment Scale* (3rd ed.). Seattle: University of Washington.

Fewell, R. R. (1984b). Assessment of preschool handicapped children. *Educational Psychologist, 19,* 172–179.

Flavell, J. H. (1982). On cognitive development. *Child Development, 53,* 1–10.

French, J. L. (1964). *Pictorial Test of Intelligence.* Boston: Houghton-Mifflin.

Furono, S., O'Reilly, A., Hosaka, C. M., Inatsuka, T. T., Allman, T. L., & Zelsloft, B. (1979). *The Hawaii Early Learing Profile.* Palo Alto, CA: VORT.

Garwood, S. G. (1983). Intelligence and cognition. In S. G. Garwood (Ed.), *Educating young handicapped children: A developmental approach* (pp. 149–201). Rockville, MD: Aspen.

Gearheart, B. R., DeRuiter, J. A., & Sileo, T. W. (1986). *Teaching mildly and moderately handicapped students.* Englewood Cliffs, NJ: Prentice-Hall.

Gelman, R. & Gaillargeon, R. (1983). A review of some Piagetian concepts. In J. H. Flavell & E. M. Markman (Eds.), *Cognitive development* (pp. 167–230). New York: Wiley.

Gerken, K. C., Hancock, K. A., & Wade, T. H. (1978). Comparison of the Stanford-Binet Intelligence Scale and the McCarthy Scales of Children's Abilities with preschool children. *Psychology in the Schools, 15,* 468–472.

Goldschmidt, M. J. & Bentler, P. M. (1968). *Manual: Concept Assessment Kit: Conservation.* San Diego, CA: Educational & Industrial Testing Service.

Goodman, J. (1981). *The Goodman Lock Box Instruction Manual.* Chicago: Stoelting.

Griffiths, R. (1979). *The abilities of young children.* London: Child Development Research Center.

Guilford, J. P. (1956). The structure of intellect. *Psychological Bulletin, 53,* 267–293.

Haeussermann, E. (1958). *Developmental potential of preschool children.* New York: Grune & Stratton.

Halle, J. W., Alpert, C. L., & Anderson, S. R. (1984). Natural environment language assessment and intervention with severely impaired preschoolers. *Topics in Early Childhood Special Education, 4,* 36–56.

Harrison, P. L. & Naglieri, J. A. (1978). Extrapolated General Cognitive Indexes on the McCarthy Scales for gifted and mentally retarded children. *Psychological Reports, 43,* 1291–1296.

Hart, B. & Risley, T. (1975). Incidental teaching of language in the preschool. *Journal of Applied Behavioral Analysis, 8,* 411–420.

Haywood, H. C., Meyers, C. E., & Switzky, H. N. (1982). Mental retardation. *Annual Review of Psychology, 33,* 309–342.

Haywood, H. C. & Switzky, H. N. (1986). The malleability of intelligence: Cognitive processes as a function of polygenic-experimental interaction. *School Psychology Review, 15,* 245–255.

Haywood, H. C. & Wachs, T. D. (1981). Intelligence, cognition, and individual differences. In M. J. Begals, H. C. Haywood, & H. Garber (Eds.), *Psychosocial influences in retarded performance, 1: Issues and theories in development* (pp. 53–69). Baltimore, MD: University Park Press.

Henderson, R. W. & Rankin, R. J. (1973). WPPSI reliability and predictive validity with disadvantaged Mexican-American children. *Journal of School Psychology, 11,* 16–20.

Hiskey, M. S. (1966). *Hiskey-Nebraska Test of Learning Aptitude.* Lincoln, NE: Author.

Hunt, J. M. (1979). Psychological development: Early experience. In M. R. Rosenzweig & L. W. Porter (Eds.), *Annual review of psychology* (pp. 103–143). Palo Alto: Annual Reviews, Inc.

Jens, K. G. (1984). Non-traditional assessment of handicapped preschool children. In S. E. Laurin (Ed.), *The preschool special child: Early identification, assessment, and management* (pp. 244–250). Chapel Hill, NC: Division of Physical Therapy, University of North Carolina.

Kaufman, A. S. (1973). Comparison of the performance of matched groups of black children and white children of the WPPSI. *Journal of Consulting and Clinical Psychology, 41,* 186–191.

Kaufman, A. S. (1975). Factor structure of the McCarthy Scales at five age levels between 2½ and 8½. *Educational and Psychological Measurement, 35,* 641–656.

Kaufman, A. S. (1979). *Intelligent testing with the WISC-R.* New York: Wiley Interscience.

Kaufman, A. S. & Kaufman, N. L. (1977). *Clinical evaluation of young children with the McCarthy Scales.* New York: Grune & Stratton.

Kaufman A. S. & Kaufman, N. L. (1983). *Kaufman Assessment Battery for Children, Interpretive Manual.* Circle Pines, MN: American Guidance Service.

Kearsley, R. (1979). Iatrogenic retardation: A syndrome of learned incompetence. In R. Kearsley & I. Sigel (Eds.), *Infants at risk: Assessment of cognitive functioning* (pp. 153–180). Hillsdale, NJ: Erlbaum.

Keith, T. Z. (1985). Questioning the K-ABC: What does it measure? *School Psychology Review, 14,* 9–20.

Kendler, H. H. & Kendler, T. S. (1975). From discrimination learning to cognitive development: A neo-behavioristic odyssey. In W. K. Estes (Ed.), *Handbook of learning and cognitive processes, 1,* (pp. 191–247). Hillsdale, NJ: Erlbaum.

Kiernan, D. W. & DuBose, R. F. (1974). Assessing the cognitive development of preschool deaf-blind children. *Education of the Visually Handicapped, 6,* 103–105.

Lerner, J., Mardell-Czudnowski, C., & Goldberg, D. (1987). *Special education for the early childhood years.* Englewood Cliffs, NJ: Prentice-Hall.

Lewis, M. & Goldberg, S. (1969). The acquisition and violation of expectancy: An experimental paradigm. *Experimental Child Psychology, 7,* 70–80.

Lidz, C. S. (1983). Dynamic assessment and the preschool child. *Journal of Psychoeducational Assessment, 1,* 59–72.

Madden, R., Gardner, E. F., & Collins, C. S. (1984). *Stanford Early School Achievement Test* (2nd ed.). New York: The Psychological Corp.

Mahoney, G., Powell, A., & Finger, I. (1986). The Maternal Behavior Rating Scale. *Topics in Early Childhood Special Education, 6,* 44–56.

Matas, L., Arend, R. A., & Sroufe, L. A. (1978). Continuity of adaptation in the second year: The relationship between quality of attachment and later competence. *Child Development, 49,* 547–556.

McCarthy, D. (1972). *Manual for the McCarthy Scales of Children's Abilities.* New York: The Psychological Corp.

McCarthy, J., Bos, C., Lund, K., Glatke, J., & Vaughan, S. (1984). *Arizona Basic Assessment* and *Curriculum Utilization System (ABACUS) for young children*. Denver: LOVE.

Neisworth, J. T. & Bagnato, S. J. (1986). Curriculum-based developmental assessment: Congruence of testing and teaching. *School Psychology Review, 15,* 180–199.

Newborg, J., Stock, J. R., Wnek, L, Guidubaldi, J., & Svinicki, J. (1984). *The Battelle Developmental Inventory.* Allen, TX: DLM/Teaching Resources.

Paget, K. D. (1986). The McCarthy Scales of Children's Abilities. In J. V. Mitchell (Ed.), *Ninth Mental Measurements Yearbook* (pp. 922–926). Lincoln, NE: Buros Institute.

Pascual-Leone, J. (1980). Constructive problems for constructive theories: The current relevance of Piaget's work and a critique of information-processing simulation psychology. In R. H. Kluwe & H. Spada (Eds.), *Developmental models of thinking* (pp. 128–149). New York: Academic Press.

Phillips, B. L., Pasewark, R. A., & Tindall, R. C. (1978). Relationship among McCarthy Scales of Children's Abilities, WPPSI, and Columbia Mental Maturity Scale. *Psychology in the Schools, 15,* 352–356.

Prescott, G. A., Farr, R. C., Hogan, J. P., & Balow, I. H. (1986). *Metropolitan Achievement Tests: Sixth edition (MAT 6), preprimer and primer.* New York: The Psychological Corp.

Ramey, C. T. & Campbell, F. A. (1979). Compensatory education for disadvantaged children. *School Review, 87,* 171–189.

Ramey, C. T., Farran, D. C., & Campbell, F. A. (1979). Predicting IQ from mother-infant interactions. *Child Development, 50,* 804–814.

Ramey, C. T., Stedman, D. S., Borders-Patterson, A., & Mengel, W. (1978). Predicting school failure from information available at birth. *American Journal of Mental Deficiency. 82,* 525–534.

Reynolds, C. R. & Clark, J. (1983). Assessment of cognitive abilities. In K. D. Paget & B. A. Bracken (Eds.), *The psychoeducational assessment of preschool children* (pp. 163–190). New York: Grune & Stratton.

Reynolds, C. R. & Gutkin, T. B. (1981). Test scatter on the WPPSI: Normative analyses of the standardization sample. *Journal of Learning Disabilities, 14,* 460–464.

Reynolds, C. R. Kamphaus, R. W., & Rosenthal, B. L. (1988). *Factor analysis of the Stanford-Binet, fourth edition, for ages 2 years through*

23 years. Manuscript submitted for publication.

Rogers, S. J. (1977). Characteristics of the cognitive development of profoundly retarded children. *Child Development, 48,* 837–843.

Rogers, S. J. (1982). Assessment of cognitive development in the preschool years. In G. Ulrey & S. J. Rogers (Eds.), *Psychological assessment of handicapped infants and young children* (pp. 45–53). New York: Thieme-Stratton.

Salvia, J. & Ysseldyke, J. E. (1985). *Assessment in special and remedial education* (3rd ed.). Boston: Houghton Mifflin.

Sanford, A. R. & Zelman, J. G. (1981). *Learning Accomplishment Profile* (rev. ed.). Winston-Salem, NC: Kaplan Press.

Sattler, J. M. (1982). *Assessment of children's intelligence and special abilities* (2nd ed.). Boston: Allyn & Bacon.

Schakel, J. A. (1986). Cognitive assessment of preschool children. *School Psychology Review, 15,* 200–215.

Siegler, R. S. (1981). Developmental sequences within and between concepts. *Monographs of the Society for Research in Child Development, 46,* (Serial No. 189).

Sternberg, R. (1981). Testing and cognitive psychology. *American Psychologist, 36,* 1181–1189.

Sternberg, R. & Powell, J. S. (1983). The development of intelligence. In P. H. Mussen (Ed.), *Handbook of child psychology* (4th ed.) (pp. 341–419): Vol. 3. New York: Wiley.

Stokes, T. F. & Baer, D. M. (1977). An implicit technology of generalization. *Journal of Applied Behavior Analysis, 10,* 349–367.

Strain, P. S. (1984). Efficacy research with young handicapped children: A critique of the status quo. *Journal of the Division for Early Childhood, 9,* 4–10.

Switzky, H. N. & Haywood, H. C. (1984). A biosocial ecological perspective on mental retardation. In N. S. Endler and J. McV. Hunt (Eds.), *Personality and the behavioral disorders, 2* (pp. 78–90). New York: Wiley.

Terman, L. M. & Merrill, M. A. (1973). *Manual for the third revision (Form L-M) of the Stanford-Binet Intelligence Scale.* Boston: Houghton-Mifflin.

Thorndike, R. L., Hagen, E. P., & Sattler, J. M. (1986a). *Technical manual Stanford-Binet Intelligence Scale: Fourth edition.* Chicago: Riverside.

Uzgiris, I. C. & Hunt, J. (1975). *Assessment in infancy: Ordinal Scales of Psychological Development.* Urbana: University of Illinois Press.

Vygotsky, L. S. (1978). *Mind in society: The development of higher psychological processes.* Cambridge, MA: Harvard University Press.

Walls, R. T., Werner, T. J., Bacon, A., & Zane, T. (1977). Behavior checklist. In J. D. Cone & R. P. Hawkins (Eds.), *Behavioral assessment: New directions in clinical psychology* (pp. 77-146). New York: Brunner/Mazel.

Wechsler, D. (1967). *Manual for the Wechsler Preschool and Primary Scale of Intelligence.* New York: The Psychological Corp.

Wellman, H. M., Ritter, K., & Flavell, J. (1975). Deliberate memory in the delayed reactions of very young children. *Developmental Psychology, 11,* 780-787.

Wertsch, J. V. (1979). From social interaction to higher psychological process: A clarification and application of Vygotsky's theory. *Human Development, 22,* 1-22.

Willoughby-Herb, S. & Neisworth, J. T. (1983). *HICOMP preschool curriculum.* Columbus, OH: Merrill.

Woodcock, R. & Johnson, B. (1977). *Woodcock-Johnson Psychoeducational Battery.* Hingham, MA: Teaching Resources.

Zelazo, P. (1981). An information processing approach to infant cognitive assessment. In M. Lewis and L. Taft (Eds.), *Developmental disabilities: Theory, assessment, and intervention* (pp. 130-155). New York: S P Medical and Scientific Books.

Chapter 13

Assessing Motor Skills

Pamela D. Smith
University of Kentucky

KEY TERMS

- Atypical Motor Development
- Motor Delays
- Developmental Milestones
- Motor Development
- Postural Control (posture)
- Movement Components
- Physical Therapist
- Occupational Therapist
- Muscle Tone (postural tone)

- Hypotonia (low muscle tone)
- Hypertonia (spasticity)
- Underlying Muscle Tone
- Range of Motion
- Predominant Muscle Tone
- Associated Reactions
- Sensory Stimuli
- Primitive Reflexes
- Automatic Reactions
- Righting Reactions
- Rotation

- Equilibrium Reactions
- Protective Reactions
- Extension
- Volitional Movements
- Transitional Movements
- Movement Patterns
- Symmetry
- Independent Movements
- Fine Motor Skills
- Integrated Therapy
- Physical Guidance
- Physical Management

Movement is the vehicle through which infants and young children interact with their environment. It is believed to be closely tied to and interrelated with perceptual and conceptual development (Ayers, 1979; Piaget, 1952). Also, movement is an integral part of tasks in other instructional domains: cognitive skills, communication skills, social skills, play, mobility, and self-help. Therefore, attainment of movement competence and development of adequate motor skills is a critical aspect of educational programs for infants and preschoolers with handicaps.

This chapter focuses on assessing infants and preschoolers with delayed and **atypical motor development** or with identified motor disabilities. The chapter includes (a) a rationale for assessing movement and motor skills, (b) a description of the domain and the dimensions of a motor evaluation, (c) a discussion of the procedural considerations when assessing the various dimensions of motor skills, (d) a discussion of available assessment instruments, and (e) guidelines for translating the results of a motor assessment into intervention goals.

Rationale

Historically, physical and/or occupational therapists have been responsible for conducting assessments of motor skills. However, there are many reasons why special educators and other professionals should be familiar with assessing motor skills:

1. Professionals who have a clear understanding of normal motor development and screening methods are better able to identify children who need a thorough motor assessment.
2. Professionals who serve as team leaders and case managers must be familiar with the best assessment practices to ensure the acquisition of quality motor assessments.
3. Professionals who are knowledgeable in motor development and assessment are better able to identify children's current abilities and needs in motor functioning and can plan more adequate instructional programs.
4. Professionals who understand neuromotor development and its application to motor skill development are better able to use equipment and apply intervention techniques across curricular domains.
5. Professionals who are knowledgeable in motor assessment are better able to document child progress, monitor intervention strategies, evaluate program effectiveness, and identify subtle changes in children's motor skills, par-

ticularly those with motor disabilities.
6. Professionals who understand and use terminology from relevant disciplines (e.g., physical therapy, occupational therapy, and adaptive physical education) are able to communicate more effectively with members of those disciplines.

Another reason for addressing motor assessment is that motor delays are common in many types of handicapping conditions. For example, the severity of mental retardation is proportionally related to motor delays and deficits (Robinson & Robinson, 1976). Blind children exhibit delays in the attainment of selected motor and locomotion behaviors, particularly those that require the child to project her body in space, such as pulling to stand, creeping, and walking (Fewell, 1983).

This chapter focuses on assessment of motor development in infants and young children with **motor delays** due to atypical muscle tone. This approach was taken because these motor problems (a) are frequently encountered by special educators and other professionals, (b) are a significant threat to attaining useful skills in other domains, and (c) are most amenable to change when intervention is implemented early. The motor problems may be caused by damage to the central nervous system (e.g., cerebral palsy) or due to a chromosomal abnormality (Down syndrome).

It is believed that 90% of infants who were later diagnosed as having cerebral palsy originally had low muscle tone (Bly, 1983; Kong, 1966). The remaining 10% is composed of infants with severe brain damage who have true, congenital high muscle tone or spasticity. Thus, increased muscle tone appears to be acquired as a means of compensating for low muscle tone to attain antigravity postures and continues to be reinforced and strengthened through constant use in performing functional tasks. Early intervention for infants and young children with deficits in motor skills is critical. Attention to young children's motor problems may prevent patterns from becoming habitual, leading to secondary problems such as muscle contractures, bone deformities, loss of function, and delays in other areas.

The results of an assessment of motor skills should be used to design intervention strategies aimed at assisting children in performing movements as normally as possible and thus experiencing and learning the sensation of normal movement. Intervention techniques can enhance children's movement competence, thus increasing their participation in activities related to mobility, self-help, communication, play, socialization, and cognitive tasks. In addition, specific physical management techniques may be designed to assist parents and significant others in the daily care of the child.

Overview of the Domain of Motor Development

In order to understand fully movement competency and assessment of motor skills, a thorough understanding of motor development is needed. However, it is not possible or appropriate to include such information within this chapter. Thus, the following section provides the reader with a brief review of terminology related to motor development and motor developmental milestones.

Movement Terminology Related to Motor Development

The first step in understanding movement terminology is to know that movement occurs in relationship to imaginary lines drawn through various parts of the body. It is helpful to keep these in mind when observing, analyzing, and describing posture and movement.

The most commonly used body line is midline, which runs in a cephalocaudal (head-to-tail) direction and divides the body into two halves. The front and back halves of the body are divided into two equal parts by another imaginary line. The front half is referred to as the anterior side, and the back half is the posterior side. Selected movement terms and definitions are contained in Table 13.1.

Normal Motor Development and Developmental Milestones

The **developmental milestones** in **motor development** and general age levels for attaining these have been described elsewhere (Chandler, 1979; Knoblock & Passamanick, 1974). Children's development can be compared to these milestones to determine if delays are present.

In general, achievement of these milestones proceeds in an orderly sequence in nonhandicapped children, although rates of acquistion will vary from child to child depending on factors such as sex, genetics, environmental stimulation, and motivation. While the age of attaining milestones varies, the principles governing motor development remain consistent. These principles are shown in Table 13.2.

The process of normal motor development should not be seen as the attainment of motor milestones. Motor development refers to the *process* of acquiring the necessary **postural control** and **movement components** to perform purposeful volitional movements. The attainment of each motor milestone is the end product of combining and recombining the components to produce a functional motor act (e.g., sitting, walking, running, jumping).

Numerous sources provide lists of gross and fine motor milestones and developmentally sequenced tests to determine delays in motor skills. However, when assessing and teaching gross motor skills, it is important to

TABLE 13.1
Movement Terminology

Term	Definition
Prone	Lying on stomach
Supine	Lying on back
Lateral	Pertaining to the side
Abduction	Movement away from the midline of the body
Adduction	Movement toward the midline of the body
Extension	Straightening a body part at the joint
Flexion	Bending a body part at the joint
External rotation	Rotation of a body joint that moves a body part away from the midline
Internal rotation	Rotation of a body joint that moves a body part toward the midline
Symmetry	Equal development of both sides of the body in size and shape and/or same position of both sides of the body while assuming postures and performing movements
Asymmetry	Unequal development of one side of the body from the other in size or shape and/or different position of one side of the body from the other while assuming postures and performing movements
Rotation	Twisting of the body along the body axis or movement between the shoulders and pelvis (trunk rotation), needed in all volitional and transitional movements (moving from one posture to another)
Dissociation	Ability to isolate and use only those body parts and muscles needed to perform independent movements
Weight bearing	Symmetrical, with weight evenly distributed over weight-bearing joints or body parts (e.g., prone on forearms or extended arms, sitting, kneeling, standing)
Weight shift	Shifting the weight of the body from a position of equal weight bearing in an antigravity posture to one side of the body to free a body part to perform independent movements, a weight shift precedes every volitional movement

determine what *components* the child lacks or is performing abnormally to plan intervention programs to facilitate the acquisition of the missing components and attain functional skills. For example, the motor milestone of head up in prone position requires that the infant use motor components of neck extension and head righting to lift the head in midline against gravity.

Dimensions of Motor Evaluation and Assessment Procedures

In general, assessments of motor skills should be conducted prior to or concurrent with assessments in other domains. The primary reasons are that (a) the results of the motor assessment may provide information on the relationship of delays in motor development

TABLE 13.2
Principles of Motor Development

Principle	Description	Purpose/Function	Example
Cephalo to caudal	Motor development begins with cephalic (head) control and progresses downward through the body to caudal control (tail/feet).	Allows for development of vertical control of the body upward against gravity.	Infants lift their heads and acquire head control before shoulders and upper trunk. Control of trunk is followed by pelvis, then lower extremities.
Proximal to distal	Motor development begins with control of proximal (nearest midline) body parts and progresses to control of distal (farthest from midline) body parts.	Allows for development of horizontal control; critical for upper extremity function and fine motor skills.	Infants develop stability and mobility of shoulder girdle; then acquire ability to use elbow, wrist, and finally the fingers for grasp, release, and object manipulation.
Flexion to extension	Motor development begins with physiological flexion (fetal position) and progresses to development of controlled extension in prone position, which is later balanced with controlled flexion in supine position.	Development of extension allows for control over the influences of gravity; assists in assuming antigravity postures. Both controlled extension and controlled flexion are needed to counterbalance each other to allow both stability (posture) and mobility (movement) for voluntary motor behaviors.	Infants develop extension in prone position first to raise head and upper body up against gravity. Later they use controlled flexion with controlled extension to maintain posture and move against gravity.
Horizontal and vertical control to diagonal control	Diagonal control is developed through the trunk and provides rotation between the shoulders and pelvis around the body axis (trunk rotation).	Active trunk rotation is needed to perform useful motor tasks (e.g., reaching, walking) and in transitional movements (e.g., from sidelying to sitting to standing).	Walking requires body alignment and balance upright against gravity (vertical and horizontal control), reciprocal weight shift from one side of body to the other requiring trunk rotation (diagonal control). To reach (horizontal) while sitting (vertical) requires the child to shift weight and use trunk rotation (diagonal).

TABLE 13.2
Continued

Principle	Description	Purpose/Function	Example
Gross motor to fine motor	Motor development proceeds from uncontrolled, undifferentiated gross movements to controlled, precise, fine movements.	Initially controlled by reflexes (gross movements), then voluntary control allows for controlled dissociation to perform specific movements.	Infants begin by moving in wide ranges of motion using large muscle groups, gain stability in proximal joints of the body through weight-bearing experiences (e.g., lying prone on forearms), then gain control of smaller muscle groups for use in midranges.
Pronation to supination	Pronation/supination refers to position of the forearm and hand. Pronation (palm facing down) of the forearm and hand precedes supination (palm facing upwards).	The acquisition of supination allows for reach and a variety of functional grasps. Supination assists in transfers from one hand to the other.	Young children initially grasp using a raking motion with the hand/forearm pronated. Later, they develop the ability to supinate for more complex and functional grasps (e.g., to grasp cup, hold pencil).
Ulnar to radial	Fine motor development begins with the ulnar (little finger) side of the hand, then proceeds to the radial (thumb) side.	Allows for a variety of functional grasps. Radial development enables dissociation and control of the thumb and index finger. Radial development allows for manipulation and transfers from one to the other.	Young children initially grasp using the ulnar side of the hand (ulnar palmer grasp). Later, they develop the ability to dissociate the thumb and index finger for more refined grasps (e.g., neat pincer grasp).

to delays in other domains, and (b) the presence of abnormal tone and movement patterns will influence how the child is handled and postioned physically when other skills are assessed, which may result in a more accurate picture of the child's capabilities in other areas of development.

Whenever possible, professionals should rely on the expertise of **physical** or **occupational therapists** in conducting motor assessments.

Children should be referred to a physical therapist for a thorough motor assessment if they exhibit poor head control or sitting posture; develop asymmetry; or demonstrate muscle weakness, delays in attaining developmental milestones, or poor balance (Esterson, 1978). Occupational therapists should be consulted to assess and work with children who demonstrate difficulty in fine motor skills (e.g., grasping, using both hands, writing) and activities of daily living (e.g., eating/drinking, dressing) (Exner, 1987). The purpose of the assessment and the child's individual needs will dictate the number and types of professionals involved.

When conducting motor assessments, several factors may have an impact on the quality and validity of the results. These include such factors as the presence of sensory impairments or associated conditions such as epilepsy. If children are taking medication, any side effects of the medication that may affect the child's behavioral state should be identified. In general, the examiner should establish rapport with the child and maintain the child in a relaxed and cooperative state throughout the testing session. A carpeted area or large therapy mat that allows for adequate floor space should be available. Prior to the testing session, the examiner should gather needed equipment such as therapy balls or rolls, vestibular board, appropriate-sized chair or other positioning devices as well as other materials such as several small and attractive toys that the child prefers.

An adequate motor assessment for the purpose of planning intervention should include an assessment of (a) postural tone under conditions of stimulation and different positions, (b) primitive reflexes and automatic reactions, (c) posture and movement patterns, and (d) functional abilities and disabilities (Bobath, 1969; Bobath & Bobath, 1972). The following sections will describe the dimensions of motor assessment and discuss the procedures commonly used for each.

Muscle Tone

The term **muscle tone** or **postural tone** refers to the degree of tension in the muscles of the body when they are at rest. This can be conceptualized as a muscle's "readiness" to perform movement. Muscle tone provides the basis for the development of normal background postures (positions) or stability against gravity to enable the acquisition of balance and voluntary movements (Campbell,

1985a; Campbell, 1987b). Normal muscle tone must be high enough to provide upright stability against gravity, yet low enough to allow mobility of the joints of the body for movement. Normal muscle tone is evenly distributed throughout the body and remains fairly constant throughout life. Muscle tone is controlled by the central nervous system, and prenatal, perinatal, or postnatal damage to the central nervous system may result in abnormal muscle tone.

Assessment of Muscle Tone. Assessment of muscle tone is a critical aspect of motor evaluation for several reasons. First, the presence of abnormal muscle tone will result in delays in developmental milestones, atypical postures, and atypical movement patterns. Children who exhibit abnormal muscle tone in conjunction with other deviations in motor development (e.g., presence of residual primitive reflexes) should begin to receive intervention to prevent reinforcement of abnormal patterns as early as possible. Second, the type of abnormal muscle tone that the child exhibits will determine intervention techniques, positioning, handling, and adaptive equipment.

Deviations in muscle tone range on a continuum from severely reduced muscle tone (**hypotonia** or **low muscle tone**) to an excess of muscle tone (**hypertonia** or **spasticity**). The possible ranges of muscle tone are depicted in Figure 13.1. Some children have fluctuating muscle tone or athetosis that is present even when the child is at rest. Fluctuating muscle tone is not only abnormal but is constantly changing, and may occur in varying degrees from hypotonic to hypertonic.

The measurement of muscle tone is generally subjective, and clinical observation is the most widely used method. Some rating scales exist (Campbell, 1987b; Bricker & Campbell, 1980; Chandler, Andrews, & Swanson, 1980), and fair to good interrater reliability has been reported (Bricker & Campbell, 1980; Harris, Haley, Tada, & Swanson,

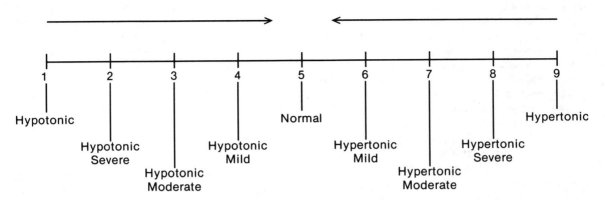

FIGURE 13.1
Two-Dimensional Representation of the Domain of Tonicity. (Source: From "Programming for Students with Dysfunction in Posture and Movement" by P. Campbell. In Systematic Instruction of Persons with Severe Handicaps (p. 191) by M. E. Snell (Ed.), 1987. Columbus, OH: Merrill. Copyright 1987 by Charles E. Merrill. Reprinted by permission.)

1984). However, rating scales also rely on observation and clinical judgment and are more useful in *identifying* children for services than in *planning* intervention.

The process of assessing muscle tone requires the examiner to feel the amount of tension in the child's muscles through hands-on procedures and to observe the child's movements while performing various motor tasks in functional situations. Reliable and accurate assessment of muscle tone requires extensive experience in working with children with a variety of movement problems. An assessment of muscle tone should be conducted under both passive and active conditions. The distribution of tone throughout body and the influences of other factors that affect muscle tone also should be determined.

Assessment of Underlying Muscle Tone. **Underlying muscle tone** is assessed when the child is passive or at rest. Underlying muscle tone can range from hypotonia to hypertonia to normal, though it is usually on the lower end of the range, particularly in the trunk

(Campbell, 1985b). The child should be positioned in either a prone, supine, or sitting position. When assessing muscle tone, particular attention should be given to proximal parts of the body such as the head and neck, shoulder girdle, trunk, and pelvis (Campbell, 1985a). The examiner should move the proximal joints or body parts passively and note presence of muscle and joint tightness or proximal fixations. Children tend to develop increased muscle tone in proximal body parts first, as they use biomechanical adjustments in an attempt to compensate for low muscle tone to attain antigravity postures. In addition, the degree of muscle tone may not be evenly distributed throughout the body. For example, muscle tone may be lower in the trunk and higher in the head/neck area, shoulders, pelvis, and/or lower extremities.

Methods of assessing underlying muscle tone include (a) feeling the *consistency* of the child's muscles particularly in the calf, thigh, and arm, (b) observing the **range of motion** or the *extensibility* of the child's joints by moving them through their full arch (consult

Fraser & Hensinger, 1983, for more detail on assessing joint range of motion), (c) determining the *passivity* of the muscles by shaking the child's wrist or ankle to determine the amount of resistance to movement, and (d) observing the child's *posture* in various positions such as prone, supine, sitting, quadruped, kneeling, and standing (Swanson, 1979). Throughout assessment, one side of the body should be compared with the other to determine any asymmetries (differences) that might be present (McCarraher-Wetzel & Wetzel, 1984). A summary of the results based on each of these methods for normal tone, hypertonia, and hypotonia are contained in Table 13.3.

Assessment of Predominant Muscle Tone. **Predominant muscle tone** is assessed when the child is actively involved in maintaining antigravity postures and moving through space (Campbell, 1985a). The examiner should gather information related to changes in muscle tone as a result of the various postures and of performing different movements such as reaching, speaking/vocalizing, and moving. The child's posture and spontaneous movements should be observed in different positions, which include prone, supine, sidelying, sitting, quadruped, kneeling, and standing.

Throughout the session, the presence of associated reactions should be noted. **Associated reactions** occur when the muscle tone increases in parts of the body that are not being used to perform a task (Bobath, 1969). This can be tested by requiring children to grasp an object with their preferred or lesser-involved hand. If associated reactions are present, the nondominant hand will increase in muscle tone or clench, indicating abnormal "overflow" of hypertonia into the nondominant hand (Levitt, 1982). The assessment of predominant muscle tone will be useful in determining the appropriate positioning and handling procedures and the specific physical guidance techniques that should be used to facilitate volitional movements.

Distribution of Muscle Tone. Diagnostic categories are based on the predominant type of muscle tone and the distribution of tone throughout the body. Topographical classification systems based on the areas of the body involved are used to describe the distribution of abnormal tone. The most well-known system was developed by the American Academy for Cerebral Palsy (Minear, 1956), and classifies physical impairment according to limb involvement (presence of abnormal tone). This system has been updated and shortened

TABLE 13.3
Results of Assessment of Underlying Muscle Tone Based on Types

Measure	Normal	Hypotonia	Hypertonia
Consistency	firm	soft, flabby	hard, stony
Extensibility	normal range of motion of joints	exceeds normal range of motion of joints (hypermobility)	joint tightness with limited range of motion (contractures)
Passivity	attempt to control movement	no resistance to movement	resistance to movement may increase, joint tightness
Posture	symmetrical, weight evenly distributed on weight-bearing surface	no resistance to gravity, "molds" to support surface, arms and legs flaccid/passive	too tightly flexed or extended

to reflect more accurately the actual anatomical distribution of abnormal muscle tone. The three major categories include the following:

Hemiplegia: involvement of one side of the body.
Quadraplegia: involvement of the trunk with equal involvement of both upper (arms) and lower (legs) extremities.
Diplegia: involvement of trunk and all four extremities, with greater involvement of the lower extremities.

The primary purpose for using these diagnostic categories is to facilitate communication among professionals. Practitioners should refrain from using these terms as labels to refer to a particular child or when interacting with the child's parents.

Factors that Influence Muscle Tone. Factors such as the child's position in relation to gravity, **sensory stimuli**, environmental factors, physical management, and child state can affect muscle tone (Campbell, 1987b). Gravitational influences are assessed by observing the child's posture in various positions under both passive and active conditions. In general, higher antigravity postures (e.g., sitting, quadruped, kneeling, standing) tend to increase muscle tone more than do low antigravity postures (e.g., prone, supine, sidelying). This information is useful in determining which positions tend to reduce or normalize hypertonus and improve posture and motor functioning.

Various auditory, visual, and tactile stimuli may cause changes in muscle tone. Children with hypertonia tend to have a low threshold for sensory input, meaning a small amount of sensory input can increase their muscle tone. On the other hand, many children with hypotonia (e.g., those with Down syndrome) have a much higher threshold, thus, large amounts of sensory stimuli are needed to produce a change in muscle tone. Loud noises and sounds with sudden onset (e.g., door slamming) may increase muscle tone, while soft or soothing sounds may decrease it. Quick, jerky movements that provide visual input may increase tone, while slow, directed movements tend to reduce it. Many children are hypersensitive to touch and may attempt to move away from and/or exhibit increased muscle tone due to tactile stimulation, thus demonstrating "tactile defensiveness." Children exhibiting tactile defensiveness are particularly sensitive to light touch and rough textures. This information is used to design programs that aim at improving the child's ability to tolerate various sensory stimuli through grading techniques (Ayers, 1979; Campbell, 1985a; 1987b). Grading techniques serve to assist the child in learning to tolerate increased sensory input. Sensory experiences are provided at the child's present level of tolerance and are increased over time to enable the child to tolerate different and greater amounts of sensory input.

Information about the effects of sensory stimuli is gathered by observing children's reactions to various sensory stimuli throughout the testing sessions and by interviewing those who know the child. Direct testing to determine sensitivity to sensory input is not recommended. The child may become overly excited, frightened, and severely hypertonic (rigid) making the remainder of the testing session virtually impossible. At the least, it will make the session unpleasant and will result in an inaccurate assessment of abilities.

Environmental factors such as time of day or difficulty of the task, as well as how the child is handled or positioned, may affect muscle tone (Bobath, 1969; Bobath & Bobath, 1984; Finnie, 1975; Nwaobi, Brubaker, Cusick, & Sussman, 1983; Nwaobi, Trefler, & Hobson, 1984). In addition, the behavioral state of the child may affect muscle tone (e.g., crying increases tone), and testing conditions should be aimed at keeping the child relaxed and cooperative.

Primitive Reflexes

A reflex is an automatic, stereotyped, involuntary response to a specific environmental stimulus. In infancy, most movements are accomplished using the whole body and are controlled by primary or **primitive reflexes**. These reflexes control the distribution of muscle tone in the infant's body and may be stimulated by the position of the head and/or body. Primitive reflexes are controlled by lower centers of the brain and diminish or become inhibited by higher centers of the brain by age 4–6 months. Inhibition of reflexes allows the development of more sophisticated skills (e.g., righting and equilibrium reactions) (Florentino, 1973). If damage to the brain has occurred, the higher centers of control may be unable to inhibit the primitive reflexes, such as is the case in children with cerebral palsy. Primitive reflexes are correlated with age ranges in which they appear and disappear or become inhibited; these are displayed in Table 13.4 (p. 312). The age ranges should be used only as a general guide because individual differences in rate will occur.

Assessment of Primitive Reflexes. It is not possible to discuss the assessment procedures for all the primitive reflexes. There are a number of references that can be consulted if additional information is needed (Capute, Accardo, Vining, Rubenstein, Walcher, Harryman, & Ross, 1978; Florentino, 1973; Powell, 1981). Reflexes are tested by presenting the required environmental stimulus and observing the resultant motor response. Table 13.4 contains selected reflexes that are commonly persistent in children with neurological damage. Each reflex is accompanied by the testing procedure used and the corresponding appearance and inhibition of the reflex in normal development. When testing primitive reflexes, child state should be considered. Children who are uncooperative or crying will have reflex responses that are less consistent than children exhibiting more

relaxed and responsive behavior (Smith, Gossman, & Canan, 1982).

In children with neurological damage, some primitive reflexes may be delayed in emergence (absent), delayed in integration (persistent), or abnormal in quality (tone). Assessment of primitive reflexes should not be limited to the presence or absence of the reflex, because this provides no information on the severity of the child's neurological impairment (Florentino, 1973; André-Thomas & Saint Anne-Dargassies, 1964). Qualitative information is critical such as the consistency and intensity of the reflex (Brazelton, 1973; Chandler et al., 1980). Questions that should be answered when conducting assessments of reflexes include: Does the reflex produce an excess of hypertonia? Does the reflexive response to the stimulus occur consistently? Does the reflex control the child's movements, that is, can the child escape the static position caused by the reflex? Constant use of these primitive reflexes can prevent the development of more sophisticated motor skills and lead to structural asymmetries (Inge, 1987; Swanson, 1979).

The asymmetrical tonic neck reflex (ATNR), for example, is tested by placing the child in a supine position and turning his head first to one side and then the other. The result is flexion of the extremities on the skull side and extension of the extremities on the face side. This reflex allows the normal infant to focus optically on and discover his hand. If the reflex is elicited every time the infant's head turns, this will prevent the attainment of hands to midline for optical convergence and hand-to-mouth exploration. Persistence of the ATNR allows the infant to practice asymmetry, which results in unequal development of both sides of the body. Eventually, the asymmetries lead to structural deformities such as spinal curvatures and dislocated hips. The results of this assessment will have implications for program planning, for the child handling and positioning, and for positioning objects and persons relative to the child. Ad-

TABLE 13.4
Primitive Reflexes

Reflex	Age in Normal Development	Stimulus	Response Description
Asymmetrical tonic neck reflex (ATNR)	0 to 4 months	Turning the head to either side while supine	Extension of arm and leg on the face side and flexion of arm and leg on the skull side
Symmetrical tonic neck reflex (STNR)	2 to 4 months	Raising the head when the child is held prone over the knees or on all fours	When head is extended, extension increases in arms and flexion increases in legs. Flexing the head results in flexion of the arms and extension of the legs.
Tonic labyrinthine reflex	1 to 4 months	Placement in prone position	*Prone:* Total flexion pattern throughout body (neck, hips, arms, legs all flexed)
		Placement in supine position	*Supine:* Total extension pattern throughout body (head pushes back, back arches, arms/legs extend)
Startle reflex	normal from birth	Push child backwards while in supported sitting position or make a loud noise	Arms and legs extend and abduct

ditional information on the detrimental effects of persistent primitive reflexes can be found by consulting Inge (1987) and Utley, Holvoet, and Barnes (1977).

Automatic Postural Reactions
Automatic reactions, also referred to as the normal postural reflex mechanism (Bobath & Bobath, 1964), are automatic postural responses of the body and limbs to changes in the body's center of gravity (midline). These reactions provide the subtle, postural adjustments necessary to maintain balance while performing movements. They serve to (a) make the postural adjustments that maintain balance during movement, (b) maintain the body in alignment with itself, and (c) provide support when balance is lost.

Assessment of Automatic Postural Reactions. Automatic reactions include righting reactions, equilibrium reactions, and protective reactions (Florentino, 1973; Swanson, 1979). They are not present at birth, but emerge in relationship to developmental milestones. A child first develops the ability to maintain a posture (prone, sitting) and, through weight shift in that position, develops and perfects the balance reactions needed to maintain postural alignment in that position. Similar to the assessment of primitive reflexes, automatic reactions also are tested by providing the environmental stimulus and observing the postural response. Table 13.5 lists the age of appearance and duration of righting and equilibrium reactions, stimulus to elicit the reactions, and a description of the response if the reaction is present. Persistent primitive reflexes and abnormal tone will interfere with the emergence of automatic reactions.

Righting reactions interact with each other and work toward the establishment of normal head and body relationship in space as well as in relation to each other. They maintain the head in a vertical position relative to the midline of the body and keep the eyes horizontal to the vertical plane (midline). Righting reactions appear, then disappear (are inhibited) as higher postural reactions emerge (equilibrium and protective reactions). They are assessed by placing the child in various postures and situations that change the relationship of the positions of the head and body. These reactions initiate rolling and **rotation** of the trunk (diagonal control).

Equilibrium reactions are compensatory movements of the trunk and limbs in

TABLE 13.5
Righting and Equilibrium Reactions

Reaction	Age in Normal Development	Stimulus	Response Description
Neck righting reaction	Birth to 4 months	Turning head to the side in supine	Body rotates as a unit toward the side to which head is turned (log roll)
Body righting reaction acting on the body	6–8 months to 36 months	Turning head to the side in supine	Body rotates in segments using trunk rotation toward the side to which head is turned
Body righting reaction acting on the head	4–6 months to 1–5 years	Place child's feet on ground or roll to side on firm surface	Head "rights" itself in space in midline
Equilibrium reaction, prone	4–6 months, normal for life	Position in prone on tilt board and tilt to one side	Head bends, body arches toward the raised side with arms/legs extended and abducted
Equilibrium reaction, supine	7–10 months, normal for life	Position in supine on tilt board and tilt to one side	Head bends, body arches toward the raised side with arms/legs extended and abducted

TABLE 13.5
Continued

Reaction	Age in Normal Development	Stimulus	Response Description
Equilibrium reaction, quadrapedal	10–12 months, normal for life	Position on hands and knees, tilt gently to one side	Arm and leg on raised side extend and abduct, other arm extends in protective reaction
Equilibrium reaction, sitting	12–14 months, normal for life	Gently push to one side in sitting position	Head moves toward raised side, arms/legs extend and abduct
		Push backward	Head, shoulders, and arms move forward; legs extend
		Push forward	Legs flex, spine and neck extend, arms extend back in protective reaction
Equilibrium reaction, standing	12–18 months, normal for life	Position in standing, extend/pull outward on either arm	Opposite arm and leg extend and abduct, head "rights" to maintain position in space
		Hold child under arms in standing position and tilt backward	Head, shoulders, and arms move forward; feet point upward flexing at ankles

response to changes in the body's center of gravity caused by displacement of the body or the body's supporting surface (Swanson, 1979). They result from "the interplay between stability [posture] and mobility [movement]" (Campbell, 1982, p. 6) and allow the body to maintain balance. In normal development, equilibrium reactions emerge during the first year and continue throughout life. Equilibrium reactions are tested by disrupting the child's balance and observing her attempts to regain and maintain balance. The best way to test for equilibrium reactions is to place the child on a tilt (vestibular) board in prone, supine, sitting, and standing positions. As the examiner tilts the board first to one side and then the other, facilitating a full weight shift, the child should exhibit flexion of the head and trunk and extension of the arm and leg on the higher (raised) side of the board. If a tilt board is not available, testing can be done by placing the child in the test positions on the floor while the examiner disrupts her balance directly.

Protective reactions are movements of the extremities that assist in preventing or breaking a fall. Protective **extension** is tested by rapidly shifting the child's weight to each side, front, and back while she is in a sitting position. The normal response is extension and abduction (movement of the limbs away from the midline) of the arms as the child attempts to break the fall by supporting herself with an open hand. This response is also seen in the lower extremities when the child is lowered rapidly to the floor feet first, when the legs show abduction (legs spread apart).

Posture and Volitional Movements

"On the foundation of normal muscle tone and postural reactions, a child builds increasingly complex volitional motor skills which are measured by many developmental scales" (Swanson, 1979, p. 88). **Volitional movements** are cognitively directed voluntary movements such as reaching, walking, and grasping, and **transitional movements** such as pulling to stand, sitting from standing, and rotation to sitting. Posture provides the antigravity background positions (stability) from which automatic and volitional movements occur.

Most assessments of motor skills focus on the number of developmental milestones that have been attained by a particular child, giving little or no attention to the way in which postures and movements are performed. The current trend in assessing children with atypical muscle tone includes a description of both the form or *quality* of posture and **movement patterns** as well as the function or purpose of the movement (Campbell, 1987b; Swanson, 1979). For example, a child may be able to maintain a sitting position (function), but may be relying on increased muscle tone or proximal joint fixations to maintain the sitting position (quality). Enabling children to make gains in motor development requires the facilitation of postures and movement patterns that are of a more normal quality.

In working with children who have neuromotor disabilities, it is important to be concerned with the quality of the postural and movement patterns. The interventionist must be able to analyze posture and movement patterns to identify missing and/or atypical components in order to plan appropriate motor programs.

Analysis of posture and movement requires an understanding of (a) normal motor development, (b) atypical motor development,

(c) the functional relationship between abnormal muscle tone and resultant deviations in posture and movement patterns, and (d) movement terminology that is used by therapists. This section of the chapter is not intended to make the reader a therapist or motor specialist. Rather, the intent is to provide special educators and other professionals with enough information about movement analysis to recognize abnormal postural and movement patterns and to request consultation services or direct therapy for identified children. In addition, an understanding of abnormal movement patterns is needed to identify and correctly implement handling, positioning, and specific intervention strategies.

Assessment of Posture and Volitional Movements. When assessing posture and movement, primary attention should be given to the way the child uses the movement components to maintain antigravity postures and perform volitional movements (Campbell, 1985a). Infants and children with abnormal posture and movement are likely to demonstrate proximal fixations to compensate for the lack of normal muscle tone. Typical patterns that are demonstrated by children with cerebral palsy are contained in Table 13.6 (pp. 316–317). This list should *not* be used to assess children for the presence of specific proximal adjustments; it is provided as a guide in describing the typical proximal adjustments that may be observed and as an example of the application of movement terminology to specific problems of posture and movement that are frequently encountered.

According to Campbell (1985a, 1987b), an assessment of posture and movement should answer the following questions:

1. What are the child's problem areas (typically proximal), such as the head/neck, shoulder, arm(s), pelvis, leg(s), and trunk, and under what gravitational conditions?
2. What are the compensatory patterns, caused by the proximal adjustments,

that are used in postural alignment and movement patterns (automatic and volitional or goal-directed movements)?

3. What components of mature movement (extension, **symmetry, independent movements,** rotation) is the child missing that prevent optimal skill performance?

4. What muscular or orthopedic changes are present or may develop in the future due to continued use of compensatory patterns?

5. What are possible intervention strategies for these problems?

These questions are answered through a movement analysis of the muscular components of postural and movement patterns while simultaneously observing changes in muscle tone. Children's spontaneous postures and movements should be observed in environments in which they usually function. If possible, it is helpful to have a familiar person (e.g., teacher, parent) assist with the assessment or act as the facilitator. The assessment should be conducted in the context of functional activities and play situations, using toys and objects that are appropriate for the child's functioning level. These items should be motivating and facilitate a variety of postures and movements for analysis. The child should be observed while moving on the floor, interacting with objects, moving from

TABLE 13.6

Examples of Typical Proximal Adjustments that Contribute to Abnormal Postures and Movement Patterns

Proximal Adjustment	Description	Compensatory Patterns	Consequences
Neck			
Neck hyperextension	Absence of head/neck flexion; cannot bring head to midline; does not tuck chin in supine or forearm propping; may push back with head	Relies on hyperextension of head/neck to raise head in prone; elevates shoulders to stabilize head in upright position in prone and from supine to sitting; prevents normal head and neck movements	Normal range of motion of scapula impaired, thus development of upper extremities is prevented; shortened neck extensors; lack of neck flexion (chin tuck); inability to close mouth, jaw juts forward
Head and Neck Asymmetry	No symmetrical use of head/neck flexors results in inability to bring or maintain head in midline, which results in continued domination by ATNR	Due to domination by ATNR, must rely on unilateral upper extremities swiping/ reaching on extension side; decreased bilateral upper extremities function; misses optical convergence and coordination that comes with midline orientation of head, forced to use lateral or uncoordinated ocular movements	Poor use of bilateral upper extremities resulting in lack of body exploration, poor hand-to-mouth play resulting in lack of normalization of oral sensitivity, and poor ocular control resulting in poor visual perception; continued ATNR sets stage for scoliosis and hip dislocation on flexed side due to constant rotation of pelvis in this position

TABLE 13.6
Continued

Proximal Adjustment	Description	Compensatory Patterns	Consequences
Shoulders	Scapular instability; scapular winging while on forearms in prone position or inability to bear weight on forearms; lack of independent/ dissociated humeral movements	In prone position, uses scapular adduction and spinal extension to elevate trunk; stabilizes humerus close to sides of trunk and bears weight on pronated forearms	Scapular instability and tightness (muscle shortening); poor development of upper extremities (forearms will be pronated or internally rotated at elbows, feeds into ulnar deviation of hand due to weight bearing in abnormal position); poor upper extremity weight bearing in prone and creeping positions; poor protective extension; poorly coordinated reach, grasp, and manipulation patterns
Pelvis/Hips			
Anterior pelvic tilt	Anterior pelvic tilt is not balanced by flexion components (posterior pelvic tilt) due to abdominals not developing to posteriorly tilted pelvis and elongated lumbar extensors (lower back); prevents practice of lateral weight shifting in prone position and interferes with development of normal righting reactions	Child maintains frog-legged position while prone to control or prevent lateral weight shifting when attempts are made to reach while lying prone	Frog-legged position while prone increases flexion, abduction, and external rotation of hips; decreases extension, adduction and internal rotation of hips (reinforces total pattern and prevents development of complimentary movement patterns) when weight shifts in prone position; normal development of lower extremities is impeded in frog-legged position
Posterior pelvic tilt	Presence of abnormally strong extension in lumbar with extension of hips and adduction of legs in prone position; limited hip mobility in flexion and abduction with inactive abdominals	Loss of function in lower extremities due to excessive extension; uses other available movements for mobility (usually upper extremities— diplegia)	Tight hip extensors prevent flexion at hips and subsequent rounding of lumbar spine and thoracic spine in sitting position; tight hip extensors also cause increased knee flexion

one place to another, moving from one posture to another (transitional movements), and while positioned in adaptive equipment.

When assessing postural control and volitional movements, consideration should be given to the children's posture and the quality of their movement patterns. The components of mature movement (symmetry, extension, independent movements, rotation) should be used as a guide in describing movement patterns. The volitional movements to be observed are shown in Table 13.7 and are organized according to the position of the child during testing. Observations should be made with the child in various positions. The examiner should focus on each body part, paying close attention to the position of the head. Proximal body parts (e.g., shoulders, hips/pelvis) should be observed before more distal body parts (e.g., arms/hands, legs/feet).

TABLE 13.7
Assessment Variables for Conducting Observations of Volitional Movements

Position	Variables
Supine	What postural asymmetries are present during active movement (head, trunk, pelvis, extremities)?
	What is the posture and movement of the arms and legs?
	Can the child raise her head? How does the child perform this movement?
	Can the child roll to prone? How does the child perform this movement?
	Can the child pull to a sitting position? How does the child perform this movement?
	Does the child have adequate hand functions in this position? How does she perform these movements?
Prone	What postural asymmetries are present during active movement (head, trunk, pelvis, extremities)?
	What is the posture and movement of the arms and legs?
	Can the child raise his head? How does the child perform this movement?
	Can the child use his forearms and/or extended arms for support? How does the child perform this movement?
	Can the child reach out using weight shift and trunk rotation? How does the child perform this movement?
	Can the child roll to supine? How does the child perform this movement?
	What mode of mobility does the child use to progress on the floor? How does the child perform this movement?
	Can the child assume an all-fours position (on hands and knees)? Can the child move from this position to sitting? How does the child perform these movements?
	Does the child have adequate hand functions in this position? How does the child perform these movements?

TABLE 13.7
Continued

Position	Variables
Sitting	What is the position of the child's pelvis, trunk/spine, shoulders, head, arms, and legs in long sitting, side sitting (check both sides), Indian sitting, and sitting in a chair (regular chair, highchair, adapted chair, wheelchair, etc.)?
	Can the child assume these sitting positions unassisted? How does the child perform these movements?
	Does the child have adequate hand functions in these various sitting positions? How does the child perform these movements?
Standing/Walking	Can the child move from all fours to upright kneeling (on both knees), half kneeling (on one knee), then to standing? How does the child perform these movements (e.g., weight shifting)?
	Can the child assume standing from the floor, squatting, chair/wheelchair?
	What is the position of the pelvis, trunk, shoulders, head, arms, and legs while standing (e.g., equal weight bearing, body alignment)?
	Can the child walk? How does the child perform this movement (e.g., weight shift, equal weight bearing, trunk rotation, body alignment, posture)?

Table 13.8 (p. 320) contains a list of questions to serve as a guide when assessing posture and is organized by areas of the body.

The results of an assessment of posture and movement are descriptive in nature and should describe how the child uses movement components to attain and maintain postures and accomplish goal-directed movements. Pictures, drawings, or slides may be included to provide additional information and documentation of postural and movement problems (Campbell, 1985a; Haring, 1976). If direct observation is not possible, reports from others can be used or an analysis can be conducted using videotaped samples of postures and motor behaviors.

Fine Motor Skills

Children with delayed gross motor development likely will be delayed in developing **fine motor skills**. Also, children with abnormal muscle tone who exhibit atypical motor development will have even more difficulties in performing fine motor tasks. Tasks, such as building block towers and putting puzzles together, which require the intergration of gross motor, fine motor, and visual and cognitive skills, will not be included here. Emphasis will be placed on those fine motor behaviors (grasp, release, reach, transport) that comprise a variety of other useful tasks (e.g., writing, turning the pages of a book, unbuttoning/buttoning a shirt).

Assessment of Fine Motor Skills. Assessments of fine motor skills are generally conducted using developmental tests and checklists. Although this information is useful in determining a child's level of proficiency in fine motor skills, no attention is given to the quality (form) of the child's fine motor pat-

TABLE 13.8
Guiding Questions to Assess Posture in Various Positions

Body areas	Observation questions
Head	Positioned in midline? Positioned predominantly to one side?
Neck	Clearly visible, front and back? Hyperextended, visible just in front?
Shoulders	Elevated? Retracted? (pulled back) Protracted? (pushed forward)
Scapula	Stabilized? Hypermobile or unstable?
Arms	Internally rotated? Externally rotated?
Elbows	Flexed, extended?
Forearms	Pronated, supinated?
Wrists	Flexed, extended?
Hands	Open, fisted?
Trunk	Symmetrical? Asymmetrical? "Short" (laterally flexed) to which side? Does asymmetry change with positioning of the head?
Pelvis/Hips	Flexed? Extended? Dislocated? (ask therapist or parent) Pelvis tilted back? (posterior pelvic tilt) Pelvis tilted forward? (anterior pelvic tilt)
Legs	Internally rotated? (scissoring) Externally rotated? (frogging)
Knees	Flexed? Extended?
Feet	Plantarflexion, neutral, dorsiflexion?
Other	Contractures and deformities?

terns. In assessing fine motor skills, the examiner should conduct a systematic observation of how well children use fine motor skills in needed tasks (e.g., play, eating/drinking). Whenever possible, assessments should be conducted in natural contexts and daily activities. Particular attention should be given to foundational skills related to the development of fine motor skills: vision, head and trunk control, and upper extremity function. The assessment of fine motor skills can be completed while conducting the assessment of posture and volitional movements and should not be conducted in isolation, separate from the total motor evaluation. The child's posture and overall movement patterns will have direct bearing on the quality of hand function. Thus, assessments should be conducted in conjuction with the assessment of posture and volitional movements. Portions of the observation methods contained in Tables 13.7 and 13.8 should be used because they relate directly to the assessment of hand function.

Vision plays a vital role in the development of fine motor skills. It allows the child to locate an object and provides vital information related to motivation to reach and grasp the object. Vision is not a precursor to the development of fine motor skills, since children who are visually impaired do acquire fine motor skills. But, the process is facilitated when vision is intact by providing a visual motivation to reach. Children with specific motor disabilities may have adequate vision, yet may be unable to use their vision functionally due to poor head control or the inability to coordinate the movements of their eyes bilaterally due to muscle imbalance. This difficulty will have an impact on their ability to locate an object visually. Thus, the variables of head and occular control should be assessed to determine their impact on fine motor development.

The ability to reach and transport an object (e.g., spoon) is more of a gross motor skill of the upper extremities than a fine motor skill. However, it is important to understand that development of hand functions such as grasp and release are dependent on the ability to reach and transport. In this case, the child must have the ability to maintain a stable background posture (using head control, trunk control, and symmetry), to control leaning forward at the trunk, to use weight shift and trunk rotation to free the reaching arm, and to dissociate the humerus (upper arm) from the shoulder girdle.

Grasp and release are critical components of fine motor skills. Figure 13.2 shows the sequential development of grasp (Erhardt, 1974; 1982). A description of each type of grasp is included to assist in assessing the components that comprise particular grasp patterns. Tests of fine motor skills do not include assessment variables related to reach and transport or quality indicators of grasp and release. The quality of grasp and release behaviors will be directly related to (a) overall muscle tone in the body, (b) overall body position and control, (c) the position and function of the shoulder girdle, and (d) the position of the forearm (pronated or supinated). The results will have direct implication for (a) how the child is to be handled and positioned to facilitate upper extremity and hand function, and (b) the specific physical guidance techniques that will be used in teaching fine motor skills. The examiner should observe how well the child uses fine motor components such as extension, flexion, and dissociation of the wrist and fingers of the hand, and adduction and dissociation of the thumb from the hand.

From the results of the assessment of fine motor skills, intervention programs will be formulated to improve hand function. However, if activities to develop fine motor skills are conducted in isolation with no attention given to the child's muscle tone and overall movement patterns, little success will be realized. Children with severe motor disabilities (e.g., severe hypertonia/spasticity) will have considerable deficits in the development of fine motor skills. An occupational therapist should be consulted when working with these children. Some children may require such adaptive equipment as hand splints

to reduce tone in the hand and to prevent the hand from being maintained in a fisted position. Also, assistive devices may be needed, such as adaptive switches used with battery-operated toys or spoons with built-up handles to aid the child with a weak grasp.

Representative Methods for Assessing Motor skills

Physical and occupational therapists have primary responsibility for assessing motor skills, particularly when the child has an identified motor disability. Several types of tests may be used to accomplish this task, including norm-, criterion-, and curriculum-referenced measures of motor skills. When assessing children with motor disabilities, these measures will need to be supplemented with qualitative information derived from direct observations that have been discussed in the previous sections.

Choosing an Appropriate Assessment Instrument

The following questions concerning the purpose of the assessment should serve to guide the examiner in determining the test instruments that will be used.

1. Is the purpose of the assessment to screen for delays in motor development so that further assessment can be conducted if needed?
2. Is the purpose of the assessment to identify and diagnose infants or children with delays in motor development so that services can be provided?
3. Is the purpose of the assessment to determine a child's present level of functioning in terms of strengths and weakness, movement problems, or functional skills to determine appropriate goals and design intervention programs?
4. Is the purpose of the assessment to evaluate child progress or for program evaluation purposes?

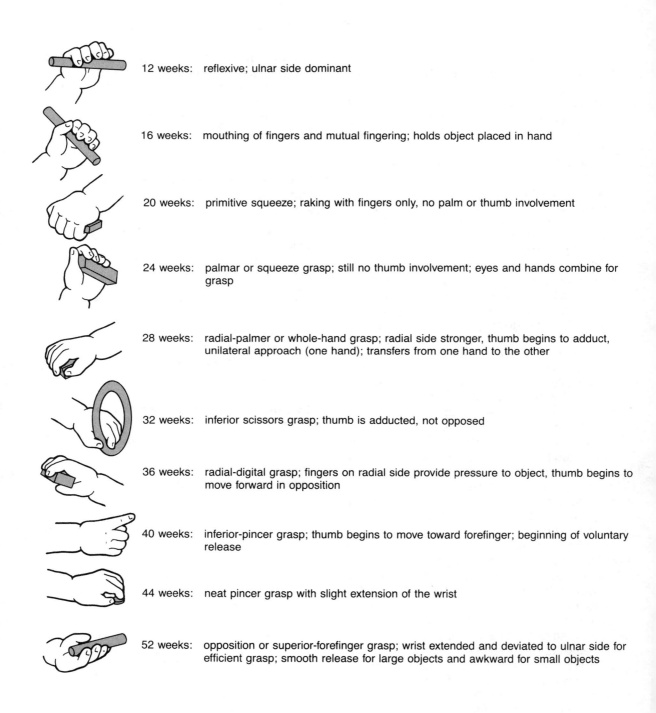

12 weeks: reflexive; ulnar side dominant

16 weeks: mouthing of fingers and mutual fingering; holds object placed in hand

20 weeks: primitive squeeze; raking with fingers only, no palm or thumb involvement

24 weeks: palmar or squeeze grasp; still no thumb involvement; eyes and hands combine for grasp

28 weeks: radial-palmer or whole-hand grasp; radial side stronger, thumb begins to adduct, unilateral approach (one hand); transfers from one hand to the other

32 weeks: inferior scissors grasp; thumb is adducted, not opposed

36 weeks: radial-digital grasp; fingers on radial side provide pressure to object, thumb begins to move forward in opposition

40 weeks: inferior-pincer grasp; thumb begins to move toward forefinger; beginning of voluntary release

44 weeks: neat pincer grasp with slight extension of the wrist

52 weeks: opposition or superior-forefinger grasp; wrist extended and deviated to ulnar side for efficient grasp; smooth release for large objects and awkward for small objects

FIGURE 13.2
Sequential Development of Grasp

Once these questions have been answered, the type of test instrument can be chosen. No test of movement or motor skills has been standardized on infants and children with motor disabilities. Table 13.9 contains a list of the most widely used assessment instruments for assessing motor skills. These tests have been organized according to the purposes of assessment. A more specific critique of a number of these tests has been outlined elsewhere (Langley, 1977).

Translating Assessment Information into Instructional Goals

Interpreting the Results of a Motor Assessment

The interpretation of a child's motor assessment requires that the information collected from developmental tests; observations of muscle tone, primitive reflexes, and automatic reactions; and analysis of posture and movements be organized to provide a clear picture of the child's abilities and needs. Also, this information should be organized to describe the child's overall development of motor skills and the attainment of useful skills in other domains. The following questions have been formulated to serve as a guide in organizing the results of the motor assessment to assist in planning instructional goals (Bobath, 1963; Bobath & Bobath, 1984; Campbell, 1985a; 1987b; Swanson, 1979):

1. What type of muscle tone does the child exhibit (both underlying and predominant), and how is it distributed throughout the body?
2. What factors appear to influence muscle tone (e.g., gravity or position, sensory stimuli, environmental factors, handling and positioning, and child state)?
3. What residual primitive reflexes are present that control the child's attempts at movement and/or prevent the attainment of higher-level motor skills such as

automatic reactions and goal-directed movements?
4. What automatic postural reactions are missing that prevent the child from maintaining postural alignment or balance while performing volitional movements?
5. What abnormal proximal adjustments and compensatory movement patterns is the child using to attain postures and perform movements? What are the consequences of these compensations on future motor development?
6. What normal movement components is the child missing? Has the child developed normal patterns of antigravity extension, and is extension counterbalanced by antigravity flexion? Is symmetry present in the development of both sides of the body? If not, what asymmetries exist? Has the child developed trunk rotation? Can the child dissociate and isolate body parts to perform independent movements?
7. What secondary changes (e.g., muscles shortening or lengthening, contractures, deformities) have occurred or are likely to occur in the future, and how will these affect motor development?
8. What other areas of development are delayed (e.g., fine motor, cognitive, communication, play, social, and self-care skills), and are these delays primarily related to the deficits in motoric functioning?
9. What critical, useful skills (e.g., head control, postural stability and balance, reach, grasp, manipulation, mobility) are missing that are needed across curricular domains?

Therapists, early childhood special educators, and parents should share assessment information and work together to determine the answers to these questions. This interaction increases the probability that all persons involved in the planning process consider the child as a whole instead of each viewing the

TABLE 13.9
Common Tests Used to Assess Motor Skills

Purpose/Instruments	Age Range (years)	Motor Areas Assessed	Unique Aspects
Screening			
Denver Developmental Screening Test (Frankenburg & Dodds, 1967)	0–6	Gross motor, fine motor–adaptive	Norm-referenced; uses observation or parent interview format; good reliability but validity questioned; profiles scored as normal, abnormal, questionable, untestable; less reliable and sensitive for children 0–30 months; includes prescreening questionnaire
Developmental Profile II (Alpern, Boll, & Shearer, 1980)	0–9	Physical age: Gross and fine motor (coordination, strength, stamina, flexibility, skills)	Standardized functional assessment for screening purposes; interview or direct testing may be used; good reliability and validity; easily and accurately completed by parent
Milani-Comparetti Motor Development Screening Test (Milani-Comparetti & Gidoni, 1967)	0–2	Postural control; active movement; primitive reflexes; righting reactions; parachute reactions; tilting reactions	Quick screening for motor delays and disabilities; intervals are provided for regular follow along; administered by therapist or trained professional
Diagnostic			
Battelle Developmental Inventory (Newborg et al., 1984)	0–8	Motor domain: Muscle control, body coordination, locomotion, fine motor, perceptual motor	Includes procedures for direct testing; interview and observation methods are included for many items; easy-to-follow instructions; norm-referenced; includes adaptations for sensory-impaired and multi-handicapped children; includes screening test
Bayley Scales of Infant Development (Bayley, 1969)	0–2½	Bayley motor scales: Gross motor, fine motor	Norm-referenced; provides developmental motor age; norms established for 2–30 months; widely used to determine developmental delays;

324

TABLE 13.9
Continued

Purpose/Instruments	Age Range (years)	Areas Assessed	Unique Aspects
			provides no information on quality of movement; good reliability and validity; requires training to administer
Early Learning Accomplishment Profile (Glover, Preminger, & Sanford, 1978)	0–3	Gross motor; fine motor	Criterion-referenced; indicates presence, absence, or emergence of skills; widely used in interdisciplinary settings; developmentally sequenced; each item includes testing procedure and description of correct response
Movement Assessment of Infants (Chandler, Andrews, & Swanson, 1980)	0–1	Muscle tone; primitive reflexes; automatic reactions; volitional movements	Provides quantitative information on the degree of motor dysfunction related to test items; used to identify motor dysfunction in infants and at-risk infants; includes easy-to-follow, step-by-step procedures for each item; administered by therapist or trained interventionist
Programming Adaptive Performance Instrument (CAPE, 1980)	0–9	Reflexes and reactions; physical intactness; gross motor; fine motor	Assessment adaptations included for motorically sensory impaired; includes a section that describes deformities
Brigance Diagnostic Inventory of Early Development (Brigance, 1978)	0–6	Preambulatory motor skills and behaviors; gross motor skills; fine motor skills	Criterion-referenced; provisions for tracking progress; skill sequences are task analyzed; easily administered
Callier-Azusa Scale (Stillman, 1978)	0–6	Motor development: Postural control, locomotion; fine motor, visual motor	Based on longitudinal observation of child behavior; specifically for use with deaf/blind and multihandicapped children; criterion-referenced; developmentally sequenced

325

TABLE 13.9
Continued

Purpose/Instruments	Age Range (years)	Areas Assessed	Unique Aspects
Carolina Curriculum for Handicapped Infants (Johnson-Martin, Jens, & Attermeier, 1979)	0–2	Tactile integration and manipulation; feeding; reaching and grasping; object manipulation; bilateral hand activity; gross motor: Prone, supine, and upright	Curriculum-referenced check-sheet; curriculum sequences provided for each skill; good task analyses of skills arranged in developmental sequences
Developmental Programming for Infants (Revised) (Schafer & Moersch, 1981)		Gross motor; perceptual/fine motor	Curriculum-referenced; includes stimulation activities to be used by teacher or parents; includes curriculum adaptations for motorically impaired children; indicates presence, absence, or emergence of behaviors
Hawaii Early Learning Profile (HELP) (Furuno, O'Reilly, Hosaka, Inatsuka, Allman, & Zeisloft, 1979)	0–3	Gross motor; fine motor	Curriculum-referenced; provides developmental profile; useful in program planning; qualitative descriptions of each item are provided; teaching activities are provided for each item
Peabody Developmental Motor Scales (Folio & DuBose, 1974)	0–7	Gross motor; fine motor	Curriculum-referenced; five criteria are used to rate child's performance on each item (total dependence to complete independence); provides developmental motor age for both gross and fine motor skills; includes teaching activities; provides description of performance of each item
Prescriptive Behavioral Checklist for the Severely and Profoundly Retarded (Popovich, 1977)	Not applicable	Motor development: Head and trunk control, sitting, hand-knee position, standing, eye-hand coordination	Objectives, task analysis, and teaching procedures for all items; includes section on writing behavioral objectives; curriculum-referenced; checklist provides no qualitative criteria for motor performance

TABLE 13.9
Continued

Purpose/Instruments	Age Range (years)	Areas Assessed	Unique Aspects
Programmed Environments Curriculum (Tawney, Knapp, O'Reilly, & Pratt, 1979)	Not applicable	Fine motor; gross motor	Curriculum-referenced; designed specifically for children with severe or multiple disabilities; Provides objectives, skill sequences, and teaching methods for functional skills in each domain; includes some qualitative descriptions in skill sequences; behavioral approach to instruction is used
RISE: Computerized Checklist & Curriculum for the Motorically Delayed/Impaired Child (Holder, Wells, & Cook, 1985)	Not applicable	Physical management; reflex integration; reflex development; oral motor development	Curriculum-referenced; specifically designed for children with motor delays or disabilities; administered by therapists or trained early interventionist; step-by-step instructions to administer; scored on qualitative indicators; curriculum corresponds with each item on checklist; curriculum stresses equipment usage, positioning, handling, direct intervention activities aimed at tone normalization, inhibition of persisting primitive reflexes, and facilitation of automatic and voluntary movements
The Teaching Research Curriculum for Moderately and Severely Handicapped (Fredericks et al., 1976, 1980)	Not applicable	Gross motor (1980); fine motor (1980); Motor development skills (1976)	Curriculum-referenced; used with infants and children with delays, motor disabilities, and multiple disabilities; includes placement test and corresponding behavioral objectives and skill phases to be taught; skill phases provide useful instructional methods and activities; behavioral approach used in instructional procedures

child from her particular perspective and that an appropriate and comprehensive intervention plan is developed.

Identifying Appropriate Goals for Intervention

General Goals of Intervention. The general goals of intervention for children with movement disorders are as follows:

1. To obtain more normal muscle tone as a foundation for developing more normal movement: reduce, increase, or regulate muscle tone.
2. To inhibit primitive reflexes, abnormal postures, and abnormal movement patterns or compensatory movements.
3. To facilitate the development of automatic reactions, more normal postures, and movement patterns.
4. To develop and/or improve the performance quality of important voluntary movement patterns (e.g., head control, sitting, manipulation), thus increasing the acquisition of useful skills and promoting independence and skill performance across domains.
5. To interrupt the sequence of abnormal motor development, including the prevention of secondary muscle changes, contractures, and deformities.
6. To teach others the necessary handling, positioning, facilitation techniques, and physical guidance procedures to ensure optimal and consistent management of the child.

These goals of intervention for children with movement disorders are primarily based on the neurodevelopmental treatment (NDT) approach or "the Bobath method" (Bobath, 1963; 1969; Bobath & Bobath, 1964; 1984) and related works (Campbell, 1982; 1985b; Finnie, 1975; Harris, 1980; 1981; Harris & Tada, 1983). The NDT approach is the most

widely used method in treating children with various types of cerebral palsy and is based on many years of clinical intervention. It is also appropriate for use with infants and children who exhibit hypotonia related to Down syndrome (Hanson & Harris, 1986; Harris, 1981), severely retarded children (Ellis, 1967), as well as blind or deaf children (Bobath & Bobath, 1964).

There is no "cure-all" therapy; intervention programs may be drawn from a number of approaches including sensorimotor (Rood, 1954; 1956), sensory integration (Ayers, 1979), and proprioceptive neuromuscular facilitation (Knott & Voss, 1968). However, the approach used should both relate directly to the acquisition of motor skills that build on the attainment of useful skills across curricular domains and include intervention methods that are easily integrated into daily routines in the classroom and at home. If an intervention method is recommended that does not logically relate to improving performance in the children's daily environments, the practicality and feasibility of the intervention should be questioned.

Specific Goals of Intervention

Each child's program must be designed individually based on his unique needs. A physical or occupational therapist is most qualified to make these decisions. Having the services of a well-trained developmental therapist should be a funding priority for early intervention and preschool programs that serve children with motor disabilities.

Because the motor behavior and movement problems of different infants and children are very dissimilar, it is impossible to describe the goals of intervention for each specific problem. However, it is important to have a general understanding of the treatment goals based on a child's particular movement problems. Table 13.10 contains the goals of intervention based on type and distribution of abnormal muscle tone. Again,

TABLE 13.10
Goals of Intervention Based on Motor Problem

Problem	Goals	Inhibit/Discourage	Facilitate/Encourage
Spastic diplegia and quadriplegia	Increase variety of postures and movements; increase movement in wide ranges; prevent muscle and joint tightness; increase interaction with objects by improving reach, grasp, and manipulation of objects; dissociation increase opportunity to experience normal movement	Hypertonia; "W" sitting; bunny hopping or commando crawling as form of mobility; total patterns of either flexion or extension of extremities; primitive reflexes; internal rotation of extremities; pronation of forearms and fisting of hands; associated reactions	Extension and active rotation of trunk; abduction and external rotation of extremities; weight bearing with good body alignment (symmetry) in all postures; weight shift in all postures and planes to develop automatic reactions; Mobility with good movement quality or provide alternate form of mobility; independent movements through dissociation; supination of forearms and open hands
Hemiplegia	Same as above for involved side; increase bilateral trunk and extremity development; increase functional use of involved side	Hypertonia in involved side; asymmetry of trunk and extremities on involved side; associated reactions of extremities on involved side; use of lateral trunk flexion on involved side, shortening of trunk on involved side; "half-run" gait (walks quickly to keep balance); volitional movements performed using uninvolved side or in direction of uninvolved side (exclusively); pronation of forearm and fisting of hand on involved side; internal rotation of extremities on involved side	Active trunk rotation and elongation of involved side; weight bearing with good alignment of involved side in all postures; weight shift to involved side in all postures to develop automatic reactions on that side; bilateral movements of extremities; volitional movements of both sides of the body performed in both directions (e.g., rolling); dissociation of involved leg from pelvis/hip to promote independent movements of lower extremity; abduction and external rotation of extremities on involved side; supination of forearms and open hand on involved side

TABLE 13.10
Continued

Problem	Goals	Inhibit/Discourage	Facilitate/Encourage
Athetosis	Increase coordination in midranges; improve trunk control; improve head control particularly in midline; minimize involuntary movements (Caution: spasticity usually increases with age); control amount of environmental/sensory stimuli; improve proximal stability and control in midranges; regulate tone; increase ability to grade movements	Associated reactions, primitive reflexes, bunny hopping, "W" sitting, tone fluctuations	Automatic reactions (particularly equilibrium reactions to assist in maintaining balance); head and trunk control; weight bearing in all positions; slow, graded weight shift when posture can be sustained; midline activities
Hypotonia	Improve head and trunk control; increase muscle tone and improve tone in trunk; increase active involvement in all activities	Hypermobility of joints; total patterns of flexion, abduction, and external rotation; primitive reflexes	Activities aimed at increasing muscle tone; proprioceptive sensation and stability in joints; proximal stability through weight-bearing experiences; active trunk extension and use of abdominals; equilibrium and protective reactions; active involvement in all activities; active extension and adduction of extremities

remember that children will exhibit a unique combination of postural and movement problems, and this information should not be used as a "cookbook" in planning motor programs based on a child's particular diagnostic label. Instead, this information has been included to provide an overall picture of common motor problems, and how they relate to intervention.

Integrating Motor Goals into Functional Activities

Motor skills should be developed within the context of purposeful activities and daily routines as much as possible. The development of motor skills within the context of functional activities is based on the following guiding principles:

1. **Integrated therapy** (incorporates therapeutic techniques into educational and daily activities) is more effective than isolated therapy (traditional therapy approach where therapeutic techniques are implemented in isolation) in acquiring useful skills (Giangreco, 1986).

2. The use of distributed trials increases the number of opportunities that children have to develop and practice particular motor skills, resulting in more rapid acquisition of some motor skills (Chasey, 1976; Holvoet, Guess, Mulligan, & Brown, 1980).

3. Teaching motor skills in context should promote generalization of the motor skills across persons, settings, and activities (Mulligan, Guess, Holvoet, & Brown, 1980).

4. The provision of naturally occurring reinforcers within functional activities (e.g., interaction with objects and persons) enhances motivation and desired consequences to produce movement (Campbell, 1987b; Campbell, McInerny, & Cooper, 1984).

5. Infants and young children with movement problems "need to acquire movement concepts rather than isolated movement skills for a movement pattern to be functional" (Campbell et al., 1984, p. 599).

6. The integration of therapeutic intervention techniques into routine caretaking activities (e.g., diapering, dressing, feeding) and activities of daily living (e.g., toileting, eating/drinking, self-dressing) is a more efficient use of instructional time (McCormick & Goldman, 1979).

7. The use of preparation techniques such as handling and positioning can normalize muscle tone (Finn, 1985; Nwaobi et al., 1983; Nwaobi et al., 1984), improve upper extremity function (Nwaobi, Hobson, & Trefler, 1985), and head and trunk control (Trefler, Nickey, & Hobson, 1983); improve performance of functional activities such as eating and drinking (Hulme, Shaver, Acher, Mullette, & Eggert, 1987) and communication (McEwen, 1987; Smith, Holder-Brown, & Nwaobi, 1988); and enhance children's general medical/physical status (Bardsley, 1984; Nwaobi & Smith, 1986).

Programming for infants and young children with movement problems should include both direct instruction and physical management programs (Campbell, 1987b). Direct instruction involves teaching the child a new skill by using specialized **physical guidance** techniques (Campbell, 1987b; Campbell & Stewart, 1986). This may occur in one-on-one interaction between the child and the early interventionist or in the context of functional activities that occur throughout the day. **Physical management** programs are implemented to handle the child in ways that normalize muscle tone and prevent the development of secondary changes of muscles, joints, and bones; to maintain body alignment, which is directly related to tone normalization; and to move and position the child in ways that facilitate carry-over of therapeutic intervention into functional activities (Campbell, 1987a). The use of physical management techniques increases the opportunities that the child has to experience more normal muscle tone, good body alignment, and the sensation of more normal movement patterns.

Three procedures that may be used to incorporate movement goals into functional activities will be presented. The first procedure involves the integration of physical management and direct instruction of motor skills into naturally occurring contexts in daily routines. The child's daily schedule (in the classroom and at home) should be analyzed to determine the age-appropriate activities (e.g., play, cognitive, readiness skills) and functional activities (e.g., self-care, mobility, communication) that occur within the child's daily routine (Holvoet et al., 1980). Physical management and direct intervention are in-

NEURODEVELOPMENTAL EDUCATIONAL PLAN

Student: _____   Teacher/Therapist: _____

Birthdate/Age: _____   Date plan initiated: _____

Learning Objective(s):_____

_____

_____

Movement Objective(s): _____

_____

_____

_____

Learning Task:	Required Movement Components:	Movement Problems:

Optimal Position:	Optimal Equipment:	Materials:	Movement Transitions:

Alternate Position:	Alternate Equipment:	Materials:	Movement Transitions:

FIGURE 13.3

Neurodevelopmental Educational Plan (Source: *From* The neurodevelopmental educational plan: A model for teachers of the movement impaired. *S. Burton and M. B. Langley, November, 1987. Paper presented at Weekend with the Experts for Teachers of the Visually Impaired, Orlando, FL. Used with permission.)*

tegrated (as much as possible) within the context and activity during which they occur. Several examples include incorporating trunk rotation in diapering, carrying, locomotion, and reaching activities; incorporating positioning procedures in activities such as eating, dressing, bathing, toileting, and table or desk activities; and incorporating special physical guidance techniques whenever possible to facilitate volitional movements in functional contexts.

Second, physical management and intervention techniques should be incorporated into identified goals from other domains using the format shown in Figure 13.3 (Burton & Langley, 1987). Using this approach, a targeted movement objective is paired with an educational objective. Specific handling procedures and positioning requirements are specified as well as any adaptive equipment (e.g., wedges, sidelyer, adaptive eating utensils) or other materials. This method can provide a framework for the special educator to discuss with therapists how therapeutic intervention can be incorporated across educational objectives.

The third method involves analyzing the target behavior in terms of antecedent conditions (including handling, positioning, and use of adaptive equipment), the required response, and the consequences (Hanna & Gallina, 1985; Campbell & Stewart, 1986). The reaching program in Table 13.11 is an example of how this method can be used. The unique aspect about this approach is that the motoric response is described in terms of the *components* of movement. Systematic intervention is designed to alter the quality of

TABLE 13.11
Instructional Program for Reaching

Antecedent conditions
    Trainer positions child in chair with neutral alignment of the pelvis, trunk, and shoulders, using the following positioning equipment:
(specified for individual child) .

    Object is placed (specified for individual child) inches away from either the right or left hand.

    Child is asked to get the object: " ___(name)___ , get the ___(object)___ ."

Response requirements
    Humeral (arm) flexion
    No humeral internal rotation
    Movement toward elbow extension
    Neutral wrist
    Fingers open
    Forearm movement toward supination
    All movement components correct
    Contacts object

Consequence conditions
    Guided (or independent, if possible) interaction with the object with social interaction provided by the therapist around the activity.

Source: From "Measuring Changes in Movement Skills with Infants and Young Children with Handicaps" (p. 156) by P. Campbell and B. Stewart, 1985, *Journal of the Association of Persons with Severe Handicaps, 11.* Copyright 1985 by The Association for Persons with Severe Handicaps. Reprinted by permission.

the motor response. The intervention consists of specific physical guidance techniques recommended by a physical or occupational therapist, which are used to facilitate the motor response and later faded as the child acquires the skill. This method provides a systematic approach to implement intervention programs, measures child progress, and contains sufficient detail to ensure consistency in implementation across persons, settings, and activities.

SUMMARY OF KEY CONCEPTS

- Movement competence and motor skills are an integral part of skills in all other domains.

- Infants and young children with various handicapping conditions exhibit delays and/or deviations in motor development.

- Achievement of motor milestones proceeds in an orderly sequence in nonhandicapped children.

- The components of mature movement include extension, symmetry, independent movement, and rotation.

- Children with atypical muscle tone demonstrate delays in the attainment of motor milestones and exhibit atypical postures and volitional movements.

- Practicing abnormal movement patterns over time may result in muscle contractures and structural deformities.

- Motor assessments should be conducted in cooperation with physical and occupational therapists.

- An adequate motor evaluation for the purpose of planning intervention should include an assessment of (a) postural tone, (b) primitive reflexes and automatic reactions, (c) posture and volitional movement patterns, and (d) functional abilities and disabilities.

- Muscle tone can range from hypotonia to hypertonia and is generally subjective.

- Assessment of underlying muscle tone is conducted with the child at rest.

- Methods to assess underlying tone include (a) feeling the consistency of the muscles, (b) observing the extensibility of the joints, (c) determining the passivity of the muscles, and (d) observing the child's posture.

- Assessment of predominant muscle tone is conducted while the child is maintaining antigravity postures and performing volitional movements.

- Factors that can influence tone should be assessed: child's position in relation to gravity, sensory stimuli, environmental factors, and physical management.

- Assessment of primitive reflexes involves presenting the environmental stimulus and observing the absence or the persistence and intensity of the specific response.

- Assessment of automatic postural reactions includes observing for the presence, absence, or proficiency of righting, equilibrium, and protective reactions.

- When assessing posture and volitional movements, particular attention should be given to quality indicators related to (a) appropriate use of the components of movement and missing components, (b) adverse effects of posture and movements on muscle tone, (c) use of proximal adjustments and compensatory movement patterns, and (d) consequences of habitual compensatory patterns.

- When assessing fine motor skills, the quality of grasp and release behaviors will be directly related to (a) overall muscle tone in the body, (b) overall body position and control, (c) the position and function of the shoulder girdle, and (d) the position and function of the forearm.

- Choosing an assessment instrument should be based on the purpose of the assessment: screening for motor delays, diagnosis of motor delays and/or disabilities and eligibility for services, planning motor development programs, or evaluating the effects of intervention.

- The goals of intervention should be designed individually based on children's particular motor problems.

- Motor skills should be developed within the context of purposeful activities and daily routines as much as possible.

- Programming for infants and young children with movement problems should include both direct instruction using specific physical guidance techniques and physical management programs, including handling and positioning techniques, and using adaptive equipment.

REFERENCES

Alpern, G., Boll, T., & Shearer, M. (1980). *Developmental Profile II.* Aspen, CO: Psychological Development Publications.

André-Thomas, Y. & Saint Anne-Dargassies, S. (1964). *The neurological examination of the infant.* London: Heinemann.

Ayers, A. J. (1979). *Sensory integration and the child.* Los Angeles: Western Psychological Services.

Bardsley, G. I. (1984). The Dundee seating programme. *Physiotherapy, 70*(22), 59–63.

Bayley, N. (1969). *Manual for the Bayley Scales of Infant Development.* New York: Psychological Corp.

Bly, L. (1983). *The components of normal movement during the first year of life and abnormal motor development.* Chicago: Neurodevelopmental Treatment Association.

Bobath, B. (1963). A neuro-developmental treatment of cerebral palsy. *Physiotherapy, 49,* 242–244.

Bobath, B. (1969). The treatment of neuromuscular disorders by improving patterns of coordination. *Physiotherapy, 55,* 18–22.

Bobath, K. & Bobath, B. (1964). The facilitation of normal postural reactions and movements in the treatment of cerebral palsy. *Physiotherapy, 50,* 246–252.

Bobath, K. & Bobath, B. (1972). Cerebral palsy. In P. H. Pearson & C. E. Williams (Eds.), *Physical therapy services in the developmental disabilities* (pp. 31–185). Springfield, IL: Charles C. Thomas.

Bobath, K. & Bobath, B. (1984). *Motor development in the different types of cerebral palsy.* London: Heinemann.

Brazelton, T. (1973). *Neonatal Behavioral Assessment Scale.* Philadelphia: J.B. Lippincott.

Bricker, W. A. & Campbell, P. H. (1980). Interdisciplinary assessment and programming for multihandicapped students. In W. Sailor, B. Wilcox, & L. Brown (Eds.), *Methods of instruction for severely handicapped students* (pp. 3–45). Baltimore, MD: Paul H. Brookes.

Brigance, A. H. (1978). *Brigance Diagnostic Inventory of Early Development.* North Billerica, MA: Curriculum Associates.

Burton, S. & Langley, M. B. (1987, November). *The neurodevelopmental educational plan: A model for teachers of the movement impaired.* Paper presented at Weekend with the Experts for Teachers of the Visually Impaired, Orlando, FL.

Campbell, P. (1982). *Introduction to neurodevelopmental treatment.* Akron, OH: Children's Hospital Medical Center.

Campbell, P. H. (1985a). *Assessment of posture and movement in children with severe movement dysfunction.* Akron, OH: Children's Hospital Medical Center.

Campbell, P. H. (1985b). *Neurodevelopmental treatment—An integrated treatment approach.* Akron, OH: Children's Hospital Medical Center.

Campbell, P. H. (1987a). Physical management and handling procedures with students with movement dysfunction. In M. E. Snell (Ed.), *Systematic instruction of persons with severe handicaps* (3rd ed.) (pp. 174–187). Columbus, OH: Merrill.

Campbell, P. H. (1987b). Programming for students with dysfunction in posture and movement. In M. E. Snell (Ed.), *Systematic instruction of persons with severe handicaps* (3rd ed.) (pp. 188–211). Columbus, OH: Merrill.

Campbell, P. H., McInerny, W. F., & Cooper, M. A. (1984). Therapeutic programming for students with severe handicaps. *The American Journal of Occupational Therapy, 38,* 594–602.

Campbell, P. H. & Stewart, B. (1986). Measuring changes in movement skills with infants and young children with handicaps. *Journal of the Association for Persons with Severe Handicaps, 11*(3), 153–161.

CAPE (Consortium on Adaptive Performance Evaluation). (1980). *Adaptive Performance Instrument.* Moscow, ID: Department of Special Education, University of Idaho.

Capute, A. J., Accardo, P. J., Vining, E. P. G., Rubenstein, J. E., Walcher, J. R., Harryman, S., & Ross, A. (1978). Primitive reflex profile: A pilot study. *Physical Therapy, 58,* 1061–1065.

Chandler, L. (1979). Gross and fine motor development. In M. Cohen & P. Gross (Eds.), *The developmental resource: Behavioral sequences for assessment and program planning (vol. 1)* (pp. 119–152). New York: Grune & Stratton.

Chandler, L. S., Andrews, M. S., & Swanson, M. W. (1980). *Movement assessment of infants: A manual.* Rolling Bay, WA: Authors.

Chasey, W. C. (1976). Distribution of practice, learning and retention. *Perceptual and Motor Skills, 43,* 159–164.

Ellis, E. (1967). Physical management of developmental disorders. *Clinics in Developmental Medicine* (No. 26). London: Heinemann.

Erhardt, R. P. (1982). *Developmental hand dysfunction: Theory, assessment, treatment.* Laurel, MO: RAMSCO.

Erhardt, R. P. (1974). Sequential levels in development of prehension. *The American Journal of Occupational Therapy, 28*(10), 592–596.

Esterson, S. H. (1987). Physical therapy. In M. M. Esterson & L. F. Bluth (Eds.), *Related services for handicapped children* (pp. 79–88). Boston: College-Hill.

Exner, C. (1987). Occupational therapy. In M. M. Esterson & L. F. Bluth (Eds.), *Related services for handicapped children* (pp. 53–68). Boston: College-Hill.

Fewell, R. R. (1983). Working with sensorily impaired children. In S.G. Garwood (Ed.), *Educating young handicapped children: A developmental approach* (2nd ed.) (pp. 235–280). Rockville, MD: Aspen.

Finn, D. M. (1985). *The efficacy of two treatment techniques for children with spastic cerebral palsy as measured by electromography and thermal information.* Unpublished doctoral dissertation. University of Alabama, Tuscaloosa. (ERIC Document Reproduction Service No. ED 270 918)

Finnie, N. R. (1975). *Handling the young cerebral palsied child at home* (2nd ed.). New York: E.P. Dutton.

Florentino, M. R. (1973). *Reflex testing methods for evaluating CNS development* (2nd ed.). Springfield, IL: Charles C. Thomas.

Folio, R. & DuBose, R. F. (1974). *Peabody Developmental Motor Scales* (rev. experimental ed.). Nashville, TN: Institute on Mental Retardation and Intellectual Development, George Peabody College of Vanderbilt University.

Fraser, B. A. & Hensinger, R. N. (1983). Normal movement. In B. A. Fraser & R. N. Hensinger, *Managing physical handicaps* (pp. 67–82). Baltimore, MD: Paul H. Brookes.

Frankenburg, W. K. & Dodds, J. B. (1967). *Denver Developmental Screening Test.* Denver: University of Colorado Medical Center.

Fredericks, H. D., et al. (1976). *The teaching research curriculum for moderately and severely handicapped.* Springfield, IL: Charles C. Thomas.

Fredericks, H. D., et al. (1980). *The teaching research curriculum for moderately and severely handicapped: Gross and fine motor.* Springfield, IL: Charles C. Thomas.

Furuno, S., O'Reilly, K. A., Hosaka, C. M., Inatsuka, T. T., Allman, T. L., & Zeisloft, B. (1979). *The Hawaii Early Learning Profile.* Palo Alto, CA: VORT.

Giangreco, M. F. (1986). Effects of integrated therapy: A pilot study. *Journal of the Association for Persons with Severe Handicaps, 11*(3), 205–208.

Glover, M. E., Preminger, J. L., & Sanford, A. R. (1978). *Early learning accomplishment profile for developmentally young children.* Winston-Salem, NC: Kaplan.

Hanna, L. & Gallina, B. (1985, December). *Data based motor programming for infants and preschoolers.* Paper presented at the 12th annual convention of The Association for Persons with Severe Handicaps, Boston, MA.

Hanson, M. J. & Harris, S. R. (1986). *Teaching the young child with motor delays: A guide for parents and professionals.* Austin, TX: Pro-Ed.

Haring, N. G. (1976). Infant identification. In M. Thomas (Ed.), *Hey, don't forget about me* (pp. 16–35). Reston, VA: The Council for Exceptional Children.

Harris, S. R. (1980). Transdisciplinary therapy model for the infant with Down's syndrome. *Physical Therapy, 60*(4), 420–423.

Harris, S. R. (1981). Effects of neurodevelopmental therapy on improving motor performance in Down's syndrome infants. *Developmental Medicine and Child Neurology, 23,* 477–483.

Harris, S. R., Haley, S. M., Tada, W. L., & Swanson, M. W. (1984). Reliability of observational measures of the movement assessment of infants. *Physical Therapy, 64*(4), 471–477.

Harris, S. R. & Tada, W. L. (1983). Providing developmental therapy services. In S. G. Garwood & R. R. Fewell, *Educating handicapped infants* (pp. 343–365). Rockville, MD: Aspen.

Holder, L., Wells, B., & Cook, M. (1985). *RISE: Computerized checklist and curriculum for the motorically delayed/impaired child.* Tuscaloosa, AL: Area of Special Education, The University of Alabama.

Holvoet, J., Guess, D., Mulligan, M., & Brown, F. (1980). The individualized curriculum sequencing model (II): A teaching strategy for severely handicapped students. *Journal of the Association for the Severely Handicapped, 5,* 337–351.

Hulme, J. B., Shaver, J., Acher, S., Mullette, L., & Eggert, C. (1987). Effects of adaptive seating on the eating and drinking of children with multiple handicaps. *The American Journal of Occupational Therapy, 41*(2), 81–89.

Inge, K. J. (1987). Atypical motor development and cerebral palsy. In F. P. Orelove & D. Sobsey (Eds.), *Educating children with multiple disabilities: A transdisciplinary approach* (pp. 43–65). Baltimore, MD: Paul H. Brookes.

Johnson-Martin, N., Jens, K. G., & Attermeier, S. M. (1986). *The Carolina curriculum for handicapped infants and infants at risk.* Baltimore, MD: Paul Brookes.

Knoblock, H. & Passamanick, B. (1974). *Gesell and Amatruda's Developmental Diagnoses: The evaluation and management of normal and abnormal neuropsychologic development in infancy and early childhood.* New York: Harper & Row.

Knott, M. & Voss, D. E. (1968). *Proprioceptive neuromuscular facilitation: Patterns and techniques* (2nd ed.). New York: Harper & Row.

Kong, E. (1966). The very early treatment of cerebral palsy. *Developmental Medicine and Child Neurology, 8,* 198–202.

Langley, M. B. (1977). Functional assessment of the brain-damaged physically handicapped child: Cognitive, communication and motor variables. *Diagnostique, 2*(2), 31–37.

Levitt, S. (1982). *Treatment of cerebral palsy and motor delay* (2nd ed.). Boston: Blackwell Scientific Publications.

McCarraher-Wetzel, A. P. & Wetzel, R. C. (1984). A review of the Amiel-Tison neurological evaluation of the newborn and infant. *American Journal of Occupational Therapy, 38*(9), 585–593.

McCormick, L. P. & Goldman, R. (1979). The transdisciplinary model: Implications for service delivery and personnel preparation for the severely and profoundly handicapped. *American Association for the Education of the Severely and Profoundly Handicapped Review, 4*(2), 152–161.

McEwen, I. R. (October, 1987). *Effect of position on communication board use by students with cerebral palsy.* Paper presented at the 14th annual convention of The Association of Persons with Severe Handicaps, Chicago, IL.

Milani-Comparetti, A. & Gidoni, E. A. (1967). Routine developmental examination in normal and retarded children. *Developmental Medicine and Child Neurology, 9,* 631–638.

Minear, W. L. (1956). A classification of cerebral palsy. *Pediatrics, 18,* 841.

Mulligan, M., Guess, D., Holvoet, J., & Brown, F. (1980). The individualized curriculum sequencing model (I): Implications from research on massed, distributed, or spaced trial training. *Journal of the Association for the Severely Handicapped, 5,* 325–335.

Newborg, J., Stock, J. R., Wnek, L., Guidubaldi, J., & Svinicki, J. (1984). *Battelle Developmental Inventory.* Allen, TX: DLM Teaching Resources.

Nwaobi, O. M., Brubaker, C. E., Cusick, B., & Sussman, M. D. (1983). Electromyographic investigation of extensor activity in cerebral palsied children in different seating positions. *Developmental Medicine and Child Neurology, 25,* 174–183.

Nwaobi, O. M., Hobson, D. A., & Trefler, E. (1985). Hip angle and upper extremity movement in time in children with cerebral palsy. *Proceedings of the Eighth Annual Conference of the Rehabilitation Engineering Society of North America, 8,* 39–41.

Nwaobi, O. M. & Smith, P. D. (1986). Effect of adaptive seating on pulmonary function in children with cerebral palsy. *Developmental Medicine and Child Neurology, 28,* 351–354.

Nwaobi, O., Trefler, E., & Hobson, D. (1984). Body orientation in space and tonic muscle activity in patients with cerebral palsy. *Proceedings of the Second International Conference on Rehabilitation Engineering* (pp. 481–483). Ottawa, Ontario, Canada.

Piaget, J. (1952). *The origins of intelligence in children.* New York: Norton.

Popovich, D. (1977). *A prescriptive behavioral checklist for the severely and profoundly retarded.* Baltimore, MD: University Park Press.

Powell, M. L. (1981). *Assessment and management of developmental changes and problems in children* (2nd ed.). St. Louis, MO: C. V. Mosby.

Robinson, N. M. & Robinson, H. B. (1976). *The mentally retarded child* (2nd ed.). New York: McGraw-Hill.

Rood, M. S. (1954). Neurophysiological reactions as a basis for physical therapy. *Physical Therapy Review, 34,* 444–449.

Rood, M. S. (1956). Neurophysiological mechanisms utilized in the treatment of neuromuscular dysfunction. *American Journal of Occupational Therapy, 10,* 220–225.

Schafer, D. S. & Moersch, M. S. (Eds.). (1981). *Developmental programming for infants and young children* (rev. ed.). Ann Arbor: University of Michigan Press.

Smith, P. D., Holder-Brown, L. F., & Nwaobi, O. M. (1988). *Comparative effects of adaptive and unsupported seating on speech intelligibility in children with cerebral palsy.* Manuscript submitted for publication.

Smith, S. L., Gossman, M. R., & Canan, B. C. (1982). Selected primitive reflexes in children with cerebral palsy: Consistency of response. *Physical Therapy, 62*(8), 1115–1120.

Stillman, R. D. (1978). *Callier-Azusa Scale.* Reston, VA: Council for Exceptional Children.

Swanson, M. W. (1979). Early motor development: Assessment and intervention. In B. L. Darby & M. J. May (Eds.), *Infant assessment: Issues and applications* (pp. 79–101). Seattle: Western States Technical Assistance Resource.

Tawney, J. W., Knapp, D. S., O'Reilly, C. D., & Pratt, S. S. (1979). *Programmed environments curriculum.* Columbus, OH: Merrill.

Trefler, E., Nickey, J., & Hobson, D. A. (1983). Technology in the education of multiply-handicapped children. *The American Journal of Occupational Therapy, 37*(6), 381–387.

Utley, B., Holvoet, J., & Barnes, K. (1977). Handling, positioning, and feeding the physically handicapped. In E. Sontag (Ed.), *Educational programming for the severely and profoundly handicapped* (pp. 279–299). Reston, VA: Division on Mental Retardation, Council for Exceptional Children.

Wolery, M. & Dyk, L. (1984). Arena assessment: Description and preliminary social validity data. *Journal of the Association for Persons with Severe Handicaps, 9*(3), 231–235.

Chapter 14

Assessing Communication Skills

Joanne Erwick Roberts
Elizabeth R. Crais
University of North Carolina at Chapel Hill

KEY TERMS

- Communication
- Language
- Mode
- Pragmatics
- Communicative
  Intentions
- Discourse
- Role Taking
- Phonology
- Phoneme

- Syntax
- Morpheme
- Semantics
- Standardized Tests
- Nonstandardized
  Measures
- Augmentative
  Communication
- Decision Trees
- Communicative Event
  Perspective

- Developmental
  Perspective
- Individual Differences/
  Disordered Perspective
- Etiological Perspective
- Communication Sample
- Naturalistic
  Observation
- Structured Elicited
  Interactions

Communication is integral to everyday functioning. Through it people exchange ideas, information, and feelings; achieve goals (i.e., obtain a desired object, elicit attention); and share the events of the past and make plans for the future. Basic communication skills are crucial for accessing and enjoying others and for managing everyday activities. For many young children with handicaps, however, learning to communicate is not an easy or naturally occurring task; therefore, assessing communication skills and planning intervention for communication difficulties becomes a very important part of the intervention process.

This chapter is devoted to the assessment of communication skills for the purpose of determining appropriate instructional goals for infants and preschool children with handicaps. First, the nature of communication development is described. Next, testing and observational procedures are discussed, and finally, a protocol for translating assessment information into instructional goals is presented. This chapter does not provide a guide for an in-depth assessment of communication, as such an assessment is typically the responsibility of a speech-language pathologist (SLP). Instead, the aim is to acquaint the interventionist with a framework for examining communication when planning for intervention programs.

Rationale for Assessing Communication

Professionals working with young exceptional children need to be familiar with basic communicative assessment procedures, so they can set and implement their own intervention goals more effectively and integrate these goals with those of other professionals. Several other reasons exist for early interventionists being familiar with communication assessment. First, communication develops in accordance with a child's social, cognitive, and motor skills (McLean & Snyder-McLean, 1978). Therefore, early interventionists must look at communication in relation to the overall development and needs of the child, as well as the intervention targets of other professionals. The SLP working with a young child with cerebral palsy who has poor hand movements may teach the child to point as she vocalizes to request an object, while the occupational therapist may work on developing a pincer grasp. The physical therapist, on the other hand, may work on trunk stability dur-

ing reaching, while the special educator works on using the hand to sort puzzle pieces as an educational activity.

Second, interventionists should be familiar with procedures for communication assessment because all professionals interact and intervene with children through communication. They should be knowledgeable of the child's level of communication (e.g., the child's comprehension skills) and modify their own communication and task demands to that level.

Third, interventionists should be familiar with communication because a large number of the preschool children served as the result of P.L. 99-142 and of P.L. 99-457 will have communication needs. Of the 183,021 children aged 3-5 years who received services under P.L. 94-142 in 1984–1985, 70% were classified as having a speech or language impairment as their primary handicapping condition (U.S. Department of Education, 1986). Based on the prevalence of communication disorders among other handicapping conditions, one can assume that a large number of the children with other primary handicapping conditions also have communication problems.

Fourth, interventionists should be familiar with communication assessment because communication difficulties typically cannot be remedied with a few hours of speech therapy per week. Additionally, unless the environment where communication skills are taught is very similar to the environment where they are used, most handicapped children will not generalize the newly acquired skills (Leonard, 1981; Stokes & Baer, 1977; Rogers-Warren & Warren, 1984). Recent research (Warren & Kaiser, 1986; Rogers-Warren & Warren, 1984; Halle, Alpert, & Anderson, 1984), therefore, has recommended that most communication assessment and teaching be taken out of highly structured and isolated instructional settings and moved to more natural communication environments such as the home or classroom where a child actually uses communication. In the classroom, children have many opportunities to interact with their teacher and peers, as do children at home with their families. Thus, it makes sense to transfer assessment and intervention to the classroom and home.

In summary, all early interventionists can play an important role in the assessment and intervention of communication skills for infants and preschoolers, especially by sharing information on a child's communication and other related skills across different contexts, and by mutually planning an integrated program to meet each child's individualized needs.

Dimensions of Communication Assessment

A basic understanding of the normal course of communication development is needed for assessment of communication and for the subsequent planning of intervention. A description of the major components of communication and language follows.

Definitions of Communication, Language, and Speech

Communication is the process of exchanging information, ideas, and feelings between individuals. It is usually an active process that requires a sender who encodes or formulates a message and a receiver who decodes or comprehends the message. Communication is essentially a social act, the primary function of which is interaction with another living being. However, communication also can occur without either the intent or the knowledge of the sender; for example, the sender who, because of an inadvertent frown, communicates to others "Do not disturb." Communication can occur between and among many species (e.g., dogs, bees, and humans). For communication to be considered language, however, a mutually understood symbol system is necessary. **Language** is a socially shared code used to communicate and is composed of arbitrary symbols and rules for combining those symbols. English, Spanish, and Japanese are all languages, yet each has its own symbol system.

Communication and language also require a mutually understood **mode** or system of motor acts for expressing language. Although speech is a common mode of human communication, a variety of modes exist: (a) nonverbal (gestures, body-part movement, and facial expression); (b) verbal (speech, writing, and signing); and (c) vocal (speech sounds such as "baba" and nonspeech sounds such as laughter).

Components of Language

When acquiring any language, children must learn rules about its sounds, grammar, meanings, and uses. These rules are reflected in the four components of language: phonology, syntax, semantics, and pragmatics. The following section focuses on the four components of language followed by an example of the rules acquired across the four components. Because many researchers (Miller, 1981, McLean & Snyder-McLean, 1978) have argued that pragmatics has the greatest implications for the interventionist, it is discussed in considerable detail. In addition, the importance of the relationships between communicative, cognitive, social, and motor skills are discussed as well as the relationship between language comprehension and production.

Pragmatics. **Pragmatics** refers to the use of language in social contexts and includes the rules that govern how language is used for the purpose of communication. Three different levels of pragmatics are commonly assessed: intentions, conversational discourse, and role taking. **Communicative intentions** are the reasons a speaker talks (e.g., to request a desired object or to protest not getting it). Bates, Camaioni, and Volterra (1975) and Golinkoff (1983) suggest a progression in the development of communicative intentions as children move from prelinguistic to one-word to multiword expressions of these intentions. In the interactional stage during the first few months of life, caretakers respond to infants' unintentional signals (e.g., eye gaze, facial expressions, and body movements) as if they were purposeful communicative attempts. For example, early infant crying or repetitive sucking movements appear to be reflexive reactions rather than intentional communication, but caretakers typically interpret these behaviors as purposeful expressions of hunger or a desire to be picked up. As noted by Goldberg (1977), "readability," or the ability of caretakers to recognize and respond to the infant's behaviors, is an important part of the infant learning the effects these behaviors can have on others.

By approximately 9 months, an infant will consistently use a number of nonverbal behaviors (e.g., extending arms to be picked up) in such a fashion that the parent understands what the infant is intentionally communicating. These earliest-appearing communicative intentions, shown in Table 14.1, include requests for objects and actions (e.g., child points to a desired ball), attention seeking (e.g., child pats mother's arm), protests (e.g., child pushes adult's hand away), and comments on objects and actions (e.g., child holds up toy car and smiles at parent).

At approximately 12–15 months, children begin to use words (e.g., up, mama) to express the same intentions expressed in the prelinguistic stages (see Table 14.1). In addition, Harding and Golinkoff (1979) note that the goals of infants' nonverbal (gesture and vocalization) signals are now easier to interpret, and if signal is not understood, the infant repeats and varies the communication. Many taxonomies have been proposed to account for the range of communicative intents. See Chapman (1981), Roth and Spek-

man (1984) and McLean and Snyder-McLean (1978) for a review of these taxonomies. The communication intentions typically expressed by children at the prelinguistic, one-word, and multiword stage are shown in Table 14.1.

To be an effective conversationalist, a child must acquire the rules for conversational **discourse,** that is, how to participate in a conversation by taking a turn and moving from one topic to another. According to Bruner (1978), the early nonverbal interchanges between a child and a caretaker during the first few months of life form the basis for later conversational turn taking. Consider the example of a baby who smiles in response to a tickle from her mother. The mother smiles and says "tickle, tickle, tickle" and tickles the child again. The baby then vocalizes and smiles in pleasure, and the interactive routine continues. At about 16–22 months, children learn to use words to express intentions in relation to preceding utterances in conversation. As shown in Table 14.1 these discourse functions include requesting information (e.g., "What is that?"), answering (e.g., child says "juice" in response to "What do you want?"), and acknowledging (e.g., child says "ok" as he listens to the speaker).

To participate in a conversation, the child must also learn to integrate the rules. For example, to initiate a topic, a child must: (a) elicit a listener's attention, (b) speak clearly, (c) provide sufficient information to enable the listener to identify the topic, and (d) provide sufficient information for the listener to determine intended semantic relations between the words (Keenan & Schieffelin, 1976). The first three steps are typically performed by children at the one- and two-word stage; however, only older children are able to specify clearly the semantic relations in their conversational discourse.

Children also must learn how to maintain a topic of conversation over several speaking turns. The ability to maintain a conversation is typically established within the second year of life, and as children mature, the ability to

TABLE 14.1

Communicative Intentions Expressed in the Prelinguistic, One-word, and Multiword Utterances

Intention	Definitions	Prelinguistic	One Word	Multiword
Attention seeking	Solicits attention to self or aspects of the environment; has no other intent	Child tugs on her mother's skirt	"Mommy," as she tugs on skirt	"You know what?"
Request object	Demands desired tangible object; includes requesting consumable and nonconsumable objects	Child points to a dog he wants	"Dog"	"Give me dog."
Request action	Commands another to carry out an action; includes requesting assistance and other actions involving another person or between another person and an object	Child puts adult's hand on lid of jar while looking at the adult	"Open," while giving jar to adult	"Mama, open bottle."
Request information	Finds out something about an object or event; includes *wh*-questions and other utterances having the intonation contour of an interrogative		"Shoe?" as he points to shoe box	"Where shoe?"
Protest	Commands another to cease an undesired action; includes resisting another's action and rejection of object that is offered	Child pushes the adult's hand away when an undesired food item was offered	"No," in response to undesired food	"No peas, Mama."

TABLE 14.1
Continued

Intention	Definitions	Prelinguistic	One Word	Multiword
Comment on object	Directs another's attention to an object; includes pointing, show-ing, describing, informing, and interactive labeling	Child holds up toy car toward the adult and smiles while looking at the adult	Child points to the car in his hand and says, "Car"	"My car."
Comment on action	Calls listener's at-tention to the movement of some object or action of others or self	Laughs and looks at adult while adult falls down	"Down," as adult falls	"Bobbie fall down."
Greeting	Communicates salutation and offers conversa-tional rituals "hi," "bye," "please," and "thank you"	Child waves as mother leaves	"Bye"	"Bye, mom."
Answering	Responds to request for information		Child says "nose" in response to "Where's your nose?"	"Here my nose."
Acknowledgement of other's speech	Acts or ut-terances used to indicate that the other's ut-terance was received, not in response to a question; in-cludes repeti-tion of an utterance		Child says "yea" when favorite song is men-tioned	"My song."
Other	Tease, warn, alarm, exclaim, or convey humor	Child giggles as she takes a turn in a tickle routine	Child says "no" as she sticks her tummy out to be tickled	"No tickle me."

Source: Adapted from Coggins and Carpenter (1981), Dore (1974), and Roth and Spekman (1984).

maintain a topic for a greater number of turns, adding new information in each turn, is developed (Bloom, Rocissano, & Hood, 1976). Bloom et al. (1976) found that at 21 months, children maintained topic 50% of the time; however, by age 3 years, they main-tained topic 75% of the time.

In addition to initiating and maintaining a topic, a child must also learn to recognize the need to take turns in the conversation (Sacks,

Schegloff, & Jefferson, 1974). The length of the turn, how to take a turn, when it is acceptable to take a turn, as well as when it is not acceptable for turn taking are all part of these "rules for conversation."

The third component of pragmatic skills is the ability to take the perspective of the listener, a skill typically called **role taking**. Children learn to monitor portions of the conversational interchange by analyzing what the listener is comprehending. The child as speaker must pay attention not only to what he is saying and to whether the listener follows and understands what is said, but also to monitoring his own comprehension of what the other participant is saying. In regard to children's monitoring of their own comprehension, Patterson and Kister (1981) argue that listener skills in preschool children are relatively poorly developed and show considerable improvement over the elementary school years.

Phonology. **Phonology** refers to the rules for the formation of speech sounds, or phonemes, and how phonemes are joined together into words. A **phoneme** is the smallest linguistic unit of sound that signals a difference in meaning. The words *cat* and *bat* differ from each other in their initial sound, hence both *c* and *b* are different phonemes. English has between 40 and 45 phonemes; the number of phonemes varies from language to language. Speech sounds generally develop in a predictable sequence at certain ages, as noted by Sander (1972). Phonological rules govern what sounds can appear in various positions within a word (e.g., in English *ft* occurs in the final position of words and never in the initial position) and also in what sequences they can occur (e.g., *sl* is a permissible sequence and *sd* is not).

During the first year of life, children produce many different vocalizations that include both nonspeech-like and speech-like sounds. At about age 6 months, children begin to babble and repeat consonant-vowel combinations such as mamma, bababa. As children acquire adult speech, they often fail to produce it in accordance with the adult form and thereby produce phonological errors. For example, a child may consistently say *wabbit* for *rabbit*, not having acquired the initial *r* sound. These errors have been described recently as resulting from phonological processes, which are patterns of simplifications children use when learning words. For example, omitting the final *g* in *dog*, *r* in *car*, and *s* in *house* are all instances of the phonological process of deletion of final consonants. Examples of phonological processes common in young children are: deletion of final consonant (dog→do, car→ca); cluster reduction (bred→bed, sleeping→eeping); stopping (sun→tun, shoe→do); gliding (red→wed, light→wight). Ingram (1976), Shriberg and Kwiatkowski (1980), and Stoel-Gammon and Dunn (1985) provide further descriptions of the development of phonological processes.

Syntax. **Syntax** is the rule system for combining words into phrases and sentences. These rules specify parts of speech (e.g., noun, adjective, adverb), word order, and constituents of a sentence (noun phrase, verb phrase). For example, a competent speaker knows that "The boy throws the ball," is an acceptable sentence and "The ball throws boy the," is not.

The rules of syntax are acquired gradually as the child learns to put words together. Children begin to use one-word utterances at about age 12 months, and combine words into two- and three-word utterances at about 18 months. A child must also learn basic sentence structure (subject clause + verb clause) and basic sentence forms: questions, imperatives, or negatives (see Miller, 1981, for a discussion of the development of sentence structure). At about age 3, children begin to learn complex sentence structure so that clauses can be joined and embedded into one another. The development of complex sentences continues well into the school years. Both type and frequency of complex sentences acquired can be additional guides to children's level of linguistic development (Paul, 1981).

Another means of looking at grammatical complexity is through morpheme development. A **morpheme** is the smallest meaningful element of language. For example, in the word *boys*, both *boy* and the plural marker *s* are each one morpheme; the sentence *The / boy/s pull/ed / hard* contains six morphemes. Brown (1973) has identified 14 grammatical morphemes (e.g., present progressive *ing*, plural *s*, possessive *s*) that occur frequently and in some sequential order in young children's speech. Although there is variability in the acquisition of the 14 morphemes (de Villiers & de Villiers, 1973), children begin to acquire them between approximately 24 and 30 months and generally take several years to master them.

An estimate of young children's syntactical complexity is mean length of utterance (MLU) in morphemes or words. The MLU is computed by dividing the number of morphemes or words in a language sample by the number of utterances in the sample (150 morphemes/ 50 utterances = 3.0 MLU). As shown in Table 14.2, MLU in morphemes corresponds to chronologial age as well as to stages of linguistic development described by Brown (1973). MLU in morphemes is a valid index of language development when the MLU is between 1.0 and 4.5 morphemes. However, as children get beyond this upper MLU level, complex sentence structure is a more appropriate index of language development.

Semantics.   **Semantics** refers to the rules for meanings of individual words and their joint

TABLE 14.2
Predicting Chrononlogical Age from Mean Length of Utterance

Brown's stage	MLU	Predicted chronological age[a]	Predicted age ± 1 SD (middle 68%)
Early Stage I	1.01	19.1	16.4-21.8
	1.50	23.0	18.5-27.5
Late Stage I	1.60	23.8	19.3-28.3
	2.00	26.9	21.5-32.3
Stage II	2.10	27.7	22.3-33.1
	2.50	30.8	23.9-37.7
Stage III	2.60	31.6	24.7-38.5
	3.00	34.8	28.0-41.6
Early Stage IV	3.10	35.6	28.8-42.4
	3.50	38.7	30.8-46.6
Late Sate IV-Early Stage V	3.60	39.5	31.6-47.4
	4.00	42.6	36.7-48.5
Late Stage V	4.10	43.4	37.5-49.3
	4.50	46.6	40.3-52.9
Post Stage V	4.60	47.3	41.0-53.6
	5.10	51.3	42.9-59.7
	5.60	55.2	46.8-63.6
	6.00	58.3	49.9-66.7

[a]Age is predicted from the equation: age (in months) = 11.199 + 7.857 (MLU)
Computed from obtained standard deviations

Source: From *Assessing Language Production in Children* by J. Miller, 1981, Baltimore: University Park Press. Copyright 1981 by University Park Press. Adapted by permission.

relationship to one another. A particular word has many characteristics that establish its meaning, and a child's task is to learn which factors are critical in acquiring the use of a word. As children get older, the total number and the variety of words increase, as do the individual relationships among words and the complexity of their meanings. Words (e.g., glasses) take on very different meanings depending on the context in which they are uttered (eye glasses, drinking glasses).

Semantics provides a way to examine relationships among words. Just as the words in the utterance "Johnny jumps" can be described as noun and verb in a syntactic approach, they can also be described as agent (Johnny) and action (jumps) in a semantic approach. Other "semantic relations" are location (up), negation (no), and recurrence (more). Retherford, Schwartz, and Chapman (1981) describe a complete list of the 21 semantic categories in children's early language. Children's initial combination of words into multiword utterances consists of combinations of semantic categories such as agent-action ("Doggie bark") and agent-action-object ("Mommy eat cookie"). The particular relations children use in their prelinguistic communication and their one-word and multiword utterances are shown in Table 14.3 (p. 348).

Learning the Rules of Language Across Components

Children learn language by abstracting the rules of language from the ongoing stream of speech surrounding them. That is, they acquire language while they interact with people and objects in their environment. No marker identifies which word is a noun, subject, or agent of a sentence or indicates that a sentence such as "Cakes eat the door," is nonsensical. Rather, word classes are created and the rules for syntax, semantics, pragmatics, and phonology evolve as children observe organizational similarities across utterances that they hear and attempt to use.

To understand the complexity of the rules a child must learn about language, consider the following example. Imagine that you observe two Zorks on planet Zoff using the utterances listed below. See how many rules you can identify that describe the phonology, syntax, semantics, and pragmatics of this language.

Zork A: "Zto to"	(points to toy truck Zork B is holding)
Zork B: "Zo to"	(shakes head and jumps up and down)
Zork A: "Zto ho"	(points to man driving truck)
Zork B: "Ho"	(gives Zork A the man)
Zork A:	(takes the man and smiles)

You observed for this language that there are: (a) four phonological rules—four phonemes, z, h, o, and t, can occur; each word-unit consists of two or three phonemes; z, h, or t can occur in the initial position; and only o occurs at the end of words; (b) two syntactical rules—each utterance consists of one or two words, and no sentence ends with a z word; (c) four semantic rules—the word zto means want, to means truck, ho means man, and zo means no; and (d) two pragmatic rules—if you want something you request it verbally or point ("zto to"), and if you do not like something, you protest it verbally ("zo, zo") or shake your head. There are other rules that could be determined from this sample, but what is important is that, based on the "rules" derived from the language of the two Zorks, you could process and produce novel utterances that were never previously heard (e.g., "zo ho" meaning "no man"). Similarly, by acquiring the rules for a language, a child can generate an endless number of utterances never heard directly by the child.

TABLE 14.3
Semantic Relations Expressed in Prelinguistic, One-word, and Multiword Utterances

General relationship	Function/meaning	Prelinguistic	One Word	Multiword
		Child Behavior		
Agent	States the individual performing the action	Throws ball to teacher and smiles proudly	Throws ball and says "Me"	"Me throw"
Action	Requests action	Holds hands up to be picked up	"Up," to indicate pick me up	"Up Mommy"
Object	Comments on the object of action	Points to ball being pushed	"Ball," as ball is pushed	"Ball go"
Recurrence	Requests/comments on repetition of activity/object	Drinks milk and holds up empty bottle	"More," to indicate more milk	"Me more milk"
Nonexistence	Comments on nonexistence/disappearance of object or person	Points to missing wheel on car	"Wheel," while pointing to car	"No wheel"
Cessation	Comments on cessation of activity	Points to top that stopped spinning	"Stop," to indicate top is no longer spinning	"Top stop"
Rejection	Protests/comments on undesired action or something forbidden	Turns head away from food	"No," in response to peas	"No peas"
Location	Comments on spatial location	Holds truck and points to box	"Box," while pointing to toy box	"Put box"
Possession	Comments on possession of object	Reaches for own shoes among others' shoes and points	"Mine," while getting own shoes	"My shoes"
Agent action[a]	Comments on agent and action			"Boy hit"
Action object[a]	Comments on action and object			"Kick ball"
Agent action object[a]	Comments on agent, action, and object			"Mommy throw ball"
Action object location[a]	Comments on agent, action, and location			"Put ball chair"

[a]These are more commonly used examples of relational combinations; many possibilities exist.

Relationship of Language to Social, Motor, and Cognitive Skills

When planning assessment and intervention for infants and young children, the interventionist should consider the mutual influences of social, motoric, and cognitive development on the child's efforts to communicate and learn language. The infant's interactions with people and objects in the environment set the stage for the development of many nonverbal behaviors considered to be the antecedents of language (Carlson & Bricker, 1982; Seibert & Hogan, 1982a). For example, eye gaze, touch, and attention getting are important antecedents of social and communicative development in the first two years of life. Holdgrafer and Dunst (1986) have organized many of these early behaviors into seven sequential levels of "communicative competence": behavior state, recognitory, contingency, instrumental, triadic, verbal contextualized, and verbal decontextualized. Seibert and Hogan (1982a) have presented a five-level model of the development of social and object skills including: responsive, simple voluntary undifferentiated, complex differentiated, regulation by feedback, and anticipatory regulation.

A recent trend in communication assessment is to incorporate into the overall assessment nonstandard measures of nonverbal cognitive skills (Gill & Dihoff, 1982) as well as scores of nonverbal (performance) mental ages on standardized intelligence tests (Chapter 11). This practice typically allows for comparison between verbal and nonverbal skills and between cognitive and other developing skill areas. Although there is disagreement as to the exact relationship between language and cognitive development, the correlation between measures of cognition and language takes on particular importance when assessing children whose development appears to be delayed (Miller, Chapman, Branston, & Reichle, 1980). A child's level of cognitive and language skills should be examined for major discrepancies between the two areas, based on the belief that cognition and language are generally developing in a parallel and correlated fashion. Gill and Dihoff (1982) suggest that when a child's language level is significantly below that of her cognitive level, the early interventionist should suspect the presence of a disorder such as a hearing impairment, an auditory processing problem, or a potential learning disability. For pratical guides to cognitive development and assessment within the framework of an overall communication assessment, see Miller et al. (1980) and Gill and Dihoff (1982).

Relationship Between Language Comprehension, Production, and Imitation

In recent years, the commonly held view that language comprehension *always* precedes language production has come under attack. A number of children have been reported to *produce* some words, phrases, and syntactical structures before they *comprehend* them (Chapman & Miller, 1975; de Villiers & de Villiers, 1973). For example, a 2-year-old may produce correctly the sentences "Girl hits boy" and "Boy hits girl" but due to confusion in comprehension of word order will not be able to identify correctly pictures depicting those actions until age 5. This inconsistency can be explained by the fact that young children depend in part on the situation and their experience in this context, rather than sentence structure, to help them produce or comprehend utterances. Thus, the early interventionist should focus on the child's productions and determine whether or not the child comprehends those words and structures when contextual support and object-and-task familiarity are varied. For a more complete description of the development of comprehension skills, see Chapman (1977) and Paul (1987).

The relationship of children's imitation skills to their production skills is also controversial. Although some studies have reported that spontaneous multiword productions may be better than imitative productions (Bloom, 1974; Slobin & Welsh, 1971), others have argued that children typically imitate only the structures that appear in their spontaneous utterances (Bloom, Hood, & Lightbown, 1974). As noted by Owens (1984), although the nature of the relationship between imitation and language development is not clear, it appears that imitation is often used by the child for items that the child is in the process of learning. See Owens (1984) for an overview of imitation skills and their role in language development.

Procedural Considerations in Assessing Communication

The advantages and disadvantages of standardized and nonstandardized assessment prodecures will be discussed first, and then the variables influencing a child's performance will be presented.

Standardized vs. Nonstandardized Procedures

Traditionally, assessment procedures have been classified into two categories, those described as *standardized* assessment measures and those termed *nonstandardized*. As the terms imply, each represents differences in administration modes, settings, materials, response expectations from the child, and judgments as to the child's success or failure. **Standardized tests** require specific instructions and procedures to elicit behavior and include standards or norms for scoring and interpretation. **Nonstandardized measures** differ from standardized procedures in not having well-established norms, and they may not have standardized procedures for test administration and interpretation. Nonstandardized measures include developmental scales, checklists, and observational samples,

as well as structured situations or procedures designed to elicit particular behaviors.

Standardized testing is particularly useful for screening, subsequent diagnosis, and documentation of communication delays. This type of testing, however, may not be useful for identifying specific instructional targets. Also, standardized testing typically does not describe how the child actually uses language to communicate (both verbally and nonverbally). Furthermore, no standardized tests are available for examining all aspects of language. Indeed, a number of researchers (Leonard, Prutting, Perozzi, & Berkley, 1978; Miller, 1981; Muma, 1978) argue against the sole use of standardized testing and suggest various combinations of observational and informal assessment measures. A blend of standardized testing, nonstandardized testing including direct observation, interaction with the child, and parent interview is suggested as the best assessment procedure for intervention planning. For interventionists who have naturalistic contexts in which to observe and assess their children informally, nonstandardized tests are particularly appropriate for analyzing a child's communicative skills.

Variables Influencing Performance

Many of the assessment issues discussed in earlier chapters apply to assessment of communication skills. These include validity, reliability, choice of which behaviors to measure, and certainty that the measured behaviors represent typical communicative interaction. It is important to confirm assessment results by testing with different procedures (i.e., speech sample and informal test) across multiple measurement occasions.

Other assessment issues particularly relevant in assessing infants and preschoolers at risk for communication difficulties are: (a) context or setting of assessment, (b) child's mode of communication (speech, sign, gesture), (c) the expected type of response (pointing, answering) and type of stimulus materials (pictures, objects) for the assessment task, and (d) level of parental participation in the assessment. Children, unlike most adults, may not be willing or capable of talking freely to an unfamiliar adult, and making them feel comfortable in a new and possibly threatening setting is not easy. Figure 14.1 is a list of suggestions on how to manage the context and setting to engage children in interactions.

In addition to setting, the child's typical mode of communicating needs consideration. Some children with severe retardation or sensory and/or motor impairments may lack the cognitive or motor capabilities necessary for speech. In assessing these children, alternate or augmentative modes of communication

(gestures, signing, communication systems) may be necessary. The term **augmentative communication** refers to a general classification of procedures that are designed and utilized to supplement whatever vocal skills an individual possesses (American Speech-Language-Hearing Association, 1981). Augmentative systems are of primary importance for severely impaired children and have been implemented with infants as young as 4–6 months (Hanrahan, Ferrier, & Jolie, 1987). Typical variables for consideration in determining candidacy for augmentative use are cognitive and sensory functioning, motor ability, imitation skills, social/interative and language ages, chronological age, motivation of the child, and caregivers' attitudes about an augmentative communication system.

FIGURE 14.1
Guidelines for
Interactions with
Children

1. Choose developmentally appropriate toys and materials. Use play and motor scales to help in the selection.
2. Limit your own talking, especially questions. Pause often to encourage the child to initiate communication and take a turn.
3. Watch for and encourage any mode of communication demonstrated by child (eye gaze, point, shrug, word, etc.).
4. Parallel play with the child, mimicking her actions. Play animatedly with object or toy and occasionally comment on an object or action.
5. Place a few items within eye gaze but out of reach; partially hide a few objects as well. If necessary, point to or comment on objects to encourage a comment or request by the child.
6. Let the child choose objects and/or activities, particularly in the beginning (and throughout the interaction if possible). Be prepared to watch and interact/comment when the child shows interest.
7. Include parent or another child to help break the ice. Stay in the background and slowly get into the interaction.
8. Begin interaction with activities that require little or no talking, and gradually move to more verbal tasks.
9. Be genuine in your questions, and stay away from asking what is obvious to both you and the child.
10. Follow the child's lead in the interaction by maintaining the child's focus on particular topics and meanings.
11. Show warmth and positive regard for the child, and value his comments.

Because of the complex nature of the factors influencing the candidacy decision and the type of system to be used, an interdisciplinary team is necessary (see Blackstone, 1986, for detailed discussion of criteria and guidelines for use of augmentative communication).

Consideration should also be given to the response required of the child by the assessment task and the stimuli used to elicit that response. Some children, although capable of speaking, may be more comfortable communicating nonverbally. In this case, the administration of nonverbal tasks first in the assessment process may be useful. Children's responses also may vary depending on the type of stimuli used. For very young children, objects may be more interesting and may elicit better responses than pictures. For all assessments, the type of stimuli used, the nature of the accompanying instructions, and the mode of communication should be noted in the protocol and report.

The final consideration in the assessment process is the level of parental involvement. It is often helpful for the parents of young children to be physically present and at times to assist with the assessment itself. Parents are indispensable when the interventionist needs information on the child's level of mastery of communication skills as well as the child's likes, dislikes, typical behaviors, and capabilities. Parents can also be asked to play with the child to allow the interventionist to view a typical interaction, or they could be employed as confederates or models for the child during a direct-testing phase. The parents can also provide direct feedback on the representativeness of the child's performance.

Representative Methods for Assessing Communication

In this section, three decision trees as well as four perspectives of communication are presented to guide the assessment process. In addition, the use of nonstandardized instruments and methods as well as standardized measures are discussed. The information in this section should be useful in both assessing children's communication and planning instructional programs.

Decision Trees

To help the interventionist initiate the assessment process, three **decision trees** are provided for children functioning at the prelinguistic, one-word, and multiword levels (Figures 14.2, 14.3, and 14.4, respectively). The decision trees incorporate questions to be used to identify a child's level of communication functioning and can later be used to guide intervention planning. The key points in assessing young children are whether a child communicates and when, what, and how that information is transmitted. For prelinguistic children, the focus is on early-developing social and interactive aspects of communication. For example, if a child uses only gestural and vocal behaviors, the focus in assessment primarily would be on determining whether those behaviors represent functional communication. For verbal children, although words are important, the focus still remains on functional and interactive aspects; thus, assessments of semantics and pragmatics rather than phonology or syntax are highlighted. Furthermore, the decision trees were designed for use with children functioning to a developmental age of 3. For children functioning at a higher level, the assessment tools listed in Table 14.4 (beginning on page 359) can guide the assessment process.

Each decision tree includes three major skill areas: pragmatics, comprehension, and production. For practical purposes, production has been divided into two areas: semantics/syntax and imitation, although imitation crosses each of the other areas. Within each skill area is a list of behaviors that children may or may not exhibit. The individual behaviors generally are listed in a developmental sequence from early developing to later developing; however, because some behaviors develop simultaneously, the sequence may vary. Although each skill area is presented as discrete, any one behavior within a skill area may incorporate aspects of the other skill areas.

The interventionist generally should move vertically through each list of behaviors, stop-

FIGURE 14.2

Decision Tree for Child at the Prelinguistic Stage

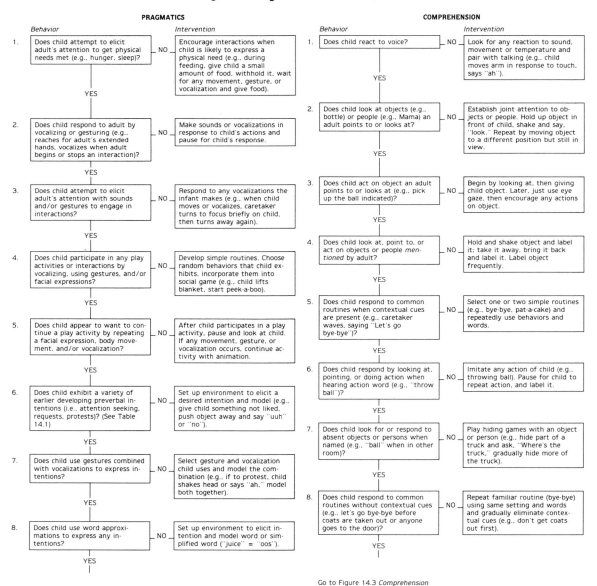

Go to Figure 14.3 *Pragmatics*

Go to Figure 14.3 *Comprehension*

FIGURE 14.2
Continued

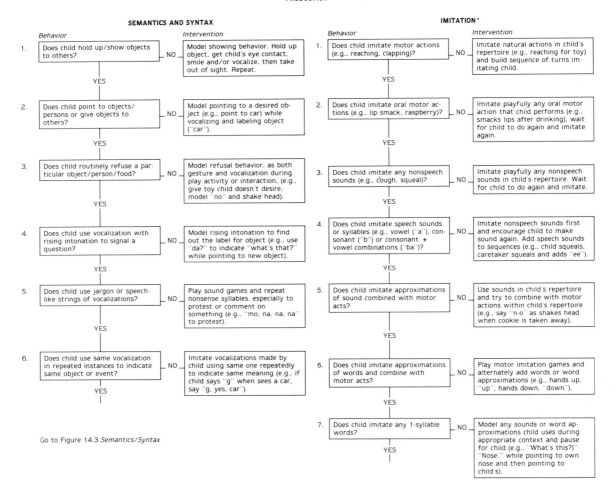

PRODUCTION

SEMANTICS AND SYNTAX

	Behavior		Intervention
1.	Does child hold up/show objects to others?	NO	Model showing behavior. Hold up object, get child's eye contact, smile and/or vocalize, then take out of sight. Repeat.
	YES		
2.	Does child point to objects/persons or give objects to others?	NO	Model pointing to a desired object (e.g., point to car) while vocalizing and labeling object ("car").
	YES		
3.	Does child routinely refuse a particular object/person/food?	NO	Model refusal behavior, as both gesture and vocalization during play activity or interaction. (e.g., give toy child doesn't desire, model "no" and shake head).
	YES		
4.	Does child use vocalization with rising intonation to signal a question?	NO	Model rising intonation to find out the label for object (e.g., use "da?" to indicate "what's that?" while pointing to new object).
	YES		
5.	Does child use jargon or speech-like strings of vocalizations?	NO	Play sound games and repeat nonsense syllables, especially to protest or comment on something (e.g., "mo, na, na, na" to protest).
	YES		
6.	Does child use same vocalization in repeated instances to indicate same object or event?	NO	Imitate vocalizations made by child using same one repeatedly to indicate same meaning (e.g., if child says "g" when sees a car, say "g, yes, car").
	YES		

Go to Figure 14.3 *Semantics/Syntax*

IMITATION*

	Behavior		Intervention
1.	Does child imitate motor actions (e.g., reaching, clapping)?	NO	Imitate natural actions in child's repertoire (e.g., reaching for toy) and build sequence of turns imitating child.
	YES		
2.	Does child imitate oral motor actions (e.g., lip smack, raspberry)?	NO	Imitate playfully any oral motor action that child performs (e.g., smacks lips after drinking), wait for child to do again and imitate again.
	YES		
3.	Does child imitate any nonspeech sounds (e.g., cough, squeal)?	NO	Imitate playfully any nonspeech sounds in child's repertoire. Wait for child to do again and imitate.
	YES		
4.	Does child imitate speech sounds or syllables (e.g., vowel ("a"), consonant ("b") or consonant + vowel combinations ("ba")?	NO	Imitate nonspeech sounds first and encourage child to make sound again. Add speech sounds to sequences (e.g., child squeals, caretaker squeals and adds "ee").
	YES		
5.	Does child imitate approximations of sound combined with motor acts?	NO	Use sounds in child's repertoire and try to combine with motor actions within child's repertoire (e.g., say "n-o" as shakes head when cookie is taken away).
	YES		
6.	Does child imitate approximations of words and combine with motor acts?	NO	Play motor imitation games and alternately add words or word approximations (e.g., hands up, "up", hands down, "down").
	YES		
7.	Does child imitate any 1-syllable words?	NO	Model any sounds or word approximations child uses during appropriate context and pause for child (e.g., "What's this?)" "Nose," while pointing to own nose and then pointing to child's).
	YES		

Go to Figure 14.3 *Imitation*

*For children with severe motor, cognitive, and/or sensory impairments, alternative communication modes may be necessary, therefore, referral to a speech-language pathologist is advised.

ping where the child either does not exhibit a few consecutive behaviors or does so in a limited or inconsistent manner. Once this point—which is the child's current level of functioning—is established, the interventionist should then move through the other two areas of the decision tree. At any point in the process, further analysis in any of the

FIGURE 14.3
Decision Tree for Child at the One-word Utterance Stage

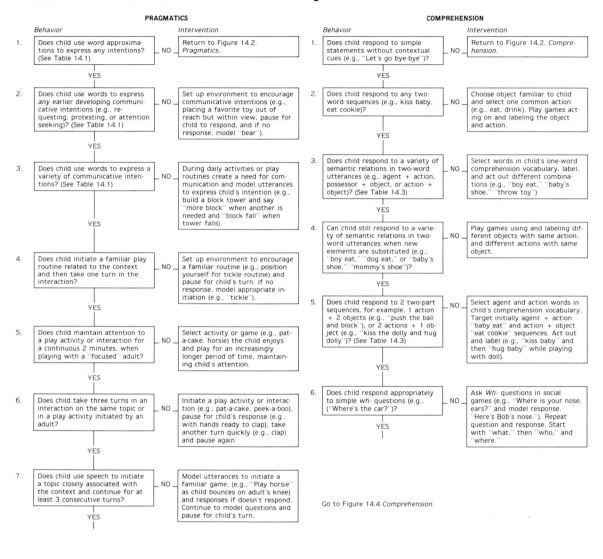

PRAGMATICS

Behavior — *Intervention*

1. Does child use word approximations to express any intentions? (See Table 14.1) — NO — Return to Figure 14.2. *Pragmatics.*

    YES

2. Does child use words to express *any* earlier developing communicative intentions (e.g., requesting, protesting, or attention seeking)? (See Table 14.1) — NO — Set up environment to encourage communicative intentions (e.g., placing a favorite toy out of reach but within view, pause for child to respond, and if no response, model "bear").

    YES

3. Does child use words to express a variety of communicative intentions? (See Table 14.1) — NO — During daily activities or play routines create a need for communication and model utterances to express child's intention (e.g., build a block tower and say "more block" when another is needed and "block fall" when tower falls).

    YES

4. Does child initiate a familiar play routine related to the context and then take one turn in the interaction? — NO — Set up environment to encourage a familiar routine (e.g., position yourself for tickle routine) and pause for child's turn. If no response, model appropriate initiation (e.g., "tickle").

    YES

5. Does child maintain attention to a play activity or interaction for a continuous 2 minutes, when playing with a "focused" adult? — NO — Select activity or game (e.g., pat-a-cake, horsie) the child enjoys and play for an increasingly longer period of time, maintaining child's attention.

    YES

6. Does child take three turns in an interaction on the same topic or in a play activity initiated by an adult? — NO — Initiate a play activity or interaction (e.g., pat-a-cake, peek-a-boo), pause for child's response (e.g., with hands ready to clap), take another turn quickly (e.g., clap) and pause again.

    YES

7. Does child use speech to initiate a topic closely associated with the context and continue for at least 3 consecutive turns? — NO — Model utterances to initiate a familiar game, (e.g., "Play horsie" as child bounces on adult's knee) and responses if doesn't respond. Continue to model questions and pause for child's turn.

    YES

Go to Figure 14.4 *Pragmatics*

COMPREHENSION

Behavior — *Intervention*

1. Does child respond to simple statements without contextual cues (e.g., "Let's go bye-bye")? — NO — Return to Figure 14.2. *Comprehension.*

    YES

2. Does child respond to any two-word sequences (e.g., kiss baby, eat cookie)? — NO — Choose object familiar to child and select one common action (e.g., eat, drink). Play games acting on and labeling the object and action.

    YES

3. Does child respond to a variety of semantic relations in two-word utterances (e.g., agent + action, possessor + object, or action + object)? (See Table 14.3) — NO — Select words in child's one-word comprehension vocabulary, label, and act out different combinations (e.g., "boy eat," "baby's shoe," "throw toy")

    YES

4. Can child still respond to a variety of semantic relations in two-word utterances when new elements are substituted (e.g., "boy eat," "dog eat," or "baby's shoe," "mommy's shoe")? — NO — Play games using and labeling different objects with same action, and different actions with same object.

    YES

5. Does child respond to 2 two-part sequences, for example, 1 action + 2 objects (e.g., "push the ball and block"), or 2 actions + 1 object (e.g., "kiss the dolly and hug dolly")? (See Table 14.3) — NO — Select agent and action words in child's comprehension vocabulary. Target initially agent + action "baby eat" and action + object "eat cookie" sequences. Act out and label (e.g., "kiss baby" and then "hug baby" while playing with doll).

    YES

6. Does child respond appropriately to simple *wh*- questions (e.g., ("Where's the car?")? — NO — Ask *Wh*- questions in social games (e.g., "Where is your nose, ears?" and model response. "Here's Bob's nose."). Repeat question and response. Start with "what," then "who," and "where."

    YES

Go to Figure 14.4 *Comprehension*

---

areas should be initiated. Developmental charts and scales, described in the next section, can be used to identify additional behaviors between achieved and unachieved behaviors. Most of the behaviors can be elicited through interaction with the child or gained from parent or caregiver interviews.

When moving through the decision trees, the interventionist should remember that each child is unique and, therefore, should be

FIGURE 14.3
Continued

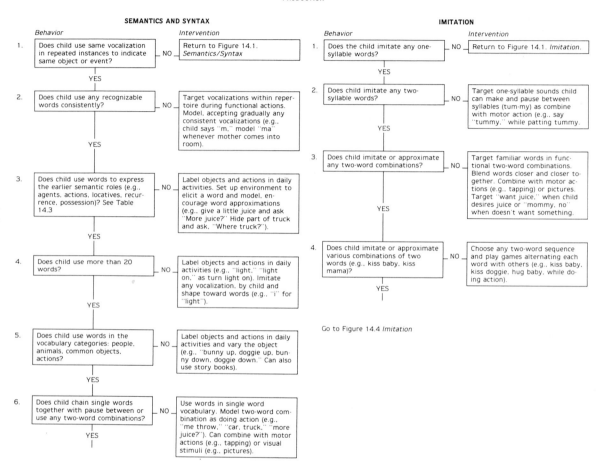

PRODUCTION

Go to Figure 14.4 *Semantics and Syntax*

expected to display some degree of individual variability. The decision questions are basic guidelines and are not presented as hard-and-fast rules for each child's absolute progression of skills. Although the three decision trees are presented separately, interventionists may need to move back and forth among the trees to explore a child's full range of communication skills. It is also important to remember that opportunity plays a part in which skills will be exhibited by an individual child. The type and number of interactions that are initiated, responded to, and encouraged by a child's parents or teachers can shape the kinds of behaviors displayed by the child. It is often helpful to observe the

FIGURE 14.4
Decision Tree for Child at the Two-word Utterance Stage and Above

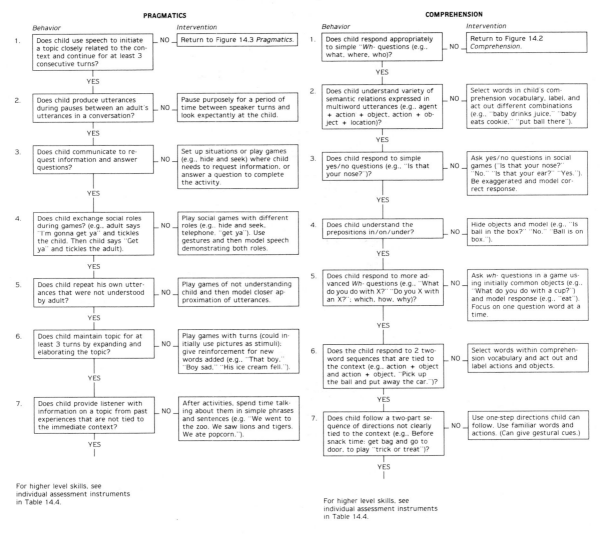

PRAGMATICS

Behavior — Intervention

1. Does child use speech to initiate a topic closely related to the context and continue for at least 3 consecutive turns? — NO — Return to Figure 14.3 *Pragmatics.*

YES

2. Does child produce utterances during pauses between an adult's utterances in a conversation? — NO — Pause purposely for a period of time between speaker turns and look expectantly at the child.

YES

3. Does child communicate to request information and answer questions? — NO — Set up situations or play games (e.g., hide and seek) where child needs to request information, or answer a question to complete the activity.

YES

4. Does child exchange social roles during games? (e.g., adult says "I'm gonna get ya" and tickles the child. Then child says "Get ya" and tickles the adult). — NO — Play social games with different roles (e.g., hide and seek, telephone, "get ya"). Use gestures and then model speech demonstrating both roles.

YES

5. Does child repeat his own utterances that were not understood by adult? — NO — Play games of not understanding child and then model closer approximation of utterances.

YES

6. Does child maintain topic for at least 3 turns by expanding and elaborating the topic? — NO — Play games with turns (could initially use pictures as stimuli); give reinforcement for new words added (e.g., "That boy." "Boy sad," "His ice cream fell.").

YES

7. Does child provide listener with information on a topic from past experiences that are not tied to the immediate context? — NO — After activities, spend time talking about them in simple phrases and sentences (e.g. "We went to the zoo. We saw lions and tigers. We ate popcorn.").

YES

For higher level skills, see individual assessment instruments in Table 14.4.

COMPREHENSION

Behavior — Intervention

1. Does child respond appropriately to simple "Wh- questions (e.g., what, where, who)? — NO — Return to Figure 14.2 *Comprehension.*

YES

2. Does child understand variety of semantic relations expressed in multiword utterances (e.g., agent + action + object, action + object + location)? — NO — Select words in child's comprehension vocabulary, label, and act out different combinations (e.g., "baby drinks juice," "baby eats cookie," "put ball there").

YES

3. Does child respond to simple yes/no questions (e.g., "Is that your nose?")? — NO — Ask yes/no questions in social games ("Is that your nose?" "No." "Is that your ear?" "Yes."). Be exaggerated and model correct response.

YES

4. Does child understand the prepositions in/on/under? — NO — Hide objects and model (e.g., "Is ball in the box?" "No." "Ball is on box.").

YES

5. Does child respond to more advanced Wh- questions (e.g., "What do you do with X?" "Do you X with an X?"; which, how, why)? — NO — Ask wh- questions in a game using initially common objects (e.g., "What do you do with a cup?") and model response (e.g., "eat"). Focus on one question word at a time.

YES

6. Does the child respond to 2 two-word sequences that are tied to the context (e.g., action + object and action + object, "Pick up the ball and put away the car.")? — NO — Select words within comprehension vocabulary and act out and label actions and objects.

YES

7. Does child follow a two-part sequence of directions not clearly tied to the context (e.g., Before snack time: get bag and go to door, to play "trick or treat")? — NO — Use one-step directions child can follow. Use familiar words and actions. (Can give gestural cues.)

YES

For higher level skills, see individual assessment instruments in Table 14.4.

parent(s) or teacher(s) interacting with the child to get an idea of the typical opportunities the child may have available.

An example of a way one might use the decision trees to assess communicative behavior in a child at a prelinguistic level is demonstrated for the Pragmatics category.

The interventionist could set up a play setting or a direct-interaction context and watch for or elicit a variety of communicative intentions from a child (Table 14.1 provides a list of possible intentions). By setting up situations to elicit specific communicative intents (as described later, in the section on language

FIGURE 14.4
Continued

PRODUCTION

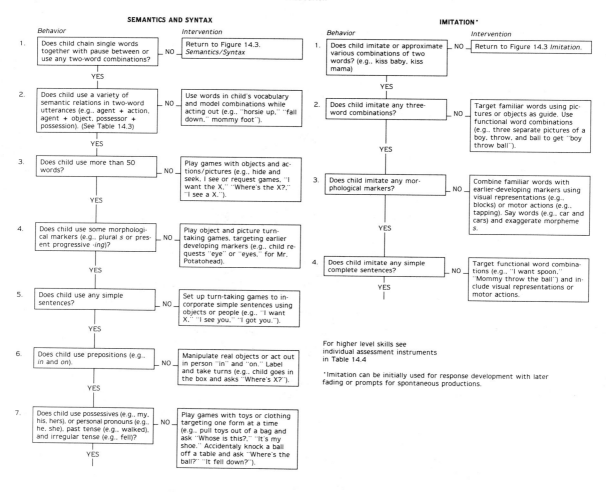

SEMANTICS AND SYNTAX

Behavior		*Intervention*
1.	Does child chain single words together with pause between or use any two-word combinations?	— NO —	Return to Figure 14.3. *Semantics/Syntax*

YES

| 2. | Does child use a variety of semantic relations in two-word utterances (e.g., agent + action, agent + object, possessor + possession). (See Table 14.3) | — NO — | Use words in child's vocabulary and model combinations while acting out (e.g., "horsie up," "fall down," "mommy foot"). |

YES

| 3. | Does child use more than 50 words? | — NO — | Play games with objects and actions/pictures (e.g., hide and seek, I see or request games, "I want the X," "Where's the X?," "I see a X."). |

YES

| 4. | Does child use some morphological markers (e.g., plural *s* or present progressive -*ing*)? | — NO — | Play object and picture turn-taking games, targeting earlier developing markers (e.g., child requests "eye" or "eyes," for Mr. Potatohead). |

YES

| 5. | Does child use any simple sentences? | — NO — | Set up turn-taking games to incorporate simple sentences using objects or people (e.g., "I want X," "I see you," "I got you."). |

YES

| 6. | Does child use prepositions (e.g., *in* and *on*). | — NO — | Manipulate real objects or act out in person "in" and "on." Label and take turns (e.g., child goes in the box and asks "Where's X?"). |

YES

| 7. | Does child use possessives (e.g., my, his, hers), or personal pronouns (e.g., he, she), past tense (e.g., walked), and irregular tense (e.g., fell)? | — NO — | Play games with toys or clothing targeting one form at a time (e.g., pull toys out of a bag and ask "Whose is this?" "It's my shoe." Accidentally knock a ball off a table and ask "Where's the ball?" "It fell down?"). |

YES

For higher level skills, see individual assessment instruments in Table 14.4.

IMITATION *

Behavior		*Intervention*
1.	Does child imitate or approximate various combinations of two words? (e.g., kiss baby, kiss mama)	— NO —	Return to Figure 14.3 *Imitation.*

YES

| 2. | Does child imitate any three-word combinations? | — NO — | Target familiar words using pictures or objects as guide. Use functional word combinations (e.g., three separate pictures of a boy, throw, and ball to get "boy throw ball"). |

YES

| 3. | Does child imitate any morphological markers? | — NO — | Combine familiar words with earlier-developing markers using visual representations (e.g., blocks) or motor actions (e.g., tapping). Say words (e.g., car and cars) and exaggerate morpheme *s.* |

YES

| 4. | Does child imitate any simple complete sentences? | — NO — | Target functional word combinations (e.g., "I want spoon," "Mommy throw the ball") and include visual representations or motor actions. |

YES

For higher level skills see individual assessment instruments in Table 14.4

*Imitation can be initially used for response development with later fading or prompts for spontaneous productions.

sampling), the interventionist can observe those intents that are readily used by the child and look for evidence of those not yet developed. The interventionist could also rely on teacher or parental report through the use of a form like that shown in Figure 14.5 (p. 366). With the help of the interventionist,

the teacher or parent describes: (a) what intentions the child uses, does not use, or is learning to express (e.g., requests for object or actions, or protests); (b) how those intentions are typically expressed: nonverbally (gesture, body movement, and facial expression), verbally (speech or signing), or vocally

TABLE 14.4
Summary of Speech and Language Instruments

A. *Standardized Language Diagnostic Instruments:*

Test Name	Areas Assessed	Age (years: months) Range	Format	Scores Obtained	Unique Aspects
Assessment of Children's Language Comprehension (Foster, Giddan, & Stark, 1973. Palo Alto: Consulting Psychologists Press)	Comprehension of word combinations of varying length and complexity	3:0–6:11	Picture identification, object manipulation, parent report, best choice	Percentage of accuracy on four subtests	Can be adapted for children with motor impairments
Carrow Elicited Language Inventory (Carrow, 1974. Austin, TX: Learning Concepts)	Grammatical form and structure	3:0–7:11	Elicited imitation	Percentile, stanine, age equivalent	
Detroit Tests of Learning Aptitude—Primary (Hammill & Bryant, 1986. Austin, TX: Pro-Ed)	Cognitive, attention, linguistic, and motor	3:0–9:0	Picture identification, object identification, object manipulation, observation, drawing	Percentile and standard score for general intelligence and specific skills	Embedded subtests correspond conceptually to composites on DTLA-2
Expressive One-Word Picture Vocabulary Test (Gardner, 1979. Novato, CA: Academic Therapy Publications)	Expressive vocabulary	2:0–11:11	Picture identification	Mental age, percentile, stanine, IQ	
Miller-Yoder Language Comprehension Test (Miller & Yoder, 1984. Baltimore, MD: University Park Press)	Comprehension of grammatical form and structure	4:0–8:0	Picture identification	Receptive developmental age and error analysis by grammatical form	

TABLE 14.4
Continued

Test Name	Areas Assessed	Age (years: months) Range	Format	Scores Obtained	Unique Aspects
Peabody Picture Vocabulary Test— Revised (Dunn & Dunn, 1981. Circle Pines, MN: American Guidance Service)	Receptive vocabulary	1:9–33:8	Picture identification	Receptive vocabulary age, standard score, percentile, stanine	Adaptable for children with motor impairment; Spanish translation
Preschool Language Assessment Instrument (Blank, Rose, & Berlin, 1978. New York: Grune & Stratton)	Discourse, general language ability	3:0–5:11	Responses to pictures, questions	Profile of discourse skills; qualitative rating of language adequacy	Can be used with children who have poor school performance & whose language skills are questionable (up to age 10)
Reynell Developmental Language Scales (Reynell, 1969. NFER Publishers)	General expressive and receptive language skills	1:0–5:0	Observation, picture identification, object identification, object manipulation	Communication age equivalent	
Sequenced Inventory of Communicative Development— Revised (Hedrick, Prather, & Tobin, 1984. Seattle: University of Washington Press)	Sound awareness and discrimination, comprehension; motor, vocal, and verbal expressions (i.e., responses, initiations, imitations)	0:4–4:0	Parent report, object manipulation, picture identification, following directions	Receptive communication age, expressive communication age	Assesses prelinguistic skills
Test for Auditory	Comprehension of	3:0–9:11	Picture identification, ob-	Percentile rank, com-	Percentile ranks for

TABLE 14.4
Continued

Test Name	Areas Assessed	Age (years: months) Range	Format	Scores Obtained	Unique Aspects
Comprehension of Language— Revised (Carrow-Woolfolk, 1985. Allen, TX: DLM Teaching Resources)	grammatical form and structure, content, and vocabulary		ject manipulation, best choice	prehension age equivalent	grade equivalents
Test of Early Language Development (Hresko, Reid & Hammill, 1981. Austin, TX: Pro-Ed)	Receptive and expressive grammatical forms, content of language, and word knowledge	3:0–7:11	Picture identification, answering questions, object manipulation, imitation, picture description, best choice, sentence completion, synonyms, sentence formulation, defining words	Percentile, language age, language quotient	
Test of Pragmatic Skills (Shulman, 1985. Tucson, AZ: Communication Skill Builders)	How children verbally adapt to various communicative contexts	3:0–8:11	Four guided-play interactions	Summary sheet for normative data	
The Test of Language Development— Primary (Newcommer & Hammill, 1984. Austin, TX: Pro-Ed)	Grammatic understanding; receptive and expressive vocabulary; expressive grammatical structure	4:0–8:11	Picture identification, imitation, grammatic completion, defining words, word discrimination, word articulation	Language ages for each subtest, standardized global index of language ability	

TABLE 14.4
Continued

B. *Standardized Language Screening Instruments:*

Test Name	Areas Assessed	Age (years: months) Range	Format	Scores Obtained	Unique Aspects
Bankson Language Screening Test (Bankson, 1977. Baltimore, MD: University Park Press)	Vocabulary, grammatical form, content, and visual and auditory perception	4:1–8:0	Picture identification, object identification, best choice, imitation, sequencing, matching	Standard deviation scores, percentiles	
Compton Speech and Language Screening Evaluation (Compton, 1978. San Francisco: Carousel House)	Articulation, vocabulary, colors, shapes, fluency, voice, oral mechanism, auditory-visual memory, expressive grammatical structure, and grammatical understanding	3:0–6:0	Object identification, object labeling, oral mechanism exam	Pass/fail	
Fluharty Preschool Speech and Language Screening Test (Fluharty, 1978. Hingham, MA: Teaching Resources)	Articulation, vocabulary, receptive and expressive language	2:0–6:0	Object identification, picture identification, sentence repetition	Cut-off scores for each age group	
Preschool Language Screening Test (Hannah & Gardner, 1974. Northridge, CA: Joyce Motion Picture)	Visual and auditory perception, motor skills, basic concepts	3:0–5:6	Picture identification, following directions	Percentiles for general language ability and for specific skills	Toddler screening to determine if basal can be established (2:6–3)

TABLE 14.4
Continued

Test Name	Areas Assessed	Age (years: months) Range	Format	Scores Obtained	Unique Aspects
Northwestern Syntax Screening Test (Lee, 1971. Evanston, IL: North-western University Press)	Receptive and expressive grammatical form and structure	3:0–7:11	Picture identification, imitation	Age equivalent	
Pragmatics Screening Test (Prinz & Weiner, 1987. Columbus, OH: Merrill)	Maintaining topic, formulating speech acts, politeness, establishing a referent for listener, narration, revising a directive when listener does not understand	3:5–8:5	Gamelike tasks (ghost trick, absurd requests, referential communication)		
Preschool Language Scale— Revised (Zimmerman, Steiner, & Pond, 1979. Columbus, OH: Merrill)	Developmental aspects of auditory comprehension, articulation, grammatical form and structure, basic concepts	1:0–6:7	Responses to pictures; object manipulation; picture identification; following directions	Auditory comprehension and verbal ability ages; language quotient; profile of language use	Spanish translation
Receptive-Expressive Emergent Language Scale (Bzoch & League, 1970. Baltimore, MD: University Park Press)	Prelinguistic skills	0:1–3:0	Parent report	Receptive and expressive communication age	

TABLE 14.4
Continued

C. *Developmental Profiles of Speech and Language*:

Test Name	Areas Assessed	Age (years: months) Range	Format	Scores Obtained	Unique Aspects
Birth to Three Developmental Scales (Bangs & Dodson, 1979. Hingham, MA: Teaching Resources)	Problem solving, personal-social skills, motor skills, general receptive and expressive language	0:0–3:0	Observation, following directions, motor and verbal imitation, picture identification, naming body parts, object identification, parental report	Age equivalent for each subtest, scores indicating emerging behaviors; profile of skills across areas	
Communicative Evaluation Chart (Anderson, Miles, & Matheny, 1963. Cambridge, MA: Educators Publishing Service)	Overall language development	0:3–5:0	Observation, following directions, verbal and motor productions, drawing, answering questions	Checklist to mark present, absent, or inconsistently present behaviors	
Environmental Prelanguage Battery (Horstmeier & MacDonald, 1978. Columbus, OH: Merrill)	Prelinguistic skills (functional play, imitation, turntaking)	criterion norms 1:0–2:6	Observation, play, verbal and gestural imitation, object identification, picture identification, following directions	Nonverbal and verbal percentage scores	Assesses early communication skills
Environmental Language Intervention Program (MacDonald, 1978. Columbus, OH: Merrill)	Expressive grammatical forms and structure	norms for 1:1–4:9	Conversation, imitation, play	Rankings, length of responses, intelligibility	Adaptable for many different populations
Infant Scale of Communicative Intent (Sacks & Young, 1982.	Prelinguistic skills	0:0–1:6	Observation	Checklist to mark pass/ fail, inconsistent behaviors	

TABLE 14.4
Continued

Test Name	Areas Assessed	Age (years: Months) Range	Format	Scores Obtained	Unique Aspects
Philadelphia: St. Christopher's Hospital for Children)					

D. *Standardized Speech Diagnostic Instruments:*

Test Name	Areas Assessed	Age (years: Months) Range	Format	Scores Obtained	Unique Aspects
Arizona Articulation Proficiency Scale (Fudala, 1970. Los Angeles: Western Psychological Services)	Determining misarticulations and total articulation proficiency	any age, norms for 3:0–11:11	Picture identification	Total score, weighted for percentage each error sound is used in English	
Compton-Hutton Phonological Assessment (Compton & Hutton, 1978. San Francisco: Carousel House)	Broad patterns of articulation errors and linguistic analyses of misarticulation	any age	Picture identification	Summary of phonological processes used, phonological pattern analysis, phonological rule analysis	
Goldman-Fristoe Test of Articulation (Goldman & Fristoe, 1986. Circle Pines, MN: American Guidance Service)	Articulation errors and stimulability for correct production of error sounds	2:0–16:0 +	Picture identification, story retell, imitation	Percentage of speech in error	
Khan-Lewis Phonological Analysis (Khan & Lewis, 1986. Circle Pines, MN: American Guidance Service)	Diagnosis and description of articulation or phonological disorders	any age, norms for 2:0–5:11	Uses stimulus material from *Goldman-Fristoe Test of Articulation*, test yields error scores, percentage ranks	Developmental phonological process rating	

FIGURE 14.5
Communication Report Form

Instructions: Please check under level of use each communicative function and write in the communication mode.

	Level of Use			Communication Mode Used[a]		Situations	
Functions	Yes does this	Is learning this	Does not do this	Most often	Least often	In what situations?	Give example
1. *Requests objects*— Does your child communicate that he wants an object that is out of reach? (e.g., pushes adult's hands toward a cookie or says, "cookie")							
2. *Requests action*— Does your child communicate that she wants help doing something? (e.g., hands adult a jar to open or says, "open")							
3. *Attention seeking*— Does your child communicate that he wants you to attend to him or to something in the environment? (e.g., tugs on mother's pants or says, "mama")							
4. *Comment on object*—Does your child communicate that she wants you to notice or comment on an object? (e.g., points to "dog" and smiles or says, "dog")							

FIGURE 14.5
Continued

Functions	Level of Use			Communication Mode Used[a]		Situations	
	Yes does this	Is learning this	Does not do this	Most often	Least often	In what situations?	Give example
5. *Comment on action*—Does your child communicate that he is interested in something another person or object has done or does he try to get you to notice (e.g., flies plane in air and claps or says, "up")							
6. *Protests*—Does your child communicate that she does not like or does not want something (e.g., pushes your hand away or says, "no")							
7. *Requests information*—Does your child ask for names and locations of things, animals or people? (e.g., points to picture in book and looks at adult or asks "What that?")							
8. *Answers*—Does your child respond to your questions about names and locations of things, animals, or people? (e.g., when asked, "What do you want?" points to chocolate cookie or says, "cookie")							

FIGURE 14.5
Continued

| Functions | Level of Use | | | Communication Mode Used[a] | | Situations | |
	Yes does this	Is learning this	Does not do this	Most often	Least often	In what situations?	Give example
9. *Acknowledges*—Does your child do something to indicate that he has heard you speaking to him? (e.g., nods his head or says, "ok")							
10. *Social routines*— Does your child communicate routines such as "please," "thank you," "hi," and "bye"? (e.g., to indicate "bye bye" waves or says "bye")							

[a]GE = gesture, SP = speech, SO = sounds, SI = signing, BM = body movements, and FE = facial expressions.

(speech sounds or nonspeech sounds); and (c) in what situation the child expresses these intentions.

A Framework for Communication Assessment

Once having established through the decision trees how the child typically communicates in the areas of pragmatics, comprehension, and production, a number of questions should be considered: (a) How does this child compare with other children of the same chronological age? (b) Should this child be diagnosed as belonging to a particular etiological group? (c) Is this child "delayed" or "disordered"? (d) How does the child function across the domains of language (semantics, syntax, phonology, pragmatics)? and finally, (e) what

communicative skills should be expected of this child? The answers to most of these questions typically involve the SLP working in conjunction with other interventionists performing both formal and informal tests and observations. Other professionals have many opportunities to observe and interact with the child in a natural setting and therefore can supplement the findings of the SLP by performing additional informal assessment techniques as well as providing additional intervention planning and implementation.

To help the interventionist both ask and answer questions pertinent to a particular child, a framework for looking at communication, suggested by R. S. Chapman (personal communication, March 3, 1986), is provided.

The framework includes four perspectives: (a) communicative event, (b) developmental, (c) individual differences or disordered, and (d) etiological. Each perspective has its own set of questions, particular behaviors to sample, and judgments to be made when evaluating a child's communication skills. Chapman suggests the integrated use of all four perspectives when assessing communication skills in children. In this section, a brief overview of each perspective will be presented, followed by a discussion of the assessment tools and practices specific to each of the four perspectives. In addition, the use of the four perspectives in assessment and remediation planning for an individual child is demonstrated.

Communicative Event Perspective. The **communicative event perspective** is based on the adult model of communication and asks, "What does a child need to know and do to be a successful communicator?" This perspective draws heavily from work in the area of pragmatics. Thus, communication is viewed as an act of problem solving for both the speaker and listener as they work together to carry on conversations. Once the decision trees have been used to determine the child's typical mode of communicating, the way a child elicits a listener's attention, and the way he takes turns in a conversation, this perspective is used to focus on whether the child is successful in his attempts to communicate and on what kind of success/failure ratio is demonstrated. Usually the more nonverbal a child, the less successful the child will be, at least in a traditional communicative environment. If there are unsuccessful communication attempts, the interventionist should question how and why the child is unsuccessful and how the success rate can be improved.

From the communicative event perspective, it is also necessary to examine communicative efforts with different speakers and across different situations. Do communication difficulties appear to be external

to the child (e.g., cultural or foreign language differences or extremely high expectations by the parents or caretakers), or are they child-related (e.g., not knowing the rules of discourse or having a limited vocabulary)? Additionally, are the difficulties specific to interactions with speakers (e.g., teacher, caretakers, or peers) or situations (e.g., structured classroom activity, mealtime, or free play)? The interventionist making judgments about a child's communicative interactions also needs to consider and evaluate how typical these interactions are for the child and whether they represent a changeable dimension for the child.

Due to the recent focus on pragmatics in the field of child language, the communicative event perspective has the fewest formal and informal measures for assessment. A few standardized instruments that assess pragmatic skills are described in Table 14.4. In a practical sense, however, the interventionist can be guided by her own knowledge of the rules and behaviors necessary to achieve successful communication. Roth and Spekman (1984) review informal measures of pragmatic development.

Developmental Perspective. Because all children lack some communication skills when compared to adults, it is necessary to look at a second perspective, taking into account the developmental nature of communication. The **developmental perspective,** as its name implies, considers the child's current communication skills in comparison to the skills of children of the same chronological age. The focus is also on the child's level of development across skill areas (i.e., motor, cognitive) to get a picture of the child's overall developmental level.

The developmental perspective is based on the belief that children generally perform similarly across many skill areas and that a major discrepancy between skill levels is indicative of developmental problems. The first task of the interventionist is to look across the skill areas relevent to communication (motor, social/emotional, cognitive, self-help, play and academic achievement) and decide which ones should be assessed. Once these areas have been selected and evaluated, the interventionist should look across the components of language (phonology, semantics, syntax, and pragmatics) for both the comprehension and production skills available to the child in each domain.

Once all the skill areas are chosen and assessed, the interventionist compares developmental levels across skill areas. First, for each area, she must decide whether the skills displayed (and the developing behaviors preceding those skills) have followed a normal developmental sequence. Is this child performing like a younger normally developing child? Second, she should look for discrepancies between areas that may indicate particular difficulties for the child. For normally developing children, most skill areas will generally develop in parallel with the child's chronological age with relatively little discrepancy between areas. For children with communication and/or other problems, the discrepancies between skill areas may be much larger. For these children it is often better to use the child's nonverbal cognitive age level as a guide to the type and level of behaviors that can be expected from that child (Miller et al., 1980). The developmental perspective has been the basis of most currently available assessment tools and a variety of these measures are given in Table 14.4.

Individual Differences/Disordered Perspective. The **individual differences/disordered perspective** is used to examine the child who exhibits unusual or developmentally nonsequential behaviors. This perspective focuses on the individual differences exhibited by a child and attempts to determine the characteristics of those behaviors. The perspective asks, "Are there particular behaviors that do not disappear or improve with age and thus should be considered

disordered?" Certain behaviors and mannerisms, for example, the echolalia and pronoun reversals displayed by individuals with autism or mental retardation, are not representative of younger normally developing children. Additionally, there are individuals who display such discrepancy between skill areas that they are considered to be disordered; for example, children with learning disabilities who typically have normal intelligence yet still experience academic difficulties.

Few assessment measures, however, give any indication of "delay" vs. "disorder" in their results, and typically this decision is left to the clinician and/or interventionist. The most practical way to come to such a decision is by using developmental scales and focusing on the sequence of development followed by the child. The educator should look especially to the skills and behaviors exhibited by younger, normally developing children for evidence of a particular child's behaviors. Traditionally, if the child either is out of sequence in development or exhibits behaviors not typically seen in younger children, then the child's skills in that area are assumed to be disordered.

Etiological Perspective. The fourth perspective for assessing communication difficulties is based on etiological categorization. The **etiological perspective** stresses the similarities among children who have been diagnosed as being in the same etiological group. Typically when assessing and diagnosing children, we first note their language difficulties and then attempt to fit them into one of our existing diagnostic or etiological categories, such as hearing impairment, mental retardation, or aphasia. If the child has enough characteristics representative of a particular diagnosis, then the assumption is made that this child has a similar diagnosis.

Etiological categories can be especially useful when trying to predict what skill levels and behaviors to expect from an individual child. Each diagnostic category provides us with a set of assumptions (based on the development of other children in that category) that can guide both our assessment and treatment of a particular child. Although a given child may differ from other children in the same etiological group, there will also be a number of similarities.

Using the Decision Trees and Four Perspectives

As a guide to implementing and integrating the information gained from the decision trees and the four perspectives, a description of a child with communication difficulties follows. Take for example, an 18-month-old child named Susan, who, as was determined through using the decision tree in Figure 14.2, plays two social interaction games (e.g., tickle and peek-a-boo), elicits adult attention by vocalizing, looks at objects mentioned, reacts to "bye-bye" when context cues are present (e.g., coat, car keys), imitates some sounds when she is the initiator of the sounds, and exhibits vocally the intentions of requesting and protesting.

Considering each of the four perspectives for communication assessment, the communication event perspective is used first to rule out any event-related or environmentally related problems affecting the child's current level of communication functioning. Susan is observed with her parents, other caretakers, and the examiner in three situations (e.g., free-play, mealtime, bathtime) to look for difficulties in interactional style and for ways to increase and improve interaction patterns. After considering factors external to the child, child-related issues are examined, including the child's conversational skill level and functioning with different speakers and situations.

The interventionist can now use the developmental perspective to look at Susan's performance in communication as well as in cognitive, motor, and social skills as compared to children of the same chronological or cognitive level. From the use of developmental scales, Susan appears to be functioning at approximately the 12- to 14-month level in prelinguistic, cognitive, motor, and play skills and is approximately 5 months below age level in all areas. Although her skills are delayed, they display a "flat" or even profile, thus the individual differences/disordered perspective will not be necessary at this time.

Considering that Susan had delayed but normally sequenced skills, the next step is to look for causal or etiological factors such as mental retardation, metabolic disorder, or brain injury. The interventionist uses the etiological perspective for verification or for sample behaviors indicative of a particular etiological group. If, for example, Susan was identified after genetic testing as having Down syndrome, several characteristics associated with Down syndrome that put this child at risk for language deficits should be considered. As noted by Miller (1987), Down syndrome children have an increased incidence of otitis media, hearing loss, speech/motor control problems, and cognitive deficits. Further, there are often differences in the expectation for performance of these children. With this etiological information in mind, the examiner may take certain actions for testing, such as allowing longer response times and gearing testing instructions to Susan's particular cognitive and language levels.

Finally, using the decision trees and all four perspectives, the examiner comes full circle and returns to asking and answering questions about ways in which modifications can be made in both the assessment procedures and the examiner's expectations. The observations and parent reports acquired from the decision trees now can be compared with the information gained from use of the four perspectives to look for patterns of strengths and weaknesses in and across skill areas. The use of the decision trees and the perspectives, however, involves only brief interactions between the child and other individuals. The next section explores additional assessment alternatives, particularly those which involve continuous sampling of a child's communicative attempts.

Communication Sampling Strategies

A frequently used method for obtaining information about children's communication is to collect a spontaneous **communication sample**, which is a running record of the communication efforts by a child during a set period of time. Most samples can be collected in a natural setting and are useful for assessing the frequency and manner in which children communicate in their daily environment. The ultimate goal of the data gathering is to achieve a sample representative of a child's usual communicative performance.

Two broad categories of communication sampling are available to the interventionist. The first is a detailed or formal analysis covering all language domains (phonology, syntax, semantics, and pragmatics) and is typically performed by the SPL. The interventionist can, however, play an important role in the data collection and analysis of a formal sample, particularly when the focus is on specific language behaviors. Several structured and computerized techniques are available to assist in formal analysis and are listed in Table 14.4. The second category of communication sampling includes informal methods often used to gather information about a specific language structure or intention. In this method, the interventionist chooses a behavior to sample, sets up the environment to elicit the behavior, and then keeps a record of the communicational exchanges between the participants.

Before the interventionist decides which type of sample to collect, four important issues should be considered. First, what is the purpose of the assessment? Is it to document the child's development across all language domains or to document only specific language behaviors (i.e., use of requests for objects and actions)? Second, how much detail is needed; for example, is it necessary to examine all aspects of pragmatic communication or only one or two categories of communicative intent? Third, how much time is available to collect and analyze the sample? For a formal sample, Miller (1981) suggests at least two 15-minute sampling sessions with a minimum of 50–100 utterances recorded. An informal sample, on the other hand, could last 5 minutes and could include only the child's nonverbal behaviors. Finally, what are the resources available for collecting and analyzing the sample? A formal sample, for example, typically requires more elaborate recording, coding, and analysis procedures than does an informal sample.

Collecting the Sample.   The collection of the sample is very important because the context, elicitation technique, and nature of the interaction will influence the representativeness of the sample. The context should include activities that are both age appropriate and interesting to the child, and it is particularly important that the sample be collected during genuine communication where the child is communicating for a purpose. The sample can be collected almost anywhere (e.g., classroom, home, playground), although certain settings, (e.g., playtime, mealtime) are more accessible than others. It is advantageous to sample more than one context within a setting, for example, by changing the communicative partner or activity.

Once the context is selected, the technique for eliciting the sample should be identified. One technique available is **naturalistic observation**, in which the interventionist only observes the behavior and does not provide any structure during the observation. With naturalistic observation, however, certain types of communicative behaviors (i.e., question asking) may occur infrequently or not at all. Therefore, a second technique, **structured elicited interaction**, may be used, in which the interventionist structures the situation to increase the probability of particular types of behaviors occurring. This structured technique can be used to elicit specific intentions such as requests or protests as well as to elicit specific language structures such as negatives or complex sentences. For example, if the interventionist desires information about a child's requesting behavior, the child can be given a tightly closed plastic jar with a cookie inside to see whether the child requests assistance and how she requests it. The child also can be given a dried-out marker to encourage requesting another marker. Creaghead (1984), Fey (1986), and Miller (1981) describe specific procedures that can be used during structured elicited interactions.

Finally, the nature of the interaction between the child and other participants in the sample should be outlined. Children talk more when their conversational partners use facilitative strategies such as pausing for the child to take a turn, being responsive to any communicative attempts, and using open-ended rather than close-ended questions. Additionally, as noted by Cazden (1970), children converse more readily and with a greater number of exchanges when conversation is initiated by the child rather than the adult. See Figure 14.1, Miller (1981) and Lund and Duchan (1988) for suggestions on how to engage children in conversation during language samples.

Recording the Sample. An accurate account of the communicative interaction is important for specifying appropriate instructional targets. Language samples can be recorded using videotape, audiotape, or the "on line" method, that is, with the observer writing down the sample verbatim. Although videotaping is the optimal way to record the sample, it is often impractical. Audio recording with notes about the context and the child's nonverbal behavior are typically considered adequate. When video or audio recording are not available or practical, however, on-line

transcription of a child's communication can be performed. The interventionist can either write down everything the child says that relates to the language dimension of focus or use interval sampling techniques where the examiner intermittently records behavior (e.g., 1 minute of recording, 30 seconds nonrecording, 1 minute recording). An example of a form for collecting a sample is shown in Figure 14.6 (p. 374). The form's first column identifies the speaker; the second column, the transcription of the communication; the third column, the type of turn; the fourth column, the type of intention; and the last column, the mode used to communicate. Nonverbal behaviors and other contextual notes are in parentheses and are often necessary because the meaning of an utterance may differ depending on the context in which it was emitted (Bloom, 1970).

Analyzing the Sample. Just as the data-collection and recording procedures depend on the assessment goals, so do the analysis strategies. For the interventionist who is primarily interested in an overview of a child's communicative behavior (e.g., whether a child can initiate and respond in interactions), the collected sample itself may provide adequate and interpretable information. For some children, however, more detailed analyses are necessary to focus on specific behaviors in the areas of pragmatics, semantics, syntax, and phonology.

In analyzing pragmatic behavior, children's intentions can be coded into specific categories using a taxonomy such as the one in Table 14.1. The language sample can then be examined for three indices: the frequency of communication, the diversity of intentions expressed, and the diversity of forms used to express the communicative intentions. Intentions can also be analyzed to determine the typical mode of communication and whether intentions are expressed using different modes. For example, requests may be expressed with speech, but protests with gestures only.

FIGURE 14.6
Communication
Sample Analysis

Child: <u>Bob (B)</u>   Other Participant: <u>Teacher (T)</u>   Setting: <u>Classroom</u>   Date: <u>7/7/87</u>

Activity: <u>Snack</u>   Length of observation: <u>10</u>   Observer: <u>J R</u>

Notes: <u>Bob appears tired</u>

Speaker	Communication Behavior	Turn[a]	Intentions[b]	Mode[c]
T	"It's snack time. Look." (teacher puts cookies wrapped in tin foil on table and pauses)			
B	"Want." (reaches for package)	I	RO	GE
T	"What do you want?"			
B	"Want that." (pointing to tin foil package)	R	AN	SP&GE
T	"What *is* that?" (teacher models question and waits)			
B	(reaches for package)	R	RO	GE
T	"What *is* that? I don't know." (teacher again models question and answer and waits)			
B	"What that?" (pointing to package)	R	RI	SP&GE
T	"I don't know. Let's look." (teacher opens tin foil, briefly shows edge of cookie, and then closes foil)			
B	"Cookie?"	R	RI	SP
T	"Yes, it's a cookie."			
B	"Want cookie."	I	RO	SP
T	"I want a cookie."			
B	"Me want cookie."	R	RO	SP
T	"Good, I want a cookie too." (gives one to each of them)			
B	"More cookie." (pointing toward others in package)	I	RO	SP

[a] *Turn*—I = Initiation, R = Response
[b] *Intention*—RO = Request for object, RI = Request for information, AN = answer
[c] *Mode*—SP = speech, GE = gesture

The sample can also be analyzed for the frequency of use of discourse skills in conversation. Determining the percentage of time a child responds to or initiates an overture, as well as to whom the child speaks (e.g., adults only and never to peers) can provide important information on the effectiveness of the child's conversation skills. The average number of turns over which a child maintains interaction in routines such as pat-a-cake or vocal play and in conversational exchanges can be useful. Additional information in specific categories of discourse such as answering, acknowledging, and requesting information, along with their form of communication can also be useful. Figure 14.6 shows how intentions and turn-taking can be coded in a communication sample. For additional information on pragmatic behaviors to be coded, see Roth and Spekman (1984) and Paul (1987).

When coding any aspect of pragmatic behavior, it is important to examine the context to determine if an opportunity existed for the child to produce a particular communicative intention or discourse strategy. It may be possible that a specific behavior did not occur (i.e., protesting or responding) because there was not opportunity for the behavior to occur. Also intentions must be inferred from a child's behavior. Although various sources of information (context, verbal and nonverbal behavior, and effect of the behavior) can be used when inferring communicative intent, one cannot always be certain that the interpretation was the speaker's intent.

For semantic abilities, the analysis can include the number and type of semantic relations, the total number of words, and the number of different words expressed in the sample. Using Table 14.3, each utterance can be examined to determine the semantic relationship categories used in any prelinguistic, one-word, and multiword utterances, as well as whether a variety of semantic roles is used to express communicative intents. If, for intervention purposes, the interventionist is interested in a specific category of words such as common foods or animals, these words can be included in the analysis. A further index of vocabulary diversity can be computed by using a Type Token Ratio (TTR), which is the number of different words used in a 50-utterance sample divided by the total number of words. A TTR of .45–.50 is common in children between the ages 3 and 8 and shows a reasonable amount of vocabulary diversity within the sample. A low ratio, .10 for example, on the other hand, indicates that a child is using only a few words, although repeatedly, and is thus limited in vocabulary diversity.

When analyzing the sample for syntactic knowledge, the interventionist should look first at both the child's overall utterance length or the MLU (as described earlier, p. 346) and the basic sentence structure used. For a child using only one- or two-word utterances, syntactic analysis is not necessary. For a child using constructions of three words or more, the analysis could include the use of the 14 grammatical morphemes (de Villiers & de Villiers, 1973), negatives, questions, and simple vs. complex sentence structures. Detailed procedures for syntactic analysis are described in Miller (1981).

In analyzing the sample for phonological skills, the interventionist can note the sounds the child is and is not producing and then use developmental information to identify the child's approximate developmental level. Although a language sample can be analyzed for specific sounds and simple error patterns, a detailed analysis is typically carried out by the SLP.

For more detailed analysis of syntax, semantics, and pragmatic skills, several standardized language analysis procedures are available. Procedures that include a computerized analysis program are: *Systematic Analysis of Language Transcripts* (Miller & Chapman, 1985), *Lingquest Language Sample Analysis* (Mordecai, Palin, & Palmer, 1985), and *Developmental Sentence Analysis* (Lee, 1974).

Analysis Illustrated. An example of how language sample information can be analyzed is illustrated in Figure 14.6 for a 4-year-old child, Bob, who has cerebral palsy. The language sample was collected during two 10-minute classroom activities, one during snack and the other during free-play. A portion of the snack-time sample is shown in Figure 14.6. Bob communicated 50 times during the two observations, using speech most frequently and gestures on occasion. His speech consisted primarily of one- and two-word utterances and an occasional three-word utterance. He responded appropriately to many adult requests by answering questions using words and gestures (especially grabbing), and when frustrated, cried rather than verbalized his desires. Except for very structured settings such as snack time, Bob infrequently initiated communication to his teacher and less frequently to peers. If an adult started and controlled the interaction, however, Bob would respond by taking as many as five turns using speech. He often used repetition of the adult's utterance as a means for continuing the interaction.

The semantic analysis indicated that Bob used a total of 64 words and that there were 32 different words, for a TTR of .50. Bob expressed a range of semantic relations at the two-word level, such as agent + object, action + object, recurrence + object, and one type at the three-word level (agent + action + object). The words he used were the names of people and common objects, actions, social words, and modifiers. The syntactic analysis on 40 utterances indicated that Bob's MLU in morphemes was 1.75 although this figure should be interpreted cautiously. As recommended by Miller (1981), MLU should be based on at least 50 utterances. The morphemes used included plural *s*, pronoun *me*, and the present progressive *-ing*. The phonological analysis indicated that Bob used age-appropriate initial and medial consonants but omitted most final consonants.

In summary, the information derived from a language sample can provide important information about the way a child communicates during everyday situations and can be a working basis for later intervention decisions. In addition to the nonstandard methods described above, there are also standardized measures to consider in the assessment, and ultimately the treatment, processes.

Standardized Tests of Language

As noted previously, standardized testing is particularly useful for screening communication skills and for documenting communication levels, but less useful for identifying instructional targets. Standardized tests, however, can be used to supplement the information gained from the decision trees, four perspectives, and a language sample. Table 14.4 contains a list of selected standardized speech and language diagnostic and screening tests that can be used to assess the communication of infants and preschoolers. Indicated for each test are the areas assessed, age range, format of the test, type of score obtained, and unique aspects.

Developmental Scales

Developmental scales, unlike standardized tests, are typically not standardized and are often a compilation of developmental information taken from other developmental charts and scales. Although this information can be very helpful in an assessment and later for intervention purposes, care should be taken when using developmental charts as anything more than rough guidelines to development. Table 14.4 shows a listing of commercially available instruments to diagnose and screen a child's speech and language. Other developmental scales that assess communication also assess social, cognitive, and motor skills. Examples are the Battelle Developmental Inventory (Newborg, Stock, Wnek, Guidubaldi, & Svinicki, 1984), Hawaii Early Learning Profile (Furuno, O'Reilly, Hosaka, Inatsuka, Allman, & Zeisloft; 1979), and Developmental Programming for Infants and Young Children (Roger, Donovan, D'Eugenio, Brown, Whiteside-Lynch, Moersch, & Schafer, 1981). Several other developmental scales, although not commercially available, may be very useful in the assessment process. These include: Early Communicative Competence Scale (Holdgrafer & Dunst, 1986), Procedures Manual for Early Social Communication Scales (Seibert & Hogan, 1982b), Generic Skills Inventory, Parsons Preschool Curriculum (Snyder-McLean, Sack, & Solomonson, 1985), and Assessing Prelinguistic and Early Linguistic Behaviors in Developmentally Young Children (Olswang, Stoel-Gammon, Coggins, & Carpenter; 1987).

Synthesizing the Assessment Information

Once the interventionist has used the decision tree, formulated and answered questions from the four perspectives of communication, taken a language sample (if necessary), administered standardized tests, and/or used the developmental scales, then instructional goals in communication can be selected. The information gained from these procedures will not only give some indication of how the child currently communicates but also typically reveals the child's strengths and weaknesses.

Translating Assessment Information into Instructional Goals

This section focuses first on several guidelines for planning communication goals for intervention. Although many of the guidelines can be applied to any type of educational intervention, some are specific to communication abilities. Following these guidelines is a discussion of how to use the information from the decision trees, the perspectives of communication, and the language sample in planning instructional goals. Finally, a demonstration of how to translate the assessment information into instructional goals is provided.

Intervention Guidelines

Start at Go. Children cannot be expected to achieve skills beyond their cognitive, motor, social, or communicative levels, and yet somehow many interventionists forget this fact. A concrete example of starting at an inappropriate level is when the parent, teacher, or interventionist prompts the child, who typically only produces vocalizations, to use entire words. Although prompting words or structures that are slightly beyond the child's current capabilities is initially appropriate, it is also important to meet the child at her level of functioning and to provide a bridge to the next higher skill level. An example of bridging for this child would be to: (a) model an entire word, (b) reduce the whole word to shortened form on successive productions, (c) guide the child to make closer and closer approximations of the word, and (d) encourage and reinforce the child for any communication attempts. In essence, be aware of the child's overall developmental and communicative skills, and balance instructional goals to encompass both the child's current level of functioning and her behaviors at a slightly higher or more complex level.

Move Vertically and Horizontally. When planning intervention, consider both vertical and horizontal movement in various skill areas. As the previous example illustrates, if the child is not ready or able to move vertically to the next level (from vocalization to verbalization), the interventionist should consider either smaller vertical behaviors or other horizontal skills that can be encouraged and developed. Thus, vocalization could be paired with a gesture (vertical move) or vocalization could be encouraged across communicative intents (horizontal move). For practical guides to communication development, the interventionist can turn to the developmental scales listed in Table 14.4 and to the decision trees, Figures 14.2–14.4.

Focus on the Child for Cues. *Readability*, or the ability of the interventionist to recognize and respond to the child's behaviors, is an important part of the intervention process (Goldberg, 1977). The better the adult is at "reading" the infant, the more likely is the adult's response to get or keep an interaction going. In addition, reading cues more accurately can help the interventionist establish the child's level of communication functioning. Clearly, interventionists need to orient their own skills to reading infants and also, at times, to helping the parents develop or expand these abilities. It is also important to look for many types of communication (gestures and vocalizations) from the child and to take the focus off words. Refer to Goldberg (1977), Dunst (1981), and Dunst and Wortman-Lowe (1986) for ideas for recognizing communicative efforts in young children.

Be Functional. Use naturalistic settings, materials, and procedures as often as possible. As described in earlier chapters, the acquisition and generalization of newly acquired skills are greater when the context for training is closest to the setting in which the behavior actually occurs. With communication skills, for example, the context for teaching a child to request actions should occur at the time and in the place when the child actually needs someone to perform an action. Language is typically acquired in a context in which the child is motivated to communicate to achieve a desired response from others; therefore, always provide the child with a reason to communicate. In this way, the achievement of the desired response often becomes its own reinforcement. Hart and Rogers-Warren (1978) and Fey (1986) are excellent guides to the use of naturalistic contexts for language intervention.

Follow the Interest of the Child. Use developmental and play scales as a guide to toys,

materials, and activities that are of interest to children of different developmental levels. As noted previously, the closer the match between a child's cognitive and developmental levels and the tasks and materials, the more likely is the child to succeed and enjoy the activity. A major tenet of incidental teaching that has considerable empirical support in increasing children's communication (Warren & Kaiser, 1986; Hart & Risley, 1978) is following a child's interest in selecting communication targets. Sources such as Dunst (1981), Fey (1986), and Westby (1980) are useful for guiding decisions about children's interests and developmental skills.

Go for Success. Target either frequently occurring behaviors that need modification or desired but nonexisting behaviors that have many opportunities for practice and reinforcement. Clearly, behaviors that are required often are more likely to be acquired. For example, modeling vocalizations to request objects that the child likes and is exposed to frequently is an appropriate target for a child who vocalizes to protest actions but not to make requests.

Consider the Content of the Activities. Be sure to keep in mind the developmental levels and functionality of the topics chosen for intervention. Many preschool programs for children with developmental delays continue to focus on colors or shapes or the days of the week, when more functional skills such as requests for information or how to ask a peer for a toy would be more useful targets. In other words, when planning content for intervention consider how and when that content could be used by the child. Choose topics the child can benefit from in everyday life.

Be Efficient. Plan individual goals in order to work on more than one skill area or aspect of an area at one time. As an example, plan goals that focus on language as well as cognitive skills and embed them both in a play activity. Or, while focusing on single-word imitation and requests for objects, you might use particular words with a *b* sound for concurrent articulation work.

Check Comprehension in Relation to Production. Keep in mind that if a child produces a particular syntactic form, it does not ensure that the child automatically comprehends it, or vice versa. For example, a child's use of temporal order ("we ate lunch then we played") in productive language does not necessarily mean the child comprehends that structure when used by others. Before working on production goals, test the task or skill in comprehension.

Use Direct Training at Times. Remember that many children with handicaps have had difficulty learning some skills in an incidental manner, that is, through naturalistic interactions with people and objects in their environment. Therefore, it may be appropriate to train some skills more directly. This may be true, for example, of articulation skills (*s*) or syntactic structures (use of *is*) for some children. In addition, the use of imitation, particularly for sound, word, phrase, or morphological learning can be extremely productive. As noted previously, imitation is often used by the child for items that the child is in the process of learning (Owens, 1984). Thus, the use of imitation training and later generalization to more "natural" and spontaneous contexts has empirical support from the language acquisition literature.

Be Facilitative. Use techniques to facilitate interaction such as modeling desired verbal and nonverbal behaviors, describing your own or a child's actions, expanding communications used by the child, allowing the child time to take a turn, and occasionally revising a child's communications. Nonverbal behaviors and vocalizations can be modeled as easily as verbalizations. For example, you could hold a toy to "trade" while vocalizing "uh?" and pointing to the desired toy, or you could model only what you want the child to *say*,

such as "That's mine," while demonstrating a pulling away gesture with the toy, rather than using, "Say, that's mine." Remember that you are a model of communication for the child, and therefore consider carefully what you say and how. As often as possible, use phrases and sentences that the child would be likely to use in her own interactions. Fey (1986) is an excellent source for a variety of facilitation techniques.

Selection of Goals

With these guidelines in mind, the next step is to look across the skill areas and identify both the broad and the immediate instructional goals. For infants and young children with communication difficulties, the focus should primarily be on the pragmatic and semantic aspects of communication rather than the syntactic and phonological. The interventionist must also decide what skill areas other than communication will be intervention targets. When choosing and ranking goals for intervention, the following list of factors should be considered:

- What goal would have the most effect on communication?
- What skill areas or behaviors are being worked on by other professionals?
- Which goal will have the largest effect on other skill areas?
- What behaviors have the best possibility of generalization?
- Which behavior is the most easily modified?
- On which goal will the child be most successful?
- What goal would be the most motivating for the child?
- What goals are most important to the caretaker?

Illustration of Goal Planning

There are two major methods of planning intervention. The first is to focus on the child's weaknesses compared with other children of the same chronological age level. In this method, the interventionist primarily examines developmental charts and scales to identify those skills and behaviors the child does not exhibit. Intervention planning then consists of working on teaching those deficient skills in order to get the child closer to age level.

The other, and preferable, method of planning is to focus on what the child can do and then begin expanding the already available skills. In this way the interventionist "starts at go" and builds in an upward and outward fashion from where the child is currently functioning. The latter method of planning instructional goals will be illustrated for the two example children previously discussed (see Figures 14.7 and 14.8). Several of the goals are briefly described; however, for the pragmatic and semantic areas more detail as to explict activities is provided.

The first child, Susan, is 18 months old, although her communication age and other developmental levels are approximately 12–14 months. In Figure 14.8, the first goal for pragmatics focuses on encouraging variation in existing routines, while shaping and developing new routines. The interventionist should engage Susan in any type of routine that can be repeated and ultimately initiated by the child. For example, the interventionist should watch for naturally occurring motor acts such as patting, tapping, or nonspeech sounds (e.g., squeals, snorts), playfully and explicitly imitate the action or sound (e.g., tapping, giggling), and encourage the child to repeat the behavior. The interventionist can also encourage social routines through sound games by acting on one item of a toy (e.g., a ring toy with graduated ring sizes, blocks thrown into or taken out of a bucket, or puzzles), while vocalizing a sound within the child's repertoire. As the child does the motor action combined with vocalizations, the vocalizations are gradually shaped to new sounds. See Dunst (1981), Fey (1986), and

Hart and Risley (1978) for suggestions on developing infants' and young children's early social routines.

The second pragmatics goal focuses on the area of communicative intentions. As can be seen in Figure 14.8, many of the "intention" objectives can be incorporated into the activities suggested for the first goal. Clearly, Susan needs to increase both the frequency and diversity of intentions as well as to learn to express other intentions nonverbally.

Under production, the semantic goal focuses on expanding Susan's production vocabulary to include more object, agent, and action words and to increase the number of semantic relation categories expressed. The comprehension goal focuses on expanding her comprehension vocabulary and developing her ability to indicate recognition through eye gaze or choosing a named object. Because Susan's comprehension skills appear at a slightly higher level than her production, this goal also focuses on increasing comprehension of additional categories (e.g., locations, attributes, greeting). At this time, syntax and phonology are seen as secondary goals and targeted through work on goals in other areas (e.g., semantics and pragmatics).

The second example is of the other child, Bob, presented in Figure 14.7. The pragmatics goal is to increase Bob's initiations of interactions with adults and peers. A number of activities could be designed that required Bob's interaction with other children. For instance, the children could take turns turning over a card, calling each other by name, and saying, "What's this?" The interventionist could also set up activities where the children must ask each other for pieces of a puzzle. See Fey (1986) for other suggestions on how to modify the classroom and home environment to increase a child's initiations. The classroom environment could be set up so that Bob must request an object or action from another to get what he wanted. For example, the interventionist could hand out different kinds

GOALS AND OBJECTIVES FOR
INTERVENTION WITH BOB

I. PRAGMATICS
Social Interaction/discourse
Total number of turns = 50
Number of consecutive turns = up to
5 verbally, interaction lasts 1
minute
Initiations = 6 gestures (e.g., pointing
to cookie package, toy)
8 speech (e.g., "want
cookie," "more
cookie")
Responses = 4 gestures (e.g., head
nod)
32 speech (e.g., "want
that," "cookie?")

Intentions
Diversity and mode of intentions:
Attention seeking = 4 speech (e.g.,
"look")
Requests   = 5 gestures (e.g.,
pointing to object)
8 speech (e.g., "more
cookie," "what
that?")
Protests   = 2 gestures (e.g., grabbing another child's
cookie)
Comments = 4 speech (e.g., "big
cookie")
Answers   = 3 gestures (head nod)
24 speech ("cookie,"
"juice")

II. PRODUCTION
Semantics
Total number of words: 64
Total number of different words: 32
Type token ratio: .50
Semantic relations: agent + object
("me fall," "me want"), ac-
tion + object ("eat cookie"),
agent + action + object ("me want
cookie")

I. PRAGMATICS
Social Interaction/discourse
1. Increase number and diversity of initiations to adults.
   a. Increase number of initiations during
   structured activities.
   b. Increase diversity of initiations in
   unstructured activities.
2. Increase number and diversity of initiations with peers.
   a. Increase number of initiations.
   b. Increase diversity of initiations.

Intentions
1. Increase number and diversity of
intentions.
   a. Increase number of requests for objects (want X, I want X)
   b. Increase number of requests for information (what, who, where,
   with books, pictures, objects)
   c. Increase number of requests for action (push swing, pick up)
   d. Increase number of comments on objects (dirty hands, toy broken)
   e. Increase number of verbal protests
   (no, mine)

II. PRODUCTION
Semantics
1. Expand production vocabulary
   a. Increase number and diversity of
   items in word classes (animals,
   food, clothing, etc.)
   b. Increase number and diversity within
   semantic relation categories (actions, attributes, locations,
   possession)

FIGURE 14.7
Continued

Word categories: names of people, common objects, simple actions, few modifiers (big, hot), social words ("hi," "bye")

Syntax
MLU: 1.75 in morphemes (70 morphemes, 40 utterances)
Distribution of utterances: 19 one-word, 18 two-word, 3 three-word
Morphological markers: 3 plural -*s*, 1 -*ing*, 1 *me*, 1 past irregular verb, "fell"

2. Expand use of semantic relations
  a. Increase diversity in semantic relations in multiword utterances (attribute + object/agent, possession + object)
  b. Increase combinations of existing semantic relation categories (agent + different actions, action + different objects)

Syntax
1. Increase mean length of utterance
  a. Increase use of self as agent (I/me + want/go/eat)
  b. Increase use of action + object (want + cookie)
  c. Increase use of agent + action + object (boy + kick + ball)
  d. Increase use of question forms (who, what, where)
  e. Increase use of past tense (irregular past: broke, ate)

III. COMPREHENSION (Information gained from responses to communications during language sample)
Semantics
Semantic relations correctly responded to: 6 agent, 5 object, 2 recurrence, 1 agent + action, 1 action + object, 1 possession + object

Syntax
Question forms correctly responded to: 3 "What is that?," 2 "Where is X?," 2 "What do you want?," 5 "Who is that?"

IV. PHONOLOGY
Sound inventory: /p/, /b/, /w/, /m/, /n/, /g/, /t/, /d/, /n/, /ng/, /k/, /g/
Error patterns: deletes all final sounds, sound substitutions on later developing sounds

V. OTHER SKILLS
Hearing checked under earphones
Appears normal for development of speech and language

III. COMPREHENSION
Semantics
1. Expand comprehension vocabulary
  a. Increase recognition of less typical category members (animals: goat, hamster)
  b. Increase recognition of less common objects and actions (parachute, rolling)

Syntax
Increase recognition of multiword utterances
  a. Increase appropriate responses to questions ("What does X say?," "What do you do with X?")
  b. Increase appropriate responding to combinations of existing semantic relation categories (agent + different actions, action + different objects)

IV. PHONOLOGY
Increase use of final consonant sounds

V. OTHER SKILLS
Recheck hearing every six months

GOALS AND OBJECTIVES FOR
INTERVENTION WITH SUSAN

I. PRAGMATICS
Social interactions/discourse
Turns: nonverbal = up to 5 turns within
social routines
vocal = up to 3 turns if self-initiated
Social interactions: peek-a-boo, tickle

Total number of communicative intentions:
8
Diversity and mode of intentions:
Attention seeking = squeals, laugh
Requests = vocalization "uh uh,"
gestures (e.g., pointing to objects &
people), vocalization + gesture (e.g.,
some foods & actions)
Protests = vocalization (e.g., when food
taken away), gestures (e.g., pushing
away unwanted foods)

I. PRAGMATICS
Social Interaction/discourse
1. Increase number, length, and diversity
of social interactions
a. Increase number of interactive
games (e.g., this little piggie, got-
cha, bounce on knee = horsie)
b. Increase number of games incorporating recurrence (e.g., child
bounces for "more," holds up
blanket for more actions)
c. Incorporate vocalizations into games,
choose same word or syllable to
express the game (e.g.,
pee = peek-a-boo)
d. Expand imitation of motor acts (e.g.,
begin with imitation of acts
already in child's repertoire, try to
incorporate into social games, for
example, wave "bye bye" as part
of peek-a-boo)
e. Encourage child's vocalization of
sounds already in repertoire that
you produce first. Start game
where child begins vocalizing.
After interchange begins, introduce another sound within
child's repertoire.

Intentions
1. Increase frequency, diversity and use of
vocalizations and word approximations to express communicative
intentions
a. Increase number of nonverbal intentions expressed (e.g., comment-
ing = pointing to unusual
happening)
b. Expand existing vocalizations to
other intentions (e.g., protests)
c. Expand requests to new objects and
agents (e.g., first within comprehension vocabulary, later new
items)
d. Expand requests to different actions
(e.g., go, up, bounce on knee)

383

FIGURE 14.8
Continued

e. Expand protests to combine vocalization + gesture (e.g., when someone takes toy away)
f. Introduce "no" with nonverbal gestures

II. PRODUCTION
Semantics
Semantic relations: Recurrence = gesture by holding out cup, Rejection = vocalizes to refuse food

Syntax
Not applicable

II. PRODUCTION
Semantics
1. Expand production vocabulary
   a. Increase use of word approximations for common objects, agents, actions, and encourage use of these by child (e.g., "bo" = "boat")
   b. Increase use of semantic relations (e.g., recurrence, rejection)

Syntax
Work on through semantic relations
Increase comprehension of word combinations (e.g., agent + action)

III. COMPREHENSION
Semantic relations: 3 agents = Mama, Daddy, doggie
   6 objects = ball, juice, cookie, car, cup, boat
   2 actions = go, bye bye

III. COMPREHENSION
Semantics
1. Expand comprehension vocabulary
   a. Increase identification of objects, actions, agents: play games of hiding, finding different items and label
   b. Introduce locations, attributes (e.g., hot, big) into games
   c. Increase comprehension of different actions on objects already in comprehension vocabulary (e.g., patting, kissing, holding, pushing, giving)

Syntax
1. Increase comprehension of word combinations
   a. Increase use of different action + object combinations (e.g., kiss baby, hug baby)
   b. Develop new recognition responses (e.g., eye gaze, pick up, imitate) for familiar agents, objects, actions in different combinations

IV. PHONOLOGY
Sound inventory: /m/, /b/, /g/, /d/ with some vowels; babbling of consonant-vowel combinations

IV. PHONOLOGY
1. Increase imitation of sounds in play activities
   a. Increase imitation of nonspeech sounds

FIGURE 14.8
Continued

Nonspeech sounds: raspberries, play cough,
tongue clicks, laugh
Sound imitation: Only sounds in repertoire
and only when self-initiated

V. OTHER SKILLS
Hearing checked in sound-field (i.e.,
without earphones), appears adequate
for normal development of
speech/language

   b. Increase imitation of sounds within
      speech repertoire
   c. Increase imitation of new sounds
      and sound combinations

V. OTHER SKILLS
Recheck hearing every six months
Watch for signs of otitis media

of cookies and ask children to choose one. If Bob points to the raisin cookie, the interventionist could model "want raisin."

A major production goal in the area of intentions would be to increase the number of requests and comments expressed verbally by Bob. Another goal would be to increase Bob's use of verbal protesting in the place of crying or grabbing. The interventionist could identify a situation when Bob displays nonverbal protesting and model for him an appropriate verbal response to accompany the nonverbal one. For example, as another child grabs a truck from Bob, the interventionist could model "No, my truck."

The semantic goal in the area of production is to increase the amount and variety of Bob's vocabulary. Frequent labeling of objects and ongoing activities in the child's environment is very helpful. The syntactic goal includes increasing the number of two- and three-word utterances through combining existing agents, actions, objects, and so forth, in Bob's vocabulary. The interventionist should model short utterances describing activities in the environment as well as expand the child's utterances by repeating his utterance and adding an additional word or words. The goals for comprehension are similar to those for production and focus primarily on the expansion of Bob's comprehension vocabulary and his appropriate response (whether verbal or nonverbal) to multiword utterances. The

phonological goal focuses on increasing use of final sounds by exaggerating the production of these sounds in contrasting words (*bow* vs. *boat*).

Conclusion

In this chapter, various "nonstandard" ways of looking at communication assessment and intervention planning have been presented with a few "hows" for going about these activities. In closing, there are a few final suggestions for the interventionist. First, use continuous "reality checking" to remember the "real world." Keep asking: (a) Is this goal important to the child's development; (b) will it improve communication in a substantial manner; and finally, (c) why should this goal be selected for intervention above all others possible? If the answers are "yes," "yes," and a worthwhile "because . . .," then follow through with the goal. If the answers are "no," "no," and "I'm not sure," then rethink the implementation of this goal.

Second, children will usually try to communicate the best way they know how. Interventionists, families, and other professionals need to be aware of the many and varied means through which children communicate. For children with communication difficulties, the interventionist must discover what the child's best mode of communication is and then help the child to expand and develop her communication efforts from that base. Third, remember that you serve as a model for the child in an interaction, so think carefully about what you want to model and how you will do it. And finally, remember that you are an experienced communicator and therefore you can use your own knowledge of what promotes or hinders communication to guide the assessment and goal planning process.

SUMMARY OF KEY CONCEPTS

- *Communication* is the exchanges of information between individuals; *language* is the symbol system used in communication; and *mode* refers to the motor movements used to convey symbols.

- Interventionists should be familiar with communication assessment because communication skills occur within the context of other developmental domains, and are used in interactions with children; communication deficits are common in many preschoolers, and such deficits cannot be remedied in isolated therapy sessions.

- Components of language include pragmatics, phonology, syntax, and semantics; pragmatics and semantics are the components that should receive the largest emphasis in intervention. Furthermore, the rules of language and comprehension and production of language are key assessment targets.

- Standardized and nonstandardized assessment procedures should be used in assessing communication skills.

- Several variables influence communication performance during assessment, including the context or setting, the child's mode of communication, stimulus characteristics, and the level of parental participation.

- Three separate decision trees were described for guiding assessment efforts; their use should be viewed from at least four perspectives (communicative event, developmental, individual differences, and etiological perspectives).

- Collection and analysis of communication samples is a primary method used in the assessment of children's communication abilities.

- Information gathered during the assessment of communication skills should be used for planning intervention; guidelines for that intervention are (a) starting intervention at children's levels, (b) focusing on children's cues, (c) providing functional intervention, (d) following the interests of children, (e) targeting behaviors that will result in success, (f) considering the content of activities, (g) using efficient strategies, (h) checking for comprehension in relation to production, (i) using direct teaching when necessary, and (j) using techniques that facilitate children's use of language.

REFERENCES

American Speech-Language-Hearing Association. (1981). Ad Hoc Committee on Communication Processes and Non-speaking Persons. Committee position paper. *American Speech and Hearing Association, 23,* 267–272.

Bates, E., Camaioni, L., & Volterra, V. (1975). The acquisition of performatives prior to speech. *Merrill-Palmer Quarterly, 31,* 205–226.

Blackstone, S. (Ed.). (1986). *Augmentative communication: An introduction.* Rockville, MD: American Speech, Language and Hearing Association.

Bloom, L. (1970). *Language development: Form and function of emerging grammars.* Cambridge, MA: MIT Press.

Bloom, L. (1974). Talking, understanding, and thinking. In R. Schiefelbusch & L. Lloyd (Eds.), *Language perspectives: Acquisition, retardation and intervention* (pp. 285–312). Baltimore, MD: University Park Press.

Bloom, L., Hood, L., & Lightbown, P. (1974). Imitation in language development: If, when and why. *Cognitive Psychology, 6,* 380–420.

Bloom, L., Rocissano, L., & Hood, L. (1976). Adult-child discourse: Developmental interaction between information processing and linguistic knowledge. *Cognitive Psychology, 8,* 521–552.

Brown, R. (1973). *A first language.* Cambridge, MA: Harvard University Press.

Bruner, J. (1978). The role of dialogue in language acquisition. In A. Sinclair, R. J. Jarvella & W. J. M. Leveit (Eds.), *The child's conception of language* (pp. 241–256). Berlin: Springer-Verlag.

Carlson, L. & Bricker, D. (1982). Dyadic and contingent aspects of early communicative intervention. In D. Bricker (Ed.), *Intervention with at-risk and handicapped infants: From research to application* (pp. 291–309). Austin, TX: Pro-Ed.

Cazden, C. (1970). The neglected situation in child language research and education. In F. Williams (Ed.), *Language and poverty: Perspectives on a theme* (pp. 81–101). Chicago: Markham.

Chapman, R. (1977). Comprehension strategies in children. In J. Kavanagh & P. Strange (Eds.), *Language and speech in the laboratory, school, and clinic* (pp. 308–327). Cambridge, MA: MIT Press.

Chapman, R. (1981). Exploring children's communicative intents. In J. F. Miller (Ed.), *Assessing language production in children* (pp. 111–136). Baltimore, MD: University Park Press.

Chapman, R. & Miller, J. (1975). Word order in early two and three word utterances: Does production precede comprehension? *Journal of Speech and Hearing Research, 18*(2), 355–371.

Coggins, T. & Carpenter, R. (1981). The Communicative Intention Inventory: A system for coding children's early intentional communication. *Applied Psycholinguistics, 2,* 235–252.

Creaghead, N. (1984). Strategies for evaluating and targeting pragmatic behaviors in young children. *Seminars in Speech and Language, 5*(3), 241–252.

de Villiers, J. & de Villiers, P. (1973). Development of the use of word order in comprehension. *Journal of Psycholinguistic Research, 2,* 331–341.

Dore, J. (1974). A pragmatic description of early language development. *Journal of Psycholinguistic Research, 4,* 343–350.

Dunst, C. (1981). *Infant learning.* Hingham, MA: Teaching Resources.

Dunst, C. & Wortman-Lowe, L. (1986). From reflex to symbol: Describing, explaining, and fostering communicative competence. *Augmentative and Alternative Communication, 2,* 11–16.

Fey, M. (1986). *Language intervention with young children.* San Diego: College-Hill Press.

Furuno, S., O'Reilly, K., Hosaka, C., Inatsuka, T., Allman, T., & Zeisloft, B. (1979). *The Hawaii Early Learning Profile.* Palo Alto: VORT.

Gill, G. & Dihoff, R. (1982). Nonverbal assessment of cognitive behavior. In B. Campbell & V. Baldwin (Eds.), *Severely handicapped/hearing impaired students: Strengthening service delivery* (pp. 77–113). Baltimore, MD: Paul H. Brookes.

Goldberg, S. (1977). Social competence in infancy: A model of parent-infant interaction. *Merrill-Palmer Quarterly, 23,* 163–177.

Golinkoff, R. (1983). *The transition from prelinguistic to linguistic communication.* Hillsdale, NJ: Erlbaum.

Halle, J., Alpert, C., & Anderson, S. (1984). Natural environment language assessment and intervention with severely impaired preschoolers. *Topics in Early Childhood Special Education, 4*(2), 36–56.

Hanrahan, L., Ferrier, L., & Jolie, K. (1987, November). *Infants, caregivers and augmentative communication: We must intervene earlier.* Paper presented at the American Speech-Language-Hearing Association Annual Convention, New Orleans.

Harding, C. & Golinkoff, R. (1979). The origins of intentional vocalizations in prelinguistic infants. *Child Development, 50,* 33–40.

Hart, B. & Risley, T. (1978). Promoting productive language through incidental teaching. *Educational Urban Society, 10,* 407–432.

Hart, B. & Rogers-Warren, A. (1978). A milieu approach to teaching language. In R. Schiefelbusch (Ed.), *Language intervention strategies* (pp. 193–236). Baltimore, MD: University Park Press.

Holdgrafer, G. & Dunst, C. (1986). Communicative competence: From research to practice. *Topics in Early Childhood Special Education, 6*(3), 1–22.

Ingram, D. (1976). *Phonological disabilities in children.* New York: American Elsevier.

Keenan, E. & Schieffelin, B. (1976). Topic as a discourse notion: A study of topic in the conversations of children and adults. In C. Li (Ed.), *Subject and topic* (pp. 337–384). New York: Academic Press.

Lee, L. (1974). *Developmental Sentence Analysis.* Northwestern University Press, Evanston, IL.

Leonard, L. (1981). Facilitating linguistic skills in children with specific language impairment. *Applied Psycholinguistics, 2*(2), 89–118.

Leonard, L., Prutting, C., Perozzi, J., & Berkley, R. (1978). Nonstandardized approaches to the assessment of language behaviors. *American Speech and Hearing Association, 20*(5), 371–379.

Lund, N. & Duchan, J. (1988). *Assessing children's language in naturalistic contexts.* Englewood, NJ: Prentice-Hall.

McLean, J. & Snyder-McLean, L. (1978). *A transactional approach to early language training.* Columbus, OH: Merrill.

Miller, J. (1981). *Assessing language production in children: Experimental procedures.* Baltimore, MD: University Park Press.

Miller, J. (1987). Language and communication characteristics of children with Down syndrome. In S. Pueschel, C. Tinghey, J. Rynders, A. Crocker & D. Crutcher (Eds.), *New perspectives on Down syndrome* (pp. 233–262). Baltimore, MD: Paul H. Brookes.

Miller, J. & Chapman, R. (1985). *Systematic Analysis of Language Transcripts.* Language Analysis Lab, Madison, WI.

Miller, J., Chapman, R., Branston, M., & Reichle, J. (1980). Language comprehension in sensorimotor stages V and VI. *Journal of Speech and Hearing Research, 23,* 284–311.

Mordecai, D., Palin, M., & Palmer, S. (1985). *Lingquest Language Sample Analysis I.* Columbus, OH.

Muma, J. (1978). *Language handbook: Concepts, assessment, intervention.* Englewood Cliffs, NJ: Prentice-Hall.

Newborg, J., Stock, J. R., Wnek, L., Guidubaldi, J., & Svinicki, J. (1984). *The Batelle Developmental Inventory.* Allen, TX: DLM/Teaching Resources.

Olswang, L., Stoel-Gammon, C., Coggins, T., & Carpenter, R. (1987). *Assessing prelinguistic and early linguistic behaviors in developmentally young children.* Seattle, WA: University of Washington Press.

Owens, R. (1984). *Language development.* Columbus, OH: Merrill.

Patterson, C. & Kister, M. (1981). The development of listener skills for referential communication. In W. P. Dickson (Ed.), *Children's oral communication skills* (pp. 143–166). New York: Academic Press.

Paul, R. (1981). Analyzing complex sentence development. In J. Miller (Ed.), *Assessing language production in children* (pp. 36–40). Baltimore, MD: University Park Press.

Paul, R. (1987). A model for the assessment of disorders in infants and toddlers. *National Student Speech Language Hearing Association Journal, 15,* 88–105.

Retherford, K., Schwartz, B., & Chapman, R. (1981). Semantic roles and residual grammatical categories in mother and child speech: Who tunes into whom? *Journal of Child Language, 8*(3), 583–608.

Roger, S., Donovan, C., D'Eugenio, D., Brown, S., Whiteside-Lynch, E., Moersch, M. & Schafer, D. (1981). Early intervention developmental profile. *Developmental programming for infants and young children* (rev. ed.). Ann Arbor: University of Michigan Press.

Rogers-Warren, A. & Warren, S. (1984). The social basis of language and communication in severely handicapped preschoolers. *Topics in Early Childhood Special Education, 4*(2), 57–72.

Roth, F. & Spekman, N. (1984). Assessing the pragmatic abilities of children: Part I. Organizational framework and assessment parameters. *Journal of Speech and Hearing Disorders, 49,* 2–11.

Sacks, H., Schegloff, E., & Jefferson, G. (1974). A simplest systematics for the organization of turn-taking for conversation. *Language, 50,* 696–735.

Sander, E. (1972). When are speech sounds learned? *Journal of Speech and Hearing Disorders, 37,* 55–63.

Seibert, J. & Hogan, A. (1982a). A model for assessing social and object skills and planning intervention. In D. McClowry, A. Guilford & S. Richardson (Eds.), *Infant communication, development, assessment, and intervention* (pp. 21–53). New York: Grune & Stratton.

Seibert, J. & Hogan, A. (1982b). *Procedures manual for the early social-communication scales (ESCS).* Unpublished manuscript, University of Miami Mailman Center for Child Development, Miami, FL.

Shriberg, L. & Kwiatkowski, J. (1980). *Natural process analysis: A procedure for phonological analysis of continuous speech samples.* New York: John Wiley & Sons.

Slobin, D. & Welsh, C. (1971). Elicited imitation as a research tool in developmental psycholinguistics. In C. Lavatelli (Ed.), *Language training in early childhood education.* Urbana: University of Illinois Press.

Snyder-McLean, L., Sack, S., & Solomonson, B. (1985). *Generic Skills Inventory.* Parsons: University of Kansas, Bureau of Child Research.

Stoel-Gammon, C. & Dunn, C. (1985). *Normal and disordered phonology in children.* Baltimore, MD: University Park Press.

Stokes, T. & Baer, D. (1977). An implicit technology of generalization. *Journal of Applied Behavior Analysis, 10,* 349–367.

U.S. Department of Education, Office of Special Education and Rehabilitation Services. (1986). Report submitted to the Subcommittee on Select Education of the U.S. House of Representatives.

Warren, S. & Kaiser, A. (1986). Incidental language teaching: A critical review. *Journal of Speech and Hearing Disorders, 51*(4), 291–299.

Westby, C. (1980). Assessment of cognitive and language abilities through play. *Language, Speech, and Hearing Services in Schools, 11*(3), 154–168.

Chapter 15

Assessing Social Interaction Skills

Samuel L. Odom
Peabody College of Vanderbilt University
Scott R. McConnell
University of Minnesota

KEY TERMS

- Social Development
- Social Interaction
- Social Behavior
- Social Competence
- Attachment
- Social Reciprocity
- Reciprocity One (R1)
- Reciprocity Two (R2)
- Duration of Interactions

- Peer Preferences
- "Strange Situation"
- Performance-based Measure of Competence
- Anecdotal Notes
- Rating Scales
- Behavioral Anchor
- Time Sampling
- Scan
- Interval Sampling

- Discontinuous Interval Systems
- Continuous Interval Systems
- Event Recording Systems
- Focal Child System
- Sociometric Assessment
- Peer Nominations
- Peer Ratings
- Norm-Referenced Measures
- Criterion-Referenced Measures

SCENE 1: A mother of a 9-month-old girl with cerebral palsy is depressed because her baby does not relax in her arms during breast feeding and never responds to her attempts to play. She sees herself as a failure as a mother and is very unhappy with the relation- ship that she feels has not developed with her baby.

SCENE 2: Matt, a 4-year-old boy who is mild- ly mentally retarded, waits patiently at his table for free-play to begin. He is one of the two children in the school district who has been selected for a mainstream placement, and in fact he has quickly learned the rules of the classroom. When the teacher gives the signal, he sprints for the puppet box and pulls out the P. Mooney and Ernie puppets. He takes the puppets to a place by the window and carries on an imaginary conversation between the two for the entire 20-minute free-play period. At different times during the free-play, two boys come over and talk to him about trading the puppets and building a block tower, but he ignores them. They lose interest and leave. The teacher reports that Matt has played this same type of puppet game during free-play ever since he came to the class five weeks ago. He rarely plays with peers and usually ignores them when they try to play with him.

These scenarios illustrate the breakdown in the **social development** process. Infants and young children with handicaps frequently have delays or disorders in social development severe enough to suggest that intervention should occur. Such problems require that programs promoting social interaction skill development should be incorporated into individualized educational plans for many children enrolled in early childhood special education programs.

A first step in creating instructional programs for social development is, of course, assessment; but, to date, there have been few appropriate or useful assessment instruments (Guralnick & Weinhouse, 1983) and few guidelines for using the assessment data for building intervention programs. In this chapter, we describe a number of ways in which information can be collected on the social interaction skills of infants with handicaps and their caregivers and preschool-aged children with handicaps and their peers. The social developmental process for normally developing children and delays in development that seem to occur for infants and young children with handicaps are described, followed by a description of the dimensions

of social assessment for young children with handicaps and the procedural considerations to which the assessor must attend. Representative methods for assessing children and ways the assessment data can be used for designing, monitoring, and evaluating social development intervention programs for infants and young children with handicaps are discussed in detail.

Nature of the Social Interaction Development

Social interaction is a transactional event in which the **social behavior** of one partner is intentionally directed to the second partner, and often the second partner will respond by directing an intentional social behavior back to the original partner. The partners in social interactions will be infants or preschoolers with handicaps, their parents, caregivers, and peers. Social development is the acquisition of skills necessary for interacting competently with adults—particularly parents—and peers, and **social competence** is the competent use of those skills in appropriate contexts. (A more detailed discussion of social competence will follow.) Most social behavior is learned through observing or participating in social interactions with others. Also, relationships between parents and infants, or between peers, develop at least in part through the ongoing interactions that occur between these social partners.

This view of social development suggests that breakdowns in the acquisition of social interaction skills may result from several causes. First, the infant or child may lack the prerequisite skills for participating in successful social interactions. For example, infants with cerebral palsy may not have the motor skills to respond quickly enough to the social messages provided by the mother. Similarly, preschool children may not have learned how to share or trade their toys with their peers.

Because social interaction involves two partners, it is possible that the partner does not have sufficient skills for participating in successful interactions. A mother whose infant has Down syndrome may try to get her to play yet never give her a chance to respond. Similarly, a preschooler with autism who is placed in a class with other autistic children may be unable to engage his peers in mutually satisfying social interactions because the peer group does not have the necessary skills.

Finally, a situation may arise where both partners have some social skills, but there is a mismatch between the skills involved. For example, an infant will often explore his mother's face with his eyes; this visual regard sets the context for social exchanges. However, blind infants explore their mothers faces with their hands, without orienting their faces toward their mothers (Fraiberg, 1977). Although such manual exploration is a social skill, mothers may not understand and respond to it as such. Similarly, preschoolers with handicaps who are enrolled in classes with a range of developmental levels may have the skills necessary for engaging peers of similar developmental levels in social interaction but may not be able consistently to engage in interactions with more advanced peers.

A Sketch of Early Social Development

During infancy and early childhood, human beings must accomplish two tasks related to social development; failure to accomplish either will have negative implications for future development (McConnell & Odom, 1986). Behavioral aspects of these developmental tasks are presented in Table 15.1. First, humans must establish a positive and working relationship, an **attachment**, with at least one primary caregiver. This relationship begins to form as early as age 3–4 months, solidifies around 12–18 months, develops and changes forms through the preschool years,

and, for many of us, extends through adulthood (Ainsworth, Blehar, Waters, & Wall, 1978; Main, Kaplan, & Cassidy, 1985). Attachment appears to be based on predictable, positive, and mutually satisfying social interactions that occur between the infant and the caregiver, usually the mother, although strong attachments also develop with fathers and siblings. Aimsworth and co-workers (1978) and Bretherton (1987) provide a fuller description of the development of attachment.

A second developmental task is to establish oneself as a viable member of a social network of peers. Although there is evidence of peer social interaction (Mueller & Vandell, 1979) and peer preferences (Howes, 1983) in the infant and toddler years, peer interactions do not increase substantially in frequency or cohesion until the preschool years (Hartup, 1983). By age 3, children will show a preference for playing with peers rather than playing with objects alone, although peer social interactions will not be well coordinated. By age 5, most normally developing children who have had peer group experiences will be fairly sophisticated social interactors. They know many social rules for interacting with a partner, although they may not be able to articulate them, and they can carry on sustained and reciprocal social interactions with their peers. The hallmark of this developmental task is social acceptance by peer groups and at least a small circle of identified reciprocal friendships (i.e., friendship choices in which two children each choose the other as a friend).

Social Development of Infants and Young Children with Handicaps

Some infants with handicaps experience disrupted social relationships with their parents, and preschoolers with handicaps display delayed peer social interaction skills and achieve less social acceptance by peers than

TABLE 15.1
Development of Social Interaction in Infants and Young Children

Age	Social Development
Birth–3 months	Infant born with predispositions toward social behavior (attends selectively to faces, some imitation abilities, crying as a natural elicitor of adult behavior, endogenous smiles).
3–6 months	Infant develops social smile.
6–9 months	Infant participates in adult/infant social games with adult as elicitor.
9–15 months	Infant/toddler increasingly becomes the imitator in parent/infant games. Developing motor skill allows infant/toddler to maintain physical proximity to mother or other attachment figure. Begins to discriminate unfamiliar adults (stranger anxiety). Some low rates of peer interaction begin to occur.
15–24 months	Increasing language skills allow parent/infant interactions to become increasingly verbal and more sophisticated. Increasing cognitive skills allow child to represent attachment figures in their absence.
24–36 months	Interest in peers increases. Sociodramatic play skills become more refined, allowing inclusion of peers in symbolic play. Parent/child interactions maintain.
36–48 months	Children become frequent social interactors with peer group. Elaboration of sociodramatic play skills continues. Child moves to attachment relationship involving mutual understanding between child and attachment figure about their absence.
48–60 months	Children typically are competent social interactors with peers. They are learning to play positively with peers and negotiate conflicts, and are beginning to learn responses to aggression.

normally developing children in their peer group.

Parent/Infant Relationship

Several factors may contribute to disruptions or delays in the development of successful parent/infant interactions or relationships. For infants who are developing normally, their behavior (e.g., being alert, smiling at the parent, reaching to the parent) often signals the parent that they are ready to interact or that they are responding to the parent's social overtures. For infants with handicaps, par-ticularly motoric handicaps, the behavioral signals are sometimes unclear and may not provide enough information to the mothers about when their infants are ready to interact (Yoder, 1986).

Some infants with handicaps are delayed in the development of behavioral cues that are important for social interaction. For example, mothers of infants with Down syndrome report disappointment in the social smiles that their infants portray during playful encounters (Emde, Katz, & Thorpe, 1978; Sroufe, 1979). Similarly, the muted smiles that blind infants develop and the absence of eye contact early in life are often distressful for parents (Fraiberg, 1975).

The development of the attachment relationship (i.e., identification of one or two adults as significant security figures) may be affected by children's handicaps. For some children with handicaps, it appears that attachment does develop, although it may be delayed or expressed in a manner different from that of normally developing children (Berry, Gunn, & Andrews, 1980; Sigman & Ungerer, 1984). For other children with handicaps, insecure and ambivalent attachment relationships sometimes develop (Spieker, 1986).

It should be noted that the relationship that develops between infants/toddlers and parents, as reflected in their social interactions, exists within a dynamic family system. Factors within the family but outside the parent/infant relationship may at times influence the responsiveness of the parents or the infant. For a description of the way an infant with handicaps affects the family system and how families may be assessed, the reader is referred to Barber, Turnbull, Behr, and Kerns (1988) and Bailey and Simeonsson (1988).

Peer Relationships

Preschool-aged children with handicaps exhibit substantial social interaction deficits. When observing children in integrated groups, Guralnick (1980) noted that children with moderate and severe handicaps interacted significantly less often with their peers than did children with mild handicaps and normally developing children. Similarly, Strain (1983), in a study of severely handicapped children in mainstreamed settings, found that children with handicaps who were chosen as "friends" on a sociometric measure exhibited a number of positive social behaviors that less-preferred children with handicaps did not display (e.g., a range of different positive social initiations, responding to the social behavior of a peer).

Although initial research seemed to indicate that children with mild developmental delays did not suffer as greatly from social skills deficits as their peers with moderate and severe handicaps, research by Guralnick and Groom (1985; 1987) suggests that these deficits are clearly evident. Mildly handicapped children in play groups are less successful in peer social interactions than their younger and same-aged normally developing peers. In fact, in one study, the success with which the children with mild handicaps participated in social interaction in integrated play groups *decreased* across the time that they were in the play group, suggesting that deficits in social skills led to impaired interaction patterns as the group became more familiar with its members (Guralnick & Groom, 1987). These patterns of interactions were confirmed by lower preference scores that the children with mild handicaps received on peer-rating assessments. Together, these data suggest that most preschool-aged children with handicaps have social interaction delays that exceed their developmental delay. When placed in peer groups with normally developing children, children with handicaps may not automatically establish positive peer relationships. However, the development of peer relationships in nonintegrated settings, such as a preschool special education class, has yet to be investigated.

Dimensions of Social Interaction Assessment

Assessment of social interaction skill development may take place at different levels of analysis. Like viewing a mountainside through a telescope and adjusting the focus to obtain a clear picture of the details of the landscape, one can adjust the focus of an assessment to provide different views of children's social development. One can choose assessment approaches that provide information at the most detailed, microscopic level (i.e., individual social behavior), at a less microscopic level (i.e., social interactions), at a more macroscopic level (i.e., relationship/social status) and at the most macroscopic level (i.e., norm-referenced assessment). These levels of specificity may, in turn, be related to the purposes of assessment noted in Chapter 1. For example, the most microscopic assessment approaches might be used for monitoring intervention programs, with the macroscopic approaches being used more often for diagnostic or program evaluation purposes.

Individual Social Behaviors

When professionals assess the single social behaviors of infants and children, there are several aspects of social behavior to which they attend. Most often, they count the *frequency* with which a social behavior occurs within a given time frame. Usually some judgment of the *affective quality* of the social behavior (e.g., positive or negative) occurs. Some systems state the specific type of behavior being assessed. For example, Guralnick and Groom (1985) used specific categories such as "leads peer," "displays affection," or "gains attention." Other systems use a single, global definition of social interaction, which includes all interactions that occur (Greenwood, Walker, Todd, & Hops, 1981). Last, many assessment systems at the single-behavior level indicate whether the child initiated the behavior or was responding to the social behavior of another (Strain & Timm, 1974).

Interactional Level

At the interactional level, the concept of **social reciprocity** becomes significant. Social reciprocity has been defined in two ways. One definition, called **reciprocity one** (R1), refers to the immediate response of a social partner to a social behavior from the partner (Strain

& Shores, 1977). In analyzing social behavior at this level, the *sequence* or order of behaviors in an interaction is most important. Social behaviors that produce a response from a peer are reciprocal, while those that do not produce a response are not. If social interactions are viewed as a chain of social behavior directed back and forth between social partners, all social interactions, by definition, will have some element of R1. In their investigation of peer-related social behaviors that would be appropriate for intervention programs, Tremblay, Strain, Hendrickson, and Shores (1980) identified the positive social behaviors that were most likely to result in a positive response from a peer. Similarly, in their analysis of mother/infant interaction, Bakeman and Brown (1977) examined the conditional probabilities of mothers and infants responding, given a certain set of conditions.

A second type of reciprocity, called **reciprocity two** (R2), is assessed at a slightly less microscopic level of social interaction. R2 refers to the direction and frequency of social interactions with potentially available partners. Preschool-aged children who direct the most positive social behaviors to peers are also the recipients of the most positive social behavior from peers (Hartup, Glazer, & Charlesworth, 1967; Kohler & Fowler, 1985). R2 in this sense means that the net effect of being positively social with a partner will be that the partner will probably be positively social in return. To assess this type of reciprocity at the preschool level, one would look at the number of social behaviors that a child directs to his peers and the number directed to him from his peers. At the parent/infant level, particularly after the child has attained the developmental age of 9 months, one might observe the amount of positive social exchanges that the infant attempts to direct to the parent and the number that the parent initiates.

A last dimension related to assessment of social behavior at the interaction level is the notion of **duration of interactions.** Like reciprocity, duration has also been interpreted in two slightly different ways. First, it may refer to the length of time an interaction continues. To measure duration in this way, a teacher might begin a stopwatch when an interaction began and turn it off when the interaction ended. For example, Brown, Ragland, and Fox (in press) measured the number of seconds that children were engaged in interactions. Second, duration may also refer to the number of behaviors in a social interaction chain. For example, if a mother began a social game with her infant, and the infant responded, the mother made another verbalization to the infant, and the infant responded again, a 4-unit chain of interaction would have occurred. To measure duration in this way, an interventionist would record and then count the number of behaviors in each interaction. In their studies of peer interaction, Odom and Strain (1986) and Rubenstein and Howes (1979) assessed the duration of the interactions by determining the number of behaviors in each social interaction sequence.

At the interactional level, one can also examine **peer preferences** or relationships, at least for toddlers and preschoolers. Typically, when a child interacts frequently with a peer and the peer in turn directs a large percentage of his interactions back to the original child, the development of a friendship is reflected. Friendships identified by observing social interaction have been shown to correlate with teacher ratings of peer preferences (Howes, 1983; Roopnarine & Field, 1984) and mother's identifications of their children's preferred play partners (Hinde, Titmus, Easton, & Tamplin, 1985).

Social Relationships

Assessment of social relationships of infants and young children with handicaps occurs at a macroscopic level and may signify the success with which children achieve the benchmark social developmental tasks: attachment and social acceptance within a peer group. *Attachment* refers to the relationship that develops between infants and their caregivers. The purpose of behaviors related to attachment (e.g., smiling, crying, locomotion to mother, talking to mother) is to ensure that the child will stay in close proximity to the attachment figure, especially at times when the child feels insecure (Bowlby, 1969; Ainsworth et al., 1978). Assessment of attachment usually occurs through a laboratory procedure called the **strange situation.** In this assessment, the infant is exposed to several conditions in which the mother is present or absent (Ainsworth & Bell, 1970). The critical indicator of the attachment relationship is the infant's behavior when the mother and child are reunited. Research has revealed a number of types of attachment relationships, from secure to insecure and ambivalent (Ainsworth et al., 1978). Unfortunately, the strange situation is mainly an experimental assessment, and professionals have yet to develop a reliable and valid clinical assessment of attachment.

At the preschool level, social relationships with peers are most often measured by the use of a sociometric assessment. These assessments may reveal the popularity of the child as well as the level of acceptance that the child has achieved in the peer group (Asher & Taylor, 1981). Moreover, peer acceptance as measured by sociometrics has fairly substantial predictive validity (McConnell & Odom, 1986). A range of sociometric assessments, described in a later section, have been used with preschool-aged children, and some evidence of reliability exists.

Normative Level

For certain assessment purposes, such as diagnosis or classification of children, it is necessary to judge a child's social behavior against an established norm. In such situations, an assessor would be less concerned about specific interaction patterns or relationships than about the general performance of the child as it relates to the performances of other children. A number of assessment instruments described in a later section can be useful in providing this information.

Social Competence vs. Social Skill

Professionals have used the term *social competence* in many ways. It has been referred to as a myriad of skills that could be grouped under general competence (Anderson & Messick, 1974; Zigler & Trickett, 1978), as successful social behavior (Bailey & Simeonsson, 1985; Foster & Ritchey, 1979), or as interpersonal social problem solving (Spivak & Shure, 1974). In a previous conceptualization of social competence, we have followed the lead of Hops (1983) in identifying social competence as competent social behaviors in appropriate settings and have incorporated McFall's (1982) concept of "performance" as the ultimate measure of competence. Performance implies that social behaviors are judged appropriate by significant social agents, who are in unique positions to render an opinion (Odom & McConnell, 1985). Social competence is a summary dimension of social interaction skills, in that it incorporates information from the behavior, interaction, relationship, and possibly the normative levels.

Procedural Considerations in Assessing Social Interaction

Assessment of social interaction skills differs from assessment of most other developmental areas in that specific tests are not given to infants or children. Rather, the social interaction skills are usually observed in natural contexts and recorded by an observer or reported by the parent. The opportunity for conducting the type of standardized assessment useful for measurement of cognitive or language development (e.g., individual administration of test items, standard presentation of items) is not available or appropriate for the assessment of social interaction skills. As such, a number of aspects of the natural setting in which assessors observe infants or young children may affect the information obtained by the assessment (e.g., the home or preschool vs. a clinic setting, presence of toys with high social value vs. those with low social value). Similarly, the manner in which assessments are chosen or employed will affect the ultimate usefulness of the information obtained.

Setting of the Social Interaction

The setting in which assessment information is collected will affect the social behavior of infants and children. For infants, social interactions with parents are typically of most interest. Some observational assessments of parent/infant interaction are conducted at centers or clinics and may involve the use of videotapes. The assessor may or may not ask the parents to "get their child to play." These assessments may create demand characteristics (e.g., the parents may interact in a way that they think will please the assessor) that influence the information collected. Similarly, if preschool children are observed in an unfamiliar setting or with novel play objects, their attention and activity will probably be directed more to the objects than to peers. Unless the assessor is interested in information that can be collected only in a specific situation (e.g., the strange situation), then the most representative sample of social behavior will occur in the natural setting for the child. This may be in the home at feeding time or a play time for the parents and infants, or a free-play time at school for preschoolers. However, even in natural settings, the observer's presence may cause the children to act in nonrepresentative ways, so observers may wish to delay collecting data until children or mother and infant have become used to their presence.

Participants in the Social Interaction

Because social interaction is a reciprocal process, the children's behavior will be affected by the partners with whom they may interact. Information collected about a child's social behavior will also reflect the immediate history of social interactions. Thus, infants' social interactions with their mothers reflect not only their social skills but also the mothers' skills as social partners. Moreover, infants' social behavior would probably be quite different with their fathers (Power & Parke, 1986). Similarly, when children with handicaps are assessed in situations that contain only peers with handicaps, the resultant social information reflects the child's skills and the peers' ability to be responsive social partners (Strain & Shores, 1983). Assessors must report the social context in which they collect assessment information and consider this context when they interpret the information.

Use of Multiple Measures

The **performance-based measure of competence** implies that multiple sources of information would be collected on children's social performance and that different informants would provide this information. The advantage of this approach is that it provides evidence of agreement or disagreement on socially competent behaviors from different perspectives and from different instruments (e.g., direct observation, teacher ratings, peer ratings, parent ratings).

If agreement exists across assessments, then more confidence can be placed in the information provided. For example, direct observation of a child's social interactions and teacher ratings might indicate the same performance level. However, it is probable that assessment information will not always agree. For example, the teacher's ratings of social interactions and the parent's ratings might differ substantially. In such cases, differences may be due to different behaviors the child exhibits in the home and school settings or to different standards imposed by each of the raters. In either case, differences provide unique information about the child's social skills across settings. A comprehensive evaluation should include multiple assessment sources.

Methods for Assessing Social Interactions

Several techniques exist for assessing the social interaction development of infants and young children with handicaps. Each provides slightly different information. Assessment information may be collected through (a) observation of infants and children in a social context, (b) rating scales, (c) sociometric nominations or ratings by peers, (d) criterion-referenced assessments, and (e) norm-referenced tests. Examples of each of these assessments are provided in Table 15.2.

Observation of Children's Social Behavior

The most direct way of collecting information on social interactions is to observe and record them in a social context (i.e., with social partners and when social interaction is appropriate). These observations may occur in single settings where the teacher steps away from the interaction and watches the child. (In this and subsequent references, *teacher* refers to the classroom teacher or any other professional interested in conducting assessments of a child.) The teacher also may record some types of observational data after an activity terminates, possibly one in which he was interacting with the child.

Anecdotal Data Collection.   When observing infants or young children, teachers some-

TABLE 15.2
Assessment of Social Behavior and Interaction of Infants and Young Children with Handicaps

Type/Instruments		Age Range	Behaviors Assessed	Description
Anecdotal	Systematic Anecdotal Assessment of Social Interaction (Odom, McConnell, Kohler, & Strain, 1987)	Open	Behaviors generated by the teacher	A structured anecdotal recording system for collecting social interaction information
Direct Observation	Social Interaction Scan (Odom et al., 1988)	Preschool	Isolate/unoccupied Proximity Interactive Negative Teacher interaction	A system for scanning classrooms of children. Designed to measure both interaction play and social integration.
	Observational Assessment of Reciprocal Social Interaction (McConnell, Sisson, & Sandler, 1984)	Preschool	Initiations (five behaviors listed) Response (four behaviors listed) Summative (four behaviors listed) Teacher behavior (two behaviors listed)	An interval-sampling system designed to measure components and durations of social interaction of peers
	Scale of Social Participation (Parten, 1932)	Preschool	See Table 15.3	An interval-sampling system designed to measure young children's participation in social interaction
	Parten/Smilansky Combined Scale (Rubin, 1983)	Preschool	See Table 15.3	An interval-sampling system designed to measure cognitive play within a social context
	Bakeman & Adamson (1984)	Infancy	Unengaged Onlooking Persons Objects Passive Joint Coordinated Joint	Event-recording systems for measuring mother/infant interactions

TABLE 15.2
Continued

Type/Instruments		Age Range	Behaviors Assessed	Description
	Guralnick & Groom (1987)	Preschool	Gains peer attention Uses peer as resource Leads peer in activity—positive Leads peer in activity—negative Imitates peer Expresses affection to peer Expresses hostility to peer Competes for adult attention Competes for equipment Shows pride in product Follows peer's activity without specific direction	Event-recording system for measuring peer interactions
	Odom, Silver, Sandler, & Strain (1983); Strain (1983); Tremblay, Strain, Hendrickson, & Shores (1980)	Preschool	Play organizer Share request Share Assistance Assistance request Affection Complimentary Negative Motor Gestural Negative Vocal Verbal	Event-recording system for measuring peer social interactions
Teacher Rating	Social Interaction Rating Scale (Hops et al., 1979)	Preschool-Elementary	Summary score	Eight items with 7-point Likert scale
	Teacher Rating of Social Interaction (Odom et al., 1988)	Preschool	Summary scores Positive and negative subscores	Eight items with a 5-point Likert scale
	Preschool Behavior Questionnaire (Behar & Stringfield, 1974)	Preschool	Summary score Hostile subscore Angry subscore Hyperactive subscore	30 items with a 3-point Likert scale

TABLE 15.2
Continued

Type/Instruments		Age Range	Behaviors Assessed	Description
	Social Competence Scale (Kohn, 1977)	Preschool	Participation vs. disinterest subscore Cooperation vs. defiance subscore	
	Carolina Record of Individual Behavior (Simeonsson, Huntington, Short, & Ware, 1982)	Infant/ Preschool	State rating score Eight items related to orientation and communications Eight items related to task performance and responsiveness	Rating scale completed after 15–30 minute observation of infant/child
	Carey Infant Temperament Scale (Carey & McDevitt, 1978)	Infant	Allows the classification of several patterns of infant temperament	95-item questionnaire completed by parents; items are scored on a 6-point scale
	Teacher Rating of Intervention Behavior (Odom, McConnell, Kohler, & Strain, 1987)	Preschool	Rating scores on 14 behavioral outcomes of intervention	Rating scale for measuring social interaction target for intervention
Sociometric	McCandless & Marshall (1957)	Preschool	Summary score of peer nominations as friends	Peer nomination sociometric using photographs
	Asher, Singleton, Tinsley, & Hymel (1979)	Preschool	Summary score of peer rating by whole class	Peer rating scale using photographs
Criterion-Referenced	Learning Accomplishment Profile (LAP) Early LAP (LeMay, Griffin, & Sanford, 1977)	Infancy- Preschool	Criterion items in the social strand	Criterion-referenced items provided in strands across developmental areas
	Battelle Developmental Inventory (Newborg, Stock, Wnek, Guidubaldi, & Svinicki, 1984)	Infancy- Preschool	Criterion items in the personal social strand, also provides norms	Assessment across developmental areas

401

TABLE 15.2
Continued

Type/Instruments		Age Range	Behaviors Assessed	Description
	Portage Guide to Early Education (Bluma, Shearer, Frohman, & Hillard, 1976)	Infancy-Preschool	Criterion items in social abilities strand	Criterion-referenced items provided across developmental areas
Norm-Referenced	Vineland Adaptive Behavior Scale (Sparrow, Balla, & Cicchetti, 1984)	Preschool and above	Age scores and percentile ranks for social age	General adaptive behavior scale with social competence subscale
	California Preschool Social Competency Scale (Levine, Elzey, & Lewis, 1969)	Preschool	36-item rating scale that yields raw score and percentile ranked norms	Scale designed to measure social competence of preschool children

times keep notes on an infant's or child's social behavior. These **anecdotal notes** should describe the context and the overall behavior of the child and should be concise, clear, and descriptive. If possible, they should be written while the teacher is directly observing the child; however, if the notes are taken during the "heat of the social interaction," the teacher should review the notes at a quieter time later in the day to make sure that they reflect clearly the social interactions that occurred.

To give some structure to anecdotal recording of social interaction, Odom, McConnell, Kohler, and Strain (1987) created an anecdotal prodedure called the Systematic Anecdotal Assessment of Social Interaction (SAASI). In this system, the teacher observes one child and her peers and writes down the behaviors that occur in the interaction. On the recording form (Figure 15.1) blocks are provided for the teacher to record the name of the social partner(s) and each social behavior that occurred in the interaction.

An example of the use of this approach is given in Figure 15.1. Using this system, the teacher can collect information on who starts the interaction, how long it goes, the quality of the interaction, and the specific behavior. If the teacher has an interest in a specific behavior, she may summarize its frequency from the SAASI.

Rating Scales. **Rating scales** are more sophisticated ways for collecting information about children's social behavior. The specific scales discussed in this section will be those that describe social interaction but do not include norms. Rating scales are also discussed in a later section on sociometric and norm-referenced assessments.

Rating scales require teachers to make a summary judgment about the degree of social behavior or set of behaviors. Teachers complete a social interaction rating scale after they have interacted with an infant or child or after a series of observations. Rating measures differ from the direct observational systems described in the next section in that the teacher incorporates a range of observations and experiences with a specific child into the ratings (Cairns & Green, 1979).

FIGURE 15.1
Systematic Anec-
dotal Assessment
of Social Interac-
tion. (Source. From
Social Interaction
Skill Curriculum
[1987] by S. L.
Odom, S. R. McCon-
nell, F. Kohler, and
P. S. Strain.
Reproduced by per-
mission of the
authors.)

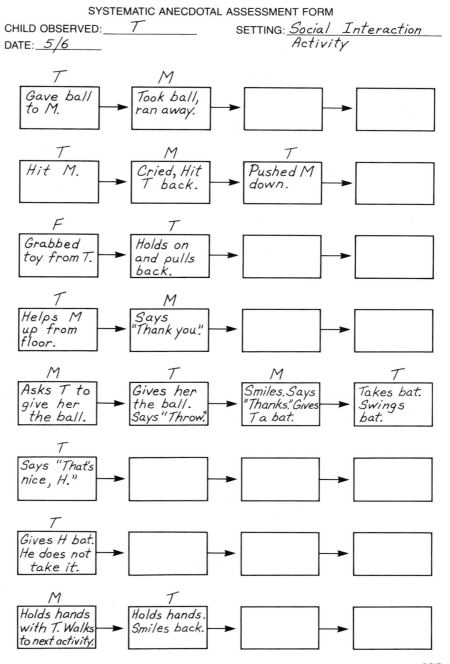

SYSTEMATIC ANECDOTAL ASSESSMENT FORM

CHILD OBSERVED: T   SETTING: Social Interaction Activity
DATE: 5/6

T — Gave ball to M.
M — Took ball, ran away.

T — Hit M.
M — Cried, Hit T back.
T — Pushed M down.

F — Grabbed toy from T.
T — Holds on and pulls back.

T — Helps M up from floor.
M — Says "Thank you."

M — Asks T to give her the ball.
T — Gives her the ball. Says "Throw."
M — Smiles. Says "Thanks." Gives T a bat.
T — Takes bat. Swings bat.

T — Says "That's nice, H."

T — Gives H bat. He does not take it.

M — Holds hands with T. Walks to next activity.
T — Holds hands. Smiles back.

403

Rating scales are based on the assumption that the teacher has the same understanding about the behavior or trait being rated as did the scale developer. For that reason, items on rating scales must be very explicit. Most individual rating-scale items contain a description of the behavior to be rated and provide a continuum on which the rater must indicate the degree to which a social behavior is present or absent. This continuum most often contains 5–7 points and may be arranged in a Likert-scale fashion. For example, the Social Interaction Rating Scale (Hops, Guild, Fleishman, Paine, Street, Walker, & Greenwood, 1979) in Figure 15.2 gives teachers 7 points on a continuum to make their choice of ratings of a specific item.

The reliability of the rating scale is enhanced if each point contains a separate description, called a **behavioral anchor.** These behaviorally anchored points give the teacher more information upon which to make a judgment about the item. In Figure 15.3 (p. 406), the first item from the Parent Behavior Progression, Form 2 (Bromwich, 1981) illustrates the advantage of providing behaviorally anchored items. For each point, a description of the rating choice is stated in behavioral terms; such specificity reduces the inference teachers make and should thus increase reliability.

Most rating scales include procedures for summarizing the ratings on individual items. This summary is done by adding the ratings and computing a total score, or, if the individual items are designed to measure different behaviors or attributes, specific subscale scores are calculated. For example, on the Maternal Behavior Rating Scale (Mahoney, Powell, & Finger, 1986), a rating scale of parent/infant interaction, the individual item's scores may be grouped into subscales indentified as child-oriented/maternal pleasure, quantity of stimulation, and control. Whereas the two exemplary scales noted were ratings of parents' behavior or parent/child interaction, other scales exist for measuring infant behavior (Barnard, Booth, Mitchell, & Telzrow, 1982; Farran, Kasari, & Jay, 1984; Simeonsson, Huntington, Short, & Ware, 1982).

A variation on the rating-scale theme is the checklist, which requires the observer to determine whether a behavior or set of behaviors occurred during an observation. These checklists typically require a yes/no response about the occurrence of the behavior but do not require finer judgments. The Home Observation for Measurement of the Environment (HOME) (Caldwell & Bradley, 1978) is an example of such a scale. Although the major purpose of the scale is to measure aspects of the physical environment of homes, several subscales measure mothers' responsivity and maternal involvement with the child.

The advantages of rating-scale measures of social interaction are that they usually (a) are quick to complete, (b) do not require the training necessary for direct observational systems, and (c) do not require frequent reliability checks. Rating scales yield global information about social interaction development. As such, they may be useful for measuring general levels of social interaction, as the teacher might need when screening children for possible problems, identifying current functioning level, or measuring change in behavior across the year. However, rating scales provide less-detailed information about the specific processes of development, such as day-to-day interactions in social settings.

Direct Observation of Social Interaction. Observational systems that require the assessor to observe directly and record immediately infants' or children's social interactions provide detailed assessment information. Direct observational systems are similar to anecdotal systems in that they depend on observation of the child in a social context, but are different in that the categories for observation are predetermined and the observations are made within a temporal frame

Peers Program
Social Interaction Rating Scale

Child's Name _____ Teacher _____

School _____ Grade _____

Date _____ Consultant _____

	Not descriptive or true	Moderately descriptive or true	Very descriptive or true
1. Verbally responds to a child's initiation.	1 . . . . 2 . . . . 3 . . . . 4 . . . . 5 . . . . 6 7		
2. Engages in long conversations (more than 30 seconds).	1 . . . . 2 . . . . 3 . . . . 4 . . . . 5 . . . . 6 7		
3. Shares laughter with classmates.	1 . . . 2 . . . . . 3 . . . . 4 . . . . 5 . . . 6 7		
4. Spontaneously contributes during a group discussion.	1 . . . . 2 . . . . 3 . . . . 4 . . . . 5 . . . . 6 7		
5. Volunteers for "show and tell."	1 . . . . 2 . . . 3 . . . . 4 . . . . 5 . . . . 6 7		
6. Freely takes a leadership role.	1 . . . . 2 . . . . 3 . . . . 4 . . . . 5 . . . 6 7		
7. Spontaneously works with a peer(s) on projects in class.	1 . . . . 2 . . . . 3 . . . . 4 . . . . 5 . . . . 6 7		
8. Verbally initiates to a peer(s).	1 . . . . 2 . . . . 3 . . . . 4 . . . . 5 . . . . 6 7		

TOTAL SCORE: ☐

FIGURE 15.2
Social Interaction Rating Scale. (Source. From Peers: Procedures for Establishing Effective Relationship Skills by H. Hops, J. Guild, D. H. Fleishman, S. Paine, A. Street, H. Walker, and C. Greenwood. Copyright 1979 by CORBEH. Reproduced by permission.)

PARENT BEHAVIORS

I. **Level I:** **The parent enjoys her infant.**

A. PLEASURE IN WATCHING INFANT

1. Parent shows or reports pleasure in watching infant at least some of the time. (O-R)
2. Parent shows or reports pleasure in infant's physical appearance or attributes. (O-R)
3. Parent shows pride in the infant in connection with some area of his behavior; ascribes qualities to him that parent values. (O-R)
4. Parent spontaneously talks about the things her infant does that please her. (R)
5. Parent shows or reports pleasure in watching infant play with other caregiver or other adults. (O-R)
6. Parent shows or reports pleasure in watching infant play by himself or with other infants or children. (O-R)
7. Parent shows or reports pleasure in infant's *enjoyment of his own activities.* (O-R)

FIGURE 15.3
Parent Behavior Progression, Level 1, Item A. (Source. From **Working with Parents and Infants: An Interactional Approach** *by R. Bromwich. Copyright 1981 by PRO-ED. Reproduced by permission.)*

(i.e., a specific point in time or within a time interval). They also differ from rating scales in that ongoing entries are recorded as the assessor observes the social interaction, while in rating scales only a summary score is provided. A detailed discussion of direct observation systems is provided in Chapter 4.

Three types of direct observational systems exist for coding social interaction information. **Time-sampling** systems require that the observer record at a specific point in time whether the infant, child, or parent is engaged in a specific social behavior or interaction (Sackett, 1978). Multiple data points are collected to gain a representative level of social interaction in which the infant or child engages.

In a time-sampling system, called the Social Interaction Scan (SIS) (Odom, Bender, Stein, Doran, Houden, McInnes, Gilbert, DeKlyen, Speltz, & Jenkins, 1988), the teacher observes a child for 2 seconds and then in the subsequent 4 seconds records the behavior in which the child was engaged. As can be seen from the coding sheet in Figure 15.4, the observer circles one of the letters that indicates a category of play behavior. These categories, based loosely on Parten's (1932) pioneering work, included isolate/unoccupied (I/U), proximity (P), interactive play (I), negative interaction (N), and teacher interaction (T). For the I and N categories, superscripts and subscripts indicated whether the child was playing with a handicapped (H) or nonhandicapped child (N).

FIGURE 15.4 *(opposite)*
Social Interaction Scan. (Source. From **Integrated Preschool Curriculum** *by S. L. Odom, M. Bender, M. Stein, L. Doran, D. Houden, M. McInnes, M. DeKlyen, M. Speltz, and J. Jenkins. Copyright 1988 by University of Washington Press. Reproduced by permission.)*

Social Interaction Scan

Classroom/Teacher:_____ Time Started:_____

Observer:_____ Activity:_____

Date:_____

Child's Name	T^c_t I^h_n N^h_n P I/U	T^c_t I^h_n N^h_n P I/U	T^c_t I^h_n N^h_n P I/U	T^c_t I^h_n N^h_n P I/U	T^c_t I^h_n N^h_n P I/U	T^c_t I^h_n N^h_n P I/U	T^c_t I^h_n N^h_n P I/U	Child's Name	T^c_t I^h_n N^h_n P I/U	T^c_t I^h_n N^h_n P I/U	T^c_t I^h_n N^h_n P I/U	T^c_t I^h_n N^h_n P I/U	T^c_t I^h_n N^h_n P I/U	T^c_t I^h_n N^h_n P I/U	T^c_t I^h_n N^h_n P I/U
Child's Name	T^c_t I^h_n N^h_n P I/U	T^c_t I^h_n N^h_n P I/U	T^c_t I^h_n N^h_n P I/U	T^c_t I^h_n N^h_n P I/U	T^c_t I^h_n N^h_n P I/U	T^c_t I^h_n N^h_n P I/U	T^c_t I^h_n N^h_n P I/U	Child's Name	T^c_t I^h_n N^h_n P I/U	T^c_t I^h_n N^h_n P I/U	T^c_t I^h_n N^h_n P I/U	T^c_t I^h_n N^h_n P I/U	T^c_t I^h_n N^h_n P I/U	T^c_t I^h_n N^h_n P I/U	T^c_t I^h_n N^h_n P I/U
Child's Name	T^c_t I^h_n N^h_n P I/U	T^c_t I^h_n N^h_n P I/U	T^c_t I^h_n N^h_n P I/U	T^c_t I^h_n N^h_n P I/U	T^c_t I^h_n N^h_n P I/U	T^c_t I^h_n N^h_n P I/U	T^c_t I^h_n N^h_n P I/U	Child's Name	T^c_t I^h_n N^h_n P I/U	T^c_t I^h_n N^h_n P I/U	T^c_t I^h_n N^h_n P I/U	T^c_t I^h_n N^h_n P I/U	T^c_t I^h_n N^h_n P I/U	T^c_t I^h_n N^h_n P I/U	T^c_t I^h_n N^h_n P I/U
Child's Name	T^c_t I^h_n N^h_n P I/U	T^c_t I^h_n N^h_n P I/U	T^c_t I^h_n N^h_n P I/U	T^c_t I^h_n N^h_n P I/U	T^c_t I^h_n N^h_n P I/U	T^c_t I^h_n N^h_n P I/U	T^c_t I^h_n N^h_n P I/U	Child's Name	T^c_t I^h_n N^h_n P I/U	T^c_t I^h_n N^h_n P I/U	T^c_t I^h_n N^h_n P I/U	T^c_t I^h_n N^h_n P I/U	T^c_t I^h_n N^h_n P I/U	T^c_t I^h_n N^h_n P I/U	T^c_t I^h_n N^h_n P I/U
Child's Name	T^c_t I^h_n N^h_n P I/U	T^c_t I^h_n N^h_n P I/U	T^c_t I^h_n N^h_n P I/U	T^c_t I^h_n N^h_n P I/U	T^c_t I^h_n N^h_n P I/U	T^c_t I^h_n N^h_n P I/U	T^c_t I^h_n N^h_n P I/U	Child's Name	T^c_t I^h_n N^h_n P I/U	T^c_t I^h_n N^h_n P I/U	T^c_t I^h_n N^h_n P I/U	T^c_t I^h_n N^h_n P I/U	T^c_t I^h_n N^h_n P I/U	T^c_t I^h_n N^h_n P I/U	T^c_t I^h_n N^h_n P I/U
Child's Name	T^c_t I^h_n N^h_n P I/U	T^c_t I^h_n N^h_n P I/U	T^c_t I^h_n N^h_n P I/U	T^c_t I^h_n N^h_n P I/U	T^c_t I^h_n N^h_n P I/U	T^c_t I^h_n N^h_n P I/U	T^c_t I^h_n N^h_n P I/U	Child's Name	T^c_t I^h_n N^h_n P I/U	T^c_t I^h_n N^h_n P I/U	T^c_t I^h_n N^h_n P I/U	T^c_t I^h_n N^h_n P I/U	T^c_t I^h_n N^h_n P I/U	T^c_t I^h_n N^h_n P I/U	T^c_t I^h_n N^h_n P I/U

407

For the teacher category, the observer indicated whether the child was talking to the teacher (C) or the teacher was talking to the child (T).

This system is called a **scan** because, after the observer records the behavior for one child, he moves on to the next child, and, when the behavior of the final child on the list is recorded, the observer begins again with the first child. This technique provides a more representative picture of the children's social behavior across a play session than does a single block of observations. An alternative way of using this system is to observe a single child for a certain number of observations before moving on to the next child.

An advantage of time sampling is that it is usually less difficult to learn than either interval sampling or event recording (described in the following sections). In this system, one could collect information on frequency of interactive play, the type of child involved in the interaction, and frequencies of other data (e.g., proximity, teacher interactions). In addition, information may be collected for the whole class in a relatively brief amount of time. The SIS is a relatively simple scanning system, and more detailed and descriptive categories of social interaction could be developed.

Time-sampling systems typically do not allow the observer to collect information about the sequential nature of a child's social interaction (i.e., how many turns occurred in the interaction). Also, because the behavior is collected either instantaneously or within a very short interval, high frequency behaviors tend to be overrepresented in the data, and low frequency behaviors tend to be underrepresented unless a substantial amount of data are collected for the assessment (Sackett, 1978). For example, the authors of the SIS recommend that the teacher collect at least 100–150 data points per child in order to obtain a representative sample of children's behavior (Odom et al., 1988).

Interval-sampling measures of social interaction require the observer to watch an infant or young child for a short period of time, usually between 6 and 15 seconds, and record whether the behavior occurred anytime during that interval. In **discontinuous interval systems,** a short interval is provided after the observation interval to allow the observer to record the social behavior. In **continuous interval systems,** the observer records the behavior as it occurs and moves to the next observation interval without pausing to record. Usually an auditory tone (e.g., from an audiotape) cues the observer to change recording intervals.

An interval sampling system for coding the social interactions of preschool children is provided in Figure 15.5 (McConnell, Sisson, & Sandler, 1984). This system is based on continuous 6-second intervals. When an interaction occurs in an interval, the observer records (a) whether the target child being observed (T) or a peer (P) initiated the interaction, (b) the type of initiation (affection, starts, shares, share request, play organizers, entries, or negatives), (c) whether there was a response (yes, no, negative, or ignores), (d) what general kind of social behavior occurred during the interval (parallel, social interaction, inappropriate social interaction, or nonsocial), and (e) any teacher interaction (correction, prompt, or praise). The coding sheet in Figure 15.5 contains enough intervals for 2 minutes of data. All of the data are collected on the same child. Samples of from 5 to 15 minutes are collected on a child during a single session. After data are collected, the observer transfers those data to a summary coding sheet. From there, data may again be summarized across a number of samples.

The advantage of the interval-sampling system is that it is less difficult to learn than the event recording system (noted next), but it is more difficult than the time-sampling system. Interval-sampling systems may provide more information about the reciprocal nature of social interactions than time-sampling systems because the observer

Target _____   Observer _____

Date _____   Tmt. Cond. _____

Setting _____   Session No. _____

	Initiations (Target & Peers)							Response (Target & Peers)				Summative (Target Only)		Teacher Atn to Target	
1	#	T	Aff	Sta	Sha-R	PlaO	Ent	Neg	T	Yes	No	Neg	Ign	Parallel	Inapp-SS	Corr/Prom	1
		P	Aff	Sta	Sha-R	PlaO	Ent	Neg	P	Yes	No	Neg	Ign	SocInter	NonSoc	Praise	
2	#	T	Aff	Sta	Sha-R	PlaO	Ent	Neg	T	Yes	No	Neg	Ign	Parallel	Inapp-SS	Corr/Prom	2
		P	Aff	Sta	Sha-R	PlaO	Ent	Neg	P	Yes	No	Neg	Ign	SocInter	NonSoc	Praise	
3	#	T	Aff	Sta	Sha-R	PlaO	Ent	Neg	T	Yes	No	Neg	Ign	Parallel	Inapp-SS	Corr/Prom	3
		P	Aff	Sta	Sha-R	PlaO	Ent	Neg	P	Yes	No	Neg	Ign	SocInter	NonSoc	Praise	
4	#	T	Aff	Sta	Sha-R	PlaO	Ent	Neg	T	Yes	No	Neg	Ign	Parallel	Inapp-SS	Corr/Prom	4
		P	Aff	Sta	Sha-R	PlaO	Ent	Neg	P	Yes	No	Neg	Ign	SocInter	NonSoc	Praise	
5	#	T	Aff	Sta	Sha-R	PlaO	Ent	Neg	T	Yes	No	Neg	Ign	Parallel	Inapp-SS	Corr/Prom	5
		P	Aff	Sta	Sha-R	PlaO	Ent	Neg	P	Yes	No	Neg	Ign	SocInter	NonSoc	Praise	
6	#	T	Aff	Sta	Sha-R	PlaO	Ent	Neg	T	Yes	No	Neg	Ign	Parallel	Inapp-SS	Corr/Prom	6
		P	Aff	Sta	Sha-R	PlaO	Ent	Neg	P	Yes	No	Neg	Ign	SocInter	NonSoc	Praise	
7	#	T	Aff	Sta	Sha-R	PlaO	Ent	Neg	T	Yes	No	Neg	Ign	Parallel	Inapp-SS	Corr/Prom	7
		P	Aff	Sta	Sha-R	PlaO	Ent	Neg	P	Yes	No	Neg	Ign	SocInter	NonSoc	Praise	
8	#	T	Aff	Sta	Sha-R	PlaO	Ent	Neg	T	Yes	No	Neg	Ign	Parallel	Inapp-SS	Corr/Prom	8
		P	Aff	Sta	Sha-R	PlaO	Ent	Neg	P	Yes	No	Neg	Ign	SocInter	NonSoc	Praise	
9	#	T	Aff	Sta	Sha-R	PlaO	Ent	Neg	T	Yes	No	Neg	Ign	Parallel	Inapp-SS	Corr/Prom	9
		P	Aff	Sta	Sha-R	PlaO	Ent	Neg	P	Yes	No	Neg	Ign	SocInter	NonSoc	Praise	

FIGURE 15.5
Observation Assessment of Reciprocal Social Interactions. (Source. *From* Category Definitions for Observational Assessment of Reciprocal Social Interactions *by S. R. McConnell, L. Sisson, and S. Sandler. Reproduced by permission.)*

watches the interaction longer. However, interval sampling may be problematic when an interaction stretches across an interval, unless the code has a specific category for continuation.

The disadvantage for some interval systems is that more than one behavior may occur in an interval. When this happens, the assessment data will actually underestimate the level of social interaction. Code developers sometimes make their intervals short (i.e., 6 seconds) so that the likelihood of more than one social interaction occurring per interval is reduced.

In time-sampling and interval-sampling systems, a teacher records one occurrence of a social behavior or interaction whether it occurs once or several times during the observation point or interval. **Event recording systems** differ in that the teacher records all social behaviors or interactions that occur. As with the other systems, these behaviors may be recorded within a specific time frame or interval, so that when interobserver agreement is collected, the teacher can determine on which specific behaviors there is agreement or disagreement. However, within the time frame the assessor records all the behaviors that occur rather than just the fact that the behavior occurred.

A coding sheet for an event recording system of preschool children's social interactions with peers is presented in Figure 15.6. This system was based on the work of Tremblay and co-workers (1980), Strain (1983), and Odom, Silver, Sandler, and Strain (1983). The system is called a **focal child system** because one child is observed for a period of time, and all social behaviors the focal child directs to peers and all social behaviors directed to the focal child are recorded. This system contains nine behavioral categories (e.g., complimentary, assistance request), and within each category is a space to mark whether the behavior is an initiation or a response. The numbered rows represent 10-second intervals, and the teacher records all social interactions that occur within an interval. The focal child's behavior is denoted by a checkmark; the peers' behavior is identified by the initial of their first name. In the data presented in Figure 15.6, Sam (S) first suggested a play organizer and the focal child responded. In interval 3, the focal child gave a toy to Sam, Sam responded by taking the toy, then he gave another toy to Sam, and finally, Sam responded by taking the toy from the focal child. In interval 4, the focal child asked a peer for assistance, and the peer did not respond.

The relative accuracy of the event recording system, as compared with time- and interval-sampling systems, is a major advantage. By coding all behaviors (i.e., within the coding system) that occur, the teacher gains more information about the child's social interaction performance. For coding chains of social interactions, event-recording systems are essential because they allow the teacher to see the specific sequence of initiations and responses occurring within an interaction.

The disadvantage of event recording systems is that they are more difficult than the other systems to learn and use. For example, for the complex system such as the one described above, a number of weeks may be required for training observers. Such detailed information may be more than is needed for designing and monitoring social interaction intervention programs for young children with handicaps and their peers. More often, complex event-recording systems are used for research or very systematic program evaluations.

A Note on a Classic Observational System. Any discussion of measuring children's social interaction would be incomplete without an acknowledgment of Mildred Parten's work (1932). The Parten Scale of Social Participation was one of the earliest social interaction observational assessments and has served as a basis for many other systems that have been developed (e.g., the SIS scale previously described). The behavioral categories, presented in Table 15.3 (p. 412), denote the range of children's behavior from unoccupied to highly sophisticated cooperative play. In recent years, researchers have combined Parten's original social categories with Smilansky's (1968) measures of cognitive play to obtain an even more detailed description of the quality of children's social participation (Odom, 1981; Rubin, 1982; Rubin, Maioni, & Hornung, 1976; Rubin, Watson, & Jambor, 1978).

Sociometric Assessments

Sociometric assessment procedures are those in which children are asked to provide general qualitative evaluations of the social acceptance, social preference, or likability of other children. Typically, teachers gather sociometric information from intact groups of children, such as all children enrolled in a particular class or all children in a particular play group. As a result, sociometric measures are not useful for children who have little interaction with peers outside of their home.

There are four general types of sociometric assessment instruments: (a) peer nominations, (b) peer ratings, (c) peer assessments, and (d) paired comparisons. Given the level of

Focal Child: _____ Setting Arrangement: _____

Class: _____ _____

Date: _____ Observer: _____

Page _____ of _____

BEHAVIORAL CATEGORIES

	Compli-mentary		Assist-ance Request		Assist-ance		Affection		Play Or-ganizer		Share Request		Share		Negative M/G		Negative V/V	
	I	R	I	R	I	R	I	R	I	R	I	R	I	R	I	R	I	R
1																		
2																		
3																		
4																		
5																		
6																		

	Compli-mentary		Assist-ance Request		Assist-ance		Affection		Play Or-ganizer		Share Request		Share		Negative M/G		Negative V/V	
	I	R	I	R	I	R	I	R	I	R	I	R	I	R	I	R	I	R
1																		
2																		
3																		
4																		
5																		
6																		

FIGURE 15.6
Direct Observation of Social Behavior. (Source. From Direct Observation of Social Behavior Manual by S. L. Odom, F. Silver, S. Sandler, and P. S. Strain. Copyright 1983 by Early Childhood Research Institute. Reprinted by permission.)

411

TABLE 15.3
Abbreviated Behavioral Categories of the Parten Scale of Social Participation and the Smilansky Scale, as defined in Odom (1981)

Scale/Category	Definition
Parten Scale	
Unoccupied	Glancing around the room but not focusing on an activity
Onlooker	Observing other children, but not interacting
Solitary	Playing alone with toys different from those being played with by children in the general proximity, not conversing
Parallel	Playing with toys similar to those used by children in the subject's vicinity
Associative	Playing with other children without role assignment, loosely organized
Cooperative	Playing with other children in an organized manner, roles assigned
Smilansky Scale	
Functional	Simple muscular activities, manipulating play objects
Constructive	Creative activities, appropriately manipulating academic materials
Dramatic	Manipulating objects in a symbolic manner
Games with rules	Playing games with prearranged rules

resources needed and the limited scope of their application, peer assessments and paired comparisons have little relevance to work in applied settings and will not be discussed further in this section. Instead, procedural descriptions of peer nominations and ratings are given.

Peer Nominations. **Peer nominations** are sociometric assessment procedures in which children are asked to identify those of their classmates who meet some general criterion. Children may be asked to identify classmates they, for example, consider their best friends, like to play or work with, or like the least. All children are asked to complete this nomination by selecting from the list of classmates' names or, for preschoolers, from a set of pictures of classmates (Marshall, 1957). Peer nomination scores are calculated as the pro-

portion of nominations a child receives from all peers in her class or play group.

By using both positive (e.g., "Name your three best friends") and negative (e.g., "Name three children you don't like") nomination criteria, children can be classified into sociometric groups. These groups typically include: (a) "stars," who receive many positive and few, if any, negative nominations; (b) "neglected" children, who receive few positive or few negative nominations; (c) "rejected" children, who receive few positive and many negative nominations; and (d) "controversial" children, who receive high numbers of both positive and negative nominations. It must be noted that the use of negative criteria in any sociometric assessment procedure, including nomination measures, is at times controversial. While there is no evidence children change their interactions with peers after negative nomination assessments, little research has been conducted in this area (McConnell & Odom, 1986). Until such research is available, users of negative nomination sociometric procedures should be particularly attentive to concerns of parents and administrators and to the possible effects of these assessment procedures on the behavior of young children.

Peer Ratings. Unlike peer nominations, **peer ratings** require children to provide general qualitative ratings for each child in their classroom or play group. These ratings, typically 3-point to 7-point Likert-type scales, provide scores for each child in a particular group with that score based on evaluations by all other children in the group. Like peer nominations, specific criteria vary as a function of the purpose of assessment; however, all ratings are completed to reflect general statements of preference (e.g., "How much do you like to play with _____?" or "How much do you like to talk with _____?"). A child's sociometric rating score is typically calculated as the sum or average rating received from all raters; however, other scoring procedures (e.g., sum of ratings by same-sex classmates, number of highest-preference ratings) are also used.

Peer ratings provide one way for avoiding the use of negative evaluations by children. All children in a group are rated on a common dimension; as a result, individual scores can be rank-ordered, and children can be sorted from most highly rated to least highly rated on a single dimension. However, as noted earlier, without negative nominations, specific sociometric subgroups cannot be formed.

Peer rating sociometrics also have been adapted for use with preschool children. Asher, Singleton, Tinsley, and Hymel (1979) developed and evaluated a picture rating procedure in which children sorted photographs of their individual classmates into marked boxes to indicate their relative ratings. This procedure proved to be quite useful and is now widely accepted as a standard for collecting peer ratings among young children.

A Note On Reliability. After reviewing stability analyses from a variety of investigations, McConnell and Odom (1986) concluded that sociometric measures cannot necessarily be expected to offer stable estimates of social preference when completed by young children and that reliability estimates should be obtained each time sociometric procedures are used in research and, where possible, applied settings. The authors of this chapter, and others, are currently trying to develop procedures that will increase the reliability of these procedures when used with preschool children (ages 3 and 4) in classroom settings (e.g., teaching children to rate preferences for foods and toys before rating peers). Until such procedures have been developed and evaluated, teachers should be cautious in interpreting information obtained from these instruments.

Norm-Referenced Assessment

A variety of **norm-referenced measures** are available for assessing social interaction skills as well as the broader assessment of social competence of young children with handicaps. As with other measures, the development of norm-referenced measures in this domain appears to have been influenced by our recent attention to school-based treatment for 3- to 5-year-old children; the vast majority of norm-referenced measures of social skill and competence has been designed for use by teachers or for description of school-based behaviors.

Norm-referenced assessments of social behavior and competence for infants and toddlers with handicaps typically describe the child's performance on broad dimensions of social development. Rather than describing specific skills that can be selected for intervention (as criterion-referenced measures), these normative measures tend to describe social functioning across a broad, relatively undifferentiated spectrum. These measures are used to compare the behavior, performance, or development of an individual child to the overall status of other children at similar ages, thus providing relative information regarding a child's current level of development. Typically, the norm-referenced assessment of social development and competence is seen as one part of a broader assessment of development or adaptive behavior of infants and preschool children with handicaps. Norm-referenced measures of social development are included in several commonly used scales of development and adaptive behavior, including the Battelle Developmental Inventory (BDI) (Newborg, Stock, Wnek, Guidubaldi, & Svinicki, 1984), the recently revised Vineland Adaptive Behavior Scales (Sparrow, Balla, & Cicchetti, 1984), and the AAMD Adaptive Behavior Scale (Nihira, Foster, Shellhaas, & Leleand, 1974). Additionally, several teacher rating scales have been developed for describing the social competence of preschoolers with handicaps, including the California Preschool Social Competency Scale (Levine, Elzey, & Lewis, 1969).

Norm-referenced measures of social skill and competence often rely on teachers' or parents' ratings. In both instances, adults are asked to provide behavior-specific ratings or evaluations of an individual child, and these ratings are scored into one or more scales for normative comparisons. Normative measures of problem behaviors include the Child Behavior Checklist (Achenbach & Edelbrock, 1983) and the Walker Problem Behavior Identification Checklist (Walker, 1983). However, rather than being at different ends of a common continuum, these measures of social competence and problem behaviors may represent overlapping yet fairly distinct concepts (Walker & McConnell, in press). For this reason, these latter measures of problem behaviors will not be discussed further in this section.

Norm-referenced measures of social skill and competence are of two types: parent or caregiver ratings, often completed in interview formats, and teacher ratings, completed in classroom situations. Examples of each type of measure are described briefly in the following sections. Other measures are listed in Table 15.2.

Parent Ratings

Vineland Adaptive Behavior Scales. The Vineland Adaptive Behavior Scales (Sparrow et al., 1984) were originally developed in 1935 to provide measures of adaptive behavior and "social competence" among children and adults with mental retardation. The scales were fully revised and restandardized in 1984. The current edition of the Vineland scales includes three versions: an interview edition: survey form; an interview edition: expanded form; and a classroom edition. Each edition provides scores in four domains, including socialization.

The Vineland Scales were designed for use with children from birth to age 18 years 11 months. Both the survey and the expanded editions are completed during interviews with a child's parent (or other informed adult). These two scales differ primarily in the number of items included in each domain. The socialization domain of the Vineland Scales is made up of three subdomains: interpersonal relations (descriptions of how the individual interacts with others), play and leisure time (quality of the child's play), and coping skills (descriptions of the child's ability to assume responsibility or to be sensitive to others). Items in each of these three domains are included for toddlers; items in interpersonal relationships and play and leisure time extend down to birth. However, in spite of the Vineland's presentation of these subdomains, most norm-referenced assessments of children with this instrument primarily will focus on the composite score for the socialization domain. The Vineland Scale offers age-level norms for children from birth, with raw scores being converted to standard scores (mean of 100 and standard deviation of 15), percentile ranks, stanines, and age equivalents.

Battelle Developmental Inventory. The BDI (Newborg et al., 1984) is an individually administered instrument for children from birth to age 8 that was specifically designed for use in the assessment of children with handicaps. The BDI is composed of five scales, including the personal-social scale, which is designed to be completed either by directly observing the child's behavior or by interviewing the child's parent, primary caregiver, or teacher. The scale includes 85 items divided into 6 subdomains: adult interaction, expression of feelings/affect, self-concept, peer interaction, coping, and social role. In three instances (i.e., adult interaction, expression of feelings/affect, and self-concept) these subdomains include items with developmental ages at birth; however, in all instances but adult interaction, few items are included for developmental ages below 12 months. All items are scored as 0—child cannot or does not perform specified behavior; 1—child attempts behavior but does not demonstrate mastery; and 2—child exhibits behavior as described. Scores in each of the 6 subdomains are summed to obtain a total domain score for the personal-social section, and age-level norms are then used to obtain standard scores, percentile ranks, or age equivalents.

Teacher Ratings

Despite the increased attention paid to social interaction and development during the preschool years, there are surprisingly few technically adequate and well-established norm-referenced teacher rating measures of social skill and competence for preschool children. While this situation may change in coming years due to increased attention to social skill development for young children

with handicaps and the increased need for teachers and administrators to document children's progress during intervention, professionals currently interested in teacher-provided, norm-referenced evaluations have few tests from which to select. One of the most common teacher ratings of social competence is the California Preschool Social Competency Scale.

California Preschool Social Competency Scale. The California Preschool Social Competency Scale (CPSCS) (Levine et al., 1969) is a 30-item rating scale that provides a total score and percentile rankings by age, sex, and socioeconomic class. The CPSCS has been demonstrated to detect changes in the social behavior of children with handicaps who have been socially integrated with normally developing peers (Jenkins, Odom, & Speltz, in press). However, in a content analysis of the CPSCS conducted by the authors of this chapter, a group of 21 professionals who work with handicapped preschoolers identified approximately 25% of the CPSCS items as measures of adaptive behavior rather than social competence. At this point, then, the overall content validity of the CPSCS may be unknown, but the scale appears to be one of the few options for assessing teachers' norm-referenced ratings of the social skill and competence of their students.

Comments on Norm-referenced Measures

Several norm-referenced measures of social skill and competence are available for use with handicapped preschool children. However, most of these measures are designed to use parents as primary sources of data and are parts of larger measures of developmental status or adaptive behavior. Currently, there are few widely available, well-standardized instruments that rely on teacher evaluation of the social skills of preschool children with handicaps.

As noted previously, norm-referenced measures are used primarily to evaluate a child's eligibility for services according to some set of administrative criteria. To perform this task adequately, norm-referenced instruments must demonstrate adequate levels of reliability and validity with respect to the assessment of social skill; that is, they should offer consistent information that provides believable data about a child's relative level of social development. These measures, however, may offer little, if any, evidence regarding the specific behaviors in which a child demonstrates competence or deficits and may not be of great use in the design of preventive or remedial programs for that child. This latter type of assessment, planning for intervention, typically requires the use of criterion-referenced measures, which are discussed next.

Criterion-Referenced Measures

Criterion-referenced measures of social skill and competence are those that provide behavior-specific information regarding a child's current level of performance. Unlike norm-referenced measures, criterion-referenced (or curriculum-referenced) measures provide highly specific information regarding a child's level of performance for multiple individual skills.

Currently, there are several commercially published tests for assessment of social skills and competence of handicapped preschool children that are criterion-referenced and offer direct information for the planning of individual interventions. For instance, the BDI (Newborg et al., 1984) presents developmental age-level scores for each item in the personal-social scale, presents items in a hierarchical order, and offers recommendations for translating test results into IEP or IFSP objectives. Other criterion-referenced assessments that contain social strands and are appropriate for infants and young children with handicaps include the Carolina Cur-

riculum for Handicapped Infants (Johnson-Martin, Jens, & Attermeier, 1986), the Hawaii Early Learning Profile (Furuno, O'Reilly, Inatsuka, Hosaka, Allman, & Zeisloft-Falbey, 1985), the Early Learning Accomplishment Profile (Glover, Preminger, & Sanford, 1978), and the Portage Guide to Early Development (Bluma, Shearer, Frohman, & Hillard, 1976).

The varying, somewhat idiosyncratic features of criterion-referenced measures of social interaction skill restrict the utility of reviewing characteristics of individual tests. Rather, criterion-referenced tests must be carefully selected based on the specific needs of their intended application. For this reason, teachers should look for several desirable characteristics of the instruments when selecting assessment measures.

First, criterion-referenced measures must provide for direct and detailed assessment of a child's behavior across the range of situations or settings. Whenever possible, this assessment should be based on direct observation of the child; if necessary, analogue situations can be created so that teacher or peer prompts can be provided for low-frequency but important social behaviors.

Second, assessment must focus on discrete social skills and behaviors. Rather than assessing current levels of social interaction or other composite aspects of the child's development (e.g., total social scores), criterion-referenced measures must capture a child's performance on the component behaviors that constitute social interaction. For instance, criterion-referenced assessment of social initiations may include attention to the child's use of eye contact, proximity to peers during play, presence of appropriate toys or materials, and demonstration of a specific verbal or gestural bid to peers. The focus on discrete skills or behaviors is essential for obtaining assessment data that can be used in planning future intervention.

Third, criterion-referenced measures must arrange skills in a natural progression or hierarchy. This hierarchy may be based on task analysis of social interaction or on evidence of typical developmental progressions, but in any case, the validity of this hierarchy should be evaluated directly. The hierarchy of skills helps teachers arrange assessment data to plan intervention more carefully and efficiently.

Fourth, criterion-referenced measures must be linked carefully to curricula or other intervention programs for children. Outside of the context of treatment, criterion-referenced assessment has little meaning. Rather, measures of this type identify the social interaction skills a child has yet to master and help teachers mark progress toward this mastery. Lack of concordance between assessment information and intervention goals reduces the efficiency of both efforts.

Finally, criterion-referenced measures must be sensitive to small changes in behavior. After identification of treatment needs, one major application of criterion-referenced assessment is to monitor progress. When children are exposed to effective intervention procedures in well-organized classrooms, it is likely that their behavior will begin to change rapidly. To monitor children's development and plan for revisions in intervention programs, teachers must apply measures often to detect subtle changes for individual children. For this reason, criterion-referenced measures must be sensitive to minor changes in the social skill or competence of individual children (Hops, Finch, & McConnell, 1986).

Using Social Interaction Assessment Information

Assessment information of children's social interaction is commonly used for several purposes: screening, diagnosing social problems, designing instructional programs, monitoring instruction, program evaluation, and research

(see Chapter 1). The social interaction assessment approaches just discussed are important for different purposes. Outlined in Table 15.4 (p. 418) is the interface between different assessment approaches and different purposes for conducting assessments. Each of these purposes is discussed in the following sections.

Screening

Professionals conduct screenings in order to identify infants and children who might be at risk for social interaction problems. When the teacher determines that a problem might exist, the infant or young child would then be referred for more intensive assessment of social development. The information collected from a screening test is not sufficient for designing a social interaction intervention program; it should only be used for determining whether further assessment is needed.

Formal screening measures for infants and parents are not available. More often, information about interactional problems may arise from parents' reports that their child does not respond consistently to their attempts to play, or the professional may notice that the parent rarely attempts to interact with the child. Also, the parents may report that the child sometimes wants attention, but when they try to give it, the infant turns away. This type of information may be seen as a *red flag* for a potential social interactional problem, and indicates that the professional needs to concentrate assessment efforts on the pattern of social interaction that exists between the infant and the parent and on the social relationship that has developed. The teacher may depend on anecdotal information collected through observations or interviews with the parent. Also, the Parent Behavior Progression (Bromwich, 1981) may serve as a guide for collecting initial screening information.

For preschool children, teachers may take a different approach to screening for social

TABLE 15.4
Social Interaction Assessment, Approaches, and Purposes

Purposes	Anecdotal	Direct Observation	Teacher Ratings	Peer Ratings	Criterion Referenced	Norm Referenced	Comments
Screening		X	X				
Diagnosis	X	X	X	X	X	X	Multimethod Assessment Important
Program Design	X	X	X		X		
Program Monitoring	X	X	X		X		
Program Evaluation		X	X	X		X	Multimethod Assessment Important
Research		X	X	X		X	Multimethod Assessment Important

interaction problems. First, teachers, more than most other adults, are able to observe preschool children with their peer group, and they are very good at picking up problems through these observations. To confirm their concerns, teachers may use rating scales or observational systems to collect screening information on specific children. Second, if they work with a group of children for whom there is a risk of developmental or social problems (e.g., children from low-income families, physically or sexually abused children),

teachers might routinely collect screening information on all the children in the class. Third, from what we know about the development of children with handicaps (Guralnick & Groom, 1985), there is reason to suspect that these children will have delays in social development. Presence of a handicapping condition should be enough of a screening indicator for the teacher to plan for a more detailed assessment.

Teacher rating scales seem to be the most efficient assessment approach for screening preschool aged children. The Social Interaction Rating Scale (Hops et al., 1979), the Child Behavior Questionnaire (Behar & Stringfield, 1974), the Teacher Rating of Social Interaction (Odom et al., 1988) are examples of teacher rating measures that can be completed quickly and can identify potential social problems. Teacher rating scales routinely provide guidelines for interpreting the scores and identifying children who are at risk.

The teacher also may use direct observational measures for screening. When screening a whole class, a time-sampling/scanning system like the SIS may be the most efficient method. When screening one child, the teacher may use any of the direct observational methods mentioned previously. Behavioral indicators that might represent a problem for 3- to 5-year-old children are (a) infrequent interactions with other children during play sessions (i.e., on the average less than one or two interactions per five minutes of play), (b) consistently turning away or ignoring other peers when they attempt to play, (c) frequent aggression toward peers (i.e., consistently once or twice per play session), and (d) standing at the edge of a group and watching others as they play, yet never joining the group. All children engage in these behaviors at some time. However, if the observational data suggest that these behaviors occur frequently across several weeks, the teacher should consider referring the child for more extensive testing.

Diagnosing Social Interaction Difficulties

Social interaction assessment information may also be used for documenting children's current functioning level in order to diagnose a problem. To diagnose social problems and particularly to qualify children for special services, teachers often use norm-referenced tests. These assessments, such as the Vineland Adaptive Behavior Scale (Sparrow et al., 1984) or the CPSCS (Levine et al., 1969), provide normative information for comparing the child's social performance to that of children of a similar age or for documenting the presence of social problems. In addition, sociometric information, which would yield information about the child's social status within the peer group, would also be important for this assessment purpose.

Unfortunately, few norm-referenced assessments are available for identifying social interaction problems for mothers and infants. Formally identifying social interaction deficits for infants will require the teacher to interview the parents and observe the parents and infant during both caregiving and playful situations. In such instances, anecdotal information or rating scale information, such as is provided by the Maternal Behavior Rating Scale (Mahoney et al., 1986), may be useful. With this information, the assessor would attempt to document the discrepancy between normal and atypical development.

Organizing a Diagnostic Assessment Session. To collect information on parent/infant interaction to be used for diagnostic purposes, the teacher should observe the parent and child in a setting that is natural and comfortable for both. The home is often the best place for such observations, although they sometimes also occur at centers. Unless the teacher is particularly interested in observing feeding skills, the observations may occur in a playful setting with toys and other activities. It is particularly important that the child is as active and alert as possible, so the observations should be scheduled around lunch and nap time. Also, it would be useful for the observation to occur in a room that contains toys but that is otherwise free from distractions.

The teacher should begin the diagnostic sessions by putting the parent at ease and trying to build rapport. In the early part of the session, teachers may direct the conversation around information that they want to collect for any checklist or norm-referenced instruments that they may be using (e.g., the

HOME Scale, Caldwell & Bradley, 1978). As the parent becomes more at ease and the infant becomes familiar with the teacher, the teacher may tell the parent that she wishes to watch a typical "play time" (e.g., if using the Maternal Behavior Rating Scale) or she may ask the parent to try to teach the infant a skill (e.g., if using the Teaching Skills Inventory). The requests that the teacher makes of the parent depend completely on the type of information that she wants to collect for the parent (e.g., parent-teaching skills, parent/infant interaction). However, information about the parent's discomfort with the infant, parent's lack of knowledge about how to play with the infant, and the infant's responsivity to parent social initiation are best obtained during the initial rapport-building session and during the subsequent play time. If feasible, information should be collected over several play time sessions on different days.

Collecting diagnostic assessment information on peer interaction should occur in a setting in which the child is familiar with the peer group and has an opportunity to play freely with peers. Observations seem to work best in free-play times in daycare centers or the preschool in which the child is observed. If a child has not had exposure to a preschool peer group for at least a month prior to the assessment, then little information will be obtained about his peer social interaction skills. The peer group should consist of children who are about the same age and who are not exclusively of the opposite sex (i.e., boys should never be observed in a peer group containing all girls, and vice versa).

Most rating scales have specific instructions for collecting the needed information. If the teacher collecting the assessment information is not the child's regular teacher and has not observed over several free-play sessions, then the regular teacher should complete the scale. Norm-referenced information, from adaptive behavior scales for example, may be collected by interviewing the child's regular teacher or parent. Direct observation information should be collected over three to five play sessions that last 20 to 30 minutes each, although the specific amount of information needed will depend on the specific observational instrument used. Observational systems should have some guidelines for the amount of data needed. Often, specific criteria (i.e., norms) for observational instruments are not available and the teacher may have difficulty interpreting the assessment information. A solution is to establish "local norms" by collecting identical assessment information on one or two children in the class who are competent social interactors. The regular classroom teacher may nominate these children. The referred child's data may then be compared with the data from the competent peers.

Designing Instructional Programs

A teacher may use assessment information as a way of identifying the starting point of an intervention program. Although normative data could be important for identifying goals, information obtained through other assessment approaches is often more useful. Many of the broad-based criterion-referenced assessments, such as the Learning Accomplishment Profile, the Portage Guide to Early Development or the BDI, provide social development strands. From these assessments the teacher may determine general goals and specific objectives for children.

Several teacher rating scales may also be useful. For infants, McCollum and Stayton (1985) described the use of a rating scale for assisting a teacher in designing social interaction interventions for infants and parents. With this system, called the Social Interaction Assessment/Intervention (SIAI), the teacher also includes other data (e.g., parent interviews) in selecting the social objectives. The Parent Behavior Progression, Form 1, is also a helpful rating measure for determining the type of goal a teacher should emphasize (i.e., social interaction vs. a didactic goal) as well as identifying specific objectives. The Teaching Skills Inventory (Rosenberg, Robinson, & Beckman, 1984) is a particularly useful scale for determining parental interactive behavior when the goal of the program is for parents to teach skills to their infant or toddler. The Parent-Caregiver Interaction Scale (Farran et al., 1984) has also been a useful guide for developing intervention programs.

Direct observation systems can provide useful information for determining the types of social interactions in which the parents and infants or the preschool child and the peer group are currently engaging. Such information should reveal how reciprocal the social interactions are (i.e., is an initiation followed by a response; who is the consistent initiator), the quality of the interaction (i.e., is it positive or negative), the specific nature of the social behaviors that occur (e.g., game playing, sharing), or the specific participants in the interaction (Comfort, 1988).

However, a last point on assessment at this level deserves emphasis. For diagnosing children's problems and establishing current functioning level, the multimethod assessment approach would be important to follow. This approach would provide important assessment data from several sources that could support or refute the diagnosed problem or, more importantly, the goals and objectives selected.

Monitoring Intervention Programs

Social interaction assessment information that is useful for screening, diagnosing, and selecting objectives may not be as useful for monitoring the intervention program once it has been implemented. Monitoring information must be collected efficiently and frequently (e.g., daily, weekly) by the teacher. Anecdotal records, teacher ratings, and direct observation information seem to be the most useful for monitoring. Anecdotal information can be recorded by the teacher while an in-

tervention session is occurring or shortly after the session. For infants and parents, it should reflect the nature and quality of the interactive episodes. For preschool children, it should describe the setting, type of interaction, quality and length of interactions, and the peers involved. As noted before, the SAASI may be useful for collecting these types of anecdotal data.

Social interaction data for monitoring may also be collected with more systematic observational systems. Time-sampling, interval-sampling, or event-sampling systems can provide very precise information about children's social behavior. Such systems are more sensitive than most other measures to behavioral changes in social interaction that may result from the intervention. A wide variety of social observational systems are available. When using direct observational systems it is important to observe the infant and mother or the preschool children in natural settings. Summary scores of the frequency of social interactions, the percentage of reciprocal interactions, or the occurrence of particular behaviors may be graphed, and the teacher may use these graphs to determine when an objective has been met, when the program should be changed because it is not having a positive effect, or when the child has met the objective and should move on to something else. As noted before, the disadvantages of the direct observational system are that it requires more time than other forms of assessment and interobserver agreement should be collected.

Rating scales may help the teacher monitor intervention programs. Some rating scales, such as the Teaching Skills Inventory for infants and the Social Interaction Rating Scale for preschool children can be administered frequently and can provide some consistent feedback to teachers on parents' (for infants) and children's success in the intervention. Rating scales are most useful for monitoring when the individual items give information on targeted social behaviors rather than providing a summary score across items. For example, the Teacher Rating Scale of Intervention Behavior (Odom et al., 1987) is designed to allow teachers to rate the frequency of several target behaviors that occur during daily intervention sessions. It should be noted, however, that when single items of rating scales are used, the reliability of this assessment may be questioned.

Program Evaluation

Program evaluation may be either formative or summative. In formative evaluation, assessment information is used to reorganize the program. The assessment information described for monitoring intervention programs would also be appropriate for use in formative evaluations.

Summative program evaluations of early intervention programs typically require that assessment information of children's social behavior be collected at the beginning and the end of the year. Evaluators compute the differences between the pretest and posttest assessments and then compare this information to either the changes that occurred for similar children who were not in the program, or the expected changes (i.e., based on preprogram rate of development) that would have occurred if the infants or young children had not been enrolled in the program (Odom, 1988). To conduct this type of evaluation, assessment information must be quantifiable. Direct observational data that can be summarized into one or a few scores, teacher rating scales that produce global scores, peer ratings scores, perhaps criterion-referenced information (i.e., number of criterion items passed), and scores from norm-referenced assessments can be used to conduct summative evaluations for programs designed to teach social interaction skills. It should also be noted that naturalistic or ethnographic evaluation approaches might also use anecdotal information (Lincoln & Guba, 1985). As we note in Table 15.2, and as a number of leaders in program evaluation have noted, collection of data from multiple data sources is important. The data sources will allow the evaluator to include multiple perspectives in evaluating the worth of the program (Casto, 1988; Cronbach, 1982; Karnes & Johnson, 1988).

Research

In conducting research on infants' and young children's social behavior, researchers have tended to use direct observation (Greenwood et al., 1981; Tremblay et al., 1980), teacher rating scales (Jenkins et al., 1987), and peer rating assessment information (Strain, 1983; 1985). Anecdotal procedures have rarely been used in research, possibly because reliability procedures are not well developed for this type of assessment. Researchers use criterion-referenced and norm-referenced assessment information to describe subjects, but they rarely use it to describe the outcomes of studies on social interaction training. Again, if the objective of the research is to investigate the social competence of infants or young children, then we propose that the investigators use a performance-based approach to assessment that would include multiple measures collected from different perspectives.

SUMMARY OF KEY CONCEPTS

- The social development process can break down in infants' interactions with their parents or in children's interactions with their peers.

- Infants and preschoolers with handicaps may be at risk for attachment problems with parents and social interaction problems with peers.

- Assessment of social interaction can occur at the individual-child behavior level, interactional level, social relationship level, and at the normative level. At each level, the information gathered can be used for different purposes.

- The social reciprocity (R1 and R2), frequency of social interactions, duration of interactions, and peer preferences are all important dimensions of assessment of interaction.

- A performance-based assessment of social competence involves obtaining judgments from multiple sources about the adequacy of children's social behaviors.

- The setting, materials, and participants will influence the information obtained from social interaction assessment, as will the measure used to obtain that information.

- Several observational methods can be used to obtain information on social interactions, including anecdotal recording; rating scales; and time, interval, and event sampling.

- Sociometric methods using peer nominations or peer ratings can be used with preschoolers who have handicapping conditions.

- Norm-referenced measures, although few exist, can be used for diagnosis and determining program eligibility; criterion-referenced measures, if selected appropriately, can be used for identifying social skills that should receive instruction.

- Assessment of social interactions can be used for making decisions relative to screening; diagnosis; program planning, monitoring, and evaluation; and research. Measures must be selected carefully to answer the questions being asked.

REFERENCES

Achenbach, T. M. & Edelbrock, C. S. (1983). *Manual for the Child Behavior Checklist.* (Available from T.M. Achenbach, University of Vermont, Burlington VT 05405.)

Ainsworth, M. D. & Bell, S. M. (1970). Attachment, exploration, and separation: Illustrated by behavior of one year olds in a strange situation. *Child Development, 41,* 49–67.

Ainsworth, M. D., Blehar, M. C., Waters, E., & Wall, S. (1978). *Patterns of attachment: A psychological study of the strange situation.* Hillsdale, NJ: Erlbaum.

Anderson, S. & Messick, S. (1974). Social competency in young children. *Developmental Psychology, 10,* 282–293.

Asher, S. R., Singleton, L. C., Tinsley, B. R., & Hymel, S. (1979). A reliable sociometric measure for preschool children. *Developmental Psychology, 15,* 443–444.

Asher, S. R. & Taylor, A. R. (1981). Social outcomes of mainstreaming: Sociometric assessment and beyond. *Exceptional Education Quarterly, 1,* 13–30.

Bakeman, R. & Adamson, L. B. (1984). Coordinating attention to people and objects in mother-infant and peer-infant interaction. *Child Development, 55,* 1278–1289.

Bakeman, R. & Brown, J. V. (1977). Behavioral dialogues: An approach to assessment of mother-infant interaction. *Child Development, 49,* 195–203.

Bailey, D. B. & Simeonsson, R. J. (1985). A functional model of social competence. *Topics in Early Childhood Special Education, 4*(4), 20–31.

Bailey, D. B. & Simeonsson, R. J. (1988). *Family assessment in early intervention.* Columbus, OH: Merrill.

Barber, P. A., Turnbull, A. P., Behr, S. K., & Kerns, G. M. (1988). A family systems perspective on early childhood special education. In S. Odom & M. Karnes (Eds.), *Early intervention for infants and children with handicaps: An empirical base* (pp. 179–198). Baltimore, MD: Paul H. Brookes.

Barnard, K., Booth, C., Mitchell, S., & Telzrow, R. (1982). *Newborn nursing models.* Seattle: Department of Parent and Child Nursing, School of Nursing, University of Washington.

Behar, L. & Stringfield, S. (1974). *The Preschool Behavior Questionnaire.* Chapel Hill: University of North Carolina.

Berry, P., Gunn, P., & Andrews, R. (1980). Behavior of Down's syndrome infants in a strange situation. *American Journal of Mental Deficiency, 85,* 213–218.

Bluma, S. M., Shearer, M. S., Frohman, D., & Hillard, J. M. (1976). *Portage Guide to Early Education.* Portage, WI: The Portage Project.

Bowlby, J. (1969). *Attachment and loss: Attachment (Vol. 1).* New York: Basic Books.

Bretherton, I. (1987). New perspectives on attachment relations: Security, communication, and internal working models. In J. Osofsky (Ed.), *Handbook of infant development (2nd ed.)* (pp. 1061–1100). New York: John Wiley.

Bromwich, R. (1981). *Working with parents and infants: An interactional approach.* Baltimore, MD: University Park Press.

Brown, W. H., Ragland, E. U., & Fox, J. J. (in press). Effects of socialization procedures on social interactions of preschool children. *Research in Developmental Disabilities.*

Cairns, R. B. & Green, J. A. (1979). How to assess personality and social patterns: Observations or ratings? In R. Cairns (Ed.), *The analysis of social interactions: Methods, issues, and illustrations* (pp. 209–226). Norwood, NJ: Erlbaum.

Caldwell, B. M. & Bradley, R. H. (1978). *Home Observation for the Measurement of the Evironment.* Little Rock: University of Arkansas at Little Rock.

Carey, W. B. & McDevitt, S. C. (1977). Revision of the infant temperament questionnaire. *Pediatrics, 60,* 621–624.

Casto, G. (1988). Research and program evaluation in early childhood special education. In S. Odom & M. Karnes (Eds.), *Early intervention for infants and children with handicaps: An empirical base* (pp. 51–62). Baltimore, MD: Paul H. Brookes.

Comfort, M. (1988). Assessing parent-child interactions. In D. Bailey & R. Simeonsson (Eds.), *Family assessment in early intervention* (pp. 65–94). Columbus, OH: Merrill.

Cronbach, L. J. (1982). *Designing evaluations of educational and social programs.* San Francisco: Jossey-Bass.

Emde, R. N., Katz, E. L., & Thorpe, J. K. (1978). Emotional expression in infancy: II. Early deviations in Down's syndrome. In M. Lewis & L. Rosenblum (Eds.), *The development of affect* (pp. 125–148). New York: Plenum Press.

Farran, D., Kasari, C. & Jay, S. (1984). *Parent-child Interaction Scale: Training manual.* Chapel Hill, NC: Frank Porter Graham Child Development Center.

Foster, S. L. & Ritchey, W. L. (1979). Issues in the assessment of social competence in children. *Journal of Applied Behavior Analysis, 12,* 625–638.

Fraiberg, S. (1975). The development of human attachments in infants blind from birth. *Merrill-Palmer Quarterly, 21,* 315–324.

Fraiberg, S. (1977). *Insight from the blind: Comparative studies of blind and sighted infants.* New York: Basic Books.

Furuno, S., O'Reilly, K., Inatsuka, T., Hosaka, C., Allman, T., & Zeisloft-Falbey, B. (1985). *The Hawaii Early Learning Profile, 1985 Edition.* Palo Alto: VORT.

Glover, M. E., Preminger, J. L., & Sanford, A. R. (1978). *The Early Learning Accomplishment Profile for Developmentally Young Children.* Winston-Salem, NC: Kaplan Press.

Greenwood, C. R., Walker, H. M., Todd, N. M., & Hops, H. (1981). Normative and descriptive analysis of preschool freeplay social interaction rates. *Journal of Pediatric Psychology, 4,* 343–367.

Guralnick, M. J. (1980). Social interaction among preschool handicapped children. *Exceptional Children, 46,* 248–253.

Guralnick, M. J. & Groom, J. M. (1987). The peer relations of mildly delayed and nonhandicapped preschool children in mainstreamed playgroups. *Child Development, 58,* 1556–1579.

Guralnick, M. J. & Groom, J. M. (1985). Correlates of peer-related social competence of developmentally delayed preschool children. *American Journal of Mental Deficiency, 90,* 140–150.

Guralnick, M. J. & Weinhouse, E. (1983). Child-child social interactions: An analysis of assessment instruments for young children. *Exceptional Children, 50,* 268–271.

Hartup, W. W. (1983). Peer relations. In M. Heatherington (Ed.), *Handbook of child psychology, Vol IV* (pp. 103–196). New York: John Wiley.

Hartup, W. W., Glazer, J., & Charlesworth, R. (1967). Peer reinforcement and sociometric status. *Child Development, 38,* 1017–1024.

Hinde, R. A., Titmus, G., Easton, D., & Tamplin, A. (1985). Incidence of friendship and behavior toward strong associates versus nonassociates in preschoolers. *Child Development, 56,* 234–245.

Hops, H. (1983). Children's social competence and skill: Current research practices and future directions. *Behavior Therapy, 14,* 3–18.

Hops, H., Finch, M., & McConnell, S. R. (1986). Social skills deficits. In P. H. Bornstein and A. E. Kazdin (Eds.), *Handbook of child behavior therapy* (pp. 543–598). New York: Dorsey.

Hops, H., Guild, J., Fleishman, D. H., Paine, S., Street, A., Walker, H., & Greenwood, C. (1979). *Peers: Procedures for establishing effective relationship skills.* Eugene, OR: CORBEH.

Howes, C. (1983). Patterns of friendship. *Child Development, 54,* 1041–1053.

Jenkins, J. R., Odom, S. L., & Speltz, M. L. (in press). Effects of integration and structured play on the development of handicapped preschoolers. *Exceptional Children.*

Johnson-Martin, N., Jens, K. G., & Attermeier, S. M. (1986). *The Carolina Curriculum for Handicapped Infants and Infants at Risk.* Baltimore, MD: Paul H. Brookes.

Karnes, M. B. & Johnson, L. J. (1988). Considerations and future directions for conducting research with young handicapped and at-risk children. In S. Odom & M. Karnes (Eds.), *Early intervention for infants and children with handicaps: An empirical base* (pp. 287-298). Baltimore, MD: Paul H. Brookes.

Kohler, F. W. & Fowler, S. A. (1985). Training prosocial behaviors to young children: An analysis of reciprocity with untrained peers. *Journal of Applied Behavior Analysis, 18,* 187–200.

Kohn, M. (1977). *Social competence, symptoms, and underachievement in childhood: A longitudinal perspective.* Washington, DC: Winston.

Lemay, D., Griffin, P., & Sanford, A. (1977). *Learning Accomplishment Profile—Diagnostic Edition.*

Chapel Hill, NC: Chapel Hill Outreach Project.

Levine, S., Elzey, F. F., & Lewis, M. (1969). *California Preschool Social Competency Scale.* Palo Alto, CA: Consulting Psychologist Press.

Lincoln, Y. S. & Guba, E. G. (1985). *Naturalistic inquiry.* Beverly Hills: Sage.

Mahoney, G., Powell, A., & Finger, I. (1986). The Maternal Behavior Rating Scale. *Topics in Early Childhood Special Education, 6*(2), 44–56.

Main, M., Kaplan, K., & Cassidy, J. (1985). Security in infancy, childhood, and adulthood: A move to the level of representation. In I. Bretherton & E. Waters (Eds.), Growing points of attachment theory and research. *Monographs of the Society for Research in Child Development, 50*(1-2, Serial No. 209), 66–104.

Marshall, H. R. (1957). An evaluation of sociometric-social behavior research with preschool children. *Child Development, 28,* 131–137.

McCandless, B. R. & Marshall, H. R. (1957). A picture sociometric for preschool children and its relation to teacher judgments of friendship. *Child Development, 28,* 139–147.

McCollum, J. A. & Stayton, V. D. (1985). Infant/parent interaction: Studies and intervention guidelines based on the SIAI model. *Journal of the Division for Early Childhood, 9,* 125–145.

McConnell, S. R. & Odom, S. L. (1986). Sociometrics: Peer-referenced measures and the assessment of social competence. In P. Strain, M. Guralnick & H. Walker (Eds.), *Children's social behavior: Development, assessment, and modification* (pp. 215–286). New York: Academic Press.

McConnell, S. R., Sisson, L., & Sandler, S. (1984). *Category definitions for observational assessment of reciprocal social interactions.* Unpublished observer training manual. University of Pittsburgh.

McFall, R. M. (1982). A reformulation of the concept of social skill. *Behavioral Assessment, 4,* 1–33.

Mueller, E. & Vandell, D. (1979). Infant-infant interaction. In J. Osofsky (Ed.), *Handbook of infant development* (pp. 591–622). New York: John Wiley.

Newborg, J., Stock, J., Wnek, F., Guidubaldi, J., & Svinicki, A. (1984). *The Battelle Developmental Inventory.* Dallas: DLM Teaching Resources.

Nihira, K., Foster, R., Shellhaas, M., & Leleand, H. (1974). *AAMD Adaptive Behavior Scale.* Washington, DC: American Association for Mental Deficiency.

Odom, S. L. (1981). The relationship of play to developmental level in mentally retarded children. *Education and Training of the Mentally Retarded, 16,* 136–141.

Odom, S. L. (1988). Research in early childhood special education: Methodologies and paradigms. In S. Odom & M. Karnes (Eds.), *Early intervention for infants and young children with handicaps: An empirical base* (pp.1–21). Baltimore, MD: Paul H. Brookes.

Odom, S. L., Bender, M., Stein, M., Doran, L., Houden, P., McInnes, M., Gilbert, M., DeKlyen, M., Speltz, M., & Jenkins, J. (1988). *Integrated Preschool Curriculum.* Seattle: University of Washington Press.

Odom, S. L. & McConnell, S. R. (1985). A performance-based conceptualization of social competence of handicapped preschool children: Implications for assessment. *Topics in Early Childhood Special Education, 4*(4), 1–19.

Odom, S. L., McConnell, S. R., Kohler, F., & Strain, P. S. (1987). *Social interaction skill curriculum.* Unpublished curriculum manuscript. Pittsburgh: Early Childhood Research Institute, University of Pittsburgh.

Odom, S. L., Silver, F., Sandler, S., & Strain, P. S. (1983). *Direct Observation of Social Behavior Manual.* Pittsburgh: Early Childhood Research Institute.

Odom, S. L. & Strain, P. S. (1986). Using teacher antecedents and peer initiations to increase reciprocal social interactions of autistic children: A comparative treatment study. *Journal of Applied Behavior Analysis, 19,* 59–71.

Parten, M. B. (1932). Social participation among preschool children. *Journal of Abnormal and Social Psychology, 27,* 243–269.

Power, T. G. & Parke, R. D. (1986). Patterns of early socialization: Mother-infant and father-infant interaction in the home. *International Journal of Behavioral Development, 9,* 331–341.

Roopnarine, J. L. & Field, T. M. (1984). Play interactions of friends and acquaintances in nursery school. In T. Field, J. Roopnarine & M. Segal (Eds.), *Friendships in normal and handicapped children* (pp. 89–98). Norwood, NJ: Ablex.

Rosenberg, S., Robinson, C., & Beckman, P. (1984). Teaching skills inventory: A measure of parent performance. *Journal of the Division for Early Childhood, 8,* 107–114.

Rubenstein, J. L. & Howes, C. (1979). Caregiving and infant behavior in day care and in homes.

Developmental Psychology, 15, 1–24.

Rubin, K. (1982). Nonsocial play in preschoolers: Necessarily evil? *Child Development, 53,* 651–657.

Rubin, K. H., Maioni, T. L., & Hornung, M. (1976). Freeplay behaviors in middle- and lower-class preschoolers: Parten and Piaget revisited. *Child Development, 47,* 414–419.

Rubin, K. H., Watson, K., & Jambor, T. (1978). Freeplay behaviors in preschool and kindergarten children. *Child Development, 49,* 534–539.

Sackett, G. P. (1978). Measurement in observational research. In G. Sackett (Ed.), *Observing behavior: Data collection and analysis methods, Vol. II* (pp. 25–44). Baltimore, MD: University Park Press.

Sigman, M. & Ungerer, J. A. (1984). Attachment behaviors in autistic children. *Journal of Autism and Developmental Disorders, 14,* 231–244.

Simeonsson, R. J., Huntington, G. S., Short, R. J., & Ware, W. B. (1982). The Carolina Record of Individual Behavior: Characteristics of handicapped infants and children. *Topics in Early Childhood Special Education, 2*(2), 43–55.

Smilansky, S. (1968). *The effects of sociodramatic play on disadvantaged children: Preschool children.* New York: Wiley.

Sparrow, S. S., Balla, D. A., & Cicchetti, D. V. (1984). *Vineland Adaptive Behavior Scales.* Circle Pines, MN: American Guidance Service, Inc.

Spieker, S. J. (1986). Pattern of very insecure attachment found in samples of high-risk infants and toddlers. *Topics in Early Childhood Special Education, 6*(3), 86–99.

Spivak, G. & Shure, M. B. (1974). *Social adjustment of young children: A cognitive approach to solving real-life problems.* San Francisco: Jossey-Bass.

Sroufe, L. A. (1979). Socioemotional development. In J. Osofsky (Ed.), *Handbook of infant development* (pp. 462–516). New York: John Wiley.

Strain, P. S. (1983). Identification of social skill curriculum targets for severely handicapped children in mainstreamed preschools. *Applied Research in Mental Retardation, 4,* 369–382.

Strain, P. S. (1985). Social and nonsocial determinants of handicapped preschool children's social competence. *Topics in Early Childhood Special Education, 4*(4), 47–59.

Strain, P. S. & Shores, R. E. (1977). Social reciprocity: A review of research and educational implications. *Exceptional Children, 43,* 526–530.

Strain, P. S. & Shores, R. E. (1983). A reply to

"Misguided Mainstreaming." *Exceptional Children, 50,* 271–272.

Strain, P. S. & Timm, M. A. (1974). An experimental analysis of social interaction between a behaviorally disordered preschool child and her classroom peers. *Journal of Applied Behavior Analysis, 7,* 583–590.

Tremblay, A., Strain, P. S., Hendrickson, J. M., & Shores, R. E. (1980). Social interactions of normal preschool children. *Behavior Modification, 5,* 237–253.

Walker, H. M. (1983). *Walker Problem Behavior Identification Checklist: Test and manual (2nd ed.).* Los Angeles: Western Psychology Services.

Walker, H. M. & McConnell, S. R. (in press). *The Scale of Social Competence and School Adjustment: Test and manual.* Austin, TX: Pro-Ed.

Yoder, P. (1986). Clarifying the relation between the degree of infant handicaps and maternal responsivity to infant communicative cues: Measurement issues. *Infant Mental Health Journal, 7,* 281–293.

Zigler, E. & Trickett, P. K. (1978). IQ, social competence, and evaluation of early childhood intervention programs. *American Psychologist, 33,* 789–798.

Chapter 16

Assessing Play Skills

Mark Wolery
University of Kentucky
Donald B. Bailey, Jr.
University of North Carolina at Chapel Hill

KEY TERMS

- Object Manipulation
- Interactive Games
- Exploration
- Play
- Practice Play

- Symbolic Play
- Games with Rules
- Functional Play
- Constructive Play

- Dramatic Play
- Physical Play
- Manipulative Play
- Low-Structure
  Situations

As described in the previous chapter, social interactions are an important part of young children's social development. A related but distinctly separate domain is play. Nearly everyone agrees that children spend large amounts of time in play; disagreement, however, has existed over the definition of play, why children play (cf. Johnson, Christie, & Yawkey, 1987), the value of play, adults' roles in children's play, and whether play should be assessed and taught. Play has been given more value in recent years, and in this chapter it is viewed as a legitimate curricular domain for infants and young children with handicaps. The chapter (a) provides the rationale for assessing play skills, (b) discusses issues in defining play, (c) describes methods

for assessing play, and (d) provides suggestions for using play assessment information when planning intervention. Because play frequently involves motor, cognitive, communication, and social skills, the assessment of play should also consider children's development in these other areas.

Rationale for Assessing Play Skills

Several rationales exist for assessing and facilitating play skills, and these can be categorized into four general statements: (a) play is an enjoyable activity, (b) play may facilitate development of other behaviors, (c) play normalizes children's interactions with the environment, and (d) play has practical value.

As an Enjoyable Activity

Weisler and McCall (1976) characterized play behaviors as "intrinsically motivated and apparently performed for 'their own sake' and . . . are conducted with relative relaxation and positive affect" (p. 494). Simply stated, one reason children engage in play activities is that they are fun, or inherently reinforcing. Given that young children with handicaps often show delayed or inadequate play skills (e.g., Li, 1981), one rationale for assessing and teaching play skills is to increase the quality of life for children by providing them with skills needed to engage in enjoyable activities.

To Facilitate Development

Piaget (1962, 1963) suggested that children's interactions with and actions upon the physical and social environment influence their cognitive development. In fact, those interactions along with neurological maturation were viewed as the primary sources of developmental progress. Many of those interactions occur during play and serve as a means to practice and consolidate new cognitive abilities. The relationships between play and cognitive development are not totally clear; however, there appears to be a correlation between some types of play and various measures of cognitive abilities. For example, as children acquire more symbolic abilities, their play appears to reflect those abilities (Lowe, 1975). Specific types of play may promote cognitive development more than other types. For example, training in sociodramatic play may increase children's play skills and their performance on cognitive tasks (Johnson et al., 1987), and play with materials similar to test problems may result in greater problem-solving abilities (Bruner, 1972; Pepler & Ross, 1981). The availability

of toys is related to cognitive development during early childhood and appears particularly important for infants and toddlers (Bradley, 1985). Furthermore, the responsivity of toys and having a variety of toys appear to be related to development (Wachs, 1985).

Play also is thought to promote emotional and social growth; however, the relationship between play and social skills appears to be a two-way street. As children play, they learn and practice new social skills, and as they learn new social skills, their play becomes more complex and advanced (Johnson et al., 1987; Musselwhite, 1986). This fact is particularly true of social play rather than solitary toy play. Play is also thought to be an activity whereby children can test social hypotheses, learn roles, take others' perspectives, acquire persistence, and develop creativity (Fewell & Kaminski, 1988, Johnson et al., 1987).

Play also may influence the development of gross and fine motor behaviors by providing a context for trying new behaviors and gaining practice in others. In fact, some studies suggest that training in play can be designed to enhance specific motor skills (Musselwhite, 1986).

Finally, play may influence communication skills. It appears to provide a time for children to learn the rules of conversation and try new pragmatic functions. Further, children appear to play with different linguistic structures, and, apparently, this practice contributes to their acquisition of competent communication skills (Johnson et al., 1987).

To Increase Opportunities for Normalized Interactions

During infancy, play involves both **object manipulation** and **interactive games** with others. Young children who interact with objects in a nonstereotypic manner (i.e., play with toys) are perceived as doing what young children should be doing. Thus, appropriate object manipulation may increase the opportunity of normalized interactions with other persons. Interactive games are seen as particularly important in promoting appropriate social interactions and relationships. Initially, an infant's role in interactive play tends to be both responsive and somewhat passive; however, as the infant learns to play games and take turns, she becomes the initiator of the play and also assumes a more active role in that play (Odom, 1983). Odom (1983) suggests that infants and their parents may play several games each day. Furthermore, positive interactions may occur around appropriate toys (Langley, 1985). Thus, normalized interactions between infants with handicaps and their families probably will include frequent game and toy playing. Assessing episodes of parent/infant play allows the interventionists to develop appropriate social-interaction interventions (cf., Bromwich, 1981; Mahoney & Powell, 1984).

In addition, play is an important part of child/child interactions and relationships. It is clear that as children grow older, their play becomes progressively more social (Fewell & Kaminski, 1988; Johnson et al., 1987), although they will continue to engage in independent toy play. For young children with handicaps, play with toys may be a prerequisite for social play. If this is the case, then assessing and facilitating children's play skills may be an initial means of securing more social play with peers, including nonhandicapped peers (cf. Kohl, Beckman, & Swenson-Pierce, 1984). Play-organizing behaviors (e.g., child saying, "Let's play with ____ ") and highly rated toy play skills appear to result in higher sociometric ratings by nonhandicapped peers (Strain, 1985).

Play may also be a viable alternative to socially unacceptable or maladaptive behaviors. Teaching play skills can result in decreases in stereotypic (self-stimulatory) and self-injurious behaviors (Wehman, 1978). Furthermore, teaching play to socially withdrawn children may produce increases in social contacts and decreases in social isolation (Strain, 1975). Thus, to behave in a socially acceptable manner, young children with handicaps should engage in play.

The Practical Value of Play

In several chapters in this text, authors have suggested that assessment of particular skills should occur in low-structured situations that set the stage for naturally occurring routines and interactions. The chief activity of such situations is play. Fewell and Kaminski (1988) suggest that assessment during play may result in valid information about children's typical skills and may lead to more useful information than does standardized testing. Similarly, many authors have suggested that intervention activities should be initiated during play episodes (cf., Bailey & Wolery, 1984; Dunst, 1981; Fewell & Vadasy, 1983). Thus, play has practical value because assessment of other skills (e.g., social interaction, communication) may occur while children play, and many interventions can be embedded into play. Therefore, it appears reasonable to assess children's play.

Play may be of value because it occupies time in an adaptive manner and allows family members to engage in tasks other than caregiving. Even if play did not facilitate more positive social interactions nor the development of other behaviors, its adaptive, time-occupying characteristics suggest that play is a viable intervention target. Most parents report that when their child learned to play appropriately for a few minutes, their own lives became more manageable. They had time to read the newspaper, prepare dinner, and attend to other chores.

Furthermore, Musselwhite (1986) suggests that including play in the curriculum may lead to the development of adequate leisure skills. A recurring problem with secondary-aged students and adults with moderate to severe handicaps is lack of adequate leisure-time activities; in fact, those skills constitute a large part of the secondary curriculum. Implementing a play curriculum during early childhood may lead to enduring leisure skills in older students.

Dimensions of Play

In this section, the issue of defining play is mentioned briefly, the characteristics of play are described, and various types of play are discussed. The developmental sequence of play and the effect of various handicapping conditions on play are presented in several sources (Bradley, 1985; Brooks-Gunn & Lewis, 1982; Fewell & Kaminski, 1988; Mindes, 1982).

Definition
Definition is one of the first steps in serious scientific study and a key step in assessing a given construct or skill. Writing a workable definition of play has been difficult because play occurs in such variety. Play can take on many forms; thus it is not form specific. Individuals play throughout their lives; thus, it is not age specific. Play occurs in almost all settings; thus, it is not setting specific. Additionally, a given behavior may be interpreted as play at one time but not at another. The perceived intentions of an individual also influence whether an episode is considered play (Musselwhite, 1986). Thus, play represents such a broad array of behavior and activities that a single definition is almost impossible to write.

In an attempt to define play, investigators have differentiated play from exploration (cf., Johnson et al., 1987; Weisler & McCall, 1976). Johnson and colleagues indicate that **exploration** occurs prior to play, involves unfamiliar objects as compared to familiar ones, is done to gain information about an object rather than use it for stimulation, focuses on the external reality of the object rather than on

what it can be used to represent, is stereotypic in form rather than highly variable, results in a serious rather than joyful affect, and produces low variability in heart rate rather than the high variability noted in play. While these distinctions appear real, we will focus on assessment of exploration and play because both are important, and exploration appears to precede play.

In addition, some authors have attempted to discriminate play from games. Games are viewed as restrictive and involving compliance with externally imposed rules, whereas play involves lack of restriction and freedom from external rules. While this distinction may be relevant, we will employ a broad perspective of play that would include games. For purposes of this chapter, **play** is defined as active engagement and interaction with an object or in an activity that appears to be intrinsically motivated, spontaneously performed, flexible, and accompanied by positive affect.

Characteristics
To solve the difficulties in defining play, authors have attempted to define the characteristics of play (Fewell & Kaminski, 1988; Johnson et al., 1987). Several characteristics have been proposed and are shown in Table 16.1 (p. 432); for more complete discussions see Johnson et al. (1987); Garvey (1977); Rubin, Fein, and Vandenberg (1983); and Weisler and McCall (1976). Authors, however, do not agree even on these characteristics; some consider them to be too broad, or too restrictive or redundant. Smith and Vollstedt (1985) attempted to determine whether some of these general characteristics could be used to measure the occurrence of play reliably. In short, they found that nonliterality, positive affect, and flexibility could be reliably measured, as could means/ends and intrinsic motivation, to a lesser extent. Furthermore, it appears that if an episode of behavior includes multiple char-

TABLE 16.1
Characteristics of Play

Characteristic	Description
Intrinsic motivation	Play is not motivated by biological drives (e.g., hunger) but comes from within the child and not from the stimulus properties of the play objects.
Spontaneous and voluntary	Play involves free choice; children engage in play because they want to, not because someone assigns it to them.
Self-generated	Play involves the child actively generating the activities.
Active engagement	Play involves active attention to the activities of play.
Positive affect	Play involves pleasurable or enjoyable activities or results in pleasurable and enjoyable consequences.
Nonliterality	Play involves activities that are carried out in a pretend or "as-if" nature—less serious or real.
Flexibility	Play involves variability in form or context and can be done in a variety of ways or situations.
Means more than ends	Play involves emphasis on the activity itself rather than on the goal of the activity.

acteristics of play, then it is more likely to be judged as play by observers. The application of these characteristics to assessment of children's play in general seems appropriate. However, as will be described later, most assessment procedures adopt various taxonomies of play and attempt to determine the occurrence or nonoccurrence of the included categories.

Types

Numerous types of play have been described and, for purposes of assessment and intervention, partly solve the definitional problem. By defining types of play, interventionists can apply specific behavioral definitions for each type, compare children's behaviors to those definitions, and make statements about children's play. Thus, rather than attempting to provide a broad definition that would include all instances of play, and only play, the interventionist can focus on specific types of play that seem relevant to given infants and children and their unique ecologies.

At the most basic level, play can be divided into two types: independent toy play and social play. However, to be meaningful, these types of play have been divided into many subcategories. Piaget (1962) initially described three categories of play: practice play, symbolic play, and games with rules. **Practice play**, which predominates during the sensorimotor period, involves repetitive motor manipulations on objects. **Symbolic play**, which occurs during the preoperational period, involves the use of symbols to represent absent objects and the use of objects to substitute for other objects. **Games with rules**, occurring during the concrete operations period, involve children restricting their play to conform to the constraints and rules involved in games. Since Piaget's (1962) original description, numerous authors have offered other classifications of play. For example, Smilansky (1968) retained Piaget's games with rules, and added three other types: **functional play** where repetitive movements are made on objects, **constructive play** where objects are used to make something, and **dramatic play** where the child engages in pretend play. Chance (1979) retained games with rules and symbolic play, and added two categories: **physical play** where actions are frequently social and competitive and includes rough-and-tumble activities, and **manipulative play** where actions are made to gain control of various objects. These classifications and others are shown in Table 16.2 to illustrate the variety of ways in which play has been classified and to suggest that

each can be defined operationally and used for assessing play. It is important to note that these categories of play do not necessarily represent developmental sequences. Young children engage in different types of play throughout early childhood, and a progression of four types of play are shown in Table 16.3 (p. 435). Types of social play also have been developed; as described in Chapter 15, Parten's (1932) taxonomy is one of the most frequently used (See Table 15.3).

Methods of Assessing Play

The primary method by which play skills are assessed is direct observation of play sessions; however, some scales also exist. In this sec-

TABLE 16.2
Examples of Different Taxonomies of Play

Author and Play Types (categories)	Description
Smilansky (1968)	
Functional play	Repetitive movements that appear playful and frequently involve objects
Constructive play	Use of objects to make or create something
Dramatic play	Use of pretend play with or without objects, frequently involving the child assuming a given role
Games with rules	Engagement in activities that involve compliance with the conventions and requirements of games and may involve competition with others
Chance (1979)	
Physical play	Action that is frequently social, may be competitive, and includes rough-and-tumble activities
Manipulative play	Actions on objects, designed to gain control of those objects
Symbolic play	Pretend play that may include objects being used to represent other objects
Games	Engagement in activities that involves compliance with the conventions and requirements of games and may involve competition with others

TABLE 16.2
Continued

Author and Play Types (categories)	Description
Wehman (1977)[a]	
Exploration	
Level I—Orientational responses	Relatively abrupt behavioral changes that occur as a result of external stimulation and appear to redirect the child's attention
Level II—Locomotor exploration	Movement about an environment that produces sensory feedback
Level III—Perceptual investigation and manipulation	Movements on objects that appear to provide the child with information about the characteristics of the object
Level IV—Searching	Seeking a new stimulus for exploration
Toy Play	
Level I—Repetitive manual manipulation/ oral contacts	Repetitive actions on objects with attention to sensory consequences
Level II—Pounding, throwing, pushing/ pulling	Repetitive actions on objects that frequently involve gross motor movements and a beginning awareness of cause/effect relationships
Level III—Personalized toy use	Use of toys to perform actions on the child's body, frequently uses miniatures of real objects to imitate common routines
Level IV—Manipulation of movable parts of toys	Movements on movable parts of objects; objects are viewed as having parts rather than being a whole
Level V—Separation of parts of toys	Movements on objects that result in separation of parts or of taking things out of containers
Level VI—Combinational use of toys	Movements on toys where two or more different objects are used together or where parts of objects are put back together
Sutton-Smith (1970)[b]	
Imitation	Copying the motor and/or verbal behavior of others
Exploration	Investigating what can be done with objects, and how they work
Prediction	Testing the effects of various actions on objects and the effects of different behaviors
Construction	Movements on objects to make or create something

[a]This classification is based on an adaptation of Wehman's (1977) hierarchies by Bailey and Wolery (1984).

[b]This categorization of play describes common modes of play seen throughout early childhood.

TABLE 16.3
Example of Developmental Sequences for Four Types of Play

Age (months)	Exploration/ Manipulation	Construction	Dramatics	Games
12–24	Sensorimotor/ perceptual examination of objects; modes of exploration include banging, inserting in and pulling out, tasting, creeping and crawling through, emptying and filling, tasting and scribbling	Simple towers with blocks, primarily exploration and manipulation	Imitates own behavior but in different situations; themes center on simple adult routines; late in this year child begins to perform activities with doll	Appearance/ disappearance (peek-a-boo); strange appearance, chase and capture
24–36	Exploration becomes integrated with other types of play such as construction and dramatics; child can manipulate and observe the results of behavior at the same time	Block building, painting, pasting, clay, puzzles; child is pleased with whatever she makes	Assumes more complete adult roles, usually pretending to be adult doing things to other children; a toy can symbolize another object	Participation in story telling; rhyme games
36–48	Becomes very interested in exploring new places, although usually prefers to have an adult companion; field trips begin to be meaningful and exciting experiences	Drawing, cutting, advanced puzzles, coloring, diverse structures with blocks	Increased variety of themes, creation of imaginary characters; wants some outstanding prop (shoes, hat) to aid in role play; enjoys puppet play	Imaginary monsters, friends and enemies, singing and chanting
48–60	Enjoys exploring increasingly greater range of experiences and places	Collages, painting, complex puzzles; child begins to be critical of own workmanship	Dramatic play becomes very social and at times cooperative; more advanced themes; child is more likely to want more than one prop or piece of clothing to aid in role play	Simple board games, hunts for hidden treasures, prisoners, hide-and-seek

Source: From *Teaching infants and preschoolers with handicaps*, 1984 (p. 212) by D. B. Bailey and M. Wolery. Copyright 1984 by Merrill, Columbus, OH. Used with permission.

tion, the goals of an assessment of toy play for instructional planning are described, and assessment strategies are discussed. Emphasis is placed on assessing play with toys rather than social play because social play was addressed, in part, in Chapter 15. In this section, the word *toys* will be used for both commercially available toys and any objects children use as toys whether they are daddy's shoes, the box in which a toy came, or pots and pans.

For obvious reasons, norm-referenced measures of toy play do not exist. We should note that many developmental scales assess the cognitive or motor skills necessary to engage in many play activities. For example, items may assess skills such as transferring objects from one hand to another, stacking, throwing, or assembling. The assessment of these skills probably is a necessary but insufficient step in targeting play skills, inasmuch as play requires use of these skills in certain ways. Thus, it is important to determine what constitutes competent toy play for young children. In short, young children who are competent players interact with a variety of toys, play for extended durations, and display a variety of different types of play that become progressively more complex. As a result, the assessment of toy play for instructional program planning should focus on at least three goals: (a) describing children's general contact with toys, (b) identifying children's reactions to and preferences for specific toys, and (c) assessing children's levels and types of play.

General Contacts with Toys/Objects

When attempting to assess the general level of contact the child has with toys, the interventionist should gather information on (a) the number of objects contacted, (b) the types of objects contacted, and (c) the duration of each contact. This information can be collected by observing the child when there are a number of toys available, writing down which ones are contacted, and timing the

duration of each contact. These observations should occur in familiar environments, and the length should vary depending upon the child, but 10–15 minutes frequently is sufficient. Ideally, multiple sessions would occur.

From the data collected in these sessions, the interventionist should determine what type of toys the child contacts. For example, do the toys provide visual or auditory feedback, do the toys have movable parts and does the child manipulate those parts, do the toys involve multiple parts that are separated or combined by the child, did the child use two or more toys together, do the toys need to be activated to be used (e.g., turn handle of jack-in-the-box, turn key of wind-up toys, manipulate switch on battery-operated toys) and does the child activate them or seek help from others? The interventionist also should attempt to determine whether the duration of play episodes is greater with some types of toys than with others.

Reactions to and Preferences for Toys

Although an indication of children's toy preferences and reactions to various toys may be found from observing their toy contacts in free-play situations, lack of contact does not indicate lack of preference. It is possible that the child did not notice the toy and thus did not interact with it. Further, if children do not have experience with a given toy, then they may unintentionally avoid it. Other children may not play with the toys when given free access, may play with only one or two toys, or simply may carry them rather than play with them. Therefore, systematic presentation of toys is needed to gain more information on preferences and reactions to toys.

To assess preferences of children who have few experiences with toys, the interventionist should present four or five toys one at a time and allow the child a brief time to play with each. After presenting them separately, they should be presented as a group. Over repeated trials, children frequently will show preferences for some toys or types of toys and show avoidance or lack of interest in others. Preferences may be shown by consistently choosing a toy, playing with it for long durations, and protesting when it is removed. If children have experience with toys, then presentation of four toys at once may be appropriate (Musselwhite, 1986). This information is useful in selecting materials for intervention. While children are playing with the toy, the interventionist should observe what the child does with it. Specifically, the interventionist should determine how children explore the object (orally, manually, visually) and what actions they make on the object (e.g., bang, throw, shake). Three data-collection forms are shown in Figure 16.1 (pp. 438–439) for recording children's reactions to the toys. Each of these sheets suggests collecting slightly different types of data, but they deal with children's reactions to and actions upon toys.

Selecting toys for assessment and intervention requires considering issues other than children's preferences and reactions. Musselwhite (1986) and Langley (1985) describe several variables that should be considered when selecting toys. For young children, toys should be selected that are (a) related to children's needs, (b) safe to use, (c) durable, (d) realistic replications of their real world counterparts, (e) attractive, and (f) reactive or responsive.

Guidelines for Assessing Children's Play
In addition to children's contact with toys, preferences for given toys, and reactions to toys, interventionists should assess the types of play displayed, the complexity of that play, and any themes that exist in the play. To do this, however, interventionists should consider several factors when setting up a play assessment session.

Space and Structure of the Play Session. The nature of play requires that children be free to select various toys, have adequate space to play, and have peers available if social play is being assessed. **Low-structure situations** in which children can choose toys and materials and can expand and change their play without constraints from adults should be used. Although more research is needed, it appears that decreases in available space may result in more dramatic play and more observation of other children's play (Rubin & Howe, 1985); likewise, it may result in more social contacts (Odom & Strain, 1984). However, overcrowded conditions may lead to higher frequencies of aggressive behaviors and children interfering with the play of peers.

Peers in the Play Session. When conducting the assessment, the nature of the available peers is important. Generally, children are likely to show higher levels of social and cognitive play if they are with familiar, as opposed to unfamiliar, peers (Johnson et al., 1987). In addition, the sex of the available peers may influence the type of play observed. For example, children appear more likely to play with toys generally related to their sex (e.g., dolls for girls, trucks for boys) if they are in the presence of same-sex peers than if only opposite-sex peers are available (Rubin & Howe, 1985). Undoubtedly, the competence of peers to engage in social interactions also will influence the type and amount of social play.

Activities in the Play Session. Odom and Strain (1984) suggest that the type of activities in which children are engaged will influence the amount of positive social interactions or play. Structured free-play results in more positive social interaction than table-top activities and learning centers, and the types of activities in structured play (e.g., playing grocery store as compared to playing with blocks) influence the amount of positive social interactions. In short, when assessing social play, the space should be small, peers should be available, and structured free-play activities should occur.

FORM A

Child's Reactions to Toys

TOYS	Visually attends	Touches	Vocalizes	Self-stimulates	Explores mouth	Explores hands	Bangs	Shakes	Drops	Manipulates approximately (Describe)	Length of interaction	Offers to adult	When all 5 offered as a group, child's preference	Other observations
1.														
2.														
3.														
4.														
5.														

FIGURE 16.1
**Three data-collection sheets for recording children's exploration and use of toys/objects (Sources:
Form A from** *"Assessing Handicapped Infants"* **by R. R. Fewell in Educating Handicapped Infants,
ed. S. G. Garwood and R. R. Fewell, 1983, Rockville, MD: Aspen. Forms B and C from Teaching
Infants and Preschoolers with Handicaps by D. B. Bailey and M. Wolery, 1984, Columbus, OH:
Merrill.)**

Toys and Materials in the Play Session. Some toys and materials are *social* while others are *isolate*. For example, social play is more likely with dress-up clothes, balls, sand, house and dolls, dishes, and games such as "Don't break the ice"; social play is less likely with crayons, paint, puzzles, playdough, and beads (Odom & Strain, 1984). Similarly, the number of toys available appears to influence the amount of social play; that is, more social play occurs when there are fewer toys. Thus, if the purpose of assessment is to identify children's social play, social materials should be available and a limited number of materials should be used.

The type and number of available materials also will influence the nature of play (Rubin & Howe, 1985). For example, realistic toys (e.g., dolls) appear to produce more pretend play than abstract toys for young preschoolers. Furthermore, provision of dolls, doll house, and furniture will produce more pretend play than dolls alone, at least for young children (about age 3). Materials such as paints and crayons will produce more constructive play and less pretend play. Materials such as puzzles are likely to produce isolate, constructive play, but provision of puzzle pieces alone without the form into which they fit will produce constructive and pretend play. Thus, when the goal is to assess children's pretend play, certain materials and toys should be used: when the goal is to assess constructive play, then other materials should be available. Fewer toys produce more social contacts, and more toys produce isolate play.

FORM B

Child: __Eddie__
Date: __8/1/82__
Time: __9:00-9:30__

Description of environment: __Block and toy centers__
__in classroom__

Observer: __DB__

	Exploratory play			Toy play						
Orientational responses	Locomotor exploration	Perceptual investigation and manipulation	Searching	Repetitive manipulations/oral contacts	Pounding/through pushing pulling	Personalized toy use	Manipulation of movable parts of toys	Separation of parts of toys	Combinational use of toys	Other
Looks at visual changes in environment ℍ11 Responds to sounds 111	Moves to another area of center 111	Rubs carpet 11	Looks for rattle 11	Shakes rattle ℍ Bangs block on floor 111	Pushes car 1					
9 Total number	3	2	2	8	1					
36 Percentage of behaviors	12	8	8	32	4					

Notes: _____

Favorite objects: __Rattle, blocks__

Any interactions with peers? __None__

FORM C

Child: __Eddie__
Date: __8/3/82__
Time: __9:00-9:30__

Description of environment: __Block and toy centers__

Observer: __DB__

Touches	Grasps	Holds	Carries	Shakes	Pounds	Squeezes	Pushes	Pulls	Turns	Other
11	111	1	11	1111 1111	1		1	1		
Total number 2	3	1	2	9	1		1	1		
Percentage of behaviors 10%	15	5	10	45	5		5	5		

Notes: _____

Favorite objects: __Rattle, blocks__

Any interactions with peers? __None__

FIGURE 16.1
Continued

Repeated Observations of Children's Play. When assessing children's play for instructional program planning, use of a single play session for establishing goals is inappropriate. As noted above, children's play is influenced by a number of factors such as space, peers, activities, and toys/materials. Thus, information from one observation is likely to give a rather unrepresentative picture of children's play skills. Thus, observations over a few days should be used.

Level-of-Assistance Assessment. When children exhibit few play skills, the interventionist may need to conduct a levels-of-assistance analysis as part of the assessment process. This strategy, as described in Chapter 4, involves using a series of successive prompts to determine the level of help needed before a child will engage in play behaviors. For example, some children will not play independently, but may do so if requested to play. Others may only play after observing a model, or receiving some physical prompts.

For children with motor impairments, interventionists should recognize that some may have the cognitive and social skills to engage in play activities, but do not play because of motor limitations. A variety of battery-operated and computer-activated toys and switches have been developed in recent years to assist motorically impaired children in interacting with toys. A comprehensive assessment of such children should seek to determine the mechanisms needed to help children play with minimal or no adult assistance. When conducting such assessments, interventionists should (a) identify positions that allow the child to make reliable volitional movements, (b) identify switches that can be activated easily by the child, (c) identify switch positions that allow efficient activation, and (d) identify children's toy preferences (Musselwhite, 1986; Schaeffler, 1988).

Procedures for Assessing Social and Cognitive Play

To determine the level and type of play, two strategies have been used: direct observation with interventionist-devised taxonomies of play behavior and play assessment scales that use direct observation. When using either strategy, the guidelines listed previously should be considered.

In the past, interventionists have assessed children's cognitive and social play separately. However, based on the lead of Rubin, Watson, and Jambor (1978), these two types of play can be assessed simultaneously (Johnson et al., 1987). An example showing a combination of Smilansky's (1968) levels of cognitive play and Parten's (1932) levels of social play is shown in Figure 16.2. This form allows for 12 combinations of social/cognitive play to be recorded and also allows the observer to record whether the child is unoccupied, watching others, or in transition, and whether the child is in a nonplay activity. Johnson and co-workers (1987) recommend using a separate sheet for each child, observing each child for 15 seconds, noting the type of play, placing a tally mark in the appropriate space on the form, and then observing another child. They suggest that having 20–30 observations on a child will provide an adequate pattern of the child's levels of play. Similar direct observation procedures can be developed for the other taxonomies presented in Table 16.2.

A useful scale for assessing toy play is Fewell's (1986) *Play Assessment Scale.* This scale uses a variety of readily available toys and objects to assess the play of children during the first three years of life. The toys are divided into eight developmentally more advanced sets, and assessment is conducted in two conditions. In the first condition, about four sets of toys are presented to the child, and the child's spontaneous play with the toys is recorded. The scale has a list of 45 items depicting various types of play. Ex-

Name: _____   Observation Dates: _____

COGNITIVE LEVEL

	Functional	Constructive	Dramatic	Games with Rules
Solitary				
Parallel				
Group				

SOCIAL LEVEL

UNOCCUPIED/ONLOOKING/TRANSITION   ACTIVITIES

Nonplay	

FIGURE 16.2
Data-collection form for the combination of Smilansky's cognitive play and Parten's social play developed by Johnson, Christie, and Yawkey (1987). (Source: From Play and early childhood development [p. 152] by J. E. Johnson, J. F. Christie, and T. D. Yawkey. Copyright 1987 by Scott, Foresman and Company. Reprinted with permission.)

amples are: (a) explores toys with mouth/ tongue for sensory pleasure (b) places toys near other toys, (c) performs single act on a doll, (d) uses one object for two different purposes, (e) verbalizes play plan for assigned roles. The number of times each item is displayed is recorded. In the second condition, the interventionist attempts to elicit more advanced play from the child by providing verbal, model, and verbal plus model prompts.

The level of assistance needed to elicit more advanced levels of play is recorded. In the current version of the scale, an estimated play age can be calculated. Probably the most appropriate use of this scale, however, is for identifying instructional goals for play. Information is collected on children's actions on various toys, their need for support with given skills, and their cognitive levels of play. Fewell and Rich (1987) demonstrate the utility of the instrument in a study of 17 deaf/blind preschoolers. They found high correlations between play observational data and measures of cognitive, language, and social behaviors. They suggested that because social, cognitive, motor, and communication skills rarely are used in isolation, play provides a useful context for assessing these skills.

Another scale that assesses symbolic play is Westby's (1980) Symbolic Play Scale Checklist. This scale divides symbolic play into 10 stages from ages 9 months to 5 years. The scale is completed by parent or teacher interview and direct observation and includes two columns, one for symbolic play and one for language skills. The play column includes a number of different examples of symbolic play at each age level. The language column assesses corresponding language functions (pragmatic and semantic). This organization assists in targeting language and play skills that are related to each other.

A scale that is useful in assessing social play is Howes's (1980) Peer Play Scale. This scale is an adaptation of Parten's (1932) categories, but provides a finer analysis of play. Five levels are used: *simple parallel play*, where children play near one another but do not engage in eye contact or other social interactions; *parallel play with mutual regard*, where children play near each other, are aware of the other's presence, watch the peer play, but do not engage in social interactions; *simple social play*, where children play near each other, initiate some social behavior, but do not engage in reciprocal or joint social interactions; *complementary/reciprocal play with mutual awareness*, where children play near each other, demonstrate some awareness of roles (e.g., may take turns), but no conversation occurs; and *complementary/reciprocal social play*, where children participate in joint play with roles, reciprocal social interactions, and conversation. Johnson and colleagues (1987) devised a data-collection sheet using these categories and added categories of (a) nonplay activities, (b) onlooking, unoccupied,

and transition, (c) teacher involvement, and (d) type of objects used. Data are collected with this scale in a manner similar to that described for the combined Parten/Smilansky form (Figure 16.2).

In addition to these scales, a number of other scales exist. Listings and brief descriptions of these can be found in several sources (e.g., Fewell & Kaminski, 1988; Johnson et al., 1987; Musselwhite, 1986). Some of these assess very narrow play skills, such as imaginative doll play, or were used for specific research projects.

Using Assessment Information When Planning Intervention

Information based on assessment from children's play can be used to play intervention activities for other curricular domains or to target play skills that should be facilitated.

Using Play as a Context for Teaching Other Skills

When using play to teach skills from other domains, the targeted nonplay skills should be listed along with the child's play abilities, usual play patterns, and play preferences. Times for integrating instruction on the target skills into the play patterns should be identified. Dunst (1981) provides excellent examples of this type of program for infants and cognitive, language, and social skills. Langley (1985) lists numerous considerations for selecting toys that would facilitate acquisition of target skills from other developmental areas. Musselwhite (1986) provides excellent examples of using play to facilitate communication skills. Intervention programs that focus on parent-infant/child interaction frequently use play activities as the context for implementing intervention. For information on these issues see Mahoney and Powell (1984) and Bromwich (1981).

Using Assessment Information on Play to Facilitate Play Skills

When play skills are targeted for instruction, the interventionist should consider several issues for using the assessment information. These are discussed in this section.

Establishing Functional Play Targets. *Functional* as used here refers to play skills that are likely to be used by the child. Because play is a child-initiated activity, establishing functional play targets requires consideration of children's current play patterns and preferences. Children are not likely to engage in generalized play unless those play activities hold some reinforcement value. In general, however, the targets should focus on a type of play (e.g., visual and manual exploration, repetitive manipulations of toys that provide auditory feedback, personalized use of realistic toys, specific play themes) rather than on specific toys. By focusing on the type of play or toy manipulation, the child can be taught to play with a variety of toys rather than one or two toys. Such training is likely to lead to more enduring use of play skills. Increasing the duration of play frequently is a functional outcome of play intervention.

Selecting and Adapting Appropriate Toys. As mentioned earlier, several issues should be considered when selecting toys, such as child preferences, child needs, durability, safety, availability, and cost. Musselwhite (1986) and Langley (1985) provide guidelines for selecting toys, and they both provide information on adapting toys for specific children. Musselwhite (1986) describes procedures for using adaptive switches to allow physically involved children to play.

Structuring Environmental Variables to Facilitate Play. As noted previously, several factors such as space, materials, peers, and activities will set the stage for particular types of play (cf., Odom & Strain, 1984; Rubin & Howe, 1985). For example, if social play is

to be increased, then the play space should be restricted, the number of children in the space increased, structured free-play activities initiated with materials to facilitate dramatic play. If constructive play is to be increased, then the play space should be increased, the number of children in the space decreased, and play initiated with materials that are more isolate.

The Adult's Role in Play. In addition to these factors, the adult's role in the play should be identified. Johnson and co-workers (1987) describe four adult roles: parallel player, co-player, play tutor, and spokesman for reality. In intervention programs, the parallel player, co-player, and play tutor are appropriate. The spokesman-for-reality role is used primarily with children having highly advanced play skills and is used to stop or redirect sociodramatic play that is getting repetitious or antisocial. The parallel-player role involves play near a child with similar materials, but without any interaction. Although this role may result in longer durations of play, research has yet to establish its benefits. In the co-player role, the adult assumes a role in the play but allows children to control the flow of play. It is primarily useful in dramatic and constructive play. This type of play appears to facilitate persistence and may be used to increase the level of play (Johnson et al., 1987).

In the play-tutor role, the teacher is quite involved in the play and attempts to influence children's play. At the most intrusive level, the adult structures the situation and provides prompts and reinforcement for engaging in toy play (cf., Wehman, 1978). This is most appropriate when teaching toy-play skills to children who have extremely limited toy interactions. Johnson and colleagues (1987) describe three other variations of the play-tutor role: outside intervention, inside intervention, and thematic-fantasy training. In the *outside-intervention* role, the teacher does not join the play but observes it and makes comments and suggestions. The adult may suggest new or different roles, suggest variations of the theme of the play, encourage social interactions and verbalizations, and encourage persistence in play. In the *inside-intervention* role, the teacher joins the play and provides similar suggestions but also has the advantage of modeling new or different roles, variations of themes, and social and verbal interactions. In *thematic-fantasy* training, the adult tells a story, assigns children to roles from the story, assists them in performing the roles, and assigns exchanges of roles and reenactment of the story. The role of play tutor appears to be responsible for some of the cognitive gains seen in children's play (Johnson et al., 1987). Johnson and co-workers suggest there are

three times when the play-tutor role is appropriate: (a) when children are not engaged in pretend play, (b) when children are having difficulty playing together, and (c) when pretend play becomes repetitious or seems to be breaking down.

Musselwhite (1986) adds two other roles: entertainer and observer, and each may be of value at different times. The entertainer role should be used sparingly but is appropriate when telling stories or securing children's attention prior to group activities. The observer role is important during assessment; however, it is also important when intervening in children's play. Ideally, adults will observe the play, enter and engage in it appropriately, and then move away and observe again (Johnson et al., 1987).

SUMMARY OF KEY CONCEPTS

- The rationale for assessing play is that play may facilitate development in other areas, normalize children's interactions, and serve as a context for assessment and intervention of other skills.

- Play is difficult to define, but characteristics have been listed and types of play have been described.

- Several taxonomies of play exist and are helpful in assessing children's play and later intervention in that play.

- Play is frequently assessed using direct observation with various taxonomies or play scales.

- Assessment information from children's play can be used to understand the context into which intervention on other skills will be provided or to identify targets that will facilitate children's play.

- When planning intervention to facilitate children's play, the interventionist should establish play targets that are functional, select and adapt toys appropriate to the targeted play, structure environmental variables to facilitate play, and consider the adult's role in play.

REFERENCES

Bailey, D. B. & Wolery, M. (1984). *Teaching infants and preschoolers with handicaps.* Columbus, OH: Merrill.

Bradley, R. H. (1985). Social-cognitive development and toys. *Topics in Early Childhood Special Education, 5*(3), 11-29.

Bromwich, R. M. (1981). *Working with parents and infants: An interactional approach.* Baltimore, MD: University Park Press.

Brooks-Gunn, J. & Lewis, M. (1982). Development of play behavior in handicapped and normal infants. *Topics in Early Childhood Special Education, 2*(3), 14-27.

Bruner, J. S. (1972). The nature and uses of immaturity. *American Psychologist, 27,* 687-708.

Chance, P. (1979). *Learning through play.* New York: Gardner.

Dunst, C. J. (1981). *Infant learning: A cognitive-linguistic intervention strategy.* Hingham, MS: Teaching Resources.

Fewell, R. R. (1986). *Play Assessment Scale.* College of Education, University of Washington, Seattle.

Fewell, R. R. & Kaminski, R. (1988). Play skills development and instruction for young children with handicaps. In. S. L. Odom & M. B. Karnes (Eds.), *Early intervention of infants and children with handicaps: An empirical base* (pp. 145-158). Baltimore, MD: Paul Brookes.

Fewell, R. R. & Rich, J. S. (1987). Play assessment as a procedure for examining cognitive, communication, and social skills in multihandicapped children. *Journal of Psychoeducational Assessment, 2,* 107-118.

Fewell, R. R. & Vadasy, P. F. (1983). *Learning through play.* Allen, TX: Developmental Learning Materials.

Garvey, C. (1977). *Play.* Cambridge, MA: Harvard University Press.

Howes, C. (1980). Peer play scale as an index of complexity of peer interaction. *Developmental Psychology, 16,* 371-372.

Johnson, J. E., Christie, J. F., & Yawkey, T. D. (1987). *Play and early childhood development.* Glenview, IL: Scott, Foresman and Company.

Kohl, F. L., Beckman, P. J., & Swenson-Pierce, A. (1984). The effects of directed play on functional toy use and interactions of handicapped preschoolers. *Journal of the Division for Early Childhood, 8*(2), 114-118.

Langley, M. B. (1985). Selecting, adapting, and applying toys as learning tools for handicapped children. *Topics in Early Childhood Special Education, 5*(3), 101-118.

Li, A. K. F. (1981). Play and the mentally retarded child. *Mental Retardation, 19,* 121-126.

Lowe, M. (1975). Trends in the development of representational play in infants from one to three years—An observational study. *Journal of Child Psychology and Psychiatry, 16,* 33-47.

Mahoney, G. & Powell, A. (1984). *The transactional intervention program: Preliminary teachers guide.* Unpublished manuscript. Woodhaven, MI: Woodhaven School District.

Mindes, G. (1982). Social and cognitive aspects of play in young handicapped children. *Topics in Early Childhood Special Education, 2*(3), 39-52.

Musselwhite, C. R. (1986). *Adaptive play for special needs children: Strategies to enhance communication and learning.* San Diego: College-Hill Press.

Odom, S. L. (1983). The development of social interchanges in infancy. In S. G. Garwood & R. R. Fewell (Eds.), *Educating handicapped infants.* Rockville, MD: Aspen.

Odom, S. L. & Strain, P. S. (1984). Classroom-based social skills instruction for severely handicapped preschool children. *Topics in Early Childhood Special Education, 4*(3), 97-116.

Parten, M. B. (1932). Social participation among preschool children. *Journal of Abnormal and Social Psychology, 27,* 243-269.

Pepler, D. J. & Ross, H. S. (1981). The effects of play on convergent and divergent problem solving. *Child Development, 52,* 1202-1210.

Piaget, J. (1963). *The origins of intelligence in children.* New York: Norton.

Piaget, J. (1962). *Play, dreams, and imitation in childhood.* New York: Norton.

Rubin, K. H., Fein, G. G., & Vandenberg, B. (1983). Play. In P. H. Mussen (Ed.), *Handbook of child psychology: Vol. 4. Socialization, personality, and social development* (4th ed., pp. 693-774). New York: John Wiley.

Rubin, K. H. & Howe, N. (1985). Toys and play behaviors: An overview. *Topics in Early Childhood Special Education, 5*(3), 1–9.

Rubin, K. H., Watson, K. S., & Jambor, T. W. (1978). Free-play behaviors in preschool and kindergarten children. *Child Development, 49,* 534–536.

Schaeffler, C. (1988). Making toys accessible for children with cerebral palsy. *Teaching Exceptional Children, 20*(3), 26–28.

Smilansky, S. (1968). *The effects of sociodramatic play on disadvantaged children: Preschool children.* New York: John Wiley.

Smith, P. K. & Vollstedt, R. (1985). On defining play: An empirical study of the relationship between play and various play criteria. *Child Development, 56,* 1042–1050.

Strain, P. S. (1975). Increasing social play of severely retarded preschoolers through socio-dramatic activities. *Mental Retardation, 13,* 7–9.

Strain, P. S. (1985). Social and nonsocial determinants of acceptability in handicapped preschool children. *Topics in Early Childhood Special Education, 4*(4), 47–58.

Sutton-Smith, B. (1970). *A descriptive account of four modes of children's play between one and five years.* New York: Columbia University Teachers College.

Wachs, T. D. (1985). Toys as an aspect of the physical environment: Constraints and nature of relationship to development. *Topics in Early Childhood Special Education, 5*(3), 31–46.

Wambold, C. B. & Bailey, R. (1979). Improving the leisure-time behaviors of severely/profoundly mentally retarded children through toy play. *American Association for the Education of the Severely and Profoundly Handicapped Review, 4,* 237–250.

Wehman, P. (1977). *Helping the mentally retarded acquire play skills.* Springfield, IL: Charles Thomas.

Wehman, P. (1978). Play skill development. In N. H. Fallen & G. E. McGovern (Eds.), *Young children with special needs* (pp. 277–303). Columbus, OH: Merrill.

Westby, C. E. (1980). Assessment of cognitive and language abilities through play. *Language, Speech, and Hearing Services in Schools, 11,* 154–168.

Weisler, A. & McCall, R. B. (1976). Exploration and play: Resume and redirection. *American Psychologist, 31,* 492–508.

Assessing Self-Care Skills

Mark Wolery
Pamela D. Smith
University of Kentucky

KEY TERMS

- **Self-care Skills**
- **Self-help Skills**
- **Assessment Heuristic**
- **Instructional Control**
- **Latency Errors**
- **Topographical Errors**
- **Oral Motor Functioning**

- **Oral Structures**
- **Rooting Reflex**
- **Suck-swallow Reflex**
- **Gag Reflex**
- **Bite Reflex**
- **Tonic Bite**
- **Tongue Thrust**

- **Jaw Thrust**
- **Sucking**
- **Swallowing**
- **Chewing**
- **Biting**
- **Self-feeding**
- **Toilet Training**

Early interventionists frequently assess and teach skills that have not been a part of the traditional school curriculum; the abilities discussed in this chapter are a prime example. **Self-care skills,** commonly called **self-help skills,** are those abilities needed for independent functioning in relation to basic needs such as food and warmth. Examples include eating, self-feeding, dressing, undressing, toileting, bathing, grooming, and, with older students, basic housekeeping skills. This chapter describes (a) the rationale for assessing these skills, (b) important characteristics of self-care skills, (c) methods for assessing these skills, and (d) information on using assessment information for planning instruction. Although the chapter primarily focuses on skills displayed by preschool children (e.g., dressing/undressing, toileting), some attention also is given to assessment of infants. Clearly, assessment of self-care skills cannot occur separately from assessment of motor functioning; therefore, understanding the concepts and assessment procedures described in Chapter 13 is important for conducting useful assessments of self-care skills.

Rationale for Assessing and Teaching Self-Care Skills

Several rationales exist for assessing and teaching self-care skills. First, children who can feed, dress/undress, and use the toilet by themselves are more independent than children who cannot. A goal of early intervention is to increase children's adaptive, independent functioning. Thus, a primary purpose for assessing self-care skills is to identify behaviors that, if learned, would make children more independent.

Second, and closely related to the first, is that the caregiving demands placed on family members are reduced when children can perform self-care skills independently and fluently. Children place caregiving demands on their parents; these are thought to be greater when the child has a handicap, and increased stress and fatigue may occur (Dyson & Fewell, 1986). Furthermore, the duration of basic caregiving tasks usually is greater when the child is handicapped. For example, although typical children frequently are toilet-trained around 2.5 years, children with handicaps are rarely toilet-trained by this age. In addition, the caregiving tasks related to self-help skills frequently are unpleasant—few people actually enjoy changing diapers or dressing/undressing children. By assessing and teaching self-care skills, the caregiving demands placed on parents and other family members can be reduced.

Third, special infant food and diapers are expensive. Few skills taught to young children hold immediate economic benefit for families; some self-help skills, particularly toileting skills, are exceptions. While immediate economic benefit is not a usual criterion for skill selection, it is a legitimate reason for assessing and teaching self-care skills.

Fourth, children who can perform self-help skills independently appear more like non-handicapped children. Children who are 4 to 5 years old and are fed by others or wear diapers appear more handicapped than do children of a similar age who perform these skills independently. Appearing less handicapped may result in more positive social interactions.

Fifth, self-help skills frequently are obvious examples of accomplishment. Ideally, every-thing taught to infants and preschoolers with handicaps should make them more developmentally advanced and/or independent. Many of the skills, however, are not easily recognized by parents, other caregivers, and extended family members. For example, learning to recognize that objects exist even when they are out of sight, engage in social interactions for longer durations, comment on novel events, and use a pincer grasp are useful skills, yet children's mastery of these may not be noticed by others. Self-help skills such as learning to self-feed with a spoon, use the toilet, put on a coat, and wipe their noses when needed will likely be noticed by others and be viewed as major accomplishments. Thus, a reason for assessing and teaching these skills is that children and parents alike will recognize the child's success; recognition of success may increase positive interactions.

Description and Characteristics of Self-Care Skills

Self-care skills in early childhood include eating, feeding, dressing/undressing, toileting, and grooming/hygiene. Each of these skills and sample behaviors within them are shown in Table 17.1. The listing of sample behaviors in Table 17.1 is not complete, and many of these behaviors could be broken into smaller behaviors; for comprehensive listings, consult the assessment tools listed later in the chapter and various curricula (e.g., Baker, Brightman, Heifetz, & Murphy, 1976a, 1976b; Fredericks, Makohon, Fruin, Moore, Piazza-Templeman, Blaire, et al., 1980; Tawny, Knapp, O'Reilly, & Pratt, 1979; Tilton, Liska, & Bourland, 1977), and skill lists (e.g., Cohen & Gross, 1979). Although this chapter focuses on assessment of self-care skills, the experienced teacher recognizes that they are highly related to other areas of the curriculum. For example, appropriate eating skills frequently are needed in social contexts

TABLE 17.1
Major Self-Care Skill Areas and Sample Skills

Skill Area	Sample Skills
Dressing/Undressing	Cooperating with adult while being dressed/undressed
	Anticipating next step while being dressed/undressed by adult
	Taking off and putting on socks, shoes, pants, pull-on garments (t-shirts, sweaters, sweat shirts), front-opening garments (coats, button-up shirts), underwear, gloves, mittens, overshoes, hats
	Unfastening and fastening fasteners such as connected-end zippers, open-end zippers, laces, buttons, buckles, and snaps
	Selecting and matching clothing appropriate for weather conditions and specific activities or occasions
Eating/Feeding	Sucking nipples and straws
	Swallowing liquids and foods of various textures and consistencies
	Biting and chewing food of various types
	Opening mouth as food is presented
	Moving hands to mouth
	Feeding self with fingers, spoons, and forks
	Cutting and spreading substances with a knife
	Drinking from cups and glasses
	Using a napkin to wipe fingers and mouth
	Using appropriate mealtime behaviors, including social graces and complying with social expectations
Toileting	Urinating in the toilet
	Defecating in the toilet
	Anticipating need to toilet and moving to toilet
	Caring for clothing before and after toileting
	Wiping and flushing after toileting
Grooming	Cooperating while others wash and brush hair and teeth
	Washing and drying own hands and face
	Bathing self
	Brushing own teeth
	Combing and brushing own hair
	Wiping and blowing nose

where conversation is likely. Toileting skills are more than eliminating bodily wastes; cultural customs dictate how and where toileting behaviors are performed. Dressing is more than putting on a piece of clothing; it involves judgments about the front/back of garments and about the appropriateness of an item of clothing for the weather. Grooming skills involve discriminations about how the child wants to look, what changes are needed to assume that appearance, and what is and is not clean. Further, self-help skills are highly influenced by children's motor abilities. In addition, self-care skills have several important characteristics (Bailey & Wolery, 1984), and the implications of those characteristics for assessment are shown in Table 17.2.

TABLE 17.2
Characteristics of Self-Care Skills and Implications for Assessment

Characteristic	Implication for Assessment
Self-care skills are part physiological and part learned behavior	Evaluator must determine whether necessary physiological processes and structures are present.
	Evaluator must identify behaviors child needs to learn.
Self-care skills are acquired throughout the preschool period	Evaluator must be skilled in assessing skills across a broad age range.
	Evaluator must be knowledgeable of normal developmental sequences.
Self-care skills are needed in the natural environment on a regular but low-frequency basis	Self-care skills should be assessed when they are naturally needed.
	Assessment should include interviews with parents because they have information that cannot be collected easily through other measurement strategies.
	The conditions of the natural environment should be assessed.
Many self-care skills are chained behaviors (skills that involve a number of discrete behaviors tied together)	Children's ability to do the individual responses and their ability to sequence those responses into meaningful units must be assessed
	Assessment of chains should occur during times when they are needed.
Self-care skills are useful only if they are performed fluently, maintained, and generalized to the needed situations	Evaluator must assess fluency, maintenance, and generalization of targeted self-care skills.

Procedures for Assessing Self-Care Skills

This section includes four parts: (a) a summary of tests for assessing self-care skills; (b) assessment of dressing, undressing, and grooming skills; (c) assessment of eating and self-feeding skills; and (d) assessment of toileting skills. In each of these latter three sections, best practices and guidelines for assessing these skills are described.

Tests for Assessing Self-Care Skills

As noted earlier, direct observation rather than direct testing is the primary method by which assessment information is gathered on self-care skills. However, some tests exist that address these abilities. Three tests are described in the oral motor and eating section and, thus, are not discussed here.

One measure, the Balthazar Scales of Adaptive Behavior (Balthazar, 1976) is designed to assess toileting, eating, and dressing. The toileting scale is a questionnaire of 10 items about daytime and nighttime toileting. An item from the daytime section is, "How many times does the subject wet himself?" The rater is to estimate the average number of times out of 10. This scoring method is used throughout the toileting, eating, and dressing scales, leading to questions about the reliability of the measure. For instructional program planning, the toileting scale does not sample the prerequisite skills adequately. The eating section of the Balthazar scales is divided into five domains (called classes). These include dependent feeding, finger foods, spoon usage, fork usage, and drinking, and each of these has 9–13 items. This scale is more usable for instructional program planning, but does not address fluency or reasons children may not be performing each response correctly. An eating checklist also is included that has items on self-service, assistive devices, type of food fed, positioning, rate of eating, advanced utensil use, and need for supervision. These items are scored as occurring or not occurring; thus, they have limited usefulness for instructional program planning beyond identifying areas where further assessment is needed. The dressing scale includes items on taking off, putting on,

fastening, and unfastening various garments; different garments are listed for males and females. The level of information obtained from the scale is not detailed and, thus, has limited usefulness.

Several criterion-referenced measures address self-care skills. The number of items for each of the self-care domains included in some common criterion-referenced scales is shown in Table 17.3. Also, included in this table is a rating of how adequately the self-care skills are covered by the measure, the type of

TABLE 17.3
Self-Help Items on Criterion-Referenced Measures

Measure	Number of Items in Instrument[a]						Methods/ Skill Coverage[b]	Level of Measurement[c]
	Dressing	Undressing	Grooming	Eating	Self-Feeding	Toileting		
Inventory Early Development (Brigance, 1978)	13	10	22	12	23	12	Interviewing, observation, and testing; coverage = 2	Binary; criteria = 1
Early LAP (Glover, Preminger, & Sanford, 1978)	7	5	2	5	9	5	Testing and observation; coverage = 2	Binary; criteria = 1
LAP-D (LeMay, Griffin, & Sanford, 1977)	6	6	7	3	5	9	Testing; coverage = 2	Binary; criteria = 2
RISE (Holder & Cook, n.d.)	16	12	70	40	42	65	Testing and observation; coverage = 3	Rating scale criteria = 1
UPAS (Haring et al., 1981)	5	3	5	2	6	4	Testing; coverage = 2	Binary; criteria = 2
Adaptive Performance Instrument (CAPE, 1980)	10	15	9	10	11	5	Observation, testing, and interview; coverage = 4	Frequency count; criteria = 2
Battelle Developmental Inventory (Newborg, Stock, & Wnek, 1984)	5	3	2	4	9	4	Observation, and interview; coverage = 2	3-level rating; criteria = 1

[a]Items on fastening/unfastening were not counted.
[b]Coverage of skills was rated from 1 to 4, with 1 being inadequate, 2 less than adequate, 3 being adequate, and 4 comprehensive.
[c]Criteria were rated from 1 to 2 with 1 being inadequate, and 2 being adequate.

measurement used, and a rating of how well the criteria were stated. These and other similar measures serve as a useful outline for self-help skill assessment, but they alone are not adequate for program planning assessment.

The chained nature of self-care skills and the need to assess them at times they are needed limit the value of direct testing. Tests typically approach self-care skills in one of two ways: Various skills are listed (e.g., takes off shoes, puts on shoes, ties shoes), and the evaluator uses a binary system (yes/no) to record whether the child can or cannot do the behavior; or a specific task analysis is listed for various skills, and the evaluator determines whether the child can do each step of the task analysis or combines this with levels-of-assistance recording to identify precise functioning levels. Although these practices may be acceptable with some children, they will be less than adequate with others for several reasons. Recording whether a child can or cannot do a skill (e.g., puts on his shoes) does not provide much useful information for planning instruction. Two children could be scored as not putting on their shoes, but one could do all the required steps with the exception of one and the other child could do none of the required steps. Using task-analytic data-collection procedures or combining them with levels-of-assistance recording can solve some of these problems; however, two major weaknesses to this approach exist. First, the data usually do not address the fluency of the child's responses, and second, the procedure typically employs only one sequence of steps. Taking off and putting on most garments and performing many grooming skills can be accomplished using a variety of skill chains. For example, taking off a pullover shirt can be accomplished by at least four separate sequences as displayed in Table 17.4. Each of these task analyses requires different movements and a different sequence of steps. None of these sequences is inherently correct or incorrect, and all of them will produce the same effect, that is, taking off a pullover shirt. However, any of these sequences may be easier for a given child than for another. The task in assessment is to identify which sequence will allow the child to learn most quickly to take off the pullover garment. Using a predetermined task analysis does not allow this flexibility.

Assessment of Dressing/Undressing, Fastening/Unfastening, and Grooming Skills

Heuristic for Assessing Chained Skills. When assessing dressing, undressing, and grooming skills, the evaluator should be flexible as to the sequence of steps required for each skill, should attempt to identify steps the child can and cannot do, and should identify the appropriate phase of learning for which intervention can be planned. A chained-task, **assessment heuristic** for accomplishing these goals is presented in Table 17.5 (p. 454). A heuristic is a pattern or design for problem solving, and the one presented in Table 17.5 is designed for use with taking off or putting on clothing, but the idea is applicable for almost any chained task, including grooming skills, self-feeding, and non-self-care skills.

Assessment of dressing, undressing, and grooming skills should occur at natural times when these skills are needed. Prior to the assessment, the evaluator should ensure that all needed materials (clothing, grooming instruments, and supplies) and recording forms are present. Generally, it is desirable to assess children with real clothing and grooming articles rather than with toys or materials such as buttoning boards. If children have substantial movement dysfunction, they should be positioned to facilitate correct responses, to normalize muscle tone as much as possible, and to maximize volitional arm movements and range of motion. Finally, the evaluator should use task directions or other cues to be sure the child realizes what is expected.

TABLE 17.4
Sample Sequences for Taking off a Pullover Shirt

Sequence	Steps in the Sequence
Crossed-Arm Method	1. Child crosses both arms in front of his trunk 2. Child grasps bottom of shirt with each hand 3. Child raises both arms flexing at the elbows and pulling shirt off trunk 4. Child extends both arms over head and pulls shirt off neck and head 5. Child grasps opposite sleeve with one hand and pulls shirt off first arm 6. Child grasps other sleeve with other hand and pulls shirt off arm
Elbow-Tuck Method	1. Child crosses dominant arm across trunk 2. Child grasps bottom of shirt with dominant hand 3. Child pulls bottom of shirt away from trunk 4. Child flexes nondominant arm and tucks elbow into trunk 5. Child pulls bottom of shirt over nondominant elbow 6. Child raises dominant elbow over head, while maintaining grasp of bottom of shirt with the dominant hand 7. Child extends dominant arm up and away from body pulling the shirt off the nondominant arm and head 8. Child grasps sleeve of dominant arm with nondominant hand and pulls shirt off dominant arm
One-Arm-at-a-Time Method	1. Child grasps end of sleeve of nondominant arm with dominant hand 2. Child extends dominant arm, while maintaining grasp of sleeve end and flexes nondominant arm pulling the sleeve off the nondominant arm 3. Child drops nondominant arm under shirt and out the bottom 4. Child grasps bottom of shirt on nondominant side and pulls it up over nondominant shoulder 5. Child repeats process with dominant sleeve 6. Child grasps shirt and pulls over head
One-Arm-over-the-Back Method	1. Child raises dominant arm, flexed at elbow, over the shoulder 2. Child places thumb of dominant hand inside of the shirt at the collar 3. Child gathers back of shirt into grasp of dominant hand 4. Child flexes neck forward and pulls shirt off head by extending dominant arm at elbow 5. Child pulls or shakes shirt off arms

TABLE 17.5

Heuristic for Assessing Chained Dressing/Undressing and Grooming Skills

Step	Assessment Task	Question Being Asked	Dimension Being Measured	Result	Next Step in Process
1	Teacher gives child opportunity to do entire task without assistance and in any sequence that will result in desired effect (e.g., take off or put on garment).	Can child complete the entire task? (i.e., take off or put on specific garment)	Accuracy	*No.* Child cannot complete entire task correctly.	Go to Step 2
				Yes. Child completes task accurately.	Go to Step 7
2	Teacher determines whether child has prerequisite skills to do task.	Does child have prerequisite skills?	Presence of prerequisite behaviors and their adequacy	*No.* Prerequisite skills not adequate.	Go to Step 3
				Yes. Prerequisite behaviors present and adequate.	Go to Step 4
3	Teacher searches and tests for task-modifications that will eliminate need for standard prerequisite behaviors.	Can task-modifications be found to eliminate need for standard prerequisite behaviors?	Accuracy with task-modifications being used	*No.* Task modifications not found.	Teach prerequisite skills
				Yes. Need for prerequisite behaviors is eliminated, but child does not do skill accurately.	Go to Step 4
				Yes. Need for prerequisite behaviors is eliminated, and child does skill accurately.	Go to Step 7
4	Teacher observes child attempt behavior and notes what type of error keeps child	What type of error is occurring?	Type of error	Latency error— child can do steps but latency between responses is too long/short.	Identify the level of assistance needed and initiate teaching to eliminate errors.

454

TABLE 17.5
Continued

Step	Assessment Task	Question Being Asked	Dimension Being Measured	Result	Next Step in Process
	from completing entire task.			Topographical error—child incorrectly does specific responses in chain.	Go to Step 5
5	Teacher lists topographical errors and searches for and tests adaptations that will eliminate errors.	Can adaptations eliminate topographical errors?	Accuracy with adaptations being used	*No.* Adaptations cannot be found to eliminate topographical errors.	Go to Step 6
				Yes. Adaptations eliminate topographical errors.	Go to Step 7
6	Teacher searches for and tests sequences to eliminate topographical errors.	Can a different sequence eliminate topographical errors?	Accuracy with different sequence of steps	*No.* Different sequences do not eliminate errors.	Identify level of assistance needed and teach responses where errors occur
				Yes. Different sequences eliminate topographical errors.	Go to Step 7
7	Teacher observes child do skill to determine whether it is done quickly enough.	Is child fluent in doing the skill? (i.e., can child do it quickly)	Duration or rate of skill completion	*No.* Child does skill too slowly.	Teach to increase fluency
				Yes. Child does skill quickly.	Go to Step 8
8	Teacher interviews parents or observes in generalization situations.	Does child perform the skill across needed situations?	Accuracy and fluency	*No.* Child does not do skill in generalization settings.	Teach to facilitate generalization
				Yes. Child does skill in generalization situations.	Monitor for maintenance

After the initial set-up is completed, the teacher should cue the child to attempt the task being assessed. Initially, this attempt should be made without assistance to determine whether the child can do the task accurately; the fluency with which the skill is performed is not measured at this point. Teachers should be careful to provide students with sufficient time to complete the task alone. Frequently, teachers and parents provide help that is not needed. If the child can do the skill alone, than the goal of intervention may be to increase fluency. If the child does not complete the skill accurately, then the teacher should determine whether the child has the necessary prerequisite skills.

At least three prerequisite motor skills are needed for dressing, undressing, and most grooming tasks: Children should (a) maintain their balance in the positions used during dressing/undressing and make adjustments in that position as dressing/undressing progresses, (b) move their limbs (at least one arm) volitionally and accurately, and (c) maintain a relatively strong grasp while their arms move. For fasteners, children need a strong pincer grasp, but for taking off and putting on clothing, a more primitive grasp pattern is acceptable. Procedures for assessing these skills were discussed in Chapter 13. In addition to these prerequisite behaviors, two other skills are desirable: Children should be under instructional control, and they should be imitative. **Instructional control** means disruptive, maladaptive behavior occurs frequently, and children comply with directions and commands they understand. Assessment results will more likely reflect actual performance when instructional control is present; however, assessment of skills can occur in its absence. Similarly, if children are imitative, both assessment and instruction in dressing, undressing, and grooming skills will be easier. If children are not imitative, assessment and instruction is possible but difficult.

If children do not display the motor prerequisites, then modifications in the task should be sought that will eliminate the need for the prerequisite skills. For example, if sufficient balance does not exist, then the task should be modified to provide more trunk support. If such modifications eliminate the need for the prerequisite skills, then the teacher should determine if the child can do the skill correctly. If the modifications do not eliminate the need for the prerequisite behaviors, then they should be taught or further assessment should be delayed until they are displayed.

If the child has the prerequisite skills or task modifications can eliminate their necessity and she still cannot complete the task correctly, then the type of error and the steps on which errors are made should be identified. Latency errors and topographical errors are common in chained tasks. **Latency errors** refer to those that occur because the child waited too long between responses or did not wait long enough. For example, when a child is putting on a coat, one arm is placed in one sleeve and then the child should reach behind her back with the other arm to put it in the second sleeve. If the child is slow in reaching behind her back, the coat will fall limp at her side. If latency errors are present, then the level of assistance needed to eliminate the errors should be identified and teaching initiated at that point. **Topographical errors** refer to responses that are incorrect in form. For example, the child places her arm in the wrong sleeve of a coat or performs a correct step out of sequence. Teachers should determine whether different clothing or adaptations in clothing can be made to eliminate errors. Clothing such as elastic-waistband pants rather than zip or snap pants, pullover shirts rather than front opening shirts, and tube socks rather than socks with heels are examples of garments that make dressing easier. Numerous adaptations exist for fasteners, such as Velcro in place of buttons. Generally, adaptations that allow children to dress/ undress and fasten/ unfasten their clothing independently should be used rather than clothing that children cannot manage. Later in the child's school career, she can be taught to manage more difficult fasteners. If topographical errors remain present after different types of garments and adapted fasteners are used, the alternative sequences should be considered. As illustrated in Table 17.4, many sequences can be used with the same skill to produce the same effect. However, topographical errors may be present even after using alternative clothing, adaptations, and sequences. If this is the case, then the level of assistance needed to perform the skill correctly should be identified, and instruction should be initiated.

If at any point the child can do the skill correctly, then how quickly it can be done should be assessed. This assessment is accomplished by timing, usually with a stopwatch, how long it takes the child to put on an item of clothing. The recorded times should be compared with the amount of time the child will have to do the skill in the natural environment or with the times of children who do the skill fluently. For children who perform too slowly, fluency of the skill should become the instructional objective.

If children are fluent in performing the skill, then their accuracy and fluency in doing the skill in all relevant generalization settings should be assessed. If adequate generalization occurs, then the skill should be monitored for maintenance; if there is no generalization, then instruction to facilitate it should be targeted. When assessing generalization, it is ideal for the teacher to observe the child in all relevant contexts; however, this is frequently impractical. Therefore, teachers need to include parents in the assessment. Parents can be included in at least two ways: (a) They can collect observational data, and (b) they can be interviewed about typical performance. Parents can be taught to collect several types of data; for example, (a) simply recording whether a child correctly completes the skill at home, (b) recording which step results in errors, (c) recording when in a chain

the child stops attempting the skill, and (d) timing how long it takes the child to complete the skill. Data collection by parents can be facilitated if data-collection demands are reasonable, recording forms are easily completed, and skills in completing the forms are checked.

Using Parent Interviews to Assess Self-Care Skills. Parents frequently are interviewed concerning self-care skills. Interviews should serve at least three functions: (a) collecting information about children's skills, (b) validating information collected through direct testing and observation, and (c) identifying parents' values about the skills being assessed. For collecting information about child skills, the interview should be relatively structured but flexible. The teacher should have a list of questions about the child's performance on specific skills. Information on dressing can be obtained by asking the parent to describe how the child usually gets dressed, and whether the child ever dresses himself. Specific questions about what the child can and cannot do increase the probability of obtaining useful information. When parents are not sure, the teacher can ask them to observe the child at a later time, and then contact the parents about the results. This pattern of asking questions, allowing time to observe, and then asking the questions again at a later time will result in more information and may help teach parents problem-solving skills (cf., Powell, 1981). Furthermore, parents should be asked whether they have attempted to teach the child any of the self-care skills, and if so, what the results were. When parents have been unsuccessful, the reasons for it should be identified.

When interviewing parents to validate assessment results obtained from other measures, the teacher should be sure to preface the interview with the fact that children perform differently for different people and in different situations. Children may do some behaviors in informal testing situations that they do not do in usual day-to-day functioning; the reverse also is true. Therefore, validating the assessment information through interviews is an important step in determining whether and on what to initiate instruction. The teacher should describe skills the child did successfully, skills the child did not do, and where errors occurred. Parents should be asked throughout the description whether it matches usual performance at home. Discrepancies should be noted and later may become targets for instruction.

Finally parents' views about self-care skills should be solicited. Instruction in these behaviors undoubtedly will be conducted in part by the parents. Their willingness to expend effort in teaching these skills may be influenced by the value they place on those skills. The teacher should first determine how valuable these skills are, in general, to the parents, and then which skills are viewed as most important (e.g., putting on a coat as compared to lacing shoes).

Assessment of Eating and Self-feeding Skills

Assessment of eating skills should include measurement of oral motor functioning, self-feeding and utensil use, mealtime environments, and nutritional intake. These issues are discussed in this section.

Assessment of Oral Motor Functioning and Eating. Assesment of **oral motor functioning** and eating is particularly critical when working with children who are suspected or identified as having motor disabilities (e.g., cerebral palsy, Down syndrome). Children who lack oral motor control have difficulty coordinating chewing, sucking, and swallowing. For these children, mealtime can be time consuming, with the child gagging, crying, and receiving little nourishment. Often behaviors of adults can prolong feeding problems. For example, a 4-year-old child who drinks from a bottle or receives nothing but

pureed foods and is fed in someone's lap is not likely to progress beyond infantile eating behaviors.

Most children with motor disabilities have some eating problems (Gallender, 1979). The problems are primarily due to abnormal muscle tone, delayed integration of primitive reflexes, abnormal movement patterns, problems associated with oral structural abnormalities, or a combination of these. Some children have such severe problems that oral feeding is not possible. These children may be tube-fed, at least temporarily, in order to provide adequate nutritional intake. However, their oral motor development should be assessed and intervention programs designed to develop oral motor control and eating skills, because the ultimate goal is to resume oral feeding.

In order to assess oral motor functioning and eating in children with oral motor problems, a basic understanding of normal oral motor development is neccessary. In the nonhandicapped infant, oral motor development follows a predictable sequence. However, rates of acquisition will vary from child to child. The developmental milestones for eating are shown in Table 17.6. The ages listed are not exact and should only be used as a guide; this listing is not a checklist to be used for assessment purposes.

When assessing oral motor development and eating, the examiner should ask:

1. What is the child's basic underlying and predominant muscle tone? How is it distributed throughout the body? How do changes in muscle tone and its distribution interfere with oral motor control and eating?
2. How does the position of the head, neck, shoulders, and trunk affect muscle tone and movements of the child's lips, tongue, jaw, and cheeks? Do these change with the child's position?
3. What primitive reflexes or abnormal movement patterns in the body interfere with oral motor control and eating?

TABLE 17.6
Normal Sequence of Oral Motor Development and Eating

Age (months)	Skill
0–4	Strong oral reflexes (suck-swallow, rooting, gag)
	Incomplete lip closure, especially at the corner of the lips.
	Unable to release the nipple voluntarily.
1–2	Better lip closure.
	Tongue moves with jaw.
	Suckling—tongue moves up and down, in and out with sucking.
3	Mouth opens or tongue protrudes in anticipation of feeding.
4	Recognizes bottle.
	Suckling strength increases, tongue starts to raise and lower.
	More variety of tongue movements and less "reflex" movement.
	Loses liquids from sides of mouth during sucking.
	Cup drinking introduced. Messy, tongue may thrust with cup.
	Appetite may be erratic.
5	Mouth opens for spoon.
	Thrusts tongue involuntarily when spoon removed, ejects food.
6	Munches, jaw moves up and down. Biting lacks rotary chewing.
	Tongue lateralization (uses tongue to move food side to side).
	True suck, stable jaw, tongue moves up and down.
	Upper lip comes down well on spoon.
	Finger feeding begins (6–8 months).
8	Tongue elevation with stable jaw, can handle liquids.
	Transfers food well from center of mouth to sides.
	Rotary chewing begins, retains some vertical motions.
	Feeds self finger foods, messy.
	Holds own bottle.
	Makes sounds while eating.
12	Controlled bite through food.
	Chews adequately with rotary chew.
	Plays with tongue. Sticks it out experimentally.
	More choosy about food, very independent.
15–18	Begins spoon feeding, may spill.
	Drinks well from cup, stabilizes muscle around jaw.
	Licks lower lip.
21–24	Holds small glass with one hand.
	Inserts spoon without inverting it.
	Food preference stems from taste, form, consistency, or color.

Source: Adapted from *Considerations for Feeding Children Who Have a Neuromuscular Disorder* (pp. 14–15) by S. Hall, N. Cicirello, P. Reed, & J. Hylton, 1987, Portland: Oregon Health Sciences University, Crippled Children's Division.

4. What primitive oral reflexes are present? How do they interfere with eating?
5. What abnormal oral movements are present? How do they interfere with eating?
6. Are there structural abnormalities present or abnormal movement patterns that may result in future abnormalities of the oral structures?
7. What is the child's response to sensory stimulation? Does the child show signs of

hyposensitivity or hypersensitivity of the neck, face, and mouth?

8. How long does it take to feed the child? How much food and/or liquid does the child usually eat at a meal? Is the child's diet nutritionally balanced? What are the textures or consistencies of the foods that the child eats? Are there behavior problems during mealtimes?

9. How well does the child suck and swallow when eating/drinking from a bottle/breast, cup, or spoon?

10. How well does the child bite, chew, and swallow solid foods?

Oral motor and eating assessments are usually conducted by an experienced physical, occupational, or speech therapist, or a trained special educator who has a thorough knowledge of normal oral motor development, as well as an understanding of specific oral motor problems. Nutritionists also should be consulted, particularly for children who have eating problems or need special diets. Special educators require information in conducting assessments of oral motor functioning and eating to identify children who need a thorough evaluation and to be able to detect abnormal eating patterns during mealtimes.

An assessment of oral motor function and eating skills should include assessments of (a) the child's overall muscle tone, postural control, and movement patterns; (b) general information related to eating; (c) the oral structures through a visual examination; (d) oral motor reflexes; and (e) sucking, swallowing, biting, and chewing. Assessments of oral motor development and eating should be conducted in context using direct observation techniques.

An assessment of general postural tone and movement should be conducted prior to assessing oral motor development and eating. Abnormal muscle tone, either hypotonia (low muscle tone) or hypertonia (high muscle tone) exhibited in the child's body may affect the child's oral movements. Hypotonia may result

in a drooping head, jaw, and lips and weak sucking or chewing. Hypertonia may result in restricted movement of the oral mechanism, which may result in oral deformities and excessive effort in eating. In addition, primitive reflexes that affect the whole body, such as the asymmetrical tonic neck reflex (ATNR), should be noted (Gallender, 1979; Inge, 1987; Utley, Holvoet, & Barnes, 1977). The ATNR makes it difficult for the child to get food into his mouth and the asymmetrical distribution of muscle contractions generalizes to the tongue and jaw, creating structural deviations that interfere with oral motor control. The examiner should note abnormal movements of the head, neck, or shoulders, which affect the movements of the child's oral mechanism. For example, a child with abnormal head and neck extension will develop abnormal oral movements, including jaw thrusting, lip retraction, and tongue retraction as part of this abnormal movement pattern. Assessment information on posture and movement should be gathered both before and throughout the feeding situation. The reader should review Chapter 13 for specific information on assessing muscle tone, postural control, and movement.

The second aspect of the assessment is an examination of the **oral structures** (cf., CAPE, 1980). This should include inspection of the teeth, gums, and palate. The examination should be conducted with the child's head upright, in midline, and neutral with no excessive flexion or extension. The child's teeth should be examined, noting the presence of malformations, asymmetry, malocclusion (abnormal relationship of lower and upper teeth when jaw is closed), or decay that might interfere with eating or indicate nutritional problems. When examining the gums, note the presence of any swelling or discoloration. Various medications used to control seizures may cause gums to become tender, swell, or grow over teeth. Many children with hypertonia (spasticity) may have a high-arched palate, which is related to the abnormal position of the tongue (Fraser, Hensinger, & Phelps, 1987; Orelove & Sobsey, 1987). Abnormalities of the oral structures such as cleft lip and/or palate should be surgically corrected as early as possible to prevent additional oral motor and eating problems (Orelove & Sobsey, 1987).

A third aspect of the assessment involves gathering information about eating through parent interviews. This information includes length of time required to feed the child, amount of food and liquid consumed at an average meal, types of foods eaten (e.g. tastes, textures, temperatures, variety), and feeding position. The evaluator should ask parents to collect data on the length of feeding times and the amount consumed. These data should be collected over a period of several days to provide an approximate average. Ask the parents about the types and consistencies of foods that the child usually eats. Many parents and others will provide the child only pureed foods, because the child cannot chew or swallow well and chokes or gags. However, the child will not be able to improve in eating until foods with firmer consistencies are provided in a systematic manner over time.

The best position for feeding should be determined. For infants being bottle fed, the best position is to be cradled in the feeder's arms and lap. For the young child, the most preferable position is sitting facing the feeder. In the face-to-face position, the feeder can monitor overall body posture and eating and oral motor movements, apply oral control techniques with the free hand, and interact socially with the child during feeding.

While seated, the child's hips/pelvis and knees should be flexed 90 degrees, with the ankles neutral and feet well supported. Children with poor head control may need to be reclined at an angle of 45 to 90 degrees. The trunk should be at midline, and the spine should be straight without excessive rounding of the lower spine. The head should be in midline and slightly flexed. The shoulders should be forward and slightly rounded with hands in midline. These positioning guidelines can be attained with the infant cradled in the feeder's lap and arms, and with the child sitting facing the feeder using a wedge against a table for postural support. Feeding also may be done with the child positioned appropriately using a corner chair, a wheelchair with adaptive seating or positioning accessories, or other chairs adapted to facilitate appropriate positioning (cf., Hall, Cicirello, Reed, & Hylton, 1987; Mueller, 1975).

Assessing oral motor reflexes is a fourth aspect of the oral motor and eating evaluation. Primitive oral motor reflexes are present in all children; in most cases they disappear or are integrated as higher neurological levels of functioning and voluntary control emerges. In children with disabilities, these oral motor reflexes may be absent or persist past the time that they should normally disappear. Assessment of oral motor reflexes should focus on their presence or absence, *and* on how persistent they are and how they interfere with eating. These reflexes should *not* be evaluated by eliciting them artificially, but should be assessed during an actual feeding situation. A description of selected primitive oral motor reflexes such as the **rooting, suck-swallow, gag,** and **bite reflexes** is shown in Table 17.7 on page 462 (cf., Alexander & Bigge, 1982; Fraser et al., 1987; Morris, 1982a; Radtka, 1977).

In addition, abnormal oral motor patterns that are not present in typical children may be exhibited in those with handicaps. These include the **tonic bite reflex, tongue thrust, jaw thrust**, and others previously mentioned. These abnormal oral movements are described in Table 17.8 (p. 463). Also, children may be hyposensitive or hypersensitive to tactile stimulation around the neck and face and in the mouth.

During the assessment, the examiner should use foods the child prefers or ask the parents to bring samples of the foods the child usually eats. Depending on the child's

TABLE 17.7
Selected Oral Motor Reflexes

Reflex	Age in Normal Development	Stimulus	Response Description
Rooting	0–4 months	Tactile stimulation applied to the outside of the mouth outward to cheek (stroking) while child's head in midline	Head-turning from side to side, stops at side of stimulus
Sucking	0–5 months	Insert nipple or finger in the mouth and make contact with child's tongue or hard palate	Alternate sucking with resting periods noting strength of sucking, when nipple or finger is withdrawn head flexes forward toward stimulus
Suck-Swallow	0–18 months	Liquid/food makes contact with back of tongue or throat	Early lick-type suck characterized by large up-and-down movements of separated jaw, back and forth tongue movements, little lip closure; swallow between each suck, rhythmic
Gag	Normal from birth	Pressure applied to back half of tongue	Mouth opens, head extends, floor of mouth depresses
Bite	0–6 months	Tactile stimulation to teeth or gums	Rhythmical series of small up and down jaw movements

developmental level in eating, this should include something to drink from a bottle or cup, something to eat from a spoon, and something to chew. If the parents bring foods, this eliminates problems such as food preferences and possible food allergies. The parents also should bring any positioning equipment used during feeding, special bottles, cups, or utensils that are used. Begin the actual feeding session by asking the parent to position and feed the child in the usual manner. During this time, information may be gathered on the areas previously described, while also

observing communicative interactions between parent and child. Valuable information for parent training and consultation may be gathered as the parent's reaction and remedies for abnormal patterns and eating problems are observed. For example, a parent may extend the child's head back and "bird feed" the child. This may result in the parent getting food down, but does not facilitate better oral motor control and voluntary eating behaviors.

During initial observations, no special techniques or oral control should be provided.

TABLE 17.8
Abnormal Oral Movements

Type	Description
Jaw Thrusting	The abnormally strong downward extension of the lower jaw; the jaw is often stuck in an open position.
Lip Pursing	A tight purse-string movement of the lips; the corners of the lips pulled back slightly while the lips themselves appear to be puckering.
Lip Retraction	The strong pulling back of the lips so that they form a tight line across the mouth; the cheeks are also pulled back.
Tongue Retraction	The strong pulling back of the tongue; the tongue tip may touch the floor of the mouth, with the rest of the tongue humped up in the back.
Tongue Thrust	The abnormally strong forward push of the tongue; the tongue appears thick or bunched.
Tonic Biting	The abnormally strong closure of the jaw in response to tactile stimulation of the teeth or gums; attempts to remove the stimulation only result in stronger closure of the jaw; the jaw is often stuck in a closed position.

Source: From "Facilitation of Language and Speech" by R. P. Alexander & J. L. Bigge in *Teaching Individuals with Physical and Multiple Handicaps* (2nd ed.) (p. 267) ed. by J. L. Bigge, 1982, Columbus, OH: Merrill. Copyright 1982 by Merrill Publishing Company. Adapted by permission.

Later in the session, the examiner may want to experiment with the use of various oral control techniques (e.g., jaw control), different utensils, positioning techniques, different food consistencies, and adaptations in the presentation of food and utensils to observe changes in the child's eating behaviors.

When assessing **sucking** and **swallowing**, the following questions should be used as a guide (Alexander & Bigge, 1982):

1. In bottle drinking/breast feeding, can the child initiate and sustain sucking? What type of nipple is used on the bottle (old-fashioned, rounded ones are best), and has the hole been enlarged due to insufficient or weak sucking?
2. Does the child suck or suckle liquids or pureed foods from a cup or spoon? Does the child have good lip closure on the cup or spoon?
3. Is there tongue thrusting, jaw thrusting, tongue retraction, lip retraction, lip pursing, or tonic biting during bottle/cup drinking or spoon feeding? Is tongue thrusting present with swallowing?
4. Does the child use the upper lip to remove food from the spoon?
5. Does the child choke, cough, or gag on liquids or pureed foods?
6. Does the child use head extension when swallowing?
7. Can the child coordinate sucking, swallowing, and breathing?

The liquids used during this portion of the assessment should be a smooth consistency and at room temperature or a little cooler. Thicker liquids such as stirred yogurt and thinned baby food are easier to handle than thin ones. However, thinner liquids such as fruit juices may be used to determine the child's ability to handle these. Foods used for spoon feeding should be thick and hold their shape on the spoon. Recommended foods include unstirred yogurt, small curd cottage cheese, pudding, thick cooked oatmeal, mashed potatoes, and blended (not pureed) table foods. Foods that are more difficult to handle and are not recommended for spoon feeding include Jello, mashed bananas, spaghetti noodles, and rice.

When assessing **biting** and **chewing**, the following questions should be used as a guide (Alexander & Bigge, 1982):

1. Does the child use a suck or tonic bite to bite? Is there jaw thrusting or tongue thrusting during biting?
2. Does the child suck the food instead of chewing it? Does the child mouth the food instead of chewing to get it moist enough to swallow?
3. Does the child use a munching pattern?
4. Does the child use tongue lateralization to move the food from the center of the mouth to the side?
5. Does the child use a mature chewing pattern with tongue lateralization and rotary jaw movements?
6. Does the child gag, choke, or cough when swallowing chewed solids?

Foods used for this portion of the assessment should be small bite-sized pieces on which the child cannot choke. Such foods include toasted bread with peanut butter and jelly, crackers, meat sticks, steamed vegetables, fruit, and chunks of cheese cut into strips, so that the examiner can hold onto one end while the child chews on the other. Dangerous foods that may induce choking should be avoided; they include raw vegetables such as carrots and celery, peanuts, popcorn, hard candy, or any other foods that will not readily dissolve.

The results of oral motor and eating assessments are used to plan intervention programs to improve oral motor functioning and eating behaviors. The areas of concern may include

any or all of the following: appropriate positioning and use of adaptive equipment; development of good sucking, swallowing, biting, and chewing patterns through the use of special preparation techniques, oral control, and systematic increases in food consistencies; selection and use of proper eating utensils (e.g., teflon-coated spoon, cut-away cups); decreasing hyposensitivity or hypersensitivity by using appropriate preparation techniques, oral stimulation techniques, and appropriate food textures; increasing the complexity and variety of foods that the child can handle; and decreasing the amount of time required to feed the child.

Several formal tests are available for assessing oral motor development and eating. The Pre-Speech Assessment Scale (Morris, 1982b) is an indepth scale designed to assess prespeech behaviors in neurologically impaired children. It contains a thorough questionnaire for parents and four subtests related to eating: feeding behavior, sucking, swallowing, and biting and chewing. The results obtained are useful for diagnostic, programming, and program evaluation purposes. The Behavioral Assessment Scale of Oral Functions in Feeding (Stratton, 1981) provides a graded method for measuring oral motor functions. This scale includes nine eating functions, which are scored according to the child's performance using six levels from passive performance to normal. The results may be useful in diagnosing specific eating problems, program planning, and evaluation. The RISE: Computerized Checklist and Curriculum for the Motorically Delayed Impaired Child (Holder, Wells, & Cook, 1985) includes a section to assess prespeech and feeding behaviors and is accompanied by a curriculum that includes special preparation techniques, desensitization techniques, oral control techniques, and utensil selection and use.

Assessment of Self-Feeding and Utensil Use. **Self-feeding** skills such as drinking from a cup and using spoons, forks, knives, and napkins are chained responses that can be assessed using the heuristic described for assessing dressing and grooming skills. As with dressing and grooming skills, assessment of self-feeding behaviors should occur during natural times (i.e., when the child is hungry). Positioning for normal muscle tone and range of motion should precede assessment activities, and prerequisite skills (i.e., hand-to-mouth behavior and volitional grasp patterns) also should be checked. Adapted utensils should be used when necessary. If accuracy is demonstrated, fluency and generalization of skills become an important focus of measurement. In addition, the teacher should use foods the child likes. A record of the foods used during assessment should be maintained, because performance may vary depending on the foods being eaten. For example, using a spoon to eat mashed potatoes is much easier than using a spoon to eat peas.

Assessment of Eating Environments and Mealtime Behaviors. In addition to eating and self-feeding, assessment should address mealtime behaviors. Meals in our society are social events as well as a means for getting nourishment. For integration, children with handicaps should engage in the social/cultural aspects of meals. These behaviors include eating neatly, conducting conversations during meals, taking and passing food, asking for food and giving food that is requested by others, and eating at appropriate rates. Ideally, mealtime routines can be used for teaching or practicing skills such as preparing meals, eating and feeding, making choices, and interacting and communicating with others (Perske, Clifton, McLean, & Stein, 1977).

Bailey, Harms, and Clifford (1983) compared mealtime activities of programs serving typical preschoolers and programs serving preschoolers with handicaps. Their study revealed some interesting differences between the two types of programs: mealtimes for handicapped children typically did not (a) involve children in meal preparation or table setting, (b) allow choice making, (c) allow children to serve themselves, (d) pro-

mote child/child communicative exchanges, (e) include teaching of concepts other than self-care behaviors, (f) involve children in postmeal clean-up activities, and (g) encourage appropriate postmeal hygiene such as brushing the teeth. These findings suggest that a real need exists to assess the quality of mealtime routines in early intervention programs for young children with handicaps.

The measure used by Bailey et al. (1983) in their assessment of mealtimes was the Observation: Atmosphere and Environment of an Eating Experience (Harms & Farthing, 1979). This measure requires direct observation of mealtime routines and includes sections on (a) pre-eating activities, such as what activity occurred before the meal, children's role in meal preparation, and the tone of the pre-eating activities; (b) physical setting, such as whether children sat at a table while eating, with whom children ate, the number of adults and children at each table, and whether the chairs and tables were the correct size; (c) food, such as what was served and whether it was easy for children to manage it; (d) food service, such as the style of service (family, cafeteria, etc.) and manner in which second helpings were obtained; (e) mealtime interactions (adult behaviors), such as whether and where adults ate, their interactions with children, and their attempts to teach concepts during the meal; (f) mealtime interaction (child behaviors), such as whether children talked with each other, whether children could leave the table when they were finished, and the tone of the meal; and (g) post-eating activities, such as whether children helped clean up and brushed their teeth, and the tone of the post-eating activities. The measure employs (a) binary (yes/no) items, (b) frequency count items (e.g., number of adults and children at each table), and (c) rating scale items (e.g., for assessing the tone of activities). This measure can be used to identify changes that should be made in environments to make them more pleasant, more conducive to teaching, and more conducive to promoting appropriate mealtime routines. It can be used to identify the behaviors children need in a given environment, which is useful in planning transitions to that environment. Also, the measure can be used to monitor the quality of mealtimes in a program. Finally, it can be used in research on mealtime routines as a dependent measure or to identify specific factors that can be measured in other ways.

Assessment of Nutritional Intake. The need for adequate food intake is well established; however, many infants and preschoolers with handicaps are at risk for nutritional problems. Several factors may put infants and children at risk for not receiving adequate nutrition; these are shown in Table 17.9. Information on these issues is obtained by parental interviews and by collecting a record of the child's nutrient intake over a 3- to 7-day period, preferably 7 days. Parents need instruction on how to maintain the record of food intake. Pipes (1981) suggests using a data-collection

sheet that includes a separate column for the time, food, amount, and method of preparation. The following instructions accompany the data-collection sheet:

1. Record all food and beverages immediately *after* they are eaten or drunk.
2. Measure the amounts of each food carefully in terms of standard measuring cups and spoons. Record meat portions in ounces or as fractions of pounds. . . .
3. Indicate method of (food) preparation. . . .
4. Be sure to include any condiments, gravies, salad dressings, butter, margarine, whipped cream, relishes, etc. . . .
5. Be sure to include all between meal foods and drinks. . . .
6. If you eat away from home, please put a little symbol beside the foods. (p. 150)

Other measures, such as bone age and fat-fold thickness, also can be used by appropriate professionals (Hayman, 1983). The role of early interventionists in assessing nutrition is threefold. First, they should attempt to

TABLE 17.9
Indicators of Potential Nutritional Risk for Infants and Children

General Factor	Descriptions
Inappropriate Weight Gain	Lack of adequate weight gain.
	Rapid weight gain.
	Discrepancies between length and weight.
	Obese or emaciated children.
Inappropriate Nutrient Intake	Consumption of more than 32 ounces or less than 16 ounces of milk per day.
	Diluted formulas due to parents failure to understand preparation, lack of financial resources, use of skim milk, use of sugar water rather than milk.
	Infants less than 2 months old who receive more than 145 calories per kilogram or less than 110 calories per kilogram.
	Infants and children who receive inappropriate nutrient supplements such as lack of vitamin supplements, use of excessive vitamin supplements, use of high-potency vitamin supplements, use of unnecessary vitamin supplements
Parental Factors	Families of low socioeconomic status.
	Parents who do not understand or follow formula preparation instructions.

TABLE 17.9
Continued

General Factor	Descriptions
	Parents who do not have financial resources to buy formula, or ones who dilute formula, use skim milk, or use sugar water rather than milk.
	Parents who schedule feedings, but offer at intervals greater than 5 hours or less than 2 hours.
	Parents who appear to lack concern about feeding or do not know what to feed their children.
	Parents who are overanxious about children's eating.
	Parents who consistently prop bottle.
	Parents who breast feed for excessively long periods at each feeding.
	Parents who do not burp infant.
	Breast-feeding mothers who do not eat foods that contribute important nutrients during lactation
	Breast-feeding mothers who have questions about scheduling, supplementary feedings, or adequate supply of milk.
	Parents who follow faddist food rules or who have questions about such fads.
	Parents who lack home management skills.
	Parents who do not take advantage of resources available to them such as food stamps or school lunches.
	Parents who offer (a) inappropriate kinds of foods such as adding semisolids to milk, (b) foods that do not contain appropriate amounts of iron, (c) excessive amounts of high-carbohydrate foods or alcoholic beverages, (d) excessive amounts of high-calorie semisolids, and (e) infant and junior dinners to replace meat.
	Parents who drink alcohol or take drugs while breast feeding.
Infant/Child Factors	Infants who consistently fall asleep before completing adequate nutrient intake.
	Infants who refuse the breast or bottle.
	Infants and children who refuse entire food groups.
	Infants and children who have physical handicaps that intefere with the ability to eat.
	Children who have specific dietary problems.

Source: Adapted from "Assessing Food and Nutrient Intake," by P. L. Pipes. In M. L. Powell (Ed.), *Assessment and Management of Development Changes and Problems in Children* (pp. 147–161), 1981, St. Louis: Mosby. And adapted from "Nutritional Assessment of Handicapped Preschoolers," by L. Hayman, *Topics in Early Childhood Special Education*, 1983, *3*(2) 9–17.

identify infants and children who are at risk for receiving inadequate diets and refer them to dieticians or other professionals. Second, they can help parents collect and maintain a record of nutrient intake. Third, they assist parents in implementing recommendations from other professionals.

Comments on Eating/Self-feeding Assessments. Eating and feeding are important self-help skills. The oral motor functioning of children can be assessed through direct observation and informal assessment with various instruments, and self-feeding skills can be assessed using the heuristic described earlier. In addition, the environment of mealtimes should be assessed, and the Observation: Atmosphere and Environment of an Eating Experience (Harms & Farthing, 1979) is a useful tool for doing this. Finally, for many children, their nutritional intake should be evaluated.

Assessment of Toileting Skills

Toilet training is the process by which children are taught the cultural practices related to eliminating urine and feces. It traditionally has been the responsibility of families but is a legitimate educational activity with preschoolers who display handicapping conditions (Snell, 1980). Because of psychoanalytic thinking, toilet training has been feared and dreaded by parents and professionals alike. A more contemporary view of toileting is that it is a skill, similar to many others, that must be learned, but one for which the child holds some control. Specifically, the child determines (for the most part) when to toilet; adults cannot provide prompts that will ensure toileting responses. Although toileting is another skill that can be taught, it is an activity around which children and adults can develop negative interaction patterns.

Toilet Training Outcomes. The outcomes of toilet training can be conceptualized in three levels: (a) when taken to the toilet, the child

urinates and defecates in the toilet; (b) the child anticipates when toileting is needed and communicates that need to an adult; and (c) the child anticipates when toileting is needed, moves to the bathroom or communicates the need to an adult, unfastens and takes down her pants, sits on the toilet, urinates and/or defecates, wipes if necessary, pulls up her pants, fastens the pants, flushes the toilet, and washes her hands. Although this third level is the ultimate goal of toilet training, the first two levels also are of value and probably precede the third. Assessment activities for the first level address whether a child has the prerequisite skills needed for toileting; for the second level, toileting prerequisites and requesting behaviors are assessed; for the third level, toileting prerequisites, requesting, locomotion, clothing management, wiping, flushing, and hand washing are assessed.

Identification and Measurement of Prerequisite Factors for Toilet Training. The prerequisite and desirable factors for toilet training and a summary of data-collection procedures are shown in Table 17.10. Two primarily physiological skills must be present before toilet training is indicated. These are the *ability to hold urine and feces* in the bladder and bowel, and the *ability to release them* in "large" quantities at once as compared to "small" quantities more frequently. When these skills are present, the task of toilet training is to teach children to hold their bodily waste when they are not sitting on the toilet, and release it when they are. Generally, children obtain bowel control simultaneously with or before bladder control; however, nearly all training programs focus first on urination because it occurs more frequently and is easily prompted through increased liquid intake.

Snell (1987) suggests that the chronological age of 2.5 years also is a prerequisite for toilet training. However, as she indicates, the relationship between chronological age

TABLE 17.10
Summary of Prerequisite and Desirable Factors for Toilet Training

Type of Skill/Factors	Summary of Measurement Procedures
Prerequisite Factors	
Bladder control	Direct observation using a time-sample recording system to note when child urinates, defecates, and takes in liquid and food
Releases urine in large amounts at once	Direct observation using anecdotal recording about whether diaper is soaked
Sitting position on toilet	Direct observation and consultation with physical or occupational therapist to identify appropriate position
Free of interfering medical conditions	Review of medical records, interviews with parents, and knowledge of child; consultation with physician on questionable cases
Desirable Factors	
Reinforcer identification	Direct observation, interviews with parents, and use of reinforcer menu
Instructional control	Direct observation using event recording to assess compliance with adult requests, and direct observation using event recording to determine frequency of interfering behaviors
Awareness of elimination and/or discomfort	Direct observation using anecdotal recording and parent interviews about changes in child behavior related to toileting
Sitting on toilet	Direct observation timing the duration of sitting on the toilet
Parent involvement	Interview with parents to explain procedures, solicit participation, and determine ability to implement training program
Requesting skills[a]	Direct observation using anecdotal recording to determine presence of requesting function
Clothing management,[b] locomotion, and hygiene	Direct observation using event sampling to assess clothing management skills and ability to move to bathroom

[a] Assessed only if second level of toilet training outcomes is targeted.

[b] Assessed only if third level of toilet training outcomes is targeted.

and toilet training success is weak. Toilet training appears easier for typical children who are older than 2.5 years. In reality, chronological age is an indicator of central nervous system development, and with children whose central nervous systems are dysfunctional or are of questionable status, chronological age may be a poor predictor of toilet-training success.

The best method of determining whether children can hold their bodily wastes and release them periodically as compared to releasing small amounts frequently is to collect data on children's elimination patterns. The most widely accepted method of collecting these data is to use a time-sampling recording system. Children are checked periodically, usually at 20- or 30-minute intervals, throughout the day. In the simplest form, a record is made of whether children's diapers are dry or wet; however, more complete information frequently is obtained. For example, at each interval the caregiver determines and records whether (a) the diaper is dry, (b) the diaper is free of feces, (c) the child has urinated in the toilet since the last check, (d) the child has had a bowel movement in the toilet since the last check, and (e) what the

child has eaten or drunk since the last check. A data-collection sheet for recording this information is shown in Figure 17.1. Ideally, data should be collected for children's entire waking day and for 2–3 weeks; thus, parents need to be involved in collecting this data. The purpose of such extensive data collection is to document whether children *consistently* remain dry for 1–2 hours at a time and whether those dry periods appear at consistent times of day.

The amount of urine released is more difficult to measure; it is related to how well children can retain their urine as well as whether

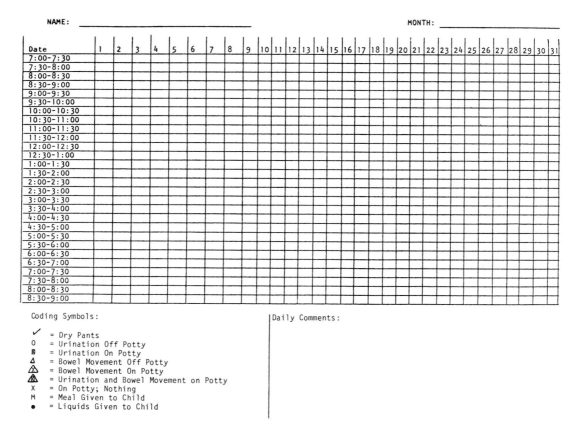

FIGURE 17.1
Data-collection sheet for collecting data on children's patterns of urination and defecation (Source: From **Toilet Training the Handicapped Child** *by H. D. Fredericks, V. Baldwin, D. N. Grove, and W. G. Moore, 1975, Monmouth, OR: Instructional Development. Copyright 1975 by H. D. Fredericks. Reprinted by permission.)*

it is released at once or is dribbled. Information on this variable can be recorded in the comments sections of the data-collection form shown in Figure 17.1. At issue is whether children soak or dampen their diapers. More frequent measurement intervals (e.g., 8–10 minutes) can be used if this is a question.

A third prerequisite for successful toilet training is proper positioning on the toilet, especially for children who display movement dysfunction. While on the toilet, children's muscle tone should be as normal as possible, and their postural alignment should facilitate maximum control of the muscles of the trunk, hips, and pelvis (Campbell, 1987). In general, children should be able to touch the floor or some adapted platform with their feet; their knees and hips should be flexed, and some children will need additional trunk support. The appropriate position can be checked through consultation with a physical or occupational therapist.

In addition to these prerequisites, children should be free of medical complications that may interfere with toilet training. For example, students with paralysis in the lower extremities also may have paralysis or partial paralysis of muscles needed for bladder and bowel control. Children with frequent urinary-tract infections may have difficulty with toilet training. Consultation with a physician should occur prior to toilet training, when medical records, parent interviews, or knowledge of the child suggest that any condition exists that may interfere with the course of toilet training.

Identification and Measurement of Desirable Factors for Toilet Training. Several factors have been identified that increase the probability that toilet training will be successful; thus, assessment of these factors should occur. Toilet training may be possible without the presence of these factors, but it will be more efficient if they exist. First, positive reinforcers should be identified through parent interviews, direct observation of the

child, and testing with reinforcement menus (see Chapter 4).

Second, children should be under instructional control, which involves compliance with adult requests and absence of disruptive, inappropriate behaviors such as tantrums, severe aggression, severe social withdrawal, and self-injurious behaviors. Children should be informally assessed on commands such as "Come here," "Look at me," "Sit here," "Touch your (eyes, nose, etc.)," and "Give me _____ ." Azrin and Foxx (1974) suggest that nonhandicapped children should comply with 8 of 10 requests before initiating toilet training. Inappropriate behaviors can be assessed through direct observation and interviews with parents and others who know the child. While some maladaptive behavior may be present, the intent of this factor is to ensure that high rates of interfering, inappropriate behavior are not being displayed.

Third, children show some awareness of toileting functions and/or displeasure with the results. Awareness may be indicated by changes in facial expressions, decreases in the amount of activity, or changes in posture. These behavioral changes may occur prior to or during urination and defecation. Children also may show discomfort with the consequences of toileting by attempting to get out of the diaper, adjusting their sitting positions, becoming fussy, or tugging on their pants. Data on these factors are collected through anecdotal recording and/or interviews with parents.

Fourth, the ability to sit on the toilet for a few minutes is necessary. When children are first learning to toilet, the latency from the time they sit down on the toilet until they release their bodily waste may be a few minutes. Thus, children need to be assessed for their ability to sit on the toilet; this should be done in addition to identifying the most appropriate sitting position. Data collection should involve timing how long children sit during a variety of activities, including actually sitting on the toilet.

Fifth, parents' cooperation in implementing toilet-training procedures should be obtained prior to training. Lance and Koch (1973) found that parents view toilet training as the most important self-care skill, but that they also viewed it as the most difficult to teach. Thus, parents' willingness to implement the toilet-training regimen and their skill in doing so should be assessed and monitored. Frequently, parents are desirous of toilet training, but have temporary circumstances that will interfere with the ability to implement a training regimen. Examples include up-coming vacations, illness of a family member, impending birth of a sibling, and visiting friends or relatives. Parental interviews are the primary method of collecting information on this issue. Specific questions about potentially interfering factors should be asked.

Sixth, when the second or third level of toilet-training outcomes is sought, the presence of requesting skills is desirable. Prior to toilet training, requests to use the toilet are unlikely; however, children should make requests for food, toys, and/or activities. Through anecdotal recording, the teacher should note occurrences of requesting behaviors. A well-established and frequently used requesting function is probably needed before the second level of toileting outcomes is targeted as an instructional goal.

Seventh, if the third level of toilet-training outcomes is targeted, then it is desirable that children have the prerequisite skills related to managing their own clothing, hand washing, and moving independently to the bathroom. Clothing management and hand washing can be assessed using the heuristic described previously and independent locomotion can be assessed through direct observation of the child's movements throughout the day.

Comments on Toileting Assessments. Children are considered ready for toilet training if they can hold their urine, release it in large amounts at once, are free of interfering medical conditions, and can be positioned appropriately on the toilet. Several factors increase the probability of toilet training being effective: (a) reinforcer identification, (b) instructional control, (c) awareness by children of toileting functions and consequences, (d) adequate durations of sitting,(e) requesting skills, and (f) clothing management and locomotion. Assessment of these factors is best accomplished through direct observation, interviews with parents, and consultation with therapists and physicians when appropriate.

Using Self-Care Assessment Information

Snell (1987) states that seven instructional decisions must be made in relation to self-care skills; including specification of (a) reinforcers, (b) procedures to control interfering behaviors, (c) self-care objectives, (d) instructional strategies, (e) monitoring procedures, (f) maintenance-facilitating procedures, and (g) generalization-facilitating procedures. Many of these decisions are made in response to assessment information from nearly all curriculum areas. However, five comments deserve special attention.

Involving Team Members
As noted in this chapter, performance of self-care skills relies heavily on children's movement skills. Thus, physical and occupational therapists should participate in the assessment and in planning instruction. Speech and language therapists frequently can assist in assessing oral motor behaviors needed in eating. Nutritionists can assess the adequacy of children's diets. Parents can provide important and unique information related to potential self-help objectives and teaching possibilities. Early childhood special educators should

have unique skills in designing and using behavioral procedures (e.g., prompting, prompt fading, and reinforcing target behaviors) used to teach many of the self-care skills. Thus, self-care is a domain for which team assessment and intervention are necessary.

Teaching at Natural Times

Because of the unique characteristics of self-care skills, instruction should occur when the self-care skills are needed. For example, if a child is learning to use a fork or spoon, then the instruction should be embedded into a mealtime rather than during isolated instructional sessions that do not involve eating. Some self-care skills must be taught at naturally occurring times; for example, toileting can only be taught when the child needs to toilet. Other skills are taught more practically at natural times (e.g., bathing). Although some self-care skills (e.g., dressing) can be taught in isolated instructional sessions, several rationales exist for teaching at natural times. If skills are taught when needed, natural reinforcers may be available for skill completion. For example, children learning to eat with a spoon have successful attempts reinforced with the food in the spoon; children who urinate in the toilet receive negative reinforcement by the removal of bladder pressure and avoidance of wet pants, which may be aversive; similarly, children who are taught to dress/undress during naturally occurring times can then become engaged in reinforcing activities. Similarly, inappropriate behaviors that occur as a result of repeated-trial, isolated, instructional sessions may be avoided if training is initiated when the skill is needed. Furthermore, because most self-help skills are performed in rather long chains of behavior, teaching in natural situations may allow the individual responses of the chains to come under the control of naturally occurring stimuli, thus facilitating maintenance and generalization.

However, teaching in natural contexts also presents difficulties. The urgency of the biological needs/results associated with some of the self-care skills may interfere with teaching in the natural context. For example, some eating skills may not be easily taught when children are very hungry or when they are getting full; therefore, the middle portions of mealtimes may be the best time for instruction; and children in the later stages of toilet training may need to urinate urgently and will not tolerate training on taking their pants down. Another difficulty of teaching at natural times is that monitoring children's performance may be more difficult because teachers or parents are attending to so many other variables. Finally, many of the naturally occurring times when these skills are needed do not occur during regular school hours. Two strategies have been used to deal with this problem: (a) assisting parents in teaching the skills and (b) structuring the environment to increase artificially the natural teaching opportunities. The issue of parent involvement is discussed later in the chapter. Examples of environmental structuring include providing several small meals when teaching self-feeding as compared to three meals (e.g., Azrin & Armstrong, 1973) and increasing liquid intake during toilet training to prompt a greater need for urination (Foxx & Azrin, 1973).

Considering All Phases of Learning

To increase children's independence, self-care instruction must target fluent responses, maintenance of acquired skills, and generalization of skills across situations and settings. The heuristic for assessing dressing and grooming skills allows specification of acquisition, fluency, maintenance, and generalization objectives. Teaching at natural times and involving parents in toilet training and feeding instruction are primary means of increasing the probability of generalization.

Using in Routines

Self-care skills occur in routines that involve many skills. Thus, to be useful to children and to increase the probability of generalization, self-care instruction should occur in routines (cf., Brown, 1987). Eating, feeding, and other mealtime behaviors should be taught during the sequences of events involved in meals. This routine may involve partial participation in meal preparation, setting the table, eating the meal, cleaning the table and dishes, and brushing the teeth. Toilet training should include the entire toileting routine—moving to the bathroom, taking down pants, sitting on the toilet, eliminating waste, wiping, pulling up pants, flushing, washing hands, and returning to the ongoing activities. Dressing frequently involves putting on all garments, not just one or two. In some cases, only a part of the routine will be chosen as the priority instructional target; however, teachers should ensure that children are engaged in each step of the routine. This system teaches the student that the skill being taught occurs within the context of other skills and increases the likelihood that completion of one step will serve as the discriminative stimulus for the next step in the routine. Teachers also should provide only the level of assistance needed by the child to be independent and at times give the child an opportunity to perform with less assistance or with no assistance. By providing the minimum level of assistance and fading that assistance, children may incidentally learn to perform some of the untargeted steps of the routines. Teaching in routines also sets the stage for children to learn appropriate hygiene and health-care habits such as washing hands after toileting or brushing teeth after meals. Bailey et al. (1983) in their comparison of mealtimes in preschools for typical and handicapped children found that in many cases programs for handicapped children did not have them brush their teeth after meals. With the higher incidence of dental problems in populations with handicapping conditions, it would seem that teaching children to brush their teeth after eating is a legitimate and socially valid practice. Teaching in routines will help establish such responses.

Involving Children's Parents

With nearly all skills, parents can be involved in (a) conducting assessment activities, (b) validating the assessment information, (c) assisting in making decisions based on assessment results, (d) planning instructional times and strategies, (e) implementing the instruction, (f) facilitating maintenance and generalization of the skills, and (g) monitoring the effects of instruction. With self-care skills, parental involvement is important because the skills are needed frequently at home, are likely to be needed more at home that in other settings, and can decrease family caregiving responsibilities if fluent generalization occurs. A number of sources have described issues related to, and procedures for involving, parents in instruction of self-care and other skills (cf., Baker et al., 1976a, 1976b; Baldwin, Fredericks, & Brodsky, 1973; Bronicki & Turnbull, 1987; Snell & Beckman-Brindley, 1984). In summary, several findings are apparent: (a) Considerable training materials exist for helping parents teach self-care skills; (b) parents can teach self-care skills to their children with handicapping conditions; (c) some parents will need special instruction in the form of verbal directions, actual demonstrations, and feedback or in the form of coaching; (d) parents' instruction of self-care skills should be integrated into the naturally occurring routines and interactions rather than being conducted in isolated sessions; and (e) not all parents are eager to teach their children, and their participation should be voluntary as compared to expected and drafted.

SUMMARY OF KEY CONCEPTS

- Self-care skills include eating, self-feeding, dressing/undressing, fastening/unfastening, grooming, and toileting and are best assessed using direct observation rather than direct testing.

- Self-care skills are (a) part physiological and part learned behavior, (b) acquired throughout the preschool period, (c) needed in the natural environment on a regular but low-frequency basis, (d) frequently chained behaviors, and (e) only useful if performed fluently, maintained, and generalized to the needed situations.

- A heuristic for assessing chained self-help skills allows measurement of accuracy, determines presence of prerequisite skills, and shows benefit of adapted materials and alternative skill sequences; it also allows specification of instructional objectives by the appropriate phase of learning.

- Assessment of oral motor development and eating should include muscle tone, postural control, and movement patterns; oral structures; general eating information and positioning; primitive oral reflexes; and sucking, swallowing, and biting and chewing.

- Children's oral motor abilities, self-feeding, and nutrient intake should be assessed when measuring eating/feeding skills.

- The mealtime environment should be considered when assessing eating and self-feeding skills.

- Toilet-training outcomes can be specified by levels: (a) Toileting is initiated by others taking the child; (b) toileting is initiated by requesting assistance from adults; and (c) toileting can be initiated by the child moving to the bathroom or by requesting assistance.

- Toilet-training prerequisite skills include children's ability to hold their urine and release it, identification of an appropriate sitting position, and absence of medical conditions that would interfere with training.

REFERENCES

Alexander, R. P. & Bigge, J. L. (1982). Facilitation of language and speech. In J. L. Bigge (Ed.), *Teaching individuals with physical and multiple handicaps* (2nd ed.) (pp. 257–289). Columbus, OH: Merrill.

Azrin, N. H. & Armstrong, P. M. (1973). The "mini-meal"—A method for teaching eating skills to the profoundly retarded. *Mental Retardation, 11,* 9–13.

Azrin, N. H. & Foxx, R. M. (1974). *Toilet training in less than a day.* New York: Simon & Schuster.

Bailey, D. B., Harms, T., & Clifford, R. M. (1983). Social and educational aspects of mealtimes for handicapped and nonhandicapped preschoolers.

Topics in Early Childhood Special Education, 3(2), 19–32.

Bailey, D. B. & Wolery, M. (1984). *Teaching infants and preschoolers with handicaps*. Columbus, OH: Merrill.

Baker, B. L., Brightman, A. J., Heifetz, L. J., & Murphy, D. M. (1976a). *Early self-help skills*. Champaign, IL: Research Press.

Baker, B. L., Brightman, A. J., Heifetz, L. J., & Murphy, D. M. (1976b). *Intermediate self-help skills*. Champaign, IL: Research Press.

Baldwin, V. L., Fredericks, H. D., & Brodsky, G. (1973). *Isn't it time he outgrew this? A training program for parents of retarded children*. Springfield, IL: Charles C. Thomas.

Balthazar, E. E. (1976). *Balthazar Scales of Adaptive Behavior, I*. Palo Alto, CA: Consulting Psychologists Press.

Brigance, A. H. (1978). *Inventory of Early Development*. North Billerica, MA: Curriculum Associates.

Bronicki, G. J. & Turnbull, A. P. (1987). Family-professional interactions. In M. E. Snell (Ed.) *Systematic instruction of persons with severe handicaps* (3rd ed.) (pp. 9–35). Columbus, OH: Merrill.

Brown, F. (1987). Meaningful assessment of people with severe and profound handicaps. In M. E. Snell (Ed.) *Systematic instruction of persons with severe handicaps* (3rd ed.) (pp. 39–63). Columbus, OH: Merrill.

Campbell, P. H. (1987). Physical management and handling procedures with students with movement dysfunction. In M. E. Snell (Ed.) *Systematic instruction of persons with severe handicaps* (3rd ed.) (pp. 174–187). Columbus, OH: Merrill.

CAPE, Consortium on Adaptive Performance Evaluation. (1980). *Adaptive Performance Instrument*. Moscow, ID: Department of Special Education, University of Idaho.

Christian, W. P. & Luce, S. C. (1985). Behavioral self-help training for developmentally disabled individuals. *School Psychology Review, 14*, 177–181.

Cohen, M. & Gross, P. (1979). *The developmental resource: Behavioral sequences for assessment and program planning (Vol. 1)*. New York: Grune & Stratton.

Dyson, L. & Fewell, R. R. (1986). Stress and adaptation in parents of young handicapped and nonhandicapped children: A comparative study.

Journal of the Division for Early Childhood, 10(1), 25–34.

Foxx, R. M. & Azrin, N. H. (1973). *Toilet training the retarded: A rapid program for day and nighttime independent toileting*. Champaign, IL: Research Press.

Fraser, B. A., Hensinger, R. N., & Phelps, J. A. (1987). *Physical management of multiple handicaps*. Baltimore, MD: Paul H. Brookes.

Fredericks, H. D., Makohon, L., Fruin, C., Moore, W., Piazza-Templeman, T., Blair, L., et al. (1980). *The teaching research curriculum for moderately and severely handicapped: Self-help and cognitive*. Springfield, IL: Charles C. Thomas.

Fredericks, H. D., Baldwin, V., Grove, D. N., & Moore. W. G. (1975). *Toilet training the handicapped child*. Monmouth, OR: Instructional Development.

Gallender, D. (1979). *Eating handicaps*. Springfield, IL: Charles C. Thomas.

Glover, M. E., Preminger, J. L., & Sanford, A. R. (1978). *Early Learning Accomplishment Profile*. Winston-Salem, NC: Kaplan School Supply.

Hall, S., Cicirello, N., Reed, P., & Hylton, J. (1987). *Considerations for feeding children who have a neuromuscular disorder*. Portland: Oregon Health Sciences University, Crippled Children's Division.

Haring, N. G., White, O. R., Edgar, E. B., Affleck, J. Q., Hayden, A. H., Munson, R. G., & Bendersky, M. (Eds.). (1981). *Uniform Performance Assessment System*. Columbus, OH: Merrill.

Harms, T. & Farthing, M. A. (1979). *Observation: Atmosphere and environment of an eating experience*. Chapel Hill: Frank Porter Graham Child Development Center, University of North Carolina.

Hayman, L. (1983). Nutritional assessment of handicapped preschoolers. *Topics in Early Childhood Special Education, 3*(2), 9–17.

Holder, L. & Cook, M. (no date). *Rural Infant Stimulation Environment: Developmental checklist and computerized curriculum*. Tuscaloosa: Area of Special Education, University of Alabama.

Holder, L., Wells, B., & Cook, M. (1985). *RISE: Computerized checklist and curriculum for the motorically delayed/impaired child*. Tuscaloosa: Area of Special Education, The University of Alabama.

Horner, R. H., Bellamy, G. T., & Colvin, G. T. (1984). Responding in the presence of nontrained stimuli: Implications of generalization error patterns. *Journal of the Association for Persons with Severe Handicaps, 9*, 287–295.

Inge, K. J. (1987). Atypical motor development and cerebral palsy. In F. P. Orelove & D. Sobsey (Eds.), *Educating children with multiple disabilities: A transdisciplinary approach* (pp. 43–65). Baltimore, MD: Paul H. Brookes.

Kohlenberg, R. J. (1973). Operant conditioning of human anal sphincter pressure. *Journal of Applied Behavior Analysis, 6*, 201–208.

Lance, W. D. & Koch, A. C. (1973). Parents as teachers: Self-help skills for young handicapped children. *Mental Retardation, 11*, 3–4.

LeMay, D. W., Griffin, P. M., & Sanford, A. R. (1977). *Learning Accomplishment Profile: Diagnostic edition (rev.)*. Chapel Hill, NC: Chapel Hill Training and Outreach Project.

Morris, S. E. (1982a). *The normal acquisition of oral feeding skills: Implications for assessment and treatment*. Central Islip, NY: Therapeutic Media.

Morris, S. E. (1982b). *Pre-speech Assessment Scale* (2nd ed.). Clifton, NJ: J. A. Preston.

Mueller, H. (1975). Feeding. In N. R. Finnie (Ed.), *Handling the young cerebral palsied child at home* (2nd ed.) (pp. 113–132). New York: E. P. Dutton.

Newborg, J., Stock, J. R., & Wnek, L. (1984). *Battelle Developmental Inventory*. Allen, TX: DLM Teaching Resources.

Orelove, F. P. & Sobsey, D. (Eds.). (1987). Mealtime skills. In F. P. Orelove & D. Sobsey (Eds.), *Educating children with multiple disabilities: A transdisciplinary approach* (pp. 219–252). Baltimore, MD: Paul H. Brookes.

Perske, R., Clifton, A., McLean, B. M., & Stein, J. I. (Eds.). (1977). *Mealtimes for severely and profoundly handicapped persons*. Baltimore, MD: University Park Press.

Pipes, P. L. (1981). Assessing food and nutrient intake. In M. L. Powell (Ed.), *Assessment and management of developmental changes and problems in children* (pp. 147–161). St. Louis: C. V. Mosby.

Powell, M. L. (Ed.). (1981). *Assessment and management of developmental changes and problems in children* (2nd ed.). St. Louis: C. V. Mosby.

Radtka, S. (1977). Feeding reflexes and neutral control. In J. M. Wilson (Ed.), *Oral-motor function and dysfunction in children* (pp. 96–105). Chapel Hill: University of North Carolina, Division of Physical Therapy.

Snell, M. E. (1980). Does toilet training belong in the public schools? A review of toilet training research. *Education Unlimited, 2*, 53–58.

Snell, M. E. (1987). Basic self-care instruction for students without motor impairments. In M. E. Snell (Ed.). *Systematic instruction of persons with severe handicaps* (3rd ed.) (pp. 334–389). Columbus, OH: Merrill.

Snell, M. E. & Beckman-Brindley, S. (1984). Family involvement in intervention with children having severe handicaps. *Journal of the Association for Persons with Severe Handicaps, 9*, 213–230.

Stratton, M. (1981). Behaviorial assessment scale of oral functions in feeding. *American Journal of Occupational Therapy, 35*(11), 719–721.

Tawney, J. W., Knapp, D. S., O'Reilly, C. D., & Pratt, S. S. (1979). *Programmed Environments Curriculum*. Columbus, OH: Merrill.

Tilton, J. R., Liska, D. C., & Bourland, J. C. (1977). *Guide to early developmental training*. Boston: Allyn & Bacon.

Utley, B. L., Holvoet, J. F., & Barnes, K. (1977). Handling, positioning and feeding the physically handicapped. In E. Sontag, J. Smith, & N. Certo (Eds.), *Educational programming for the severely and profoundly handicapped* (pp. 279–299). Reston, VA: Council for Exceptional Children.

Chapter 18

Using Assessment Information to Plan Instructional Programs

Mark Wolery
University of Kentucky

KEY TERMS

- Profile Analysis
- Function
- Form
- Long-term Goals

- Task Analysis
- Instructional Objectives
- Behavior
- Conditions

- Criterion
- Functional
- Criteria of the Next Educational Placement
- Social Validity

As defined in Chapter 1, *assessment* is the process of gathering information to make decisions, and there are a number of decisions for which assessment information can be used. For example, it can be used to identify children who need further assessment (screening), or to determine the nature and extent of disabilities and handicapping conditions (diagnosis), to determine eligibility for services, to identify the most appropriate placement, to identify goals and therapeutic and instructional strategies (instructional program planning), to evaluate the effects of the intervention program, and to monitor the effects of instructional programs. In the last seven chapters, the emphasis was placed on *collecting information* across different curricular domains; in this chapter, issues are described for *using that information* to plan instructional programs (i.e., develop Individualized Education Programs [IEPs] and Individualized Family Service Plans [IFSPs]).

Rationale for Linking Assessment Information and Instructional Program Planning

All instructional endeavors address, explicitly or implicitly, at least four major issues (Wolery & Gast, 1984). These are (a) identifying the content of the curriculum, (b) determining a match between the content and the learner's needs, (c) implementing changes in the environment to facilitate learner's acquisition of needed curriculum content, and (d) implementing procedures to facilitate fluency, maintenance, and generalization of acquired content. The content of the early childhood curriculum comes from two sources: the demands of the environments in which young children function and from normal development. Because environmental demands and normal development are such broad areas, the match between the needs of individual infants and children and the curriculum content is not obvious. To make this match, early interventionists use assessment activities. Assessments for instructional program planning should identify the following: Skills the child does independently; skills the child does with support, adaptation, or assistance; skills that the child does not do; instructional strategies that will be effective and efficient in teaching the infant or child; and variables that may influence the way intervention is implemented. Thus, the primary rationale for using assessment information to plan instructional programs is that it helps identify which environmental demands and which developmental skills are relevant instructional targets. Nearly all models of instruction and therapy include at least four major functions: assessment, program planning, program implementation, and monitoring/evaluation and program revision. Different models operationalize these four components differently or place greater emphasis on one over the other and break each into additional steps, but they include these four functions.

A basic assumption of these models is that each of these components is tied to the other: Assessment leads to program planning, program planning to program implementation, and program implementation to monitoring, evaluating, and revising the program.

In addition to using assessment information to identify what and how to teach, assessment information can be used to identify priorities for instruction. A thorough assessment of most infants and preschoolers with handicaps will identify numerous skills that could be taught. Some of these skills will be more important than others, and some will require more effort, some will require more time, and others can be learned later more quickly. Determining which skills will be taught involves value judgments by the team, including, of course, the parents. Nonetheless, information acquired during the assessment should be considered when making these judgments.

Using the results of assessment in planning instructional programs appears to be a logical and straightforward process; however, it is not as clear cut as it may seem. Early intervention teams must be competent in (a) writing reports of the assessment activities and results, (b) translating assessment information into instructional objectives, (c) translating instructional objectives into meaningful intervention plans, and (d) involving families in the process. Each of these competency areas is discussed in the remainder of this chapter.

Writing Reports from Instructional Program Planning Assessments

Writing assessment reports for instructional program planning is a skill that requires considerable work and practice. The written assessment report is a document from which instructional programs are derived, but it also serves other functions such as communicating with other team members and professionals, specifying the best estimation of a child's abilities at a given point in time, and as a record against which later performance can be compared. The report should be accurate, clear, objective, and detailed. Although numerous formats exist for writing assessment reports, some types of information are critical. (It should be noted that the information that follows is designed for instructional program planning assessments and not for screening reports, which would be briefer, or diagnostic reports, which have a different function.) Instructional program planning assessment reports should include identifying information about the child and the assessment, background information, methods of assessment, results of the assessment, and recommendations.

Identifying Information

This section gives a reader information about who was assessed, who conducted the assessment, and when and where it occurred. The section should appear first in the written report and include the child's full name; agency/client number, if applicable; and important demographic information (e.g., age; sex; date of birth; current placement, if any; diagnosis). It also should include the parents' names and addresses. The person who initiated the referral and the reason for the referral should be noted, the assessor's name and title, the setting in which the assessment occurred, dates of the assessment activities, and reference citation of tests that were used.

Background Information

This section provides historical information about the child; it should be a relatively brief, narrative summary. For diagnostic assessment reports, this section may be much more comprehensive. Three things should be addressed in this section: the child's birth and

medical history, developmental history, and educational experiences. The source of the information also should be noted in this section; for example, parental interviews or review of records. The birth and medical history section should identify whether the pregnancy was difficult and what complications, if any, occurred. It describes whether the birth was full-term or premature, whether it was characterized by any unusual events and what they were, and whether the child has a history of any medical treatment and the nature of that treatment. The developmental history should describe the age at which the child achieved important developmental milestones, and when, if appropriate, the parent suspected that difficulties may exist. The educational history section should be a record of the child's intervention contacts since birth. It should include a listing and brief description of the services the child has received.

Methods

This section should be written in narrative form and should include several subsections. The *tests and scales* used during the assessment should be listed; when they were administered and by whom should be recorded; and the purpose of each should be described. The *observational* procedures should be described in terms of who conducted observations, when and where they occurred, and what domains were observed. When the setting of observations is described, it should include a brief description of how many children were present, and so on, to give a flavor for the context in which it occurred. *Interviews* with others should be described in terms of who was interviewed and their relationship to the child, who conducted the interview, and the topic of the interview. Finally, any *environmental assessments* would be described including which environments were assessed, what measures were used, when it occurred, who conducted it, and the purpose of the assessment.

Results of Assessment Activities

This section can be the most difficult to write, and considerable care should be taken to describe the following information: skills the child does independently; skills the child does with support, adaptation, and assistance; the type of assistance, support, and adaptation needed; skills the child does not have; variables that may influence how intervention is designed; stimuli that appear to hold reinforcing value; and results of using, even briefly, any instructional or therapeutic strategies. When describing children's performance, the conditions under which it occurred or did not occur should be listed. For example, saying the "child requested cookies" is inadequate because several questions remain, such as, what was occurring when she requested the cookie, had she already eaten a cookie, were cookies visible? Describing the conditions allows a more complete and meaningful picture of the child's performance to be presented. Generally, this section should be organized by curricular area. Tables that list the three types of skills (independent, supported, did-not-do) can be included, but the conditions must be written on the tables if they are to be useful. As noted earlier, this must be an accurate, objective description of the child's performance; inferences should not be included here or should be indentified as such.

Recommendations

This section should summarize the primary abilities of the child and the areas of need. It also should include suggestions about (a) the need for additional assessment activities, (b) potential long-term goals, (c) potential intervention strategies, and (d) a listing of any variables that would influence how the intervention should be implemented.

When writing assessment reports, interventionists should write to communicate with multiple audiences including their team members, the child's parents, professionals to whom the child might be referred, and future caregivers. This requires use of clear, objective, jargon-free prose. Further, reports should be written sensitively, because they will be available to family members. This does not mean that the hard issues should be ignored but that the conclusions should be described, qualified, and supported by the information gathered in the assessment activities. Finally, clear delineation of facts from assumptions should be made. Both may be included, but assumptions should be labeled as such.

Translating Assessment Information into Instructional Objectives

Assessment results are translated into instructional programs by a systematic process of analyzing assessment results, specifying long-term goals, breaking those goals into teaching sequences through task analysis, writing instructional objectives, and translating instructional objectives into instructional reality. These steps are described in the following sections.

Analyzing Assessment Results

Analyzing information collected from assessments for instructional program planning requires appropriate interpretation of data from multiple measurement strategies (tests, observations, and interviews) and from multiple sources (child's behavior, parents' perceptions, other professionals' veiws). It is assumed that information collected from multiple disciplines would be considered when analyzing the information from any one discipline. Three issues are discussed here: profile analysis, teaching to the test, and the form-function issue.

Profile Analysis. **Profile analysis** is a method of analyzing test results in which the scores of an infant or child are compared across various subscales of a scale or test. Profile analysis is one of the first steps in analyzing test results. Many tests of child behavior and structured interview instruments include procedures and forms for completing profiles. The profile provides a pictorial representation of children's relative strengths and weaknesses in different areas. This information is helpful in communicating the results to family members and other professionals. The profile also is helpful in setting instructional priorities. A sample profile from Dunst's (1980) extention of the Uzgiris and Hunt Ordinal Scales of Psychological Development (1975) is shown in Figure 18.1. As can be seen, the child depicted in this profile shows fairly even performance of all sensorimotor skills except for the area of vocal and gestural imitation. Based on this profile, it would appear that imitation would be an intervention target of high priority.

An inherent assumption of profile analysis is that a child's performance should be conceptualized in terms of strengths and weaknesses. While this is a popularly held notion, it carries some liabilities. Perhaps the greatest liability is the practice of assuming that weaknesses should be the sole target of intervention and that strengths should be allowed to continue to develop. However, as noted throughout this text, a child's performance in one area is closely related to his performance in other areas. Lack of social skills and communication skills are related, motor skills clearly influence self-care skills, and some behaviors are simultaneously motor, cognitive, communicative, and social. Thus, with few exceptions, infants and young children with handicaps will need intervention in almost all developmental areas and across most domains within each area. For this reason, emphasis has been placed in this chapter on determining what children do, do with support, do not do, and need to learn to do rather than on identifying their strengths and weaknesses. Profile analysis, then, is a means of indentifying the relative priority that should be given to skills rather than a

means of excluding particular content from instruction.

Teaching to the Test. The question, "Should we teach to the test?" will prompt many emphatic responses. In some cases, such as screening and diagnostic tests, the answer is definitely no. In reality, the question is stated inappropriately and should be, "Should we teach from test results?" The answer to this question clearly is yes; there is no other reason to conduct assessments for instructional program planning than to use the results for planning the targets and methods of instruction. However, there are several inappropriate ways to use test results. For example, a common practice is to assess children with criterion- or curriculum-referenced tests, identify all the skills a child can do in each domain, and then target the first items the child failed as the primary instructional objectives. This practice is inappropriate for several reasons: (a) Many of the criterion-referenced tests have items that were not developed as instructional items; (b) adjacent items on many tests are not related to the same skill; (c) the sequences of items on many tests may not be the best teaching sequences, especially for children with sensory and motor disabilities; and (d) many of the sequences may have large gaps between items. Furthermore, this practice does not take into account prerequisite skills needed for some skills and the relationships of skills in one developmental area to those of another.

Appropriate use of test results involves asking many questions, some of which are:

1. What is the intent of the items the child failed, or what are these items designed to measure?
2. Are these intents important developmental constructs or skills that the child should acquire?
3. Why did the child fail these items, and what does that say about the child's

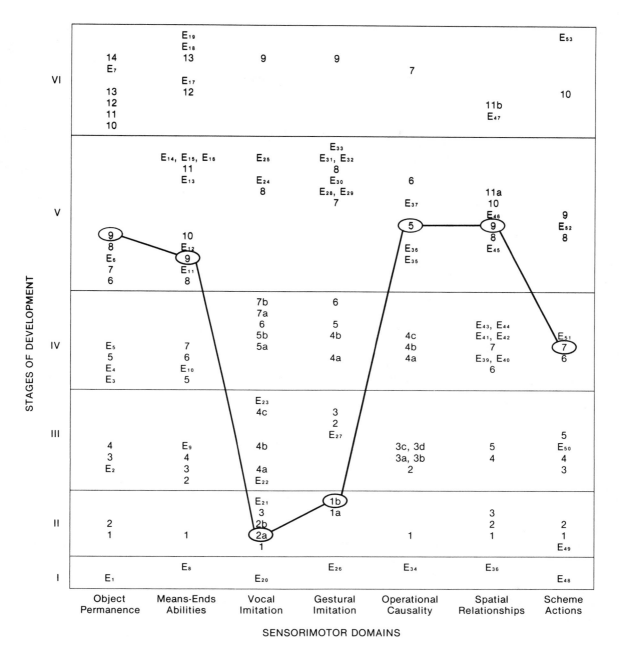

FIGURE 18.1
Profile showing a child's performance on an assessment of sensorimotor functioning (Source:
From A Clinical and Educational Manual for Use with the Uzgiris and Hunt Scales of Infant
Psychological Development (p. 45). by C. J. Dunst. Copyright 1980 by Pro-Ed. Used with per-
mission.)

overall competence in this and other areas?

4. Why are these skills important to this individual infant or child?

5. Does the infant or child need this skill to be more independent in the environments in which she functions or will soon be expected to function?

6. What are the prerequisite behaviors for performing this skill, and does the child have those prerequisites?

7. How does performance on this skill relate to other domains within this or other developmental areas?

8. Is this skill an important prerequisite to other skills?

9. Should the focus of this skill be on acquisition, fluency, maintenance, or generalization?

Answers to these and other related questions allow teams to make appropriate decisions based on assessment results. Clearly, the process is much more complex than simply teaching the next item from a test.

Form vs. Function.   Many important skills for infants and young children can be performed by multiple behaviors. For example, initiating social interactions can be performed by speaking to other people, touching them, giving a toy, or making eye contact and looking "expectantly." Frequently, the more important issue is whether children can get social interactions started rather than the precise behaviors they use to do so. This conflict between behavior and effect of behavior has been characterized by White (1980) as the form-vs.-function issue. The **function** is the effect or the results of a behavior, and the **form** is the actual behavior used. Every behavior theoretically has some effect or function, and every function or effect is actualized by some behavior. In some objectives, the function is critical and the form is less important, as in the case with initiating social interactions, social play, or making requests.

In other cases, the form used also is important. For example, to be socially acceptable, children cannot eat by placing their faces in their plates or by using their fingers with all foods. Thus, for each objective, the team should ask themselves, "What is really important with this skill? Is it the effect, the behavior(s) needed to obtain the effect, or both?"

Neel, Billingsley, McCarty, Symonds, Lambert, Lewis-Smith, and Hanashiro (1983) suggest that assessment information should address form and function, and the results should be analyzed in terms of both. They present several potential combinations that would lead to very different intervention procedures. For example, if a child's social interaction skills were analyzed, at least four functions could be identified: initiating interactions, responding to others' initiations, sustaining the interaction, and terminating the interaction. Many behaviors could be used with each of these functions. The potential combinations and resulting focus of intervention are listed in Table 18.1. By analyzing the child's performance in terms of forms and functions in each domain or activity, meaningful skills can be targeted and intervention initiated.

Establishing Long-term Objectives

Long-term goals are statements of learning outcomes that are expected over the course of several months or a year. Public Law 94-142 and P.L. 99-457 require that IEP/IFSPs contain annual goals. These goals should come directly from the analysis of assessment results and serve as a general guide for the instruction. Long-term goals frequently are written in a general way, such as "Ashley will learn to feed herself." More specificity, however, is desirable; for example, "Ashley will use a spoon to feed herself" or "Ashley will use a spoon and fork to feed herself table food without spilling for three consecutive meals." The specificity in the goals allows for

TABLE 18.1
Potential Combinations of Form and Function and Resulting Intervention Focus

Forms	Function	Potential Intervention Focus
Adequate	Multiple	Continue monitoring child's performance
Adequate	Limited	Teach new functions using existing forms and promote maintenance of existing functions
Limited	Multiple	Teach new forms for existing functions and promote maintenance of existing forms
Limited	Limited	Teach new functions with existing forms and teach new forms with existing functions
No identifiable form	No identifiable function	Teach new forms and new functions

better communication with others about the intent of instruction and makes it easier to translate the goal into instructional objectives. Ideally, goals should specify who will do the learning (Ashley), the behavior that will be learned (using a spoon), the conditions under which learning will be measured (with table food), and the criterion (three meals without spilling).

Public Law 94-142 requires review of long-term objectives annually, and P.L. 99-457 requires review every six months. In reality, review of goals should occur more frequently, such as monthly or quarterly. The number of goals that are established for each child should vary, and a balance should be found between addressing needs comprehensively and establishing realistic outcomes. Little is gained by establishing goals for which no instruction will be possible.

Task Analysis

Task analysis is a *process* by which large goals are broken into smaller objectives and sequenced for instruction. Task analysis also is a *product;* the written result from conducting a task analysis is a product called a *task*

analysis. This product is a list of short-term objectives that lead directly from the child's current level of performance to the long-term objective. It is not a set of teaching procedures or a set of activities; rather it is a list of child behaviors that lead to the more advanced behavior in the long-term objective.

Task analysis is a fundamental means of analyzing (into smaller units) curriculum content that is too large to be learned at once. Conducting task analyses is an important teacher competency and may be related to the amount children learn (Fredericks, Anderson, & Baldwin, 1979). The steps for conducting task analyses are straightforward; Wolery, Bailey, and Sugai (1988) present five.

Step 1: Specify the Long-term Objective and Look for Related Sources. The objective to be task analyzed should be specified precisely. The teacher should then look to various curricular guides for information concerning this objective. Over the past 20 years, hundreds of task analyses have been written, and many of them are found in curricula and other texts on teaching children with handicaps. While task analysis is a method for individualizing curriculum content, there is little need to write new task analyses for skills that already have been analyzed by someone else. However, teachers need the skill of analyzing objectives because published task analyses may not be available or may not be successful with a particular child on an important objective. In most cases, skills can be analyzed in a number of sequences. No one task analysis is necessarily correct, and the interventionist should attempt to find the one best suited to the child's learning patterns.

Thiagarajan (1980) has described a procedure for adapting previously written task analyses for individual children. This involves making adjustments in the entry point into a sequence of steps, adjusting the size of the steps (making them larger or smaller), adjusting the assistance children need to perform different steps, and adjusting the behaviors by which children show they have acquired the content of the task analysis.

Step 2: Break the Long-term Objective into Steps or Break the Behavior into Smaller Behaviors. At this point in the process, the teacher is not concerned with how to teach the skill or how many steps are involved in the task analysis. Rather, teachers should attempt to break the skill into a few meaningful behaviors. Several means exist for doing this.

First, find a person who can do the behavior competently, watch her do it, and write down the behaviors she does. Depending upon the complexity of the task being analyzed, the teacher may have to watch the person do the skill several times to identify all of the small subtle behaviors involved. Competent performers do skills quickly, and the teacher may have to ask the person to do the behavior more slowly. Second, the teacher can do the behavior himself and write down the steps as they are done. Again, several repetitions may be needed, and doing the task slowly may be of benefit. These two methods

are particularly useful for task analyzing skills that are composed of chains of motor responses such as playing with certain toys, dressing/ undressing, self-feeding, and riding a tricycle.

The two methods just described are not very useful for analyzing skills such as making a greeting response, matching shapes, or naming the letters of the alphabet. For such skills, teachers should use a third method: logical analysis. With logical analysis, teachers "think through tasks" to identify the behaviors and discriminations needed to perform the skill correctly. For example, a logical analysis of naming objectives would involve visual discrimination of the target objects from other similar objects, "matching" the object to the correct name from the infinite number of possible names, and then accurately saying the name.

Fourth, teachers can identify and use the sequences through which typical children acquire a given skill. The assumption of this method is that children learn complex behaviors sequentially starting with the simplest behaviors and progressively moving toward more difficult responses. Thus, teachers merely determine the course through which a skill is acquired normally, and write down the steps. Cohen and Gross (1979a, 1979b) described numerous sequences using this method across a number of different curricular domains. This method will be inappropriate when the identified sequences are impossible for the child to do because of her handicapping conditions.

Fifth, teachers can use a levels-of-assistance approach to breaking skills into steps. The process involves specifying the different amounts of help that a child might need at various points in learning a specific skill. For example, if a child can perform the target skill only when given a physical prompt, the steps of the task analysis might include doing it in response to partial physical prompts, a full model, a partial model, and without assistance. A similar approach is to increase the complexity of the conditions in which the child performs a skill. For example, if a child currently will greet one teacher, then the steps of the task analysis might specify a number of different people and situations in which a greeting response is appropriate. This method is particularly useful when analyzing generalization tasks. When using this method, all the possible situations in which the behavior might be needed should be listed.

Step 3: Eliminate Unnecessary and Redundant Behaviors. When skills are task analyzed, some unnecessary steps may be listed. In such cases, they should be eliminated in the written task analysis. Likewise, if the same behavior occurs several times, it should be listed only once.

Step 4: Sequence the Steps for Teaching. After listing behaviors and eliminating unnecessary and redundant steps, the remaining behaviors should be sequenced for teaching. There are two primary methods for sequencing skills for teaching. These methods include sequencing by temporal order and sequencing by difficulty. *Temporal order* means listing the steps in the sequence in which they will be performed when the skill is completely learned. This is a particularly useful method for chained skills (e.g., putting on clothing, brushing teeth) or for behaviors that occur during large routines (e.g., preparing to go home, mealtime routines). Because it is desirable to teach such skills during naturally occurring routines, specifying the skills to be learned in temporal order is helpful. Sequencing by *difficulty* is more useful with responses that do not occur in chains or larger routines. When sequencing by difficulty teachers must consider the difficulty in actually producing each response and the difficulty of the discriminations associated with those responses. When skills are broken into different behaviors using the levels-of-

assistance method, sequencing by difficulty can be easily accomplished.

Step 5: Specify Prerequisite Behaviors. Most task analyses include some behaviors that must be acquired before the easiest step of the task analysis can be performed. If the target child cannot perform the prerequisite behaviors, then instruction should be delayed on the task analysis until the prerequisite behaviors are acquired.

These five steps have been used repeatedly and successfully to develop task analyses of skills across different types of content. To decrease the effort expended in teaching, teachers should retain copies of successful task analyses. If a task analysis was successful with one child, it may well apply to another. Therefore, teachers should compile a task-analysis "bank." Also, teachers who use task analysis frequently begin to have several different task analysis patterns into which they can fit similar content. For example, to name pictures of common objects, the steps of the task analysis might be (a) to imitate verbally the name of the picture, (b) to match the picture to an identical picture in the presence of three distractors, (c) to identify receptively the picture when given the name, and (d) to identify the picture verbally. This structure of verbal imitation, matching, receptive identification, and expressive labeling could fit other areas, such as naming objects, naming letters of the alphabet, reading sight words, and naming numerals. When teachers are aware of these task-analysis patterns, then writing new task analyses can be accomplished quickly.

Writing Instructional Objectives
Several sources have described procedures for writing instructional objectives (Mager, 1962; Wolery et al., 1988; Vargas, 1972). Writing **instructional objectives** involves specifying the behaviors to be performed, identifying the conditions under which performance will be

measured, and identifying the level (criterion) at which the behavior must be performed before it is said to have been learned. Objectives should be written because they are required by P.L. 94-142, provide a focus for instruction, are a standard against which progress can be monitored, and can be used to communicate information to others.

As described in Chapter 4, a **behavior** is a movement, has a beginning and end, is repeatable, and can be measured reliably by two or more individuals. Also, behaviors have a variety of dimensions, such as their accuracy, rate, latency, duration, and intensity. Teams must identify the most appropriate dimension when writing objectives. Furthermore, they must identify whether the function or the form of the skill is more important. As described earlier, the form may be important with some objectives, but function may be more important with others. When function is identified, then a list of appropriate forms should be generated.

Conditions in instructional objectives refer to the materials, task directions, and situations in which the behavior must be performed. Careful specification of the conditions allows for consistent measurement of the effects of the instruction. When specifying conditions, those that will exist in the generalization setting should appear in the objective or a separate generalization objective should be written.

Criterion statements in objectives tell how well the child must perform the skill. Criterion statements serve several functions: (a) They set a goal toward which teachers, families, and children can work; (b) they tell the teacher when to move on to other skills; and (c) they provide a standard against which progress can be monitored. Too often the criterion portion of objectives is written without sufficient thought. Because of the important functions that criterion statements serve, they should be written with care. Consideration should be given to several issues. The dimension (accuracy, rate,

combination of accuracy and rate, duration, etc.) of behavior that is most important should be measured. This may change as instruction progresses. For example, initial focus may be on accuracy, and as it is established, the focus may switch to a combination of rate and accuracy. Consideration also should be given to how well the behavior must be performed before it will be useful to the child. This ability can be determined by measuring how well children who competently perform the behavior do it. An average of this measurement can then be used in the criterion statement. For example, the teacher could measure how long it takes typical children to brush their teeth, calculate an average time, and use that interval in the criterion statement for a target child. Consideration should be given to identifying the minimum level that will result in enjoyment of the skill or the minimum level needed to move on to the next skill or environment. Consideration also should be given to the form in which the criterion is written. If percentage is written into the criterion statement, then the number of opportunities on which the percentage is calculated also should be listed. For example, 100% could be one correct response out of one opportunity, or 10 out of 10, or 100 out of 100. When writing the criterion statements, teachers should always check them and ask, "What does this really mean?"

Writing Worthwhile Objectives

Many objections to writing objectives have been proposed, and one is that objectives are so precise that the result is trivial or meaningless. Unfortunately, examples of such objectives probably could be found readily. However, considering several issues will help avoid this possibility, and these considerations are described in the following sections.

Functional and Age-appropriate Objectives. **Functional,** as used here, refers to the immediate usefulness of a skill. Usefulness can have at least four distinct meanings in early intervention programs. First, the behavior should result in increased independence for the child, or the behavior should produce a needed effect for the child. To determine whether a behavior produces increased independence or a desired effect, the environment in which it is performed must be analyzed. The same skill for two different children may result in increased independence for one but not the other. For example, Jerry and Kim both learned to put on their coats without assistance. Jerry's family now expects and allows him to put on his coat each morning. As a result, his independence was increased and the skill was functional. Kim's family, however, continues to help her with the coat; therefore, the skill is not functional because it does not produce increased independence.

Second, some skills do not result in increased independence but allow the child to learn other more complex or advanced skills that will make the child more developmentally advanced or more independent. Thus, the skill is functional. For example, a student who learns to imitate can learn many new skills by observing and copying the behavior of others. Imitation does not, in and of itself, result in more independent functioning, but it does allow many skills to be learned that are more developmentally advanced or could result in greater independence.

Third, skills are functional if they allow a child to be placed in either a less restrictive environment, or more desirable environment, or allow the child to be more socially acceptable to others in those settings. Vincent, Salisbury, Walter, Brown, Gruenwald, and Powers (1980) refer to this characteristic as the **criteria of the next educational environment.** They suggest that these skills can be identified by (a) having brief try-out placements in the new setting, (b) analyzing the success of previous graduates from the child's current program who were enrolled in

the target placement, (c) asking caregivers in the next environment to list "survival skills," and (d) observing children who currently are enrolled in the target placement.

Fourth, in some cases an objective would be considered functional if it resulted in the child being more easily managed by his family and other caregivers. Many behavior problems result in increased stress and caregiving demands on families; teaching children more appropriate ways to respond may result in decreased stress and caregiving responsibilities. Similarly, when a child learns a response such as cooperating with dressing, lip closure during feeding, or toileting in the bathroom, she becomes more manageable for her family. In such cases, these behaviors would be useful.

Socially Valid Objectives. **Social validity** refers to the value or worth that others place on the goals, procedures, and effects of intervention programs (Wolf, 1978). The value placed on potential objectives by parents and caregivers in future environments should be assessed before objectives are selected for instruction. The social validity of objectives can be determined by asking parents to identify skills they want the child to learn, to rate which of several objectives are most important, or to provide reasons for wanting or not wanting a skill to be learned.

Realistic and Achievable Objectives. Because assessment activities and procedures for establishing learning outcomes are imperfect, the possibility exists that any objective could be either too easy or too difficult. Objectives are likely to be more realistic if the assessment activities take place in natural situations, occur over time, and involve familiar adults when testing is used and when assessment results are validated. Further, considering past performance patterns on similar skills may provide information on the realism of an objective. While achievable objectives should be set, the objectives also should be challenging. Some evidence suggests that for mildly handicapped school-aged children, achievement is greater when the objectives were more "ambitious" (Fuchs, Fuchs, & Deno, 1985). Clearly, a balance needs to be established between realistic and challenging objectives.

Frequent monitoring, using the procedures described in Chapter 4, will allow teachers to identify whether objectives are being met. Application of data-decision rules will allow the teacher to determine whether the intervention strategies should be altered, easier skills should be targeted, or more difficult skills should be taught (Haring, White, & Liberty, 1980; Wolery et al., 1988). Thus, assessment of learner performance is important in setting objectives that can be achieved and determining whether achievement actually occurs.

Objectives to Address All Phases of Learning and Higher-level Skills. A child's performance can be conceptualized as progressing through five phases: acquisition, fluency, maintenance, generalization, and adaptation (Haring et al., 1980). Acquisition is the first phase and refers to learning the basic requirements of a skill. Frequently, objectives that target acquisition focus on the accuracy of a response. The second phase of learning is fluency or proficiency and refers to how quickly or smoothly the child performs skills. Fluency objectives frequently have rate or duration-per-occurrence measures in the criterion statements. Maintenance refers to continued performance of a skill in conditions similar to training. Generalization refers to performance of acquired skills in situations other than the instructional conditions. For example, children need to apply skills when other people are present, in other settings, and with other materials; Billingsley (1984) analyzed IEPs of students with severe handicaps and found that few objectives targeted generalization of skills. Adaptation refers to the child's ability to modify the skill to per-

form it when the conditions in which it is needed change. A good rule of thumb is that no objective should be considered mastered until (a) it is performed fluently and over time for the person who taught it in the situation where it was taught, (b) when it is performed for some other individual at a needed time in a situation different from the instructional setting, and (c) when it is performed spontaneously when needed in a situation other than the instructional environment.

In addition to establishing, teaching, and monitoring objectives for each phase of learning, it is important to note that objectives have been taught for such high-level skills as creativity. Bloom's taxonomy (Bloom, Englehart, Furst, Hill, & Krathwohl, 1956) of learning outcomes has been used as a framework for writing objectives for levels of learning such as knowledge, comprehension, application, analysis, synthesis, and evaluation (cf., Bailey & Leonard, 1977; Vargas, 1972; Wolery et al., 1988).

Translating Instructional Objectives into Instructional Realities

After instructional objectives have been written, several steps remain before instruction can be implemented. First, the objectives should be analyzed to determine which are most important; importance here refers to the social validity of the objectives from the family's perspective and from the team's view. Ideally, priority objectives will be those that will result in maximal independence and in greater developmental progress. Second, high-priority objectives should be scheduled for instruction; this issue is discussed later. Third, the persons and resources needed to teach the objectives should be identified. Fourth, instructional strategies should be identified. In the past 20 years, considerable research on instruction with children who have handicapping conditions has occurred, and several instructional strategies have been developed and refined (cf. Halle, Alpert, & Anderson, 1984; Haring, Neetz, Lovinger, Peck, & Semmel, 1987; Wolery et al., 1988). Fifth, measurement procedures should be devised for monitoring progress on objectives. Monitoring progress almost always involves using direct observation (see Chapter 4).

Scheduling and Planning Objectives for Instruction

In the past, when objectives were identified, a time was scheduled for instruction, and teaching began. However, failure to obtain generalization of skills suggests that this isolated instructional approach is less than optimal. As a result, more attention has been given to when and how instruction is provided. Five general guidelines are discussed in this section.

Embed Instruction from Different Curricular Domains into the Same Activity or Routine. In this text, assessment procedures for cognitive, motor, social, communicative, and self-care skills have been described separately from one another. This organization allows individuals to understand the unique aspects of each skill and serves as a useful framework for remembering information about various skills. However, it should be noted that this organization may communicate unintentionally that the domains are entirely separate entities. In reality, even the simplest behaviors from each of these domains may involve components from the other domains. For example, saying and waving good-bye seems to be a communication skill, but speaking involves oral motor movements and waving involves a gross motor movement; recognizing when it is appropriate to say good-bye is a subtle cognitive discrimination and demonstrates social awareness. Thus, various target objectives from each domain are, in reality, skills that

are influenced by multiple domains. Kaczmarek (1982) provides a model for integrating communication objectives into motor activities. This model can be expanded to address other domains as well.

Embed Instruction into Naturally Occurring Routines When Appropriate. As noted throughout this text, many of the skills infants and preschoolers need are performed in routines. As much as possible, instruction should be provided on targeted objectives during those routines. For example, social interactions should be taught during play routines, self-feeding skills should be taught when children are hungry and during mealtime routines, and communication skills should be taught during times and routines where they will be used such as play, mealtime, and arrival/departure routines. Teaching in routines requires knowledge of the settings in which instruction will occur, may require modification of those settings, and requires use of special monitoring procedures (cf., Brown, 1987; Neel et al., 1983). In programs where parents are the primary interventionists (e.g., home-based programs or parent-consultation models), scheduling instruction so that it will fit into the daily routines of the home is critical. It probably increases the likelihood that the activities will be implemented, and it requires less effort than having parents conduct structured instructional sessions. Joint planning with parents will help identify routines that can be used for instruction of high-priority objectives.

Embed Instruction into Child-directed Activities Using Naturalistic Teaching Strategies. Embedding instruction into child-directed activities holds several advantages. First, preschool programs for typical children frequently spend considerable portions of the day in activities that are child-directed as compared to one-on-one or small-group, teacher-directed instruction. Preschoolers with handicapping conditions need to be able to function in such environments if they are to be integrated successfully. Second, child-directed activities allow children to make choices and learn the natural consequences of those choices. Third, child-directed activities allow families and teachers to attend to other responsibilities while the child is engaged in a meaningful activity. Several strategies have been devised for teaching in child-directed routines. These include incidental teaching, the mand-model procedure, naturalistic time delay, and their modifications (Halle et al., 1984; Haring et al., 1987). These procedures have been effective in teaching communication skills to a wide variety of children and may have application to social (cf., Charlop & Walsh, 1986) and cognitive skills as well. These procedures also can be used by families.

Distribute Teaching Opportunities throughout the Instructional Day.   Sailor and Guess (1983) describe the individualized-curriculum-sequencing model. This model involves teaching functional skills using distributed-trial formats and concurrent-task presentations. Essentially, trials on the same behavior are presented throughout the day, and trials on different skills are presented in close proximity to one another. This model allows instruction to be embedded into routines, occur during natural times, and address multiple domains within the same instructional activity.

Consider Current Skills When Planning Instructional Programs.   An old adage is, "Teaching must begin where the child is." This general guideline can be implemented by two related principles: First, use old forms to teach new functions; and second, use old functions to teach new forms. These principles are seen when children learning new semantic functions use words that were already in their vocabulary. For example, say a certain child currently expresses his ownership of objects by acting as though they were his (e.g., gets his own coat) and through one-word statements. However, he does not appear to demonstrate that the others may also own objects. If the teacher wanted to teach the child that other people could own objects, then the best approach would be to have the child express that ownership through an old form (i.e., one-word statements) rather than through a new form (i.e., two-word statements). The rule of teaching new functions by using old forms also applies to other areas. For example, if a child puts toys in her mouth to explore them (old form), then teaching the child to finger-feed would be appropriate (new function). Similarly, if a child uses the giving of toys to start social interactions and the taking of toys to respond to others' initiations, then transfer of toys (old form) may be used to teach sustaining interactions (new function). Or if the child uses pulling to activate a toy, then pulling can be used to activate another toy.

The second principle (using old functions to teach new forms) can be illustrated with the child described previously who used a one-word statement to describe ownership. Suppose a team chose to teach two-word statements, then using an existing function (i.e., personal ownership) to teach this skill is appropriate. For example, the team should teach the child two-word statements such as "my cup" or "my toy" because he already demonstrates the function of personal ownership. Thus, a new form (two words) is being taught with an old function (personal ownership). Both of these principles have applications across curricular domains. If a child initiates social interactions by giving toys, then teaching a new form (e.g., vocalizing) to do the same function (start interactions) is appropriate.

Involving the Parent in Using Assessment Information

Parental involvement in relation to assessment activities addresses three issues: their rights in relation to assessment, their participation in assessment activities, and their participation in planning intervention. Parents have distinct rights in relation to assessment activities. For example, under P. L. 94-142 and P. L. 99-457, parents must provide informed consent for the measures to be implemented, they must be allowed to participate in the assessment activities, they may seek assessments from an outside agency, and they have a right to understand what the assessment results mean. Two comments about parents' rights are noteworthy. First, parents frequently are not aware of their rights. This fact is particularly true of parents of infants or young children. Thus, the early intervention team must teach parents about their rights and how to exercise them appropriately. Second, in many cases, parents' rights are met in the letter rather than the intent of the law. In other words, parents are given notice that their child will be assessed and given a list of their rights in relation to that assessment. However, they are not fully informed of the options that are available, and their understanding of those options and the protection they receive if they exercise those options are not fully described. Thus, teams have a responsibility to inform parents of their rights and to ensure that they understand what those rights are and how to exercise them.

Beyond compliance with the law, parents should be involved in the assessment activities at a number of levels. When their consent for assessment is sought, the interventionists should be sure the parents understand the purpose of the measurement activities. Furthermore, the interventionists should provide information relevant to that purpose. When the purpose is instructional program planning, parents serve several useful functions: (a) They can provide information about their child's skills; (b) collect additional information on skills when appropriate; (c) validate the assessment results from other sources; and (d) participate in decisions based on the results. Involving parents in each of these steps increases the likelihood that they will

perceive themselves as partners with professionals in the intervention provided to their child. Brinckerhoff and Vincent (1986) compared the involvement of two groups of families in their children's IEP meetings. The control group simply received a letter telling when their child's IEP would occur. The experimental group (a) completed an assessment of their children's current developmental status, (b) provided information on their family, and (c) participated in a meeting that described the purpose of IEPs, listed participants in the IEP meeting, described roles of various persons in the meeting, and indicated how assessment data would be used to develop the IEP. The parents in the experimental group made more contributions to the meeting, generated more goals, and made more decisions about their children's instructional program.

Finally, family involvement in intervention program planning should be facilitated. Bailey (1987) suggests that five practices by interventionists can facilitate collaborative goal-setting between families and interventionists. These include (a) viewing the family as a functioning system within a society of systems, (b) assessing family needs and attempting to establish goals and interventions that accommodate those needs (cf., Bailey et al., 1986; Bailey & Simeonsson, 1988), (c) employing effective interviewing and listening skills throughout the assessment and while planning intervention, (d) negotiating goals and interventions because of potentially different values, and (e) filling the case-management role for families by helping them secure the services they need. In addition to these practices, interventionists can set the tone of cooperation and joint decision-making by preparing families for meetings and for acting on information. This may involve providing them with information about the decisions to be made prior to meetings and the options available to them, the manner in which meetings will be conducted, and conducting meetings at times and places convenient for them. Also, during interactions with families, interventionists should seek their input actively, ask for their judgment about priorities, listen to their responses, give them time to respond, and attend to their concerns. Finally, meaningful participation in program planning will occur only when interventionists clearly communicate that the decisions made will be reviewed and are open to revision.

SUMMARY OF KEY CONCEPTS

- Assessment results are used to identify skills needed by infants and preschoolers, identify intervention strategies, and identify instructional priorities.

- To use assessment results, teams must be skilled in writing clear, accurate, and objective assessment reports.

- To use assessment results teams should have competence in analyzing assessment results, establishing long-term objectives, conducting task analyses, writing short-term objectives, and translating objectives into instructional realities.

- Appropriate use of assessment results requires involving parents throughout the assessment process, attending to and teaching them about their rights, and involving them in decisions made on the assessment results.

REFERENCES

Bailey, D. B. (1987). Collaborative goal-setting with families: Resolving differences in values and priorities for service. *Topics in Early Childhood Special Education, 7*(2), 59–71.

Bailey, D. B. & Leonard, J. L. (1977). A model for adapting Bloom's taxonomy to a preschool curriculum. *Gifted Child Quarterly, 21*, 97–103.

Bailey, D. B. & Simeonsson, R. J. (1988). *Family assessment in early intervention.* Columbus, OH: Merrill.

Bailey, D. B., Simeonsson, R. J., Winton, P. J., Huntington, G. S., Comfort, M., Isbell, P., O'Donnell, K. J., & Helm, J. M. (1986). Family-focused intervention: A functional model for planning, implementing, and evaluating individualized family services in early intervention. *Journal of the Division for Early Childhood, 10*, 156–171.

Billingsley, F. F. (1984). Where are the generalization outcomes? (An examination of instructional objectives). *Journal of the Association for the Severely Handicapped, 9*, 186–200.

Bloom, B. S., Englehart, M. D., Furst, E. J., Hill, W. H., & Krathwohl, D. R. (1956). *A taxonomy of educational objectives: Handbook I, the cognitive domain.* New York: McKay.

Brinckerhoff, J. L. & Vincent, L. J. (1986). Increasing parental decision making at the individualized educational program meeting. *Journal of the Division for Early Childhood, 11*(1), 46–58.

Brown, F. (1987). Meaningful assessment of people with severe and profound handicaps. In M. E. Snell (Ed.), *Systematic instruction of persons with severe handicaps* (3rd ed.) (pp. 39–63). Columbus, OH: Merrill.

Charlop, M. H. & Walsh, M. E. (1986). Increasing autistic children's spontaneous verbalizations of affection: An assessment of time delay and peer modeling procedures. *Journal of Applied Behavior Analysis, 19*, 307–314.

Cohen, M. & Gross, P. (1979a). *The developmental resource: Behavioral sequences for assessment and program planning (Vol. 1)*. New York: Grune & Stratton.

Cohen, M. & Gross, P. (1979b). *The developmental resource: Behavioral sequences for assessment and program planning (Vol. 2)*. New York: Grune & Stratton.

Dunst, C. J. (1980). *A clinical and educational manual for use with the Uzgiris and Hunt Scales of Infant Psychological Development*. Baltimore, MD: University Park Press.

Fredericks, H. D., Anderson, R., & Baldwin, V. (1979). The identification of competency indicators of teaching of the severely handicapped. *American Association for the Education of the Severely and Profoundly Handicapped Review, 4,* 81–95.

Fuchs, L. S., Fuchs, D., & Deno, S. L. (1985). Importance of goal ambitiousness and goal mastery to student achievement. *Exceptional Children, 52,* 63–71.

Halle, J. W., Alpert, C. L., & Anderson, S. R. (1984). Natural environment language assessment and intervention with severely impaired preschoolers. *Topics in Early Childhood Special Education, 4*(2), 36–56.

Haring, N. G., White, O. R., & Liberty, K. A. (1980). *An investigation of phases of learning and facilitating instructional events for the severely handicapped, 1977-1978*. (Bureau of Education for the Handicapped, Project No. 443CH70564) Seattle: University of Washington, College of Education.

Haring, T. G., Neetz, J. A., Lovinger, L., Peck, C. A., & Semmel, M. I. (1987). Effects of four modified incidental teaching procedures to create opportunities for communication. *Journal of the Association for Persons with Severe Handicaps, 12,* 218–226.

Kaczmarek, L. A. (1982). Motor activities: A context for language/communication intervention. *Journal of the Division for Early Childhood, 6,* 21–35.

Mager, R. (1962). *Preparing instructional objectives*. Belmont, CA: Fearon.

Neel, R. S., Billingsley, F. F., McCarty, F., Symonds, D., Lambert, C., Lewis-Smith, N., & Hanashiro, R. (1983). *Impact curriculum*. U. S. Department of Education (Contract No. 300-80-0842). Seattle: University of Washington, College of Education.

Sailor, W. & Guess, D. (1983). *Severely handicapped students: An instructional design*. Boston: Houghton Mifflin.

Thiagarajan, S. (1980). Individualizing instructional objectives. *Teaching Exceptional Children, 12,* 126–127.

Uzgiris, I. C. & Hunt, J. M. (1975). *Assessment in Infancy: Ordinal Scales of Psychological Development*. Urbana: University of Illinois Press.

Vargas, J. S. (1972). *Writing worthwhile behavioral objectives*. New York: Harper & Row.

Vincent, L. J., Salisbury, C., Walter, G., Brown, P., Gruenwald, L. J., & Powers, M. (1980). Program evaluation and curriculum development in early childhood special education: Criteria of the next environment. In W. Sailor, B. Wilcox, & L. Brown (Eds.), *Methods of instruction for severely handicapped students*. Baltimore, MD: Paul H. Brookes.

White, O. R. (1980). Adaptive performance objectives: Form versus function. In W. Sailor, B. Wilcox, & L. Brown (Eds.), *Methods of instruction for severely handicapped students*. Baltimore, MD: Paul H. Brookes.

Wolery, M., Bailey, D. B., & Sugai, G. (1988). *Effective teaching: Principles and procedures of applied behavior anlaysis for exceptional students*. Boston: Allyn & Bacon.

Wolery, M. & Gast, D. L. (1984). Effective and efficient procedures for the transfer of stimulus control. *Topics in Early Childhood Special Education, 4*(3), 52–77.

Wolf, M. M. (1978). Social validity: The case for subjective measurement, or how applied behavior analysis is finding its heart. *Journal of Applied Behavior Analysis, 11,* 203–214.

Author Index

Abidin, R. R., 226, 238
Achenbach, T. M., 414
Adamson, L. B., 399
Ainsworth, M. D., 392, 396
Akeson, N., 153, 155, 159
Aldridge-Smith, J., 261
Alexander, R. P., 461, 463, 464
Allen, K. E., 15, 64
Allman, T. L., 27, 263, 290, 376, 416
Alpern, G. D., 28, 129, 134
Alpert, C. L., 292, 340, 491
Als, H., 169, 173, 174, 176, 179, 188, 189, 190, 192, 193, 194, 204–207, 210–215, 218, 233
Amatruda, L., 183
American Psychological Association, 41, 43
American Speech-Language-Hearing Association, 351
Amiel-Tison, L., 172, 182
Amochaev, A., 147, 148
Anders, T. F., 188, 189, 203, 208, 209, 211, 217
Anderson, B. J., 236, 237
Anderson, R., 485
Anderson, R. M., 364
Anderson, S. R., 292, 340, 397, 491
André-Thomas, Y., 170, 171, 311

Andrews, R., 394
Apgar, V., 180, 181
Arend, R. A., 279
Armstrong, P. M., 473
Arthur, G., 286
Asch, P., 188
Asher, S. R., 396, 401, 413
Ashton, R., 207, 213
Atkinson, J., 156, 157
Attermeier, S. A., 10
Attermeier, S. M., 32, 416
Ault, M. J., 86
Avery, G. B., 113, 177, 178
Azrin, N. H., 471, 473

Backman, J. E., 137
Bacon, A., 280
Baer, D. M., 92, 292, 340
Bagnato, S. J., 13, 33, 35, 36, 38, 290–291
Bailey, D. B., 4, 8, 11, 14, 15, 17, 26, 27, 30, 31, 32, 37, 40, 42, 65, 98, 106, 108, 109, 115, 123, 226, 230, 233, 241, 292, 394, 397, 430, 434, 435, 438, 449, 465, 474, 485, 490, 493
Baird, A. S., 155, 160, 161
Baird, S., 137
Bakeman, R., 395, 399
Baker, A., 54
Baker, B. L., 448, 474
Bakker, H. H., 208

Bakow, H., 188
Balaban, N., 280
Baldwin, V. L., 470, 474, 485
Ball, R. S., 286
Balla, D. A., 402, 414
Balow, I. H., 288
Balthazar, E. E., 450
Balzer-Martin, L., 239
Bandura, A., 277, 279, 281
Bangs, T. E., 364
Bankson, N. W., 362
Barber, L. M., 236
Barber, P. A., 394
Barnard, K. E., 218, 404
Barnes, K., 460
Barraga, N. C., 156
Barringer, U., 44, 54
Bates, E., 342
Bates, J. E., 229, 236, 237
Bauman, K. E., 94
Baumgart, D., 86
Bayley, N., 25, 27, 51, 136, 172, 173, 238, 258, 280
Beail, N., 261
Becker, P. T., 203, 205, 207, 211, 215, 216, 217, 239
Beckman, P. J., 231, 238, 239, 240, 421, 430
Beckman-Brindley, S., 474
Bee, H. L., 218
Behar, L., 400, 419
Behr, S. K., 394
Beintema, D., 171, 185, 188

Bell, S. M., 396
Belsky, J., 280
Bender, M., 406
Benowitz, S., 44, 54
Bentler, P. M., 285
Berdine, W. H., 65, 70
Berg, K. M., 208, 209, 212
Berg, W. K., 208, 209, 212
Berk, R. A., 37
Berkley, R., 350
Berlin, L. J., 360
Berliner, D. C., 106
Berrien, C., 181
Berry, P., 394
Bess, F. H., 177
Best, B., 265
Bettenburg, A., 133, 134, 136
Bidder, R. T., 261
Biggs, J. L., 461, 463, 464
Bigou, S. W., 64, 125
Billingsley, F. F., 484, 490
Birch, H. G., 228, 229, 235, 236
Bjorkman, S., 109
Blacher-Dixon, J., 14, 51, 124
Black, F. W., 265, 266
Blackstone, S., 352
Blackwell, J., 233
Blair, L., 448
Blank, M., 360
Blehar, M. C., 392
Blickman, J. G., 191, 211
Bloom, B. S., 490
Bloom, L., 344, 350, 373
Blum, L. H., 286
Bluma, A., 11
Bluma, S. M., 290, 402
Boehm, A. E., 40, 287, 294
Bohlin, G., 237
Boll, T. J., 28, 129, 134
Bolocofsky, D. B., 136
Booth, C., 404
Borders-Patterson, A., 279
Borg, W. R., 106
Bos, C., 290
Boudreault, M., 237
Bourland, B., 120, 121, 122
Bourland, J., 448
Bower, G. H., 66
Bowlby, J., 396
Boyce, V. S., 159
Boyce, W. T., 229

Bracken, B. A., 283, 284, 288, 294
Bradley, R. H., 107, 124, 125, 131, 138, 279, 404, 420, 429, 431
Brainerd, C. J., 250
Brandt, B. J., 137
Brann, B. A., 181
Bransford, J. D., 278
Branston, M., 349
Brazelton, T. B., 168, 169, 171, 173, 176, 183, 184, 185, 187, 188, 203–205, 207, 210–211, 218, 233
Bremer, D. L., 156
Bretherton, I., 392
Bricker, D., 37, 40, 42, 349
Bricker, W., 254
Brigance, A. H., 10, 290, 451
Brightman, J. A., 448
Brinckerhoff, J. L., 12, 493
Brinker, R. P., 60
Brodsky, G., 474
Broman, S., 181
Bromwich, R., 404, 405, 417, 430, 442
Bronfenbrenner, U., 16, 124, 279
Bronicki, G. J., 474
Brooks-Gunn, J., 4, 6, 49, 123, 138, 431
Brown, A. L., 278, 291
Brown, E., 191
Brown, F., 66, 474, 489, 491
Brown, J. V., 395
Brown, L., 86
Brown, P., 17, 65, 114
Brown, R., 4, 25, 346
Brown, S. L., 11, 26, 263, 377
Brown, W. H., 396
Bruder, M. B., 41, 42, 132, 137, 262
Bruner, J. S., 342, 429
Bryant, B. R., 359
Burchinal, M. R., 146
Burdy, N. B., 41, 137, 262
Burgemeister, B., 286
Burnstein, N. D., 230
Buros, O. K., 126, 285
Buss, A. H., 228
Byrne, J. M., 137
Bzoch, K. R., 363

Cadman, D., 134
Cain, R. L., 236, 237
Cairns, R. B., 402
Caldwell, B. M., 107, 124, 125, 138, 183, 279, 404, 420
Caldwell, J., 230
Cameron, J. R., 242, 243
Camp, B., 134
Campbell, C. R., 66
Campbell, F. A., 219, 279, 280
Campbell, P. H., 254, 471
Campbell, S. K., 28, 260
Campione, J. C., 278
Campos, J. J., 228
Camsioni, L., 342
CAPE (Consortium on Adaptive Performance Evaluation), 451, 460
Caperaa, P., 237
Capone, A., 290
Carey, W. B., 189, 235, 237, 242, 243, 401
Carlson, L., 349
Carpenter, M. W., 181
Carpenter, R., 344, 377
Carr, D., 259, 263
Carr, E. G., 94
Carrow, E., 359
Carrow-Woolfolk, E., 361
Carta, J. J., 106, 113
Casati, I., 249, 251, 266, 267
Case, R. S., 277
Cassidy, J., 392
Casto, G., 422
Catalpo, M. F., 106
Catlin, E. A., 181
Cattell, P., 260
Cauble, A. E., 233
Cazden, C., 373
Chambers, L. W., 134
Chambers, S., 236
Chance, P., 433
Chandler, M., 173, 181
Chapman, J. J., 177
Chapman, R., 342, 347, 349, 368, 375
Charlesworth, R., 394
Charlop, M. H., 492
Chee, F. K. W., 232
Chesney, B. H., 233
Chesni, Y., 170, 171

Chess, S., 48, 228, 229, 230, 235, 236, 237, 241
Christie, J. F., 428, 441
Cicchetti, D., 7, 59, 233, 402, 414
Cicerello, N., 459, 461
Clark, D., 232
Clark, J., 145, 146, 148, 151, 281, 284
Clarke-Stewart, A., 277
Clay, W. A., 58
Cliff, S., 259, 263
Clifford, R. M., 98, 106, 108, 109, 110, 115, 465
Clifton, A., 465
Coates, D. L., 59
Coen, C., 177
Coggins, T., 344, 377
Cohen, D. V., 280
Cohen, M., 448, 486
Cole, E., 145
Collier, A. M., 146
Colligan, R. C., 137
Collins, C. S., 289
Comeau, J., 233
Comfort, M., 230, 241, 421
Compton, A. J., 362
Cook, M., 451, 464
Coons, E. E., 125
Coons, S., 209, 210
Cooper, J. O., 68, 74, 91
Corman, H., 266, 285
Cornell, E. H., 177
Cote, K. S., 153, 157
Cote, R., 237
Creaghead, N., 373
Cress, P. J., 124, 159
Crockett, B. K., 284
Cronbach, L. J., 422
Cross, L., 120, 121
Cryer, D., 109
Cunningham, E. E., 233

Daley, S., 125
Darlow, B. A., 113
Darwin, L., 172
Das, J. P., 281
Daum, L., 177
David, T. G., 97, 98
Davidson, P., 57
Davis, C., 287
Davis, J., 265

Davis, L. J., 57
DeBriere, T. J., 124, 159
Deck, J., 233
Decker, N. T., 146
Deklyen, M., 406
Dellinger, J., 8, 26
Dement, W. C., 209
Denenberg, V. H., 205, 211, 217, 239
Deno, S. L., 490
DeRemer, P., 265
Derryberry, D., 228
DeRuiter, J. A., 292
D'Eugenio, D. B., 26, 263, 377
Devaney, B., 122
deVilliers, J., 346, 375
deVilliers, P., 346, 375
DeVivo, S., 136
Diamond, K. E., 42, 134
Dick, N. P., 132
Didhoff, R., 349
Dileo, J., 172
Divitto, B. A., 211
Docherty, E. M., 136
Dodds, J. B., 27, 129, 173
Dodson, S., 364
Dolan, A. B., 238
Donovan, C. M., 26, 263, 377
Doran, L., 406
Dore, J., 344
Dorsey, M. F., 94
Dowd, J. M., 210
Doyle, P. M., 86
Drews, J. E., 11
Dreyfus-Brisac, C., 208, 212, 215
Drinkwin, J., 218
DuBose, R. F., 7, 56, 124, 285
Dubowitz, L., 169, 181, 182, 184, 210
Dubowitz, V., 169, 181, 182, 184, 210
Duchan, J., 373
Duffy, F., 190, 191, 205, 211
Dunn, C., 345
Dunn, J., 242
Dunn, L. M., 360
Dunst, C. J., 7, 106, 112, 115, 124, 250, 253, 256, 265, 266, 267, 271, 278, 279, 280, 285, 290, 292, 349, 377, 378, 380, 430

Durand, V. M., 95
Dyk, L., 16
Dyson, L., 231, 448

Easton, D., 396
Eckerman, C. O., 211, 226
Eckerman, L., 178
Edelbrock, C. S., 414
Edgar, G., 98
Edlund, C. V., 54
Egan, D. F., 4, 25
Eichwald, J. G., 147
Eisert, D., 58
Elardo, R., 107, 138
Elliott, C. D., 287
Ellis, D., 155
Elzey, F. F., 402, 414
Emde, R. N., 393
Englehart, M. D., 490
Escalona, S. K., 266, 285
Etienne, J. E., 147
Eyberg, S., 242
Eysenck, H. J., 228
Eysenck, S. B. G., 228

Fagioli, I., 210
Fallen, N., 133
Fanaruff, A., 177, 178
Fandal, A. W., 129
Fargel, J. W., 208
Farr, R. C., 288
Farr, V., 182
Farran, D. C., 219, 279, 404, 421
Farthing, M. A., 465, 468
Featherstone, H., 233
Fein, G. G., 431
Feldman, C. M., 146
Feldman, J., 203
Feldman, R. S., 14
Feldman, W., 134
Fellows, R. R., 156
Ferber, R., 207, 208, 209, 210, 213, 214, 217, 220, 221
Ferguson, R., 134
Fernandez, P., 241
Ferrara, R. A., 278, 291
Ferrier, L., 351
Ferris, C., 233
Fetters, L., 265
Feuerstein, R., 291

Fewell, R. R., 4, 5, 13, 29, 56, 57, 134, 156, 159, 231, 234, 257, 279, 290, 291, 429, 430, 431, 438, 440, 441, 448
Fey, M., 373, 378, 379, 380
Field, T. M., 195, 214, 216, 218, 219, 220, 230, 396
Finch, M., 417
Finger, I., 279, 404
Finkler, D., 35
Fischler, R. S., 146
Fitch, J. L., 147
Flavell, J. H., 276, 277
Fleishman, D. H., 404, 405
Fluharty, N. B., 362
Ford, A., 86
Fordyce, W., 15
Forsythe, A. B., 211
Foster, R., 359, 414
Foster, S. L., 397
Fowler, S. A., 395
Fox, J. J., 397
Fox, N., 137
Foxx, R. M., 471, 473
Fraiberg, S., 56, 57, 228, 233, 392, 394
Frankenburg, W. K., 27, 125, 128, 129, 131, 132, 134, 138, 173
Fraser, B. A., 461
Fredericks, H. D., 448, 470, 474, 485
Freeland, C. A. B., 229
Freeman, R. D., 233
French, J. L., 287
Friendly, D. S., 113, 177
Fristoe, M., 365
Frohman, A., 290, 402, 416
Fuchs, D., 18, 44, 49, 54, 92, 490
Fuchs, L. S., 18, 44, 54, 92, 490
Fuin, C., 448
Fullard, W., 235, 236, 237
Furst, E. J., 490
Furuno, S., 11, 27, 263, 290, 376, 416

Gaensbauer, T. T., 239
Gaillargeon, R., 280, 290
Gaines, J. A., 229

Gaiter, J. L., 178, 193
Galambos, N. L., 230
Gallagher, J. J., 131
Gallagher, J. L., 250, 256, 265, 285
Gallagher, R. J., 233
Gallender, D., 458, 460
Gallerani, D., 124
Gardner, E. F., 289
Gardner, J. M., 193, 210
Gardner, J. O., 362
Gardner, M. F., 359
Gardner, S. M., 261
Garino, E., 236
Garrity, J., 145, 147, 151, 152
Garside, R. F., 236
Garvey, K., 431
Garwood, S. G., 5
Garwood, S. J., 280, 290
Gast, D. L., 73, 86, 479
Gaussen, T., 4
Gdowski, B. S., 146
Gearheart, B. R., 292
Gelman, R., 280, 285
Gentry, D., 259
Gerken, K. C., 255, 284
German, M. L., 134, 136, 137
Gessel, A., 172, 183
Gibes, R., 191, 211
Giddan, J. J., 359
Gieblink, G. S., 146
Gilbert, M., 406
Gill, G., 349
Ginsberg, H., 173, 250
Glass, E., 113
Glass, P., 177
Glatke, J., 290
Glazer, J., 395
Gleser, G., 188
Glover, M. E., 11, 27, 416, 451
Goldberg, A., 134
Goldberg, D., 28, 292
Goldberg, S., 101, 181, 211, 219, 226, 227, 291, 342
Goldenburg, D., 131, 136
Goldman, G. D., 227
Goldman, R., 365
Goldschmidt, M. J., 285
Goldsmith, H. H., 228
Goldstein, A. D., 134
Goldstein, M., 181
Goldstein, S., 233

Golinkoff, R., 342
Goodley, S., 203
Goodman, J., 278
Goodrich, J., 161
Gorski, P. A., 168, 177
Gottfried, A. W., 137, 177, 178, 193
Gottlieb, M., 146
Gould, J., 238, 239
Gradel, K., 14, 124
Graham, F. K., 182, 183
Grajek, S., 98, 109
Gray, C. A., 107
Gray, J., 259, 263
Gray, O. P., 261
Green, J. A., 402
Greenberg, M. T., 230, 233
Greenman, M., 183
Greenwood, C. R., 106, 113, 133, 395, 404, 405, 422
Grenier, A., 172, 182
Griffin, P., 401, 451
Griffiths, R., 28, 255, 260, 286
Grigg, N. C., 66
Groom, J. M., 394, 395, 400, 418
Gross, P., 448, 486
Grove, D. N., 470
Gruenewald, L. J., 17, 65, 114, 489
Guba, E. B., 422
Guerin, D., 137
Guess, D., 492
Guidasci, S., 211
Guidubaldi, J., 10, 26, 57, 261, 290, 376, 401, 414
Guild, J., 404, 405
Guilford, J. P., 286
Guilleminault, C., 209, 210
Gunn, P., 394
Guralnick, M. J., 391, 394, 395, 400, 418
Gutkin, T. B., 284

Haber, A., 211
Hack, M., 207, 212
Haddow, R., 203
Haeussermann, E., 285, 291
Hagekull, B., 237
Hagen, E. P., 281
Hall, J., 14

Hall, S., 459, 461
Halle, J. W., 292, 340, 491, 492
Hamilton, C., 218
Hanashiro, R., 484
Hancock, K. A., 284
Handen, B. L., 14
Hannah, E. P., 362
Hanrahan, L., 351
Hanson, M. A., 124
Hanson, R., 28, 57, 261
Harbin, G. L., 15, 17, 120, 121, 122
Harding, C., 342
Harel, J., 134
Haring, N. G., 65, 67, 68, 73, 91, 92, 451, 490, 491, 492
Harington, R. G., 124, 138
Harley, R. K., 157, 158, 159
Harms, T., 98, 106, 108, 109, 110, 115, 465, 468
Harper, R. M., 203
Harrel, L., 153, 155, 159
Harris, F. R., 64
Harris, M., 193
Harrison, H., 211, 218, 219
Harrison, P. L., 283
Hart, B., 100, 292, 378, 380
Hartman, A. F., 183
Hartup, W. W., 392, 395
Harwicke, N. J., 15
Hasenstab, M., 15, 151, 152
Haskins, R., 51
Hayden, A., 120
Hayman, L., 466, 467
Haywood, N. C., 278
Heath, C. P., 136
Hebel, J. R., 137
Hedrick, D., 136, 360
Heffernan, L., 265, 266
Heguik, R. L., 237
Heifetz, L. J., 448
Helsel-DeWert, M., 15
Hemming, A. M., 155, 160, 161
Hendersen, F. W., 146
Henderson, R. W., 284
Hendrickson, J. M., 395, 400
Henzinger, R. N., 461
Herbert-Jackson, E., 105
Heron, T. E., 68

Herrel, N., 177
Herzfeld, J., 134
Heward, W. L., 68
Hilgard, E. R., 66
Hill, W. H., 490
Hilliard, J. M., 290, 402, 416
Hinde, R. A., 396
Hiskey, M. S., 286
Hochstadt, N. J., 15
Hodgman, J., 203
Hoffman, M., 291
Hogan, A., 349, 377
Hogan, J. P., 288
Hogrenes, J. R., 233
Holaday, D., 181
Holbert, K., 112, 115, 280
Holder, L., 451, 464
Holdgrafer, G., 349, 377
Holm, V. A., 15
Holroyd, J., 231
Holvoet, J. F., 460
Honigman, A., 14
Hood, L., 344, 350
Hopkins, C., 136
Hoppenbrouwers, T., 203
Hops, H., 133, 395, 397, 400, 404, 405, 417, 419
Horner, J., 151, 152
Horner, T. M., 49
Hornung, M., 410
Horstmeier, D. S., 364
Hosaka, C. M., 27, 263, 290, 376, 416
Houden, P., 406
Howe, N., 437, 438, 443
Howes, C., 392, 396, 442
Hritcko, T., 158
Hunt, J. M., 255, 263, 265, 266, 279, 285, 482, 483
Huntington, G. S., 203, 207, 213, 230, 232, 236, 238, 239, 241, 401, 404
Hutton, J. S., 365
Hylton, J., 459, 461
Hymel, S., 401, 413

Ilg, F. L., 183
Illingworth, R. S., 177
Inatsoka, T., 27, 263, 290, 376, 416
Inge, K. J., 460
Ingram, D., 345

Ireton, H., 120, 124, 127, 128, 131, 132, 133, 136
Irwin, J., 35
Isbert, H., 170
Iwata, B. A., 94

Jacobs, P., 259
Jacobson, C. A., 148
Jacobson, J. T., 148
Jaffe, M., 134
Jambor, T., 410, 440
James, L., 181
Jan, J. E., 233
Jarman, R. F., 281
Jay, S., 279, 404
Jefferson, G., 345
Jenkins, J. R., 406, 415, 422
Jens, K. G., 10, 26, 32, 59, 233, 280, 416
Johnson, B., 287
Johnson, J. L., 124, 159, 428, 429, 430, 431, 437, 440, 441, 442, 443
Johnson, L. J., 422
Johnson, M., 58
Johnson, N. M., 10, 26, 59, 233
Johnson, R. A., 124
Johnson-Martin, N., 32, 227, 416
Johnston, M. S., 64
Jolie, K., 351
Jones, F. R., 147
Jones, M. J., 136
Jose, R. T., 153, 156, 157, 162

Kaczmarek, L. A., 491
Kahn, J. V., 265
Kahn, L., 365
Kaiser, A., 340, 378
Kaminski, R., 429, 430, 431
Kamphaus, R. W., 282
Kaplan, K., 392
Karma, P., 146
Karmel, B. Z., 192, 210
Karnes, M. B., 422
Kasari, C., 279, 404
Kastein, S., 233
Katz, E. L., 393
Kaufman, A. S., 53, 281, 282, 283, 284, 285

Kaufman, N. L., 53, 281, 282, 283, 284
Kazdin, A. E., 91, 92
Kearsley, R., 291
Keenan, E., 342
Keener, M., 211, 217
Keith, T. Z., 282, 283
Kelley, M. F., 14
Kellman, N., 177
Kendler, H. H., 280
Kendler, T. S., 281
Kendrick, C., 242
Kennedy, J. C., 233
Kenny, T. J., 137
Kenowitz, L., 98, 99
Keogh, B. K., 4, 7, 29, 125, 230, 241
Ker, L., 125
Kerns, G. M., 394
Keys, M. P., 113, 177
Kiernan, D. W., 285
King, J., 177
Kinney, P., 161
Kirby, J., 281
Kirk, S. A., 124
Kirkland, C., 146
Kister, M., 345
Klein, J. O., 146
Knapp, D. S., 448
Knobloch, H., 27, 134, 172, 173, 259
Koch, A. C., 472
Koch, J., 277
Kohl, F. L., 430
Kohler, F. W., 395, 399, 401, 402, 403
Kohn, M., 400
Kolinjavadi, N., 177
Kolvin, I., 236
Kopp, C. B., 4, 125
Korn, S. J., 241
Korner, A. F., 204, 211, 215, 218
Kositsky, A., 211, 218, 219
Kraemer, H., 211, 217
Krafchuk, E., 188
Krantz, P. J., 106
Krathwohl, D. R., 490
Kreutzberg, J. R., 232
Kurtz, P. D., 121, 122
Kwiatkowski, J., 345

Lachman, M. E., 229
Lambert, C., 484
Lance, W. D., 472
Landesman-Dwyer, S., 106, 213, 214, 217
Langley, M. B., 124, 134, 143, 153, 159, 160, 257, 265, 285, 437, 442, 443
Larsen, A., 233
Lawhon, G., 191, 211
Lawrence, G. A., 157, 158, 159
Lawson, K., 177, 218
League, R., 363
Leake, B., 203
Lee, L., 363, 375
Legouri, S. A., 57
Leguire, L. E., 156
Lelaurin, K., 100
Leleand, H., 414
Lemay, D., 401, 451
Lenard, H. G., 203, 207, 211, 212
Leonard, J. L., 490
Leonard, L., 340, 350
Lerner, J. V., 230, 241, 292
Lerner, R. M., 237, 241
Lester, B. M., 169, 173, 188, 205
Levine, M. D., 124
Levine, S., 402, 414, 415, 419
Lewis, J. M., 207, 213, 214, 216, 220, 221
Lewis, M., 4, 6, 13, 49, 60, 123, 138, 291, 402, 414, 431
Lewis, N., 365
Lewis-Smith, N., 484
Lezine, I., 249, 251, 266, 267
Li, A. K. F., 429
Liberty, K. A., 67, 490
Lichtenstein, R., 120, 124, 127, 128, 131, 132, 133, 134
Liddel, T. N., 132
Lidz, C. S., 291
Lightbown, P., 350
Lillie, D. L., 123
Lincoln, Y. S., 422
Lindhagen, K., 237
Lipsitt, L., 183
Lipton, E. L., 219

Liska, D., 448
Little, D. L., 242
Little, W. J., 181
Lockman, J. L., 153
Lombard, T. J., 121, 124
Lombroso, C. T., 211, 217
Long, J. G., 177
Lorenz, K., 171
Lorge, I., 286
Lounsbury, M. L., 229
Lovinger, L., 491
Lowe, M., 429
Lucey, J. R., 177
Lumley, J. M., 233
Lund, K., 290
Lund, N., 373
Lynch, E. W., 26, 263
Lyon, G., 15
Lyon, S., 15

McAnulty, G., 191, 211
McArthur, D., 231
McCall, R., 7, 429, 431
McCandless, B. R., 401
McCarthy, D. A., 52, 136, 283
McCarthy, J., 290
McCartney, K., 98, 109
McCarton, C., 218
McCarty, F., 484
McCauley, R., 134
McClean, M., 137
McCollum, J. A., 226, 420
McConnell, S. R., 392, 396, 397, 399, 401, 402, 403, 408, 409, 413, 414, 417
McCormick, K., 41, 137
McCormick, K., 262
McCubbin, H. I., 233
McDevitt, S. C., 235, 237, 243, 401
MacDonald, J. E., 364
McFall, R. M., 397
McFarland, W. H., 147
MacFarlane, A., 203
McGhee, L. J., 211, 226
McGinness, G. D., 120
McGinty, D. J., 203
McInnes, M., 406
McLean, J., 259, 340, 341, 342
McLean, M., 41, 262, 465
MacNamee, R., 242

McNeil, T. F., 237
MacPhee, D., 97
McWilliam, R. A., 106, 112, 115, 278, 280, 292
Madden, R., 289
Mager, R., 487
Magnano, M. A., 193
Magnus, R., 170
Mahoney, G., 43, 279, 419, 430, 442
Mahoney, T. M., 147
Main, M., 392
Maioni, T. L., 410
Makohon, L., 448
Malone, A. F., 27, 172, 173, 259
Mandell, C. J., 124
Mann, N. P., 203, 218
Mardell-Czudnowski, C., 292
Margolis, L. H., 123, 130, 134
Marshal, H. R., 401, 412
Marshal, R. M., 134
Marshall, N. R., 233
Martin, R., 237
Martin, R. J., 177
Martin, R. P., 230
Martin, S., 178
Marvin, R. S., 233
Matarazzo, R. G., 183
Matas, L., 279
Matheny, P. A., 238, 364
Matsumiya, Y., 211, 217
Mayfield, P., 137
Mayfield, S. R., 181
Maziade, M., 237
Meadow, K. P., 233
Mehrabian, A., 266, 267
Meier, J. H., 234
Meier, S. J., 125, 128
Meisels, S. J., 13, 123, 125, 130, 134
Meltzer, C. J., 124
Melville-Thomas, G., 212
Mengel, W., 279
Mengle, H., 145, 147, 151, 152
Mercer, C. D., 124
Merrifield, P., 286
Merrill, M. A., 281
Messick, S., 397
Messina, R., 86
Meyer, C., 137, 278

Meyer, S. A., 65, 70
Michaelis, R., 184, 211
Miles, M., 364
Miller, J., 14, 232, 341, 345, 349, 350, 359, 370, 371, 372, 373, 375, 376
Miller, L. J., 134
Mindes, G., 431
Mischook, M., 145
Mitchel, R. G., 182
Mitchel, S. K., 107
Mitchell, S., 404
Moersch, M. S., 263, 377
Mohan, P., 212
Monod, N., 211
Montes, F., 106
Moore, G. T., 99, 100, 109, 112
Moore, W., 448, 470
Morante, A., 184
Mordecai, D., 375
Mordock, J. B., 233
Morehouse, R. R., 148
Morgan, G. A., 49
Morris, J. E., 156
Morris, S. E., 461, 464
Morse, A. R., 153, 155, 156, 157
Mott, S. E., 13
Mueller, E., 392, 461
Muhiudeen, H. A., 212
Muma, J., 350
Munn, D., 8, 26
Murdoch, D. R., 113
Murphy, D. M., 448
Murray, D. J., 287
Musselwhite, L. R., 429, 430, 431, 437, 440, 442, 443, 444
Muzio, J. N., 209

Nagle, R. J., 124, 230
Naglieri, J. A., 32, 33, 283
Nance, S., 213, 218, 221
National Academy of Early Childhood Programs, 99, 100, 101, 102, 103
Neel, R. S., 484, 491
Neeley, C. A., 218
Neetz, J. A., 491
Neisworth, J. T., 11, 13, 33, 35, 36, 38, 290, 291

Neligan, G. A., 182
Nevin, R. S., 233
Newburg, J., 10, 26, 57, 137, 261, 290, 293, 376, 401, 414, 415, 416, 451
Newcommer, P. L., 361
New York Association for the Blind, 156, 159
Nihira, K., 414
Nijhuis, J. G., 209
Nisbet, J., 86
Northam, J. K., 124, 159
Northern, J., 152
Norton, K., 193
Nugent, J. K., 134, 195, 204, 209, 216, 219
Nymann, C., 259, 263

Oberklaid, F., 236
O'Brien, M., 105
Obrzut, J. E., 136
Odom, S. L., 14, 71, 234, 392, 395, 397, 399, 400, 401, 402, 403, 406, 408, 410, 411, 412, 413, 415, 419, 422, 430, 437, 438, 443
O'Donnell, K., 174, 206
Oehler, J. M., 178, 180, 181
Oh, W., 181
Olds, A. R., 100, 101
Olswang, L., 377
Opper, S., 173, 250
O'Regan, M., 124
O'Reilly, A., 263, 290
O'Reilly, K. A., 27, 376, 416, 448
Orelove, F. P., 451
Orlando, C., 15
Ornitz, E. M., 211
O'Sullivan, P. J., 126
Owens, R., 350, 379

Paget, K., 50, 52, 53, 124, 230, 283
Paine, R., 171
Paine, S., 404, 405
Palay, S. L., 174
Palermo, M., 247
Palin, M., 375
Palinscar, A. S., 278
Palmer, S., 375

Pappas, D., 148, 151, 152, 153
Paradise, J. L., 146
Parke, R. D., 398
Parkin, J. M., 182
Parmelee, A. H., 170, 184, 211
Parr, C. A., 28, 260
Parse, S., 203, 232
Parsonson, B. S., 92
Parten, M. B., 399, 406, 410, 433, 440, 442
Pasamanick, B., 134
Pascual-Leone, J., 277
Pasewark, R. A., 284
Patterson, C., 345
Patterson, J., 233
Paul, R., 346, 349, 375
Pearson, L. S., 287
Peck, B. F., 177
Peck, C. A., 491
Pedersen, F. A., 236, 237
Peiper, A., 170
Pennoyer, M. M., 183
Pepler, D. J., 429
Perozzi, J., 350
Perske, R., 465
Persson-Blennow, I., 237
Peterson, N. L., 65, 133, 234
Peterson, R. F., 64
Pfeffers, J., 237
Pfeiffer, S. I., 15
Phelps, J. A., 461
Philip, A. G. S., 177
Phillips, B. L., 284
Phillips, D., 98, 109
Phyfe-Perkins, E., 97
Piaget, J., 250, 252, 429, 432, 433
Piazza-Templeman, T., 448
Pierce, J. E., 51
Piper, M. C., 97, 108
Pipes, P. L., 466, 467
Platt, M., 218
Plomin, R., 228
Pokorni, J. L., 239
Pollack, D., 145, 148, 151
Polloway, E. A., 114
Pond, R. E., 363
Porterfield, J., 105
Poteat, G. M., 109
Powell, A., 279, 404, 430, 442
Powell, J. S., 280

Powell, M. L., 108, 129, 134, 136, 138, 457
Power, T. G., 398
Powers, N., 17, 65, 114, 489
Prather, E., 136, 360
Pratt, S. S., 448
Prechtl, H. F. R., 171, 184, 185, 188, 203, 207–212, 233
Preminger, J. L., 11, 27, 416, 451
Prescott, G. A., 288
Price, D., 148
Prinz, P. M., 363
Prior, M., 236
Prutting, C., 350
Puchalski, C. B., 228
Pukander, J., 146
Pullis, M. E., 230
Pumpian, I., 186
Purcell, K., 133

Quiltich, J., 100

Radtka, S., 461
Ragland, E. U., 397
Ramey, C. T., 28, 97, 146, 219, 260, 279, 280
Ramsay, M. V., 98, 108
Rand, Y., 291
Rankin, R. J., 284
Rardin, M. W., 284
Redding, S., 259, 263
Reed, P., 459, 461
Reichle, J., 349
Reid, D. K., 361
Reinhertz, H., 124
Rethford, K., 347
Reuler, E., 233
Reynell, J., 57, 262, 360
Reynolds, C. R., 281, 282, 284
Rheingrover, R. M., 7, 265, 285, 290
Riccivti, H., 49
Rice, D. C., 242, 243
Rice, R. D., 177
Rich, J. S., 13, 441
Richman, G. S., 94
Richmond, J. B., 219
Rieser-Danner, L. A., 228
Risley, T. R., 100, 105, 106, 292, 378, 380

Ritchey, W. L., 397
Ritter, K., 277
Ritvo, E. R., 211
Roberts, G., 265
Roberts, J. E., 146
Robinson, L. L., 35, 421
Robinson, R. J., 182
Rocissano, L., 344
Roeser, R., 148, 152
Roffwarg, H. P., 209
Rogers, G. L., 156
Rogers, K. D., 146
Rogers, S. J., 10, 26, 27, 50, 52, 58, 228, 263, 265, 285
Rogers-Warren, A. K., 97, 124, 340, 378
Roll, A., 257
Roopnarine, J. L., 396
Roscoe, D., 121
Rose, J. S., 35
Rose, S. A., 360
Rosenberg, S. A., 35, 421
Rosenblith, J. F., 183
Rosenshine, B., 106
Rosenthal, B. L., 282
Rosenthal, S. L., 30, 31, 123
Roskies, E., 233
Ross, H. S., 429
Rotatori, A. F., 14, 232, 237
Roth, F., 342, 344, 369, 375
Rothbart, M. K., 228, 236, 242
Rowland, C., 259
Ruben, R., 146
Rubenstein, J. L., 396
Rubin, K., 177, 399, 410, 431, 437, 438, 440, 443
Rudolph-Schnitzer, M., 134
Rutter, N., 203

Sack, S., 377
Sackett, G. P., 213, 214, 217, 406, 408
Sacks, G., 364
Sacks, H., 344
Sailor, W., 492
St. Clair, K. L., 169, 170
Sainte Anne-Dargassies, S., 170, 171, 184
Sak, R., 146

Salisbury, C., 17, 65, 114, 489
Salvia, J., 29, 281, 283, 285
Salzarula, P., 210
Sameroff, A., 173, 174, 181, 188
Sammons, W. A. H., 207, 213, 214, 216, 220, 221
Sandau, S. R., 29
Sander, E., 345
Sandler, S., 399, 400, 408, 409, 410, 411
Sanford, A. R., 11, 27, 290, 401, 416, 451
Sanger, D. D., 146
Sanson, A., 236, 237
Sanya, M. A., 146
Sarachan-Deily, A. B., 136
Sattler, J., 30, 31, 51, 52
Sattler, J. M., 281, 283, 284
Saylor, L. F., 137
Scarr, S., 98, 109
Schaeffler, C., 440
Schafer, D., 377
Schafer, S., 263
Schakel, J. A., 276, 281, 284, 289
Scharf, B., 233
Schegloff, E., 345
Schiefelbusch, R. C., 15
Schieffelin, B., 342
Schlesinger, H. S., 233
Schneider, D., 124
Schneider, P., 218
Schroeder, J., 86
Schuster, S. K., 234
Schwartz, B., 347
Schwartz, J. L., 109
Scott, D., 236
Scott, E. P., 233
Scott, R., 14
Seibert, J., 349, 377
Semmel, M. I., 491
Senior, E. M., 124
Serunian, S., 181
Sewell, J., 236
Sexton, D., 14, 232
Sexton, M. J., 137
Shah, C. P., 58
Shane, K. G., 157
Shaul, P. W., 181
Shearer, M., 28, 129, 134, 290, 402, 416

Sheehan, R., 4, 7, 14, 29, 124
Shellhass, M., 414
Sherard, E. S., 134
Sheridan, M. D., 156, 159
Sherman-Brown, S., 177
Shipe, D., 181
Shonkoff, J. P., 13
Shores, R. E., 395, 398, 400
Short, R. J., 207, 213, 232, 239, 401, 404
Shriberg, L., 345
Shure, M. B., 397
Shuster, S. K., 14, 71
Siegel, E., 28, 260
Siegler, R. S., 277
Sievel, J., 205, 211, 217, 239
Sigman, M., 265, 394
Sileo, T. W., 292
Silva, P. A., 146
Silver, F., 400, 410, 411
Simeonsson, N. E., 7
Simeonsson, R. J., 7, 13, 14, 34, 58, 98, 107, 124, 203, 204, 213, 215, 217, 226, 230, 232, 236, 238, 239, 241, 258, 265, 394, 397, 401, 404, 493
Simmer, M., 124
Simmons, F. B., 147
Simmons, M. A., 210, 218
Simpson, A., 146
Simpson, A. E., 229, 230
Singleton, L. C., 401, 413
Sipila, M., 146
Sirignano, S. W., 229
Sisson, L., 399, 408, 409
Sizemore, A. C., 124, 159
Slifer, K. J., 94
Slobin, D., 350
Smilansky, S., 410, 433, 440, 442
Smith, A. J., 153, 157
Smith, I. M., 137
Smith, J. A., 28, 261
Smith, K., 134
Smith, P. K., 431
Snell, M. E., 66, 468, 472, 474
Snow, C. W., 109
Snyder-McLean, L., 30, 35, 259, 340, 341, 342, 377
Sobsey, D., 461
Solomonson, B., 377

Sonnander, K., 14, 232
Soper, E., 58
Sostek, A. M., 113, 177, 188, 189, 203
Sparrow, S. S., 402, 414, 419
Spaulding, I., 233
Spekman, N., 342, 344, 369, 373
Spellman, C. R., 124, 159
Speltz, M. L., 406, 415
Spencer, J. E., 137
Spieker, S. J., 394
Spiro, A., 237
Spivak, G., 397
Sprong, T. A., 134, 136
Sprunger, L. W., 229
Sroufe, A., 7, 59, 233, 393
Sroufe, L. A., 279
Stanley, J. L., 38, 39
Stark, J., 359
Stayton, V. D., 226, 420
Stedman, D. J., 51, 279
Steichen, J. J., 188
Stein, J., 465
Stein, M., 406
Steiner, V. S., 363
Steinschneider, A., 219
Sterinberg, L. D., 280, 291
Sterman, M. B., 203
Stern, E., 211
Stern, R., 280
Sternberg, R., 280
Stevens, F., 172, 173, 259
Stevens, F., 27
Stevenson-Hinde, J., 229, 230
Stewart, I., 146
Stillman, R., 10
Stock, J., 10, 26, 57, 137, 401, 414, 451
Stock, J. R., 261, 290, 376
Stoel-Gammon, C., 345, 377
Stokes, L., 203
Stokes, T. F., 292, 340
Stone, N. W., 233
Stoneburner, R. L., 132
Stoner, S., 133
Stott, L. H., 286
Strain, P., 122, 290, 394, 395, 396, 397, 398, 399, 400, 401, 402, 403, 410, 411, 422, 430, 437, 438, 443
Stratton, M., 464

Street, A., 404, 405
Stremel-Campbell, K., 66, 259
Striefel, S., 92
Striker, K., 233
Stringfield, S., 400, 419
Subramanian, S., 177
Subramaniou, K. N. S., 113
Sugai, G., 485
Sugel, G. M., 65
Suinicki, J., 10, 26, 57, 261, 290, 376, 401, 414
Sullivan, M., 124
Sutton-Smith, B., 444
Sweet, M., 86
Swenson-Pierce, A., 430
Swisher, L., 134
Switzky, H. N., 278
Symonds, D., 484

Tamplin, A., 396
Tanguay, P. E., 211
Tawney, J. W., 73, 448
Taylor, A. R., 396
Telzrow, R., 404
Terestman, N., 236
Terman, L. M., 281
Teska, J. A., 132
Thelen, E., 232
Thiagarajan, S., 486
Thiele, J. E., 15, 239
Thivierge, J., 237
Thoman, E. B., 203, 205, 207, 211, 215, 216, 217, 239
Thomas, A., 48, 228, 229, 230, 235, 236, 237, 241
Thomas, P. J., 14
Thompson, H., 172
Thompson, M. S., 14, 124
Thorndike, R. L., 281
Thorpe, J. K., 393
Thurlow, M. L., 126
Thurman, S. K., 65, 70, 71
Thwing, E., 131, 136
Tilton, J. R., 448
Timm, M. A., 395
Tindall, R. C., 284
Tinkelman, S. N., 24
Tinsley, B. R., 401, 413
Titmus, G., 396
Tivnan, T., 126
Tjossem, T., 125
Tobin, A., 136

Todd, N. M., 133, 146, 395
Tremblay, A., 395, 400, 410, 422
Tricket, P. K., 397
Trief, E., 153, 155, 156, 157
Trificetti, J. J., 124
Trivette, C. M., 106
Tronick, E. Z., 169, 173, 188, 205, 233
Tucker, J., 120
Turkewitz, G., 177
Turnbull, A. P., 394, 474
Turner, S., 203
Twardosz, A., 106
Tweedle, E. G., 236

Ulrey, G., 49, 53, 57
Umansky, W., 133
Ungerer, J. A., 265, 394
U. S. Department of Education, 340
Utley, B. L., 460
Uzgiris, I., 255, 263, 265, 266, 285, 482

Vadasy, P. F., 430
Vandell, D., 392
Vandenberg, K. A., 98, 112, 113, 218
Vandenburg, B., 431
Vandenburg, S., 181
Vandiviere, P., 8, 26
Van Doorninck, W. J., 132
Vargas, J. S., 487, 490
Vaughn, S., 290
Veda, R., 134
Verghote, M., 184
Vietze, P. M., 59
Vincent, L. J., 12, 17, 65, 114, 489
Vistech Consultants, 159
Vollstedt, R., 431
Volpé, J. J., 178
Volterra, V., 342
Von Bernuth, H., 203, 207, 211
Vulpé, S. G., 11, 264
Vygotsky, L. S., 291

Wachs, T. D., 101, 102, 108, 115, 265, 278, 429
Wade, T. H., 284

Walker, H. M., 133, 395, 404, 405, 414
Wallace-Lande, P., 177
Walls, R. T., 280
Walls, S., 392
Walsh, M. E., 492
Walter, G., 17, 65, 114, 489
Walter, S. D., 134
Warburg, M., 155
Ware, W. B., 15, 207, 213, 239, 401, 404
Warren, S. F., 66, 340, 378
Wasserman, R., 124
Waters, E., 392
Watson, K., 410, 438, 440
Webster-Stratton, C., 242
Wechsler, D., 32, 284
Wedell-Monnig, J., 233
Wehman, P., 430, 434, 443
Weiner, F. F., 363
Weinhouse, E., 391
Weinmann, H. M., 208
Weinstein, C. S., 97, 98, 99
Weisbrot, I., 181
Weisler, A., 429, 431
Weisz, J. R., 265
Wellman, H. M., 277
Wells, B., 464
Welsh, C., 350
Werner, H., 174
Werner, T. J., 280
Wertsch, J. V., 281
Westby, C. E., 378, 442
White, O. R., 11, 55, 56, 65, 67, 68, 73, 91, 92, 484, 490
Whiteside-Lynch, E., 377
Widerstrom, A. H., 65, 70, 71
Widmayer, S. M., 216
Wiegerink, R., 34
Wildmayer, S. M., 195
Wilhelm, L., 58
Williams, A. R., 134
Williams, E., 134
Williams, M., 266, 267
Williams, P. D., 134
Williams, R., 181
Williams, S., 146
Williams, T. F., 147
Willoughby-Herb, S. J., 11, 290
Wilson, R. S., 238
Wilson, W. R., 124, 178

Wing, L., 238, 239
Winter, S. T., 134
Winton, P. J., 14, 241
Wiske, M. S., 134
Wnek, L., 10, 26, 57, 137,
    261, 290, 376, 401, 414
Wolery, M., 4, 16, 34, 65, 68,
    70, 86, 91, 92, 226, 233,
    292, 430, 434, 435, 438,
    449, 479, 485, 487, 490,
    491
Wolf, M. M., 489
Wolff, P. H., 207, 208, 210,
    211, 212, 215, 216, 218
Wolke, D., 98, 113

Wong, S., 35
Woodcock, R., 287
Woodson, R., 218
Woodward, M., 265
Wordbey, J., 195
Wortman-Lowe, L., 378

Yawkey, T. D., 428, 441
Yeates, K. O., 97
Yoder, D., 359
Yoder, P., 226, 393
Young, E. C., 364
Young, J., 57
Ysseldyke, J. E., 29, 126, 281,
    283, 285

Zabski, S., 241
Zane, T., 280
Zaslow, M., 237
Zehrbach, R., 134
Zeidner, L., 205, 211, 217,
    239
Zeisloft, B., 27, 263, 290, 376
Zeisloft-Falbey, B., 416
Zelazo, P. R., 60, 291
Zelman, J. G., 11, 27, 290
Zigler, E., 265, 397
Zimmerman, I. C., 363
Zinkos, P., 146
Zweibel, S., 98

Subject Index

AAMD Adaptive Behavior Scale, 414
Abbreviated Temperament Questionnaire, 276
Abduction, 304
Accessible space, 99
Accuracy, 69, 75
Activity level, 48
Adaptive Performance Instrument, 259, 324, 451
Adduction, 304
Affective development, 59
Aided response, 151
Albert Einstein Scale, 266, 267
Alertness, 220
Alternate forms reliability, 40
Analogue analysis, 94
Anecdotal records, 70, 398, 400, 402, 403
Animism, 277
Anticipatory guidance, 243
Apgar scoring system, 180–181
Arena assessment, 16
Arizona Articulation Proficiency Scale, 365
Arizona Basic Assessment and Curriculum Utilization System, 290
Arthur Adaptation of the Leiter International Performance Scale, 286
Assessing Prelinguistic and Early Linguistic Behaviors in Developmentally Young Children, 377
Assessment
  barriers to, 4–8
  characteristics of effective, 8–18
  defined, 2, 478
  rationale, 2–4
Assessment of Children's Language Comprehension, 359
Assessment of Preterm Infant Behavior, 182, 189–190, 214
Associated reactions, 309
Astigmatisms, 155
Asymmetrical tonic neck reflex, 311–312, 460
Asymmetry, 304
Athetosis, 330
Attachment, 392, 394, 396
Attention, 220, 277
Atypical motor development, 301–303
Audiogram, 150
Audiology, 145
Auditory Brainstem Response, 148
Auditory screening, 145–153
Augmentative communication, 351
Auropalpebral response, 147
Automatic postural reactions, 312–315
Awake states, 202
Balthazar Scales of Adaptive Behavior, 451
Bankson Language Screening Test, 362
Barriers to child assessment, 4–8
Battelle Developmental Inventory, 10, 16, 26, 27, 31, 32, 33, 40, 41, 42, 57, 137, 261, 262, 290, 293, 294, 324, 376, 401, 414–415, 420, 451
Bayley Scales of Infant Development, 25, 27, 28, 31, 32, 33, 51, 136, 137, 173, 226, 227, 258, 260, 261, 325
Behavior, 68
Behavior checklists, 280
Behavioral anchor, 404
Behavioral Assessment Scale of Oral Functions in Feeding, 464
Behavioral characteristics, 226, 231–232
Behavioral cues, 226–228
Behavioral Observation Audiometry, 151
Behavioral organization, 168
Behavioral states, 202–221
  application, 217–221
  defined, 203, 207

Behavioral States (*continued*)
  dimensions, 205–207
  procedural considerations,
    212–214
  representative methods
    215–217
Behavioral style, 226,
  228–231
Behavioral Style Questionnaire,
  237
Behavioral subsystems, 173
Bidirectional effects, 203
Binocularity, 157
Biological risk, 125
Birth to Three Developmental
  Scales, 364
Bite reflex, 461–462
Biting, 464
Blindness, 153
Bobath method, 328
Boehm Test of Basic Concepts,
  287, 294
Bracken Concept Development
  Series, 288, 295
Brainstem evoked response
  audiometry, 152
Brigance Diagnostic Inventory
  of Early Development, 10,
  290, 325, 451
British Ability Scale, 287

Calibrated, 73
California Preschool Social
  Competency Scale, 402,
  414, 415, 419
Callier-Azusa Scale, 27, 325
Caregiver Styles of Interaction
  Scales, 279
Carolina Curriculum for
  Handicapped and At-Risk
  Infants, 10, 32, 33, 326,
  401, 416
Carolina Record of Individual
  Behavior, 207–209, 213,
  215–217, 226, 227,
  239–240
Carrow Elicited Language
  Inventory, 359
Casati-Lezine Scale, 266, 267
Cataracts, 156
Category sampling, 80, 82, 83,
  84, 85

Cattell Infant Intelligence
  Scale, 260
Causality, 253, 269
Central nervous system, 167,
  202
Cephalo to caudal, 305
Chained skills, 88
Chewing, 464
Child Behavior Checklist, 414
Child Behavior Questionnaire,
  419
Child find, 119–139
  components of, 120–122
  defined, 119–120
  rationale for, 120
Children's Handicaps Behavior
  and Skills Schedule, 238
Clinical judgment, 232
Closed-plan facility, 99
Cochlea, 145
Cognition,
  assessment of infant skills,
    249–273
  assessment of preschool
    skills, 275–296
  defined, 276
Cognitive competence,
  278–279
  contexts, 279
  forms, 279
  types, 278–279
Cognitive skills, 9
Cognitive structures, 276–277
Color vision, 158
Columbia Mental Maturity
  Scale, 286
Combination of new means
  through mental
  combinations, 252
Communication sample,
  372–376, 381
Communication skills, 9,
  339–386
  defined, 340, 341
  dimensions of
    communication, 341–350
  procedural considerations,
    350–352
  representative methods for
    assessing 353–377
  translating assessment into
    instruction 377–386

Communicative Evaluation
  Chart, 364
Communicative event
  perspective, 369
Communicative intentions,
  341–342, 343
Comprehension, 349, 352,
  353, 355, 357
Comprehensive Developmental
  Evaluation Chart, 259,
  263
Comprehensive Identification
  Process, 134
Compton-Hutton Phonological
  Assessment, 365
Compton Speech and Language
  Screening Evaluation, 362
Concept formation, 294
Conceptual criteria for
  determining test content,
  24
Conditioned Orientation
  Response, 151
Conductive loss, 146
Conservation, 277
Considerations in assessing
  young children, 47–54
Construct validity, 42
Construction of objects in
  space, 253, 269
Constructive play, 433
Content validity, 41
Conversation, 344
Co-occurrences, 60
Coordination of secondary
  circular reactions, 251
Cortical blindness, 156
Crib-o-gram, 147
Criteria of the next
  educational environment,
  489
Criterion validity, 42
Criterion-referenced measures,
  36–38, 416–417
Criterion-referenced scoring,
  37–38
Critical function, 55
Crystallized abilities, 281
Curricular Efficiency Index,
  38

Data collection sheets, 73–89

Decibels, 146
Decile, 31
Deductive reasoning, 252
Denver Developmental
    Screening Test, 27, 42,
    129, 131, 132, 134, 137,
    173, 324
Detroit Tests of Learning
    Aptitude, 359
Developmental Activities
    Screening Inventory—II,
    134
Developmental age score, 28–29
Developmental Diagnosis, 259
Developmental Indicators for
    the Assessment of
    Learning—Revised (DIAL-
    R), 28, 131, 136
Developmental milestones
    approach, 4
Developmental perspective,
    369
Developmental Profile II, 28,
    129, 131, 134, 136, 137,
    324
Developmental Programming
    for Infants and Young
    Children, 326, 377
Developmental quotient, 30
Developmental Screening
    Inventory, 134
Developmental Sentence
    Analysis, 375
Diagnosis, 2
Difficultness, 229, 230, 235
Dimensions of Temperament
    Survey, 237
Diplegia, 310, 329
Direct observation, 13–14,
    64–95, 404–410
Direct Observations of Social
    Behavior, 410–411
Discourse, 342
Discriminative stimulus
    functions, 67
Dissociation, 304
Distractibility, 48
Dramatic play, 433
Dressing/undressing, 449,
    452–458
Duration, 69, 72, 73, 76, 396

Ear canal, 145
Early Childhood Environment
    Rating Scale, 108–111
Early Childhood Physical
    Environment Scales,
    109–110
Early Communicative
    Competence Scales, 377
Early Intervention
    Developmental Profile, 5,
    10, 27, 263
Early Learning
    Accomplishment Profile,
    11, 325, 401, 416, 451
Early Periodic Screening,
    Diagnosis, and Treatment
    Program, 121, 123
Early Screening Inventory, 134
Early Social Communication
    Scales, 377
Eating/Feeding, 449, 458–468
Ecobehavioral assessment, 106
Ecological approach, 16, 279
Ecologically valid assessments,
    16–17
Effect (of behavior), 68
Efficiency Index, 34–35, 36
Egocentrism, 277
Eliciting functions, 67
Eligibility for services, 3
Endurance, 69
Engagement, 106
Environment/Behavior
    Observation Schedule, 112
Environment, defined, 99
Environmental Language
    Intervention Program, 364
Environmental neonatology,
    113
Environmental Prelanguage
    Battery, 364
Environmental risk, 125
Environments, 97–116
Equilibrium reactions,
    313–314
Error in measurement, 38–41
Established risk, 125
Etiological perspective, 371
Eustachian tube, 145
Evaluation, 4
Evaluation and Programming
    System, 40, 42

Event-sampling, 71, 75, 76,
    77, 409–410
Exhaustive, 80
Exploration, 431
Expressive One-Word Picture
    Vocabulary Test, 359
Extended Merrill-Palmer Scale
    of Mental Tests, 286
Extension, 304–305, 314–315
External rotation, 304
Externoceptive reflexes,
    211–212
Extrapolated scores, 29, 30,
    31, 32

False negative, 130
False positive, 130
Family Day Care Rating Scale,
    109, 111
Fatigue, 220
Fine motor skills, 319–321
Flash-Card Vision Test,
    156–159
Flexibility, 49–50
Flexion, 304–305
Flexion to extension, 305
Fluharty Preschool Speech and
    Language Screening Test,
    362
Fluid-analytic abilities, 281
Focal child system, 410
Form
    of behavior, 68, 484
    of environments, 102
Frequency, 69, 72, 75
    of sound, 145
Function
    of behavior, 68, 484–485
    of environments, 102
Functional analysis, 93–94
Functional approach, 5
Functional objectives, 488–489
Functional play, 433
Functional relationship, 67
Functional vision assessment,
    158
Functional Vision Inventory,
    159, 160, 162

Gag reflex, 461–462
Games with rules, 432

Generic Skills Assessment Profile, 259
Generic Skills Inventory, Parsons Preschool Curriculum, 377
Gesell Developmental Schedules, 27, 42
Gestational age, 180–182
Goal-directed behavior, 249
Goldman-Fristoe Test of Articulation, 365
Goodness-of-fit, 241
Graham Rosenblith Behavior Test for Neonates, 182–184
Grasp, 321–322
Griffith Scales of Mental Development, 28, 260, 261, 286
Grooming, 449
Gross motor to fine motor, 306

Hawaii Early Learning Profile, 5, 11, 27, 263, 290, 326, 376, 416
Hearing impairments, 58
Hearing threshold, 146
Hemiplegia, 310, 329
Hertz, 145
Heuristic, assessment, 452
HICOMP Preschool Curriculum, 11, 290
High-interest materials, 52
High-risk register, 147
Home environments, 107–108
Home Eye Test, 159
Home Observation and Measurement of the Environment, 107–108, 138, 279, 404, 420
Horizontal and vertical control to diagonal control, 305
Hypertonia, 307, 309
Hypotonia, 307, 309, 330

Imitation, 254, 270, 349, 354, 356, 358
Impedance Audiometry, 148
Incidental teaching, 292
Individual differences/ disordered perspective, 370

Individualized Education Plan, 3, 12, 478, 484, 493
Individualized Family Service Plan, 3, 9, 17, 478, 484
Infant Behavior Questionnaire, 236, 237
Infant Behavior Record, 226, 238
Infant Characteristics Questionnaire, 236–237
Infant Psychological Development Scale, 263, 265, 266
Infant Scale of Communicative Intent, 364, 365
Infant Temperament Questionnaire, 235, 237, 401
Infant/Toddler Environment Rating Scale, 109, 111
Information-processing techniques, 59, 277
Inner ear, 145
Instructional control, 456
Instructional utility, 42
Instrumental behavior, 252
Integrated therapy, 330
Intellectual functions, 276–277
Intensity, 69, 73
of sound, 145
Interactive games, 429
Interdisciplinary team, 15–16
Interindividual sources of risk, 125
Internal consistency reliability, 40
Internal rotation, 304
Interpretability, 226–227
Interval sampling, 408
Intervention Efficiency Index, 33–34
Interviewing, 14, 257, 457
Intra-individual sources of risk, 125
Intuitive phase, 277
Irritability, 174, 219
Item difficulty level, 24–25
Item score, 27

Jaw thrust, 461, 463

Kaufman Assessment Battery for Children, 276, 282–283
Khan-Lewis Phonological Analysis, 365

Language, 341
Language sample. See Communication sample
Latency, 69, 73, 77
Latency errors, 456
Lateral, 304
Learning Accomplishment Profile, 11, 27, 290, 401, 420, 451
Learning Potential Assessment Device, 291
Least restrictive, 98
Levels-of-assistance recording, 86, 87, 88, 440
Lingquest Language Sample Analysis, 375
Linking assessment and intervention, 479
Lock Box, 278

McCarthy Scales of Children's Abilities, 31, 52, 136, 137, 276, 283–284, 293
Manipulative play, 433
Man-to-man procedure, 100
Maternal Behavior Rating Scale, 279, 404, 420
Mean Length of Utterance, 346, 375, 376
Means-ends relationships, 252–253, 269
Mediate, 203, 242
Medication, 7
Mehrabian and Williams Scales, 266
Memory, 293
Metacognition, 278
Metropolitan Achievement Tests, 288
Middle ear, 145
Milani-Comparetti Motor Development Screening Test, 324
Miller Assessment of Preschoolers, 134

Miller-Yoder Language Comprehension Test, 359
Minneapolis Preschool Screening Instrument, 134
Minnesota Child Development Inventory, 130, 136
Mixed hearing loss, 147
Mode of communication, 341, 366–368
Modified open-plan facility, 99
Molar descriptions, 106
Molecular descriptions, 106
Momentary time sampling, 74, 78
Morpheme, 346
Motor impairments, 58
Motor skills, 9
Motor skills assessment, 301–335
    rationale, 302–303
    representative methods, 321–327
Movement, 303
Movement Assessment of Infants, 325
Multidisciplinary team, 15
Muscle tone, 307–310
    distribution of muscle tone, 309–310
    predominant muscle tone, 309
    underlying muscle tone, 308
Mutually exclusive, 80

Narrative descriptions, 70–71
Naturalistic observation, 13–14, 64–95, 372
Naturalistic Observation of the Preterm Neonate, 191–192
Naturalistic research, 71
Naturalistic teaching, 292
Nebraska Test of Learning Aptitude, 286
Neonatal Behavioral Assessment Scale, 168–169, 171, 185–189, 207–209, 212, 214, 216
Neonatal Intensive Care Unit, 167
Neonatology, 178

Neurobehavioral assessment, 166–197
Neurodevelopmental treatment, 328
Neurological Assessment of the Preterm and Full Term Newborn Infant, 184–185
Neurological integrity, 191–193
Newborn assessment, 166–197
Nondiscriminatory assessment, 17
Nonstandardized administrative conditions, 285
Normal curve, 30
Normalized, 98
Normative group, 27–28
Norm-referenced scores, 28–36, 413
Norm-referenced tests, 27–36
Northwestern Syntax Screening Test, 363
Nutritional intake, 466–468
Nutritional risk, 466–467
Nystagmus, 156

Object concept, 254, 270
Object manipulation, 429
Object permanence, 252, 268, 269
Objectives, 481–490
Observation, 64–95, 256–257
Observation: Atmosphere and Environment of an Eating Experience, 465
Observational Assessment of Reciprocal Social Interaction, 399, 409
Observer bias, 91
Observer drift, 91
Occupational therapist, 306
Open-plan facility, 99
Ophthalmologist, 156
Optometrist, 156
Oral motor functioning, 458–464
Oral structures, 460
Ordinal scales, 255
Ossicles, 145
Otitis media, 146
Outer ear, 145

Paired comparisons, 410
Parallel forms reliability, 40
Parent Behavior Progression, 404, 406, 420
Parent/Caregiver Interaction Scale, 279, 421
Parent involvement in child assessment, 11–12, 14–15, 457–458, 492–494
Parent presence during testing, 51–52
Parent Temperament Questionnaire, 237
Parent Temperament Scale, 237
Parental observations of behavior, 219
Parent-child interaction, 230
Parent-Child Play Scale, 279
Parenting Stress Index, 226, 228
Parent-professional agreement, 14–15
Parsons Visual Acuity Test, 159
Parten/Smilansky Combined Scale, 399, 412
Partial-interval method, 74, 76, 78
Peabody Developmental Motor Scales, 326
Peabody Picture Vocabulary Test, 360
Peer assessments, 410
Peer environments, 100
Peer nominations, 410, 412–413
Peer Play Scale, 442
Peer preferences, 396
Peer ratings, 410, 413
Peer social interaction, 392
Percentile rank, 31
Perception of Baby Temperament, 236–237
Perceptual discrimination, 293
Performance standard, 37
Performance-based measure of competence, 398
Perkins-Binet, 57, 286
Permanent products, 71
Persistence at tasks, 277

Phoneme, 345
Phonology, 345, 347, 375
Physical guidance, 331
Physical management, 331
Physical play, 433
Physical space, 99
Physical therapist, 306
Piagetian approach, 250–254, 276–277
Piagetian-based scales of preschool cognition, 285, 290
Placement, 2–3
Planning, 50
Play, 431
Play Assessment Scale, 440–442
Play audiometry, 151
Play skills, 9, 428–444
 defined, 431
 methods and procedures for assessing, 433–442
 rationale for assessing, 428–431
Portage Project Checklist, 11, 290, 402, 416, 421
Positive reinforcement, 53–54
Postural control, 303
Postural tone. (*See* muscle tone)
Posture, 314–319, 320
Practice play, 432
Pragmatics, 341, 347, 352, 353, 355, 357, 373, 375
Pragmatics Screening Test, 363
Preconceptual phase, 277
Preferential looking procedures, 156
Preoperational stage, 277
Preschool Assessment of the Classroom Environment, 112
Preschool Behavior Questionnaire, 400
Preschool Developmental Profile, 11
Preschool Language Assessment Instrument, 300
Preschool Language Scale—Revised, 363

Preschool Language Screening Test, 362
Prescriptive Behavioral Checklist for the Severely and Profoundly Retarded, 326
Pre-Speech Assessment Scale, 464
Primary circular reactions, 251
Problem-solving skills, 294
Procedural reliability, 39
Process-oriented approaches to assessment, 291
Process-product analysis, 106
Production, 349, 352, 354, 356, 358
Profile analysis, 481–482
Program to Develop Efficiency in Visual Functioning, 162
Programmed Environments Curriculum, 327
Pronation to supination, 306
Prone, 304
Proportional Change Index, 34–35, 36
Protective reactions, 314–315
Proximal to distal, 305
Psychometric approach, 280
Public Law 94-142, 2, 11, 12, 98, 340, 484, 493
Public Law 99-457, 2, 3, 9, 17, 98, 340, 484, 493
Punishing functions, 67
Purdue Home Stimulation Inventory, 108
Pure tone, 151

Quadraplegia, 310, 329
Quartile, 31

Range of motion, 308–309
Rapid Eye Movements (REM), 207, 209, 217
Rapport, 50–51
Rate, 72
Rating scales, 400–402, 404–405
Raw score, 27
Reasoning skills, 294
Receptive-Expressive Emergent Language Scale, 43, 363
Reciprocal determinism, 278

Reciprocity. (*See* social reciprocity)
Referral systems, 121
Reflexes, 169–170, 249, 251, 311–314, 461–462
Refraction, 157
Refractive errors, 156
Reinforcer assessment, 93
Reinforcing functions, 67
Reliability, 6, 39–41, 126
Report writing, 479–481
Responsiveness, 101
Retrolental fibroplasia, 155
Reynell Developmental Language Scales, 360
Reynell-Zinkin Scales, 262
Rhythmic habit patterns, 232
Righting reactions, 313–314
RISE: Computerized Checklist and Curriculum for the Motorically Delayed/Impaired Child, 327, 451, 464
Risk categories, 125
 biological risk, 125
 environmental risk, 125
 established risk, 125
 suspect risk, 125
Role taking, 345
Rooting reflex, 461–462
Rotation, 304, 313
Running record, 70–71

Scale of Social Participation, 399
Scan, 408
Schematic, 104
Schemes, 252–254, 276
Scoring reliability, 39–40
Screening, 2, 119–139, 417
 characteristics of effective screening, 125–130
 decision models, 130–133
 defined, 2, 122
 focus of, 123–124
 representative measures, 133–137
 sensory screening, 144–162
Screening systems, 121
Secondary circular reactions, 251

Self-care skills, 9, 447–475
  defined, 447
  description and
    characteristics of,
    448–450
  procedures for assessing,
    450–472
Self-help skills. (See self-care
  skills)
Self-regulation, 173
Semantics, 346–347, 348,
  354, 356, 358, 375
Sensitivity, 127
Sensorimotor intelligence, 249
  procedural considerations of
    testing, 254–258
  rationale for assessment,
    250–251
  representative measures and
    procedures, 258–267
Sensorineural hearing loss,
  146–147
Sensory impairments, 54–58
Sequenced Inventory of
  Communication
  Development, 136, 360
Serial use, 129
Short Temperament Scale for
  Infants, 236, 237
Short-term memory, 281
Single-stage screening decision
  model, 132
Situational effect, 234
Situational specificity, 279
Six-month Temperament
  Questionnaire, 237
Sleep habits, 220
Sleep states, 202
Sleep/wake cycles, 209
Slow-to-warm-up, 230, 235
Snellen eye chart, 156, 158
Social competence, 391
Social Competence Scale, 401
Social development, 390–394
Social Interaction Assessment/
  Intervention, 420
Social Interaction Rating Scale,
  400, 404–405, 419
Social Interaction Scan, 399,
  406–407
Social interaction skills,
  390–423

defined, 39
developmental sequences,
  390–394
dimensions of, 394–397
procedural considerations,
  397–398
representative methods for
  assessment, 398–416
Social learning theory,
  277–278
Social reciprocity, 395
  reciprocity one, 395
  reciprocity two, 395
Social skills, 9
Social validity, 489
Sociometric assessment, 396,
  410
Spasticity, 307, 329
Spatial relationships, 253
Specificity, 127
Specimen descriptions, 71
Speech-language pathologist,
  340, 368
Staff-child ratios, 101
Stage of development
  approach, 5
Standard deviation, 30–31
Standard Error of
  Measurement, 41
Standard score, 30
Standardization, 23, 55
Stanford Early School
  Achievement Test, 289
Stanford-Binet Intelligence
  Test, 31, 54, 57, 276,
  280, 281–282, 283, 284,
  293
Startle reflex, 313
State. (See also Behavioral
  states), 48, 171
Statistical criteria for
  determining test content,
  24
Strabismus, 155, 156, 157
Strange situation, 396
Structured elicited interaction,
  372
Stycar Vision Tests, 156, 159
Sucking, 463
Sucking reflex, 461–462
Supine, 304
Suspect risk, 125

Swallowing, 463
Swedish Temperament
  Questionnaire, 237
Symbolic play, 432–433
Symbolic Play Scale Checklist,
  442
Symmetrical tonic neck reflex,
  312
Symmetry, 304, 316
Synactive theory, 174, 176,
  205, 210–211
Syntax, 345, 347, 354, 356,
  375
Systematic Analysis of
  Language Transcripts, 375
Systematic Anecdotal
  Assessment of Social
  Interaction, 399, 403

T score, 31
Task analysis, 485–487
Task-analytic recording, 88, 89
Task-intrinsic motivation, 278
Teacher Rating of Intervention
  Behavior, 401, 422
Teacher Rating of Social
  Interaction, 400, 419
Teacher Temperament
  Questionnaire, 230
Teaching Research Curriculum
  for Moderately and
  Severely Handicapped, 327
Teaching Skills Inventory, 421
Teaching to the test, 482, 484
Teller Visual Acuity Cards, 159
Temperament, 168, 228–230
Tertiary circular reactions, 252
Test for Auditory
  Comprehension of
  Language, 360–361
Test content, 23–27
Test of Early Language
  Development, 361
Test of Language
  Development, 361
Test the limits, 55–56
Test of Pragmatic Skills, 361
Testing, 13, 256
Test-retest reliability, 40
Tests, 22–44
Test-teach-test paradigm, 291

Time-sampling, 74, 84, 85, 406, 408–409
Toddler Behavior Questionnaire, 237
Toddler Temperament Scale, 236–237
Toilet training, 468–471
Toileting, 449, 468–472
Tone. (*See* Muscle tone)
Tongue thrust, 461, 463
Tonic bite reflex, 461, 463
Tonic labyrinthine reflex, 312
Topographical errors, 456
Transdisciplinary team, 15
Two-stage screening decision model, 132–133
Tympanic membrane, 145
Tympanogram, 148–149

Ulnar to radial, 306

Uniform Performance Assessment System, 11, 451
Uzgiris-Hunt Scales, 265–266, 267, 483

Validity, 6, 41–44, 126–127
Vineland Adaptive Behavior Scale, 402, 414, 419
Vision screening and assessment, 152–162
Visual acuity, 153
Visual field, 157
Visual impairments, 56–58, 153
Visual pursuit, 252
Visual Reinforcement Audiometry, 151
Visually evoked potential, 157
Volitional movements, 315–319

Vulpé Assessment Battery, 11, 264

Walker Problem Behavior Identification Checklist, 414
Wariness of strangers, 49
Wechsler Intelligence Scale for Children—Revised, 32
Wechsler Preschool and Primary Scale of Intelligence, 280, 283, 284, 293
Weight bearing, 304
Weight shift, 304
Whole interval, 76, 78
Woodcock Johnson Psycho-Educational Battery, 287

Z score, 31
Zone procedure, 100